THIRD EDITION

The Contemporary Asian American Experience

Beyond the Model Minority

Timothy P. Fong

California State University
Sacramento

PEARSON
Prentice
Hall

Upper Saddle River, New Jersey 07458

Library of Congress Cataloging-in-Publication Data

Fong, Timothy P.
  The Contemporary Asian American Experience: Beyond the Model Minority /
Timothy P. Fong.—3rd ed.
      p.   cm.
  Includes bibliographical references and index.
  ISBN-13: 978-0-13-185061-3 (alk. paper)
  ISBN-10: 0-13-185061-X (alk. paper)
  1. Asian Americans.   2. Asian Americans—Social conditions.   3. United States—
Ethnic relations.   I. Title.
  E184.O6F66 2007
  973'.0495—dc22

                                                                    2006101984

Editorial Director: Leah Jewell
Executive Editor: Jennifer Gilliland
Editorial Assistant: Lee Peterson
Full Service Production Liaison: Joanne Hakim
Marketing Director: Brandy Dawson
Marketing Manager: Lindsey Prudhomme
Manufacturing Buyer: Brian Mackey
Cover Art Director: Jayne Conte
Cover Design: Kiwi Design
Cover Photos: Girl in cap and gown—*David Young-Wolff/PhotoEdit Inc.;* Little girl with
flag—*Joe Sohm/Chromosohm/The Stock Connection;* Man in turban—*George Doyle/Stockbyte
Silver/Getty Images;* Man and woman—*Don Smetzer/Stone Allstock/Getty Images*
Manager, Cover Visual Research & Permissions: Karen Sanatar
Composition: TexTech International
Full-Service Project Management: Edith Bicknell/Stratford Publishing Services

Credits and acknowledgments borrowed from other sources and reproduced, with
permission, in this textbook appear on appropriate page within text.

Pearson Education LTD., London
Pearson Education Singapore, Pte. Ltd
Pearson Education, Canada, Ltd
Pearson Education–Japan
Pearson Education Australia PTY,
   Limited

Pearson Education North Asia Ltd
Pearson Educación de Mexico, S.A. de C.V.
Pearson Education Malaysia, Pte. Ltd
Pearson Education, Upper Saddle River,
   New Jersey

ISBN-13: 978-0-13-185061-3
ISBN-10: 0-13-185061-X

Contents

**3   The Right to Excel: Asian Americans
and Educational Opportunity**   76

4   Workplace Issues: Beyond Glass Ceilings   116

Preface

This book is intended primarily for college-level courses, but is written in a clear and direct narrative form that can easily reach a broader audience. In *The Sociological Imagination* (1959) C. Wright Mills chides what he calls "socspeak," the complex writing style commonly used in social sciences. Mills complains that in academic circles, anyone who writes "in a widely intelligible way" is belittled for being "a mere journalist."[1] As a social scientist, I know many colleagues who criticize the journalistic writing style for being too simple. As a former journalist, I also know that journalists criticize academic writing style for being too abstract. Despite these criticisms of each other, social scientists and journalists do share the same common goal: increasing understanding of the issues confronting today's society. Readers will find the academic/journalistic approach in this book refreshing because it combines the rigor of scholarship with the accessibility of journalism. Readers will also better appreciate the significance of the research work of scholars from a variety of academic disciplines.

This book has several major objectives. The first objective is to provide a sound academic background to better comprehend the contemporary history, culture, and social relationships that form the fundamental issues confronted by Asians in America. This book analyzes the interrelationship of race, class, and gender and explores how these factors have shaped the experiences of Asian Americans. The hope is that readers will arrive at a new level of understanding and awareness beyond the simplistic stereotype of the "model minority" through the exposure to important concerns of Asian American groups and communities.

Second, this book provides a balanced and comparative analysis of the different Asian ethnic groups, newer immigrants, and American-born Asians. While Chinese, Japanese, and Filipinos were among the earliest immigrants from Asia, attention will also be given to new immigrants such as the Koreans, Asian Indians, and Southeast Asian refugees, who have come in large numbers to the United States since 1965. With this in mind, chapters in this book are organized by specific issues rather than by specific ethnic group. In addition, this book will be balanced in terms of strong representation of how the various issues pertain to and impact Asian American women.

Third, this book analyzes competing aspects of the Asian American experience. Most of the early research on Asian Americans has focused on the "positive" cultural aspects of a strong work ethic and filial piety, amazing success in education, and enviable economic upward mobility. Since the 1970s, however, an increasing number of Asian American scholars have challenged what they feel is an overemphasis on anecdotal evidence and superficial statistical data. They have focused on issues of prejudice and discrimination, underemployment, educational problems, family and intergenerational conflict, and a host of other social concerns intended to provide a comprehensive picture of the Asian American experience.

Fourth, this book compares and contrasts various theoretical perspectives throughout the text where appropriate. This approach is unique, but necessary given the diversity of issues being covered. For example, the book will discuss different theories on immigration, immigrant adaptation and assimilation, ethnic entrepreneurship, educational achievement, ethnic identity, interracial marriage, and political incorporation, among others. Within this, recent Asian immigrants greatly differ from earlier immigrants in socioeconomic background and adjustment to American society. Clearly there is a need to review traditional concepts and theories, which are primarily based on the previous historical experiences.

Lastly, this book features an up-to-date collection of immigration, demographic, socioeconomic, and educational data on Asian Americans. Liberal use of tables highlights this information and serves as an excellent resource for the general audience, students, and researchers. In addition, an extensive bibliography of books, articles, and reports on Asian American issues is included in the book. This will be extremely useful for student papers and research projects.

ACKNOWLEDGMENTS

I believe this book could not have been written without the help of many others. I first and foremost want to thank all the academic researchers, the journalists, and the community activists who have focused their attention on Asian Americans and Asian American issues. This is evidence of the growth and maturity of Asian American studies as an academic discipline, the increased attention on Asian Americans in the media, and the importance of the issues raised on the grass-roots level. Together, their works and activities over many years have converged, and have only recently reached a critical mass. Whether directly cited or not, their works and activities are very much the core of this book. It is their insights, their analyses, and their hard work that give this book life.

I would also like to thank my colleagues in the Asian American Studies Department at California State University, Northridge, and the Social Sciences Division at Holy Names College where I taught while writing the first edition of this book. Thanks also go to my colleagues in the Ethnic Studies Department at Sacramento State, where I taught while writing the second and third editions. All of their support and encouragement were invaluable. Special thanks go to librarians Kathryn Blackmer Reyes, and Rhonda Rios Kravitz for their help locating reference materials. My highest praises go to Jennifer Gilliland, Executive Editor/Sociology at Prentice Hall, Edith Bicknell, Editorial Project Manager with Stratford Publishing Services, and copy editor Suzanne Stradley for their professional guidance on this book. My thanks also, to the following reviewers of this edition: Catherine Choy, University of Minnesota; Alex Yamato, San Jose State University; Colleen Fong, California State University–Hayward; Peter Adler, University of Denver; and George Wilson, University of Miami.

Lastly, this book is dedicated to my wife, Elena Almanzo, our sons Gabriel and Tomas, and the little one on the way. It is interesting to note that each edition of this book seems to correspond with a new addition to our family. We'll see if this trend continues.

Timothy P. Fong
California State University, Sacramento

NOTE

1. C. Wright Mills, *The Sociological Imagination* (New York: Oxford University Press, 1959), pp. 218–219.

INTRODUCTION

Changing Asian America

VISIBILITY AND INVISIBILITY

On November 20, 2004, Army Chaplin James Yee, a West Point graduate, was presented with a "Courage and Inspiration Award" by the Sacramento, California, chapter of the Council on American-Islamic Relations (CAIR). The audience of more than four hundred people gave him a rousing standing ovation. Audience members included an especially large number of Asian Americans who felt a special bond with Yee, a Chinese American Muslim, who was charged a year earlier with espionage, treason, and the mishandling of classified information while working at the U.S. military prison in Guantanamo Bay, Cuba. After his arrest on September 10, 2003, Yee was blindfolded, manacled, and given seventy-six days in solitary confinement. He became another victim of an overzealous and botched government investigation that started off with high-profile accusations that ultimately collapsed because of a lack of evidence. News of Yee's arrest was leaked to the media before the investigation was complete and *The Washington Times* was the first to publish the story on September 20, 2003, citing unidentified government sources. Eventually all charges against Yee were dropped and he resigned from the military in January 2005 with an honorable discharge. "At this time just one short year ago, I was still fasting Ramadan and praying the Ramadan prayers, alone, without the benefit or the rewards of praying in congregation, while still locked up in the naval brig down in Charleston, South Carolina," Yee said in his speech at the CAIR event. "So I'm thankful that this year is different." He expressed deep concerns about what he called "this new culture of eroding civil liberties." Many Muslims believe Yee was singled out because of his religion, but the case was also particularly important to many Asian Americans because of its similarities to another high-profile case of

1

alleged espionage involving Wen Ho Lee, a Taiwan-born U.S. citizen and former research scientist at the Los Alamos Nuclear Laboratory, who spent nine months in prison where he endured grueling government investigation, harassment, and intimidation. "My first thought was, 'This is going to be exactly like my dad's case all over again,'" explained Alberta Lee, Wen Ho Lee's daughter. "The government really painted them both to be very sinister people."[1]

In March 1999 Lee was fired from his job after the *New York Times* identified him as the prime suspect giving U.S. nuclear weapon secrets to China. He was never formally charged with espionage, but Lee was indicted on fifty-nine counts of "mishandling classified data." After months of investigation, the U.S. Justice Department acknowledged they had no credible case against Lee and allowed him to plead guilty to one charge of violating security rules in order to win his freedom. After pleading guilty to the single count, Lee was sentenced to time served and fined $100. He also received a dramatic apology from a federal judge. U.S. district judge James Parker spoke from the bench accusing government officials of abusing power and providing misleading information. "They did not embarrass me alone, but they embarrassed our entire nation and each of its citizens," Parker told the packed courtroom.[2]

The Wen Ho Lee case became the cause célèbre for Asian Americans across the nation. On June 8, 2000, a group called the Coalition Against Racial and Ethnic Scapegoating (CARES) organized rallies in New York, San Francisco, Albuquerque, Seattle, Los Angeles, and Detroit protesting the treatment of Lee. Supporters chanted loudly and carried signs reading "Asian American, Arrest Me Too!" and "I Am Not a Spy!" Some protesters even chained themselves together and blocked the U.S. Federal Building in San Francisco.[3] Many Asian Americans believed that Lee was a victim of racial profiling; that is, he was selected for persecution not for what he had done, but for what he looked like. Lee was also seen as the scapegoat for all the security lapses and mismanagement issues associated with secret military research. The pressure for a government conviction of Lee intensified after the May 2000 release of a House select committee report probing China's alleged theft of U.S. military secrets. The report, commonly referred to as the Cox Report after the committee's chair Christopher Cox, a Republican congressman from Southern California, created a tremendous furor because it stated that China identified Chinese Americans with access to sensitive information and sometimes enlisted their cooperation to transfer information. The report quickly turned into a highly partisan political issue. Republican congressional leaders such as U.S. Senate majority leader Trent Lott, a Republican from Mississippi, quickly used the report to bash President Clinton and the Democratic administration. Lott charged that the report "raises very serious questions not only about this administration's handling of China policy, but more broadly about whether it can be trusted to manage the nation's security affairs."[4] Contrary to these claims, Robert S. Norris, a senior analyst and nuclear weapons expert at the Natural Resources Defense Council, was quick to challenge the report for greatly exaggerating the facts. He pointed out that the U.S. nuclear arsenal is far superior to China's and that Chinese weapons are not copies of U.S.

weapons. "I think it's best to put some of this in perspective and context and not hyperventilate about the future of Chinese nuclear weapons."[5]

Nonetheless, scrutiny on Chinese Americans and Asian Americans in general intensified to new zealous heights. Actions against Lee were indeed egregious. For example, Lee had passed a government lie detector test well before his name was leaked to the media and he was smeared as a spy. Lee was also charged with downloading secret computer files, but the materials were reclassified as "top secret" only after they were downloaded. Note that former CIA director John Deutch was investigated for downloading top secret data on to his personal computer, but he was not charged with a crime and he never spent any time in jail.[6] To some Justice Department investigators, it may have been perfectly reasonable to consider Lee's ethnic background as a way of confirming their suspicions and in building their case. However, according to Phillip B. Heymann, a Harvard University law professor who oversaw the Justice Department's counterintelligence operations during the early 1990s, using a suspect's heritage is not only offensive to the concepts of civil rights, but can also hamper a proper counterintelligence investigation. "There are so many steps between the initial observation of someone's ethnicity and making an intelligent use of it that it's really not worth using," he said. "What you're getting out of knowing that Wen Ho Lee is Chinese is an extremely crude estimate of the larger list of factors about motive and opportunity. It comes very cheap but it isn't nearly as probative as the others."[7]

The Wen Ho Lee case shows how racial profiling against Asian Americans comes from a severe lack of understanding and only serves to create conflicting images of visibility and invisibility for Asian Americans in the minds of many in the United States today. Asian Americans are visible only in such stereotypes as "perpetual foreigners," "overachievers," and the "model minority." This often leads to irrational thoughts, acts, and resentment. Consider another example: An L.A. radio talk-show host complained about Asian American dominance in women's figure skating. "You know, I'm tired of the Kristi Yamaguchis and the Michelle Kwans!" stormed Bill Handel of station KFI-AM. "They're not American. . . . When I look at a box of Wheaties, I don't want to see eyes that are slanted and Oriental and almond shaped. I want to see American eyes looking at me."[8] The fact that both Yamaguchi and Kwan are not recognized as U.S.-born citizens is evidence of the invisibility of Asian Americans because of widespread ignorance of their distinct histories and contemporary experiences. The visibility (stereotypes) and invisibility (ignorance) witnessed in the James Yee and Wen Ho Lee cases, along with the radio host's outburst all speak to the urgency of the problem and is a recurring theme throughout this book.

It is widely acknowledged that the massive 1992 L.A. riots that erupted following the acquittal of four white police officers in the beating of black motorist Rodney King prompted a national reexamination of race relations. This time, however, the debate needed to focus beyond just black and white issues. Suddenly, Asian Americans—in this case primarily Korean Americans—could not be ignored in the race relations equation. Throughout the violent uproar,

Korean American businesses were the targets of looting and arson. After the smoke had cleared and the ashes cooled, it was discovered that more than two thousand Korean-owned businesses were either damaged or destroyed during the riots. Together Korean and other Asian American businesses suffered more than $460 million in property losses, nearly half the total of all property losses in the city.[9] Despite this cataclysmic event, it is clear that precious little is known about Asian Americans in the United States. Just one year before the Los Angeles uprising, a national poll conducted by the *Wall Street Journal* and NBC News revealed some disturbing attitudes toward Asian Americans. A majority of Americans believed that Asian Americans are not discriminated against, and one out of five African Americans even believed that Asian Americans receive "too many special advantages."[10] In August 1993 the *Los Angeles Times* reported results of a survey that found most Southern Californians admired Asian Americans for their work ethic and strong family ties. At the same time, however, the survey found a large number of people—46 percent—also thought that new Asian immigrants are a burden to the local economy.[11] In 1994, nearly two years after the urban disturbance in Los Angeles, the National Conference of Christians and Jews released the results of another national survey on race relations that also produced troubling opinions of Asian Americans. On the positive side, all groups surveyed supported the notion of cultural diversity. On the other hand, whereas Asian Americans felt the most in common with whites, both whites and blacks felt the least in common with Asian Americans.[12] An important question must be asked: How much has really changed since then?

Not much perhaps. On April 1, 2001, a U.S. spy plane and a Chinese fighter plane collided over the South China Sea resulting in the death of the Chinese pilot and the capture of the twenty-four crew members of the spy plane who landed on Chinese territory. The diplomatic tensions that arose from the incident gave rise to unabashed hostility against Chinese Americans as witnessed by a swell of racist political cartoons, radio talk show hosts calling for the internment of Chinese Americans, and "humorous" monologues on late night television shows.[13] Shortly after this international incident was finally resolved and the twenty-four crewmembers were returned to the United States, a poll sponsored by Committee of 100, a Chinese American leadership organization, found that one out of four Americans who answered the survey had "strong negative attitudes" toward Chinese Americans. Another 43 percent said they had "somewhat negative" attitudes toward Chinese Americans, leaving less than a third with "positive" attitudes toward Chinese Americans.[14]

Evidence that the Wen Ho Lee case continues to haunt Asian Americans can also be found in the survey. One third of respondents believed that Chinese Americans are more loyal to China than the United States and that Chinese have too much influence in the U.S. high technology sector. The survey of 1,216 individuals was conducted by Yankelovich Partners, in consultation with the Anti-Defamation League, and it primarily studied attitudes toward Chinese Americans, but found respondents felt virtually the same about Chinese Americans as Asian Americans in general. This reflects the relentless stereotype that Asian Americans are "all the same" and that Asian Americans are "perpetual foreigners." Among the most surprising findings was the fact that nearly a quarter of those surveyed would disapprove if a member of their family married an Asian American. The results of the survey may be shocking, but it is important to note that the study was conducted two weeks *before* the spy plane incident!

More recently on February 4, 2003, Republican Congressman Howard Coble of North Carolina said on a radio call-in program that he agreed with the internment of Japanese Americans during World War II. Coble, chairman of the Judiciary Subcommittee on Crime, Terrorism, and Homeland Security, was responding to a caller who suggested that Arab Americans in the United States be confined following the tragic terrorist attacks on September 11, 2001. His comments were immediately denounced by colleagues in Congress led by Democrat Mike Honda from California. "I'm disappointed that he really doesn't understand the impact of what he said," complained Honda, a Japanese American who spent his early childhood in an internment camp during World War II. "With his leadership position in Congress, that kind of lack of understanding can lead people down the wrong path."[15] Just days after the incident the Japanese American Citizen's League (JACL) and Muslims for a Better North Carolina called for Coble's resignation as leader of the congressional subcommittee that oversees domestic security. Pressure continued to mount as Coble steadfastly refused to resign from his chairmanship post, although he agreed to meet with the JACL and other civil rights groups. Unfortunately, Coble later reneged and refused to schedule any meeting. This led to blistering criticism from JACL National Executive Director, John Tateishi. "His continued refusal to discuss this matter with JACL and other concerned members of the civil rights community only demonstrates Rep. Coble's arrogant disregard of the Asian Pacific American community and his rejection of the concerns expressed by millions of Americans," Tateishi said in a press release. "Needless to say, we are baffled at Rep. Coble's recalcitrance, intractability and complete distain for our concerns such that he will not even discuss the issue face to face."[16] This wasn't the first time Coble confronted the treatment of Japanese Americans during World War II. As a young congressman in the mid-1980s he was assigned to lead the Republican opposition to redress and reparations legislation for Japanese Americans who were forcibly interned. Despite Coble's opposition, legislation was passed authorizing an official apology from the United States government and monetary compensation to living Japanese American internees. Then-president Ronald Reagan signed the bill into law in 1988.[17]

In June 2004, California Asian American elected officials announced they were planning to honor Wen Ho Lee on the floor of the State Assembly, but they were immediately met with attacks by a conservative group that supported the U.S. war on terrorism and military intervention in Iraq. "Move America Forward," led by former state legislator Howard Kaloogian, accused the Asian American elected officials of violating their oaths of office to defend against domestic enemies. Kaloogian charged that Lee was engaged in "very suspect, questionable activity." He added: "This is wrong on so many fronts. I wonder if they (the Asian American legislators) have ever considered whether a domestic enemy could possibly be the man that they are honoring."[18] The clash prevented efforts to introduce a resolution in the state legislature. Typically resolutions are simply ceremonial, do not require a vote, and almost never prompt controversy. To the Asian American lawmakers, Wen Ho Lee is a hero; but to "Move America Forward" and some others in the California State Assembly, Lee is a convicted felon and a threat. The Asian legislators reluctantly pulled back the resolution to spare Lee the prospect of being attacked on the floor, and instead honored Lee at a dinner outside of the State Capitol building. California State Assemblywoman Judy Chu was outraged by this whole incident. "Dr. Lee has already been victimized by an overzealous prosecution by the government," she said, "and I do not want him to be brutally victimized again." Other supporters of Lee were equally angry. The resistance to the Assembly resolution was "really bigoted or else totally ignorant," said Cecilia Chang. "I'm just shocked how anybody could have the heart to still pick on this guy."[19]

Despite the duality of visibility and invisibility, Asian Americans can no longer be considered a marginal minority group. Since 1970 Asian Americans have been the fastest growing population group in the United States. The 2000 census counted 10.2 million Asian Americans, up from 6.9 million in 1990. This represents a 48.3 percent increase during this time. For the first time the U.S. census also allowed individuals to count more than one race, which had an important impact on Asian Americans. The number of Asian Americans including those who chose more than one race was 11.9 million, an overall increase of 72.2 percent from the 1990 census. According to U.S. Census, Asian Americans made up 4.2 percent of the U.S. population. The rate of increase for Hispanics of any race was 57.9 percent and was close to Asian Americans. Both groups far outpaced the rate of growth of African Americans (21.5 percent) and whites (13.2 percent). The percentage of growth for Native Americans and Alaska Natives increased the most dramatically (110.3 percent), but their overall population (2.1 million) is still relatively low. Table I-1 shows the difference between the U.S. population by race in 1990 and the population by race in 2000. Because individuals could report only one race in 1990 and could report more than one race in 2000, the race data for 1990 and 2000 are not directly comparable. Thus the difference in population by race between 1990 and 2000 is due to both these changes in the census questionnaire and to real change in the population. The estimates for the Asian American population in 2000 were impressive, but the rate of growth is slower than what was witnessed in previous decades. The Asian American population nearly doubled between 1970 and 1980, and increased 95.2 percent between 1980 and 1990. Despite the relative slowing down of population growth among Asian Americans, demographers still project that the Asian American population could be as large as 20 million by the year 2020 and 33.4 million by 2050.[20]

Table I-2 shows details of the Asian American population by groups for 2000. It must be noted that the Census 2000 question on race included fifteen

Table I-1 Difference in Population by Race and Hispanic or Latino Origin 1990–2000

Subject	1990 Census		Census 2000		Difference between 1990 and 2000			
					Using race alone¹ or Census 2000		Using race alone or in combination for Census 2000	
	Number	Percent of total population	Race alone¹	Race alone or in combination	Numerical difference (2000 minus 1990)	Percent difference (based on 1990)	Numerical difference (2000 minus 1990)	Percent difference (based on 1990)
	(1)	(2)	(3)	(4)	(5)	(6)	(7)	(8)
RACE								
Total population³	**248 709 873**	**100.0**	**281 421 906**	**281 421 906**	**32 712 033**	**13.2**	**32 712 033**	**13.2**
White	199 686 070	80.3	211 460 626	216 930 975	11 774 556	5.9	17 244 905	8.6
Black or African American	29 986 060	12.1	34 658 190	36 419 434	4 672 130	15.6	6 433 374	21.5
American Indian and Alaska Native	1 959 234	0.8	2 475 956	4 119 301	516 722	26.4	2 160 067	110.3
Asian	6 908 638	2.8	10 242 998	11 898 828	3 334 360	48.3	4 990 190	72.2
Native Hawaiian and Other Pacific Islander	365 024	0.1	398 835	874 414	33 811	9.3	509 390	139.5
Some other race	9 804 847	3.9	15 359 073	18 521 486	5 554 226	56.6	8 716 639	88.9
HISPANIC OR LATINO AND RACE								
Total population³	**248 709 873**	**100.0**	**281 421 906**	**281 421 906**	**32 712 033**	**13.2**	**32 712 033**	**13.2**
Hispanic or Latino (of any race)³	22 354 059	9.0	35 305 818	35 305 818	12 951 759	57.9	12 951 759	57.9
Not Hispanic or Latino³	226 355 814	91.0	246 116 088	246 116 088	19 760 274	8.7	19 760 274	8.7
White	188 128 296	75.6	194 552 774	198 177 900	6 424 478	3.4	10 049 604	5.3
Black or African American	29 216 293	11.7	33 947 837	35 383 751	4 731 544	16.2	6 167 458	21.1
American Indian and Alaska Native	1 793 773	0.7	2 068 883	3 444 700	275 110	15.3	1 650 927	92.0
Asian	6 642 481	2.7	10 123 169	11 579 494	3 480 688	52.4	4 937 013	74.3
Native Hawaiian and Other Pacific Islander	325 878	0.1	353 509	748 149	27 631	8.5	422 271	129.6
Some other race	249 093	0.1	467 770	1 770 645	218 677	87.8	1 521 552	610.8

- Represents zero or rounds to 0.0

¹ One of the following six races: (1) White, (2) Black or African American, (3) American Indian and Alaska Native, (4) Asian, (5) Native Hawaiian and Other Pacific Islander, (6) Some other race.

² Alone or in combination with one or more of the other five races listed. Numbers for the six race groups may add to more than the total population and the six percentages may add to more than 100 percent because individuals may indicate more than one race. For example, a person indicating "American Indian and Alaska Native and Asian and Native Hawaiian and Other Pacific Islander" is included with American Indian and Alaska Native, with Asian, and with Native Hawaiian and Other Pacific Islander.

³ The differences between 1990 and 2000 for the total population, the Hispanic or Latino Population, and the Not Hispanic or Latino population are not affected by whether data on race alone or for race alone or in combination. The Hispanic or Latino population may be of any race.

Source: http://www.census.gov/population/www/cen2000/phc-tl.html and U.S. Census Bureau, 1990 Census.

Table I-2 Asian Population by Select Group: 2000

Group	One Asian group reported	Asian group alone or in combination
Chinese (except Taiwanese)	2,314,537	2,734,841
Filipino	1,850,314	2,364,815
Asian Indian	1,678,765	1,899,599
Vietnamese	1,122,528	1,223,736
Korean	1,076,872	1,228,427
Japanese	796,700	1,148,932
Cambodian	171,937	206,052
Hmong	169,428	186,310
Laotian	168,707	198,203

Source: Asian Population: 2000 (Issued February 2002) at http://www.census.gov/ prod/2002pubs/c2kbr01-16.pdf.

separate response categories and three areas where respondents could write in a more specific race. Data collected by Census 2000 on race can be divided into two broad categories: the race *alone* population and the race *in combination* population. People who responded to the question on race by indicating only one detailed Asian ethnic group (i.e., Chinese or Korean, etc.) are referred to as the race *alone* population. In addition, respondents who reported their race as one or more Asian detailed ethnic groups (i.e., Japanese and Filipino) but no other race, would also be included in the Asian *alone* population. Individuals who reported more than one of the six U.S. Census "race categories" (White, Black or African American, American Indian and Alaska Native, Asian, Native Hawaiian and other Pacific Islander, and Some other race) are referred to as race *in combination* population. For example, if an African American male married a Vietnamese American woman, their child would be included in the Asian *in combination* population.[21]

According to the Table I-2, Chinese Americans are the largest Asian ethnic group in the United States, both in the *alone* and the *alone or in combination* population. There were 2.3 million people who reported Chinese and more than 420,000 who reported Chinese with at least one other race or Asian group. A total of 2.7 million people reported Chinese alone or in combination with one or more other races or Asian groups. Filipino Americans are the next largest Asian group. There were more than 2.3 million people who reported Filipino alone or in combination with a least one other race or Asian group. Many may be surprised that Asian Indians make up the third largest Asian American group. A total of 1.9 million people reported Asian Indian alone or in combination. Japanese Americans were more likely than any other Asian American group to report one or more other races or Asian groups. Of all respondents who reported Japanese, 31 percent reported one or more other races or Asian groups. It is interesting to point out that the median age of the total U.S. population is 35.3 years. The overall median for people who reported Asian alone was 32.7 years, which indicates a higher percentage of younger Asian Americans. However, for those who reported Asian in combination with one or more races had a median age of 31.1, which is 4.2 years younger than the total U.S. population. This indicates that the biracial and multiracial children are a relatively new phenomenon. This will be discussed in greater detail in Chapter 7, More Than "Family Values": Asian American Families and Identities.

The population growth among the Asian American is also due to immigration. This has been especially true in recent decades since the passage of the 1965 Immigration Reform Act, which ended discriminatory immigration policies that purposely kept down the number of immigrants from Asia. In the nineteen-year time span between 1941 and 1960, relatively few Asians immigrated to the United States. In just the nine years between 1961 and 1970, more than 427,000 immigrants came to the United States from Asia. This number increased to more than 1.5 million between 1971 and 1980 and reached over 2.7 million between 1981 and 1990. From 1991 to 2003 there were close to 4 million immigrants from Asia to the United States (see Table I-3).

Who Are Asian Americans?

The lack of understanding of Asian Americans is due in part to the fact that they are an extremely heterogeneous pan-ethnic and increasingly multiethnic and multiracial group. They are composed of people whose ancestry originates from dozens of countries, who have been in the United States for generations, and those who are only recent immigrants and refugees. They are composed of people who are highly educated, professionally skilled, and relatively affluent. The Asian American population also includes a significant number of people who are completely illiterate, possess little more than subsistence farming skills,

Table I-3 Asian Immigrants to the United States, Fiscal Years 1941–2003

	All Countries	Asia*	Percentage
2003	705,827	235,039	33.2
2002	1,063,732	326,871	30.7
2001	1,064,318	337,566	31.7
2000	849,807	255,860	30.1
1991–2000	9,095,417	2,795,672	30.7
1981–1990	7,338,062	2,738,157	37.3
1971–1980	4,493,314	1,588,176	35.3
1961–1970	3,321,677	427,642	12.9
1951–1960	2,515,479	153,249	6.1
1941–1950	1,035,039	37,028	3.6

* Includes Iraq, Israel, Syria, Turkey, and other Southwest Asian countries.
Source: U.S. Office of Immigration Statistics, *Statistical Yearbook of the Immigration and Naturalization Service, 2004*, (Washington, DC: U.S. Government Printing Office, 2004), Table 2, pp.12–15.

and are extremely poor. In addition, who is considered Asian American is not consistent, nor clearly defined. The U.S. Census Bureau used the broad term "Asian and Pacific Islander Americans" in its 1990 population count, which includes native Hawaiians, Samoans, Guamanians, and so forth. In 2000, however, Asian Americans and Pacific Islanders were counted in separate categories, as was done in the 1980 census. Officially, the term "Asian" refers to people having origins in any of the original peoples of the Far East, Southeast Asia, or the Indian subcontinent. It includes people who identify themselves as Burmese, Pakistani, Thai, Malaysian, or Singaporean. At the same time the Immigration and Naturalization Service broadly counts Asian immigrants to include people from Southwest Asian countries such as Iran, Israel, and Turkey. As a result, important distinctions and qualification must be made.

First of all, this book concentrates on the most prominent Asian American ethnic groups in the United States. They are Chinese American, Japanese American, Filipino American, Korean American, Asian Indians, and Southeast Asian refugees consisting of Vietnamese, Cambodians, Laotian, and Hmong Americans. Second, this book focuses on the Asian American experience as a distinct minority in the continental United States. Although I recognize the overall importance of Hawaii in the history of Asian Americans, I do not discuss the Asian American experience in Hawaii in great detail. Asian Americans are the majority population in Hawaii, and their experience is quite different from other Asian Americans on the mainland. For example, Japanese Americans in Hawaii were not interned during World War II, whereas more than 110,000 Japanese Americans on the mainland were forcibly incarcerated.

Because I do not focus heavily on Hawaii or the Pacific Islander population, I generally prefer to use the term *Asian American,* rather than *Asian Pacific Americans* or *Asian Pacific Islander Americans.* However, some individuals quoted and some sources cited throughout this book do use the Asian Pacific terms and there are occasions when these terms will be used in the text for the sake of consistency. As stated above, the Native Hawaiian and Other Pacific Islander population was listed as a separate race category in the 2000 census. Most, but not all, general statistical tables generated from the 2000 census disaggregate Asian American and Native Hawaiian and Pacific Islander populations. Because I focus on the Asian American experience after the 1965 Immigration Reform Act, I generally refer to all persons of Asian ancestry living in the United States as Asian Americans. I do this because the overwhelming majority of Asian immigrants and refugees who have come to the United States after 1965 did so fully intending to settle down and become U.S. citizens. Despite obvious ethnic and language differences within this broadly defined group, the term Asian American *is* significant and meaningful. The Asian American groups listed above have been shaped by similar historical experiences in the United States, and today they confront a myriad of common issues. I examine many of these common issues and show that Asian Americans continue to face prejudice, discrimination, and racially motivated violence that clearly hinder their full and open participation in American society. At the same time, this book is not only about social problems. The increasing number of highly educated, motivated, and talented Asian Americans is an asset to the United States in terms of economic growth and cultural enrichment. I highlight these aspects of the Asian American experience as well. Lastly, this book shows the similarities and differences between Asian Americans and other racial, ethnic, and immigrant groups to emphasize that the post-1965 contemporary Asian American experience challenges any easy definition or theoretical analysis.

ORGANIZATION OF THE BOOK

Based on the Asian American contemporary issues course I have been teaching for the past several years, the organization of this book flows sequentially, with each chapter building on information from previous chapters. Chapter 1 starts with a history of the Asian American experience in the United States and discusses the tremendous changes for Asian Americans after 1965. A historical overview is highly instructive to show the dramatic progress made by Asian Americans, as well as disturbing trends and animosities that continue to this day. Chapter 2 provides a demographic and socioeconomic profile of Asian Americans, featuring the latest data on settlement patterns, geographic dispersion, ethnic entrepreneurship, consumer buying power, as well as a critical analysis of the popular "model minority" image of Asian Americans today. Chapter 3 examines the highly touted success of Asian Americans in education and highlights several theories for this phenomenon. It also looks beyond the generalized statistics and addresses several educational issues confronting Asian Americans in school (K–12) through college.

I then shift from the classroom to the workplace. Chapter 4 focuses on the subtleties of discrimination in the workplace, which, on close examination, are not so subtle at all. Chapter 5 details the issue of anti-Asian violence. Key to this chapter is a discussion of four factors that encourage and perpetuate anti-Asian hostility, along with a closer look at the volatile issue of Asian American and African American relations. Because much of the anti-Asian sentiment and violence stems from negative images of Asians in the media, Chapter 6 provides coverage and analysis of stereotypes of Asian Americans in film and other media. The chapter not only offers a historical perspective but also looks at very recent examples, and shows how Asian American media artists and activist groups are trying to raise awareness about these issues.

Certain images of Asian Americans are perpetuated in the media, but the realities of Asian American life are constantly changing. Chapter 7 looks at Asian American families and identities, with particular emphasis on diversity and new transformations. Important cutting-edge issues such as identity formation, interracial marriage, biracial Asian Americans, gay and lesbian Asian Americans, and international adoption are included in this chapter. Lastly, Chapter 8 addresses the issue of Asian American political empowerment. The chapter begins with an overview of electoral and nonelectoral empowerment efforts by Asian Americans, and it ends with an examination of the important role of Asian Americans in several recent national, state, and local elections.

PERSPECTIVE OF THE BOOK

This book focuses on some of the most important issues confronting Asian Americans since 1965 that are likely to continue to be seen in one form or another in the future. I highlight each of the major issues within a broader historical context and from an interdisciplinary perspective. This book also draws attention to how various issues such as images in the media, anti-immigrant sentiment, and anti-Asian violence interrelate, and I analyze how the concepts of race, class, and gender intersect throughout the Asian American experience.

The Contemporary Asian American Experience is deeply rooted in many of the ideals first articulated during the founding years of the Asian American movement following the 1968 student strike at San Francisco State College (now San Francisco State University). One of the most important ideals that emerged from the student strike was the need to make education relevant. This means taking knowledge from academic institutions that can be useful to students outside of the classroom walls and beyond the final exam. At the same time, this book is also clearly centered in the new thinking on the Asian American movement as a political force and Asian American studies as an academic discipline.

Shirley Hune, professor of urban planning at the University of California, Los Angeles, has written extensively on the changes in thinking about the contemporary Asian American experience. Within this, she has called for "paradigm shifts," which are alterations of commonly held worldviews and values among people. In her article, "Rethinking Race: Paradigms and Policy Formation" (1995), Hune raises the point that race relations in the United States have historically been very narrowly focused. She questions what she calls the "vertical" model of race relations that depicts whites on top of the socioeconomic and political hierarchy, with all other nonwhites flailing below. She prefers to view race relations in a "horizontal" fashion that recognizes not only racial factors but also the importance of class and gender factors that cut across racial lines. "The relations between Asian American small business owners and their non-Asian employees and clientele, new multiracial and multiethnic residential patterns, biracial families, the growing class disparities within racial/ethnic groups, the shift in party affiliation and voting preferences of racial groups from Democrats to Republicans and other indicators give rise to rethinking race relations," Hune writes.[22]

Second, Hune challenges the presumption that race is a relatively fixed biological phenomenon and that social inequalities experienced by racial minorities are largely determined by biological factors. Instead, Hune draws on Michael Omi and Howard Winant's "racial formation" theory that argues race is in fact a constantly changing socially constructed phenomenon. This means race relations are extremely dynamic and continually being redefined. Racial formation theory identifies the combination of both micro (discourse, meaning) and macro (government policies, social institutions) levels of conflict and cooperation. It also helps to explain why Asian Americans have experienced periods of relatively calm race relations, other periods of intense hostility, and sometimes heightened racial antagonism against one Asian American group but not another.[23]

Third, Hune points to the fact that Asian Americans for the most part have been studied separately from one another and studies on individual groups (i.e., Chinese, Japanese, Filipino, Asian Indian, Korean, and Southeast Asians) are far more numerous than studies that address Asian Americans as a whole. "This approach was a necessary beginning for Asian American studies as it sought to reclaim its historic place in American history and culture," Hune writes. "However, this paradigm results in descriptions of ethnic-specific experiences that are circumscribed, while assumed to be representative of the entire community."[24] She calls for a new paradigm that explicitly and accurately compares *and* contrasts the diverse Asian American experiences. This new paradigm called for by Hune is seen throughout this book's content and organization.

Fourth, early research on the Asian American experience has often viewed Asian Americans as victims of racial, economic, and political subjugation in the United States. Some Asian American scholars and activists have perpetuated this image in an effort to rally political unity. However, Hune argues that the historic and contemporary Asian American experience has shown a far greater tendency and willingness to confront, organize, and challenge oppressive situations they face. Asian Americans are shown throughout this book fighting against the glass ceiling, educational discrimination, anti-Asian violence, distortions in the media, and political isolation. At the same time, Hune also acknowledges what she calls "differential power and agency." She recognizes that certain groups of Asian Americans face more hardships and limitations. The difficulties of the poor, the uneducated, the limited English speakers, and recent immigrants and refugees should not be ignored.[25] Good examples from this book can be seen in detailed descriptions of the garment workers' struggle against Jessica McClintock and the abuses of the garment industry, along with the campaigns aimed at encouraging voter registration and participation among new immigrants.

Lastly, Hune addresses the need to see the new immigrant experience as fundamental to the contemporary Asian American experience. The early evolution of Asian American studies rejected any connection with Asian studies, or the study of regions of Asia, in the belief that the Asian American experience was unique and had nothing to do with what happened in Asia. Today, many Asian American studies scholars are acknowledging the importance of analyzing the Asian American experience from a global perspective. This can be seen in the transnational movement of people, capital, consumer markets, interpersonal networks, culture, and technology from Asia to the United States described in various sections in this book. This can also be seen in the dramatic impact Asian immigrants have made in the demographic, social, cultural, and political life in urban and suburban communities across the nation.

Taken together, these paradigm shifts are the mainstays for present and future thinking about Asian Americans, and I address them all in this book. The rapid growth of the Asian American population, the expanding research and scholarship on Asian American issues, and the continued commitment by Asian American artists and activists are the catalysts for tremendous change and progress. The Asian American experience, continually unfolding and redeveloping, is extremely dynamic.

COMMENTS ON THE THIRD EDITION

The third edition of this book provides the most up-to-date statistics on Asian Americans available. Much of the information provided in this book can be found on the U.S. Bureau of the Census Web site at http://www.census.gov. The Asian American experience, of course, goes far beyond statistics. Since the publication of the first edition (1998) and the second edition (2002), numerous high-profile events involving Asian Americans have taken place. The terrorist attack on September 11, 2001, is the most obvious example, but there are many more cited throughout this book. Hate crime is a major concern as Asian Americans continue to be the targets of violent incidents (Chapter 5). The 2004 election season brought Asian Americans into the forefront of political interest and activism as never before (Chapter 8). New and engaging research on the Asian American experience is highlighted throughout this third edition. Along with the updates, this edition also includes updated sections on Asian American consumer spending (Chapter 2), Asian Americans in the media and in sports (Chapter 6), and on the growing number of overseas adoptees from Korea who were raised in the United States (Chapter 7). I view the various editions of this book as fluid and living documents that chronicle the social, cultural, economic, and political changes among the various Asian American groups.

I am interested in your comments about this book and the topics covered. I also welcome any suggestions for improvement, citations for additional readings or research studies on existing topics, and recommendations for additional topics. You can e-mail me at tfong01@csus.edu. I will write back and I look forward to the exchange of new ideas.

NOTES

1. Quotes in Emily Bazar, "Ex-Spy Suspect Receives Award, Hero's Welcome," *Sacramento Bee*, November 22, 2004.
2. Quoted in Vernon Loeb, "Los Alamos Scientist Released," *Washington Post*, September 14, 2000. Two books on Wen Ho Lee have recently been published. See Dan Stober and Ian Hoffman, *A Convenient Spy: Wen Ho Lee and the Politics of Nuclear Espionage* (New York: Simon & Schuster, 2001) and Wen Ho Lee with Helen Zia, *My Country Versus Me: The First-Hand Account by the Los Alamos Scientist Who Was Falsely Accused of Being a Spy* (New York: Hyperion, 2001).
3. "APIs 'Outraged' Over Lee's Treatment," *AsianWeek*, June 15, 2000.
4. Quoted in Tom Raum, "Republicans Capitalize on Espionage Allegations," *AsianWeek*, April 1, 1999.
5. Quoted in Vernon Loeb, "China Spy Report Ignites Outcry," *Washington Post*, May 26, 1999.
6. Robert Scheer, "The Wen Ho Lee 'Case' Is Quickly Evaporating," *Sacramento Bee*, July 13, 2000. On January 20, 2001, President Clinton pardoned John Deutch. The pardon spared the former spy director any criminal charges for mishandling secret information on his home computer. Deutch had been considering a deal with the Justice Department in which he would plead guilty to a misdemeanor charge of keeping classified data on home computers.

7. Quoted in Neil A. Lewis, "Wen Ho Lee Case Exposes Flaws in Racial Profiling," *New York Times,* September 17, 2000.
8. Sam Chu Lin, "Radio Tirade," *AsianWeek,* April 5, 1996.
9. Edward T. Chang, "America's First Multiethnic 'Riots'," in Karin Aguilar-San Juan (ed.), *The State of Asian America: Activism and Resistance* (Boston: South End Press, 1994), pp. 101, 114.
10. Michael McQueen, "Voters' Response to Poll Disclose Huge Chasm Between Social Attitudes of Blacks and Whites," *Wall Street Journal,* May 17, 1991.
11. Carla Rivera, "Asians Say They Fare Better Than Other Minorities," *Los Angeles Times,* August 20, 1993.
12. Steven A. Holmes, "Survey Finds Minorities Resent One Another Almost as Much as They Do Whites," *New York Times,* March 3, 1994.
13. Marsha Ginsburg, "Crisis Inflames Bias Against Asians," *San Francisco Chronicle,* April 14, 2001 and Chisun Lee, "Fun With China," *Village Voice,* April 25–May 1, 2001.
14. K. Connie Kang, "Study Finds Persistent Negative Perceptions of Chinese Americans," *Los Angeles Times,* April 25, 2001.
15. Quoted in Associated Press State and Local Wire, "N.C. Congressman Says Internment of Japanese-Americans During World War II Was Appropriate," February 5, 2003.
16. Japanese American Citizen's League Press Release, "Rep. Coble Reneges on Agreement to Meet," July 10, 2003.
17. Jim Schlosser, "Groups Call on Cobel to Resign Chair: The Greensboro Congressman Says He Won't Apologize for Comments about Japanese Americans and Arab Americans," *Greensboro News & Record,* February 8, 2003.
18. Quoted in Steve Geissinger, "Asian Caucus to Fete Former Accused Spy: New Patriotic Group Upset with Lawmakers Honoring Wen Ho Lee," *Alameda Times-Star,* June 4, 2004.
19. Quotes in "Lee Clash Angers Caucus: Group Had Planned to Honor Lab Scientist," *San Francisco Chronicle,* June 9, 2004.
20. Paul Ong and Suzanne J. Hee. "The Growth of the Asian Pacific American Population: Twenty Million in 2020," in *The State of Asian Pacific America: Policy Issues to the Year 2020* (Los Angeles: LEAP Asian Pacific American Public Policy Institute and UCLA Asian American Studies Center, 1993), pp. 11–23 and *U.S Census Bureau News,* "Census Bureau Projects Tripling" March 18, 2004, at http://www.census.gov/Press-Release/www/releases/archives/population/ 001720.html.
21. For more details, see U.S. Census Bureau, "Overview of Race and Hispanic Origin, 2000" (March 2001) at http://www.census.gov/prod/2001pubs/c2kbr01-1.pdf.
22. Shirley Hune, "Rethinking Race: Paradigms and Policy Formation," *Amerasia Journal* 21:1&2 (1995): 29–40.
23. Ibid., pp. 31–32; also see Michael Omi and Howard Winant, *Racial Formation in the United States: From the 1960s to the 1980s* (New York: Routledge and Kegan Paul, 1986).
24. Ibid., p. 33.
25. Ibid., pp. 32–33.

1

~

The History of Asians in America

VISIBILITY AND INVISIBILITY

In November 2004, Public Television (PBS) aired a four-part series, *They Made America*, profiling sixty-four influential innovators and entrepreneurs who gave birth to commercial milestones like the steamboat and important cultural symbols like the Barbie Doll. This seemingly innocent documentary series touched a raw nerve to *AsianWeek* columnist Emil Guillermo who began a personal campaign to boycott the program. The cause of Guillermo's angst was that out of all the individuals highlighted, not one was Asian American. The series is based on the book by the same name by Sir Harold Evans, the author of the acclaimed *New York Times* bestseller *The American Century* and Editor at Large of *The Week* magazine. Evans was also the founding editor of *Condé Nast Traveler*, editorial director of *U.S. News & World Report*, and president of Random House, where he published a record number of bestsellers. "That should give you the book's perspective in a nutshell," Guillermo writes. "It's a British snob's Eastern-elitist view of American history . . . So, of course, in that context, the heroes will never be the oppressed, the workers, the slaves, the ones exploited by the boardrooms and financiers on whose labor the profits are made." Although three African Americans were highlighted in the television series, Guillermo complained, "In technology alone, the failure to include an Asian American on the list is pretty curious . . . A little perspective and balance would have been more than helpful for the show and book. It would have been accurate." Guillermo was particularly offended that the series and the book are being heavily marketed to public schools for inclusion in the core U.S. history curriculum. "An all-white history presented to schools that are majority Asian, black and Latino just makes a mockery of the diversity that's all around us."[1]

Guillermo's observations speak loudly to the fact that Asian Americans are at once visible, yet invisible. This is particularly true with regard to the history of Asians in the United States. The historical experience of Asian Americans is not at all atypical of other minority groups. As a distinct racial minority group, and as immigrants, Asian Americans faced enormous individual prejudice, frequent mob violence, and extreme forms of institutional discrimination. But Asian Americans have not merely been victims of hostility and oppression; indeed, they have also shown remarkable strength and perseverance, which is a testimony to their desire to make the United States their home.

A BRIEF HISTORY OF ASIANS IN AMERICA

Immigration

Between 1848 and 1924, hundreds of thousands of immigrants from China, Japan, the Philippines, Korea, and India came to the United States in search of a better life and livelihood. Although this period represents the first significant wave, these immigrants were by no means the very first Asians to come to America. Recent archaeological finds off the coast of Southern California have led to speculation that the West Coast may have been visited by Buddhist missionaries from China in the fifth century. Direct evidence of this claim is still being debated, but it is known that the Spanish brought Chinese shipbuilders to Baja California as early as 1571, and later Filipino seamen were brought by Spanish galleons from Manila and settled along the coast of Louisiana. Chinese merchants and sailors also were present in the United States prior to the discovery of gold in California in 1848. Most people are unaware that Asian Indians were brought to America during the late eighteenth century as indentured servants and slaves.[2]

The California gold rush did not immediately ignite a mass rush of Chinese immigrants to America. In fact, only a few hundred Chinese arrived in California during the first years of the gold rush, and most of them were merchants. However, large-scale immigration did begin in earnest in 1852 when 52,000 Chinese arrived that year alone. Many Chinese came to the United States not only to seek their fortunes but also to escape political and economic turmoil in China. As gold ran out, thousands of Chinese were recruited in the mid-1860s to work on the transcontinental railroad. Eventually more than 300,000 Chinese entered the United States in the nineteenth century, engaging in a variety of occupations. During this same period Chinese also immigrated to Hawaii, but in far fewer numbers than to the continental United States.[3]

Large capitalist and financial interests welcomed the Chinese as cheap labor and lobbied for the 1868 Burlingame Treaty, which recognized "free migration and emigration" of Chinese to the United States in exchange for American trade privileges in China. As early as 1870 Chinese were 9 percent of California's population and 25 percent of the state's work force.[4] The majority of these Chinese were young single men who intended to work a few years and then return to China. Those who stayed seldom married because of laws severely limiting the immigration of Chinese women and prohibiting intermarriage with white women. The result was the Chinese were forced to live a harsh and lonely bachelor life that often featured vice and prostitution. In 1890, for example, there were roughly 102,620 Chinese men and only 3,868 Chinese women in the United States, a male-to-female ratio of 26:1.[5] Despite these conditions, Chinese workers continued to come to the United States.

Following the completion of the transcontinental railroad in 1869, large numbers of unemployed Chinese workers had to find new sources of employment. Many found work in agriculture where they cleared land, dug canals, planted orchards, harvested crops, and were the foundation for successful commercial production of many California crops. Others settled in San Francisco and other cities to manufacture shoes, cigars, and clothing. Still others started small businesses such as restaurants, laundries, and general stores. Domestic service such as house boys, cooks, and gardeners were also other areas of employment for the Chinese. In short, the Chinese were involved in many occupations that were crucial to the economic development and domestication of the western region of the United States.[6] Unfortunately, intense hostility against the Chinese reached its peak in 1882 when Congress passed the Chinese Exclusion Act intended to "suspend" the entry of Chinese laborers for ten years. Other laws were eventually passed that barred Chinese laborers and their wives permanently.[7]

The historical experience of the Japanese in the United States is both different yet similar to that of the Chinese. One major difference is that the Japanese immigrated in large numbers to Hawaii; they did not come in large numbers to the United States until the 1890s. In 1880 only 148 Japanese were living on the U.S. mainland. In 1890 this number increased to 2,000, mostly merchants and students. However, the population increased dramatically when an influx of 38,000 Japanese workers from Hawaii arrived in the U.S. mainland between 1902 and 1907.[8] The second difference was that the Japanese were able to fully exploit an economic niche in agriculture that the Chinese had only started. The completion of several national railroad lines and the invention of the refrigerator car were two advancements that brought tremendous expansion in the California produce industry. The early Japanese were fortunate to arrive at an opportune time, and about two thirds of them found work as agricultural laborers. Within a short time the Japanese were starting their own farms in direct competition with non-Japanese farms. By 1919 the Japanese controlled over 450,000 acres of agricultural land. Although this figure represents only 1 percent of active California agricultural land at the time, the Japanese were so efficient in their farming practices that they captured 10 percent of the dollar volume of the state's crops.[9]

The third major difference was the emergence of Japan as an international military power at the turn of the century. Japan's victory in the Russo-Japanese War (1904–1905) impressed President Theodore Roosevelt, and he believed a strategy of cooperation with the Japanese government was in the best interest of the United States. Roosevelt blocked calls for complete Japanese exclusion and instead worked a compromise with the Japanese government in 1907 known as the "Gentleman's Agreement." This agreement halted the immigration of Japanese laborers but allowed Japanese women into the United States. With this in mind, the fourth difference was that the Japanese in the United States were able to actually increase in population, start families, and establish a rather stable community life.[10]

Filipino immigration began after the United States gained possession of the Philippines following the Spanish-American War in 1898. The first Filipinos to arrive were a few hundred *pensionados,* or students supported by government scholarships. Similar to the Japanese experience, a large number of Filipinos went directly to Hawaii before coming to the U.S. mainland. Between 1907 and 1919, more than 28,000 Filipinos were actively recruited to work on sugar plantations in Hawaii. Filipinos began to emigrate to the U.S. mainland following the passage of the 1924 Immigration Act, which prohibited all Asian immigration to this country, and the increasing need for agricultural and service labor.[11]

Because Filipinos lived on American territory, they were "nationals" who were free to travel in the United States without restriction. In the 1920s, more than 45,000 Filipinos arrived in Pacific Coast ports, and a 1930 study found 30,000 Filipinos working in California. These Filipinos were overwhelmingly young, single males. Their ages ranged between 16 and 29, and there were 14 Filipino men for every Filipina. Sixty percent of these Filipinos worked as migratory agricultural laborers, and 25 percent worked in domestic service in Los Angeles and San Francisco. The rest found work in manufacturing and as railroad porters. Unlike the Japanese, Filipinos did not make their mark in agriculture as farmers, but as labor union organizers.[12] Both Filipino farmworker activism and Japanese farm competition created a great deal of resentment among white farmers and laborers.

Koreans and Asian Indians slightly predated the Filipinos, but arrived in much smaller numbers. Between 1903 and 1905, more than 7,000 Koreans were recruited for plantation labor work in Hawaii, but after Japan established a protectorate over Korea in 1905, all emigration was halted.[13] In the next five years, Japan increased its economic and political power and formally annexed Korea in 1910. Relatively few Koreans lived in the United States between 1905 and 1940. Among those included about one thousand workers who migrated from Hawaii, about one hundred Korean "picture brides," and a small number of American-born Koreans. The Korean population in the United States during that time was also bolstered by roughly nine hundred students, many of whom fled their home country because of their opposition to Japanese rule. Like other Asian immigrant groups, Koreans found themselves concentrated in California agriculture working primarily as laborers, although a small number did become quite successful farmers.[14]

The first significant flow of Asian Indians occurred between 1904 and 1911, when just over 6,000 arrived in the United States. Unlike the other Asian groups, Asian Indians did not work in Hawaii prior to entering the U.S. mainland, but they did work primarily in California agriculture. Similar to the Chinese, Filipinos, and Koreans, they had an extremely high male-to-female ratio. Of the

Asian Indians who immigrated to the United States between 1904 and 1911, there were only three or four women, all of whom were married.[15] Eighty to ninety percent of the first Asian Indian settlers in the United States were Sikhs, a distinct ethno-religious minority group in India. Despite this fact, these Sikhs were often called Hindus, which they are not. Sikhs were easily recognizable from other Asian immigrant groups because of their huskier build, their turbans, and their beards. But like other Asians in the United States at the time, they also worked primarily in California's agricultural industry. Asian Indians first worked as farmworkers and, like the Japanese, they also formed cooperatives, pooled their resources, and began independent farming.[16] Immigration restrictions, their relatively small numbers, and an exaggerated male-to-female ratio prevented Asian Indians from developing a lasting farm presence. One major exception can be found in the Marysville/Yuba City area of Northern California, where Asian Indian Sikhs are still quite active in producing cling peaches.[17]

Anti-Asian Laws and Sentiment

The United States is a nation that claims to welcome and assimilate all newcomers. But the history of immigration, naturalization, and equal treatment under the law for Asian Americans has been an extremely difficult one. In 1790 Congress passed the first naturalization law limiting citizenship rights to only a "free white person."[18] During the period of reconstruction in the 1870s following the Civil War, Congress amended the law and allowed citizenship for "aliens of African nativity and persons of African descent."[19] For a while there was some discussion of expanding naturalization rights to Chinese immigrants, but that idea was rejected by politicians from western states.[20] This rejection is exemplary of the intense anti-Chinese sentiment at the time.

As early as 1850 California imposed the Foreign Miners Tax, which required the payment of $20 a month from all foreign miners.[21] The California Supreme Court ruled in *People v. Hall* (1854) that Chinese could not testify in court against a white person. This case threw out the testimony of three Chinese witnesses and reversed the murder conviction of George W. Hall, who was sentenced to hang for the murder of a Chinese man one year earlier.[22] In 1855 a local San Francisco ordinance levied a $50 tax on all aliens ineligible for citizenship. Because Chinese were ineligible for citizenship under the Naturalization Act of 1790, they were the primary targets for this law.[23]

The racially distinct Chinese were the primary scapegoats for the depressed economy in the 1870s, and mob violence erupted on several occasions through the 1880s. The massacre of twenty-one Chinese in Los Angeles in 1871 and twenty-eight Chinese in Rock Springs, Wyoming, in 1885 are examples of the worst incidents. It is within this environment that Congress passed the 1882 Chinese Exclusion Act. The act suspended immigration of Chinese laborers for only ten years, but it was extended in 1892 and 1902. The act was eventually extended indefinitely in 1904.[24] The intense institutional discrimination achieved the desired result: The Chinese population declined from 105,465 in 1880 to 61,639 in 1920.[25]

Anti-Chinese sentiment easily grew into large-scale anti-Asian sentiment as immigrants from Asia continued to enter the United States. During the same period that the Chinese population declined, the Japanese population grew and became highly visible. As early as 1910 there were 72,157 Japanese Americans compared to 71,531 Chinese Americans in the United States.[26] Japanese farmers in California were particularly vulnerable targets for animosity. One of the most sweeping anti-Asian laws was aimed at the Japanese Americans but affected all other Asian American groups as well. The 1913 Alien Land Law prohibited "aliens ineligible to citizenship" from owning or leasing land for more than three years. Initially, Japanese Americans were able to bypass the law primarily because they could buy or lease land under the names of their American-born offspring (the *Nisei*), who were U.S. citizens by birth. The law was strengthened in 1920, however, and the purchase of land under the names of American-born offspring was prohibited.[27]

Several sweeping anti-immigration laws were passed in the first quarter of the twentieth century that served to eliminate Asian immigration to the United States. A provision in the 1917 Immigration Act banned immigration from the so-called "Asian barred zone," except for the Philippines and Japan. A more severe anti-Asian restriction was further imposed by the 1924 National Origins Act, which placed a ceiling of 150,000 new immigrants per year. The 1924 act was intended to limit eastern and southern European immigration, but a provision was added that ended any immigration by aliens ineligible for citizenship.[28]

Asian Americans did not sit back passively in the face of discriminatory laws; they hired lawyers and went to court to fight for their livelihoods, naturalization rights, and personal liberties. Sometimes they were successful, but oftentimes they were not. In the case of *Yick Wo v. Hopkins* (1886), Chinese successfully challenged an 1880 San Francisco Laundry Ordinance, which regulated commercial laundry service in a way that clearly discriminated against the Chinese. Plaintiff Yick Wo had operated a laundry service for twenty-two years, but when he tried to renew his business license in 1885 he was turned down because his storefront was made out of wood. Two hundred other Chinese laundries were also denied business licenses on similar grounds, although eighty non-Chinese laundries in wooden buildings were approved. The Supreme Court ruled in favor of Yick Wo, concluding there was "no reason" for the denial of the business license "except to the face and nationality" of the petitioner.[29]

The inability to gain citizenship was a defining factor throughout the early history of Asian Americans. The constitutionality of naturalization based on race was first challenged in the Supreme Court case of *Ozawa v. United States* (1922). Takao Ozawa was born in Japan but immigrated to the United States at an early age. He graduated from Berkeley High School in California and attended the University of California for three years. Ozawa was a model immigrant who did not smoke or drink, he attended a predominantly white church, his children attended public school, and English was the language spoken at home. When Ozawa was rejected in his initial attempt for naturalization, he appealed and argued that the provisions for citizenship in the 1790 and 1870 acts did not specifically exclude Japanese. In addition, Ozawa also tried to argue that Japanese should be considered "white."

The Court unanimously ruled against Ozawa on both grounds. First, the Court decided that initial framers of the law and its amendment did not intend to *exclude* people from naturalization but, instead, only determine who would be *included*. Ozawa was denied citizenship because the existing law simply didn't include Japanese. Second, the Court also ruled against Ozawa's argument that Japanese were actually more "white" than other darker skinned "white" people such as some Italians, Spanish, and Portuguese. The Court clarified the matter by defining a "white person" to be synonymous with a "person of the Caucasian race." In short, Ozawa was not Caucasian (although he thought himself "white") and, thus, was ineligible for citizenship.[30]

Prior to the *Ozawa* case, Asian Indians already enjoyed the right of naturalization. In *United States v. Balsara* (1910), the Supreme Court determined that Asian Indians were Caucasian and approximately seventy became naturalized citizens. But the Immigration and Naturalization Service (INS) challenged this decision, and it was taken up again in the case of *United States v. Thind* (1923). This time the Supreme Court reversed its earlier decision and ruled that Bhagat Singh Thind could not be a citizen because he was not "white." Even though Asian Indians were classified as Caucasian, this was a scientific term that was inconsistent with the popular understanding. The Court's decision stated, "It may be true that the blond Scandinavian and the brown Hindu have a common ancestor in the dim reaches of antiquity, but the average man knows perfectly well that there are unmistakable differences between them today."[31] In other words, only "white" Caucasians were considered eligible for U.S. citizenship. In the wake of the *Thind* decision, the INS was able to cancel retroactively the citizenship of Asian Indians between 1923 and 1926.

Asian Americans also received disparate treatment compared to other immigrants in their most private affairs, such as marriage. In the nineteenth century, antimiscegenation laws prohibiting marriage between blacks and whites were common throughout the United States. In 1880 the California legislature extended restrictive antimiscegenation categories to prohibit any marriage between a white person and a "negro, mulatto, or Mongolian." This law, targeted at the Chinese, was not challenged until Salvador Roldan won a California Court of Appeals decision in 1933. Roldan, a Filipino American, argued that he was Malay, not Mongolian, and he should be allowed to marry his white fiancée. The Court conceded that the state's antimiscegenation law was created in an atmosphere of intense anti-Chinese sentiment, and agreed Filipinos were not in mind when the initial legislation was approved. Unfortunately, this victory was short-lived. The California state legislature amended the antimiscegenation law to include the "Malay race" shortly after the Roldan decision was announced.[32]

World War II and the Cold War Era

For Asian Americans, World War II was an epoch, but the profound impact was distinct for different Asian American groups. For more than 110,000 Japanese

Americans, World War II was an agonizing ordeal soon after Japan's attack of Pearl Harbor on December 7, 1941. The FBI arrested thousands of Japanese Americans who were considered potential security threats immediately after the Pearl Harbor bombing raid. Arrested without evidence of disloyalty were the most visible Japanese American community leaders, including businessmen, Shinto and Buddhist priests, teachers in Japanese-language schools, and editors of Japanese-language newspapers. Wartime hysteria rose to a fever pitch, and on February 19, 1942, President Franklin Roosevelt issued Executive Order 9066. This order established various military zones and authorized the removal of any-one who was a potential threat. Although a small number of German and Italian aliens were detained and relocated, this did not compare to the mass relocation of Japanese Americans on the West Coast of the United States.[33]

The order to relocate Japanese Americans because of military necessity and the threat they posed to security, was a fabrication. Even military leaders debated the genuine need for mass relocation, and the government's own intelligence reports found no evidence of Japanese American disloyalty. "For the most part the local Japanese are loyal to the United States or, at worst, hope that by remaining quiet they can avoid concentration camps or irrespon-sible mobs," one report stated. "We do not believe that they would be at least any more disloyal than any other racial group in the United States with whom we went to war."[34] This helps explain why 160,000 Japanese Americans living in Hawaii were not interned. More telling was the fact that Japanese Americans in the continental United States were a small but much resented minority. Despite government reports to the contrary, business leaders, local politicians, and the media fueled antagonism against the Japanese Americans and agi-tated for their abrupt removal.[35]

With only seven days' notice to prepare once the internment order was issued, and no way of knowing how long the war would last, many Japanese Americans were forced to sell their homes and property at a mere fraction of their genuine value. Japanese Americans suffered estimated economic losses alone of at least $400 million. By August 1942 all the Japanese on the West Coast were interned in ten camps located in rural regions of California, Arizona, Utah, Idaho, Wyoming, and Arkansas. Two thirds of the interned Japanese American men, women, and children were U.S. citizens whose only crime was their ances-try; even those with as little as one-eighth Japanese blood were interned. The camps themselves were crude mass facilities surrounded by barbed wire and guarded by armed sentries. People were housed in large barracks with each fam-ily living in small cramped quarters dubbed "apartments." Food was served in large mess halls, and toilet and shower facilities were communal. Many of the camps were extremely cold in the winter, hot in the summer, and dusty all year round. The camps remained open for the duration of the war.[36]

After the first year of the camps, the government began recruiting young Japanese American men to help in the war effort. The military desperately needed Japanese Americans to serve as interpreters for Japanese prisoners of war and translators of captured documents. But to the military's incredulity, most American-born Japanese had only modest Japanese language skills and needed intense training in the Military Intelligence Service Language School before they could perform their duties.[37] It was, however, the heroic actions of the 100th Infantry Battalion, which later merged with the 442nd Regimental Combat Team, that stand out the most to historians. The two segregated units, made up of Japanese Americans, engaged in numerous campaigns and served with distinction throughout Europe. By the end of the war in Europe, for example, the Nisei soldiers of the 442nd suffered over 9,000 casualties, and earned more than 18,000 individual decorations of honor. The 442nd was the most decorated unit of its size during all of World War II.[38]

Compared to the Japanese American experience, other Asian American groups fared far better during and after World War II. Changes for Chinese Americans were particularly dramatic. Prior to the war, the image of the Chinese was clearly negative compared to the Japanese. A survey of Princeton undergraduates in 1931 thought the top three traits of the Chinese were that they were "superstitious, sly, and conservative," whereas Japanese were considered "intelligent, industrious, and progressive."[39] Immediately after the bombing of Pearl Harbor, Chinese store owners put up signs indicating they were not Japanese, and in some cases Chinese Americans wore buttons stating, "I am Chinese." To alleviate any further identification problems, *Time* magazine published an article on December 22, 1941, explaining how to tell the difference between Chinese and "Japs." The article compared photographs of a Chinese man and a Japanese man, highlighting the distinguishing facial features of each.[40] Just months later, a 1942 Gallup Poll characterized the Chinese as "hardworking, honest, and brave," and Japanese were seen as "treacherous, sly, and cruel."[41]

Employment opportunities outside the segregated Chinatown community became available to Chinese Americans for the first time during the war and continued after the war ended. Chinese Americans trained in various professions and skilled crafts were able to find work in war-related industries that had never been open to them before. In addition, the employment of Chinese American women increased threefold during the 1940s. Leading the way were clerical positions, which increased from just 750 in 1940 to 3,200 in 1950. In 1940 women represented just one in five Chinese American professionals, but by 1950 this increased to one in three. On another level, Chinese actors suddenly found they were in demand for film roles—usually playing evil Japanese characters. Shortly after the war, writers such as Jade Snow Wong and Pardee Lowe discovered the newfound interest and appreciation of Chinese Americans could be turned into commercial success through the publication of their memoirs.[42]

On the military front, Asian Americans also distinguished themselves. Over 15,000 Chinese Americans served in all branches of the military, unlike the Japanese Americans who were placed only in segregated infantry units and in the Military Intelligence Service. Similarly, more than 7,000 Filipino Americans volunteered for the army and formed the First and Second Filipino Infantry Regiments. About one thousand other Filipino Americans were sent to the Philippines to perform reconnaissance and intelligence activities for Gen. Douglas MacArthur.[43] Equally significant was the War Bride's Act of 1945, which allowed war veterans to bring wives from China and the Philippines as nonquota immigrants. This resulted in a rapid and dramatic shift in the historic gender imbalance of both groups. For example, between 1945 and 1952, nine out of ten (89.9 percent) Chinese immigrants were female, and 20,000 Chinese American babies were born by the mid-1950s. Similarly, between 1951 and 1960 seven out of ten (71 percent) Filipino immigrants were female.[44]

On the broad international front, alliances with China, the Philippines, and India eventually began the process of changing the overtly discriminatory immigration laws against Asians. The Chinese Exclusion Law was repealed in 1943, and an annual quota of 105 immigrants from China was allotted. In 1946 Congress approved legislation that extended citizenship to Filipino immigrants and permitted the entry of one hundred Filipino immigrants annually. Also in 1946, the Luce-Cellar Act ended the 1917 "Asian barred zone," allowing an immigration quota of one hundred from India, and permitted Asian Indians to apply for citizenship for the first time since the *United States v. Thind* case of 1923. Although these changes were extremely modest, they carried important symbolic weight by helping create a favorable international opinion of the United States during and immediately after the war.[45]

Geopolitical events during the Cold War era of the 1950s and 1960s immediately following World War II continued to have important ramifications for Asian Americans. After the 1949 Communist Revolution in China, about five thousand Chinese students and young professionals were living in the United States. These "stranded" individuals were generally from China's most elite and educated families and not necessarily anxious to return to China because their property had already been confiscated and their livelihoods threatened. They were eventually allowed to stay in the United States.[46] Several other refugee acts in the late 1950s and early 1960s allowed some 18,000 other Chinese to enter and stay in the United States. Many of these refugees were well-trained scientists and engineers who easily found jobs in private industry and in research universities. These educated professionals were quite distinct from the vast majority of earlier Chinese immigrants because they usually were able to integrate into the American mainstream quickly, becoming the basis of an emerging Chinese American middle class.[47]

The Cold War affected immigration from Asian countries as well, but in a very different fashion. During and after the Korean War (1950–1953), American soldiers often met and married Korean women and brought them home to the United States. Between 1952 and 1960 more than a thousand Korean women a year immigrated to the United States as brides of U.S. servicemen. At the same time, orphaned Korean children, especially girls, also arrived in the United States in significant numbers. Throughout the 1950s and up to the mid-1960s, some 70 percent of all Korean immigrants were either women or young girls. Korea was the site of the actual conflict, but large numbers of troops were also stationed in nearby Japan. Even higher numbers of Japanese women married American soldiers, left their home country, and started a new life in the United States. Roughly six thousand Japanese wives of U.S. servicemen immigrated annually to the United States between 1952 and 1960, which was more than 80 percent of all immigrants from Japan. These Korean and Japanese war brides and Korean orphans were spread throughout the United States and, as a result, had very little interaction with other Asian Americans already living in this country.[48] These war bride families were, however, a significant part of the biracial Asian American baby boom that is discussed in greater detail in Chapter 7.

POST-1965 ASIAN IMMIGRANTS AND REFUGEES

A number of factors have clearly influenced Asian immigration and refugee policies including public sentiment toward immigrants, demands of foreign policy, and the needs of the American economy. World War II and the Cold War years were epochal for Asian Americans, but the period since the mid-1960s has proven to be even more significant. An overview of U.S. immigration statistics shows just how important recent immigration reforms and refugee policies have affected Asian Americans.

Official records on immigrants entering the United States did not exist before 1820, but since that time it is quite obvious that the largest number of immigrants come from European countries. Between 1820 and 2004, just over 40 million Europeans immigrated to the United States (see Table 1-1). In contrast, about 10 million immigrants came from Asia during the same period of time. Looking at this figure more closely, however, we find over 8.6 million immigrants from Asia arrived in the United States in the period between 1971 and 2004. Although the Chinese and Japanese have the longest histories in the United States, the largest group of Asian immigrants since 1971 has come from the Philippines. More than 1.7 million Filipino immigrants entered the United States between 1971 and 2004. It is also significant to note that over 90 percent of Filipino, Asian Indian, Korean, and Vietnamese immigrants have entered the United States since 1971.

This next section focuses on three broad events that have directly influenced both the numbers and diversity of Asians entering the United States since 1965: (1) the passage of the 1965 Immigration Reform Act, (2) global economic restructuring, and (3) the Vietnam War.

The 1965 Immigration Reform Act

Why did the dramatic increase in Asian immigration take place? What changes in the law or public attitudes facilitated such a rapid influx of immigrants from Asia? One important reason was the Civil Rights movement of the 1960s, which brought international attention to racial and economic inequality in the United States—including its biased immigration policies. This attention is the background for the passage of the 1965 Immigration Reform Act, the most important immigration reform legislation. This act, along with its amendments, significantly increased the token quotas established after World War II to allow the Eastern Hemisphere a maximum of 20,000 per country, and set a ceiling of 170,000.

Table 1-1 Immigration to the United States by Region, Fiscal Years 1820–2004

Region	Total 1820–2004	1971–2004	% of Immigrants Since 1971
All countries	69,017,450	24,956,619	36.2
Europe	40,046,794	3,641,014	9.1
Asia	10,045,332	8,608,347	85.7
China*	1,528,836	1,127,394	73.7
Hong Kong†	439,239	355,890	81.0
India	1,068,829	1,044,883	97.8
Japan	564,218	199,964	35.4
Korea	878,404	852,754	97.1
Philippines	1,731,227	1,648,912	95.2
Vietnam	864,279	859,604	99.5
North America			
Canada and Newfoundland	4,577,196	629,960	13.8
Mexico	6,850,660	5,439,816	79.4
Caribbean	4,029,581	3,025,618	75.1
Central America	1,600,894	1,386,702	86.6
South America	2,057,564	1,620,255	78.7
Africa	907,377	871,873	96.1
Oceana	280,216	173,105	61.8
Not specified	348,917	108,365	31.1

* Beginning in 1957, China includes Taiwan.
† Data not reported separately until 1952.
Source: Office of Immigration Statistics, *2003 Statistical Yearbook of the Immigration and Naturalization Service* (Washington, DC: U.S. Government Printing Office, 2004), Table 2, pp. 12–14 and *2004 Yearbook of Immigration Statistics,* Table 3 at http://uscis.gov/graphics/shared/statistics/yearbook/2004/table3.xls.

This act created the following seven-point preference system that serves as a general guideline for immigration officials when issuing visas: (1) unmarried children of U.S. citizens who are at least 21 years of age; (2) spouses and unmarried children of permanent resident aliens; (3) members of the professions, scientists, and artists of exceptional ability; (4) married children of U.S. citizens; (5) brothers and sisters of U.S. citizens who are at least 21 years of age; (6) skilled or unskilled workers who are in short supply; and (7) nonpreference applicants.

U.S. immigration policy also allowed virtually unrestricted immigration to certain categories of people including spouses, children under 21, and parents of U.S. citizens. These provisions served to accelerate immigration from Asia to the United States. The primary goal of the 1965 Immigration Reform Act was to encourage family reunification, however, a much higher percentage of Asian immigrants initially began entering the United States under the established occupational and nonpreference investment categories. In 1969, for example, 62 percent of Asian Indians, 43 percent of Filipinos, and 34.8 percent of Koreans entered the United States under the occupational and investor categories. By the mid-1970s, however, 80 to 90 percent of all Asian immigrants entered the United States through one of the family categories.[49] Studies show that most post-1965 Asian immigrants tend to be middle-class, educated, and urbanized, and they arrive in the United States in family units rather than as individuals compared to their pre-1965 counterparts.[50]

The framers of the 1965 law did not anticipate any dramatic changes in the historical pattern of immigration, but it is clear Asian immigrants have taken advantage of almost every aspect of the 1965 Immigration Reform Act. Asians were just 6.1 percent of all immigrants to the United States between 1951 and 1960; this rose to 12.9 percent between 1961 and 1970, and increased to 35.3 percent between 1971 and 1980. The percentage of Asian immigrants peaked at 37.3 percent between 1981 and 1990 but declined to 30.7 percent between 1991 and 2000 (see Table 1-2). This decline was due to the sudden increase of mostly Mexicans who were able to apply for legal status following the passage of the Immigration Reform and Control Act of 1986 (IRCA). By the late 1990s, about 3 million aliens received permanent residence status under IRCA. The percentage of immigrants has remained relatively steady since 2000, although there was an increase in 2004.

This "amnesty" provision was only a part of IRCA, which was fully intended to control illegal immigration into the United States. IRCA also required that all employers verify the legal status of all new employees, and it imposed civil and criminal penalties against employers who knowingly hire undocumented

Table 1-2 Percentage of Immigrants Admitted by Region, Fiscal Years 1901–2004

Decade/Year	Europe	Asia	North America*	South America	Africa
2004	13.5	34.8	36.0	8.9	7.0
2003	14.5	33.4	35.8	7.7	6.5
2002	16.7	30.7	38.1	6.9	5.7
2001	16.7	31.7	38.1	6.4	4.7
1991–2000	14.9	30.7	43.3	5.9	3.9
1981–1990	10.4	37.3	43.0	6.3	2.4
1971–1980	17.8	35.3	37.5	6.6	1.8
1961–1970	33.8	12.9	43.9	7.8	.9
1951–1960	52.7	6.1	36.0	3.6	.6
1941–1950	60.0	3.6	32.2	2.1	.7
1931–1940	65.8	3.1	28.8	1.5	.3
1921–1930	60.0	2.7	35.9	1.0	.2
1911–1920	75.3	4.3	19.2	.7	.1
1901–1910	91.6	3.7	3.2	.2	.1

* Includes Central America and the Caribbean.
Note: Figures may not add to 100 due to rounding. Oceana and unspecified regions are not listed.
Source: Office of Immigration Statistics, *2003 Statistical Yearbook of the Immigration and Naturalization Service* (Washington, DC: U.S. Government Printing Office), 2004, Table 2, pp. 12–14 and *2004 Yearbook of Immigration Statistics,* Table 3 at http://uscis.gov/graphics/shared/statistics/yearbook/2004/table3.xls.

workers.[51] While IRCA closed the "back door" of illegal immigration, another reform, the Immigration Act of 1990, was enacted to keep open the "front door" of legal immigration. Indeed, this law actually authorizes an *increase* in legal immigration to the United States. In response to uncertain economic stability at home, growing global economic competition abroad, and the dramatically changed face of immigration, the 1990 law sent a mixed message to Asian immigrants.

First of all, the law actually authorized an increase in legal immigration, but at the same time placed a yearly cap on total immigration for the first time since the 1920s. For 1992 to 1995, the limit was 700,000 and 675,000 thereafter. This appears to be an arbitrary limit, but it still allows for an unlimited number of visas for immediate relatives of U.S. citizens. This may not have a negative effect on Asian immigration because, as a group, Asians have the highest rate of naturalization compared to other immigrants.[52] Second, the law encourages immigration of more skilled workers to help meet the needs of the U.S. economy. The number of visas for skilled workers and their families increased sharply from 58,000 to 140,000. This was generally seen as a potential boon for Asians who, since 1965, have been among the best educated and best trained immigrants the United States has ever seen. Third, the 1990 immigration law also sought to "diversify" the new immigrants by giving more visas to countries that have sent relatively few people to the United States in recent years. This program has been popular with lawmakers who want to assist those from Western European countries at the expense of Asians. For example, up to 40 percent of the initial visas allocated for the diversity category were for Ireland. Noted immigration attorney Bill Ong Hing found sections of the Immigration Act of 1990 "provide extra independent and transition visas that are unavailable to Asians."[53]

It is clear from the descriptions of Asian American history here that the conditions for the post-1965 Asian migrants are quite distinct from pre-1965 migrants. This seemingly obvious observation reflects the fact that international migration is not a simple, stable, or homogeneous process. Even with this in mind, the most popular frame of reference for all movement to the United States continues to be the European immigrant experience throughout the nineteenth and early twentieth centuries. The popular European immigrant analogy is highlighted in these words by Emma Lazarus honoring the Statue of Liberty:

> Give me your tired, your poor,
> Your huddled masses yearning to breathe free,
> The wretched refuse of your teeming shore;
> Send these, the homeless, tempest-tost to me,
> I lift my lamp beside the golden door!

The European immigrant experience, however, is by no means universal, and it is only part of what scholars today see as a much broader picture of the international movement of people and capital. Understanding the broader dynamics of global economic restructuring is useful in comparing and contrasting post-1965 Asian immigrants with other immigrants and minority groups in the United States.

Global Economic Restructuring

What makes people want to leave their home country and migrate to another country? The most commonly accepted answer is found within what is known as the push-pull theory. This theory generally asserts that difficult economic, social, and political conditions in the home country force, or push, people away. At the same time, these people are attracted, or pulled, to another country where conditions are seen as more favorable. On closer examination, however, this theoretical viewpoint does run into some problems. Most significantly, the push-pull theory tends to see immigration flows as a natural, open, and spontaneous process, but it does not adequately take into account the structural factors and policy changes that directly affect immigration flows. This is because earlier migration studies based on European immigration limited their focus on poor countries that sent low-skilled labor to affluent countries with growing economies that put newcomers to work. The push-pull theory is not incorrect, but is considered to be incomplete and historically static. Recent studies have taken a much broader approach to international migration and insist that in order to understand post-1965 immigration from Asia, it is necessary to understand the recent restructuring of the global economy.[54]

Since the end of World War II, global restructuring has involved the gradual movement of industrial manufacturing away from developed nations such as the United States to less-developed nations in Asia and Latin America where labor costs are cheaper. This process was best seen in Japan in the 1950s through 1970s, and accelerated rapidly in the 1980s to newly industrialized Asian countries, namely Taiwan, Hong Kong, Singapore, and South Korea. Other Asian countries such as India, Thailand, Indonesia, Malaysia, and the Philippines also followed the same economic course with varying degrees of success. In the 1990s mainland China increased its manufacturing and export capacity dramatically and was steering on the same economic path of other Asian nations.

Among the effects of global restructuring on the United States is the declining need to import low-skilled labor because manufacturing jobs are moving abroad. At the same time, there is an inclining need to import individuals with advanced specialized skills that are in great demand. According to research by Paul Ong and Evelyn Blumenberg (1994), this phenomenon is evidenced in part by the increasing number of foreign-born students studying at U.S. colleges.[55] In the 1954–1955 academic year the United States was host to just 34,232 foreign exchange students; this number increased to 586,000 in 2003.[56] Of those 586,000 foreign students, 367,000 are from Asia. In 2002 foreign students earned 60.7 percent of the doctorates in engineering, 53.3 percent of doctorates in mathematics, and 53.4 percent of doctorates in computer science.[57] The National Science Foundation reported that between 1985 and 2000, students from China, Taiwan, India, and South Korea earned more than 50 percent of science and engineering doctoral degrees awarded to foreign students in the United States (see Table 1-3). Many of these foreign graduate students planned to work in the United States and eventually gained permanent immigrant status. Companies in the United States have, of course, been eager to

Table 1-3 Asian Recipients of U.S. Science and Engineering Doctorates by Field and Country of Origin: 1985–2000

Field	All Asian Recipients	China	Taiwan	India	South Korea
All fields	80,310	28,698	18,508	16,029	17,075
S&E	68,550	26,534	15,487	13,274	13,255
Physical sciences	11,987	6,356	1,923	1,856	1,852
Earth, atmospheric, and ocean sciences	1,731	972	327	180	252
Mathematics	3,585	1,954	614	438	579
Computer/information sciences	3,221	673	839	1,178	531
Engineering	25,923	7,207	7,518	6,146	5,052
Biological sciences	12,251	6,790	2,175	1,766	1,520
Agricultural sciences	2,333	901	601	316	515
Psychology/social sciences	7,519	1,681	1,490	1,394	2,954
Non-S&E[a]	11,760	2,164	3,021	2,755	3,820

[a] Includes medical and other life sciences.
Note: Foreign doctorate recipients include permanent and temporary residents.
Source: National Science Foundation, Division of Science Resources Statistics, Survey of Earned Doctorates, special tabulations, 2003 at http://www.nsf.gov/statistics/seind04/c2/c2s4.htm#c2s411.

hire foreign-born scientists and engineers. Not only are highly-skilled immigrants valuable to employers as workers, but many also start their own high-tech businesses. For example, Vinod Khosla is the co-founder of Sun-Microsystems, and Gururaj Deshpande is co-founder of a number of high-tech businesses worth around $6 billion.[58]

The medical profession is another broad area where Asian immigrants have made a noticeable impact. Researchers Paul Ong and Tania Azores (1994) found that Asian Americans represented 4.4 percent of the registered nurses and 10.8 percent of the physicians in the United States in 1990. Ong and Azores estimate that only a third of Asian American physicians and a quarter of Asian American nurses were educated in the United States. Graduates of overseas medical and nursing schools have been coming to the United States since the passage of the 1946 Smith-Mundt Act, which created an exchange program for specialized training. Although this exchange was intended to be temporary, many medical professionals were able to become permanent immigrants. A physician shortage in the United States during the late 1960s and early 1970s, coupled with the elimination of racial immigration quotas in 1965, brought forth a steady flow of foreign-trained medical doctors from Asian countries. A 1975 U.S. Commission on Civil Rights report found five thousand Asian medical school graduates entered the United States annually during the early 1970s. But, under pressure from the medical industry, Congress passed the 1976 Health Professions Educational Act, which restricted the number of foreign-trained physicians who could enter the United States. Despite the passage of this law, the American Medical Association reported there were 194,600 foreign medical graduates out of 768,500 professionally active physicians in the United States in 2002.[59]

Asia is also the largest source for foreign nurses. The Philippines, in particular, is the world leader in nurse migration. A demographic profile of registered nurses in 1990 by the Center for Immigration Studies (1998) found there were 1,896,606 registered nurses in the United States. The same study found 166,708 were foreign-born registered nurses 49,033 of whom were from the Philippines (29.4 percent). A recent survey conducted by Judith Berg and her colleagues (2004) found that Filipino nurses were generally better educated and worked more full-time hours than U.S. native-born nurses. The researchers also found that Filipino nurses had higher job satisfaction. Filipino nurses find work in the United States attractive because they can earn up to twenty times the salary they can make in the Philippines, and their English-speaking abilities make them highly desired by employers. The growth of the health care industry in the United States has resulted in a shortage of hospital nurses. As a result, employers see foreign-born nurses as the best solution and this has been supported by congressional legislation. Filipino nurses are attracted to the United States because of liberal policies that eventually allow them to stay permanently. Most foreign-trained nurses are brought to work initially on a temporary basis, but the passage of the Immigration Nursing Relief Act of 1989 allows nurses to adjust to permanent status after three years of service.[60]

According to Christine Ceniza Choy (2004), the origins of Filipino nurse migration to the United States is not a new phenomenon. Its roots lie in early twentieth-century U.S. colonialism and the "Americanized training hospital system" in the Philippines. Additionally, Choy argues that Filipino migration abroad cannot be reduced to an economic logic; rather, it must be understood as part of a larger transnational process "involving the flow of people, goods, services, images, and ideas across national borders."[61] This analysis further challenges the general explanations for the origins of migration found in the push-pull theory described earlier. Global economic restructuring is an important context for understanding not only why Asian immigrants have come to the United States but also how well they have adjusted and been accepted socially, economically, and politically. Note that not all Asian immigrants are middle-class and successful professionals; a sizable number of other Asian immigrants, especially refugees, have also found their lives in America extremely difficult. The extreme diversity among Asian Americans is due in large part to the third major event affecting migration from Asia—the Vietnam War.

The Vietnam War and Southeast Asian Refugees

Since 1975, large numbers of Southeast Asian refugees have entered the United States, and today California is the home for most of them (see Table 1-4). Roughly two thirds of all Southeast Asian refugees are from Vietnam, with the rest from Laos and Cambodia. Unlike most other post-1965 Asian immigrants

Table 1-4 States with the Largest Southeast Asian Populations, 2000*

State	Vietnamese	Cambodian	Laotian	Hmong	Total
California	484,023	84,559	65,058	71,741	705,381
Texas	163,625	8,225	11,626	422	163,625
Minnesota	20,570	6,533	11,516	45,443	84,062
Washington	50,697	16,630	9,382	1,485	78,194
Massachusetts	36,685	22,886	4,449	1,303	65,323
Virginia	40,500	5,180	3,076	55	48,811
Wisconsin	4,505	856	5,405	36,809	47,575
Pennsylvania	33,204	10,207	2,536	844	46,791
Florida	37,086	3,040	4,126	163	44,415
Georgia	31,092	3,405	5,220	1,615	41,332

* Asian detailed group alone or in any combination.
Source: Max Niedzwiecki and TC Duong, *Southeast Asian Statistical Profile* (Washington, DC: Southeast Asian Resource Action), 2004.

who came to the United States in a rather orderly fashion seeking family reunification and economic opportunities, Southeast Asian refugees arrived as part of an international resettlement effort of people who faced genuine political persecution and bodily harm in their home countries. Southeast Asian refugees to the United States can be easily divided into three distinct waves: the first arrived in the United States in 1975 shortly after the fall of Saigon, the second arrived between 1978 and 1980, and the third entered the United States after 1980 and continues to this day. The United States has accepted these refugees not only for humanitarian reasons but also in recognition that U.S. foreign policy and military actions in Southeast Asia had a hand in creating much of the calamity that has befallen the entire region.

U.S. political interests in Southeast Asia actually began during World War II, although for years efforts were limited to foreign aid and military advisers. Direct military intervention rapidly escalated in 1965 when President Lyndon B. Johnson stepped up bombing raids in Southeast Asia and authorized the use of the first U.S. combat troops to contain increasing communist insurgency. The undeclared war continued until U.S. troops withdrew in 1973 at the cost of 57,000 American and 1 million Vietnamese lives. The conflict also caused great environmental destruction throughout Southeast Asia and tremendous domestic antiwar protests in the United States.[62]

As soon as the U.S. troops left, however, communist forces in Vietnam regrouped and quickly began sweeping across the countryside. By March 1975 it was clear that the capital of South Vietnam, Saigon, would soon fall to communist forces. As a result, President Gerald Ford authorized the attorney general to admit 130,000 refugees into the United States.[63] In the last chaotic days prior to the fall of Saigon on April 30, 1975, "high-risk" individuals in Vietnam, namely high-ranking government and military personnel, were hurriedly airlifted away to safety at temporary receiving centers in Guam, Thailand, and the Philippines. This group marked the first wave of Southeast Asian refugees who would eventually resettle in the United States. The first wave is distinct in that they were generally the educated urban elite and middle class from Vietnam. Because many of them had worked closely with the U.S. military, they tended to be more westernized (40 percent were Catholics), and a good portion of them were able to speak English (30 percent spoke English well). Another significant feature is that roughly 95 percent of the first wave of Southeast Asian refugees were Vietnamese, even though the capitals of Laos and Cambodia also fell to communist forces in 1975.[64]

Once these first-wave refugees came to the United States, they were flown to one of four military base reception centers in California, Arkansas, Pennsylvania, and Florida. From these bases they registered with a voluntary agency that would eventually help resettle them with a sponsor. About 60 percent of the sponsors were families, while the other 40 percent were usually churches and individuals. Sponsors were responsible for day-to-day needs of the refugees until they were able to find jobs and become independent. The resettlement of the first wave of refugees was funded by the 1975 Indochinese Resettlement Assistance Act and was seen as a quick and temporary process. Indeed, all the reception centers closed by the end of 1975, and the Resettlement Act expired in 1977.

The second wave of Southeast Asian refugees was larger, more heterogeneous, and many believe even more devastated by their relocation experience than the first wave. The second wave of refugees were generally less educated, urbanized, and westernized (only 7 percent spoke English and only about 7 percent were Catholic) compared to their predecessors; at the same time they were much more ethnically diverse than the first wave. According to statistics, between 1978 and 1980, about 55.5 percent of Southeast Asian refugees were from Vietnam (including many ethnic Chinese), 36.6 percent from Laos, and 7.8 percent from Cambodia. The second wave consisted of people who suffered under the communist regimes and were unable to leave their countries immediately before or after the new governments took power.[65]

In Vietnam, the ethnic Chinese merchant class was very much the target of resentment by the new communist government. Many of the Chinese businesses in Vietnam were nationalized, Chinese language schools and newspapers were closed, education and employment rights were denied, and food rations were reduced. Under these conditions, about 250,000 escaped North Vietnam, seeking refuge in China. Roughly 70 percent of the estimated 500,000 boat people who tried to escape Vietnam by sea were ethnic Chinese. The treacherous journey usually took place on ill-equipped crowded boats that were unable to withstand the rigors of the ocean or outrun marauding Thai pirates. The U.S. Committee for Refugees estimates at least 100,000 people lost their lives trying to escape Vietnam by boat.[66] Along with the Chinese, others in Vietnam, particularly those who had supported the U.S.-backed South Vietnamese government and their families, were also subject to especially harsh treatment by the new communist leadership. Many were sent to "reeducation camps" and banished to work in rural regions clearing land devastated by thirty years of war.

The holocaust in Cambodia began immediately after the Khmer Rouge (Red Khmer) marched into the capital city of Phnom Penh on April 17, 1975.

That same day the entire population of the capital was ordered to the country-side. It has been broadly estimated that after three years between 1 and 3 million Cambodians died from starvation, disease, and execution out of a population of less than 7 million. In 1978 Vietnam (with support from the Soviet Union) invaded Cambodia, drove the Khmer Rouge out of power, and established a new government under its own control. Famine and warfare continued under Viet-namese occupation, and by 1979 more than 600,000 refugees from Cambodia fled the country, mostly to neighboring Thailand. In Laos, the transition from one government to another was initially rather smooth compared to Vietnam after the fall of Saigon. After over a decade of civil war, a coalition government was formed in April 1974 that included Laotian communists, the Pathet Lao. But shortly after communists took power in Vietnam and Cambodia, the Pathet Lao moved to solidify its full control of the country. It was at this time that troops from both Laos and Vietnam began a military campaign against the Hmong hill people, an ethnic minority group that lived in the mountains of Laos, who were recruited by the U.S. government to fight against communist forces in the region. The Hmong were subjected to massive bombing raids that included the dropping of napalm and poisonous chemicals. Thousands of Hmong were killed in these fierce assaults, and those who remained had little choice but to seek refuge in neighboring Thailand. The Hmong were not the only people in Laos who were persecuted. By 1979 roughly three thousand Hmong were entering Thailand every month, and as late as 1983 an estimated 75 percent of the 76,000 Laotians in Thai refugee camps were Hmong people.[67]

The world could not ignore this massive outpouring of refugees from Southeast Asia, and in 1979 President Jimmy Carter allowed 14,000 refugees a month to enter the United States. In addition, Congress passed the Refugee Act of 1980, which set an annual quota of 50,000 refugees per year, funded resettlement programs, and allowed refugees to become eligible for the same welfare benefits as U.S. citizens after thirty-six months of refugee assistance (this was changed to eighteen months in 1982).

Many of the Southeast Asians who came in the third wave are technically not considered refugees, but are in actuality immigrants. This has been facilitated by the 1980 Orderly Departure Program (ODP), an agreement with Vietnam that allows individuals and families to enter the United States. ODP was a benefit for three groups: relatives of permanently settled refugees in the United States, Amerasians, and former reeducation camp internees. By the end of 1992, more than 300,000 Vietnamese immigrated to the United States including 80,000 Amerasians and their relatives, as well as 60,000 former camp internees and their families.[68] The resettlement experience, the development of Southeast Asian communities, as well as the influx of Amerasians to the United States are respec-tively discussed in greater detail in Chapters 2 and 7.

Although most Southeast Asian Americans live in California, many are surprised to see how widely dispersed this population is. For example, the population of Hmong Americans living in Minnesota and Wisconsin is larger than the number of Hmong Americans in California. Next to California, the largest number of Cambodians can be found in Massachusetts. More than

25,000 Vietnamese American lived in Louisiana, 6,000 lived in Mississippi, and 5,000 lived in Alabama prior to the devastation wrought from Hurricane Katrina in 2005. Many former refugee Vietnamese Americans were forced to become refugees once again as they were displaced and relocated following the massive storm and flood damage to their homes and businesses. The media coverage focused overwhelmingly on the black and white victims of the hurricane so Vietnamese American communities throughout the U.S. took it upon themselves to raise money, send supplies, and offer homes to other Vietnamese Americans in the Deep South. Many Vietnamese Americans have resettled in places like Houston, Texas, as well as in San Jose and Orange County, California that already had large Vietnamese American communities.[69]

CONCLUSION

This chapter briefly describes the history and recent growth of the Asian population in the United States. Historians as well as legal scholars such as Bill Ong Hing (1993 and 2004), Angelo N. Ancheta (1998), and John S.W. Park (2005) have also examined Asian American experience and have shown the tremendous legal barriers faced by Asian Americans in the United States.[70] The notion of Asian Americans as the "perpetual foreigner" has had a distinct impact on their experiences with discrimination and violation of civil rights at the hands of the legal system. At the same time, this chapter also highlights the significance of the 1965 Immigration Reform Act, global economic restructuring, and the Vietnam War as three broad events that profoundly impacted both the number and type of migrants who have come to the United States from Asian countries. To examine post-1965 Asian Americans comprehensively, it is particularly important to look at the rapid growth of the population, personal history, nativity, length of time in the United States, premigration experiences and traumas, education, socioeconomic background, and gender. Chapter 2 details the social and economic diversity of immigrant and American-born Asians, as well as their settlement patterns and impact on various communities across the United States.

NOTES

1. Emil Guillermo, "Glaring Omissions of Masterpiece History," *AsianWeek*, November 25, 2004.
2. Shih-shan Henry Tsai, *The Chinese Experience in America* (Bloomington: Indiana University Press, 1986), p. 1; also see Stan Steiner, *Fusahang: The Chinese Who Built America* (New York: Harper & Row, 1979), pp. 24–35; Elena S. H. Yu, "Filipino Migration and Community Organization in the United States," *California Sociologist* 3:2 (1980): 76–102; and Joan M. Jensen, *Passage from India: Asian Indian Immigrants in North America* (New Haven: Yale University Press, 1988), pp. 12–13.
3. Sucheng Chan, *Asian Californians* (San Francisco: MTL/Boyd & Fraser, 1991), pp. 5–6.
4. Ronald Takaki, *Strangers from a Different Shore* (Boston: Little, Brown, 1989), pp. 79, 114.
5. Stanford Lyman, *Chinese Americans* (New York: Random House, 1974), pp. 86–88.
6. Chan, *Asian Californians*, pp. 27–33.
7. Lyman, *Chinese Americans*, pp. 63–69.

8. Yuji Ichioka, *The Issei: The World of the First Generation Japanese Immigrant's, 1885–1924* (New York: Free Press, 1988), pp. 64–65.

9. Roger Daniels, *Concentration Camps: North American Japanese in the United States and Canada During World War II* (Malabar, FL: Robert A. Kreiger, 1981), p. 7.

10. Bill Ong Hing, *Making and Remaking Asian America Through Immigration Policy, 1850–1990* (Stanford, CA: Stanford University Press, 1993), pp. 28–30.

11. Chan, *Asian Californians*, p. 7.

12. Edwin B. Almirol, *Ethnic Identity and Social Negotiation: A Study of a Filipino Community in California* (New York: AMS Press, 1985), pp. 52–59; and H. Brett Melendy, "Filipinos in the United States," in Norris Hundley, Jr. (ed.), *The Asian American: The Historical Experience* (Santa Barbara: Cleo, 1977), pp. 101–128.

13. Takaki, *Strangers from a Different Shore*, pp. 53–57.

14. Chan, *Asian Californians*, pp. 7, 17–19, 37; and Warren Y. Kim, *Koreans in America* (Seoul: Po Chin Chai, 1971), pp. 22–27.

15. Joan M. Jensen, *Passage from India: Asian Indian Immigrants in North America* (New Haven: Yale University Press, 1988), pp. 24–41; and Rajanki K. Das, *Hindustani Workers on the Pacific Coast* (Berlin and Leipzig: Walter De Gruyter, 1923), p. 77.

16. Das, *Hindustani Workers*, pp. 66–67.

17. Bruce La Brack, "Occupational Specialization Among Rural California Sikhs: The Interplay of Culture and Economics," *Amerasia Journal* 9:2 (1982): 29–56.

18. Naturalization Act of 1790, I Stat. 103 (1790).

19. Act of 14 July 1870, 16 Stat. 256.

20. Roger Daniels, *Asian Americans: Chinese and Japanese in the United States* (Seattle: University of Washington Press, 1988), p. 43.

21. Chan, *Asian Californians*, p. 42.

22. Robert F. Heizer and Alan F. Almquist, *The Other Californians: Prejudice and Discrimination Under Spain, Mexico, and the United States to 1920* (Berkeley: University of California Press, 1971), p. 129.

23. Takaki, *Strangers from a Different Shore*, p. 82.

24. Lyman, *Chinese Americans*, pp. 55–85.

25. Takaki, *Strangers from a Different Shore*, pp. 111–112.

26. Juan L. Gonzales, *Racial and Ethnic Groups in America*, 2nd ed. (Dubuque, IA: Kendall/Hunt, 1993), p. 136; and Juan L. Gonzales, *Racial and Ethnic Families in America*, 2nd ed. (Dubuque, IA: Kendall/Hunt Publishing Co., 1993), p. 3.

27. Chan, *Asian Californians*, pp. 44–45.

28. Hing, *Making and Remaking Asian America*, pp. 32–39.

29. *Yick Wo v. Hopkins*, 118 U.S. 356 (1886); and Lyman, *Chinese Americans*, p. 79.

30. *Takao Ozawa v. United States*, 260 U.S. 178 (1922); Heizer and Almquist, *The Other Californians*, pp. 192–193; and Ichioka, *The Issei*, pp. 210–226.

31. *United States v. Bhagat Singh Thind*, 261 U.S. 204 (1923); Jensen, *Passage from India*, pp. 255–260; and Gurdial Singh, "East Indians in the United States," *Sociology and Social Research* 30:3 (1946): 208–216.

32. Megumi Dick Osumi, "Asians and California's Anti-Miscegenation Laws," in Nobuya Tsuchida (ed.), *Asian and Pacific American Experiences: Women's Perspectives* (Minneapolis: Asian/Pacific American Learning Resource Center, University of Minnesota, 1982), pp. 1–37; and Takaki, *Strangers from a Different Shore*, pp. 330–331.

33. William Petersen, *Japanese Americans* (New York: Random House, 1971), pp. 66–100; Roger Daniels, *Concentration Camps, U.S.A.* (New York: Holt, Rinehart & Winston, 1971), pp. 75, 81–82; and Jacobus tenBroek, Edward N. Barnhart, and Floyd W. Matson, *Prejudice, War, and the Constitution* (Berkeley: University of California Press), pp. 118–120.

34. Cited in Commission on Wartime Relocation and Internment of Civilians, *Personal Justice Denied* (Washington, DC: U.S. Government Printing Office, 1982), pp. 52–53.

35. Takaki, *Strangers from a Different Shore*, pp. 379–392.

36. Commission on Wartime Relocation and Internment of Civilians, *Personal Justice Denied*, p. 217; tenBroek, Barnhart, and Matson, *Prejudice, War, and the Constitution*, pp. 155–177, 180–181; and Daniels, *Concentration Camps: North America*.

37. Chan, *Asian Californians*, p. 101.

38. Petersen, *Japanese Americans*, p. 87.

39. Cited in Marvin Karlins, Thomas L. Coffman, and Gary Walters, "On the Fading of Social Stereotypes: Studies of Three Generations of College Students," *Journal of Personality and Psychology* 13 (1990): 4–5.

40. *Time,* December 22, 1941, p. 33.
41. Cited in Harold Isaacs, *Images of Asia: American Views of China and India* (New York: Harper & Row, 1972), pp. xviii–xix.
42. Chan, *Asian Californians,* pp. 103–104; and Lyman, *Chinese Americans,* pp. 127, 134.
43. Takaki, *Strangers from a Different Shore,* pp. 357–363, 370–378; Manuel Buaken, "Life in the Armed Forces," *New Republic* 109 (1943): 279–280; and Bienvenido Santos, "Filipinos in War," *Far Eastern Survey* 11 (1942): 249–250.
44. Harry H. L. Kitano and Roger Daniels, *Asian Americans: Emerging Minorities,* 2nd ed. (Upper Saddle River, NJ: Prentice Hall, 1995), p. 42, Table 4-2; and Monica Boyd, "Oriental Immigration: The Experience of Chinese, Japanese, and Filipino Populations in the United States," *International Migration Review* 10 (1976): 48–60, Table 1.
45. Chan, *Asian Californians,* pp. 105–106.
46. Diane Mark and Ginger Chih, *A Place Called Chinese America* (San Francisco: The Organization of Chinese Americans, 1982), pp. 105–107.
47. Chan, *Asian Californians,* pp. 108–109.
48. Ibid., pp. 109–110.
49. Hing, *Making and Remaking Asian America,* Appendix B, pp. 189–200, Table 9, p. 82.
50. Hing, *Making and Remaking Asian America,* pp. 79–120; Luciano Mangiafico, *Contemporary American Immigrants: Patterns of Filipino, Korean, and Chinese Settlement in the United States* (New York: Praeger, 1988), pp. 1–26; James T. Fawcett and Benjamin V. Carino (eds.), *Pacific Bridges: The New Immigration from Asia and the Pacific Islands* (Staten Island, NY: Center for Migration Studies, 1987); and Herbert R. Barringer, Robert W. Gardner, and Michael J. Levine (eds.), *Asian and Pacific Islanders in the United States* (New York: Russell Sage Foundation, 1993).
51. Roger Daniels, *Coming to America* (New York: HarperCollins, 1990), pp. 391–397.
52. Office of Immigration Statistics, *Statistical Yearbook of the Immigration and Naturalization Service, 2003* (Washington, DC: U.S. Government Printing Office, 2004), pp. 4–5.
53. Hing, *Making and Remaking Asian America,* pp. 7–8.
54. Paul Ong, Edna Bonacich, and Lucie Cheng (eds.), *The New Asian Immigration in Los Angeles and Global Restructuring* (Philadelphia: Temple University Press, 1994), pp. 3–100; and Edna Bonacich, Lucie Cheng, Norma Chinchilla, Nora Hamilton, and Paul Ong (eds.), *Global Production: The Apparel Industry in the Pacific Rim* (Philadelphia: Temple University Press, 1994), pp. 3–20.
55. Paul Ong and Evelyn Blumenberg, "Scientists and Engineers," in Paul Ong (ed.), *The State of Asian Pacific America: Economic Diversity, Issues & Policies* (Los Angeles: LEAP Asian Pacific American Public Policy Institute and UCLA Asian American Studies Center, 1994), pp. 113–138. Note that I am distinguishing between foreign exchange students who are overseas nationals from Asian American students who happen to be foreign born.
56. *Ibid.,* p. 173; and U.S. Department of Commerce, *Statistical Abstract of the United States, 2004–2005* (Washington, DC: U.S. Government Printing Office, 2005), p. 171, Table 265.
57. U.S. Department of Commerce, *Statistical Abstract of the United States, 2004–2005* (Washington, DC: U.S. Government Printing Office, 2005), p. 515, Table 775.
58. "The Golden Diaspora: Indian Immigrants to the U.S. Are One of the Newest Elements of the American Melting Pot—and the Most Spectacular Success Story," *Time Select/Global Business,* June 19, 2000, pp. B26–27.
59. Paul Ong and Tania Azores, "Health Professionals on the Front-Line," in Paul Ong (ed.), *The State of Asian Pacific America: Economic Diversity, Issues & Policies,* pp. 139–164 and U.S. Department of Commerce, *Statistical Abstract of the United States, 2004–2005* (Washington, DC: U.S. Government Printing Office, 2005), p. 107, Table 150.
60. Paul Ong and Tania Azores, "The Migration and Incorporation of Filipino Nurses," in Ong et al. (eds.), *The New Asian Immigration in Los Angeles and Global Restructuring,* pp. 166–195; Mangiafico, *Contemporary American Immigrants,* pp. 42–43; Leon Bouvier and Rosemary Jenks, "Doctors and nurses: a demographic profile." Available at http://www.cis.org/article/1998/DocsandNurses.htm.; and Judith A. Berg, Daisy Rodriguez, Valerie Kading, and Carolina De Guzman, "Demographic Study of Filipino American Nurses," *Nursing Administration Quarterly* 29:3 (July–Sept., 2004): 199–207.
61. Catherine Ceniza Choy, *Empire of Care: Nursing and Migration in Filipino American History* (Durham and London: Duke University Press, 2003), pp. 7, 11.
62. Literature on the Vietnam conflict is voluminous. For an excellent and readable overview, see Stanley Karnow, *Vietnam: A History* (New York: Penguin, 1991).
63. The quota for refugees under the 1965 Immigration Reform Act was only 17,400, so President Gerald Ford instructed the attorney general to use his "parole" power to admit the

130,000 refugees. The use of parole power was also used to bring European refugees to the United States during the 1950s. For more detail, see Hing, *Making and Remaking Asian America*, pp. 123–128; and Paul J. Strand and Woodrow Jones, Jr., *Indochinese Refugees in America: Problems of Adaptation and Assimilation* (Durham, NC: Duke University Press, 1985).

64. Chan, *Asian Californians*, p. 128; and Chor-Swan Ngin, "The Acculturation Pattern of Orange County's Southeast Asian Refugees," *Journal of Orange County Studies* 3:4 (Fall 1989–Spring 1990): 46–53.

65. Ngin, "The Acculturation Pattern of Orange County's Southeast Asian Refugees," p. 49; and Ngoan Le, "The Case of the Southeast Asian Refugees: Policy for a Community 'At-Risk,'" in *The State of Asian Pacific America: Policy Issues to the Year 2020* (Los Angeles: LEAP Asian Pacific American Public Policy Institute and UCLA Asian American Studies Center, 1993), pp. 167–188.

66. For more details, see Strand and Jones, *Indochinese Refugees in America;* Barry L. Wain, *The Refused: The Agony of Indochina Refugees* (New York: Simon & Schuster, 1981); and U.S. Committee for Refugees, *Uncertain Harbors: The Plight of Vietnamese Boat People* (Washington, DC: U.S. Government Printing Office, 1987).

67. Chan, *Asian Californians*, pp. 121–138; Kitano and Daniels, *Asian Americans: Emerging Minorities*, pp. 170–191; U.S. Committee for Refugees, *Cambodians in Thailand: People on the Edge* (Washington, DC: U.S. Government Printing Office, 1985); and U.S. Committee for Refugees, *Refugees from Laos: In Harm's Way* (Washington, DC: U.S. Government Printing Office, 1986).

68. U.S. Committee for Refugees, *Uncertain Harbors*, pp. 19–20; and Ruben Rumbaut, "Vietnamese, Laotian, and Cambodian Americans," in Pyong Gap Min (ed.), *Asian Americans: Contemporary Trends and Issues* (Thousand Oaks, CA: Sage, 1995), p. 240.

69. Zen T. C. Zheng, "Mall First Stop for Evacuees; Many Finding Food, Clothing, Guidance, and Care," *Houston Chronicle*, September 8, 2005; Mai Tran and Claire Luna, "Katrina's Aftermath: Vietnamese in O.C. Fear for Gulf Relatives," *Los Angeles Times*, September 3, 2003; and Vanessa Hua, "Coats Being Collected for Hurricane Victims," *San Francisco Chronicle*, October 8, 2005.

70. Bill Ong Hing, *Making and Remaking Asian America Through Immigration Policy, 1850–1990* (Stanford, CA: Stanford University Press, 1993), Bill Ong Hing, *Defining America Through Immigration Policy* (Philadelphia: Temple University Press, 2004), Angelo N. Ancheta, *Race, Rights, and the Asian American Experience* (New Brunswick: Rutgers University Press, 1998), and John S. W. Park, *Elusive Citizenship: Immigration, Asian Americans and the Paradox of Civil Rights* (New York: NYU Press, 2004).

2

Emerging Communities,
Changing Realities

VISIBILITY AND INVISIBILITY

Ever since the September 11, 2001, terrorist attacks on New York City and in Washington D.C. there has been a marked increase in negative attitudes toward immigrants in the United States. On July 22, 2004, the Gallop Poll News Service reported that about half (49 percent) of those surveyed wanted to see a decrease in the number of immigrants, and viewed immigrants as a crime and tax burden on the nation. These findings contrast the period between 1999 and 2001 when most Americans thought the number of immigrants should be maintained or increased. The 2004 Gallop Poll found immigrants were viewed more negatively than positively with respect to the overall economy, job opportunities, and social and moral values. Only in terms of "food, music and the arts" were immigrants seen in a relatively positive light. Forty-four percent of those surveyed thought immigrants helped to improve these areas of cultural life in the U.S., while only 10 percent thought immigrants made these worse.[1]

As a largely immigrant population, Asian Americans are keenly aware of anti-immigrant sentiment and very much affected by changes in immigration laws. Chapter 1 showed the large numbers of immigrants and refugees coming from Asia since 1965, and it is no surprise that the result has been increased visibility of Asian Americans across the United States. This visibility has brought heightened concern about the impact of Asian Americans on the social, cultural, economic, and political landscape in a number of states and local regions. A great deal of attention and animosity in recent years has been focused primarily on undocumented (illegal) immigrants. Although the vast majority of Asian immigrants enter the United States legally, the public image of Asian newcomers was dramatically altered with news of the cargo ship *Golden Venture* in June 1993. The wayward freighter ran aground along the coast of New York carrying almost three

41

hundred Chinese men and women who were being smuggled into the United States. Many of the passengers panicked for fear of arrest and deportation, and ten died trying to escape from the shipwreck. It was not long before stories of smuggling rings bringing in "hundreds of thousands" of Chinese to the United States illegally were reported in the news media, and this helped create the atmosphere for state and federal lawmakers to crack down on illegal immigration.[2]

This was most dramatically seen the following year with the passage of statewide Proposition 187 in California, which called for the denial of public health, education, and social services to undocumented aliens in the state. In addition, Proposition 187 allowed the police, nurses, doctors, schoolteachers, and social workers to verify the immigration status of anyone "reasonably suspected" of being in the United States illegally. The ballot initiative passed by a wide 60 percent to 40 percent margin, but was never implemented after the courts ruled it was discriminatory and unconstitutional. Although immigration advocates warned that Proposition 187 was a precursor to much larger attacks on legal immigrants, several exit polls found 47 percent of Asian American voters in California supported the initiative. They felt they had nothing to fear because they had come to the United States legally.[3] But it was not long before calls for greater limitations and control of legal immigration began being heard. Immigration control was a hotly debated topic during the 1995–1996 congressional session. Lawmakers attempted to reduce the number of legal immigrants entering the United States drastically by eliminating visa categories for adult children and siblings of newly naturalized U.S. citizens, making it more difficult for companies to hire skilled foreign workers, and cutting the number of political refugees admitted annually. "It's a state of emergency for Asian and other immigrants of color," exclaimed immigration advocate Eric Mar during a protest in front of the Federal Building in San Francisco. Mar also led a seven-day hunger strike to draw attention to the anti-immigrant movement in Congress. "It takes a drastic action to raise awareness about the politicians' scapegoating and serious attacks on immigrants," he said.[4]

Much of the recent political debate on immigration has centered on the visible costs, as opposed to the seemingly invisible benefits, of large numbers of immigrants in the United States. As a result, a number of immigration policy "think tanks" have emerged to debate various aspects of immigration and immigration policy. One such organization is the "Center for Immigration Studies," which focuses on the costs of immigration and calls for policies limiting the number of immigrants to the United States. Another organization is "National Immigration Forum," which touts the economic benefits of immigration and advocates for fair immigration laws that welcome immigrants and refugees.[5] However, the most balanced and comprehensive study of the impact of immigrants to the U.S. was done by the National Research Council in their report, *The New Americans: Economic, Demographic and Fiscal Effects of Immigration* (1997).[6] Among the key points highlighted by the report are

- "The domestic gain may run on the order of $1 billion to $10 billion a year. Although this gain may be modest relative to the size of the U.S. economy, it remains a significant positive gain in absolute terms." (p. 6)

- "The evidence points to the conclusion that immigration has had a relatively small adverse impact on the wage and employment opportunities of competing native groups." (p. 7)
- "The difference between immigrants and the native-born in program participation and program expenditures per capita varies greatly across types of government programs. For some programs, such as Social Security and Medicare, immigrants receive proportionately lower benefits than the native-born. For other programs, such as Supplemental Security Income (SSI), Aid to Families with Dependent Children (AFDC), and food stamps, they receive proportionately more. Combining the costs of benefits from all programs, there is little difference between immigrants and the native-born." (p. 11)
- "The long-term fiscal impact also depends on his or her education . . . the net present value of the fiscal impact of an immigrant with less than a high school education is −$13,000; in contrast, the net present value for an immigrant with more than a high school education is +$198,000." (pp. 11–12)

Asian American political leaders and many other immigration support groups were active in fighting against some of the harshest aspects in the 1996 immigration reform proposals. By April both houses of Congress passed their versions of immigration reform, but neither included limits on legal immigration. The issue created interesting allies on both the Senate and House sides of Congress. For example, leading the charge for immigration restrictions in the Senate were Republican Alan Simpson from Wyoming and Democrat Dianne Feinstein from California. Senators against immigration restrictions included conservative Orrin Hatch from Utah and liberal Ted Kennedy from Massachusetts. Texas senator Phil Gramm, whose wife is Korean American, offered a deeply personal as well as a solidly economic argument in favor of maintaining the current levels of legal immigration. "The American dream is not going to fade, and not going to die, on my watch on the Senate floor," stormed the fiery conservative Republican. "I do not want to tear down the Statue of Liberty. There is room in America for people who want to work."[7]

Despite the harsh rhetoric and attempts to limit legal immigration, by the late 1990s concern over immigration fell dramatically, and it no longer seemed to be a major public policy issue. Indeed, a U.S. census report estimated that the foreign-born population in 2003 was 33.5 million, or 11.7 percent of the total population of the United States. The number of foreign-born is high, but the proportion to the rest of the population is between the highest figure of 14.8 percent reached during the period of heavy immigration from Europe in 1890 and the low of just 5 percent in 1970 (see Table 2-1). In 2005, the Bureau of Labor Statistics estimated that the number of immigrant workers in the U.S. was about 22 million, which is 15 percent of the nation's workers. "Immigrants are now a critical part of the labor force across the board," said Demetrios Papademetriou, co-director of international migration policy at the Carnegie Endowment for International Peace. "We are into a new world of immigrants basically spreading throughout the economy. This is something that is going to continue and intensify."[8]

Table 2-1 Foreign-Born Population and Percentage of
Total Population for the United States, 1890–2003

Year	Number (in millions)	Percentage of total
2003	33.5	11.7
2000	28.4	11.1
1990	19.8	7.9
1970	9.6	4.7
1950	10.3	6.9
1930	14.2	11.6
1910	13.5	14.7
1890	9.2	14.8

Source: U.S. Census Bureau, "Coming to America: A Profile of the Nation's Foreign-Born" (Washington, DC: U.S. Department of Commerce Economics and Statistics Administration, August 2000), "Foreign-Born Population Nears 30 Million, Census Bureau Estimates," *United States Department of Commerce News,* January 3, 2001, and U.S. Census Bureau, "Foreign-Born Population in the United States: 2003" (Washington, DC: U.S. Department of Commerce Economics and Statistics Administration, August 2004).

Another very important element to immigration is its impact on Social Security decades in the future. Recent reports have estimated that legal immigrants entering the United States will provide a net benefit of $611 billion to the United States Social Security system over the next seventy-five years. Any reduction in the number of immigrants will increase the projected Social Security deficit, while an increase in the number of legal immigrants will serve to decrease the deficit. According to the *2004 Annual Report of the Board of Trustees of the Federal Old-Age and Survivors Insurance and Disability Insurance Trust Fund,* "The cost rate decreases with increasing rates of net immigration because immigration occurs at relatively young ages, thereby increasing the numbers of covered workers earlier than the number of beneficiaries."[9] In addition, the Social Security Agency believes that the recent increase in its "suspense file" is due in large part to illegal immigrants who pay social security taxes using false social security numbers. The result is monies paid into the system by individuals who will never see the benefits of their contributions. It is estimated that as much as $4 billion to $7 billion a year extra is paid to Social Security in this manner.[10]

With this background information in mind, this chapter provides a demographic and socioeconomic profile of Asian Americans. The first part focuses on the settlement patterns, community formation, and diversity of Asian American newcomers. In addition, the wide geographic dispersion and suburbanization of Asian Americans today is a major feature that was not seen in the past. The second part closely examines the highly publicized and prominent phenomenon of Asian ethnic entrepreneurship. In urban areas across the nation some Asian American groups have become quite successful starting their own businesses by finding interesting and unusual economic niches in which they sometimes dominate. This section also looks at the growing consumer buying power of Asian Americans. The third part of this chapter analyzes the socioeconomic status of

Asian Americans, both immigrants and U.S.-born. Summary statistics tend to provide a very positive picture; Asian Americans have been dubbed by many as the "model minority." However, this section also provides a detailed analysis of the model minority image of Asian Americans and a critical reevaluation of this concept. The statistics data in this section are drawn from a variety of sources. For the latest census information on Asian Americans, see the Web site http://www.census.gov/pubinfo/www/NEWapiML1.html. For the latest census information on Native Hawaiians and Pacific Islanders, see http://www.census.gov/pubinfo/www/NEWnativehawML1.html. The U.S. Census statistics are the basis for the analysis formed in this chapter and serve as important background for all the chapters that follow.

SETTLEMENT PATTERNS

The settlement patterns of various post-1965 Asian Americans are distinct from each other, as well as from the pre-1965 Asian Americans. This can be seen when we examine some important demographic characteristics and the emergence of new Asian American communities.

Nativity and Geographic Distribution

The recent influx of immigrants and refugees from Asia is evidenced by the extremely high percentage of foreign-born Asian Americans. According to the latest census estimates, 68.9 percent of all Asian Americans are foreign-born. Note that in Table 2-2 there were only 11.1 percent foreign-born among the

Table 2-2 Percentage of Foreign-Born Asian Americans by Ethnic Group, 2000 and 1990

Group	2000 Percentage	1990 Percentage
U.S.	11.1	7.9
Asian or Pacific Islander	19.9*	63.1
Asian	68.9	65.6
Chinese	70.9	69.3
Filipino	67.7	64.4
Japanese	39.5	32.3
Asian Indian	75.4	75.4
Korean	77.7	72.7
Vietnamese	76.1	79.9
Cambodian	65.8	79.1
Laotian	68.1	79.4
Hmong	55.6	65.2

* Native Hawaiian and Pacific Islander alone.
Source: U.S. Census Bureau, *1990 Census of the Population, Asians and Pacific Islanders in the United States* (Washington, DC: U.S. Government Printing Office, 1993), CP-3-5, Table 1 and U.S. Census Bureau, "Profile of Selected Social Characteristics: 2000" (Census 2000 Summary File 4).

general U.S. population in 2000. Although the overall percentage of foreign-born Asian Americans is high, it does vary considerably by group. Only 39.5 percent of Japanese Americans are foreign-born, as opposed to 76.1 percent of Vietnamese Americans. A high percentage of foreign-born within a group generally means a high percentage of individuals who are not fluent in the English language. The 2000 census found 39.5 percent of all Asian Americans over the age of 5 did not speak English "very well," compared with just 6 percent of all native-born Americans over the age of 5 who do not speak English "very well" (see Table 2-3). Despite being a largely foreign-born population and self-stated concerns about English-language proficiency, Asian immigrants have had a high rate of naturalization since 1971 (see Table 2-4).

Table 2-3 Asian Americans Who Do Not Speak English "Very Well," 5 Years Old and Over, 1990 and 2000

	Percentage	
Group	2000 All	1990 All
U.S.	8.1	6.1
Asian or Pacific Islander	14.5*	38.4
Asian	39.5	39.8
Chinese	49.6	50.4
Filipino	24.1	24.2
Japanese	27.2	25.2
Asian Indian	23.1	23.5
Korean	50.5	51.6
Vietnamese	62.4	60.8
Cambodian	53.5	70.0
Laotian	52.8	67.8
Hmong	58.6	76.1

* Native Hawaiian and Pacific Islander alone.
Source: U.S. Census Bureau, *1990 Census of the Population, Asians and Pacific Islanders in the United States* (Washington, DC: U.S. Government Printing Office, 1993), CP-3-5, Table 3 and Table 1 and U.S. Census Bureau, "Profile of Selected Social Characteristics: 2000" (Census 2000 Summary File 4).

Table 2-4 U.S. Naturalization by Decade, 1961–1998

Region	1961–1970	1971–1980	1981–1990	1991–1998
Europe	62.4	30.8	15.4	11.7
North America	20.9	28.1	26.2	38.9
South America	2.2	5.3	6.5	7.6
Asia	12.9	33.5	48.8	38.1
Other	1.5	2.3	3.2	3.8

Source: U.S. Immigration and Naturalization Service, *Statistical Yearbook of the Immigration and Naturalization Service 1998* (Washington, DC: U.S. Government Printing Office, 1999). p. 126, Chart O.

Asian Americans historically have clustered in California and Hawaii, but today Asian Americans are found in significant numbers across the United States. In 2000 seven out of the top ten states with the largest Asian American population are actually outside the West Coast region (see Table 2-5). The state with the largest Asian American population is California, followed by New York. Many will be surprised that the state with the third largest Asian American population is Texas. The 2000 census separated Asian Americans from Pacific Islander Americans and this had an important impact on the state of Hawaii. In 1990 Asian and Pacific Islander Americans represented 63.3 percent of Hawaii's population. In 2000, figures show that Asian Americans represent 58.0 percent of the state's population, while Native Hawaiian and other Pacific Islander Americans represented 23.3 percent. In addition, the 2000 census allowed participants to choose more than one racial category and 21.4 percent of Hawaii's counted population took that option. There were major increases in the Asian

Table 2-5 States with the Largest Asian American Population 1990–2000

	2000*			1990**	
Asian American State	Population	Percentage of State	State	Population	Percentage of State
California	4,155,685	12.3	California	2,845,659	9.6
New York	1,169,200	6.2	New York	689,769	2.9
Hawaii	703,232	58.0	Hawaii	685,236	61.8
Texas	644,193	3.1	Texas	319,459	1.9
New Jersey	524,356	6.2	Illinois	285,311	2.5
Illinois	473,649	3.8	New Jersey	272,521	5.7
Washington	395,741	6.7	Washington	210,958	4.3
Florida	333,013	2.1	Virginia	159,053	1.6
Virginia	304,559	4.3	Florida	154,302	1.2
Massachusetts	264,814	4.2	Massachusetts	143,392	2.4
NHPI State					
Hawaii	282,667	23.3			
California	221,458	0.7			
Washington	42,761	0.7			
Texas	29,094	0.1			
New York	28,612	0.2			
Utah	21,367	1.0			
Nevada	16,234	0.8			
Oregon	16,019	0.5			
Illinois	11,848	0.1			
Colorado	10,153	0.2			

* One race or in combination with one or more races.
** Totals include Asian and Pacific Islander Americans.
Source: U.S. Census Bureau, 1990 Census of the Population, General Population Characteristics, the United States (Washington, DC: Government Printing Office, 1993), CP-1-1, Table 262.

Table 2-6 Asian Pacific Islander American Region of Residence Percent Distribution of Population,* 2000 and 1990

Group	2000				1990			
	West	Midwest	North East	South	West	Midwest	North East	South
White	20.5	25.5	19.6	34.4	20.0	26.0	21.1	32.4
Black	8.9	18.8	17.6	54.8	9.4	19.1	18.7	52.8
American Indian, Eskimo, Aleut	48	16.1	6.6	29.3	47.6	17.2	6.4	28.7
Asian American	48.8	11.7	20.7	18.8	55.7	10.6	18.4	15.4*
Hispanic	43.5	8.5	18.9	32.8	45.2	7.7	16.8	30.3
Native Hawaiian And Pacific Islander	72.9	6.3	7.3	13.5				

* The percentages may not add to 100 percent because of rounding.
Sources: U.S. Census Bureau, "The White Population: 2000" (Issued August 2001) at http://www.census.gov/ prod/2001pubs/c2kbr01-4.pdf: U.S. Census Bureau, "The Black Population: 2000" (Issued August 2001) at http://www.census.gov/prod/2001pubs/c2kbr01-5.pdf U.S. Census Bureau, The Native American and Alaskan Native Population: 2000 (Issued February 2002) at http://www.census.gov/prod/2002pubs/c2kbr01-15.pdf; U.S. Census Bureau, "The Asian Population: 2000" (Issued February 2002) at http://www.census.gov/prod/ 2002pubs/c2kbr01-16.pdf; U.S. Census Bureau, "The Hispanic Population: 2000" (Issued May 2001) at http://www.census.gov/prod/2001pubs/c2kbr01-3.pdf; U.S. Census Bureau, "The Native Hawaiian and Other Pacific Islander Population: 2000" (Issued December 1991) at http://www.census.gov/prod/2001pubs/ c2kbr01-14.pdf; U.S. Census Bureau, *Census of Population, General Population Characteristics, The United States* (Washington, DC: Government Printing Office, 1993), CP-1-1, Table 253.

American population experienced by both New Jersey and Illinois. The states of Washington, Virginia, Florida, and Massachusetts are home to over 1.3 million Asian Americans. Overall, 48.8 percent of Asian Americans live in the Western portion of the United States, but 18.8 percent live in the South, 20.7 percent live in the Northeast, and 11.7 percent live in the Midwest (see Table 2-6).

New Communities

As with other minority groups, Asian Americans historically have been marginalized and segregated from both rural communities and urban cities due to pressures from the dominant society. But complex patterns can be seen in the post-1965 era and new, dynamic communities have emerged. One pattern is the increased visibility of Asian Americans in large metropolitan areas across the country. Nationally, 97 percent of all Asian Americans live in metropolitan areas, with 45 percent living in central cities and 52 percent in the suburbs. Although Asian Americans generally congregate in major metropolitan centers in and around San Francisco, Los Angeles, and New York, other lesser

Table 2-7 U.S. Cities with the Largest Asian American and Native Hawaiian and Pacific Islander Population 2000

Asian American State	City	Population	Percentage of City's Population
NY	New York	787,047	9.8
CA	Los Angeles	369,254	10.0
CA	San Jose	240,375	26.9
CA	San Francisco	239,565	30.8*
HA	Honolulu	207,588	55.9
CA	San Diego	166,968	13.6
IL	Chicago	125,974	4.3
TX	Houston	103,694	5.3
WA	Seattle	73,910	13.1
CA	Fremont	75,165	37.0
NHPI			
HA	Honolulu	58,130	15.6
NY	New York City	19,203	0.2
CA	Los Angeles	13,144	0.4
CA	San Diego	10,613	0.9
CA	Long Beach	7,863	1.7
CA	San Jose	7,091	0.8
CA	Sacramento	6,833	1.7
CA	San Francisco	6,273	0.8
WA	Seattle	4,977	0.9
CA	Hayward	4,709	3.4

* San Francisco is both a city and a county.
Source: U.S. Census Bureau, "The Asian Population: 2000" (Issued May 2001) at http://www.census.gov/prod/2001pubs/c2kbr01-3.pdf and U.S. Census Bureau, "The Native Hawaiian and Other Pacific Islander Population: 2000" (Issued December 1991) at http://www.census.gov/prod/2001pubs/c2kbr01-14.pdf.

known cities have also become quite popular. Table 2-7 shows that in 2000 more Asian Americans lived in San Jose than San Francisco. Outside California the cities of Chicago, Houston, and Seattle have become major hubs for Asian Americans. In 2000 the city of Fremont had the tenth largest Asian American population. Another pattern is Asian American suburbanization. This is the movement of Asian American communities away from traditional urban centers into middle-class suburban settings. The result of three decades of large-scale immigration from Asia has seen the emergence of new Chinatowns, Manilatowns, Koreatowns, and Little Saigons in suburban areas across the nation. The best example of the suburbanization of Asian Americans can be seen in areas surrounding Los Angeles, San Francisco, and New York. All three cities have long been the points of entry and initial settlements for most Asian immigrants. But this pattern has been altered as relatively affluent and well-educated immigrants, and established American-born Asians, are bypassing the traditional urban centers and moving directly into outlying communities.

Table 2-8 U.S. Counties with the Largest Asian American Population 2000

State	County	Population	Percentage of Total Population
CA	Los Angeles	1,137,500	11.9
CA	Santa Clara	430,095	25.6
HA	Honolulu	403,371	46.0
NY	Queens	391,500	17.6
CA	Orange	386,785	13.6
CA	Alameda	295,216	20.4
IL	Cook	260,170	4.8
CA	San Diego	249,802	8.9
CA	San Francisco	239,565	30.8
NY	Kings	185,818	7.5

Source: U.S. Census, Fact Finder at http://factfinder.census.gov/servlet/SAFFFacts?_sse=on.

Table 2-8 shows the U.S. counties with the largest Asian American populations and is an indicator of the spread of Asian American communities beyond of the core cities.

During the 1980s the San Gabriel Valley, a region just east of downtown Los Angeles, was the scene of demographic shifts so dramatic that it surprised even experienced demographers. Asian American population more than doubled in well-to-do communities such as San Marino, Hacienda Heights, and Diamond Bar that were once the domain of white middle-class home owners. Easily the most notable location in the area is Monterey Park, which in 2000 had a population of 60,000 residents and was 61.8 percent Asian. Monterey Park's population is largely immigrant Chinese and has earned the titles of "America's First Suburban Chinatown" and "The Chinese Beverly Hills."[11] In Orange County, California, known mostly as the bastion of affluent and conservative whites, Asian Americans make up 13.6 percent of the population. Orange County is the home of one of the largest concentrations of Vietnamese Americans in the United States. The city of Westminster in Orange County, population 88,000, has a very active Vietnamese commercial district, and signs on the freeway direct visitors to this "Little Saigon."[12]

Similar changes are witnessed around the San Francisco Bay Area. According to the 2000 census, nearby Santa Clara county (Asian American population 430,095) and San Mateo County (Asian American population 141, 684) have Asian populations of roughly 25 and 20 percent, respectively. Santa Clara County, anchored by Stanford University and the high-tech mecca, Silicon Valley, can actually boast of a larger Asian American population than San Francisco. In San Mateo County, Filipinos are the largest Asian American ethnic group, and most live in Daly City. Daly City's population of 103,000 is just over 50 percent Asian—two thirds of whom are Filipinos—and is known as "Adobo City," named after the finest Filipino delicacy.[13] In both Santa Clara and San Mateo counties, commercial thoroughfares show a strong Asian presence that was once found only in the major metropolitan cities. Chinese-owned stores, supermarkets, and restaurants abound, hundreds of Filipino-run stores can be seen, and the numbers of Korean and Asian Indian businesses have increased by the score.

Flushing, New York, is technically not a suburban Asian American community because it is located in the New York City borough of Queens. However, Asian immigrants and entrepreneurs have quickly turned the previously quiet area into a bustling residential and commercial alternative to Manhattan's historic Chinatown, which is much more crowded and expensive. The area has become so popular that of the 787,000 Asian Americans who live in New York City in 2000, about half live in Queens. On weekends, thousands of Asian Americans flock to Flushing to eat, shop, bank, and do business, and many believe this robust activity has revitalized an area that was previously in economic decline. More recently, another new Chinatown has blossomed in Brooklyn, New York. Chinese immigrants were attracted to the area because of opportunity and low rents. One of those Chinese immigrants is Danny Tsoi, who arrived in Manhattan in 1977. His first job was in a Chinese restaurant in old Chinatown, but after a series of jobs he moved to Brooklyn in 1989 and opened his Ocean Palace Seafood restaurant. "When I first came here," he says, "my friends told me, 'Danny, you're stupid to waste your money.' Now they tell me, 'Danny, you're smart.'"[14]

The vast majority of Asian Americans live in urban or suburban areas in various states, but there are important exceptions. In 2000, eighty percent of California's 68,706 Hmong population lived in the state's Central Valley agricultural regions in and around Fresno, Merced, Sacramento, and San Joaquin counties. Initially, the Hmong and other Southeast Asian refugees were scattered across the country by the U.S. government in hopes they would have an easier time assimilating into American life if they were physically isolated from one another. But many of the Hmong and other Southeast Asian refugees did not like the cold weather and separation, and they migrated west or to other warm weather states. "My people never hear of snow before," explains Hmong refugee Na Vang. "We arrive at night in some place like Minnesota, wake up in the morning and suddenly whole world is white."[15] Still, two conspicuous clusters of Hmong refugees continue to make their homes in concentrated areas of Minnesota (43,156) and Wisconsin (31,010).

The overall changes in Asian American settlement patterns show the emergence of new transnational communities that serve as "gateways" for the migration of people, labor, capital, and cultural exchange in the new global economy. This phenomenon is described in the work of sociologist Jan Lin in his 1999 article "Globalization and the Revalorizing of Ethnic Places in Immigration Gateway Cities," in which he compares demographic, social, economic, and cultural changes in New York, Houston, Miami, and Los Angeles. He concludes that immigrants, in general, and Asian immigrants in particular, have rejuvenated the economies and public culture of various communities. In many localities the influx of immigrant professionals, workers, and capital led to greater partnerships with city officials who see globalization as the key to economic and cultural prosperity. This can be seen not only in the increase of small business entrepreneurship, but also in the development of world trade centers, tourist complexes, and convention centers, as well as the enlargement of port and airport facilities. Lin argues that newly revitalized "ethnic places" serve as what he calls "polyglot honeypots" for urban managers and planners pursuing aggressive growth strategies in a postindustrial society.[16]

ASIAN AMERICAN SELF-EMPLOYMENT AND CONSUMER BUYING POWER

The dramatic increase of the Asian American population throughout the United States, particularly in urban regions, is also highlighted by the proliferation of business enterprises owned and operated by Asian Americans. The latest available government figures show Asian American businesses have enjoyed a steady increase in terms of numbers and sales (see Table 2-9). Asian American businesses grew to 1,105,329 firms in 2002 up from 912,960 firms in 1997. During this same period the sales generated from Asian-owned businesses increased to $343 billion up from $303 billion. According to the 2000 census, however, Asian Americans are not overrepresented in terms of business ownership compared to the national average. Of all people in the United States 16 years and older, 6.6 percent are self-employed. Among Asian Americans the percentage of self-employment is 6.1. By far the Asian American group with the highest percentage of self-employment is Korean Americans. The 2000 census shows 14.1 percent of Korean Americans are self-employed. Filipinos, in contrast, have a relatively low self-employment rate of just 3.3 percent. Among Southeast Asian refugees, self-employment is 7.0 percent for Vietnamese, 5.3 percent for Cambodians, 2.7 percent for Laotian, and 2.6 Hmong Americans (see Table 2-10).

Ethnic entrepreneurship, in general, and Asian American entrepreneurship, in particular, is not a new phenomenon. Certain ethnic groups in the United States have historically shown a noticeable propensity toward self-employment. Among eastern European/Middle Eastern immigrants, Jews, Armenians, Syrians, and Lebanese are most noted for their business acumen. Among Latinos, Cubans have a much higher self-employment rate compared to Mexicans and Puerto Ricans. Black immigrants from the Caribbean have a far greater percentage of small business enterprises than American-born blacks. In addition, Chinese and Japanese Americans have a long history of self-employment.[17] Today, however, post-1965 Asian American business owners do stand out from other racial minority groups and do have some unique characteristics that are important to note. First, according to a U.S. census, 81.8 percent of self-employed Asian Americans are immigrants. This statistic is dramatic compared to the fact that immigrants represent only 9 percent of those self-employed in the United States.[18] Second, according to the U.S. census report, *Characteristics of Business Owners, 1992*, Asian Americans have a wider variety of sources from which to raise the capital necessary to start their own business. Personal savings, borrowing from relatives, friends, or prior business owners, as well as commercial bank loans were the methods used to raise start-up funds.[19] Lastly, according to AnnaLee Saxenian (1999 and 2002) many Asian American high-technology

Table 2-9 Business Enterprises by Race and Ethnic Group, 1992, 1997, and 2002

Race/Ethnic Group	1992		1997		2002	
	Number of Firms	Gross Receipts (in millions of $)	Number of Firms	Gross Receipts (in millions of $)	Number of Firms	Gross Receipts (in millions of $)*
All	17,253,000	3,324,300	20,821,934	18,553,243	22,977,164	22,635,000
Black	621,921	32,200	823,499	71,215	1,197,988	93,000
American Indian/ Alaska Natives	102,271	8,507	197,300	34,344	206,125	26,000
Asia	N/A	N/A	893,590	303,000	1,105,329	303,000
Native Hawaiian/ Other Pacific Islander	N/A	N/A	19,370	3,933	32,299	5,000
Asian Pacific Islander	603,426	95,713	912,960	306,933	N/A	N/A
Chinese	153,096	39,188	252,577	106,196	N/A	N/A
Filipino	67,625	4,780	84,534	11,077	N/A	N/A
Japanese	68,662	12,262	85,538	43,741	N/A	N/A
Asian Indian	93,340	19,284	166,737	67,503	N/A	N/A
Korean	104,918	16,170	135,571	45,936	N/A	N/A
Vietnamese	59,674	4,312	97,764	9,322	N/A	N/A
Hispanic	862,605	76,842	1,199,896	186,275	1,574,159	226,000

* Summary statistics only.
Sources: U.S. Department of Commerce, *1992 Economic Census: Survey of Minority-Owned Business Enterprises* (Washington, DC: U.S. Government Printing Office, 1996); U.S. Department of Commerce, *1997 Economic Census: Survey of Minority-Owned Business Enterprises* (Washington, DC: U.S. Government Printing Office, 2001); U.S. Department of Commerce, Summary Statistics for Changes in Number of U.S. Businesses and their Receipts, 1997–2002 at http://www.census.gov/Press-Release/www/releases/archives/cb05_108_table.xls.

Table 2-10 Asian American Self-Employment Persons 16 Years Old and Over by Ethnic Group and Foreign-born, 2000 and 1990

Group	Self-Employed	
	2000	1990
U.S.	6.6	6.9
Asian or Pacific Islander	4.6*	6.7
Asian	6.1	6.7
Chinese	5.6	6.7
Filipino	3.3	3.2
Japanese	7.3	7.0
Asian Indian	4.7	6.1
Korean	14.1	16.9
Vietnamese	7.0	5.7
Cambodian	5.3	4.1
Laotian	2.7	2.0
Hmong	2.6	2.2

* Native Hawaiian and Pacific Islander only.
Source: U.S. Census Bureau, Profile of Selected Economic Characteristics: 2000 Data Set: Census 2000 Summary File 4, and *1990 Census of the Population, Asians and Pacific Islanders in the United States* (Washington, DC: U.S. Government Printing Office, 1993), CP-3-5, Table 4.

entrepreneurs have a wide range of professional ties to their native countries. They regularly travel back and forth to their home countries to exchange technology, labor market information, as well as investment strategies.[20]

The types of Asian American businesses range from highly successful international high-technology research and manufacturing firms, to professional business and medical offices, to small-scale street vendors, restaurants, mom-and-pop grocery stores, as well as hotel and motel operations. Most Asian American businesses are rather modest, if not marginal, family operations. Most people are familiar with the ubiquitous Chinese or Japanese restaurant, but in recent years some Asian Americans have found other, sometimes unusual, economic niches in which they cluster and often dominate. For example, Korean Americans in New York and Los Angeles were the leaders in importing and selling wigs to African American women throughout the 1970s. In recent years, Korean Americans have expanded their business interests and now own the majority of green groceries (produce markets) in New York City. Korean Americans also own a large number of liquor stores and grocery stores in many parts of Los Angeles, and they have a strong business presence in Atlanta, Georgia, and Chicago, Illinois, among other places.[21]

One interesting area where Asian Indians have found a niche is in the hotel and motel business throughout the continental United States. As early as 1987, the *Wall Street Journal* reported that 28 percent of all motels in the United States were owned by Asian Indians, and these operations range from cheap inner-city residential hotels to well-known chain franchises found along interstate highways. Unpaid family labor, especially among the women, is a central element in keeping these businesses viable. Wives, sisters, and daughters of the owners often do all of the daily cleaning and laundry chores in these hotels and motels.[22] The continuing growth of Asian Indians in what is called "the hospitality industry" is evidenced by the formation of the Asian American Hotel Owners Association (AAHOA). Despite their overarching title, AAHOA membership is overwhelmingly Asian Indian. Today AAHOA claims almost 8,700 members who together own more than 18,000 hotels, which collectively have nearly 1 million rooms. This represents more than 50 percent of the economy lodging properties in the United States and 37 percent of all hotel properties. The market value of the hotels owned by AAHOA members is estimated at $38 billion and the amount of annual property taxes paid by AAHOA members is estimated at $665 million. As a business association, AAHOA has also created its own Political Action Committee (PAC) that allows members to pool their resources for the purpose of supporting political candidates and issues consistent with the interests of AAHOA members.[23]

Since 1988 AAHOA has sponsored an annual conference and regular programs of the association include the following:

- free educational seminars conducted throughout the year for management as well as supervisory personnel;
- free regional trade shows featuring industry speakers, timely workshops, supplier exhibits, and education courses that help members stay focused;
- free youth conferences designed to expose young people to the opportunities and the responsibilities of the industry;
- free women's leadership conferences designed to inform and motivate women to be visible in the industry rather than just a "behind-the-scenes" force in the industry;
- a scholarship fund to defray the costs for qualified students who want to pursue a college education majoring in hospitality.[24]

Most recently, AAHOA made an agreement with GenaRes Worldwide Reservation Services to create a central reservation system (CRS). The system was designed specifically for the AAHOA member properties that are independent and not affiliated with any franchise hotel company CRSs. Of the hotels owned by the 8,700 AAHOA members, approximately 6,300 are nonfranchised. "Since so many of our members own independent hotels, finding a reliable independent, nonfranchise-affiliated CRS for our members was an absolute must," said Nash Patel, AAHOA's 2004 chairman. "We had been looking at systems for three or four years, and finally came to the conclusion that GenaRes's CRS was the best system on the market for our members. The GenaRes system will undoubtedly benefit hoteliers who don't have access to a franchise hotel company CRS," Patel said.[25]

Among Southeast Asian refugees, Vietnamese women have found a niche as manicurists. It is estimated that Asian Americans comprise 40 percent of this

$6 billion industry. This type of work has become popular because it requires little or no business experience, it is an easy skill to learn, English-speaking proficiency is not necessary, it takes only a small investment of money to get started, and the licensing process is fairly simple. In addition, the average salary for a manicurist is $26,000 to $32,000. Manicurists typically start off by renting space in beauty and hair-styling shops, or they work for an established nail salon. The goal for many manicurists is to open their own business. This was the case for Anna Tran, owner of Anna Nails in Sacramento, California, who puts in sixty hours a week to keep her business operating. "I came here with empty hands, and I built the shop with the support of my husband," Tran said. However, being a manicurist is hard work that can lead to carpal-tunnel damage due to the repetitive strain. For this reason Tran does not want her children to work in her shop. "We tell our children . . . they have to be educated," she explains. "I use my own hands and strength to do this."[26] Along with the physical toll of the work of being a manicurist, many are often exposed to dangerous chemicals. The Federal Environmental Protection Agency has begun a national campaign in both English and Vietnamese to warn manicurists about the long-term risks of breathing acrylic dust, fumes from nail glues, and formaldehyde-based nail polish.[27] In addition, there is now increased attention to the unsanitary work environments in some nail salons. Entertainer Paula Abdul, best known as a judge on the television show *American Idol*, was infected with a flesh-eating fungus while getting a manicure and has been a leading advocate for legislation regulating nail salon businesses.[28]

Nonetheless, the competition among Vietnamese American nail salons is fierce. As a result, some Vietnamese Americans relocate to areas where there are few Asian Americans, nail salons, and health and safety regulations or government inspectors. Anthony Nguyen, whose mother owns a nail salon in Southern California, recently relocated to Toledo, Ohio. His business is a novelty in Toledo and there he can charge $40 for a pedicure and manicure, which is roughly twice the going rate in Southern California. Relocated nail salons advertise free room and board to manicurists who are willing to move. Among the mobile manicurists is Laurie Hoang who was working in a nail salon in Chicago, then moved to Virginia, and is now in North Dakota. "Once I make enough money, I can go home," she said.[29]

Recently, Cambodian Americans have come to dominate the doughnut shop industry in California. "Cambodian people may speak very little English, but they know how to run a doughnut shop," says Ning Yen, a doughnut entrepreneur who fled Cambodia in 1980. According to a 1995 report in the *Wall Street Journal*, Cambodian Americans and their families run at least 2,450 doughnut shops, overtaking the once omnipresent Winchell's Donut House chain. Winchell's is now franchising out to many Cambodian Americans. The undisputed founder of the Cambodian doughnut phenomenon is Ted Ngoy, the former Cambodian military attaché to Thailand, who came to the United States as a refugee in 1975. He was initially hired as a manager trainee in a Winchell's doughnut shop, and after two years of hard work and saving Ngoy purchased his own business in La Habra, California. In a few years Ngoy built a chain of thirty-two stores across the state, hired and trained many fellow Cambodian refugees, and loaned them money to start their own businesses.[30] Doughnuts have been the economic gateway for many Cambodian Americans to start their own independent family-run businesses. One such example is Toty and Winnie Hou, owners of Mr. T's Donut Shop in Modesto, California. Mr. T's is a 24-hour coffee and doughnut shop with nine employees and about $320,000 in sales a year. Mr. T's must compete with major chains like Krispy Kreme and Dunkin' Donuts and coffee shops like Starbucks, but they have been able to survive. "Freshness is the key to a good doughnut," Toty Hou said. "Our customers try other places, but they come back."[31]

In California, it is estimated that Cambodian Americans own 75 percent of the 2,500 doughnut shops. Unfortunately, not all Cambodian American doughnut shops are as successful as Mr. T's. In densely populated Southern California, Krispy Kreme opened its first store in 1999 and drew 2.5 million customers. Today there are thirty Krispy Kreme stores throughout the region, with more on the way. A typical Krispy Kreme store generates $3 million in sales, which is more than ten times the revenue of the average Cambodian American doughnut shop. The largest doughnut store chain in the United States is Dunkin' Donuts and they also are making their move on Southern California. There are more than 4,000 Dunkin' Donuts locations throughout the nation that generate $3.4 billion in sales. According to company spokesperson Cindy Gordon, the chain "wants to storm California."[32] On top of the fierce competition from corporate giants, the two most prominent Cambodian American doughnut entrepreneurs have fallen on bad times. The Cambodian "doughnut king" Ted Ngoy lost his fortune and much respect in the community due to an uncontrollable gambling habit that has left him homeless and a mere shell of himself. In a recent *Los Angeles Times* article, Ngoy was reported to have been found sleeping on the porch of a friend's mobile home and was quoted saying, "I don't know who I am right now. I say Ted, who are you? I really don't know."[33] Ning Yen, the "godfather" of Cambodian doughnut makers, has seen the profits from his doughnut supply company B&H Distributors drop dramatically over the past several years. "I'm waiting for better days," Yen said. "I hope they will come."[34]

Whatever the characteristics or type of business, self-employment assures a life of hard work, long hours, and, as seen by the examples above, no guarantee of success. There have been several attempts to explain why many groups have a relatively high percentage of self-employment and others do not. One perspective is the cultural theory, which argues that certain groups have innate cultural values similar to the Protestant work ethic and are compatible with the spirit of capitalism.[35] This perspective, however, has been criticized by social scientists for a number of reasons. The most basic criticism is that there is tremendous diversity among various entrepreneurially oriented groups. Indeed, as we see here, there is no consistency in terms of geographic location or religiocultural background for who will succeed with a small business and who will not.

For Asian Americans, the most common cultural explanation seems to focus on Confucian values as the reason for business success both in the

United States as well as in Pacific Rim countries. There is, however, a great deal of diversity and mixture within and throughout Asian countries. For example, Buddhism was founded during the sixth century BCE in northern India and spread to central and eastern Asia. Confucianism became the official state philosophy in China in the second century BCE and spread across Korea to Japan. Catholicism was brought to the Philippines after it became a colony of Spain in the early sixteenth century and introduced to Vietnam after French colonialism in the late nineteenth century. Moreover, Christian missionaries were quite successful in converting many Koreans, although they were much less successful in other parts of Asia.

It is difficult to draw any firm conclusions about Asian American propensity toward entrepreneurship solely on cultural factors. For example, why are Chinese Buddhists generally active in small business, but Laotian Buddhists less likely to be? Similarly, why are Catholic Vietnamese starting businesses more than Catholic Filipinos? Among Koreans, is the Protestant ethic the more dominant cultural influence or is the Confucian ethic more dominant? These types of questions have led other social scientists to look beyond just a cultural explanation of the Asian Americans and their entrepreneurial experience and move toward examining the social situation. Researchers who study Asian Americans have noticed that many Asian American businesses are found in inner-city locations devoid of major market chain stores. As a result, these Asian Americans have formed what is known as a "middleman" niche for themselves that no one else is willing or able to fill. The middleman minority theory has been used by James Loewen in his book *The Mississippi Chinese: Between Black and White* (1971) to examine Chinese American grocery store owners in Mississippi at the turn of the century, and by Edna Bonacich and John Modell in their book *The Economic Basis of Ethnic Solidarity: Small Business in the Japanese American Community* (1980) to examine Japanese American farmers in California prior to World War II.[36] Today, however, the best example of this phenomena is seen with Korean American-owned stores operating in predominantly black communities in urban centers across the nation.

Under this theory, middleman minorities play a buffer role between large corporations and marginalized populations. Middleman minority merchants are necessary and encouraged because they are able to sell goods and products of the corporations to people who ordinarily would not have easy access to the merchandise. According to sociologist Bonacich, middleman minorities are forced into the self-employment situation because they know societal "discrimination" limits their opportunities to do much else in the mainstream economy. Korean American sociologist Pyong Gap Min has argued against the middleman minority theory and finds little evidence that U.S. corporate interests encourage Korean Americans to start small businesses. In addition, he believes Korean Americans choose to start their own businesses and are not coerced to do so. Min surveyed Korean American merchants in Atlanta and found that a high percentage of Korean American immigrants are educated and held white-collar jobs in their home countries. Min also found that Korean Americans' perception of their own labor market "disadvantages" (primarily language) was the main reason for starting a business over anything else including awareness of host-society discrimination. In short, Min believes Korean Americans make an economic and rational choice to enter self-employment.[37]

Whether by coercion or choice, the situations faced by immigrants in a new society appear to be far more a factor in starting up small businesses than cultural factors. But this still does not explain why some Asian American groups tend to have higher self-employment rates than others, nor does it explain why other "disadvantaged" groups (e.g., other racial minorities) have not taken the self-employment option more than they currently do. More recently, other social scientists have looked at the clustering of large numbers of Asian American businesses that together form ethnic "enclave economies." Enclaves appear to function quite well separate from, but also in competition with, the local mainstream economy. The positive aspects of the enclave economy are most developed by Alejandro Portes and Robert Bach (1985) in their research on Cubans in Miami, Roger Waldinger (1985) in his research on immigrant enterprise, and Min Zhou (1992) in her study of New York's Chinatown.[38]

This theory contends that enclaves develop through the transplantation of a significant number of people from the professional and entrepreneurial classes who migrate (either through immigration or as refugees) into the United States. For example, in her book *Chinatown: The Socioeconomic Potential of an Urban Enclave,* Zhou contends that Chinese immigrants with high levels of education, professional skills, and some capital find operating a small business within an enclave is preferable to working in the mainstream economy. This is particularly true for those with no English-speaking ability but also for those who do speak English. Success within the enclave depends on several factors. First, there is an ethnic population and consumer market large enough to support a number of ethnic businesses; second, enclave businesses tend to pay workers less and make them work longer hours, thus providing themselves with a competitive edge; third, ethnic solidarity within the enclave forms the basis for a mutually beneficial relationship between ethnic business owners and workers. In the enclave, the owner–worker relationship is viewed more like an apprenticeship than as exploitation. Ethnic enclave workers gain valuable work experience that will eventually lead to their own businesses, often with the help of their employers. In addition, the ethnic enclave businesses provide jobs and opportunities for less privileged immigrant workers who would likely face even greater discrimination and dead-end work outside in the mainstream labor market.[39]

This theory, however, does have its critics. Sociologists Jimy Sanders and Victor Nee (1987) and economist Don Mar (1991) have acknowledged that ethnic enclaves do provide entry-level jobs, but they question whether or not these usually low-paying jobs truly offer immigrant workers the long-term opportunities for upward mobility that enclave theorists claim. More broadly, critics of the enclave economy charge that the theory diverts attention away from the problems facing less educated, non-English-speaking immigrant workers.[40] Whether these immigrant workers are in an enclave or not, critics contend, their wages and opportunities are extremely limited. Through these criticisms, it does appear that individual human capital is an important factor to consider. Human capital is often referred to as personal factors or achieved characteristics. For example, education, skills (either professional or technical), work experience, and English-language proficiency are usually regarded as the most important and easily transferable human capital characteristics. As a general rule, the higher the level of education and skills available to the individual, the smoother his or her transition into the social and economic mainstream of the United States. This is true both for self-employment as well as for wage earners.[41]

It is also necessary to understand ethnic entrepreneurship from a broader structural perspective and show its connection with global economic restructuring. In their book *The New Asian Immigration in Los Angeles and Global Restructuring* (1994), editors Paul Ong, Edna Bonacich, and Lucie Cheng contend that the arrival of many educated, middle-class and above Asian immigrants and their resulting ethnic entrepreneurship are not merely a local phenomenon. They argue that it is very much a part of the fluid flow of people, skills, and financial capital brought together by a dramatically changing global economy. "The large-scale immigration from Asia after 1965 not only coincided with economic restructuring, but was affected by and contributed to these structural changes," the editors write in their introductory chapter. "As their numbers grow and their influence increases, Asian immigrants are not merely filling the positions that are being created as a result of restructuring. They are helping reshape the economic landscape by creating new and alternative ventures."[42] At the same time, it is important to remember that only a small percentage of Asian Americans own their own businesses. Indeed, most Asian Americans, like most other Americans, earn their money by working for someone else. For this reason we must look beyond self-employment to examine how well Asian Americans are doing socially and economically.

Asian American Consumer Buying Power

How and why some Asian American groups have come to dominate some small business niches is controversial and challenging to explain. However, the overall consumer buying power of Asian Americans is very clear. According to the Selig Center for Economic Growth, a research organization at the University of Georgia, Asian Americans' estimated disposable income in 2004 was $363 billion, up from the 2000 figure of $269 billion and up from the 1990 figure of $118.2 billion. This represents a 207 percent increase in buying power from 1990 to 2004, which is more than double the 101.1 percent increase in buying power for the United States as a whole. Between 1990 and 2004 Hispanic American buying power increased 209.3 percent (up $686.3 billion from $221.9 billion) and African American buying power increased 127.1 percent (up $723.1 billion from $318.3 billion).[43]

The Selig Center report ties in well with another study that found tremendous growth in ethnic media outlets (e.g., newspapers, magazines, radio, broadcast television, and cable television) and its impact on consumer buying power. A recent survey conducted by New California Media, an association of more than five hundred ethnic media outlets, estimated the ethnic media reaches 29 million adults who are "primary consumers" and another 22 million who prefer the mainstream media but also access ethnic television, radio, or newspapers on a regular basis. The survey also found that media consumption varies from group to group. For example, 80 percent of all Latino adults access Spanish-language television, radio, or newspapers on a regular basis. A substantial majority of African American adults listen to ethnic radio stations on a regular basis. Approximately 80 percent of all Korean, Chinese, and Vietnamese adults read an ethnic newspaper on a regular basis. In addition, access to the Internet is very high (67 percent) among all Asian Americans and half of them prefer ethnic Web sites to mainstream Web sites.[44]

There is general consensus within the ethnic media that their impact and reach is growing, but many corporations and advertisers are still learning about the diverse and increasingly complex ethnic consumer market. There are multiple markets among Asian Americans with regional and local ethnic media historically addressing their needs. Mainstream publishers, advertisers, and broadcasters have difficulty determining if this diverse population prefers to be reached in English, their native languages, or both. As a result Asian American consumers continue to be overlooked by the mainstream advertisers, experts say. According to Eliot Kang of New York-based Kang and Lee Advertising, only about $3.6 billion was put into 17,000 ethnic media outlets, a tiny fraction of the $200 billion spent on advertisements in 1998. However, this budget for ethnic media was more than double the amount spent in 1993, and many expect the growth trend to continue slowly but surely.[45]

Today it is estimated that still only 4 percent of advertising dollars are spent on the ethnic media. In an effort to increase attention to the ethnic media, New California Media organized the first National Expo of Ethnic Media that was held in New York City in June 2005. The response was overwhelming. More than 1,400 editors, corporate sales representatives, and others were there eager to make inroads in this vastly untapped market. "These media are only going to get more important," said Sandy Close, executive director of New California Media. She said that while most of the mainstream media tend to view issues through a predominantly provincial and monocultural point of view, "these media have tremendous capacity to open things up. You're talking about a new sensibility in a globalized world. This is the new America."[46] As a result, companies have emerged providing specialized consulting to corporations on how best to reach the Asian American market. "[C]orporations don't even come close to what they do for the African [American] and Hispanic [American] markets," complains Atsuko Watanabe, executive vice president and general manager of Admerasia, a leading multicultural communications agency. "Marketers are finally starting to understand that Asian Americans are one of the most lucrative markets." Bill Imada, president and chief executive officer of Imada-Wong Communications, agrees. "A vast majority of the Fortune 500 (corporations) are not involved in any way, shape or form," he said. "But I see a lot of companies getting into the market now."[47]

SOCIOECONOMIC PROFILE

The relatively high rates of self-employment and consumer spending power provide some indication of Asian American socioeconomic "success." Readers should be cautious about this impression, however, as there is also some contradictory evidence. In February 1992 the U.S. Commission on Civil Rights produced a report entitled *Civil Rights Issues Facing Asian Americans in the 1990s.* The report was immediately lampooned in an April 26, 1992 article, "Up from Inscrutable," published in *Fortune* magazine. The article began with this statement: "Easily the strangest document produced by the U.S. Commission on Civil Rights in recent years is its just-released report on the predicament, if that is the word, which we doubt, of Asian Americans." The article went on to cite general statistical data indicating that Asian Americans, as a whole, are more educated, have better jobs, and have higher family incomes than the average American. "So what's the problem?" the reporter asked incredulously.[48] Like many people, this reporter's image of Asian Americans was of an untroubled "model minority" that other racial minority groups should emulate if they want to "succeed." A closer and more critical examination of the data, however, shows tremendous diversity among various Asian ethnic groups, as well as some important invisible factors that raises serious questions about exactly how well Asian Americans really are doing in terms of their socioeconomic status.

The Model Minority: Myth or Reality?

The emergence of Asian Americans as the model minority became prominent in 1966 when two articles in national magazines praised the achievements of the two largest Asian American groups at that time. The first article, "Success Japanese-American Style," was written by sociologist William Petersen and published in the *New York Times Magazine* on January 9, 1966. The article lauded Japanese Americans for overcoming harsh racial antagonism and internment to enter successfully into the American mainstream. That same year, Chinese Americans were also highly commended for their good behavior and economic success in the article, "Success Story of One Minority Group in the United States," published in *U.S. News and World Report.*[49] Numerous other articles published since that time also focused on the virtues and accomplishments of Asian Americans, especially in terms of exceptional educational achievements and phenomenal economic upward mobility. Although flattering, the model minority image has proven to be more of a burden than a breakthrough for Asian Americans.

The 1992 report by the U.S. Commission on Civil Rights discussed four ways in which the model minority myth is indeed harmful to Asian Americans. First, the model minority image diverts attention from real and very serious social and economic problems that plague many segments of the Asian American population. Second, it distracts public attention away from continued, often times overt, racial discrimination faced by Asian Americans. Third, the model minority stereotype places undue pressure and anguish on young Asian Americans who think they have to achieve in school. This has been linked with mental health issues for teenagers and even suicides. Fourth, the model minority image serves to fuel competition and resentment between groups, particularly among other racial minorities who are asked, if Asian Americans can succeed, why can't they?[50]

Many have argued that the emergence of the model minority stereotype in the mid-1960s, and its persistence, has had important political and public policy ramifications. Attention to Asian American success first appeared at a time of an increasingly militant black power movement, which called for increased government intervention to remedy historical and contemporary racial discrimination. But the quiet self-sufficiency of Asian Americans has often been held up in contrast to active African American calls for greater government action and support for social service programs. According to the 1966 *U.S. News and World Report* article, "At a time when it is being proposed that hundreds of billions be spent to uplift Negroes and other minorities, the nation's 300,000 Chinese-Americans are moving ahead on their own, with no help from anyone else."[51] Since that time, conservative political pundits, including some African Americans, have used the model minority image to show that the United States is the land of opportunity and contend that government programs such as welfare and affirmative action are unnecessary. Conservatives claim that all racial minority groups can succeed just like Asian Americans if they work hard, don't cause trouble, and assimilate into mainstream American life.

Given the political and public policy attention surrounding the model minority stereotype, it is necessary to see if the image is indeed true. At the heart of the model minority claim are several general statistics that are used as "facts" proving Asian American "success." It is important to look closely at the evidence to better judge its validity. The three most commonly cited statistics used to "prove" that Asian Americans are the model minority are educational achievement, employment status, and median family and per capita income.

Education   Summary statistics do show that Asian Americans are a highly educated group. According to the U.S. Census Bureau report "Educational Attainment in the United States: 2003," 49.8 percent of Asian Americans 25 years of age and over have completed at least four years or more of college education. This figure exceeds the 30 percent average for non-Hispanic whites (see Table 2-11). These figures also show educational achievement for Asian Americans differs among males and females. We see in Table 2-11 that 53.8 percent of Asian American males completed four years of college or more compared to 46.1 percent of Asian American females. Although impressive, it is quite evident that educational achievement by Asian Americans is far from uniform. Table 2-12 (p. 65) provides the latest comparable data in 2000 and shows only 19.4 percent of Vietnamese, 9.2 percent of Cambodians, 7.7 percent of Laotians, and 7.5 percent of Hmong 25 years old or over earned a four-year college degree or more.

Table 2-11 Education by Sex, Ethnic Group, and Foreign-born
25 Years Old and Over, 2000 and 1990

Group	2003 4+ College	1990 4+ College
Non-Hispanic Whites	30.0	21.5
Male	32.3	25.0
Female	27.0	18.4
Black	17.3	11.4
Male	16.7	11.0
Female	17.8	11.7
Asian American	49.8	36.6
Male	53.8	41.9
Female	46.1	31.8
Hispanic	11.4	9.2
Male	11.2	10.0
Female	11.6	8.3

Sources: U.S. Census Bureau, *Educational Attainment in the United States,* 2003, Table A, p. 3 at http://www.census.gov/prod/2004pubs/p20-550.pdf; U.S. Census Bureau, *1990 Census of the Population: Education in the United States* (Washington, DC: Government Printing Office, 1993), CP-3-4, Table 1; *1990 Census of the Population, Asians and Pacific Islanders in the United States* (Washington, DC: U.S. Government Printing Office, 1993).

Employment   High rates of education generally translate into better employment opportunities. Table 2-13 (pp. 66–68) shows how various Asian American groups are well represented in the managerial and professional occupation ranks. Overall, 44.6 percent of Asian Americans are involved in management, professional, and related occupations. This is a higher percentage than non-Hispanic Whites (35.6 percent), African Americans (25.2 percent), and Hispanics (18.1 percent). As with education, there is variation from group to group among Asian Americans within this occupational category. The range is as high as 59.9 percent for Asian Indians and as low as 13.4 percent for Laotian. Less than 20 percent of Cambodians, Hmong, and Laotians were employed in management, professional, and related occupations. At the same time, these Southeast Asian groups were more than 35 percent employed in production, transportation, and material moving jobs.

Family and Per Capita Income   Asian Americans, on average, do enjoy a higher family income compared to all other Americans. The 2000 census found median family income level for the nation was $50,046. The median income was the highest ever recorded for non-Hispanic white ($53,356), African American ($33,255), and Hispanic ($34,397) families. At the same time, the Asian American median family income in 2000 was $59,324, the highest median income of any group. Like everything else, the median family income does vary for each Asian American group. In 2000 Japanese Americans had the highest

Table 2-12 Asian American Educational Attainment by Ethnic Group, 25 Years Old and Over, 2000 and 1990

Group	2000 4+ College	1990 4+ College
Chinese	48.1	40.7
Male	52.6	46.7
Female	44.0	34.9
Filipino	43.8	39.3
Male	40.2	36.2
Female	46.4	41.6
Japanese	41.9	34.5
Male	49.4	42.9
Female	36.2	28.2
Asian Indian	63.9	58.0
Male	69.6	65.9
Female	57.1	48.7
Korean	43.8	34.5
Male	53.4	50.6
Female	37.0	23.3
Vietnamese	19.4	17.4
Male	22.3*	22.3*
Female	16.7	12.2
Cambodian	9.2	5.7
Male	12.1	8.6
Female	6.8	3.2
Laotian	7.7	5.4
Male	8.5	7.0
Female	6.9	3.5
Hmong	7.5	4.9
Male	10.2	7.0
Female	4.8	3.0

* Percentage for Vietnamese Males did not change from 1990 to 2000.
Source: U.S. Census Bureau, *1990 Census of the Population, Asians and Pacific Islanders in the United States* (Washington, DC: U.S. Government Printing Office, 1993), CP-3-5, Table 3 and U.S. Census Bureau, "Sex by Educational Attainment for the Population 25 years and Over," Summary File 4.

median family income at $70,849, compared to Hmong Americans who have a median family income of just $32,384 (see Table 2-14, p. 69).

The most recent data from the 2000 census also found that among year-round full-time workers, the median earnings of Asian American males was 9 percent higher than those of all males and is slightly higher than non-Hispanic white males. Asian American women were found to make 14 percent higher than those of all women, and about 10 percent higher than non-Hispanic white females. Asian Indian men had the highest median per capita income at $51,904 followed by Japanese American males at $50,876. The median per capita income

Table 2-13 Occupation: Employed Civilian Population 16 Years and Over, 2000

Group	Percent
Non-Hispanic White	
Management, professional, and related occupations	35.6
Service occupations	13.4
Sales and office occupations	27.0
Farming, fishing, and forestry occupations	0.6
Construction, extraction, and maintenance occupations	9.8
Production, transportation, and material moving occupations	13.6
Black	
Management, professional, and related occupations	25.2
Service occupations	22.0
Sales and office occupations	27.3
Farming, fishing, and forestry occupations	0.4
Construction, extraction, and maintenance occupations	6.5
Production, transportation, and material moving occupations	18.6
Asian	
Management, professional, and related occupations	44.6
Service occupations	14.1
Sales and office occupations	24.0
Farming, fishing, and forestry occupations	0.3
Construction, extraction, and maintenance occupations	3.6
Production, transportation, and material moving occupations	13.4
Chinese	
Management, professional, and related occupations	52.3
Service occupations	13.9
Sales and office occupations	20.8
Farming, fishing, and forestry occupations	0.1
Construction, extraction, and maintenance occupations	2.6
Production, transportation, and material moving occupations	10.4
Filipino	
Management, professional, and related occupations	38.2
Service occupations	17.5
Sales and office occupations	28.1
Farming, fishing, and forestry occupations	0.5
Construction, extraction, and maintenance occupations	4.1
Production, transportation, and material moving occupations	11.5
Japanese	
Management, professional, and related occupations	50.7
Service occupations	11.9
Sales and office occupations	26.9
Farming, fishing, and forestry occupations	0.4
Construction, extraction, and maintenance occupations	4.3
Production, transportation, and material moving occupations	5.9

Table 2-13 *continued*

Group	Percent
Asian Indian	
Management, professional, and related occupations	59.9
Service occupations	7.0
Sales and office occupations	21.4
Farming, fishing, and forestry occupations	0.2
Construction, extraction, and maintenance occupations	2.1
Production, transportation, and material moving occupations	9.4
Korean	
Management, professional, and related occupations	38.7
Service occupations	14.8
Sales and office occupations	30.2
Farming, fishing, and forestry occupations	0.2
Construction, extraction, and maintenance occupations	3.9
Production, transportation, and material moving occupations	12.2
Vietnamese	
Management, professional, and related occupations	26.9
Service occupations	19.3
Sales and office occupations	18.6
Farming, fishing, and forestry occupations	0.6
Construction, extraction, and maintenance occupations	5.9
Production, transportation, and material moving occupations	28.8
Cambodian	
Management, professional, and related occupations	17.8
Service occupations	15.9
Sales and office occupations	23.5
Farming, fishing, and forestry occupations	0.5
Construction, extraction, and maintenance occupations	5.5
Production, transportation, and material moving occupations	36.8
Laotian	
Management, professional, and related occupations	13.4
Service occupations	14.5
Sales and office occupations	19.1
Farming, fishing, and forestry occupations	0.5
Construction, extraction, and maintenance occupations	5.8
Production, transportation, and material moving occupations	46.6
Hmong	
Management, professional, and related occupations	17.1
Service occupations	15.6
Sales and office occupations	20.6
Farming, fishing, and forestry occupations	0.4
Construction, extraction, and maintenance occupations	4.5
Production, transportation, and material moving occupations	41.7

(Continued)

Table 2-13 *continued*

Group	Percent
Hispanic	
Management, professional, and related occupations	18.1
Service occupations	21.8
Sales and office occupations	23.1
Farming, fishing, and forestry occupations	2.7
Construction, extraction, and maintenance occupations	13.1
Production, transportation, and material moving occupations	21.2
Native Hawaiian and Pacific Islander	
Management, professional, and related occupations	23.3
Service occupations	20.8
Sales and office occupations	28.8
Farming, fishing, and forestry occupations	0.9
Construction, extraction, and maintenance occupations	9.6
Production, transportation, and material moving occupations	16.5

Source: U.S. Census Bureau, "Profile of Selected Economic Characteristics: 2000," Summary File 4.

for Japanese American females was highest at $35,998 followed by Asian Indian females at $35,173. At the other end of the scale we see the median per capital incomes for Cambodians, Laotians, and Hmong Americans to be the lowest among all the Asian Americans (see Table 2-15, p. 70).

Beyond the Model Minority

Many people look at general statistics and conclude that Asian Americans either do not face any discrimination relative to other racial minority groups or, if they did, they have overcome them. This image is not completely false for some Asian Americans, but is a rather deceptive overstatement for all Asian American groups. Detailed statistics on Asian American education, employment, and median family income show the difficulty in creating a clear picture of the average Asian American. Even among those relatively successful Asian American groups, several factors must be taken into consideration before we make any broad assumptions. Many have argued that socioeconomic "success" for Asian Americans can be understood only within the context of (1) a high percentage of urbanization, (2) the poverty rate, and (3) analyzing income based on education. By examining these factors we find that most Asian Americans are indeed advantaged relative to blacks and Hispanics, but are still disadvantaged relative to whites.

First of all, national statistics of median family incomes are a very poor indicator of relative Asian American success. This is because they not only compare Asian Americans living in urbanized areas that naturally have a higher cost of living with whites who live in the same areas, but also with whites living in lower cost-of-living regions across the country. A much better comparison

Table 2-14 Median Family Income and Poverty Status by Race/Ethnic Group, 2000 and 1990

Group	2000		1990	
	Median Family Income	Percentage Below Poverty	Median Family Income	Percentage Below Poverty
U.S.	$50,046	9.2	$30,056	10.0
Non-Hispanic White	$53,356	6.3	$37,152	7.0
Black	$33,255	21.6	$22,429	26.3
Asian American	$59,324	9.7	$41,251	11.6*
Chinese	$60,058	10.3	$41,316	11.1
Filipino	$65,189	4.7	$46,698	5.2
Japanese	$70,849	4.2	$51,550	3.4
Asian Indian	$70,708	6.7	$49,309	7.2
Korean	$47,624	13.2	$33,909	14.7
Vietnamese	$47,103	14.2	$30,550	23.8
Cambodian	$35,621	34.8	$18,126	42.1
Laotian	$43,542	16.6	$23,101	32.2
Hmong	$32,384	34.8	$14,327	61.8
Hispanic	$34,397	20.0	$25,064	22.3
Native Hawaiian and Pacific Islander	$45,915	14.6	N/A	N/A

* Asian Americans and Pacific Islanders.
Sources: U.S. Census Bureau, "Profile of Selected Economic Characteristics: 2000," Summary File 4; U.S. Census Bureau, *1990 Census of the Population, Asians and Pacific Islanders in the United States* (Washington, DC: U.S. Government Printing Office, 1993), CP-3-5, Table 5; *1990 Census of the Population, Social and Economic Characteristics, Metropolitan Areas* (Washington, DC: Government Printing Office, 1993), CP-2-1B, Tables 6–7, 9–10.

would be Asian American family incomes compared with white family incomes in the same city. With this in mind, 2000 census figures from five cities that have large Asian American populations show how misleading national statistics can be. The median family income for whites was $55,541 in Chicago, $53,442 in Houston, $52,317 in Los Angeles, $55,400 in New York, and $81,891 in San Francisco. By contrast, median family income for Asian Americans was $47,838 in Chicago, $45,454 in Houston, $46,469 in Los Angeles, $42,199 in New York, and $56,679 in San Francisco (see Table 2-16, p. 71).

Second, it should be noted that although Asian Americans generally have a higher median family income and per capita than the average American, they also have a higher rate of poverty. In 2000 Asian Americans had a 9.7 percent family poverty rate. This figure is low compared to the 21.6 percent poverty rate for African Americans and 20.0 percent for Hispanic Americans, but it is slightly higher than the 9.2 poverty rate for non-Hispanic whites. You might be surprised to learn that even more established Asian American groups such as the Chinese and Korean American families have poverty rates of 10.3 percent and 13.2 percent, respectively, both above the national average. At the same time, all

Table 2-15 Median Per Capita Income for Full-Time
Year-Round Workers by Sex and
Race/Ethnic Group, 2000

Group	Income
Non-Hispanic white	
Male	$39,235
Female	$27,878
African American	
Male	$30,000
Female	$25,589
Asian American	
Male	$40,650
Female	$31,049
Chinese	
Male	$44,831
Female	$34,869
Filipino	
Male	$35,560
Female	$31,450
Japanese	
Male	$50,876
Female	$35,998
Asian Indian	
Male	$51,904
Female	$35,173
Korean	
Male	$38,776
Female	$28,403
Vietnamese	
Male	$31,258
Female	$24,028
Cambodian	
Male	$28,706
Female	$21,911
Laotian	
Male	$26,664
Female	$21,857
Hmong	
Male	$25,187
Female	$20,237
Hispanic	
Male	$25,400
Female	$21,634
Native Hawaiian and Pacific Islander	
Male	$31,030
Female	$25,694

Source: U.S. Census Bureau, "Profile of Selected Economic Characteristics: 2000," Summary File 4.

Table 2-16 Median Family Income by Select Cities, 2000

Group	Chicago	Houston	Los Angeles	New York	San Francisco
White	$55,541	$53,442	$52,317	$55,400	$81,891
African American	$32,776	$31,007	$32,500	$35,409	$35,943
Asian	$47,838	$45,454	$46,469	$42,199	$56,679
Hispanic	$37,166	$29,584	$28,155	$28,949	$46,809

Source: PCT113. Median Family Income, Census 2000 Summary File 4 (SF 4).

Southeast Asian refugee groups suffered higher than average rates of poverty. Among Vietnamese American families the poverty rate was 14.2 percent, and among Laotians the poverty rate was 16.6. However, 34.8 percent of Cambodian, and 34.8 percent of Hmong Americans live below the poverty line (see Table 2-14, p. 69).

Because of the mass exodus following the Vietnam War, Congress passed the Refugee Act of 1980, which formalized a policy for refugees and regularized assistance for the resettlement of Southeast Asian refugees. Basic refugee assistance included food, shelter, clothing, mental health services, English language and vocational training, and job placement for up to thirty-six months (reduced to eighteen months in 1982). After this period of refugee assistance, "time expired" refugees became eligible for welfare just like U.S. citizens. Southeast Asian refugees were, of course, encouraged to find work and avoid welfare. However, many refugees arrived in the United States with few possessions and they often lacked both transferable vocational and English-language skills. As a result, adjustment to the United States was very difficult for many. What also made their adjustment particularly arduous was the fact that many faced tremendous hardships leaving their home countries. One 1985 study found 83.3 percent of Cambodian refugees were separated from their families, and 56.3 percent had lost at least one family member. Among Vietnamese refugees, 39.5 percent had lost family members and 30 percent were assaulted during their escape.[52]

Then, between 1986 and 1992, federal funding for refugee assistance declined 27 percent, which only served to channel Southeast Asians and others into state welfare systems more rapidly.[53] As late as the 1990 census, extremely high poverty rates were seen among Southeast Asian groups. By comparison, the welfare utilization rate for other immigrant groups, many of whom were admitted to the United States as permanent residents under various refugee acts, was equally high. For example, welfare utilization was 45 percent for Afghans, 34 percent for Iranians, 30 percent for Ethiopians, and 50 percent for immigrants from the former Soviet Union.[54] High rates of poverty and welfare dependency among Southeast Asians is a major factor for the widely bifurcated socioeconomic portrait of Asian Americans, although there has been marked improvement for the 2000 census.

A third important factor to consider is that, even though Asian Americans invest in their education in hopes of achieving a higher standard of living, this strategy appears to have only limited returns. It is easy to assume that the incomes

Table 2-17 Income in 2002 by Educational Attainment, Year-Round Full-Time Workers, 25–64 Years and Over

Group	Degree			
	Bachelor's	Master's	Professional	Doctorate
Non-Hispanic White	$51,832	$60,417	$95,831	$81,263
African American	$42,385	$49,328	$56,154	(B)
Asian	$48,167	$63,391	$85,733	$80,379
Hispanic	$40,733	$50,435	$75,507	(B)

Note: The symbol B means that the base is too small to show the derived measure.
Source: http://www.census.gov/population/www/socdemo/education/cps2003.html, Table 8.

of Asian Americans should be higher because they typically live in urban areas and have high levels of education. However, data from the 2000 census show something quite different. Table 2-17 compares educational income and attainment and shows salaries are not equal for everyone despite college, graduate, and professional degrees. For example, looking at different groups of people all with bachelor's degrees, non-Hispanic whites earn on average $51,832. People with college degrees are expected to earn more than those without the same education, but why should some people make more than others with the same level of education? Asian Americans with a bachelor's degree average $48,167 while African Americans with a bachelor's degree earn $42,385 and Hispanics with a bachelor's degree average only $40,733. As the educational level increases, earning power also increases. Yet for the most part the income disparity persists. Asian Americans with a master's degree do earn more than all groups with the same education, but Asian Americans with professional degrees (doctors, lawyers, pharmacists, veterinarians, etc.) and with doctoral degrees earn less than non-Hispanic whites with the same advanced degrees.

CONCLUSION

Seeing Asian Americans only as a "model minority" may seem complimentary at first, but it serves only to homogenize unfairly an extremely diverse group of people. The model minority myth completely ignores important historical and socioeconomic realities about Asian Americans. The notion that Asian Americans are the model minority is somewhat similar to the European immigrant analogy described in Chapter 1, which views success in terms of poor immigrants who work hard to pull themselves up by their own "bootstraps" and advance socially and economically in the United States. Within this narrow context, the model minority label may seem valid. However, a more critical perspective on the Asian American experience recognizes the role of broader structural forces and policy changes that served to encourage the immigration of highly educated and well-to-do Asian immigrants, as well as the arrival of desperately poor Asian refugees to the United States. Those immigrants and refugees with the most human capital advantages are, along with their children, clearly doing the best socially and economically. They not only support their own families but also contribute greatly to the overall U.S. economy. Asian American immigrants and refugees with the fewest human capital advantages are, along with their children, generally doing worse socially and economically than any other group in the United States.

The post-1965 Asian immigrants are generally more geographically dispersed, better educated, and better off economically than pre-1965 Asian immigrants. At the same time, ample evidence shows that inequality persists even for Asian Americans with the highest levels of education and skills (human capital). Ongoing anti-immigrant sentiment described at the beginning of this chapter shows the contributions and achievements of Asian Americans are not often appreciated. Moreover, the model minority image of Asian Americans is a dubious concept that does more harm than good—it distracts attention from less affluent and less educated segments of the Asian American population, minimizes the negative impact of discrimination and inequality confronted by Asian Americans, places undue pressure and anguish on young Asian Americans, and creates tremendous resentment against Asian Americans. These issues are addressed in greater detail in the chapters ahead.

NOTES

1. Lydia Saad, "Americans Divided on Immigration," *Gallop Poll News Service,* July 22, 2004.
2. Bill Wong, "Human Cargo," *AsianWeek,* April 26, 1996.
3. Ignatius Bau, "Immigrant Rights: A Challenge to Asian Pacific American Political Influence," *Asian American Policy Review* 5 (1995): 7–44.
4. Quoted in Bert Eljera, "Mixed Reactions on Immigration Moves," *AsianWeek,* March 29, 1996.
5. See www.cis.org and www.immigrationforum.org for details.
6. National Research Council, *The New Americans: Economic, Demographic and Fiscal Effects of Immigration* (Washington, D.C.: National Academy Press, 1997).
7. Quoted in Louis Freedberg, "Feinstein Fails to Limit Legal Immigration," *San Francisco Chronicle,* April 26, 1996.
8. United States Department of Labor Bureau of Labor Statistics News. "Foreign-Born Workers: Labor Force Characteristics in 2005," April 14, 2006, at http://www.bls.gov/news.release/pdf/forbrn.pdf and Steven Greenhouse, "Foreign Workers at Highest Level in Seven Decades," *New York Times,* September 4, 2000.
9. Board of Trustees of the Federal Old-Age and Survivors Insurance and Disability Insurance Trust Fund, 2004 Annual Report of the Board of Trustees of the Federal Old-Age and Survivors Insurance and Disability Insurance Trust Fund (Transmitted to Congress March 23, 2004), p. 151 at www.ssa.gov/OACT/TR/TR04. Also see David E. Rosenbaum and Robin Toner, "To Social Security Debate, Add Variable: Immigration," *New York Times* February 16, 2005, and Stuart Anderson, "The Contributions of Legal Immigration to the Social Security System" at www.nfap.net.
10. Ruben Navarrette, Jr., "Illegal Immigrants and Social Security," *San Diego Union-Tribune,* April 10, 2005.
11. Timothy P. Fong, *The First Suburban Chinatown: The Remaking of Monterey Park, California* (Philadelphia: Temple University Press, 1994).
12. Chor-Swan Ngin, "The Acculturation Pattern of Orange County's Southeast Asian Refugees," *Journal of Orange County* 3:4 (Fall 1989–Spring 1990): 46–53.
13. Dexter Waugh and Steven A. Chin, "Daly City: New Manila," *San Francisco Examiner,* September 17, 1989.

14. Quoted in E. S. Browning, "A New Chinatown Grows in Brooklyn," *Wall Street Journal*, May 31, 1994.
15. Quoted from Frank Viviano, "Strangers in the Promised Land," *Image*, August 31, 1986, pp. 15–21, 38.
16. Jan Lin, "Globalization and the Revalorizing of Ethnic Places in Immigration Gateway Cities," *Urban Affairs Review* 34, 2 (November): 313–339.
17. Ivan Light, *Ethnic Enterprise in America* (Berkeley: University of California Press, 1972); Thomas Sowell, *The Economics and Politics of Race: An International Perspective* (New York: Quill, 1983); and Alejandro Portes and Ruben G. Rumbaut, *Immigrant America: A Portrait* (Berkeley and Los Angeles: University of California Press, 1990).
18. U.S. Bureau of the Census, *1990 Census of the Population, Asians and Pacific Islanders in the United States* (Washington, DC: U.S. Government Printing Office, 1993), p. 110, Table 4.
19. U.S. Bureau of the Census, *Characteristics of Business Owners, 1992* (Washington, DC: Government Printing Office, 1992), Tables 9, 14, 17. Asian Americans represented 94.3 percent of the category "Other minority-owned businesses."
20. AnnaLee Saxenian, *Silicon Valley's New Immigrant Entrepreneurs* (San Francisco, CA: Public Policy Institute of California, 1999) and AnnaLee Saxenian with Yasuyuki Motoyama and Xiaohong Quan, *Local and Global Networks of Immigrant Professionals in Silicon Valley* (San Francisco, CA: Public Policy Institute of California, 2002).
21. Illsoo Kim, *New Urban Immigrants: The Korean Community in New York* (Princeton, NJ: Princeton University Press, 1981); Edna Bonacich and Ivan Light, *Immigrant Entrepreneurs: Koreans in Los Angeles* (Berkeley and Los Angeles: University of California Press, 1988); Pyong Gap Min, *Ethnic Business Enterprise: Korean Small Business in Atlanta* (New York: Center for Migration Studies, 1988); and Eui-Hang Shin and Shin-Kap Han, "Korean Immigrant Small Businesses in Chicago: An Analysis of the Resource Mobilization Process," *Amerasia Journal* 16:1 (1990): 39–60.
22. James P. Sterba, "Indians in U.S. Prosper in Their New Country, and Not Just in Motels," *Wall Street Journal*, January 27, 1987; and Sucheta Mazumdar, "South Asians in the United States with a Focus on Asian Indians: Policy on New Communities," in *State of Asian Pacific America: Policy Issues to the Year 2020* (Los Angeles: LEAP Asian Pacific American Public Policy Institute and UCLA Asian American Studies Center, 1993), pp. 283–301.
23. See the AAOHA Web site at http://www.aahoa.com.
24. *Ibid.*
25. Quoted in "AAHOA—Asian American Hotel Owners Association—Selects GenaRes as the Preferred Reservations Service for its 6,300 Independent Hotels; AAHOA Members can now use GenaRes for CRS, GDS, Internet and Voice Reservations," *Business Wire*, May 10, 2005.
26. Quoted in Thuy-Doan Le and Garance Burke, "Getting a Toehold Cleaning Nails Opens Doors for Many Vietnamese," *Sacramento Bee*, September 12, 2004.
27. Garance Burke and Thuy-Doan Lee, "Cutting Edge of Danger: Programs Warn Manicurists of Salon Perils," *Sacramento Bee*, October. 24, 2004.
28. "Abdul Backs Bill for Cleaner Nail Salons," *San Francisco Chronicle*, June 28, 2005.
29. Anh Do, "Viet Manicurists Leave Southern California to Start Salons Elsewhere," *Los Angeles Times*, October 25, 1999.
30. Jonathan Kaufman, "How Cambodians Came to Control California Doughnuts," *Wall Street Journal*, February 22, 1995; and John Flynn, "Success the Old Fashioned Way," *San Francisco Examiner*, April 30, 1995. Note: "Doughnut" is the proper spelling, although "Donut" is the commonly used commercial spelling.
31. Todd Milbourn, "Tasty Treats Build Dreams: Mr. T's Doughnuts are key to Family's Success," *Modesto Bee*, August 2, 2004.
32. Quoted in Marc Ballon, "A Hole in Their Dreams," *Los Angeles Times*, April 7, 2002.
33. Quoted in Sam Quinones, "From Sweet Success to Bitter Tears," *Los Angeles Times*, January 19, 2005.
34. Quoted in Bellon, *op. cit.*
35. Thomas Sowell, *Race and Culture: A World View* (New York: Basic, 1994).
36. James W. Loewen, *The Mississippi Chinese: Between Black and White* (Cambridge: Harvard University Press, 1971); and Edna Bonacich and John Modell, *The Economic Basis of Ethnic Solidarity: Small Business in the Japanese American Community* (Berkeley: University of California Press, 1980).
37. See Edna Bonacich, "The Social Costs of Immigrant Entrepreneurship," *Amerasia Journal* 14:1 (1988): 119–128; Pyong Gap Min, "The Social Costs of Immigrant Entrepreneurship: A Response to Edna Bonacich," *Amerasia Journal* 15:2 (1989): 187–194; and Min, *Ethnic*

Business Enterprise: Korean Small Business in Atlanta (New York: Center for Migration Studies, 1988).

38. Alejandro Portes and Robert Bach, *Latin Journey: Cuban and Mexican Immigrants in the United States* (Berkeley: University of California Press, 1985); Roger Waldinger, "Immigrant Enterprise and the Structure of the Labor Market," in Bryan Roberts et al. (eds.), *New Approaches to Economic Life* (Manchester: Manchester University Press, 1985), pp. 66–88; and Min Zhou, *Chinatown: The Socioeconomic Potential of an Urban Enclave* (Philadelphia: Temple University Press, 1992).

39. Zhou, ibid.

40. Jimy Sanders and Victor Nee, "Limits of Ethnic Solidarity in the Enclave Economy," *American Sociological Review* 52 (1987): 745–767; and Don Mar, "Another Look at the Enclave Economy Thesis," *Amerasia Journal* 17:3 (1991): 5–21.

41. See Gary S. Becker, *Human Capital: A Theoretical and Empirical Analysis*, 2nd ed. (Chicago: University of Chicago Press, 1980); Barry Chiswick, *Income Inequality* (New York: Columbia University Press, 1974); and William A. Scott and Ruth Scott, *Adaptation of Immigrants: Individual Differences and Determinants* (Oxford: Pergamon Press, 1989).

42. Paul Ong, Edna Bonacich, and Lucie Cheng (eds.), *The New Asian Immigration in Los Angeles and Global Restructuring* (Philadelphia: Temple University Press, 1994), pp. 23–24, 29.

43. Jeffrey M. Humphrey, "The Multicultural Economy 2004:America's Minority Buying Power" *Georgia Business and Economic Conditions* (University of Georgia: Selig Center for Economic Growth, Vol. 64, No. 3, Third Quarter 2004).

44. Mitra Kalita, "A Dollar in Any Language, *Washington Post,* June 10, 2005. The full report can be found at http://expo.ncmonline.com/news/.

45. Dwight Cunningham, "One Size Does," *Media Week,* November 15, 1999.

46. Mitra Kalita, *op. cit.*

47. Quoted in Lenora Chu, "A Coveted Market," *Asian Week,* March 23, 2000.

48. "Up from Inscrutable," *Fortune,* April 6, 1992, p. 120.

49. William Petersen, "Success Story, Japanese-American Style," *New York Times Magazine,* January 9, 1966, pp. 20–21, 33, 36, 38, 40–41, 43; and "Success Story of One Minority Group in the U.S.," *U.S. News and World Report,* December 26, 1966, pp. 73–78.

50. U.S. Commission on Civil Rights, *Civil Rights Issues Facing Asian Americans in the 1990s* (Washington, DC: U.S. Government Printing Office, 1992), p. 19.

51. Petersen, "Success Story," p. 73.

52. Ruben Rumbaut, "Mental Health and the Refugee Experience," in Tom C. Owen (ed.), *Southeast Asian Mental Health: Treatment, Prevention, Services, Training and Research* (Rockville, MD: National Institute of Mental Health, 1985), pp. 433–486.

53. Paul Ong and Evelyn Blumenberg, "Welfare and Work Among Southeast Asians," in Paul Ong (ed.), *The State of Asian Pacific America: Economic Diversity, Issues & Policies* (Los Angeles: LEAP Asian Pacific American Public Policy Institute and UCLA Asian American Studies Center, 1994), pp. 113–138.

54. Ngoan Le, "The Case of the Southeast Asian Refugees: Policy for a Community 'At-Risk'," in *The State of Asian Pacific America: Policy Issues to the Year 2020*, pp. 167–188.

3

*The Right to Excel:
Asian Americans and
Educational Opportunity*

VISIBILITY AND INVISIBILITY

On January 26, 2005, Intel Corporation announced the forty finalists in their Intel Science Talent Search. This contest is the oldest and most prestigious precollege science competition, often considered the "Junior Nobel Prize." Alumni of this contest hold more than hundred of the world's most coveted science and math honors including six Nobel Prizes, three National Medals of Science, and ten MacArthur Foundation Fellowships. The selected finalists vie for the top prize, a $100,000 scholarship. The second-place finalist receives a $75,000 scholarship and the third-place finalist receives a $50,000 scholarship. Among the forty finalists, seventeen were Asian American. They included the following:

- June-Ho Kim, 17, of Cupertino, California, studied the ability of antibodies to reduce the symptoms of experimental autoimmune encephalomyelitis (EAE), a murine model of multiple sclerosis (MS). He is on the debate team and co-president of the Future Physicians of America Club at Monta Vista High School. An accomplished pianist, June-Ho is a founding member of both the Perfect 5th Ensemble and the Appassionato Club, which entertains senior citizens, and he is Youth Committee co-chairman for the Santa Clara Valley Red Cross. June-Ho is the son of Dr. Youngbae and Jiyeon Kim.
- Pooja Sunil Jotwani, 17, of Pembroke Pines, Florida, researched the effects of a quark matter core on neutron star cooling. Her observations of cooling

neutron stars, as well as their physical properties such as neutrino emission processes and the heat quantities of the interior and exterior, provide information about the states of matter at supernuclear densities. A student of Charles W. Flanagan High School, Pooja is active in both the math club and debate team. The daughter of Sunil and Kiran Jotwani, she was born in India and is head of the youth group in the Sindhi Association of South Florida.

- Po-Ling Loh, 18, of Madison, Wisconsin, explored finite group theory in mathematics. The group H is said to be a *closed* subgroup of a finite group G provided any homomorphism of H into G extends uniquely to all of G. Po-Ling studies the group D_{2p} of symmetries of a regular polygon with p sides, where p is an odd prime number. Ranked first in her class of 523 students at James Madison Memorial High School, Po-Ling has perfect SAT scores. She has been a gold prize winner in the USA Math Talent Search for three consecutive years, has won awards in music and forensics, and is copy editor of the school newspaper. The daughter of Dr. Wei-Yin Loh and Theresa Loh, she enjoys singing, cross-stitching, and playing frisbee.

- Albert Tsao, 17, of Brookline, Massachusetts, designed, fabricated, and studied the optical properties of silicon nanofiber ring resonator loops that are thinner than the wavelength of light and almost long enough to fit around a strand of human hair for his materials science project. Albert is one of only a handful of researchers worldwide who can pull ultrathin silica nanofibers with a diameter smaller than hundred nanometers. He hopes one day to find a way to manipulate nanofibers using magnetic bacteria. He hopes to attend Caltech. His hobbies include football, violin, and reading. The son of Dr. Thomas Tsao and Susan Chung, Albert cites his sister as the most influential person of his scientific career.[1]

Although Sho Yano and Devi Sridhar were never finalists in the Intel Science Talent Search—they are equally, if not even more, precocious. Yano became a full-time premed student at Loyola University in Chicago at age 9. He is the youngest student ever at the school and perhaps the youngest full-time college student in the United States. Standard tests cannot measure Yano's IQ because the tests cannot measure past 200. He made worldwide headlines in 2003 when he was accepted to medical school at the University of Chicago at the age of 13. Yano lives with his mother and 7-year-old sister in graduate student housing on campus and has adjusted to life at medical school. In one celebrated media event, Yano met with Dr. James Watson, who was just 15 when he was accepted to the University of Chicago in 1943. In 1953 Watson and colleague Francis Crick discovered DNA double helix, and both shared a Nobel Prize in Physiology in 1962. Watson told Yano: "You should concentrate on making a big discovery and not getting a girlfriend. The main thing is to have dreams. You should concentrate on something that no one has solved. Forget about being a prodigy and just try and find people you can learn from."[2]

At the age of 18, Sridhar became the youngest U.S. Rhodes Scholar in the organization's one hundred-year history. Rhodes Scholarships are among the most prestigious academic awards, which provide two to three years of study at Oxford University in England and are the oldest international study awards given to U.S. students. Selection of Rhodes Scholars is based not only on intellectual distinction but potential for leadership and greater service to the world. Among the many famous Rhodes Scholars are former President Bill Clinton and Supreme Court Justice David Souter. Before her Rhodes Scholarship Sridhar was in the Medical Honors Program at the University of Miami (which offers early admission to medical school). Her career aspiration includes medical school as well as international health policy. Fluent in five languages, she is also an accomplished solo violinist and a ranked tennis player. She was captain of her high school varsity tennis team, which won two state championships as well as three regional titles. In addition she has written a children's book on Indian myths and is working on a book of short stories exploring the confusion of growing up in two cultures.[3]

All these are just a few recent high-profile examples of what *Time* magazine has called "The New Whiz Kids." The seemingly phenomenal success of Asian Americans in education from kindergarten through graduate school has humbled other students, impressed their teachers, fascinated researchers, and drawn tremendous media attention. Asian American over achievers was a particularly popular topic in major newspapers and magazines throughout the 1980s. A small sample of these news stories shows the use of provocative titles such as "Confucian Work Ethic" (*Time*, 1983); "A Formula for Success" (*Newsweek*, 1984); "An American Success Story: The Triumph of Asian Americans" (*New Republic*, 1985); "Why Asians Are Going to the Head of the Class" (*New York Times Magazine*, 1986); "When Being Best Isn't Good Enough" (*Los Angeles Times Magazine*, 1987); "The New Whiz Kids" (*Time*, 1987); and "The Model Minority Goes to School" (*Phi Delta Kappan*, 1988).[4] Today, such stories are almost passé.

Much of the early mainstream media coverage made comparisons between the experiences of Asian American students of the 1980s and Jewish American students of the 1920s and 1930s. During this latter period, there was noticeable educational mobility among second- and third-generation Jewish Americans, compared to other ethnic groups. For example, by the late 1930s nearly half of all Jewish students in New York City completed high school, a remarkable achievement that only a quarter of all other students were able to accomplish at the time. In addition, although Jewish Americans represented just 3.7 percent of the U.S. population at the time, they represented 9 percent of all college students in the nation.[5]

The recent phenomenon of Asian American success in schools is very much a result of the large influx of post-1965 Asian immigrants from Asia and the 1975 first-wave Southeast Asian refugees who were largely middle class and educated in their home countries. It is generally the offspring of these immigrants and refugees who are doing so well in school. According to the U.S. Census report, *Educational Attainment in the United States: 2003*, just over 50 percent of foreign-born persons from Asia are college graduates, compared to 27.2 percent of all U.S. foreign-born (see Table 3-1). "Foreign-born professionals have been a double gift to the United States," writes Leon F. Bouvier and David Simcox,

Table 3-1 Educational Attainment of the Population 25 years and Over by Nativity, Race, and Hispanic Origin 2003

	High School Graduate or more	Some College or more	Bachelor's Degree or more
Total Population			
Native	87.5	54.2	27.2
Foreign-born	67.2	42.7	27.2
Non-Hispanic Whites			
Native	89.6	56.4	29.7
Foreign-born	86.1	56.8	37.6
Black			
Native	80.3	44.4	16.3
Foreign-born	77.3	47.6	25.4
Asian			
Native	91.8	72.7	48.3
Foreign-born	86.6	66.1	50.1
Hispanic			
Native	73.5	40.4	13.5
Foreign-born	44.7	21.5	9.8

Source: U.S. Census Bureau, "Educational Attainment in the United States: 2003," issued June 2004 at http://www.census.gov/prod/2004pubs/p20-550.pdf.

authors of the report *Foreign-born Professionals in the United States* (1994). "They have helped meet the needs of under-served populations and enriched scientific research and education. Moreover, they tend to have children who perform well academically and in many cases will themselves become professionals."[6]

This sentiment is confirmed in the research work of University of Chicago researchers Marta Tienda and Grace Kao. The two researchers conducted a national survey of nearly 25,000 eighth graders and found that Asian, Latino, and African American children with immigrant parents indeed out-perform other racial minority groups whose parents were born in the United States. The study showed that first- and second-generation Asian Americans had the highest achievement levels when compared to third-generation Asian Americans. First- and second-generation Asian American eighth graders tended to have higher grade point averages, and scored about five points higher on standardized reading and math tests than their more Americanized third-generation Asian American peers. Similar, but less spectacular, findings were true for first- and second-generation blacks, primarily immigrants from the Caribbean. Conversely, Latino immigrants did not show significant scholastic achievement compared with third-generation Latinos. However, the first- and second-generation Latinos did express a greater desire to graduate from college.[7]

Scholastic Aptitude Test (SAT) scores have often been used as evidence that Asian Americans are, in fact, the "model minority" when it comes to

Table 3-2 SAT Average Scores by Race/Ethnicity 2002–2004

Group	2002	2003	2004
Verbal			
African American	430	431	430
Asian American or			
Pacific Islander	510	508	507
Hispanic or Latino Background			
Mexican or Mexican American	446	448	451
Puerto Rican	455	456	457
Latin American, South American,			
Central American, or Other			
Hispanic or Latino	458	457	461
White	527	529	528
Math			
African American	427	426	427
Asian American	569	575	577
Hispanic			
Mexican or Mexican American	457	457	458
Puerto Rican	451	453	452
Latin American, South American,			
Central American or Other			
Hispanic or Latino	464	464	465
White	533	534	531

Source: The College Board at http://www.collegeboard.com/about/news_info/cbsenior/yr2004/reports.html.

academic achievement. Results from the 2004 SAT showed Asian Americans scored an average of 1084 (out of a total of 1600) on the combined verbal and mathematics sections. Compare this to the 1059 average for whites, 857 average for African Americans, and overall 915 average for Hispanic or Latino Americans (see Table 3-2). Although the high SAT scores for Asian Americans is the result of tallying a low verbal score (507) with a high mathematics score (577), some claim the SAT scores of Asian Americans show the objective and unbiased nature of the test, and the inherent fairness of the U.S. educational system. "Before throwing out in toto America's schools as we have known them, it would be productive to look at how and why these very schools seem to work so well for what can only be considered a most singular and unlikely minority, the Asian Americans," writes Daniel B. Taylor, former vice president of the College Board. In a rather twisted compliment to Asian Americans, Taylor adds, "It is more than a little ironic . . . that American schools seem to serve best the *most inherently alien* of their clientele. . . . 'Miraculous' might be a more apt descriptor,"[8] (emphasis mine).

Although overall educational achievement among immigrant and native-born Asian Americans is impressive, this does not mean there are no serious issues that need to be confronted and addressed. This chapter will first focus on the contrasting theoretical perspectives that try to answer the vexing question why Asian Americans seem to do so well in school. Second, this chapter will examine some of the most important educational issues for Asian Americans in primary school (K–12). These issues include students with limited English proficiency, parental pressure and stress on young Asian American students trying to live up to the "model minority" image, and racial violence against Asian Americans in school. Lastly, this chapter will highlight the backlash against Asian American educational "success" that emerged on college campuses across the nation. Particular emphasis here will be on alleged quotas in elite colleges and universities that became the biggest issue in higher education throughout the 1980s. It is important to note that all of these issues are closely related to, and often manifested in, all levels of education. For example, the lack of services for limited English proficient Asian American immigrant students in primary school just a few years ago has made it all the more difficult for these students to perform successfully in college today—if they've gotten there at all. Also, alleged quotas against Asian Americans in higher education in the 1980s have been ironically revisited today but this time on the high school level.

WHY ASIAN AMERICANS DO SO WELL IN SCHOOL

There have been many scholarly attempts to explain what appears to be an uncanny Asian American mastery of the American educational system. Theories in this matter can easily be broken down into three general categories: (1) nature, or innate genetic superiority; (2) nurture, or cultural advantages versus cultural disadvantages; and (3) relative functionalism, or a complex combination of primarily both situational and structural forces. All three perspectives have been hotly debated and are by no means limited to just Asian Americans. However, these three perspectives do offer distinct philosophical and practical challenges to education policy in the United States.

Nature/Genetics

For centuries both biological and social scientists have made attempts to "prove" genetic superiority and inferiority of certain racial groups. "Scientific racism" can be traced back to the work of Count de Gobineau, Houston Chamberlin, Madison Grant, Samuel Morton, and many others in the nineteenth and early twentieth centuries. These writers tried to argue that physical differences were a reflection of intellectual differences. In 1849, for example, Morton collected eight hundred crania from all over the world and attempted to show that cranial size equated intelligence. He filled each cranium with sand, measured the capacity, calculated the average, and came up with the following hierarchy: English (96 cubic inches); Americans and Germans (90 cubic inches); African Americans (83 cubic inches); Chinese (82 cubic inches); and American Indians (79 cubic inches). Because the English had the largest average cranial capacity,

Morton theorized, they must be the most intelligent. Conversely, Chinese had a much smaller average cranial capacity, so they must be generally less intelligent. Flawed as Morton's research was, attributing the inferiority of certain racial groups to inherent genetic deficiencies was used to help justify the institution of slavery, the spread of European colonialism throughout the world, and restrictive immigration laws.[9]

This theoretical perspective of genetic superiority/inferiority is not an anomaly of the past, but is a contemporary issue that continues to gain attention. In *Educability and Group Differences* (1973), University of California educational psychologist Arthur Jensen speculated that differences in Intelligence Quotient (IQ) scores between blacks and whites was due in substantial part to biological inheritance. Jensen, however, did not stop at looking at just blacks and whites. Although Samuel Morton may have concluded that Chinese were intellectually inferior because of their smaller cranial capacity, Jensen's research found "Orientals" (mostly Chinese) to be highly intelligent. Jensen tested nearly ten thousand children in kindergarten through fourth grade in twenty-one California schools and found "Orientals" exceeded all other groups.[10] Since the publication of his book and in other studies, Jensen's work has been thoroughly criticized on many counts. One area of criticism focuses on the methodological flaws in Jensen's research in that he failed to consider important variables such as historical disadvantage, cultural bias, social class, and geography. Another area of criticism comes from Jensen's heavy reliance on IQ test scores that are generally acknowledged to be very ineffective and inconclusive measures of anything that could be considered innate intelligence.

Despite these criticisms, others have followed Jensen's research and tried to control for variables in hopes of presenting better evidence of genetically based intelligence. One of the most notable is Richard Lynn, from the University of Northern Ireland, whose research claims that Chinese, Japanese, and Koreans score higher on standardized IQ tests than whites. For example, in his article, "The Intelligence of Mongoloids: A Psychometric Evolutionary and Neurological Theory" (1987), Lynn cited a number of studies that confirmed his conclusions.[11] The one work that did not agree that Asians had a higher mean IQ score was a six-year study headed by University of Michigan psychologist Harold Stevenson (1985). Stevenson and his colleagues' research is significant, however, because it carefully compared kindergarten, first-grade, and fifth-grade students of similar socioeconomic backgrounds in three similar sized cities—Minneapolis, Sendai (Japan), and Taipei (Taiwan). "This study offers no support for the argument that there are differences in the general cognitive functioning of Chinese, Japanese, and American children," the authors wrote. "Positing general differences in cognitive functioning of Japanese and Chinese children is an appealing hypothesis for those who seek to explain the superiority of Japanese and Chinese children's scholastic achievement, but it appears from the present data that it will be necessary to seek other explanations for their success."[12]

The genetic superiority/inferiority debate was rekindled with the publication of two controversial books: *Race, Evolution and Behavior* (1995) by J. Philippe

Rushton and *The Bell Curve* (1994) by Richard J. Herrnstein and Charles Murray. *The Bell Curve* received the most media attention and critical response with its provocative assertions. The authors have five interrelated arguments. First they claim 60 percent of every individual's IQ is genetic in origin; second, IQ is a reliable predictor for social, economic, and educational success or failure; third, blacks have the lowest average on IQ tests relative to other groups; fourth, it is unlikely that environmental factors can account for racial group differences in IQ; and lastly, any attempts to improve group performance on IQ tests by making environmental changes will fail.

While *The Bell Curve* focuses primarily on blacks and whites, the authors could not avoid studies that looked at Asian IQ scores. Herrnstein and Murray freely cite Lynn's studies that show Asians consistently have higher IQ scores than whites, but they are contradictory about what the findings really mean. On one hand, Herrnstein and Murray believe Asians "probably" have higher IQs because they tend to do better in "visual/spatial" versus verbal abilities. This is exaggerated for non-English-speaking immigrants but tends to be true even for Asian Americans who are monolingual English speakers. According to Herrnstein and Murray, this is why Asian immigrants and Asian Americans tend to abound in fields such as engineering, medicine, and the sciences, rather than literature, law, or politics. On the other hand, the authors acknowledged that the Asian/white IQ differences are small and any general comparisons are subject to error without proper controls. Within this, Herrnstein and Murray agreed with the work of Harold Stevenson that when you do control for socioeconomic differences, the distinctions between Asian and white IQ scores disappear.[13]

Overall, like the work of Arthur Jensen twenty years earlier, *The Bell Curve* created controversy but proved nothing. The book's faulty logic, overreliance on problematic studies, uncritical faith that IQ test scores equate to general intelligence, and ignorance of studies showing the important value of early educational intervention in raising educational performance and achievement levels are all pointed out in numerous reviews.[14] Innate ability is obviously an area of heated argument. A less controversial—and more accepted—reason why Asians and Asian Americans seem to perform well academically is quite simple: Asians work harder.

Data from a 1980 national survey of 58,000 students in 1,015 high schools conducted by the U.S. Department of Education show that roughly half of Asian American sophomores spend five or more hours per week on homework. Only about a third of the white students and a quarter of the black students put as much time into their homework. In addition, the survey found that 45 percent of the Asian Americans never missed a day of school, and 42 percent said they were never late.[15] A follow-up survey of 25,000 eighth graders, their parents, teachers, and school administrators throughout the nation was conducted in the spring of 1988, and it came up with very similar results. Researchers Samuel S. Peng and DeeAnn Wright (1994) analyzed the follow-up information in detail and concluded that home environments and educational activities account in large part for the differences in student achievement between Asian Americans and other minority students. They found that Asian

Americans were more likely to come from stable, two-parent home environments, spent more time at home doing their homework, and spent less time
watching television. Asian Americans were also found to be involved in educational activities that are more conducive to learning outside of school (e.g., language, art, music), and took part in more educational activities (e.g., visiting
the public library and going to museums) than other minority students. Lastly,
Peng and Wright found that Asian American parental expectations were the
highest of any other group. The average Asian American parents expected
their child to complete 16.7 years of education, which means education beyond
a baccalaureate degree (see Table 3-3). The researchers highlighted the fact
that about 80 percent of Asian American parents expected their children to
have at least a bachelor's degree compared with 62 percent of white, 58 percent
of black, and only half of the Hispanic parents.[16]

Nurture/Culture

Studies show that Asian Americans do work harder, so the question now
becomes *why* do Asian Americans work harder? A great deal of attention has
been focused on Asian cultural values that place a high priority on education,
hard work, and family honor as the main reason for Asian American academic
success. Anthropologists William Caudill and George DeVos (1956) described
how Japanese American students excelled in school, despite the overt prejudice

Table 3-3 Percentage or Average Score on Select Variables by Race/Ethnicity

Variable	Asian	Hispanic	Black	White	Native American
Demographics					
% living with both parents	79.4	65.2	38.8	68.2	53.5
% of parents with > BA+	22.2	5.5	5.5	13.9	4.2
% with income < $15,000	17.8	37.5	47.0	18.1	40.1
Discipline					
Hours per week doing homework	6.8	4.7	5.2	5.7	4.7
Hours per week watching TV	20.6	22.0	26.7	20.3	22.7
Additional Lessons/Activities					
% having outside lessons	65.6	44.6	45.1	61.6	42.6
% having outside activities	91.5	79.9	83.2	91.1	78.4
Educational Expectations/ Pressure					
Number of years of education	16.70	15.25	15.24	15.32	15.11

Source: Samuel S. Peng and DeeAnn Wright, "Explanation of Academic Achievement of Asian American Students," *Journal of Educational Research* 87:6 (1994): 349, Table 2. Reprinted with permission of the Dwight
Reed Educational Foundation. Published by Heldref Publications, 1319 Eighteenth St. N.W., Washington, DC
20036-1802.

and discrimination they faced during World War II. The authors pointed to the strength and persistence of Japanese culture, as well as strong parental involvement, as the two main reasons for this phenomenon. Sociologist Betty Lee Sung also underscored the importance of culture in academic success. "Chinese respect for learning and for the scholar is a cultural heritage," Sung writes in her book *The Story of the Chinese in America* (1967). "Other minorities have not had the benefit of this reverence for learning."[17]

Research conducted by Nathan Caplan, Marcella H. Choy, and John K. Whitmore (1989, 1991) focused on recent Southeast Asian refugees, and their conclusions serve to further reinforce the cultural argument. The University of Michigan team surveyed 6,750 Vietnamese, Laotian, and Chinese-Vietnamese in five urban areas (Orange County, Seattle, Houston, Chicago, and Boston). The survey population represented the second wave of refugees from Southeast Asia and generally had limited exposure to Western culture, had virtually no English-language proficiency, and often arrived in the United States with little more than the clothes on their backs. From the large sample, two hundred nuclear families and their 536 school-age children were randomly chosen to be part of more intensive interviews.[18]

The researchers concentrated on the children's academic achievements including grade-point averages (GPA) and standardized test scores. Despite the fact that many of the Southeast Asian children faced traumatic situations leaving their home countries, faced language barriers, and often lived in poverty after they arrived in the United States, their grades and test scores were generally superior to other American students. It was found that 27 percent of the Southeast Asian immigrant students had a GPA in the A range, and 52 percent were in the B range. Just 17 percent of the GPAs were in the C range and only 4 percent had a GPA below the C range. On standardized tests, 27 percent of the Asian immigrant students scored in the top ten in math.[19]

However, the researchers did not believe that the high GPAs and test scores occurred in a vacuum. Caplan, Choy, and Whitmore credit Asian cultural values that are deeply rooted in Confucian and Buddhist traditions for the success of Southeast Asian immigrant students. Central to these traditions, they argue, is the family. The researchers found that both the parents and the children have a strong sense of obligation to the entire family. One example the researchers cite is how homework time served as a mutually satisfying family affair in many of the Southeast Asian households studied. After dinner, the table is cleared and parents encourage their children to study. In most of these cases, older siblings helped younger siblings while doing their own homework. The researchers were also impressed by the fact that Southeast Asian high school students spent an average of three hours and ten minutes on their homework on weeknights, while Southeast Asian junior high school students averaged two hours and five minutes.[20]

Caplan, Choy, and Whitmore also found that Southeast Asian students seemed to have a high sense of completion gratification, which the researchers attribute to traditional Asian culture. At the same time, both the parents and children believed that learning came from hard work and effort, rather than from innate intelligence. This attitude differs considerably from findings in a 1992 U.S. Department of Education study, *Hard Work and High Expectations: Motivating Students to Learn*. The study concluded that most American students attributed academic achievement with intelligence and that success in school is easy if you are smart. Conversely, if you do not do well in school you must not be smart and, therefore, there is no use in trying. Most students said they preferred to be seen as smart rather than as hardworking because if you have to put a lot of effort into your work, it is a sign of being a slow learner.[21]

Recent works by Asakawa and Csikszentmihalyi (1998 and 2000) offer confirmation of earlier studies. In a study of 1,109 randomly chosen sixth, eighth, tenth, and twelfth graders, the researchers found Asian American adolescents had more positive experiences when they were engaged in activities perceived to be more work-like and future-oriented (doing homework, studying, listening to the teacher, etc.); Asian Americans were significantly happier, enjoyed themselves more, and felt better about themselves than their white counterparts. The internalization of cultural values was suggested as a factor for promoting the educational success of Asian American students. The researchers also found Asian American parents "structured" their children's lives for academic success more than white parents. Structured activities for academic success included planning where the child should go to college, discussing ACT/SAT preparation, limiting TV and video games, and assigning fewer household chores. Asian American parents also tended to leave their children alone when engaged in academic related activities, but overtly exercised control when engaged in nonacademic related activities.[22]

The cultural perspective is the most commonly cited and easy to understand reason for Asian American academic achievement. However, the cultural perspective does have its own controversial aspects. The most important is the logical extension in the cultural argument: If Asian Americans have the "right" cultural values, does it mean that other minority groups are culturally "deficient"? This prickly side of the cultural argument can be divided into two types. First, there is cultural deficiency based on *socioeconomic* status, known as the "culture of poverty." This was the thesis Edward Banfield focused on in his book *The Unheavenly City* (1970), in which he argues that "lower class" culture includes having an extreme present orientation rather than a future outlook on life, lack of self-discipline, and a heightened sense of hopelessness and powerlessness. People in this "culture" tend to do poorly in school, are unable to maintain steady employment, and live in poverty. While the culture of poverty may be a phenomenon with a long history of prejudice and discrimination for some groups, this is not the center of Banfield's work.[23]

The other type of cultural deficiency argument is based on the idea that *certain groups* of people either lack the right kind of cultural values, or they accentuate the wrong parts of their culture, which would inhibit their social, economic, and educational mobility. A key proponent of this notion is prominent conservative African American economist Thomas Sowell. This argument was forwarded in his book *Ethnic America* (1981), where he writes, "cultural inheritance can be more important than biological inheritance, although the latter is more controversial." In terms of education, for example, Sowell believes history shows that Chinese, Japanese, and Jews have different attitudes toward educational achievement than Mexicans, blacks, and Puerto Ricans. At the same time, some aspects of culture are best kept under wraps. He writes: "Some groups (such as Jews and the Japanese) have enjoyed and maintained their own special culture, but without making a public issue over it (as blacks and Hispanics have)." Although Sowell makes a point that cultures are neither "superior" nor "inferior," he does believe they need to be flexible and appropriately adapted to different circumstances. Some cultural groups, according to Sowell, are more adept at this than others. Sowell's arguments have remained unchanged over the years and are highlighted in his more recent publication *Race and Culture* (1994).[24]

Relative Functionalism

Attitudes and values are clearly emphasized within the cultural perspective, but are they enough to explain Asian American educational achievement? The cultural perspective has been criticized for being ahistorical, relying too heavily on stereotypes, and lacking in any acknowledgment of social context. With this in mind, two Asian American psychologists, Stanley Sue and Sumie Okazaki, have developed a third theoretical perspective they call "relative functionalism." Relative functionalism does not deny the influence of culture, but it does add other *structural* factors that also deserve attention. In their article "Asian-American Educational Achievements: A Phenomenon in Search of an Explanation" (1990), Sue and Okazaki contend that Asian American educational achievement is a result of limited opportunities in noneducational areas. In other words, education becomes important when there are great limitations in noneducational areas. This is particularly true for groups that are culturally oriented toward education and have a history of academic success.[25]

Relative functionalism takes a broad interdisciplinary approach to explain Asian American educational achievement and draws from the work of sociologist Stephen Steinberg, education specialist Bob Suzuki, and anthropologists John Ogbu and Maria Matute-Bianchi. Sue and Okazaki first cite from Steinberg's book *The Ethnic Myth* (1981) because he significantly undermines the thesis that certain ethnic groups succeed because they possess innately superior cultural values. Steinberg argues that socioeconomic class factors in the home country, economic necessity, and historical accident in the new host country converge to move ethnic groups up or down the economic and educational ladder. In the chapter "The Jewish Horatio Alger Story," Steinberg examines the Jewish experience in the United States in the 1880s during the industrial revolution.

Steinberg agrees that thousands of Eastern European Jews arrived in the United States materially poor. At the same time, however, many Jewish immigrants were literate and brought with them a variety of occupational skills that corresponded remarkably well to the needs of an expanding American economy. These factors gave Jewish immigrants an advantage over other immigrants in the labor market and in public school at the time. Steinberg asserts that literacy was a valuable asset for Jewish immigrants for three reasons. First, the fact that many Jewish immigrants were literate in their language helped to facilitate the acquisition of a new language. Second, being literate obviously helped Jews enter into business and more lucrative occupations that required an ability to read and write. Third, literacy provided an educational head start for Jewish children. "In terms of their European background, Jews were especially well equipped to take advantage of the opportunities they found in America," writes Steinberg. "It is this remarkable convergence of factors that resulted in an unusual record of success."[26]

This parallels the situation for the highly educated and skilled middle-class Asian American immigrants' experiences in the United States since 1965. In addition, the types of skills brought by Asian immigrants do tend to be science and technology oriented, which offer the best opportunities for gainful employment and upward mobility in a highly competitive, postindustrial economy. This attention to education, and to professions that are in demand, does not go unnoticed in the children of immigrants.

Sue and Okazaki next refer to Bob Suzuki's provocative article, "Education and the Socialization of Asian Americans: A Revisionist Analysis of the 'Model Minority' Thesis" (1977), where he posits that Asian Americans pursue a narrow education and professional training because of their "status as a minority group." In other words, Asian Americans gravitate to quantitative fields such as engineering, medicine, and the sciences because of their own perceived (whether conscious or not) limitations. These limitations may be linguistic, in the case of Asian immigrants, or racial, as in the case of more assimilated Asian Americans. In short, Suzuki believes that Asian Americans excel in education because they believe it will get them a better job, higher income, and higher status. According to Suzuki, Asian Americans realize they would have difficulty in other avenues for advancement because of discrimination. Suzuki's thesis contradicts Herrnstein and Murray's argument that Asians and Asian Americans are genetically more inclined to enter the science and technology fields. Suzuki also challenges the widely accepted idea that Asian Americans do not face discrimination, have achieved middle-class status, and have almost completely assimilated into the American mainstream.[27]

But the fundamental question arises, "Why don't other racial minority groups adopt education as a means of socioeconomic mobility?" Sue and Okazaki confront this question by stating that different minority groups have different historical and contemporary experiences. Here they cite the work of John Ogbu and Maria Matute-Bianchi (1986), who have forwarded the idea that individuals and groups develop "folk theories" of success. For example, it is generally assumed that if one works hard and gets a good education, one will get a good job and succeed. However, this belief is not true for everyone. Folk beliefs are influenced by a variety of factors such as past history of success, past history of discrimination, availability of successful role models, cultural values, and the like. As a result, some may develop a folk belief that "it doesn't matter how hard I work or how much education I receive, I will still be discriminated against." Sue and Okazaki contend that different racial minority groups have different folk beliefs about education. They cite the work of Roslyn Arlin Mickelson (1990), who found that African Americans generally believe in the importance of education, but they are less likely than whites to believe in the value of education in their own lives. Sue and Okazaki argue that the folk belief for Asian Americans may very well be: "If I study hard, I can succeed, *and* education is the best way to succeed" (emphasis theirs).[28] Sue and Okazaki's relative functionalism theory takes into consideration the complex factors of class (Steinberg), race (Suzuki), and sociohistorical context (Ogbu and Matute-Bianchi) in their analysis of Asian American academic achievement.

Criticisms of Sue and Okazaki's relative functional theory were published in the August 1991 issue of the *American Psychologist.* One writer, David Fox, from the California School of Professional Psychology and the Loma Linda University School of Medicine, even advanced a theory that Asians and Jews excel in education because their native languages are read and written from right to left. According to Fox, right-to-left writing leads to increased and flexible cerebral functioning that affects intellectual performance. Richard Lynn also wrote a sharp rebuttal to Sue and Okazaki's conclusions and reiterated his own arguments in favor of innate biological differences. In their response to the critics, Sue and Okazaki dismissed Fox's views as "speculative," highlighted many of the "problematic" assumptions of Lynn's genetic research, and maintained that relative functionalism is an "important consideration" in the debate over Asian American educational achievement.[29]

EDUCATIONAL ISSUES FACING ASIAN AMERICANS

Theoretical questions aside, the relative "success" of Asian Americans in education does give the impression that Asian Americans do not face any significant educational and personal issues. However, limited English proficiency, parental pressure and stress, and racial violence in school are three issues that are especially acute for Asian American students. These three issues impact all Asian Americans from all socioeconomic lines to some degree. Of course, limited English proficiency is particularly important to the increasing number of Asian immigrant students entering public schools across the country.

Limited English Proficiency (LEP)

As early as 1982 the U.S. Department of Education estimated there were 3.6 million school-aged limited English proficient (LEP) students across the nation and the 2005 U.S. Department of Education "Title III LEP Biennial Report to Congress" estimated approximately 5.1 million LEP students nationwide.[30] Asian Americans are not the majority of LEP students in the United States, but because of the large influx of Southeast Asian refugees and continued immigration from Asia, there is an overrepresentation of Asian American LEP students based on their percentage in the population. Dramatic statistics from the latest available Language Census Summary from the California Department of Education showed just 53 certified bilingual Vietnamese-speaking teachers and 41,456 Vietnamese-speaking students, a ratio of 1 to 113. There were 44 certified Hmong-speaking teachers to 29,474 Hmong students, a ratio of 1 to 670. Lastly, there were just 2 certified Khmer-speaking teachers to 17,637 to Khmer-speaking Cambodian students, a ratio of 1 to 8,818![31]

The most important legal precedent related to the rights of all LEP students goes back to the U.S. Supreme Court case *Lau v. Nichols* (1974). The case involved a San Francisco student, Kinney Lau, who was failing school because he could not understand the language of instruction. A class action lawsuit was filed in 1970 on behalf of Lau and about 1,800 other Chinese American students. At the time of the case, the San Francisco Unified School District was serving more than 100,000 students, 16,574 of whom were Chinese American. Almost 3,000 Chinese American students in San Francisco were in need of special help in English, but the district had fewer than two dozen remedial teachers who were fluent in both Cantonese and English. The suit originally lost in a federal district court but was appealed all the way to the U.S. Supreme Court. In 1974 the high court ruled unanimously to overturn the lower court's decision, finding that the San Francisco Unified School District failed to provide equal opportunity for LEP students. After the Lau decision, the impact on LEP students has been mixed. The primary problem has been inconsistent implementation and enforcement of programs intended to benefit immigrant students.[32]

Certainly there have been success stories of remarkable acquisition of English as a second language by some Asian American immigrant and refugee students. This was the case for A-Bo, who emigrated from Taiwan to San Jose, California, when she was 15 years old. She had been an exceptionally gifted student in her home country, but was immediately placed in the English as a Second Language program because of her inability to read and write English. Fortunately, A-Bo was very well educated in all basic subjects prior to entering the United States, and she was able to learn very quickly. Her advanced knowledge of mathematics was obvious and she soon started helping her teacher solve problems. Within just one year she became quite comfortable in English and even joined the debate team. A-Bo's success can be explained by studies that show students with a strong educational background in their own primary language (speaking, reading, and writing) can more readily transfer that information, and this forms a solid foundation for learning a new language.[33]

This example, however, cannot be generalized and may be misleading because there is a great range of educational experience among Asian immigrant and refugee students, and their own abilities to acquire a second language. It is important to remember that not all Asian American immigrant children come from well-educated, urbanized, middle-class and above families, nor do all Asian Americans glide effortlessly through school. Indeed, many Asian American immigrant children, especially those who come from families at the lower end of the socioeconomic levels, face considerable educational and acculturation challenges throughout their educational careers. Nonetheless, many LEP students face tremendous struggles, whatever their backgrounds.

The case of Shia-chi is illustrative of this fact. Shia-chi was also 15 years old when she arrived in Los Angeles from Taiwan. Her parents were well-to-do owners of a clothing factory in Taipei who sent Shia-chi to live with an aunt in order to have a good education in the United States. Shia-chi was not an exceptional student in Taiwan, and her solo relocation to the United States only exacerbated her academic troubles and low self-esteem. Even though she took three years of English in a Taiwanese school, Shia-chi was unable to speak, read, or write adequately enough and was unable to adjust to her new situation. She did attend English as a Second Language classes but continued to have difficulty mastering a new language. Although Shia-chi graduated from high school, she is considered "LEP-forever," ill-prepared for the rigors of college and lacking in the language skills needed for meaningful employment.[34]

Concerns over Asian American LEP students prompted an early call for action by the U.S. Commission on Civil Rights (1992). "Our investigation has revealed that these needs of Asian American LEP students are being dramatically under-served," the report stated. "They need professional bilingual/bicultural counseling services to help them in their social adjustment and academic development."[35]

However, on June 2, 1998, California voters overwhelmingly approved Proposition 227, which mandated an end to bilingual education in favor of English immersion, or English-only, instruction for LEP students. The vote was decisive—61 percent of voters supported the measure, while just 39 percent opposed it. On one hand, Proposition 227 reflected anti-immigrant sentiment among California voters that had been boiling since the mid-1980s when voters passed Proposition 63, declaring English the official language of the state.[36] Since that time public schools have become a prominent battleground, as the enrollment of LEP students more than doubled over the past decade.[37] By 1998 one quarter of California public school students and one third of first graders were LEP. Voters in the election were overwhelmingly white and resentful about paying taxes for "other" people's children.[38] An exit poll by the *Los Angeles Times* showed 69 percent of the voters statewide were white, 14 percent were African Americans, 12 percent were Latino, and 3 percent Asian American. As expected, 67 percent of whites voted in favor of Proposition 227, while 52 percent of African Americans and 63 percent of Latinos were opposed. Asian American voters, it is interesting to note, supported Proposition 227 by a 57 to 43 percent margin.[39]

The results are in from standardized tests required by all students in grades two through eleven since California ended bilingual education. Overall, the percentage of students scoring at or above the 50th percentile was greater in 1999 than 1998, and the results would generally be seen as "better." Continued improvements were seen in the 2004 test results. Opponents of bilingual education claim success in the scores and credit Proposition 227. Proponents of bilingual education are not so sure of the results and say there are several factors to be considered before deciding that the differences are real and not random fluctuations. Table 3-4 shows the improvements for LEP students, but also highlights the wide achievement gap between LEP students

Table 3-4 Score Summary Reports for State of California, Spring 1999, 1998, and 2004 Percentage Scoring at or Above 50th National Percentile Rank

Spring 2004 Grade Level	2	3	4	5	6	7	8	9	10	11
Reading										
LEP	28	13	11	14	14	10	7	12	12	11
Non-LEP	57	45	46	49	55	54	51	57	57	53
Math										
LEP	46	37	29	26	25	17	19	17	23	18
Non-LEP	65	60	55	57	60	55	55	52	57	50
Language										
LEP	26	22	21	17	11	11	12	15	13	12
Non-LEP	51	52	53	54	51	51	52	55	56	53

LEP Students Tested: 1,194,998

Spring 1999 Grade Level	2	3	4	5	6	7	8	9	10	11
Reading										
LEP	19	12	11	9	9	7	8	3	3	4
Non-LEP	56	53	53	53	54	54	57	41	39	41
Math										
LEP	33	28	21	19	22	16	15	19	20	22
Non-LEP	57	56	52	53	59	52	52	55	49	50
Language										
LEP	24	19	20	19	18	17	12	15	7	11
Non-LEP	58	54	57	57	58	60	57	57	45	53

LEP Students Tested: 911,489

Spring 1998 Grade Level	2	3	4	5	6	7	8	9	10	11
Reading										
LEP	15	9	9	8	7	7	7	3	3	4
Math										
LEP	26	21	17	16	18	14	13	19	17	19
Language										
LEP	19	14	18	17	15	15	12	14	6	10

LEP Students Tested: 806,419

Source: California Department of Education, California STAR State Summary Reports 1998, 1999, 2004 at http://star.cde.ca.gov/.

and non-LEP students. At this time there are no separate results or studies focusing specifically on Asian American LEP students.

Parental Pressure and Stress

The research of Peng and Wright cited earlier touched upon the fact that Asian American parents have higher academic expectations for their children compared with other parents. Although high expectations are important in encouraging excellence, excessive high expectations can create undue pressure and unhealthy levels of psychological and emotional stress on young students. One case involved a 17-year-old Korean high school student who was reportedly beaten by her father because her grade-point average dropped below a perfect 4.0. The father was arrested for child abuse and pled not guilty.[40] This is an extreme example, of course, but several studies have shown many Asian American parents commonly express their displeasure when their children bring home anything less than a straight-A report card.[41] When one Asian American student showed her parents a report card with all As except for one B, the parents focused only on the B grade and chastised their child for not working harder. The student became resentful because she had brought home a report card of which any other parent would be proud.[42]

For many Asian American children growing up in traditional Asian families, filial piety—respect and obedience toward one's parents—is expected. Although more acculturated Asian American parents do allow their children greater independence and freedom than immigrant Asian parents, studies show that Asian American parents do tend to exercise more control over their children's lives than non-Asian parents. Parental control may extend as far as choosing what courses to take in school, what school they should go to, and what their college major should be. In addition, Asian American parents are far more controlling of their children's social lives. A comprehensive 1992 survey of high school seniors found only 40 percent of Asian American students dated at least once a week, compared with 64 percent of whites, 52 percent of blacks, and 58 percent of Hispanics.[43] Asian American parents use guilt and shame rather than physical abuse to keep their children in line and to reinforce the fact that their children have strong obligations to the family. Their children often feel extremely self-critical and alienated when they fail in their parents' eyes. In some cases, young Asian Americans become so distraught they attempt suicide. This is what happened to young Paula Yoo, whose parents saved her just before she slit her wrists with a razor blade. "I wasn't class valedictorian and yes, I flunked calculus," Yoo wrote in a very personal essay published in *A Magazine*. "I was stupid because I didn't make all A's. I was absolutely convinced I was destined for failure."[44] Conversely, Asian American parents feel extremely responsible for their children's success in school and in their future careers. Their children's successful academic achievements are a direct reflection of their own parenting abilities. If their children do well in school, then they have been good parents; if their children do poorly in school, then the parents are to blame because they didn't do enough. A volatile situation may erupt when the young student's desires do not match his or her parents' high and sometimes rigid expectations. A good example of this can be seen in Audrey Teoh's experience after she told her father she didn't want to study engineering like he wanted her to. After a heated argument, Teoh's flustered father finally said, "You have given up!" She sadly recalls the way her father said those words "just made me feel so small." For his part, Teoh's father believes his "lifetime of experience" gives him the right to tell his daughter what is best for her. At the same time, the episode did leave Mr. Teoh very distraught. He asks, "Was I too strict on my children? Do I overreact? I really have no reference by which to compare my child-rearing methods, and I will never really know for sure what I'm doing is right."[45]

Recent attention on the pressures placed on young Asian Americans by their parents came in the form of the biographical book *An Extreme Asian-American Upbringing* (2003), written by Emily Guey under the pseudonym Mei Jyu-Chwang Lee. Guey was a former National Spelling Bee contestant and accomplished musician who graduated with honors from the University of Florida. In her book Guey describes her mother as physically and emotionally abusive in an obsessive drive to make her daughter a superachiever. Although the names of the family members were changed, Guey has been increasingly open about the issue of child abuse and neglect in Asian American homes. She wrote an online essay on the topic where she wrote: "Depression, suicide, and performance anxieties should not permeate Asian Americans to such a frightening degree. Surely they should respect and honor their parents after all of the hard sacrifice they have made for them, but respect should not mean bowing down to extremely unrealistic expectations, pressures that can permanently damage their mental health."[46]

Some Asian American parents not only will pressure their children to excel in school, but also may go through extreme hardships to ensure the very best educational opportunities. One Chicago-area study found more than eight out of ten Asian American parents said they would sell their house and give up their own future financial security to support their children's education. Only three out of ten white parents were willing to make this sacrifice.[47] In Fullerton, California, Sunny Hills High School is recognized as one of the truly elite public schools in the United States. The school has been nicknamed "high pressure high" and is known for its zero dropout rate, the fact that students compete for A+ grades, and as a place where all-night study sessions are considered a badge of honor. Sunny Hills is affiliated with the International Baccalaureate (IB) Organization, a Swiss foundation with headquarters in Geneva, Switzerland. The IB diploma program is a comprehensive, rigorous pre-university course of study for the academically talented. Students in the program are required to pass three higher and three subsidiary level exams that are graded externally. Students are also required to take the course "Theory of Knowledge" that culminates in a twenty-page research paper. In addition, students in the IB program are required to perform one hundred fifty hours of community service.[48]

Sunny Hills High has also seen a dramatic increase of Asian American students in recent years. In 1985, whites represented 72 percent of the student population, while Asian Americans represented 18 percent. Today, the Asian

American student population at Sunny Hills High is over 50 percent, while the white population has declined to just over 20 percent. The percentage of Asian American students at Sunny Hills is remarkable considering Asian Americans represent less than 20 percent of the school district's population. Korean Americans are the largest Asian ethnic group at Sunny Hills, and many Korean parents pay a steep price—sometimes as high as $1 million—to buy a home within Sunny Hills' boundaries. Other parents are known to stay in Korea but send their children to live in Fullerton and attend the school. Still other parents borrow addresses from people who live within the district to make their children eligible. "There are Korean parents here who don't even speak English but know the SAT cutoff to get into Stanford," exclaims astonished English teacher Kimberley Stein. "When I was in high school, my parents didn't even know what the SAT was."[49]

Asian American parents not only sacrifice but also some are willing to fight for their children's education. In San Francisco, an extremely contentious situation emerged at the city's academic preparatory school, Lowell High. Lowell High School was founded in 1856 and is the oldest public high school west of the Mississippi River. In 1978, the National Association for the Advancement of Colored People (NAACP) sued the San Francisco Unified School District (SFUSD), charging racial segregation. A U.S. district judge issued a consent decree in 1983 after an agreement was reached between the two parties that no ethnic group exceed more than 45 percent of enrollment at any one school. Chinese American parents long denounced the enrollment cap because it forced a limit on the number of Chinese American students who could go to Lowell High. Since 1978, the Chinese American student population has grown to 25 percent of the SFUSD, which makes it the largest single racial group in the district and an important constituency to reckon with. Chinese American parents became especially outraged in 1993 when they learned that higher entrance standards were placed on their children applying to Lowell relative to other groups. The initial plan required Chinese American students to score 66 out of 69 points on a scale that was based on a combination of grade-point average and standardized test scores in order to gain admission to the school. Meanwhile, 59 was the cutoff score for whites, and 56 for African Americans and Hispanics. The following year, the Chinese American Democratic Club (CADC) filed a class action lawsuit against the California Board of Education and the San Francisco Unified School District challenging the 1983 consent decree.[50]

The lawsuit created a firestorm of debate within the Chinese American community. On one hand, Roland Quan, vice president of the Chinese American Democratic Club, argued that the admission criteria for all students should be based solely on merit, which simply means that those with the highest point totals should be accepted to Lowell High regardless of race. "Opportunities and success based on individual dedication and hard work are the hallmark of America," Quan said. "Unfortunately, the public education system in this country sets its standard at mediocrity."[51] On the other hand, long-time civil rights activist Henry Der looked beyond the issue of individual merit and standard test scores. "Chinese Americans are too hung up on these basic-skills test scores," he argued. "(T)he difference between a student who scores a 59 and another who scores a 64 is practically negligible. There's nothing magical about these point scores. . . . There's such an inordinate amount of pressure being placed on these Chinese kids by their parents to get into Lowell that when they get rejected, they feel so debased."[52]

Der prefers to focus attention on the broader issue of educational fairness and equity in a society stratified by both race *and* class. He contends that a strict merit-based system serves only to perpetuate inequality among students who are forced to attend inferior schools, who have limited English skills, and who are poor. Der conducted a study of the Chinese students in San Francisco and found that three quarters of Chinese applicants to Lowell High School in 1993 lived in the most affluent parts of San Francisco. Der contends these students have more options in terms of school choice, access to alternative schools, and associations with high-achieving students than most other students. "Asian Americans can and should acknowledge internal class differences that impede low-income Asian Americans from achieving success," Der writes. "To the extent that low-income Asian students are bused or assigned to other low-income racial minority schools, the educational needs of all low-income racial minorities deserve the highest public priority and diverse set of remedies."[53]

The arguments of both Quan and Der were apparently taken into consideration when the San Francisco school board voted in a new admission policy for Lowell High School. In February 1996, the city school board voted unanimously to use a single cutoff score of 63 out of 69 to apply to all ethnic groups beginning in the 1996–1997 school year. However, to comply with court-monitored desegregation, the new policy allows for up to 30 percent of the incoming class to be reserved for low-income students. Students in this group will be allowed to enter Lowell even if they score less than 63 points, but no student will be admitted if they score below 50. The new admissions policy at Lowell High is generally acknowledged to be a compromise offer, and not everyone is completely happy. Roland Quan of the CADC complemented the board for moving "in the right direction," but made it clear that his organization, which represents the parents suing the school district, will continue on with their lawsuit.[54]

In February 1999, the Chinese American plaintiffs reached a settlement in their case over Lowell High School's admission policies. The SFUSD agreed not to use race as a primary factor in school admissions and assignments and would eventually phase out the 1983 consent decree altogether. Despite the settlement, the controversy is far from over, and the war of words continues. On November 24, 1999, the SFUSD submitted its revised plan to U.S. District Judge William Orrick that did not include race as a primary factor for admission, but did include race as a factor among several others. Amy Chang of the Asian American Legal Foundation, a group that supports the plaintiffs in this case, complained that the alternative policy "is an incredible disappointment."[55] Henry Der is particularly concerned that the lawsuit and continued fighting over the settlement make Chinese Americans look short-sighted and selfish. He sees some Chinese American parents being "obsessive" and acting "as if students of other racial backgrounds cannot or do not deserve to benefit from a Lowell education."[56]

Implementation of a new school admissions plan began in 2001. Parents were allowed to choose five schools they wanted their children to attend, but a "diversity index" formula of six socioeconomic factors determined a student's school placement: family income, the primary language spoken at home, mother's education, preschool experience or standardized test scores, and the student's prior school's ranking would determine the final placement. Problems began from the very beginning, including a "computer glitch" that eliminated the preference of keeping siblings together at one school. By far the loudest complaints were from Chinese American parents who did not get assigned to a school of their choice, saying their children would have to commute for hours across town to get to school. The pressure peaked in 2003 when a group of Chinese American parents called for a boycott of the schools. One of the group's leaders was John Zhao, an immigrant from Shanghai, China, working two jobs as a cook, and a parent of a then-13-year-old daughter. In a blistering editorial published in the May 29, 2003, issue of *Asian Week* Zhou wrote: "My daughter was assigned to Philip and Sala Burton High School, which is about 10 miles from my residence. I live just a few blocks away from Lincoln High School. I decided to rally the community, parents, students and relatives so we can collectively demonstrate to the San Francisco Unified School District and the school board that their decisions are wrong and unjust. . . . I certainly feel that I speak out because I am a responsible parent who cares for the health and well-being of my daughter. If the SFUSD expects me to shut up and look the other way, they are asking me not to be a parent."[57]

While parent indignation over the school admission plan is not unreasonable, some of the Asian American students did not feel the arguments focused on the root of the problem, which is to have their children attend only the prestigious and high-performing schools in the city. "Many Asian parents don't want their kids going to schools that don't have the words Lowell, Lincoln or Washington in them," said 17-year-old high school senior Delores Lee. "They think that if their kids go to a school with a perceived bad reputation, then their kids will be looked down upon and lose face." Another high school senior, Crystal Cao, agreed. "It's not the distance they're worried about," she said noting that parents would not complain if they lived far away from Lowell or Lincoln high schools. "Why do they want to send their kids to Harvard or UC Berkeley or faraway schools?" Social worker and school counselor Yen Dinh adds that protesting parents may create even more stress for their children and some may begin to act out. "(T)hese kids can only take so much that something bad is going to happen," she explained. "These kids are not only trying to juggle school, but also trying to fit in and cope with puberty and, if they've recently immigrated to the United States, learning the new language and culture."[58]

The stress created by parental pressure is significant, but it is by no means the only source of conflict for Asian Americans in school. Another cause comes from the school environment itself. This leads to the third major educational issue facing Asian Americans. A major survey of eighth-, tenth-, and twelfth-grade students found a high percentage of Asian American students did not feel safe in school and often witnessed fights between different racial or ethnic groups. Just under 16 percent of Asian American students surveyed did not feel safe in school. This figure is second only to black students (16.1 percent), but is higher than Hispanics (14.7 percent) and whites (8.6 percent). More than 30 percent of Asian American students often witnessed fights between different racial or ethnic groups, which was second only to Hispanics (31.9 percent), but higher than blacks (22.2 percent) and whites (20.9 percent).[59]

Racial Tensions and Violence in Schools

Daily verbal and physical clashes have, unfortunately, become a part of life for many Asian American youth. Although anti-Asian sentiment and violence will be covered in greater detail in Chapter 5, special attention on racial tension and violence in schools is placed here. Because Asian Americans are racially different, sometimes speak with an accent, are viewed as perpetual foreigners, and are seen as clannish overachievers by jealous schoolmates, they have become targets of harassment and bigotry.

The most horrific example of racial violence against Asian Americans in schools did not come from another student or a teacher. It came from an outside intruder wearing military camouflage clothing and armed with an AK-47 style assault rifle, who opened fire into a schoolyard full of children in Stockton, California. On the morning of Tuesday, January 17, 1989, one day after the Martin Luther King, Jr., holiday, Edward Patrick Purdy came to the Cleveland Elementary School and fired off 105 rounds into a playground filled with children on recess break. Five children were shot and killed, and thirty-one others were wounded. Of the children who died, the oldest was 9 and the youngest was 6. Four of the children were Cambodian and one was Vietnamese. After a few minutes of mayhem, Purdy heard police sirens. He dropped his rifle, pulled out a 9-mm pistol, and killed himself with a single shot in the head.[60]

For several years prior to the killings, the city of Stockton witnessed a large increase in the number of Southeast Asian refugees. At the time of the shooting, about one out of six residents in Stockton were born in Southeast Asia, which is one of the highest proportions of Southeast Asian refugees in the country. The Cleveland Elementary School's enrollment was more than 70 percent Southeast Asian and was a reflection of the broader changes in the community. An October 1989 report to the California State Attorney General concluded that Purdy "focused a particular dislike on Southeast Asians," and the selection of Cleveland Elementary School for the site of the attack was not a random choice. Indeed, Purdy had once attended Cleveland Elementary School, which was by 1989 "dominated by Southeast Asian children, the offspring of those who were the current target of his resentment."[61] The Stockton schoolyard killings are an extreme example of how anti-immigrant and anti-Asian resentments infiltrate the primary and secondary schools.

The above incident confirms what was highlighted in three of the most often cited studies on immigrant students in public schools. The research of John Willshire Carrea (1988), Laurie Olsen (1988), and Ruben G. Rumbaut and Kenji Ima (1988) all found racial and ethnic hostility, as well as anti-immigrant sentiment, to be a part of the social environment in many schools and communities.[62] Although most of the abuse toward immigrants is from other students, sometimes teachers also openly express their antagonism and bigotry. In addition, there are serious conflicts between native-born and foreign-born students of the same racial and/or ethnic group. American-born Asian Americans often look down upon, and want to disassociate themselves from, immigrant "FOB" (fresh off the boat) students. The immigrants, of course, are not immune to nor ignorant of these attitudes around them. "Almost every student in our sample reported the first school year included incidents of being called names, pushed or spat upon, deliberately tricked, teased and laughed at because of their race, language difficulties, accent or foreign dress," Olsen writes. "Comments like, 'they look down at us,' 'they think we are going to take over,' 'they wish we'd go back where we came from,' or 'they think we are taking their jobs and money' were most common."[63]

Incidents of racial intolerance occur against both immigrant and U.S.-born Asian Americans, and in crowded inner-city schools as well as in seemingly secure suburban schools. Unfortunately, taunting and fighting between students are frequently dismissed by school administrators either because of their insensitivity, or because they do not want to raise the specter of serious racial problems on or near their campuses. In the summer of 2003 a group of fifteen to twenty high-school-aged white youths brutally beat five Asian American teenagers on the streets of San Francisco. The assault was not only physical but included the use of racial slurs against the victims. Despite the seemingly obvious hate-motivated nature of the crime, it wasn't until community organizations applied public pressure to force an investigation by the San Francisco Police Department and finally a district attorney prosecution. Only one of the fifteen to twenty assailants, "Matthew M.," was officially identified and charged with a crime and he refused to identify any of the others involved in the attack. It took a year before the case went to trial and in the end "Matthew M." was convicted of two felony assaults with felony-hate crime enhancements. He was sentenced to a year of probation and hundred hours of community service.[64]

The negative reaction to the soft sentence was sharp and swift. "This case has caused me to become disheartened with the community that I live in," said one of the victims, Ken Zeng. "I have never seen such hate out of anyone's eyes like Matthew M. It has left me wondering if I will be safe at all, even at my own church."[65] The last comment referred to the fact that Matthew M. was a student at Sacred Heart Cathedral Preparatory, an elite private high school in San Francisco, and the irony of the light sentence for a serious hate-motivated violence was not lost to *AsianWeek* columnist, Emil Guillermo. Guillermo argued that the Sacred Heart had a vested interest in a light sentence for Matthew M. to protect the school's image among its affluent student body and governing board members. In addition, it was Sacred Heart that recommended Matthew M. do his hundred hours of community service at On-Lok, a senior care facility servicing primarily Asian Americans. It turned out that Matthew M. is related to a member of the San Francisco Health Commission. "Smell any potential conflict here?" Guillermo asked. "Connections count in San Francisco when it comes to rehabbing an upper-crust hate criminal. The lesson in this hate crime seems to be: You can get away with one fairly easily if you're rich, white and know the right people." Guillermo also quoted the victims' attorney Edwin Prather, who said, "Yeah, I'm upset. It's San Francisco. It's the haves and the have-nots."[66]

This incident in San Francisco and its results highlight the need for communities and students to organize and force change away from entrenched denial by school administrators, law enforcement, and some parents. Along with interracial conflicts, there is also increasing attention to youth violence among Asian and Pacific Islanders in schools. The Asian & Pacific Islander Youth Violence Prevention Center (API Center), a partnership between the University of Hawaii and the National Council on Crime and Delinquency (NCCD) is the leader on research, evaluation, and training in this area. The aims of the API Center are to

1. Mobilize and collaborate with community-based organizations, social services agencies, educational institutions, and juvenile justice agencies to develop a comprehensive strategy and community plan to reduce API youth violence.
2. Develop and conduct research on prevention of API youth violence using sophisticated methods and state-of-the-art technology, in collaboration with human and social service agencies.
3. Disseminate research findings and provide a national resource for prevention research, and promising effective prevention programs for API youths.
4. Train and develop new researchers in the area of violence prevention research.
5. Develop a training curriculum for health professionals on API youth violence prevention.[67]

Asian American and Pacific Islander youth violence and victimization have not been seen as significant problems to law enforcement or academic researchers. There are a number of factors for this including the image of Asian Americans, especially the youth, as the "model minority," the broad diversity that make up the Asian American and Pacific Islander communities, the under-utilization of social services, and limited interaction with law enforcement and the judicial system. In a comprehensive review of thirty-four studies on Asian American and Pacific Islander delinquency (Le, 2001), it was concluded that researchers have only begun to examine this issue, and recommendations were made for future studies. Among the recommendations was the need to focus on the relationship between culture (both an individual group's culture and the culture of the dominant society) and delinquency: "What we do know about the sociocultural aspects of delinquency is mostly based on findings from research conducted on White, African American and some Hispanic youths. In fact, in three of the largest longitudinal studies on risk/protective factors related to delinquency . . . not only was culture egregiously omitted, but APIs were not even considered in the sample pool."[68]

The API Center is fully aware of the diversity among Asian American and Pacific Islander groups and has been examining the idea of "cultural competence" commonly used in mental health, social work, and health care, and applying it to the area of youth violence and prevention. "Cultural competency" is defined as "a set of congruent behaviors, attitudes, and policies that come together in a system, agency or among professionals" specifically addressing various needs in a cross-cultural environment for a variety of services and treatments.[69] The projects the API Center concentrates on are collaborative efforts with community-based organizations, policymakers, and law enforcement in specific cities (Honolulu, Oakland, and San Francisco) to assess the needs, issues, and possible solutions to Asian and Pacific Islander youth violence. Along with an impressive body of academic research, there have been other important results from this work. For example, in Hawaii the emphasis has been placed on developing a curriculum for health care professionals on all levels of higher education (undergraduate, graduate, and post-graduate). The curriculum emphasizes culturally effective care and application of knowledge gained from reviewed research on violence prevention.[70]

The report "Culture Counts: How Five Community-Based Organizations Serve Asian and Pacific Islander Youth (2003)," identified in Oakland and San Francisco culturally competent characteristics of programs whose primary clientele was Asian Pacific Islander youth. The studied programs provided a model of best practices that (1) increased the understanding of a variety of issues pertaining to Asian and Pacific Islander youth violence; (2) enhanced communication among clients, staff, and parents; (3) implemented interventions that truly address the needs, interests, growth and development, and perspectives of youth; and (4) produced outcomes that contribute to Asian and Pacific Islander health and welfare.[71] Most recently the API Center partner, the NCCD, and the California State Attorney General sponsored a Statewide Dialogue on Asian and Pacific Islander Youth Violence on August 17, 2005. The event facilitated discussions that address the diversity of Asian and Pacific Islander groups and promote dialogue among youth, community members, advocates, law enforcement, legislators, media, and foundations. Through these efforts of the API Center, risk and protective factors for Asian and Pacific Islander youth violence and victimization is becoming an important issue in today's society.[72]

This section has shown examples, from Stockton schoolyard killings to the violence in the streets of San Francisco, that both anti-immigrant and anti-Asian resentments as well as co-ethnic conflicts, infiltrate primary and secondary schools. Unfortunately, the same types of attitudes and structural inequalities have also reached deep into higher education in both overt and covert ways. Foremost among them have been concerns of alleged quotas against Asian American applicants to the most elite and prestigious college campuses in the country.

BACKLASH IN HIGHER EDUCATION

At the State University of New York-Binghamton, three Korean American students and one Chinese American student were attacked outside their dormitory allegedly by a group of white students. During the attack racial slurs like "You damn chinks!" and "This is what you get for being a chink!" were made. The incident took place on February 27, 2000, and resulted in one student, John Lee, suffering a fractured skull. Angered by what they considered to be the university's slow response to the assault, more than three hundred students staged a rally and a sit-in to call attention to the case. The demonstrations were led by the Asian Student Union (ASU), an umbrella organization of several Asian American groups on campus. ASU also demanded an apology from the school and the immediate expulsion of the suspected attackers. ASU's efforts helped to hold attention on the case and several months later two white Binghamton students pled guilty to charges stemming from the attack. Nicolas Richetti pled guilty to attempted assault and was sentenced to eight consecutive weekends in prison and five years probation. He also agreed to make financial restitution to the victims. Christopher Taylor pled guilty to disorderly conduct and was sentenced to fifty hours of community service and a $250 fine. A third student, Chad Scott was charged with just a misdemeanor in the incident. Richetti was expelled from the university, Taylor was suspended for two years, and Scott was allowed to remain in school. "My friends and I were singled out and attacked because of the color of our skin," said an angry John Lee during a press conference following the announcement of the plea bargains and what many considered to be light sentences. "(H)ad I been white, this would not have happened to me." Lee continues to suffer from his injuries and requires on-going medical treatment.[73]

In March 1992, a small group of Asian American students at Pomona College, an expensive and exclusive liberal arts college in Claremont, California, unveiled a banner that read: "Asian American Studies Now!" That evening, under the cover of darkness, the banner was defaced and altered to read: "Asian Americans die Now!" This message of hate shook the tiny campus and in one swift move undermined six years of work by Asian American students to bring an Asian American perspective to the college community and into the general curriculum. This incident is indicative of a backlash that had been brewing against the increasingly conspicuous presence of Asian Americans on college campuses throughout the United States for several years. Despite the setback, Pomona College now houses part of what is known as the Intercollegiate Department of Asian American Studies. The program offers a rich interdisciplinary curriculum that is available to students within the Claremont Colleges (Claremont McKenna, Harvey Mudd, Pitzer, Scripps, and Pomona).[74]

Another notable incident occurred in December 1987 at the University of Connecticut (UConn) when four Asian American couples boarded a bus to attend a formal dance. The couples were humiliated throughout the ride by taunts and threats and were spat upon by a rowdy group of four male students sitting in the back of the bus. Two of the students reported the terrible episode to campus police, university administration, and the local law enforcement authorities, but felt they were given the "run around." The incident was given attention only when the two students threatened to contact the press. Eventually, one of the offending students was expelled from the school for one year.

The other student, a star football player, was mildly punished and was still allowed to play for the football team. The handling of the case so enraged Asian Americans on campus that one Asian American faculty member, Paul Bock, staged a one-person demonstration at UConn's commencement in May 1988 holding a picket sign reading, "Please Reduce Institutional Racism at UConn." Professor Bock also held an eight-day hunger strike to draw attention to what he felt was continuing anti-Asian sentiment on campus.[75]

Bock later resigned his position at UConn and formed the Asian American Council of Connecticut. In 1990 Bock filed a complaint with the U.S. Department of Education's Office of Civil Rights (OCR), charging that Connecticut illegally excluded Asian Americans and American Indians from a program to recruit and retain minority students and faculty. The OCR ruled in Bock's favor in 1993, and the Connecticut Board of Governors for Higher Education agreed to comply with recommended changes. Asian American leaders across the nation applauded the OCR's ruling, and said the decision sets an important precedent against many colleges that exclude Asian Americans for stereotypical reasons. "Connecticut had the worst record against Asian Americans in higher education of any state," Bock said.[76]

Alleged Quotas in Higher Education

Universities and colleges across the nation historically have welcomed a small number of the most privileged young people from Asian countries. The goal of these foreign students was to obtain the best education available and return to their home countries as government officials, educators, business, military, and church leaders. Following World War II, many foreign graduate students in the United States, especially those studying in science and engineering fields, chose to stay in this country because of the opportunities for gainful employment in industry and at research universities. Their skills were in great demand during the Cold War-era competition with the then-Soviet Union. Since the late 1970s, Asian Americans have made tremendous inroads into the most prestigious centers of post-secondary education. Although Asian Americans today represent only about 4 percent of the U.S. population, they made up 13 percent of the undergraduate population at Princeton (2004), 16 percent of the undergraduate population at Harvard (2003), and 24 percent of the undergraduate population at Stanford (2004). In California, where Asian Americans represent about 12 percent of the state's population, the percentage of Asian American undergraduate enrollment is even more impressive. As early as 1981 Asian Americans at the University of California, Berkeley, represented 21.5 percent of the undergraduate class, while whites represented 65.0 percent of the class. By 2004, Asian Americans made up 41.0 percent of the undergraduates at UC Berkeley compared to just under 30 percent white.[77]

Despite these seemingly positive statistics, it was not long ago that American-born Asian students confronted subtle discrimination policies that had the very real effect of limiting their numbers and participation. A major controversy erupted in 1983 when the Asian American Students Association at

Brown University (AASA) issued a statement claiming "a prima facie case of racial discrimination against Asian Americans."[78] The primary focus of the group's charge was the clear decline in the admissions rate of Asian American applicants to Brown relative to the university as a whole. The AASA had been monitoring Brown University admissions since 1979 and was deeply disturbed by several findings. Chief among them was that in 1975 the admit rate for Asian Americans at Brown was 44 percent, but by 1983 the admit rate for Asian Americans was just 14 percent. During this same period, the number of Asian Americans applying to Brown increased eight-and-a-half times. The AASA's report also found that Asian American and white applicants were comparable in their academic qualifications, and saw no reason to "justify such a drastic decrease in the admit rate."[79]

Across the country, UC Berkeley professor L. Ling-chi Wang happened to be scanning the university's fall 1984 admissions figures and was taken aback by what he saw. To his surprise, Wang found that the absolute numbers of first-year Asian Americans dropped from 1,303 in 1983 to 1,031 in 1984. This drop of 21 percent was quite an anomaly considering the numbers and percentages of Asian American freshmen at Berkeley had been rising steadily for several years, and this was projected to continue through 1990. Wang began reviewing admissions figures after attending several meetings in which disparaging comments were made about the number and quality of Asian American students at UC Berkeley. "I began to feel very uncomfortable that all these people from different departments are saying things about Asians," Wang admitted. "(S)ome English department professor said that we should do something about these Asian students who are really deficient in the English language."[80] What began as an uneasy feeling quickly gathered momentum and became one of the most heated controversies in higher education in years.

Soon the specter of quotas against Asian Americans spread across the country. "I don't want to say it was a conspiracy, but I think all of the elite universities in America suddenly realized they had what used to be called a 'Jewish problem' before World War II, and they began to look for ways of slowing down the admissions of Asians," Wang told the *New York Times*. "As soon as admissions of Asian students began reaching 10 or 12 percent, suddenly a red light went on."[81] The "Jewish problem" Wang refers to is the restrictive quotas placed on Jewish Americans at a number of elite colleges and universities from the 1920s through the 1950s. During this period, the percentage of Jewish admissions dropped and even the most qualified Jews were excluded from faculty positions in higher education. As greater media attention began to focus on the Asian American admissions issue in the mid-1980s, universities such as Yale, Princeton, Cornell, Stanford, UCLA, among others, came under close scrutiny and even federal investigation.

Not surprisingly, no university admitted to any conscious wrongdoing or deliberate quotas against Asian Americans. However, Brown University acknowledged a "serious problem," and Stanford found "unconscious bias." In 1989, UC Berkeley chancellor Ira Michael Heyman publicly apologized for admissions policies that caused a decline in Asian American undergraduate enrollments.

"It is clear that decisions made in the admissions process indisputably had a disproportionate impact on Asians," Heyman said to a gathering of Asian American leaders. "That outcome was the product of insensitivity. I regret that occurred."[82] In 1993, UCLA was cleared of any wrongdoing by the U.S. Department of Education's Office of Civil Rights, but the school was ordered to offer admission to five Asian American students who were unfairly denied entrance into the mathematics department.[83] Investigations at Ivy League schools like Harvard and Princeton found admission rates for whites were indeed higher than for Asian Americans. The differences, however, were not interpreted as bias. In both cases, the lower admission rate for Asian Americans was due primarily to high admission rates to legacy students (children of alumni) and athletes, which are not illegal. Harvard and Princeton argued that legacy privileges are necessary because they serve the institutional goal of obtaining financial and service support from alumni.

A report from the U.S. Department of Education, Office for Civil Rights agreed that if the children of Harvard alumni are rejected, "affection" for the college could decline. If children of alumni were admitted, however, alumni "involvement" will be "renewed." This relationship is deemed crucial to a private, tuition-driven institution of higher education. The discrepancy between white and Asian American admits to Harvard was not extremely high, but did vary from year to year. For example, in 1983 the admission rates ranged from just 1.8 percent higher for whites (16.9 percent) than for Asian Americans (15.1 percent), to 6.3 percent higher for whites (17.6 percent) than for Asian Americans (11.3 percent) in 1990. However, admissions differences between whites and Asian Americans disappeared at Harvard when legacies and athletes were removed from the statistical analysis. These findings were verified in the research work of Stephen S. Fujita and Marilyn Fernandez (1995) using a rigorous and sophisticated statistical analysis.[84]

An even more dramatic case of special privileges given to children of alumni occurred at Princeton University. Between 1981 and 1985 the admission rate for legacy students at Princeton was approximately 48 percent, compared with a 17 percent overall admission rate for whites and 14 percent rate for Asian Americans. A 1985 internal student-and-faculty investigation at Princeton found Asian American applicants were rated higher than whites in terms of academic qualifications in four out of the five years between 1981 and 1985. During these years Asian Americans were rated "below average" in terms of the school's nonacademic criteria (legacy, athletics, affirmative action, extracurricular activities). Like most elite private universities, Princeton based its admission decisions not only on objective factors like grades and test scores but also on subjective and arbitrary factors, which, again, are not illegal and not deemed as an indicator of bias.[85]

Problems with Subjectivity

How poorly do Asian Americans rate in terms of the "subjective," nonacademic criteria? In "Diversity or Discrimination? Asian Americans in College," authors

John H. Bunzel and Jeffrey K. D. Au (1987) cited one study of 30,000 Asian American and white high school sophomores and 28,000 seniors that found minimally lower participation differences in sports and artistic activities among Asian Americans and whites. For varsity athletics, the participation rate of Asian Americans was 30 percent compared to 34 percent for whites. Similarly, 9 percent of Asian Americans participated in debating and drama, compared to 13 percent of whites. At the same time, Asian Americans tended to participate more than whites in other extracurricular activities like honorary clubs, school newspapers, and specific subject matter clubs (i.e., science club, math club, history club, French club, etc.). This was also the case for participation in social, ethnic, and community organizations. Bunzel and Au concluded there was no evidence to "support the common stereotype that Asian Americans have significantly lower rates of participation in extracurricular activities than do Caucasians."[86] This conclusion is confirmed in the most recently available major survey of high school seniors that found Asian Americans are, indeed, quite active in school and community-related extracurricular activities (see Table 3-5).

Bunzel and Au's report also found other forms of racial stereotyping against Asian Americans by some university officials. Comments like Asian

Table 3-5 Percent of High School Seniors in Extracurricular Activities by Race/Ethnicity, 1992

Activity	White	Black	Hispanic	Asian	Native American
Athletics					
Interscholastic team sport	30.8	32.3	25.8	28.3	30.4
Interscholastic individual sport	20.9	21.2	14.9	21.6	20.7
Intermural team sport	22.3	25.8	20.8	24.9	27.9
Intermural individual sport	12.5	16.7	14.0	14.7	18.2
Performance					
Cheerleading	7.4	10.6	6.7	5.1	11.9
Band/Orchestra	19.6	24.4	16.9	17.7	16.8
Play/Musical	16.1	15.9	10.6	13.7	14.0
School					
Student government	15.4	16.7	14.7	14.6	14.3
Honor society	19.6	14.0	12.5	27.2	13.6
Yearbook/Newspaper	19.7	14.3	16.8	18.9	21.2
Service clubs	13.6	13.6	14.4	19.3	11.6
Academic clubs	25.8	20.7	22.6	32.3	17.7
Community					
Religious	31.4	33.7	26.9	30.4	14.6
Youth groups	22.5	23.3	18.5	26.4	22.1
Community service	11.1	12.1	10.9	14.0	9.2

Source: National Center for Education Statistics, *Digest of Educational Statistics, 1995* (Washington DC: U.S. Department of Education, Office of Research and Improvement, 1995) Tables 140 and 142.

Americans lack an appreciation for a "well-rounded liberal education," were made. Bunzel and Au heard statements like Asian Americans lack an interest in "public service," indicating a perception of greater selfishness and career-orientation among Asian Americans compared to whites, which is not confirmed in the survey cited above. When Bunzel and Au asked administrators why Asian American admission rates tend to be so low, the frequent response was that Asian Americans were an "over-represented minority" relative to their national population. Within this, admissions officers also acknowledge that "diversity" on their campuses was an important goal. This line of thinking is dangerous for three reasons. First and foremost, this statement shows an obvious ignorance of the tremendous social, economic, and ethnic diversity among Asian Americans, which has already been detailed in this and in earlier chapters.

Second, the notions of diversity and overrepresentation are selectively applied against Asian Americans. For example, there was never any talk about limiting the numbers of children of alumni at elite private universities such as Harvard or Princeton, even though they represent only a small percentage of the U.S. population. The Asian American Students Association at Brown University directly confronted this stereotype in its original 1983 report: "(T)ry limiting the number of alumni sons and daughters in the University to their overall national representation. The point here is not that we wish to cut (the number of) alumni children, but that this argument which Brown used to justify limiting acceptance of Asian Americans is invalid and inconsistent. . . . Indeed, such an argument for limiting admissions to reflect the national population levels only reinforces the idea that there exists an unwritten quota for Asian Americans at Brown."[87]

Third, and easily most controversial, conservative politicians and pundits saw the admissions controversy as a convenient vehicle to dismantle liberal affirmative action policies. Conservatives argued that admissions policies should be based only on merit, and framed the issue as Asian Americans fighting against blacks and Hispanics over limited space in the nation's most prestigious universities. "(A)ffirmative action discriminated against Asian-Americans by restricting the social rewards open to competition on the basis of merit," wrote conservative political columnist George Will. "(I)t is lunatic to punish Asian-Americans for their passion to excel."[88] This argument may seem persuasive at face value, and it is precisely the same argument used by Chinese American parents in the Lowell High School controversy in San Francisco. However, Asian American leaders in higher education flatly rejected eliminating affirmative action, and rejected the idea that the issue was a competition between racial minority groups. They said the real issue was that changes in, and subjective interpretations of, admission policies at various universities were used primarily to benefit whites. "I am not opposed to the use of additional criteria to bring in promising students, especially those who were currently underrepresented," wrote L. Ling-chi Wang. "(But) the admission of larger numbers of whites under various color-blind, but protected, categories in fact account for the disparity between white and Asian American students at UC-Berkeley and other elite private institutions."[89]

By the early 1990s admissions policies at many college and university campuses were reviewed and changed in response to challenges raised by Asian Americans. Constant vigilance must be maintained, however, to prevent any repeat of past problems. "If Asian American admissions should suddenly rise at a university," concluded Bunzel and Au, "it would be essential for all to understand that such an increase is not the result of 'unfair advantages' being given to Asian Americans, but rather the effect of unfair disadvantages being removed."[90]

The Admissions Controversy Continues

By the mid-1990s direct attacks on affirmative action swept the nation creating tremendous polarization of Asian Americans, especially in higher education. In 1995 the Board Regents of the University of California passed two resolutions eliminating the use of race, religion, sex, color, ethnicity, or national origins in its admission process, contracting, and employment. The following year, California voters passed Proposition 209, which prohibited the state from using most affirmative action programs. The passage of these policy measures had an immediate impact on freshman enrollments. There were 222 new African American, 531 Hispanic (Chicano/Latino Americans), and 63 Native American new freshman registrants at UC–Berkeley in fall 1995. By 2000 there were 148 African American, 320 Hispanic, and 20 Native American freshman registrants. During the same period, Asian American freshman increased from 1,268 to 1,629 and the number of white freshman increased from 1,018 to 1,122. Interestingly, the number of unidentified students or those with no ethnic data increased from 151 in 1995 to 341 in 2000. Table 3-6 provides figures from 1995 to 2004 and shows the number of African American, Mexican American, and Native American registrants continue to lag. UC–Berkeley is considered the flagship station for the UC system and, as a result, is the most competitive institution to gain admission to.

Table 3-6 University of California, Berkeley, New Freshman Registrants by Ethnicity Fall 1995, 2000–2004

UC–Berkeley	1995	2000	2001	2002	2003	2004
African American	222	148	143	141	149	108
Native American	63	20	22	14	16	16
Hispanic Chicano Latino	531	320	388	401	393	340
Asian American	1268	1629	1688	1639	1598	1611
White	1018	1122	1134	1062	1050	1168
Unknown No Ethnic Data	151	341	343	276	299	282
Other	47	63	54	32	44	49

Source: University of California, Berkeley, at http://www.berkeley.edu/news/media/releases/2004/12/02_enroll_table.shtml.

At UC–Berkeley the freshman admission rate, or the percentage of applicants actually being accepted, is 30 percent. The freshman admission rate for the UC system overall is 80 percent. As a result, figures from the entire UC system do not show as dramatic a change as with UC–Berkeley. The controversy over affirmative action and access to elite institutions of higher education is far from over.

This is evidenced by the boisterous 1998 debate between UC Regent Ward Connerly, who successfully led the effort to end affirmative action programs in the state, and Ethnic Studies professor Ronald Takaki, who is leading an effort to reinstate race-conscious social policy. Connerly argued that improving kindergarten through twelfth-grade education is the only fair way underrepresented minorities can successfully enter the university system. He said that university enrollment should be based solely on merit and objective criteria, such as grades and test scores. Takaki agreed that improvement in K–12 is necessary, but in the meantime, affirmative action is still needed especially for underrepresented minorities, many of whom lack the opportunity for college advance placement and test preparation classes that more privileged and affluent students take for granted. He noted that SAT scores only reliably predict family income rather than college preparedness.

During the debate Takaki announced that he is attempting to gather one million signatures to support what he called the "California Equality Initiative." The initiative states: "To act affirmatively in promoting equality of opportunity, it shall be lawful for the state to consider race, gender or socioeconomic class disadvantages in the selection of qualified individuals for university admission, employment and contracting." Connerly scoffed at the notion saying: "Professor Takaki opposed the action of the regents. He lost. He opposed 209. He lost. . . . At some point I would think he would get the message that the voters of California want to end preferential treatment." Takaki responded quickly to Connerly's challenge. "Let's put it out there. I might be able to prove you wrong."[91]

In response to the end of affirmative action and its effect on student enrollments, the University of California system has developed several proposals to change admissions policies that may serve to increase student diversity. One plan has been to eliminate the SAT requirement and give extra weight to applicants who participate in the university's outreach and academic preparation programs for low-income and first-generation students. There are also calls for UC campuses to admit more students based on factors such as a student's educational opportunities and socioeconomic background rather than focus only on grades and test scores. Nonetheless, many African American, Hispanic, and Native American students see the University of California as a hostile environment and are choosing to go elsewhere.[92]

Broad Enrollment Trends in Higher Education

Although the focus of this section has been on the rights of Asian American students in the elite universities, it is important to remember that many Asian Americans do not fit the model minority stereotype. Indeed, many Asian Americans are from poor and working-class backgrounds who must struggle for access to a basic college education necessary to survive in a competitive job market. Their road is far afield from the students in elite institutions of higher education described above. For example, the San Francisco Bay Area has one of the largest concentrations of Asian Americans and is the location of two of the most prestigious universities in the United States. But while Asian American enrollments are high at both UC–Berkeley and Stanford University, they pale compared to City College of San Francisco (CCSF).

CCSF is a two-year community college that serves more than 110,000 full-time and part-time students through an Associate of Arts program and the city's adult education system. Asian Americans make up about half the students at CCSF. Lower-income students are drawn to the publicly funded community college that charges only a modest amount per academic unit. Students are most interested in attaining general education credits to transfer to a four-year college, obtaining job training or retraining, and learning English as a Second Language (ESL). In fact, the largest single block of Asian American students are enrolled in ESL classes. In 2004, CCSF was honored for its excellent service to immigrant students and at the same time the college opened a first-of-its-kind Asian Pacific American Student Success Center (APASS) aimed at working with students "at risk" for dropping out of the school. "APASS will provide API students with additional bilingual and bicultural counselors, instructors and tutors," explains Lawrence Wong, president of the CCSF board of trustees.[93] According to the latest available online figures, there are far more Asian American students in the community college system, and in the California State University (CSU) system, relative to the University of California system (see Table 3-7). A special report on Asian Americans in the CSU system also highlighted the need to address ESL needs of immigrant students. "While the issue of ESL support for students is a major concern on all CSU campuses, response to the needs of ESL students are just being initiated on many campuses and have not yet been addressed by others," the report states. "With notable exceptions, campuses of the CSU have not approached the language skill needs of immigrant students in a systematic manner that reflects the increased presence and importance of these students in the CSU."[94] The high numbers of immigrant students entering

Table 3-7 Total College Enrollment in California Public Colleges and Universities by System and Ethnicity, Fall 2004

Group	University of California	California State University	Community Colleges
White	79,145	148,443	603,395
African American	6,103	22,585	116,686
Hispanic/Latino	24,771	84,179	454,536
Asian American	60,520	69,843	261,317
Native American	1,232	2,904	13,996
Not Stated/Unknown/Other	14,516	N/A	124,585

Source: University of California, California State University, and California Community College Web sites.

the CSU system with limited English proficiency is very much related to the lack of programs in K–12 to help these students improve their English language skills. Other serious issues raised by the CSU report include problems in campus climate and racial harassment and the need to diversify and incorporate multicultural and international perspectives into the curriculum. The report also highlighted the lack of Asian Americans in the faculty and in administrative or management positions, as well as the need for greater outreach to, and retention of, underrepresented Asian American groups.

In his article, "Trends in Admissions for Asian Americans in Colleges and Universities" (1993), L. Ling-chi Wang finds these enrollment patterns to be representative of the socioeconomic realities within the Asian American population, and the class hierarchies present in higher education. That is, students from upper-middle-class and above families tend to be drawn to the elite public and private universities. More often than not, students from poor, working-, and middle-class backgrounds head for the options that best suit their academic abilities, career aspirations, and their family's financial abilities to pay.[95]

CONCLUSION

This chapter has shown that the super-achieving Asian Americans in education present a prominent but superficial image that needs to be analyzed in much more detail. Attention to Asian American "whiz kids" continues today, and is still drawing as much scorn as praise. Attention is only now being given to the issues and concerns of many Asian Americans in education as witnessed by the creation of the "Asian Pacific Islander American Scholarship Fund" (APIASF), a coalition of corporate and community organizations that have come together with the goal of raising and giving away $3 million in scholarships. In 2005 APIASF awarded $330,000 in scholarships to first-year college-bound students. APIASF leaders have set a goal to see all APIAs who wish to pursue higher education have that opportunity, regardless of their cultural backgrounds or economic means. Furthermore, APIASF leaders hope to encourage students to become future leaders in their respective communities, which, in turn, will help to strengthen the leadership of the country. Federal legislation has been proposed to authorize grants for colleges and universities that serve a high number and percentage of Asian and Pacific Islander American students to improve and expand their capacity to serve this specialized population. Colleges and universities that serve primarily low-income Asian and Pacific Islander American students would have preference in the grant approval process. This legislation would add an Asian and Pacific Islander American designation in the Higher Education Act that is already approved for colleges and universities that serve large numbers of African American and Hispanic students.[96]

This chapter focused on a variety of important educational issues facing Asian Americans from primary to post-secondary education. The controversy of affirmative action in enrollment at Lowell High School and at the University of California has served to polarize Asian Americans and pit them against other groups. The "success" of Asian Americans in education has been, and continues to be, a complex and vexing issue for educators, social scientists, and political leaders. This notwithstanding, this chapter has shown that both race and class are important factors in understanding the relative success and difficulties faced by Asian American students in all levels of education. It is true that many Asian Americans have performed amazingly well in school and have a great deal to be proud of. At the same time, this should not take away from those Asian Americans who work extremely hard to accomplish what they have, and who must continue to struggle to make it through. Asian Americans, like most Americans, generally believe in education as the key to get ahead, believe in hard work and meritocracy, and believe that people should recognize their accomplishments. The experiences of Asian Americans described in this chapter challenge an uncritical faith in these beliefs.

NOTES

1. For information on the Intel Science Talent Search finalists see http://www. sciserv.org/sts/64sts/finalists.asp.
2. See "Student 9, in College," *Sacramento Bee*, October 2, 2000; and quote in Cheryl L. Reed, "One Child Genius to Another," *Chicago Sun-Times*, January 20, 2004.
3. "Indian American Woman Youngest Rhodes Scholar," *AsianWeek*, December 19, 2002, and Mala Ashok, "On the Road to Success," *The Hindu*, January 17, 2004.
4. See "Confucian Work Ethic," *Time*, March 28, 1983; Dennis Williams, "A Formula for Success," *Newsweek*, April 23, 1984, pp. 77–78; David Bell, "An American Success Story: The Triumph of Asian Americans," *New Republic*, July 1985, pp. 24–31; Fox Butterfield, "Why Asian Americans Are Going to the Head of the Class," *New York Times Magazine*, August 3, 1986, pp. 19–24; Linda Mathews, "When Being Best Isn't Good Enough," *Los Angeles Times Magazine*, July 19, 1987, pp. 22–28; David Brand, "The New Whiz Kids," *Time*, August 31, 1987; and Diane Divoky, "The Model Minority Goes to School," *Phi Delta Kappan*, November 1988, pp. 219–222.
5. Joe R. Feagin and Clairece Booher Feagin, *Racial and Ethnic Relations*, 4th edition (Englewood Cliffs, NJ: Prentice Hall, 1994), Chapter 6.
6. Quoted in Robert Suro, "Study of Immigrants Finds Asians at Top in Science and Medicine," *The Washington Post*, April 18, 1994.
7. Grace Kao and Marta Tienda, "Optimism and Achievement: The Educational Performance of Immigrant Youth," *Social Science Quarterly* 76:1 (1995): 1–19.
8. Daniel B. Taylor, "Asian-American Test Scores: They Deserve a Closer Look," *Education Week*, October 17, 1990, p. 23. Harold W. Stevenson, J. W. Stigler, S. Lee, G. W. Lucker, S. Kitamura, and C. Hsu, "Cognitive Performance and Academic Achievement of Japanese, Chinese, and American Children," *Child Development* 56 (1985): 718–734.
9. Ruth Benedict, *Race: Science and Politics* (New York: Viking Press, 1959); Thomas F. Gossett, *Race: The History of an Idea in America* (New York: Schocken Books, 1965); and Winthrop D. Jordan, *White Over Black* (Baltimore: Penguin, 1969).
10. Arthur Jensen, *Educability and Group Difference* (New York: Harper & Row, 1973), p. 304.
11. Richard Lynn, "The Intelligence of Mongoloids: A Psychometric Evolutionary and Neurological Theory," *Personality and Individual Differences* 8:6 (1987): 813–844. Also see Richard Lynn, *Educational Achievement in Japan* (London: Macmillan, 1988); and Richard Lynn, "IQ in Japan and in the United States Shows Great Disparity," *Nature* 297 (1982): 222–226.
12. Harold W. Stevenson, J. W. Stigler, S. Lee, G. W. Lucker, S. Kitamura, and C. Hsu, "Cognitive Performance and Academic Achievement of Japanese, Chinese, and American Children," *Child Development* 56 (1985): 718–734.
13. Richard J. Herrnstein and Charles Murray, *The Bell Curve: Intelligence and Class Structure in American Life* (New York: The Free Press, 1994), pp. 272–277, 298–301.
14. Claude Fischer et al., *Inequality by Design: Cracking the Bell Curve Myth* (Princeton, NJ: Princeton University Press, 1996). Also see Russell Jacoby and Naomi Glauberman (eds.), *The Bell Curve Debate: History, Documents, Opinions* (New York: Random House, 1995). Also see reviews

by Robert M. Hauser, Howard F. Taylor, and Troy Duster, "Symposium," *Contemporary Sociology* 24:2 (March 1995): 149–161. For one of the best comprehensive reviews of *The Bell Curve*, see Stephen Jay Gould, "Curveball," *New Yorker*, November 28, 1994, pp. 139–149.

15. Samuel Peng et al., "School Experiences and Performance of Asian American High School Students," paper presented at the Annual Meeting of the American Educational Research Association, New Orleans (April 1984).

16. Samuel S. Peng and DeeAnn Wright, "Explanation of Academic Achievement of Asian American Students," *Journal of Educational Research* 87:6 (1994): 346–352.

17. William Caudill and George DeVos, "Achievement, Culture and Personality: The Case of Japanese Americans," *American Anthropologist* 58 (1956): 1102–1126; and Betty Lee Sung, *The Story of the Chinese in America* (New York: Macmillan, 1967), pp. 124–125.

18. Nathan Caplan, Marcella H. Choy, and John K. Whitmore, *The Boat People and Achievement in America: A Study of Economic and Educational Success* (Ann Arbor: University of Michigan Press, 1989); and Nathan Caplan, Marcella H. Choy, and John K. Whitmore, *Children of the Boat People: A Study of Educational Success* (Ann Arbor: University of Michigan Press, 1991).

19. Caplan, Choy, and Whitmore. *Children of the Boat People*, pp. 6–7, 11.

20. *Ibid.*, pp. 105–106.

21. Tommy Tomlinson, *Hard Work and High Expectations: Motivating Students to Learn* (Washington, DC: U.S. Government Printing Office, 1992).

22. Kiyoshi Asakawa and Mihaly Csikszentmihalyi, "The Quality of Experience of Asian American Adolescents in Activities Related to Future Goals," *Journal of Youth and Adolescence* 27:2 (1998): 141–164; and Kiyoshi Asakawa and Mihaly Csikszentmihalyi, "Feelings of Connectedness and Internalization of Values in Asian American Adolescents," *Journal of Youth and Adolescence* 29:2 (2000): 121–146.

23. Edward Banfield, *The Unheavenly City* (Boston: Little, Brown and Company, 1970).

24. Thomas Sowell, *Ethnic America* (New York: Basic Books, 1981), pp. 284, 295; also see Thomas Sowell, *Race and Culture: A World View* (New York: Basic Books, 1994).

25. Stanley Sue and Sumie Okazaki, "Asian-American Educational Achievements: A Phenomenon in Search of an Explanation," *American Psychologist* 46:8 (1990): 913–920.

26. Stephen Steinberg, *The Ethnic Myth: Race, Ethnicity, and Class in America* (Boston: Beacon Press, 1981), p. 103. The second edition of Steinberg's book (1989) includes a provocative epilogue that focuses on the Asian American experience.

27. Bob H. Suzuki, "Education and the Socialization of Asian Americans: A Revisionist Analysis of the 'Model Minority' Thesis," *Amerasian Journal* 4:2 (1977): 23–51.

28. Sue and Okazaki, "Asian-American Educational Achievements," p. 919.

29. David Fox, "Neuropsychology, Achievement, and Asian-American Culture: Is Relative Functionalism Oriented Times Three?" *American Psychologist* 46:8 (1991): 877–878; and Stanley Sue and Sumie Okazaki, "Explanations for Asian-American Achievements: A Reply," *Ibid.*, pp. 878–880.

30. *The Condition of Bilingual Education in the Nation, 1982: A Report from the Secretary of Education to the President and the Congress* (1982), p. 2; and see U.S. Department of Education Office of English Language Acquisition, "Executive Summary of Title III LEP Biennial Evaluation Report to Congress (2005) at http://www.ed.gov/ about/offices/ list/oela/index.html.

31. California Department of Education, "Language Census Summary Report 1998–1999" at http://www.cde.ca.gov/ds/sd/lc/reports.asp#s.

32. James Crawford, *Bilingual Education: History, Politics, Theory, and Practice* (Trenton, NJ: Crane Publishing Company, Inc., 1989), pp. 35–37; L. Ling-chi Wang, "Lau v. Nichols: History of a Struggle for Equal and Quality Education," *Ameriasia Journal* 2:2 (1974): 16–45.

33. Henry T. Trueba, Lilly Cheng, and Kenji Ima, *Myth or Reality: Adaptive Strategies of Asian Americans in California* (Washington, DC: The Falmer Press, 1993), pp. 61–62, 65.

34. *Ibid.*, p. 65.

35. U.S. Commission on Civil Rights, Civil Rights Issues Facing Asian Americans in the 1990s, pp. 76–80.

36. Proposition 63, also known as the "English-only" initiative, was passed by California voters on November 6, 1986, by a 3 to 1 margin.

37. California Department of Education, Educational Demographics Unit, *Language Census*, 1997–1998.

38. Peter Schrag, *Paradise Lost: California's Experience, America's Future* (New York: New Press, 1998).

39. "Profile of the Electorate," *Los Angeles Times*, June 4, 1998.

40. John E. Rigdon, "Asian-American Youth Suffer a Rising Toll from Heavy Pressures," *Wall Street Journal*, July 10, 1991.

41. See Laurence Steinberg et al., "Ethnic Differences in Adolescent Achievement: An Ecological Perspective," *American Psychologist* 47:6 (1992): 723–729; Chin-Yau Lin and Victoria Fu, "A Comparison of Child-Rearing Practices American Chinese, Immigrant Chinese, and Caucasian-American Parents," *Child Development* 61:1 (1990): 429–433; Barbara Schnider and Yongsook Lee, "A Model for Academic Success: The School and Home Environment of East Asian Students," *Anthropology & Education Quarterly* 21:4 (1990): 358–377; and Rosina Chia, "Pilot Study: Family Values of American versus Chinese American Parents," *Journal of Asian American Psychological Association* 13:1 (1989): 8–11.
42. Laura Uba, *Asian Americans: Personality Patterns, Identity, and Mental Health* (New York: The Guilford Press, 1994), p. 4.
43. National Center for Education Statistics, *Digest of Educational Statistics, 1995* (Washington, DC: U.S. Department of Education, Office of Research and Improvement, 1995), Table 142, p. 138.
44. Paula Yoo, "Troubled Waters," *A Magazine,* 1:4 (1992): 14, 53–54.
45. Quoted in Sharon Yen-Ling Sim, "Parent's Wishes and Children's Dreams Are Sources of Conflict," *Asian Week,* September 2, 1995.
46. See Mei Jyu-Chwang Lee, An Extreme Asian-American Upbringing (Authorhouse, 2003), and Emily Guey, "Child Abuse Among Asian Americans," at http://modelminority.com/article469.html.
47. Cited in Jayjia Hsia, "Asian Americans Fight the Myth of the Super Student," *Educational Record,* Fall 1987–Winter 1988, pp. 94–97.
48. See http://www.sunnyhills.net/SchoolDescription.pdf.
49. Quoted in Jodi Wilgoren, "High-Pressure High," *Los Angeles Times,* December 4, 1994.
50. See the series of articles on Lowell High School: Nanette Asimov, "A Hard Lesson in Diversity," *San Francisco Chronicle,* June 19, 1995; Tara Shioyo, "Recalling Insights—and Slights," *San Francisco Chronicle,* June 20, 1995; Nanette Asimov and Tara Shioya, "A Test for the Best Public Schools," *San Francisco Chronicle,* June 21, 1995.
51. Quoted in "Questions and Answers on Lowell High Series," *San Francisco Chronicle,* June 29, 1995.
52. Gerard Lim, "Lawsuit Over Chinese American HS Enrollment: Class Warfare by the Bay?" *Asian Week,* August 19, 1994.
53. Henry Der, "Clash Between Race-Conscious Remedies and Merit: School Desegregation and the San Francisco Chinese American Community," *Asian American Policy Review* 4 (1994): 65–91.
54. Nanette Asimov, "Single Standard for Admissions at Lowell High," *San Francisco Chronicle,* February 28, 1996.
55. Jason Ma and Joyce Nishioka, "SFUSD Overseer Sends Mixed Signals on Race," *AsianWeek,* November 11, 1999, p. 12.
56. Jeff Chang, "On the Wrong Side: Chinese Americans Win Anti-diversity Settlement—and Lose in the End," *Colorlines,* Summer 1999, pp. 12–14.
57. John Zhao, "A Parent's Fight Against S.F. Schools," *AsianWeek,* May 29, 2003.
58. Quoted in "S.F. Schools Assignment Controversy Continues," *AsianWeek,* April 17, 2003.
59. National Center for Education Statistics, *Digest of Educational Statistics,* 1995, Table 138, p. 136.
60. The students killed at Cleveland Elementary School were Ram Chun, 8; Thuy Tran, 6; Rathanan Or, 9; Sokhim An, 6; and Oeun Lim, 8.
61. Nelson Kempsky, *A Report to Attorney General John K. Van de Kamp on Edward Patrick Purdy and the Cleveland School Killing* (Sacramento: California Department of Justice, 1989), p. 13.
62. John Willshire Carrea, *New Voices: Immigrant Students in U.S. Public Schools* (Boston: National Coalition of Advocates for Students, 1988); Laurie Olsen, *Crossing the Schoolhouse Border: Immigrant Students and the California Public Schools* (San Francisco: California Tomorrow, 1988); and Ruben G. Rumbaut and Kenji Ima, *The Adaptation of Southeast Asian Refugee Youth: A Comparative Study, Final Report to the U.S. Department of Health and Human Services, Office of Refugee Resettlement* (January, 1988).
63. Olsen, *Crossing the Schoolhouse Border,* p. 35.
64. Vannessa Hua, "Teen Tied to Hate Crime Must Do Public Service: White Student Assaulted Group of Asian Americans," *San Francisco Chronicle,* October 22, 2004.
65. Quoted in "Judge Imposes 100 Hours, Probation for Anti-Asian Gang Assault," *AsianWeek,* October 28, 2004.
66. Emil Guillermo, "Being White and Right in S.F. Hate-Crime Sentence," *AsianWeek,* November 4, 2004.
67. Gregory Yee Mark, "Director's Report," *API Currents Newsletter* (April 2001), pp. 1, 4.
68. Thao Le, "Delinquency Among Asian/Pacific Islanders: Review of Literature and Research," *The Justice Professional* 15:1 (2002): 57–70.

69. Isami Arifuku, et al., "Culture Counts: How Five Community-Based Organizations Serve Asian and Pacific Islander Youth" (2003), p. 1 at http://www.apicenter.org/documents/culture_counts.pdf.
70. See the API Center Web site at www.api-center.org/health_professional_curriculum.html.
71. Arifuku, et al., "Culture Counts" (2003).
72. See the National Council on Crime and Delinquency Web site at www.nccdrc.org/nccd/n_apidialog_main.html.
73. Jason Ma, "Korean Suffers Cracked Skull in Hate Crime," AsianWeek, March 30, 2000, p. 9; quotes in "Heather Harlan, "SUNY Binghamton Wrestler Pleads Guilty to Attempted Assault," *Asian Week,* June 8, 2000, p. 11.
74. See the department's Web page at www.idaas.pomona.edu.
75. U.S. Commission on Civil Rights, *Civil Rights Issues Facing Asian Americans in the 1990s,* pp. 41–44; also see Sucheng Chan, "Beyond Affirmative Action," *Change* (November–December 1989), pp. 48–51.
76. Quoted in Scott Jaschik, "Affirmative-Action Ruling on Connecticut Called a 'Big Step' for Asian Americans," *The Chronicle of Higher Education,* May 19, 1993.
77. Fall enrollment information from these universities can be easily obtained on the Internet at http://registrar1.princeton.edu/data/oe_items/ug_by_race_ethn.pdf; http://search.harvard.edu:8765/query.html?qt=undergraduate+enrollment+by+ethnicity; http://www.stanford.edu/home/stanford/facts/undergraduate.html; http://www.berkeley.edu/news/media/releases/2004/12/02_enroll_table.shtml.
78. Asian American Students Association of Brown University, "Asian American Admission at Brown University," October 11, 1983, p. 1.
79. *Ibid.,* p. 7.
80. Quoted in Dana Y. Takagi, *The Retreat from Race* (New Brunswick, N.J.: Rutgers University Press, 1992), p. 25.
81. Quoted in Robert Lindsey, "Colleges Accused of Bias to Stem Asian's Gains," *New York Times,* January 21, 1987.
82. Quoted in "UC Berkeley Apologizes for Policy that Limited Asians," *Los Angeles Times,* April 7, 1989.
83. Sandy Banks, "UCLA Is Cleared in Bias Case," *Los Angeles Times,* August 27, 1993.
84. U.S. Department of Education, Office for Civil Rights, "Statement of Findings" (for Compliance Review No. 01-88-6009 on Harvard University), October 4, 1990, cited in U.S. Commission on Civil Rights, *Civil Rights Issues Facing Asian Americans in the 1990s,* p. 127; and Stephen S. Fujita and Marilyn Fernandez, "Asian American Admissions to an Elite University: A Multivariate Case Study of Harvard," *Asian American Policy Review* 5 (1995): 45–62.
85. Takagi, *Retreat from Race,* pp. 67–68.
86. John H. Bunzel and Jeffrey K. D. Au, "Diversity or Discrimination? Asian Americans in College," *The Public Interest* 87 (Spring 1987): 56.
87. Asian American Students Association of Brown University, "Asian Admission at Brown University," p. 20.
88. George F. Will, "The Lunacy of Punishing Those Who Try to Excel," *Los Angeles Times,* April 16, 1989.
89. L. Ling-chi Wang, "Meritocracy and Diversity in Higher Education: Discrimination Against Asian Americans in the Post-Bakke Era," *The Urban Review* 20:3 (1991): 202–203.
90. Bunzel and Au, "Diversity or Discrimination?" p. 62.
91. Quoted in Janet Dang, "UC's Connerly, Takaki Debate Race," *AsianWeek,* October 1, 1998, pp. 12–13.
92. Tanya Schevitz, "UC System Struggles to Attract Minorities," *San Francisco Chronicle,* May 5, 2005.
93. See the College of San Francisco Web site at www.ccsf.edu; May Chow, "CCSF Wins Excellence Award for Immigrant Work, *AsianWeek,* May 6, 2004; and quoted in "CCSF launches First At-Risk APA Student Center," *AsianWeek,* October 21, 2004.
94. "Asian Pacific Americans in the CSU: A Follow-Up Report," a report of the Asian Pacific American Education Advisory Committee (August 1994), p. 12.
95. L. Ling-chi Wang, "Trends in Admissions for Asian Americans in Colleges and Universities: Higher Education Policy," *The State of Asian Pacific America: Policy Issues to the Year 2020* (Los Angeles: LEAP Asian Pacific American Public Policy Institute and UCLA Asian American Studies Center, 1993), pp. 49–60.
96. See the National Asian Pacific Islander American Scholarship Fund Web site at www.apiasf.org; also see "Legislation to Improve Higher Education for APAs," *AsianWeek,* January 16, 2003.

4

Workplace Issues:
Beyond Glass Ceilings

VISIBILITY AND INVISIBILITY

The December 30, 1996, edition of *Time* magazine named AIDS researcher Dr. David Ho its "Man of the Year." Ho was the first scientist since the 1960s and the first Asian American given this honor. Ho pioneered the treatment protocol using protease inhibitors in combination with standard antiviral medications at the very early stages of AIDS infection. The HIV in Ho's patients' blood dropped so low it could no longer be measured.[1] His research into antiviral "cocktails" placed him in the media limelight. Another high profile success story is Jerry Yang who, as a graduate student at Stanford University in 1994, became the co-creator of Yahoo! Internet navigational guide. The following year Yang and his partner David Filo co-founded Yahoo! Inc. and became billionaires when the company went public in 1996. With a net worth of $2.6 billion, Yang was ranked in *Forbes Magazine*'s 2005 list of the world's richest people. Yang currently serves on the board of directors of Yahoo! Inc., where he develops business strategies and guides future direction for the company. According to the Yahoo! Inc. biography, Yang is "on leave of absence" from Stanford's Ph.D. program in electrical engineering.[2] While these well-known examples show Asian Americans at the top of their profession, there are other stories that need to be told about the realities of the workplace.

In March 1995 the Glass Ceiling Commission released a report that found among the top one thousand U.S. industrial firms and the five hundred largest businesses only 3 percent of senior managers were persons of color, and only 3 to 5 percent were women. The twenty-member panel of legislators and business officials formed in 1991 by then-President George Bush, Sr., was quite blunt about its assessment. "Serious barriers to advancement remain—such as persistent stereotyping, erroneous beliefs that 'no qualified women or minorities are out there,' and plain old fear of change."[3] The term "glass ceiling" refers to an invisible, but very real, barrier for qualified women and people of color to move upward into managerial ranks (especially upper management) within both private and public institutions.

This chapter focuses on the experiences of, and issues confronted by, Asian Americans in the workplace. The single workplace issue that was raised most frequently by participants in the U.S. Civil Rights Commission's 1989 Roundtable Conferences on the concerns of Asian Americans, and continues to be a major concern today, is the glass ceiling.[4] This chapter will first examine the glass ceiling phenomenon as it applies to Asian Americans in a variety of occupations. Second, this chapter will highlight the attempts by Asian Americans to fight back against discrimination in the workplace. This section will focus on the important precedent-setting cases of Bruce Yamashita and Rosalie Tung, and the class-action lawsuit against clothing retailer Abercrombie & Fitch to show how Asian Americans fought their job discrimination cases in court even in the face of seemingly impossible odds. Third, this chapter will look at a much less publicized, but increasingly pressing, problem in the workplace—language discrimination. Since the influx of immigrants from Asia after 1965, greater numbers of Asian Americans whose primary language is not English have entered the workforce. Many are feeling held back because of their accents and some employers have gone as far as initiating "English-only" work rules. Lastly, this chapter will focus on the Asian American working class and working poor, and the conditions they face in their struggles to support themselves and their families.

GLASS CEILING

As we learned in the previous chapters, Asian Americans generally have a high regard for education, have far higher levels of education compared to other groups, and have a "folk belief" that education equates with high income and professional advancement. The images of Asian Americans in school are that they are hard working, eager to learn, and achievement-oriented. The educational stereotypes of Asian Americans, however, seem to disappear when they enter the workplace. Among the new images of Asian Americans that have emerged include unfair stereotypes that they are unassertive and passive, poor leaders, lacking social skills, and too technically oriented. As discussed in Chapter 1, Asian American efforts in education reap only limited returns in the workplace. There are, of course, some notable Asian Americans who have excelled in their professions, and have moved into high-profile positions of corporate leadership.

Naomi Hirahara's book, *Distinguished Asian American Business Leaders* (2003), profiles ninety-six individuals including: James J. Kim, founder and CEO of Amkor Technologies (semiconductor packaging); William Mow, founder and CEO of Bugle Boy Industries (sportswear for men and boys); Josie Cruz Natori, founder and president of The Natori Company (lingerie and evening fashion); Masayuki Tokioka, founder and chairman of Island Insurance Co./National Mortgage & Finance; Andrea Jung, president and CEO of Avon Products, Inc., and Jeanette Chang, publisher of *Harper's Bazaar*. However, the vast majority of the people in the book were successful because they started their own—most often high-tech—businesses rather than climb the mainstream corporate world.[5]

The invisibility of Asian Americans in the highest levels of corporate America was highlighted in a "Report Card" by the Committee of 100, a group of prominent Chinese Americans, who found Asian and Pacific Islanders represented barely 1 percent of U.S. Fortune 500 companies' boards of directors. The report added that 79 percent of the U.S. Fortune 1000 companies had at least one woman on their board of directors, 44 percent had at least one African American director, 17 percent had at least one Latino director, but only 10 percent had an Asian American or Pacific Islander director. The U.S. Fortune 500 and 1000 are made up of the largest and most established companies in the United States including Wal-Mart, ExxonMobil, Chevron, ConocoPhillips, General Motors, Ford Motor, IBM, and General Electric. By contrast, the Committee of 100 also found that 31 percent of firms listed on the Nasdaq 100, which typically consists of newer computer, software, or biotech companies, had at least one Asian Pacific American member on their board of directors. "We believe this Report Card makes a compelling case for corporate America to diversify its boards with APA members," said Bob Lee, chairman of the Committee of 100. "As with all considerations of gender, race and ethnicity, we advocate the inclusion of 100 percent of the talent pool here in American, and APA's are very much part of that."[6]

Science, Engineering, and High Technology

Areas of employment where Asian Americans would appear to have a very strong foothold and mobility would be in science, engineering, and high-technology fields. According to the National Science Foundation, Asian Americans are 4 percent of the U.S. population but they are 14 percent of the total science and engineering workforce.[7] This figure should not be a surprise since the National Science Foundation also reported that Asian Americans earned 43.9 percent of all doctorate degrees in science and engineering.[8] Talented individuals in this area are in great demand, and they are key to maintaining U.S. dominance in an increasingly competitive global economy. Table 4-1 shows data from the National Science Foundation's report *Women, Minorities, and Persons with Disabilities in Science and Engineering*, which provides an interesting picture for Asian Americans in the technical fields.

The salaries of Asian/Pacific Islander men and women working in engineering are higher than whites for those with a bachelor's degree and a Ph.D., and are equal for those with a master's degree. In the general science field, salaries for Asian/Pacific Islanders are higher for those on the bachelor's and master's degree level, and are equal on the Ph.D. level. However, in the more

Table 4-1 Engineers and Scientists, Median Annual Salary by Field and Race/Ethnicity, 2001

	Bachelor's Degree	Master's Degree	Ph.D. Degree
Engineers			
White	$48,000	$60,000	$71,000
Asian/Pacific Islander	$51,000	$60,000	$75,000
Scientists			
White	$30,000	$40,000	$45,000
Asian/Pacific Islander	$36,000	$60,000	$45,000
Computer/Information Sciences			
White	$53,000	$68,000	$88,000
Asian/Pacific Islander	$50,000	$65,000	$80,000

Source: National Science Foundation, Division of Science Resource Statistics, *Women, Minorities, and Persons with Disabilities in Science and Engineering: 2004*, NSF 04-317 (Arlington, VA, 2004), Tables H-13, H-14, H-15 at http://www.nsf.gov/statistics/wmpd/employ.htm.

popular area of computer and information sciences we see Asian/Pacific Islanders earn less at every educational level. Table 4-2 provides detailed data on scientists and engineers with doctorates disaggregated by sex, age, and race/ethnicity. For all engineers, scientists, and computer/information scientists, Asian/Pacific Islanders in the younger age bracket consistently earn the highest salaries. However, the reverse is true for older cohorts. For example, Asian/Pacific Islander engineers 29 and younger generally earned $75,000 compared to $71,000 earned by whites of the same age group. But whites between the ages of 40 and 49 made $90,000, slightly more than the $89,500 earned by Asian/Pacific Islanders. The gap increases for whites 50 years old and above, who made $100,000 compared to $93,000 earned by Asian/Pacific Islanders. This trend stays consistent for white males and Asian/Pacific Islander males primarily because the sciences and engineering are male-dominated professions. However, the earning power of Asian/Pacific Islander women in science and engineering is more mixed. Asian/Pacific Islander women scientists consistently earn more than white women scientists at all age levels, whereas older Asian/Pacific Islander women computer/information scientists earn less than older white computer/information scientists. The salary levels for Asian/Pacific Islander and white women engineers are mixed. How can this salary inconsistency for Asian/Pacific Islanders with the highest education, seemingly in their professional primes, be explained?

The relatively high salaries for Asian/Pacific Islander scientists and engineers in Table 4-2 is primarily due to the fact that they have the highest percentage working in business and industry, relative to government and education.[9] The National Science Foundation reported 56 percent of Asia/Pacific Islander

Table 4-2 Median Annual Salary of Science and Engineering Doctorate Holders Employed Full-Time by Sex, Age, and Race/Ethnicity, 2001

Sex, Occupation, and Age in Years	White	Asian/ Pacific Islander	Black	Hispanic
All Engineers				
29 and younger	$71,000	$75,000	S	S
30–39	$78,000	$84,000	$80,000	$74,000
40–49	$90,000	$89,500	$71,900	$75,000
50 and older	$100,000	$93,000	$85,000	$85,800
Scientists				
29 and younger	$43,900	$62,000	S	S
30–39	$54,000	$76,000	$52,000	$55,000
40–49	$70,000	$72,500	$57,000	$63,500
50 and older	$80,000	$80,000	$73,000	$78,000
Computer/Information Scientists				
29 and younger	$50,000	$80,000	S	S
30–39	$72,000	$84,000	$73,000	$75,800
40–49	$80,000	$85,000	$72,000	$90,000
50 and older	$85,000	$83,200	$67,000	$70,000
Male Engineers				
29 and younger	$72,000	S	S	S
30–39	$78,000	$84,000	$80,000	$72,000
40–49	$90,000	$89,500	$71,900	$75,000
50 and older	$100,000	$95,000	$86,000	$85,800
Scientists				
29 and younger	$44,500	$62,000	S	S
30–39	$59,000	$70,000	$60,000	$58,000
40–49	$74,000	$75,000	$59,000	$67,000
50 and older	$82,000	$80,000	$75,000	$83,000
Computer/Information Scientists				
29 and younger	$50,000	S	S	S
30–39	$75,000	$84,000	S	$81,000
40–49	$82,100	$88,000	$75,000	$90,000
50 and older	$85,000	$85,000	$67,000	$70,000
Female Engineers				
29 and younger	S	S	S	S
30–39	$79,800	$75,000	S	S
40–49	$85,000	$87,000	S	S
50 and older	$87,000	S	S	S
Scientists				
29 and younger	$40,000	$60,000	$36,300	$30,000
30–39	$48,500	$56,000	$48,000	$47,100

Table 4-2 *continued*

Sex, Occupation, and Age in Years	White	Asian/ Pacific Islander	Black	Hispanic
40–49	$60,500	$70,000	$53,200	$57,000
50 and older	$68,000	$70,000	$72,000	$56,000
Computer/Information Scientists				
29 and younger	S	S	S	S
30–39	$65,000	$80,000	S	S
40–49	$75,000	$72,000	S	S
50 and older	$75,000	$74,600	S	S

S=suppressed because fewer than 200 weighted cases.
Source: National Science Foundation, Division of Science Resource Statistics, *Women, Minorities, and Persons with Disabilities in Science and Engineering: 2004*, NSF 04-317 (Arlington, VA, 2004), Tables H-17 at http://www.nsf.gov/statistics/wmpd/employ.htm.

science and engineering Ph.D.s work in business and industry. This figure compares to 31 percent for whites, 24 percent for blacks, 27 percent for Latinos.[10] On the other side of the scale, the generally lower salaries of older Asian/Pacific Islander scientists and engineers may be explained by several studies showing that Asian Americans in the high-tech occupations confront a glass ceiling that limits the advancement of their careers into managerial positions. The National Science Foundation has acknowledged that racial/ethnic groups differ in some respects in their primary work activity. For example, both African American and Asian American scientists and engineers are more likely to engage in primarily solitary computer applications than whites. In addition, Asian Americans are the least likely of any group to be in management or administration.[11] In her book *Doing Engineering: The Career Attainment and Mobility of Caucasian, Black, and Asian-American Engineers* (2000), Joyce Tang argues that both Asian Americans and African Americans are particularly disadvantaged in career mobility with engineering, and they do not have an equal chance of gaining access to management positions. "(T)here is no indication of a diversity in the rungs of management," Tang writes. "If joining the managerial ranks remain the ultimate career goal for most engineers, minority engineers may want to re-evaluate their career objectives."[12]

Both the NSF and Tang studies are based on generalized national data. Could the same findings be true in Silicon Valley, the high-technology capital of the world, in which Asian Americans represent 30 percent of the high-tech professionals (i.e., engineers)? A study by the Pacific Studies Center looking at the ethnic and gender stratification of work in Silicon Valley provides a more localized perspective. The Pacific Studies Center found that whites held 80 percent of the 25,000 management jobs, compared to Asian Americans who held only 12.5 percent of the management positions.[13] It is important to note that these statistics only amplify what many Asian American professionals already know. In a separate survey of 325 Asian American professionals in Silicon Valley, 80 percent of the respondents perceived Asian Americans to be underrepresented in upper-level management positions. The same survey found 53 percent saying that promotional opportunities were inadequate. In fact, 66 percent of the respondents felt their own chances for promotion were limited because of their race.[14]

Dissatisfied with being limited to the lab or low-level management, some Asian Americans have decided simply to leave and try advancing their careers elsewhere. "We are beginning to lose them in the technical area in the four-to-seven-year range, when they start to think about promotion," notes Hughes Aircraft vice president David Barclay. "And if those promotions are not occurring, they consider moving on."[15] Similar situations are seen at other top research and development centers such as AT&T Bell Laboratories in Murray Hill, New Jersey. Asian Americans are 22 percent of the company's 22,000 employees, but they are leaving at twice the rate of white males. The main reason for this rapid turnover, according to systems engineer David Chai, is the fact that promotions for Asian Americans take three to five years longer than for white males.[16]

In the case of immigrant scientists and engineers, many have decided to pack their bags and leave the United States altogether. Taiwan, for example, has been offering high salaries, generous research grants, and other perks to entice overseas graduate students and professionals to come back home. Thousands of scientists and engineers with advanced degrees obtained from U.S. universities have returned to Taiwan within the past several years. This is significant since historically more than 90 percent of these highly trained professionals have chosen to remain in the United States. "Most of them can get high-level jobs in Taiwan," said Yaw-Nan Chen, director of Taiwan's science division at its Los Angeles diplomatic mission. "They have some kind of frustration that they do not have an equal chance here."[17]

A special November 1994 issue of *BusinessWeek* reported that more than a hundred of AT&T Bell Laboratories' prized researchers have returned to Taiwan to begin new careers with greater responsibilities. One such AT&T Bell Labs alumni is Lance Wu, who returned to Taiwan to help head the government's computer research laboratory. One major figure who recently returned to Taiwan is Yuan T. Lee, the Nobel Prize-winning chemist from UC–Berkeley. Lee left his prestigious research position at Berkeley to take on the challenge of running Taiwan's Academia Sinica, an impressive collection of twenty-one research institutes. Taiwan and other Asian countries are investing billions of dollars into becoming leaders in high-technology research, development, and production. In Pohang, South Korea, $180 million was spent to build state-of-the-art equipment that would help them compete with any high-technology research center in the world. In Bangalore, India, returning scientists, engineers, and entrepreneurs are quickly creating what many see as the Silicon Valley of South Asia.[18]

Increasingly, however, many Asian Americans who felt restricted in their careers have decided to make the big leap and start their own businesses. The National Science Foundation found that Asian and Pacific Islander scientists and engineers were more than twice as likely to be self-employed than whites (14.8 percent versus 6.1 percent) and much more likely than blacks (2.8 percent) and Hispanics (4 percent). One example is the case of Narpat Bhandari, a former electrical engineer in a Silicon Valley semiconductor firm. Bhandari realized after years of hard work that he was not getting any opportunities to move higher into the executive ranks. So he struck out on his own and started a company in 1986, naming himself president. The company, Aspen Semiconductor, was a rapid success and after just two years he sold the firm for a hefty profit. In 1992, Bhandari and a small group of other successful Asian Indian entrepreneurs founded The IndUS Entrepreneurs, or TiE, dedicated to providing mentoring and venture capital for Asian Indians who want to start their own business. Today TiE claims 8,000 members and has opened offices throughout the United States, as well as in Canada, England, and India. Every year TiE hosts a conference that draws more than 1,500 participants. "The interaction, the mentoring, the networking for these new generations is needed to start companies," said Devendra Verma, a TiE co-founder. "In order to be in the market as a company, you need more people and TiE helps provide those advisors."[19] The growth of TiE is reflective of the growth in immigrant-owned and -run businesses in Silicon Valley. According to the report by AnnaLee Saxenian, *Silicon Valley's New Immigrant Entrepreneurs* (1999), Asian Indians are chief executive officers of 778 Silicon Valley firms, which constitute 7 percent of all high-tech companies formed in the area between 1980 and 1998. In 1998 these Asian Indian-led firms employed more than 16,000 people and accounted for more than $3.5 billion in sales.[20]

The same report found 2,001 Chinese-run businesses were founded in Silicon Valley during the same period. In 1998 these firms employed 41,684 workers and produced $13.2 billion in sales (see Table 4-3).[21] Like Asian Indians, Chinese immigrant entrepreneurs rely heavily on highly organized social and professional associations. One such association is Monte Jade Science & Technology Association (named after Taiwan's highest peak), which promotes the cooperation and mutual flow of technology and investment between Taiwan and the United States. These associations are among the most vibrant and active in the region. Common activities for these associations focus on providing advice and support to highly educated technical professionals who want to gain business and management skills. These associations and networks they initiate, along with rapidly advancing technology, have allowed immigrant

Table 4-3 1998 Sales and Employment of Silicon Valley High-Technology Firms Led by Chinese or Indian CEO

	# of Firms	% of Firms	Total Sales ($ M)	Total Employment
Indian	774	7	$ 3,588	16,698
Chinese	2,001	14	$13,237	41,684
Total	2,774	21	$16,825	58,282

Source: Dun & Bradstreet database, 1998. Cited in AnnaLee Saxenian, *Silicon Valley's New Immigrant Entrepreneurs* (San Francisco, CA: Public Policy Institute of California, 1999), p. 23.

professionals who have faced the glass ceiling to build international businesses in a relatively short span of time. Details of these activities are found in Saxenian's follow-up report, *Local and Global Networks of Immigrant Professionals in Silicon Valley* (2002). She concludes that immigrants' business start-ups will likely continue as long as there is a rich pool of skilled professionals and workers both in the United States and in their home countries.[22]

Federal Government Employment

There is also evidence that Asian Americans earn lower salaries and are less likely to be in management positions than comparably educated and experienced whites in all levels of government. This is based on an analysis of Asian Americans in the federal government service that was conducted by Pan Suk Kim and Gregory B. Lewis (1994). Their work is particularly interesting for two reasons. First, they focused on Asian Americans in federal service when most other studies on employment focused primarily on blacks and whites, and on men and women. Second, they compared Asian American men and women with non-Hispanic white men and women from 1978, 1985, and 1992 federal government employment statistics in order to view changes over time.[23]

As seen in Table 4-4, white males generally held a higher mean grade level (salary scale) than Asian American men in 1992 (10.9 versus 10.4), and this gap was wider than in 1978 (10.2 versus 9.8) but narrower than in 1985 (10.5 versus 9.8). In addition, white males were nearly twice as likely to hold supervisory positions than were Asian American men (27 versus 15). This was a continuation of the situation seen in 1985, but a reversal of the situation in 1978. These factors were true even though the median level of education for Asian American men has always been higher than the median education for white males. One area where Asian American men have consistently been deficient is in the mean years of federal service. This has even declined since 1978 while white males' median years of federal service have increased. This might indicate that Asian American men leave government service at a higher rate than white males.

More detailed analysis by Kim and Lewis found that in 1992 well-educated Asian American men (e.g., those with bachelors and graduate degrees) generally had higher grades than comparably educated white males, and this has steadily improved since 1978. At the same time, Asian Americans were less likely to be in supervisory positions even if they had the same years of education, federal experience, age, and veteran and handicap status as white men. "In sum," say Kim and Lewis, "as a group, well-educated Asian men face little or no discrimination in achieving high grade positions and salaries, but they are less successful in attaining supervisory or managerial authority."[24]

For Asian American women in federal government employment, however, Kim and Lewis found their status to be, "more complex and troubling." The relative standing of Asian American women in terms of mean grade and supervisory status declined between 1978 and 1992, despite the fact that Asian American women generally had higher levels of education. These discrepancies continued even when adjusting for similar education, seniority, age, veteran, and handicap status. Interestingly, Asian American women with a graduate

Table 4-4 Characteristics of Asian Americans and White Non-Hispanics in Federal Service 1978, 1985, 1992

Characteristics	Asian American Females	Non-Hispanic White Females	Asian American Males	Non-Hispanic White Males
Mean Grade				
1992	7.7	8.1	10.4	10.9
1985	6.9	6.7	9.8	10.5
1978	6.7	5.9	9.8	10.2
% with Supervisory Authority				
1992	7.0	12.0	15.0	27.0
1985	9.0	8.0	15.0	26.0
1978	8.0	6.0	23.0	19.0
Mean Years of Education				
1992	14.4	13.7	15.3	15.2
1985	14.1	13.3	15.2	15.0
1978	13.6	12.9	15.0	14.6
Mean Years of Federal Service				
1992	10.2	12.4	11.6	14.1
1985	9.5	11.0	11.7	13.8
1978	12.5	10.4	12.9	13.2

Source: Pan Suk Kim and Gregory B. Lewis, "Asian Americans in Public Service: Success, Diversity, and Discrimination," *Public Administration Review* 54:3 (May–June, 1994): 285–290, Table 2.

school education were shown to be 1.9 grades below white women with similar education. This is a significant discrepancy and was a larger gap than what was seen in 1978 and 1985. In addition, Asian American women in 1992 were less likely to hold supervisory positions than white women, even with comparable levels of education and experience. This is a complete reversal of the situation found in 1978 and quite an anomaly considering the general societal trend toward greater equality for all racial minority groups and women. "The most likely explanation is that white women are the group that has gained most from affirmative action in recent years," explain Kim and Lewis. "Asian women have gained on white men, but not as rapidly as white women have, leading Asian women to fall behind relative to white women."[25]

The findings of Kim and Lewis were challenged in an article by Christopher Daniel (1997), who questioned whether discrimination of Asian Americans in federal service was widespread, and tried to explain the grade differentiation between Asian Americans and whites. Daniel offered an alternative analysis and raised three important points commonly used when analyzing the glass ceiling phenomenon for Asian Americans in the public sector. Daniel's first point was based on the fact that two thirds of Asian Americans in the general population are foreign-born and he makes the assumption that most Asian Americans in federal service are immigrants. If that is true, he argues, one explanation for why Asian Americans are less likely to move into supervising positions is their lack of fluency in English. Daniel does not dispute that individual immigrants can perform effectively, but emphasizes that linguistic competency is important. With this in mind, Daniel's second point centers on what he calls the "occupational choice hypothesis." This means that an individual's occupational choices are not random, but limited by family members and ethnic counterparts. A high percentage of Asian Americans in federal service majored in engineering in college, which would place them in more technical positions. However, relatively few Asian Americans in federal service majored in the social sciences, law, or public affairs, which is more typical for supervisors and administrators. Lastly, Daniel noted that Kim and Lewis exclusively used general statistical data and lacked evidence that Asian Americans actually perceived discrimination in federal government work.[26]

Kim and Lewis re-examined and expanded their study in response to Daniel's challenge. Their updated results served only to strengthen their original argument. To confront the supposed English-language deficiency of Asian Americans, Kim and Lewis analyzed a sample of male military veterans in federal service because almost all veterans are assumed to be native or near-native speakers of English. If Daniel's contention that lack of English-language proficiency harms Asian Americans, an analysis of veterans with the same level of education, federal experience, and age should show little, if any, employment discrepancy between whites and Asian Americans. The results showed an employment grade gap that actually tripled in size! Immigration status and English-language competency could not explain why the grade gap was wider in this subsample of federal employees.[27]

Next, Kim and Lewis addressed the issue of "occupational choice." They acknowledged that many Asian Americans in the federal government work in technical fields. That being the case, they reanalyzed data concentrating only on employees with engineering degrees. Interestingly, white women and African American men who earned engineering degrees held positions at about the same grade as white men. On the other hand, Asian American men lagged 0.3 and women lagged 1.3 grades below comparable white men. In addition, 32 percent of white men with engineering degrees held supervisory or management positions, while Asian American men and women held 8 and 9 percent, respectively. Kim and Lewis ask, "Did Asians turn down more promotions and supervisory opportunities or did those making promotion decisions advance whites ahead of Asians?"[28]

Lastly, Kim and Lewis acknowledged that their earlier work did not have any evidence that Asian Americans actually perceived discrimination in their federal jobs. This was a weakness they were able to correct. The results from an Office of Personnel Management Survey of Federal Employees (1992) report found that Asian Americans were twice as likely as whites to feel they were discriminated against. Although feelings of discrimination are less frequent in the higher grade levels, Asian American men in the mid-levels of their careers were more likely to feel they faced discrimination than any other group surveyed. The

Table 4-5 Percentage Responding "Yes" to the Statement, "If I am dissatisfied with my federal career perspectives, it is because I believe I am being discriminated against"

	Asian American	African American	Hispanic	Native Indian	White
Total	16	16	14	12	9
Women	10	14	10	12	8
Men	20	23	18	13	9
GS1-GS4	5	14	28	18	12
GS5-GS8	23	17	11	10	9
GS9-GS12	12	16	13	14	9
GS/GM13	18	18	13	7	7
Sample Size	785	3,251	1,102	314	20,875

Source: Computed from U.S. Office of Personnel Management, "Survey of Federal Employees," November 1991. Cited in Gregory B. Lewis and Pan Suk Kim, "Asian Americans in the Federal Service: Education, Occupation, Choice, and Perceptions of Discrimination: A Reply," *Public Administration Review* 57:3 (May–June 1997).

perception of a glass ceiling is most prevalent during this time (see Table 4-5). The results of this survey were also seen in the Merit Principles Survey, where 36 percent of both Asian American and African American men felt they had been denied a job, promotion, or other job benefit during the previous two years due to racial discrimination.[29]

Although these studies may seem a bit dated, the findings are still relevant today. This is seen by the December 1999 claim of racial bias in hiring, salaries, and promotions filed by nine long-time Asian American employees at the Lawrence Livermore Laboratory, which conducts research for the federal government. The allegations emerged after U.S. Energy Department set up a Task Force Against Racial Profiling following the indictment of Wen Ho Lee, the scientist who was investigated for three years, fired, and eventually charged with mishandling nuclear secrets. Perceptions of an unfriendly work environment and suspicions of bias had long been brewing among scientists and engineers who work at labs involved in nuclear defense research. The task force offered Livermore workers the opportunity to share their concerns and analyzed salary data that reportedly revealed an average gap of almost $1,000 a month between white males and Asian American men and women. The average salary gap widened for older employees due to the lack of Asian Americans in management positions.[30]

In January 2000, the U.S. Energy Department released their report and found an "atmosphere of distrust and suspicion" toward Asian Americans at nuclear weapons labs. The report found that while specific incidents and examples of racial profiling may differ from site to site, the general concerns and issues were virtually identical departmentwide. Supervisors and managers at nuclear research labs (Los Alamos, Sandia, and Lawrence Livermore) and other Department of Energy facilities were found to question "the loyalty and patriotism of some employees based upon racial factors." The report acknowledged that Asian Americans believed they faced a hostile work environment and speculated that their opportunities for promotions, choice job assignments, and developmental training have been greatly reduced.[31] Shortly thereafter a class-action lawsuit was filed on behalf of 460 Asian American scientists and engineers alleging discrimination in pay and promotion against Lawrence Livermore National Laboratory. The case was formally settled in March 2005, allowing for up to $765,000 to the class members and $350,000 in legal fees and costs. In entering the agreement the laboratory avoided admission of wrongdoing; both sides wanted to avoid a long and expensive legal battle.[32]

Given the historical concerns over employment discrimination against Asian Americans in federal service, the Federal Asian Pacific American Council (FAPAC) was formed in 1985. According to the organization's mission statement, "FAPAC is an organization that promotes equal opportunity and cultural diversity for APAs within the Federal and District of Columbia governments. FAPAC encourages the participation and advancement of APAs in the Government work force." The most important event sponsored by FAPAC is their Asian Pacific American Federal Career Summit, which began only in 2002. The summit was developed to address the shortage of Asian Pacific Americans in senior executive and management positions in the federal government. The summit specifically focuses on providing management insights, skills training, and other career opportunities to help Asian Pacific American government employees maximize their potential.[33] FAPAC is also part of the National Coalition for Equity in Public Service (NCEPS), which also includes Blacks in Government, Federally Employed Women, and Hispanic National Image. NCEPS jointly monitors and represents minorities and women on such issues as equal employment opportunity policies and practices, as well as executive candidate development programs and other federal recruitment initiatives, workforce management, outsourcing, and civil rights in general, such as monitoring the Government's service to and treatment of minority Americans and immigrants.[34]

ASIAN AMERICANS FIGHTING BACK

Confronting the glass ceiling is a major workplace concern for Asian Americans, but this issue does not often gain very much sympathy from non-Asians. One reason for this is the "model minority" stereotype, which plays a large part in maintaining an image that Asian Americans are untroubled and economically successful. Much more attention seems to be placed on how well some Asian Americans are doing relative to other racial minorities in the United States. Another reason why glass ceiling concerns of Asian Americans do not garner much attention is that many believe traditional Asian culture is simply antithetical to Western corporate culture. This is based on broad generalizations about Asian culture that are again used to explain both personal behavior and social results for Asian Americans. "(T)he successful manager has the get-up-and-go to grab the bull by the horns and wrestle it to the ground," explains Frances M.

Namkoong, who works for the Mid-America Consulting Group in Ohio. "In contrast, the Asian is perceived to be passive, non-aggressive."[35]

While most Asian Americans don't deny that Asian and Western cultures differ, they also feel that the rapid economic growth in Asian countries and the growth of Asian immigrant entrepreneurship in high technology contradicts the core of the cultural argument that Asians don't make good managers. Leadership exercised by Asians in the Pacific Rim tends to be much more group-oriented and consensus-driven. Interestingly, this team concept is a growing trend in U.S. corporations as we move into a more competitive economic climate in the twenty-first century. "What is misunderstood is the nature of leadership exercised by Asians," Namkoong adds. "Is the team approach the best way to operate? Certainly the Pacific Rim countries have demonstrated dramatically that the concept has worked for them." In short, the cultural conflict argument in terms of management skills is a moot point.[36]

At the same time, it is not surprising that Western corporate culture cultivates potential managers among employees who best fit its own image. Because of this, many Asian Americans recognize that they need to be better at promoting and asserting themselves if they hope to get the kinds of employment opportunities they want. It is with this in mind that Diana Ting Liu Wu wrote her book *Asian Pacific Americans in the Workplace* (1997). On one hand, the book is intended to provide business leaders a better cultural understanding of Asian American employees and colleagues. On the other hand, the book also provides basic advancement strategies for Asian Americans such as participating in business-sponsored social events, cultivating mentor relationships, following etiquette and protocol, and even advice on personal appearance as ways to improve the chances for advancement. Wu acknowledges workplace discrimination and the presence of a glass ceiling, but the emphasis of the book is clearly on "how a variety of resourceful individuals used different strategies to transform themselves, develop professionally, and transcend undesired circumstances."[37] This book is well meaning and possibly somewhat helpful, but it places most of the responsibility for change on the individual employee. This focus on individual responsibility with relatively little attention given to institutional accountability or oversight has many limitations.

Civil rights leader Henry Der, former executive director of Chinese for Affirmative Action in San Francisco, calls for more active strategies to break through the glass ceiling. Der recognizes the fact that hiring and promotional practices are not necessarily rational, nor merit-based. He says Asian Americans need to develop strong employee organizations that will serve to guide and monitor the implementation of affirmative action goals. Even with affirmative action policies, or perhaps because of them, Der thinks it is all the more important for Asian Americans to collectively organize and not let their concerns get lost in the competition for entry-level and advancement opportunities. Der also maintains that Asian Americans should make every effort to educate and inform employers about unrecognized biases against Asian Americans. The stereotype that Asian Americans lack necessary managerial and leadership skills, for example, is an unacceptable generalization and should be openly challenged at every opportunity. Finally, Der wants to see Asian Americans "cultivate a heightened sense of social responsibility." This means extending efforts to interact cooperatively with other groups at work to share common experiences, difficulties, and rewards. This is all a part of making plurality and true integration in the workplace a meaningful reality. Der's ideas are not new and are not intended to be adversarial to the employer. However, they do recognize that the responsibility for genuine and fundamental change is on both the individual and the workplace.[38]

Three Celebrated Court Cases

Self-improvement and efforts to amicably educate employers about biased attitudes is all well and good, but Asian Americans still need to take the decisive step of going to court. Historically, Asian Americans have been reluctant to openly challenge employers through the legal system, and the former vice chair of the federal Equal Employment Opportunity Commission (EEOC), Paul M. Igasaki, has lamented that Asian American employees are reluctant to file complaints.[39] A lawsuit against an employer is an action of last resort primarily because it is a long, drawn-out, expensive, and painful process that, win or lose, could have dire long-term consequences for an individual's career. This is particularly true for employees who continue in their job even after they have filed discrimination charges. In these cases, the work environment is usually quite tense because these employees often feel under extreme scrutiny by supervisors and co-workers, and may be potential victims of reprisal. In addition, it is extremely difficult to prove intentional discrimination because of its subjective nature and, as a result, the vast majority of cases settle out of court long before anything can be clearly proven, admitted, or resolved.

A settlement out of court is not necessarily bad. It often provides the employee a cash payment while avoiding the risks involved in a jury trial. At the same time, it helps the employer get rid of a problem without admitting any wrongdoing. When an employment discrimination case is successfully followed through to the end, however, the impact is far greater than just the single case. A court or jury decision that finds wrongdoing often serves as an important precedent for similar cases that are waiting to be heard or may emerge in the future. This is what happened with Bruce Yamashita, Rosalie Tung, and the class-action lawsuit against Abercrombie & Fitch.

In March 1993, Bruce I. Yamashita, a third-generation Japanese American attorney, was finally commissioned a captain in the Marine Corps reserves after a five-year legal battle that sought to prove racial discrimination. Yamashita had to fight for his commission after being drummed out of the Marine Corps' Officers Candidate School in 1989 because he had shown "leadership failure." His victory resulted in an official apology and, more importantly, an overhaul in the Marine Corps officer-training procedures. In a ceremony held at the House Armed Services Committee room in Washington, DC, Yamashita spoke of how much he longed for this moment. "It is with great pride that I wear this uniform today," he said. "It means so much more to me now than ever I could have imagined five years ago." The event was hailed as a decisive moment for Asian Americans and another important step toward equal opportunity in the U.S. military.[40]

Born and raised in Hawaii, Yamashita claims he did not experience any racism prior to taking the Marine Corps training. But throughout his ten-week officers' training, he was the target of intense racial slurs and harassment. Yamashita recalled a staff sergeant telling him on the very first day of the ten-week course, "We don't want your kind here. Go back to your own country!" During his training tour, another sergeant confronted Yamashita about World War II and spat, "We whipped your Japanese ass." Still another sergeant spoke to Yamashita only in broken English and never referred to him by name—only calling Yamashita by the names of well-known Japanese consumer products and automobiles. Just two days before graduation, Yamashita and four other officer-candidates were forced out of the program.[41]

Yamashita pondered for six months before finally deciding to challenge the Marine Corps' decision. During that long period of indecision, Yamashita met with veterans of the Japanese American 442nd Regimental Combat Team, whose military exploits made them one of the most decorated fighting units during World War II. More than four decades after the war's end, both Yamashita and the 442nd veterans found that Japanese Americans still had to prove their loyalty to the United States. Before making his final decision to fight the Marine Corps, Yamashita told a group of 442nd veterans: "If you folks do not support this case, then I will not pursue it. Your sacrifices give me the moral legitimacy to fight back." The veterans, some of whom were in tears, told Yamashita he had their support.[42]

Yamashita and his attorneys gathered evidence that showed between 1982 and 1990 a clear "pattern of discrimination" in the officers' training program and racial minorities were dismissed at a far-higher rate than white candidates. In 1991, after two internal military investigations, the Marine Corps issued a formal apology and offered to allow him to retake the training. Yamashita flatly rejected the offer because it was a denial of the commission he believed he already earned. In 1993 Yamashita was offered an apology and a commission of second lieutenant. The Marine Corps offer was conditional on Yamashita taking an additional six months of officer's training. Again, he rejected the offer. This time he said the commission was too low and did not recognize the four years that had passed since his dismissal. Yamashita stood firm in his belief that he deserved his commission from the very beginning and did not receive one because of racial discrimination. Later the Pentagon offered Yamashita a commission as captain, which was a rank commensurate with the amount of time he would have earned had he not been dismissed from officer's training. Yamashita decided to accept the commission, although it was in the Marine reserves and not active-duty status. This compromise was acceptable because he retained the right to apply for active-duty status if he wished.[43]

Yamashita wore a crisp green Marine officer's uniform and sported a military-style crewcut at his commissioning. It was clearly an emotional moment when he took his oath of office and had his captain's bars pinned on his collar. Yamashita called the confrontation with the Marine Corps a principled struggle and expressed his hope that abuses he faced would not be faced by anyone else again. "His commissioning today is a tribute to his dedication, a tribute to his courage," said Japanese American congressman Norman Y. Mineta (D-San Jose), one of many attendees at the ceremony. Absent from the event was General Carl E. Mundy, Jr., commandant of the Marine Corps, who was invited to the ceremony but claimed he had a scheduling conflict. Mundy created his own controversy when he appeared on the CBS News program *60 Minutes* and said that minorities failed in officers' training because they could not shoot, swim, or use compasses as well as whites. With this difficult chapter in his life behind him, Yamashita has had the opportunity to reflect on what it all means to him. Top among them has been the emergence of a stronger sense of identity. "I was an idiot before all this," he admits. "Before this I was just an American. Now I'm an Asian American."[44] A documentary film on the Yamashita case, "A Most Unlikely Hero," has recently been produced and information can be found at http://www.unlikelyhero.org.

Another long and hard-fought discrimination case involved Rosalie Tung, a professor who was denied tenure by the University of Pennsylvania Wharton School of Business in 1985.[45] Tung's case is particularly significant because it went all the way to the U.S. Supreme Court and in 1990 she won a unanimous decision from the court that set an important precedent for other employment discrimination cases in higher education. The University of Pennsylvania is a highly respected and elite private institution of higher education. It operates twelve schools including the Wharton School of Business, the oldest business school in the nation. When Tung joined the Wharton School in 1981 she was well regarded for her teaching, publication record, and community service. But when a new person was appointed chair of the management department at Wharton in 1983, her dream job quickly turned into a nightmare.

In her charge, Tung stated the new chair began making unwanted sexual advances toward her. When she made it clear to him that she wanted to keep their relationship professional, he became furious and, according to Tung, began a campaign to drive her out of the school. While both Asian American men and women face employment discrimination, the U.S. Civil Rights Commission has acknowledged that Asian American women face the extra burden of sexual harassment on the job. According to the 1992 commission report on Asian American civil rights issues, "the stereotypic expectation of compliance and docility, a formal complaint from an Asian American woman might (be) considered as a personal affront or challenge."[46]

In February 1985 the chair summoned Tung into his office, told her that the personnel committee had denied her tenure, and did not give any reason for the decision. Tung immediately filed a grievance with the University of Pennsylvania, as well as a complaint with the Equal Employment Opportunity Commission. Tung recalls the dean of the Wharton School offered her a cash settlement to drop her EEOC complaint and also threatened to make it difficult for her to find employment elsewhere. He warned her that if she continued with her complaint, they would fight her all the way to the Supreme Court. Tung refused to be intimidated and pursued her actions. The internal grievance commission within the University of Pennsylvania reviewed the personnel files of thirteen other faculty members who were granted tenure, found that Tung was indeed discriminated against, and forwarded its report to the EEOC. It was during the grievance commission hearing that Tung learned there were three negative evaluation letters in her file, two of which were written by the chair himself. It was at this point the EEOC issued a subpoena for Tung's personnel file and the file of five other tenured faculty members for their investigation. However, the University of Pennsylvania refused to turn over the files, claiming special privilege for confidential peer review materials and First Amendment principles of academic freedom.

The dean of the school made good on his threat to Tung, and the university challenged the subpoena all the way to the U.S. Supreme Court. Tung knew the university was trying to force her into giving up the fight and had the financial resources to do it. "The (university) could afford to drag the victim through years and years of emotional and financial stress and strain," she said. "I could not have survived this ordeal without the strong moral conviction that what I did was right. It would have been easier for me to leave the university quietly with the money offered by the dean of the Wharton School." Tung also knew that stereotypes of Asian women also played a major part in the university's underestimation of her strength and determination. She recalls reading a newspaper article in which colleagues at the University of Pennsylvania described her as "timid, and not one of those loud-mouthed women on campus" and "the least likely person to kick over the tenure-review apple cart." The 1990 U.S. Supreme Court ruling forced the University of Pennsylvania to submit to the EEOC subpoena, thus allowing Tung the opportunity to compare her files with others and to directly challenge any discrepancies or inconsistencies. The decision was both a relief and a vindication for Tung, and for many others who have faced employment discrimination. "I fought the University of Pennsylvania for principle and I'm glad I won," Tung announced to an enthusiastic gathering of supporters shortly after the high court's decision. "I'm glad I fought, and I'm proud of what I've accomplished for myself and other minorities and women in this country."[47] Tung has long since left the University of Pennsylvania and is currently professor of International Business at Simon Fraser University (Canada). A biographical profile of Professor Tung can be found at http://www.sfu.ca/~tung/.

Another important case involving cultural stereotypes and irrational judgments affecting hiring and promotional decisions of Asian Americans is seen in *U.S. Equal Employment Opportunity Commission (EEOC) v. Abercrombie & Fitch Stores, Inc.*, which was filed on November 10, 2004.[48] Abercrombie & Fitch (A&F), the clothing retailer that caters to the young, trendy, and upscale with more than six hundred stores nationally, was accused of racial discrimination through its corporate policy requiring salespeople to represent a virtually all-white "A&F" look. With nearly $2 billion in sales, A&F has been highly successful at marketing its image to the customers they want. However, a company is not allowed to use the marketing image as part of an effort to exclude or discriminate against its employees. According to Anthony Ocampo, a Filipino American who was one of the plaintiffs in the case, this is exactly what A&F had done. "The greeters and people that worked in the in-season clothing, most of them, if not all of them, were white," said Ocampo. "The people who worked in the stock room, where nobody sees them, were mostly Asian American, Filipino, Mexican and Latino." Jennifer Lu, a former A&F employee claimed she was fired after a corporate official visited the store and was unhappy with the sales clerks. Lu told CBS news, "A corporate official had pointed to an Abercrombie poster and told our management at our store, 'You need to have more staff that looks like this.' And it was a white Caucasian male on that poster."[49]

Abercrombie & Fitch already had a negative reputation among Asian Americans before the lawsuit. In 2002 a fire storm of protest emerged when the company began selling T-shirts featuring what many considered negative stereotype cartoons of Asian men. One T-shirt had two Asian men in rice-paddy hats with the slogan: "Wong Brothers Laundry Service—Two Wongs Can Make It White." Another T-shirt featured a caricature Buddha saying: "Abercrombie and Fitch Buddha Bash—Get Your Buddha on the Floor." Still another T-shirt had on it an Asian man pulling a rickshaw with the slogan: "Rick Shaw's Hoagies and Grinders. Order food by the foot. Good meat. Quick feet." It was highly ironic for a company that relies heavily on an image of sex and physical perfection with its white models (i.e., tall, blond, and muscular) photographed in perfect locations (posing on a beach, laying on the lawns of mansions, or frolicking in a meadow), depicting Asian men as short and squat, dressed like peasants, working as servants, and as comical Buddha figures. Michael Chang, vice president of Stanford University's Asian American Students' Association, was not amused. "It's really misleading as to what Asian people are," Chang said. "The stereotypes they depict are more than a century old. You're seeing laundry service. You're seeing basically an entire religion and philosophy trivialized." A&F apologized for offending shoppers, but their rational for selling the T-shirts in the first place shows how little they know or care about anyone outside of its own narrow image of reality. "We personally thought Asians would love this T-shirt," said Hampton Carney, spokesperson for Paul Wilmot Communications, a public relations firm hired by A&F to handle the outcry of complaints. The T-shirts were eventually pulled from the stores.[50]

Less than a week after the EEOC filed its 2004 lawsuit, A&F agreed to pay more than $40 million plus lawyer's fees to settle this and two other private class-action lawsuits filed against the company. A federal judge formally approved the settlement in April 2005. While A&F did not admit any guilt, it did agree to pay damages to those who were denied jobs, and back-pay to those who were denied promotions and sent to the back of the store to work instead of working in the front. A&F also agreed to institute various policies to prevent future discrimination and promote diversity among its employees and managers. In a National Public Radio interview Bill Lann Lee, lead attorney in one of the private class-action lawsuits and a former U.S. Assistant Attorney General for Civil Rights, commended A&F for entering the settlement quickly and for agreeing to make changes in how it does business. "Here's a major icon of American style, and it was perpetuating a look that was supposed to be cool, collegiate, preppie, but white," Lee told interviewer Travis Smiley. "You can do business in this country in a way that is creative, is cutting-edge, but you cannot violate our civil rights laws and you cannot discriminate against individuals on the basis of color, race, ethnicity."[51]

LANGUAGE RIGHTS

Of course, rejection from a job, denial of a promotion, or a layoff is not always the result of discrimination. But, as we have seen in the Yamashita, Tung, and Abercrombie & Fitch cases, Asian Americans, like other racial minority groups and women, often face that lingering question in their minds about what factors played into their loss of opportunity, career mobility, and livelihood.

Another issue of particular importance for Asian Americans on the job has to do with language rights. Because there is a large portion of immigrants and nonnative English speakers among the Asian American population, language discrimination is a growing trend and cause of great concern. "The main thing for us is how to overcome the language problems," admits Savio L. C. Woo, a molecular genetics specialist at the Baylor University College of Medicine and past president of the Society of Chinese Bioscientists in America. "The only difference between the foreign-born and the native-born is the mastery of the language."[52]

Concerns over English fluency do have some validity for both employers and employees. Certainly employers want managers and workers who can communicate clearly and without trouble. On the other hand, employees don't want to be unfairly handicapped in a competitive job market.

Accent Discrimination

While Asian American immigrants acknowledge their English may not be perfect, they feel that it should not be the only stumbling block in advancing their careers and that their other qualities should not be overlooked. This frustration can be found in all fields, of course, and is not limited to professionals. "There is no doubt that communication skills are very important," said Wayne Liauh, during testimony in Houston to the U.S. Commission on Civil Rights. "However, adopting a standard that is unreasonably high may be tantamount to allowing an employment practice that is prejudicial against foreign-born Asian American employees."[53] Ironically, even Asian Americans without accents often confront employers who expect a language problem. One Korean American woman was stunned when she found out an employment counselor placed a note in her file saying, "Chinese but speaks good English." According to the woman, the most troublesome part of this episode is that the counselor did not see a competitive job candidate, but "an Asian woman with a potential language problem."[54] Language, like physical features, is an easy target to single out a person or a group for unfair treatment. Recently twelve Asian American police officers sued the New York and New Jersey Port Authority for discrimination, alleging they were harassed and denied promotions. The Asian American officers were subjected to both racial slurs and the mocking of Asian accents over the radio by non-Asian officers, which created a hostile work environment and perpetuated anti-Asian prejudice.[55]

Discrimination in employment and promotion based on a person's English-language proficiency, accent, or the desire to speak another language while at work are illegal. The EEOC enforces the federal prohibition against national origin discrimination in employment under Title VII of the Civil Rights Act of 1964, which covers employers with fifteen or more employees. The only exception to language rights protection is in cases where a person is clearly unable to perform the responsibilities of the job because of his or her inability to speak and be understood in English. But since the early 1990s, serious concerns have been raised about subjective assessments of the workers' abilities to communicate, and the impact it has on the workplace. As a result, in 1995 the American Civil Liberties Union (ACLU) of Northern California and the Employment Law Center (ELC) of the Legal Aid Society in San Francisco created a nationwide "Language Rights Hotline" to meet the needs of increased reports of discrimination based on accent and English-only rules.[56]

Out of this emerged the Language Rights Project, which is dedicated to advocate for workers confronting language discrimination at their places of employment. "We have encountered many people who have been told not to speak any language other than English at work, have been denied credit or insurance because they do not speak English well, or even denied promotions because they have a foreign accent," said ACLU attorney Ed Chen. "Many of these workers are unaware that federal and state laws prohibit discrimination on the basis of language and national origin, yet their legal rights may have been violated."[57] Many attorneys who defend language rights believe the rise in the "official" English or "English-only" movement in the 1980s, along with increased anti-immigrant sentiment in the 1990s, together have fueled the flames of intolerance that has generated a growing number of language discrimination cases. Indeed, language may be used as a less direct way to vent antagonism against immigrants of different races and national origins. "There's a backlash against immigrants . . . that is expressed not in out-and-out racism but in language discrimination," explains Chen.[58]

The most publicized case of accent discrimination involved five Filipino American security guards in San Francisco who filed suit against American Mutual Protective Bureau (AMPB) and the United States government in May 1992. The case took on great significance because the five guards were removed from their posts after a Federal Protection Service official in the U.S. Treasury Building complained about having trouble communicating with an unidentified guard over the phone. The official assumed the guard was Filipino and ordered "all the Filipino guards removed from the site." AMPB officials followed orders from the federal government and removed the guards. Attorneys for the guards said AMPB made no attempt to determine whether or not any of the men were actually involved in the phone incident, nor determine whether or not the men were able to perform their jobs.[59]

Until this incident, all the guards had worked for AMPB for between three and six years and no one had complained about their work performances or their English. All except one of the guards had attended college in the Philippines, where the language of instruction is English. The five guards, Cayetano Decena, Perfecto Estrada, Teodolfo Loyola, Florentino Ramirez, and Cabrito Rose, were all devastated by their removal. "We felt embarrassed among friends, co-workers and relatives because we were removed for not being able to speak English," said Perfecto Estrada. He added that "(a)ll of us had emotional, mental, and physical distress. We have also suffered from financial hardships and family problems caused by the loss of income." Estrada himself was laid off for six months before he was eventually reassigned to swing, graveyard, and weekend shifts at another post. Of all the guards, Estrada thought he had the least to fear. During his employment at AMPB he was steadily promoted up the ranks to sergeant, then first lieutenant, captain, and eventually to deputy chief. His natural leadership abilities were also reflected in his twenty-eight years of experience in the Philippine military and as a district commander of the Philippine Constabulary highway patrol. "I had worked with AMPB for over five years without any complaints," Estrada said proudly. "I knew I didn't have any problem communicating in English."[60]

In June 1994, a settlement was reached in which the five guards received $87,500 from the U.S. General Services Administration and an undisclosed amount from AMPB. In return, however, no one conceded any wrongdoing. The importance of the case is witnessed by the fact that attorneys from the Asian Law Caucus (ALC) in San Francisco, the ACLU, the ELC, and a private law firm all joined forces on the side of the Filipino American guards. During a press conference following the settlement, Lora Jo Foo, an attorney with the Asian Law Caucus said: "When these five security guards came to ALC in March of 1992 for assistance, we were disturbed that federal government officials could even issue the removal of all Filipinos from the workplace and that [American Mutual Protection Bureau] could obey the order without batting an eye, without questioning the wisdom of the order. Had the [U.S. General Services Administration] ordered the removal of all blacks from the Department of Treasury, I am sure the reaction would have been, 'But that's discrimination; we can't do that.'"[61]

Attention to national origin discrimination has received renewed scrutiny in recent years following the tragic events on September 11, 2001. "With American society growing increasingly diverse, protection against national origin discrimination is vital to the right of workers to compete for jobs on a level playing field," said EEOC Chair Cari M. Dominguez. "Immigrants have long been [assets] to the American workforce. This is more true than ever in today's increasingly global economy. Recent world events, including the events of September 11, 2001, only add to the need for employers to be vigilant in ensuring a workplace free of discrimination."[62]

"English-Only" Rules

A second area of language discrimination is seen in "English-only" rules at work. One of the earliest cases of this type involved Adelaida Dimaranan, a Filipino American former assistant head nurse with Pomona Valley Hospital

Medical Center in Southern California. The evening she was caught speaking her native Filipino language of Tagalog during a dinner break with two co-workers began a series of events that would eventually thrust her into the center of national attention. Notes from a staff meeting just four months after the incident reported the head nurse saying, "The use of Filipino language . . . won't be tolerated." Although the hospital denied that a blanket "English-only" rule was ordered, the Filipino nurses worried if they were ever caught speaking Tagalog during breaks, on the phone with families, or informally during meals it might be cause for disciplinary action. This policy was especially difficult for Dimaranan because, as an assistant supervisor, she was expected to support the administration. "There was no way I was going to enforce the policy," admitted Dimaranan. "They didn't like that."[63]

Not only did Dimaranan refuse to enforce the policy, she was reprimanded a number of times for continuing to speak Tagalog. According to Dimaranan, this brought on further adverse actions against her. Other assistant head nurses began writing her up on minor infractions that reflected on her work and these began to show up on her performance reports. Dimaranan had received excellent work reviews prior to the Tagalog-speaking incident and had no problems after she was first promoted to assistant head nurse. But after her language troubles began, her reviews were critical and she was said to have "created tensions" and caused "division" among the staff. Based on these work evaluations, Dimaranan was demoted and relocated to another unit in the hospital. Nine nurses who were supervised by Dimaranan signed a letter of support and one of them declared, "I think the supervisors were trying to punish her because she defended herself on the language issue." Just as she fought against what she thought was an unfair English-only work rule, Dimaranan did not take her demotion and transfer quietly. With a twenty-five-year nursing career, thirteen years of service to Pomona Valley Hospital, and her dignity to protect, she filed a civil rights lawsuit in both state and federal courts.[64]

The federal Equal Employment Opportunity Commission has held that an English-only work policy is legal if it is justified by a business necessity. Blanket English-only rules that include workers' breaks or free time, though, are almost always illegal because the business necessity argument cannot be justified. The EEOC also agrees with civil rights advocates who insist the prohibition of speaking a person's native language can create an atmosphere of inferiority, isolation, and intimidation, which could result in a discriminatory working environment. The Dimaranan lawsuit was given a boost when the EEOC decided to intervene on her behalf. However, an earlier federal court's decision was not favorable in Dimaranan's case. In the *Garcia v. Gloor* (1981) case, the Fifth Circuit found English-only policies were not discriminatory because the employees in this particular instance were bilingual and could speak English if ordered to do so. The court ruled a person who is fully capable of speaking English and chooses not to do so was not a victim of discrimination. "Mr. Garcia could readily comply with the speaking-English-only rule," the ruling read. "In some circumstances, the ability to speak or the speaking of a language other than English might be equated with national origin, but this case concerns only a requirement that persons capable of speaking English do so while on duty."[65]

Before the case went to trial, the hospital did go on public record opposing English-only work rules. Dimaranan pressed on with her suit, demanded her old job back, and wanted the removal of the negative evaluations from her record. In early 1993 Dimaranan and the hospital reached an out-of-court settlement in which she was paid an undisclosed amount and the hospital admitted no wrong-doing. The Dimaranan case had the potential for setting a legal precedent of when employees are free to speak their native language, but she and her lawyers cannot be faulted for accepting a settlement. As discussed earlier in this chapter, there is never any guarantee of winning a lawsuit. To highlight this point, the following year the U.S. Supreme Court refused to hear an appeal by Latino employees at a South San Francisco meat-packing plant who challenged an English-only work policy. The decision left intact a ruling by the U.S. Court of Appeals in San Francisco, and allowed employers to impose English-only rules where and when they see fit. The earlier Court of Appeals ruling declared that English-only work policies were merely an "inconvenience" for workers.[66]

National origin discrimination is one of the fastest growing types of charge filings with EEOC nationwide, increasing from 7,035 filings in 1995 to 9,046 in 2002. This represents a 28 percent increase over that span of time. Although the number of filings based specifically on English-only work rules is relatively small, they have increased by more than 600 percent from 32 filings in 1996 (when EEOC began separately tracking them) to 228 filings in 2002. "We see it as a growing trend," said EEOC spokesman, David Grinberg. "We're trying to strike a balance between business and employees speaking their native language."[67] While some businesses may feel languages other than English to be problematic, forcing or discriminating against workers because they are not speaking English in a situation unrelated to workplace necessity has proven to be expensive. In 2003 the EEOC settled one English-only case for $1.5 million in Colorado, which made headlines across the nation.[68] Since then several other high profile English-only lawsuits have been filed including one in July 2005 against the Hartsfield-Jackson International Airport in Atlanta, which allegedly instituted an English test for all its workers to pass before they could obtain a security badge. The suit charged that the new policy resulted in the firing of a number of Somali, Mexican, and Vietnamese American workers.[69]

Arbitrary and capricious English-only rules have also been seen in areas outside the workplace. In May 2005, a group known as "ProEnglish" filed suit in Alabama trying to get the state to stop giving driver's license exams in any language other than English. Alabama gives driver's license exams in thirteen languages.[70] That same summer, another controversy was stirred up when a Little League umpire in Massachussetts halted a game because a coach yelled instructions to a pitcher in Spanish. "He (the umpire) told me, 'English only',," said coach Chris Mosher. "He said it loudly. . . . He told me if anyone speaks one more word in Spanish, they'll be ejected. It was sickening." The game was played under protest. The Little League officals later issued a statement stating the "incident could have been avoided" and the umpire "made an incorrect decision." The unidentified umpire was not allowed to work any more games for the rest of the season.[71]

ASIAN AMERICAN WORKING-CLASS AND LABOR MOVEMENT

There has been relatively little focus on the plight of the working poor Asian American women and men who live below or just above the poverty level threshold. Asian Americans have generally placed a great deal of attention on the glass ceiling problem, a primarily middle-class and professional issue. Recently, increased attention has been drawn to language rights, which impacts both middle- and working-class Asian Americans. Civil Rights organizations, however, have long helped working-class Asian Americans in their struggles against job discrimination. Often times the most egregious acts of discrimination and exploitation are committed by Asian American employers. In 2003 the owners of a Chinese restaurant were ordered by a federal district court judge in New Jersey to pay $150,000 in unpaid wages and over $3.2 million in compensatory and punitive damages to two waitresses who claimed they were forced to work eighty-hour work weeks and live in a squalid apartment with up to seventeen other people. The American Civil Liberties Union staff attorney Jennifer Arnett Lee believes there are many more workers facing similar conditions, but very few ever speak out and even fewer take the extra step to file a claim. "Employers feel they have the upper hand and they use scare tactics," Lee told the *New York Times*. "They tell them, 'If you complain, we'll have you deported.'"[72]

It is unfortunate that both the plight and the contributions of the Asian American working class have been largely ignored in U.S. labor history. If mentioned at all, Asian Americans were seen as foreign threats to the American workingman and as scabs that bore the brunt of the mainstream labor movement's wrath. Asian Americans were also seen as the victims of labor's hostile union antagonism, calls for exclusion, and ugly anti-Asian racism. The most notable scholar focusing on the contemporary Asian American working class is Peter Kwong. His three well regarded books, *Chinatown, New York: Labor and Politics, 1930–1950* (1979), *New Chinatown* (1987), and *Forbidden Workers: Illegal Chinese Workers and American Labor* (1997), have taken a critical look at racial discrimination and class exploitation particularly in the Chinese American community. Since a new wave of Asian immigrants has entered the United States starting in 1965, the labor movement has had to confront changes in the makeup of the workforce and has recognized the increase in Asian American workers. A 1991 report to the AFL-CIO's Executive Council acknowledged that Asian American communities and the labor movement shared common concerns for "economic and political justice, equal opportunity, and an improved quality of life for all working people." In addition, the AFL-CIO established a formal support organization for Asian American labor unionists.[73] The result of this effort was the creation of Asian Pacific American Labor Alliance (APALA), which held its founding convention in Washington, DC, on May 1, 1992. More than five hundred Asian American unionists from across the nation attended the conference and it was a clear pronouncement of a joint effort to increase the participation between Asian Americans and the American labor movement.[74]

APALA's eighth biennial convention was held in Las Vegas, Nevada, August 26–28, 2005. Highlights from the convention included the following:

- Addresses from national union and political leaders, Executive Vice President of the AFL-CIO Linda Chavez Thompson, Chair of the Change to Win Coalition Anna Burger, Congressman Michael Honda, and other leaders of the Asian and Pacific Islander American community.
- A panel of representatives from the Labor Coalition on Community Action including the Coalition of Black Trade Unionists, the A. Philip Randolph Institute, Coalition for Labor Union Women, and the Labor Council for Latin American Advancement joined APALA in discussing the challenges facing constituency groups, women, and people of color in the labor movement.
- Trainings in legislative action, community action, organizing, and communications and leadership skills.
- Passage of resolutions on Diversity in AFL-CIO Leadership and Staff, Condemning Raiding and Fostering Trade Union Solidarity, Supporting Chinese Daly News Workers, Supporting the University and Professional Technical Staff at the University of California, Supporting Justice for James Yee, and Condemning the Hacienda Luisita Workers Massacre in the Philippines.[75]

The formal creation of APALA, the first national Asian American labor organization established within the ranks of the AFL-CIO, was long overdue. Asian American workers historically have faced tremendous hardships and exploitation by non-Asian, as well as from Asian, employers. As a result, there have been many attempts in recent years to organize Asian American workers in the various sectors in which they are clustered. Important efforts were made to unionize garment workers, hotel and restaurant employees, electronic manufacturing workers, janitors, food processing and cannery laborers, and hospital workers, among many others. These recent efforts by unions have had only modest success, and unionization among Asian Americans remains quite low. The process has been difficult for a number of reasons. First, there has been a general decline in the labor movement since the early 1980s. In the 1960s about 35 percent of workers in the United States were represented by a union. By the early 1990s this figure was reduced to just 16 percent. According to labor statistics only about 12 percent of Asian American workers are union members.[76] Second, there continues to be deep-seated stereotypes among some union leaders that Asian Americans are clannish and uninterested in being organized. This creates frustration for the organizers as well as those who need to be organized. Third, because Asian Americans have only recently been welcomed into unions, there are relatively few Asian American union leaders, shop stewards, or organizers. Organizing Asian American workers is difficult for established unions because of the lack of cultural sensitivity, language fluency, and access to ethnic enclave businesses. Many of the workers who are most exploited and most in need of union support are immigrants and are not native English speakers.

Because of these challenges, Asian American labor activists have come together in several communities to help the unionization movement. The first president of APALA, Kent Wong, sees an increase in labor campaigns and the growth of a new generation of Asian American activists taking a leadership role in worker rights issues. "That's a development that we wouldn't have seen five to 10 years ago," Wong said.[77] An example of what Wong is referring to is the October 2003 "Celebrating America's Immigrants" day in New York City where 300,000 union workers and community supporters joined with 1,000 immigrant workers calling for greater national attention to immigrant rights and workplace issues. Executive director of APALA Gloria T. Caoile addressed the audience saying: "Hard work should be rewarded. Immigrants, like other hard working American families, should have fair and equal access to opportunities, and be allowed to go as far as their talents will take them. If we don't remove the barriers that force people to live in underclass status, we will have an underachieving society and a future that doesn't bode well for all of us."[78]

This festive event was the culmination of a two-week campaign where immigrant workers traveled more than 20,000 miles in eighteen buses and stopped in more than a hundred cities to promote justice and freedom for all workers. The immigrant workers met with more than 120 members of Congress and lobbied for citizenship and civil rights for all immigrant workers, immigrant family reunification, and protections for immigrants in the workplace. One of the participants of the campaign was Grace Manawatao, a Filipino immigrant home care worker who recounted the treatment she and her co-workers faced. "My supervisors make fun of my accent," she explained. "We are also underpaid and overworked but we are afraid to say anything because we might get fired." Another was Rena Wong, a Chinese-Mexican American labor organizer for the American Federation of State, County and Municipal Employees (AFSCME). Wong was moved by the stories shared in the bus by workers who represent some twenty-one countries. "Despite the differences in language and in how they got here, these workers all have one thing in common: they are not being treated with dignity and respect."[79]

APALA's work continues today as Asian American workers, many of them immigrants strive to achieve the American dream. Nearly half a million Asian American workers have joined unions as a way to seek better pay, improve benefits, earn dignity on the job, and have a voice in the workplace. With a national office in Washington, DC, and chapters throughout the country, APALA is waging a fight to organize the unorganized into unions, to promote the civil rights of Asian Americans, and to seek economic justice for all. "APALA's greatest strength has been the commitment of its leaders and members to working together to build an inclusive and participatory labor movement," said Antonio J. Saguibo, who was elected the new national president of

APALA at its 2005 conference. I look forward to working with everyone to ensure that APALA remains the national organization for all Asian and Pacific Islander American union members and their supporters and continues to be a strong and unified voice for worker rights, civil rights, and immigrant rights."[80]

Community-Based Labor Organizing

The linking of union and community organizing efforts is now increasingly common, but it has taken on a life of its own. According to writer and worker rights advocate Glen Omatsu, community-based labor organizing has been labeled "pre-union formations" by early labor scholars and union officials. It is generally assumed that community organizing is just part of a greater labor union movement, and union membership should eventually be the ultimate goal for Asian American workers. However, Omatsu believes the community organizing efforts may in fact be "post-union formations" that have emerged because of the decline of the overall labor union movement in recent years and its difficulties in successfully organizing Asian American workers. "The first trend (pre-union formations) is national in scope and spotlights workers in high-profile occupations such as automobile manufacturing, aerospace, and industries with long histories of labor organizing," Omatsu writes. "The second trend (post-union formations) deals with a collage of diffuse and localized struggles involving largely 'marginal' workers—new immigrants and refugees, people of color, women, and employees in the so-called service occupations, light manufacturing, and 'peripheral' industries, like garment work."[81]

There are a number of examples of community-based organizing groups, which are part of the second trend of labor organizing and have made a significant impact on the lives of Asian American workers. One of the most notable of these is Asian Immigrant Women Advocates (AIWA), based in Oakland, California. AIWA began in 1983 in response to tremendous abuses within the garment industry in the San Francisco Bay Area. Since that time AIWA has engaged in a number of activities aimed at educating and empowering Asian immigrant women, as well as community-based organizing efforts intended to bring about social change. AIWA's philosophy is focused on the belief that workers know best what they need, and want to improve the quality of their lives. This worker-centered approach is reflected in AIWA's "Seamstress Survey" that was carried out to find what the priority issues were for the workers. More than five hundred Chinese language surveys were distributed and volunteers were used to staff phone banks to help explain the questionnaire. Of the surveys sent out, 166 were returned and the results became the basis for AIWA's future efforts. Some of the major findings included the following:

- English-language proficiency was very low among the women workers. Few had ever taken an English-language class primarily because they did not have time.
- Respondents varied considerably in age. However, a significant number (26 percent) of the seamstresses were 50 years old or older. All of the women had children.

- More than 90 percent of the women stated their husbands worked as unskilled or semiskilled laborers. Their occupations included waiters, busboys, day laborers, and gardeners.
- Wages for the women were generally quite low. A third of the women worked for less than minimum wage and half worked at minimum wage.
- More than half the respondents (57 percent) worked six days a week or more, and more than a quarter (27 percent) was paid by the piece, rather than by a set hourly wage.
- A high percentage of the seamstresses lacked, or were unaware of, basic employee benefits. For example, more than 80 percent did not know their hiring and firing procedures, receive sick pay, or have any worker's compensation.
- More than three quarters of the respondents did not receive salary increases, vacation leave, or overtime pay. Almost 70 percent did not get paid holidays or health insurance, and more than half did not get any break periods.[82]

Understanding that English-language fluency is a basic survival skill, AIWA started workplace literacy classes in the evenings and on Sundays to accommodate the work schedules of the women. AIWA also sponsors leadership classes primarily aimed at garment workers. A variety of topics are covered in these training sessions, including: (1) the history of Asian immigration; (2) garment industry structure and Garment Workers Justice Campaigns; (3) how to read wages, hours, and deductions on their paycheck; (4) knowing their rights for worker's compensation and state disability insurance; and (5) occupational health and safety issues.[83] Another activity AIWA sponsored was a trip to El Paso, Texas, to attend the First Congress of Working Women. Attendance at this gathering served to establish a network of Latina, African American, Native American, and Asian American working women's rights organizations from across the nation, and to share experiences. "We were all feeling isolated," explained AIWA executive director Young Shin. "So we got together . . . and talked about the development of a new workers' movement made up of workers who had not been unionized, immigrants, people of color who work in the most marginal sectors of the economy, and workers who are not part of the elite, of any aristocracy of labor."[84]

AIWA's most publicized activity is their role in a national boycott campaign against the Jessica McClintock clothing line. The issue emerged in mid-1992, when a group of twelve seamstresses from the Lucky Sewing Company came to the AIWA office and complained their paychecks had bounced. The total amount of money owed to the workers was relatively small—just $15,000—but this represented important income to women barely able to make ends meet. AIWA initially confronted the owners of Lucky Sewing, but the company claimed complete bankruptcy and said they could not pay the workers. Jessica McClintock Inc. had contracted with and paid Lucky Sewing to sew a new line of clothes for sale in major department stores across the country. But after the dresses were made, Lucky Sewing abruptly went out of business and left its workers unpaid. Jessica McClintock Inc., a corporation that grossed $145 million in sales in 1992, denied any responsibility for workers who made their garments, flatly refused to pay the workers' back wages, and defends itself by saying the practice of contracting out work is common throughout the garment industry. AIWA knew that McClintock was not legally liable for the workers' salaries or working conditions, but wanted the company to set a new standard for the industry by making up for the workers' lost wages. AIWA saw McClintock perpetuating the much bigger problem of labor contracting within the garment industry. "Jessica McClintock knows this is not really a money issue," says AIWA's Young Shin. "It's about the working conditions of the workers who sew her dresses. . . . Fundamentally, it's a human-rights issue."[85]

Ironically, Jessica McClintock is generally recognized as a leading role model for working women because of her own personal rags-to-riches story, her work ethic, her philanthropic activities, and her generosity to her corporate employees. Other garment industry leaders such as Esprit, Levi Strauss, Banana Republic, and the Gap, among others, are also known for their socially conscious image, as well as their trendy clothing lines. Unfortunately, the public image belies some of the behind-the-scenes realities. For example, in 1992 Esprit was nominated for a Corporate Conscience Award by the Council on Economic Priorities, but between 1992 and 1993 the Department of Labor (DOL) raided nine sewing contractors in the San Francisco Bay Area that were engaged in illegal labor practices. Four of the contractors cited for their abuses worked for Esprit. In particular, one of these sweatshops contracted by Esprit paid seamstresses only $3.75 an hour with no overtime (minimum wage was $4.25 at the time) and owed the workers $127,000 in back wages.[86] These activities are allowed to continue because brand-name garment industry giants ignore the conditions of the workers who make their clothing. Technically, many apparel companies are "marketeers" who design and sell products, but don't actually own any factories that make the goods. The companies instead hire out to the lowest bidding "contractor" who agrees to sew a certain amount of clothes and deliver them at an agreed upon time. This allows companies like McClintock, Esprit, and others to distance themselves from labor practices on the shop floor.[87]

These corporations know that competition among sewing contractors is fierce. There are more than six hundred sewing contractors in the San Francisco Bay Area alone, and some of them do bid unrealistically low just to get the job. The work may get done, but workers are overworked and underpaid—if they get paid at all. There are contractors who claim bankruptcy and go out of business, then reappear just months later under another name. DOL investigator Harry Hu recalls one sewing contractor company, Kin Hing, that closed and reopened again with the new name, Hing Kin.[88] Yet another layer of separation away from garment workers comes from apparel industry leaders who say they should be commended, not condemned, because they have been keeping jobs in the United States when the general trend in all areas of manufacturing is to shift jobs overseas where workplace rights are practically nonexistent. Within this, the threat of closing shop and moving to another country is always an available weapon the garment industry uses against its detractors. Garment industry giants also place the final blame on consumers who demand good quality clothes but at affordable prices. There is little more that can be done, they say, but follow the realities of the marketplace.

AIWA insists that exploitation of garment workers does not have to continue and has spearheaded an aggressive campaign to achieve three goals: (1) to educate the public about garment industry abuses; (2) to boycott Jessica McClintock products; and (3) to push for legislative reform. The public education and boycott strategy is seen in pickets held in front of major department stores in thirteen cities across the nation, including Los Angeles, New York, Chicago, Boston, Atlanta, and even in front of McClintock's home in San Francisco. AIWA has also paid for a series of full-page ads in the *New York Times* national edition calling attention to the plight of the twelve unpaid seamstresses, while at the same time highlighting the fact that garment workers earn about $5 to sew a Jessica McClintock dress that retails for $175. A February 14, 1994, *New York Times* ad clearly stated the purpose of the boycott campaign: "Garment manufacturers are now on notice that sweatshop abuses will no longer be tolerated. . . . The campaign will continue until there is justice for the hundreds of thousands of immigrant women who suffer from the endless cycle of abusive sweatshop conditions. Not until Jessica McClintock and other manufacturers sign a Covenant of Fairness giving the women who sew our clothing a shot at fair wages, job security and decent working conditions will we declare victory."[89] Along with the education and boycott campaign, AIWA has actively lobbied for reform laws that would make garment manufacturers jointly liable with contractors for abuses of sewing factory workers. In September 1994, California's Governor Pete Wilson vetoed such a bill that was passed by both houses of the state legislature. Garment manufacturers, including Jessica McClintock, fought vigorously against the bill. Not surprisingly, industry leaders threatened to move garment production to other states or foreign countries if the bill were passed.[90]

Jessica McClintock also struck back against AIWA and its campaign. In August 1994, McClintock's lawyers were successful in obtaining an injunction against picketers at her San Francisco boutique and residence. The court ordered protesters to march at least six feet away from the entrance of McClintock's boutique and only two people at a time could march in front of McClintock's home. Similar court motions were heard in other cities where protests have been organized. "Is this justice?" asked an angry protesting seamstress. "She uses profits from our labor to pay expensive lawyers to shut us up."[91] McClintock also paid for a full-page ad in the *New York Times*, defending her position in the dispute and declaring she is the victim of a "blatant shakedown." In addition, McClintock was accused of being behind some rather unseemly tactics intended to divide the Asian American community against the AIWA's efforts. McClintock hired Lynne Choy Uyeda and Associates, an Asian American public relations firm who brought in Asian American students to counter-leaflet at boycott demonstrations in San Francisco and Los Angeles. Plus, the Northern California Chinese Garment Contractors Association—most of whom are McClintock contractors—offered a "charitable gift" to the twelve unpaid seamstresses provided they sign a document stating that the gift is not wages "and the money you are receiving does not represent wages due you from Lucky Sewing."[92] Five of the twelve seamstresses accepted the offer. Lastly, Jessica McClintock made donations to several San Francisco Bay Area Asian American community organizations "in the spirit of generosity and support." The Asian Women's Shelter returned the check and the Asian Community Health Services said it was going to donate the money back to the community or to the garment workers' cause. "We appreciate the $1,000 check, but I hope that she would focus her efforts on the retribution to garment workers and negotiating a settlement," said Asian Women's Shelter director Beckie Masaki.[93]

AIWA's direct action tactics and high-profile campaign were highly effective. In March 1996, AIWA announced it had reached a settlement in its three-year dispute with Jessica McClintock Inc. JMI did not pay any back wages but was willing to donate money to establish a garment workers' education fund for the Lucky garment workers, sponsor scholarships for students and garment workers, provide garment workers with bilingual state and federal publications to better educate them on fair labor standards, and to provide two toll-free numbers (one in English and one in Cantonese) for JMI contractors and employees to facilitate better reporting of and compliance with federal labor laws. Lastly, JMI agreed to work with other groups to explore alternative methods for worker wage protection and the viability of an independent monitoring program. According to U.S. Secretary of Labor Robert Reich, the settlement was significant in its call for cooperative efforts by both parties to insure workers' rights as well as to promote awareness of fair labor practices. "I commend both parties for reaching this agreement," Reich said.[94]

AIWA's struggle on behalf of workers has been an inspiration to many across the nation. But for all of their protest efforts, the greatest attention to the plight of garment workers and sweatshop conditions came from a very unexpected source. In April 1996, singer and daytime television talk-show host, Kathie Lee Gifford, was shocked and embarrassed when she found out that the line of clothes bearing her name sold at Wal-Mart stores were being made by underpaid workers in Honduras and New York City. Gifford was particularly upset to learn that exploited young teenage laborers were making her garments. Kathie Lee Gifford, and her husband, sports announcer Frank Gifford, have since become crusaders against sweatshops.[95] Their public denouncements of labor abuses and their celebrity status were utilized successfully by Secretary of Labor Reich in his "No Sweat" campaign aimed at eradicating wage and safety violations in sewing shops. Within a few short months this effort resulted in President Clinton announcing an agreement with ten major manufacturers to inform consumers that their clothes were made "under decent and humane working conditions." Among the well-known companies that agreed to these terms included Liz Claiborne, Nike, L. L. Bean, and Patagonia. Conspicuously absent was Levi Strauss & Co., the world's largest clothing manufacturer, who declined to sign the agreement. A spokesperson for Levi Strauss & Co. complained that the agreement was too vague and inflexible, but did agree that companies should monitor contractors for labor violations. Garment worker advocacy groups like AIWA realize that the agreement is not perfect. There are many more manufacturers who have not signed the agreement than have, and there is still plenty of work that needs to be done to correct the abuses throughout the entire industry.[96]

This is evident by news the following year that Kathy Lee Gifford's clothing line continued to be made in abusive New York City sweatshops. Gifford's spokesperson acknowledged that her line was made in three factories where Chinese immigrants allegedly worked for less than minimum wage, and for up to twenty-four hours straight without overtime pay. Some workers were reportedly not paid for several months. Gifford hired her own independent monitors to inspect the factories, but the monitors failed to turn up any abuses because they couldn't speak or understand Chinese. It was not until complaints were raised by the Chinese Staff and Workers Association, a Chinatown group that fights for workers' rights, and the Union of Needle and Industrial Textile Employees that the New York state labor authorities began an investigation.[97]

Nonetheless, the AIWA "Garment Workers Justice" national campaign is still the foundation for continued activism against unfair labor practices in the clothing industry. Most significantly, the Ninth Circuit Court of Appeals ruled in favor of nineteen workers who labored in six different Los Angeles sweatshops alleging the parent retail company, Fashion 21, Inc. (otherwise known by the label "Forever 21"), violated state wage and hour laws, engaged in unfair and unlawful business practices under state law, and was negligent in its use of sweatshops. Much like in the case of Jessica McClintock, Fashion 21 made the same argument that they were not liable for the abuses of the sewing contractors. An initial court decision upheld Fashion 21's claim stating that garment workers could state no valid legal claims against a clothing retailer for sweatshop abuses. The March 2004 Ninth Circuit Court reversed the lower court's decision. "This decision is a tremendous step forward in the fight against garment sweatshops," said Julie Su, Litigation Director of the Asian Pacific American Legal Center (APALC), a nonprofit civil rights organization that represents the workers in the lawsuit. "The Ninth Circuit has affirmed that the workers' claims against Forever 21 are alive and kicking. The decision sends the message that retailers like Forever 21 who create, perpetuate and demand sweatshop labor could ultimately be held responsible for workplace abuses," commented Su.[98]

This ruling may well have a ripple effect throughout the retail-clothing world. "The workers' lawsuit reveals that the use of sweatshop labor by Forever 21 is not an isolated occurrence, nor is it an accident, but is a matter of business choice—an unfair and unlawful one," explained Christina Chung, staff attorney at APALC. "Retailers exercise tremendous power over the garment production process and then turn a blind eye to workplace abuses. Although Forever 21 obviously does not want the public to hear this, the Ninth Circuit decision makes clear that workers who attempt to hold retailers liable for sweatshop abuses deserve their day in court." It may be many more years before this matter is finally settled in the highest levels of the court system.[99]

CONCLUSION

This chapter has shown a variety of employment issues confronted by Asian Americans. Many of these issues were also highlighted in a special issue of *The Journal of Applied Behavioral Science* focusing on Asian Americans in organizations. The journal featured articles on the impact of the model minority image for Asian Americans in the workplace, lower rates of return to education for Asian American employees, participation of Asian Americans in labor unions, among others. One particularly interesting article by Katherine Xin examined how Asian Americans tend to focus almost exclusively on their job tasks, with little attention to promoting themselves and developing positive social relationships with co-workers and supervisors. According to Xin, this creates an "impression gap" that leads to lower career mobility (i.e., glass ceiling) for Asian Americans.[100]

Although most of the media attention has been placed on the primarily middle-class issue of the glass ceiling, this chapter also provided a look at a number of other important issues that impact Asian American men and women from every socioeconomic strata. Most importantly, this chapter showed that Asian Americans are not accepting workplace discrimination passively. Rather, Asian Americans are working to change personal career strategies as well as challenge some of the workplace practices that negatively affect their careers. The issues raised in this chapter are particularly noteworthy as the Asian American population continues to grow, mature, and make its mark throughout the workforce.

NOTES

1. Christine Gorman, "The Disease Detective," *Time*, December 30, 1996, pp. 56–62.
2. See profiles of Jerry Yang at http://www.forbes.com/static/bill2005/LIRR 4Q2.html?passListId=10&passYear=2005&passListType=Person&uniqueId=R4Q2&datatype=Perso and http://docs.yahoo.com/docs/pr/executives/yang.html.
3. Robert A. Rosenblatt, "'Glass Ceiling' Still Too Hard to Break, U.S. Panel Finds," *Los Angeles Times*, March 16, 1995.
4. U.S. Commission on Civil Rights, *Civil Rights Issues Facing Asian Americans in the 1990s* (Washington, DC: Government Printing Office, 1992), pp. 131–132.
5. Naomi Hirahara, *Distinguished Asian American Business Leaders* (Westport, CN: Greenwood Press, 2003).
6. Quoted in Committee of 100, "Asian Pacific American (APA) Corporate Board Report Card," p. 8 at http://www.committee100.org/publications/initiative_corporate.htm.
7. National Science Foundation, Division of Science Resource Statistics, *Women, Minorities, and Persons with Disabilities in Science and Engineering: 2004*, NSF 04-317 (Arlington, VA, 2004), p. 74, Table H-1.
8. *Ibid.*, p. 137, Table F-5.
9. Thomas B. Hoffer, "Employment Sector, Salaries, Publishing and Patenting Activities of S&E Doctorate Holders," *InfoBrief*, NSF 04-328/June 2004 at http://www.nsf.gov/statistics/infbrief/nsf04328/.
10. National Science Foundation (2004), pp. 239–240, Table H-19.
11. National Science Foundation, *Women, Minorities, and Persons with Disabilities in Science and Engineering: 1998*, NSF 99-338 (Arlington, VA, 1999), Chapter 5, pp. 3–4.
12. Joyce Tang, *Doing Engineering: The Career Attainment and Mobility of Caucasian, Black, and Asian American Engineers* (Boulder, CO.: Rowman & Littlefield Press, 2000), p. 198.
13. Tom Abate, "Heavy Load for Silicon Valley Workers," *San Francisco Examiner*, May 23, 1993.
14. Elisa Lee, "Silicon Valley Study Finds Asian Americans Hitting the Glass Ceiling," *AsiaWeek*, October 8, 1993.

15. Quoted in Stanley Karnow and Nancy Yoshihara, *Asian Americans in Transition* (New York: The Asia Society, 1992), p. 40.
16. Catherine Yang, "In Any Language, It's Unfair," *BusinessWeek,* June 21, 1993, p. 11.
17. Quoted in Ralph Varabedian, "Aerospace Careers in Low Orbit," *Los Angeles Times,* November 16, 1992.
18. "Have Skills, Will Travel—Home," *BusinessWeek,* November 18, 1994, pp. 164–165; and J. Madeleine Nash, "Tigers in the Lab," *Time,* November 21, 1994, pp. 86–87.
19. Jack Chang, "Indian American's Powerful Tech Presence," *AsianWeek,* April 20, 2000, pp. 18–19. For more information see http://www.tie.org/. For details on the glass ceiling and Asian Indians see Marilyn Fernandez, "Asian Indian Americans in the Bay Area and the Glass Ceiling," *Sociological Perspectives* 41:1 (Spring 1998): 119–150.
20. AnnaLee Saxenian, *Silicon Valley's New Immigrant Entrepreneurs* (San Francisco, CA: Public Policy Institute of California, 1999), p. 23.
21. *Ibid.* The report refers to ethnic Chinese from either mainland China, Taiwan, or throughout the Chinese diaspora.
22. AnnaLee Saxenian, *Local and Global Networks of Immigrant Professionals in Silicon Valley* (San Francisco, CA: Public Policy Institute of California, 2002). For more information on Monte Jade at http://www.mtjade.org/.
23. Pan Suk Kim and Gregory B. Lewis, "Asian Americans in Public Service: Success, Diversity, and Discrimination," *Public Administration Review* 54:3 (May–June 1994): 285–290.
24. *Ibid.,* p. 288.
25. *Ibid.,* p. 289.
26. Christopher Daniel, "Diminishing Returns from Statistical Analysis: Detecting Discrimination in Public Employment" (a response to Pan Suk Kim and Gregory B. Lewis), *Public Administration Review* 57:3 (1997): 264–267.
27. Gregory Lewis and Pan Suk Kim, "Asian Americans in the Federal Service: Education, Occupational Choice, and Perceptions of Discrimination: A Reply," *Public Administration Review* 57:3 (1997): 267–270.
28. *Ibid.*
29. *Ibid.;* U.S. Office of Personnel Management, "Personnel Systems Oversight Group, Personnel Research Highlights: Survey of Federal Employees," (Washington, DC: U.S. Government Printing Office, 1992); U.S. Merit Systems Protection Board, "Working for America: An Update" (Washington DC.: U.S. Government Printing Office, 1994).
30. Bernadette Tansey, "9 Asians at Lab File Bias Claim," *San Francisco Chronicle,* December 24, 1999.
31. Department of Energy, "Richardson Releases Task Force Against Racial Profiling Report and Announces 8 Immediate Actions" (January 2000), see press release at http://www.fas .org/irp/news/2000/01/000119-pr00011.htm. The full report can be found at http:// www.fas.org/irp/news/2000/01/rprofilerpt.pdf.
32. "Tentative Settlement of Asian Scientists and Engineer Class Action" at http://www.llnl .gov/pao/news/news_releases/2005/NR-05-03-06.html.
33. For more information see http://www.fapac.org/.
34. For more information see http://www.fapac.org/m_partners.php.
35. Frances M. Namkoong, "Stereotyping Is Holding Asian-Americans Back," *Cleveland Plain Dealer,* May 17, 1994.
36. *Ibid.*
37. Diana Ting Liu Wu, *Asian Pacific Americans in the Workplace* (Walnut Creek, CA: AltaMira Press, 1997), p. 27.
38. Henry Der, "Affirmative Action Policy," *The State of Asian Pacific America: Policy Issues to the Year 2020* (Los Angeles: LEAP Asian Pacific American Public Policy Institute and UCLA Asian American Studies Center), pp. 215–232.
39. Edward I. Lin, "On Challenging the Glass Ceiling," *AsianWeek,* October 16, 1997, p. 9.
40. Quoted in "Marine Wins Bars After Fight Over Bias," *San Francisco Chronicle,* March 19, 1994.
41. Benjamin Pimentel, "One Man's War Against Marines," *San Francisco Chronicle,* February 5, 1994.
42. *Ibid.*
43. Eric Schmitt, "Asian-American Proves Marine Bias," *New York Times,* January 21, 1994.
44. Quoted in Pimentel, "One Man's War."
45. Tenure is the achievement of permanent status within a university's faculty. Tenure is granted after a period of six to seven years of demonstrated excellence in teaching, research, and university/community service, as well as rigorous review by colleagues within

one's academic field. When a person is denied tenure, that person is, in essence, fired from his or her faculty position.

46. U.S. Commission on Civil Rights, *Civil Rights Issues Facing Asian Americans in the 1990s*, pp. 155–156.

47. Quotes in "Tung Case Pries Open Secret Tenure Review," *The Berkeley Graduate*, April 1990.

48. "EEOC Agrees to Landmark Resolution of Discrimination Case Against Abercrombie & Fitch," November 18, 2004, at http://www.eeoc.gov/press/11-18-04.html.

49. Quotes in CBS News, "Look of Abercrombie & Fitch," November 24, 2004 at http://www.cbsnews.com/stories/2003/12/05/60minutes/main587099.shtml.

50. Quotes in Jenny Strasburg, "Abercrombie & Glitch," *San Francisco Chronicle*, April 18, 2002.

51. Bill Lann Lee quoted on the Travis Smiley Show, November 18, 2004 at http://www.npr.org/templates/story/story.php?storyId=4176534.

52. Quoted in Myrna E. Watanabe, "Asian American Investigators Decry 'Glass Ceiling' In Academic Administration," *The Scientist*, 9:11 (May 29, 1995) at http://www.the-scientist.com/1995/5/29/1/3.

53. Wayne Liauh, Statement at the U.S. Commission on Civil Rights Roundtable Conference on Asian American Civil Rights Issues for the 1990s (May 27, 1989) cited in U.S. Commission on Civil Rights, *Civil Rights Issues Facing Asian Americans in the 1990s*, p. 132.

54. Quoted in "The Asian American Dream?" *A Magazine* 2:3 (December 1993): 70.

55. Larry Neumeister, "Asian Officers Allege Discrimination in Lawsuit Against Bi-State Agency," *Associated Press*, April 15, 2005.

56. Samuel R. Cacas, "Language Rights Hotline Established," *Rafu Shimpo*, February 8, 1995.

57. *Ibid.*

58. Quoted in Yang, "In Any Language, It's Unfair," p. 110.

59. Erin McCormick, "Filipino Guards Sue Over 'Accent Discrimination,'" *San Francisco Examiner*, April 15, 1993.

60. Quoted in Richard J. P. Cavosora, "Discrimination Spoken Here," *Filipinas*, July 1993, pp. 16–18, 46.

61. Quoted in Samuel R. Cacas, "Accent Discrimination Case by Five Filipino American Security Guards Is Settled," *Asian Week*, June 10, 1994.

62. Quoted in Equal Employment Opportunity Commission, "National Origin Discrimination," March 2, 2005 at http://www.eeoc.gov/origin/index.html.

63. Quoted in Sarah Henry, "Fighting Words," *Los Angeles Times Magazine*, June 10, 1990, p. 10.

64. *Ibid.*, pp. 10–11.

65. *Garcia v. Gloor*, 618 Fed.2d 264, 270 (1981).

66. Jim Doyle, "High Court Lets English-Only Job Rules Stand," *San Francisco Chronicle*, June 21, 1994.

67. Quoted in Jeremy Meyer, "Workers Fighting English-only Rules," *Denver Post*, November 18, 2004.

68. Equal Employment Opportunity Commission, "Central Station Casino To Pay $1.5 Million in EEOC Settlement for National Origin Bias," July 18, 2003 at http://www.eeoc.gov/press/7-18-03a.html.

69. Mary Lou Pickel, "Ruling Backs Somali Refugees Fired at Airport," *Atlanta Journal-Constitution*, July 20, 2005.

70. Stan Bailey, "English-only Driver Test Likely to Fail, Lawyers Say," *Birmingham News*, May 20, 2005.

71. Quotes in Mark Zeigler, "Ump Out—Told Massachusetts Little Leaguers: English Only," *San Diego Union*, July 30, 2005. Also see Christina M. Silva and Raja Mishra, "Umpire's Call Gets Unheard-Of Result: Youth Baseball Team Told to Speak English," *Boston Globe*. July 30, 2005.

72. Maria Newman, "Restaurant Is Ordered to Pay Ex-Waitresses $3.4 Million," *New York Times*, September 27, 2003.

73. Alex Hing, "Organizing Asian Pacific American Workers in the AFL-CIO: New Opportunities," *Amerasia Journal* 18:1 (1992): 141–154.

74. Kent Wong, "Building an Asian Pacific Labor Alliance: A New Chapter in Our History," in Karin Aguilar-San Juan (ed.), *The State of Asian America: Activism and Resistance in the 1990s* (Boston: South End Press, 1994), pp. 335–349.

75. Asian Pacific American Labor Association, "APALA Convention Elects New Officers; Action Plan to Organize APA's into Unions," APALA Press Release, September 6, 2005, see http://www.apalanet.org/pr_090605.html.

76. Bert Eljera, "APA Unionists Voice Optimism." *AsianWeek*, August 8, 1997, p. 11.

77. Ji Hyun Lim, "Report Released on Plight of the Asian Pacific American Worker," *AsianWeek*, August 15, 2005.
78. Quoted in Jon Melegrito, "Freedom Riders Demand Justice, Mobilize Support," APALA Press Release, October 5, 2003 at http://www.apalanet.org/pr_100503.html.
79. *Ibid.*
80. Asian Pacific American Labor Association, "APALA Convention Elects New Officers" September 6, 2005.
81. Glen Omatsu, "Expansion of Democracy," *Amerasia Journal* 18:1 (1992): v–xix.
82. Miriam Ching Louie, "After Sewing, Laundry, Cleaning and Cooking, I Have No Breath Left to Sing," *Amerasia Journal* 18:1 (1992): 1–26.
83. "Leadership Training Wraps Up," *AIWA News* 10:2 (Fall 1994): 3.
84. Quoted in Louie, "After Sewing," p. 20.
85. Quoted in Sarah Henry, "Labor & Lace," *San Francisco Chronicle*, September 5, 1993.
86. Laurie Udesky, "Sweatshops Behind the Labels," *The Nation*, May 16, 1994, pp. 665–668.
87. Richard P. Appelbaum and Gary Gereffi, "Power and Profits in the Apparel Commodity Chain," in Edna Bonacich et al. (eds), *Global Production: The Apparel Industry in the Pacific Rim* (Philadelphia: Temple University Press, 1994), pp. 42–62.
88. Udesky, "Sweatshops Behind," p. 667.
89. "Jessica McClintock Just Doesn't Get It," *New York Times*, February 14, 1994.
90. "Governor Wilson Vetoes Garment Manufacturers' Joint Liability Bill," *AIWA News*, 10:2 (Fall 1994): 7.
91. *Ibid.;* "McClintock Attacks Free Speech Rights," *AIWANews* 10:2 (Fall 1994): 1, 6.
92. "Jessica McClintock Just Doesn't Get It," February 14, 1994.
93. Yumi Wilson, "Designer's Largesse Questioned," *San Francisco Chronicle*, February 16, 1994; and Steven A. Chin, "Garment Workers Fight for Back Pay," *San Francisco Examiner*, February 16, 1994.
94. Asian Immigrant Women Advocates Letter and Press Release, March 20, 1996.
95. Bill Wong, "Sweatshop Fame," *AsianWeek*, June 21, 1996.
96. Victoria Coliver, "Clinton Cuts 'Sweatshop-Free' Deal," *Oakland Tribune*, August 3, 1996.
97. "New Gifford Sweatshop Charge," *San Francisco Examiner*, December 6, 1997.
98. Quoted in "Garment Workers Victorious in Ninth Circuit Sweatshop Decision Against Forever 21," Asian Pacific American Legal Center Press Release, March 10, 2004 at http://apalc.org/pressr_march_10_2004.htm.
99. *Ibid.*
100. Katherine R. Xin, "Asian American managers: an impression gap? An investigation of impression management and supervisor-subordinate relationships," in Cliff Cheng and Tojo Joseph Thatchenkery, *The Journal of Applied Behavioral Science* 33:3 (1997): 335–356.

5

Anti-Asian Violence: Breaking the Silence

VISIBILITY AND INVISIBILITY

Anti-Asian sentiments and violence against Asian Americans has a long history in the United States. An individual racist, hate groups, and xenophobic lawmakers together created a hostile environment during the late nineteenth and early twentieth centuries that served to severely limit the numbers of immigrants from Asia and forced most Asian Americans to retreat into segregated communities that were out of harm's way. Since the passage of immigration reforms in 1965 and the influx of refugees after the Vietnam War, the increasing Asian American population has become more and more conspicuous across the nation. This increased visibility in recent years has also created periodic renewals of angry anti-Asian sentiment that is manifested in incidents of violence against Asian Americans. Despite the more positive images of Asian American students, professionals, and business entrepreneurs, there is growing concern over what many see as an ongoing and ugly trend. Asian American leaders commonly cite the brutal 1982 killing of Vincent Chin in Detroit, Michigan, as the crucial incident that raised the issue of anti-Asian violence to the forefront of public attention. Chin was a 27-year-old Chinese American who was bludgeoned to death with a baseball bat by two men who allegedly blamed Japan for problems in the U.S. economy and thought Chin was Japanese. The two assailants pled guilty to manslaughter, but a Michigan judge sentenced them each to just three years' probation and a fine of $3,780. Shocked by the senselessness of the killing and the lenient sentence, Asian Americans saw Chin as a martyr whose death galvanized the Asian American community and led to a nationwide call for federal intervention. After intense pressure, the U.S. Department of Justice brought federal civil rights charges against Ronald Ebens, an auto plant supervisor, and his un-employed stepson, Michael Nitz. In June 1984 Nitz was acquitted of the civil rights charge, but Ebens was found guilty and sentenced to twenty-five years in prison. Two years later, Ebens' conviction was overturned on appeal. The case was retried in Cincinnati because of the tremendous amount of publicity Chin's killing received in Detroit. The second trial ended in April 1987 with an acquittal for Ebens.[1]

The acquittal sent a chill throughout the Asian American community. For many, the message was that Asian Americans are second-class citizens—tolerated as long as they remain a quiet and passive "model minority," but patronized, or worse, when they attempt to exercise their rights. Since that time Asian American activists have called for federal, state, and local law enforcement authorities to keep statistics on reported cases of hate bias incidents, and for laws that would carry stronger penalties for those convicted of hate-related crimes. Recently, the National Asian Pacific American Legal Consortium (NAPALC), an organization made up of Asian American legal and civil rights organizations across the United States, began to document and monitor incidents of hate violence.[2] In addition, NAPALC works to educate the Asian Pacific American community, law enforcement, and the general public about the problem of anti-Asian violence. NAPALC has published an *Audit of Violence Against Asian Pacific Americans* since 1993, and has come up with some powerful findings.

The highest number of reported anti-Asian hate incidents occurred in 1995 with 534 incidents, and the numbers spiked again in 2001 with 501 incidents. NAPALC attributed the 2001 rise of hate incidents to the backlash against not only Arab Americans and Muslims, but also against immigrants in general and anyone who looked like they might be a Muslim or of Middle Eastern heritage. One of the first known bias-motivated murders after 9/11 was Balbir Singh Sodhi, a Sikh American who was mistaken for Muslim because of his turban and beard. When police arrested the alleged suspect he screamed, "I am a patriot!"[3] Interestingly, the 2002 audit saw a dramatic decline in reported anti-Asian incidents, which NAPALC attributed to law enforcement's overwhelming focus on terrorism and general hostility to immigrants and anyone who looks like "a foreigner" after September 11, 2001. "As a whole, underreporting is a growing trend that makes it more and more difficult to get accurate numbers on hate crimes and incidents," said Karen K. Narasaki, President and Executive Director of NAPALC. "The combination of disappearing resources and immigration and national security policies that are hostile to immigrants have come together at a particular point and really fostered a climate where individuals and law enforcement agencies don't report hate crimes or can't respond effectively."[4] An even more stark example of the inaccuracy of reported hate incidents can be seen in the over 1,500 cases of hate-related incidents reported to the Council of American Islamic Relations in 2002 and the mere 155 anti-Islamic hate-related incidents reported by the Federal Bureau of Investigation (FBI) that same year.[5]

The issue of anti-Asian violence is a major concern for Asian Americans, even though it is met with considerable ignorance and insensitivity among the general public and law enforcement authorities. Nonetheless, Asian Americans are keenly aware of the potential for being victims of violence simply because of their racial distinctiveness. This chapter concentrates first on definitions, distinctions, and examples of the types of anti-Asian violence confronted by Asian Americans. It next takes a close look at four factors that encourage and perpetuate anti-Asian sentiment and violence. Lastly, this chapter examines the volatile issue of Asian American and African American relations. Racial violence is not limited to just whites against people of color. In an increasing multiracial and multicultural society, the concern over antagonism between and among all groups is an issue that must be directly addressed. Particular emphasis will be placed on the high-profile tensions between Korean Americans and African Americans in major urban centers across the nation. The rebellion in Los Angeles in 1992—where predominantly Korean businesses were targeted for looting and arson—is the most prominent example of large-scale interracial conflict involving Asian Americans, but roots of the discontent are complex and deserve special attention.

ANTI-ASIAN HATE INCIDENTS

Most Asian Americans have experienced the pain caused by direct verbal abuse, subtle put-downs, unconscious insults, and thoughtless comments, as well as stereotypical portrayals in mainstream mass media. In addition, Asian Americans are becoming targeted victims of racially motivated assaults and vandalism. NAPALC acknowledges the harm caused by all of the above and has included them in its audit of anti-Asian *hate incidents*. In contrast, the 1990 Federal Hate Crime Statistics Act was enacted to develop and implement a uniform system of collecting accurate data on *hate crimes*. A *hate crime* is defined as a "violation of a criminal or penal statute" in which the primary motivation, actual or perceived, is based on race, ethnicity, national origin, immigration status, religion, gender, sexual orientation, or age. Despite laudable intentions, there are limitations that severely hamper the act's ability to be effective.

First, hate crime reports collected by state law enforcement agencies continue to be inconsistent and incomplete. Data on hate crimes are not always broken down by race, and often are not broken down by specific ethnic subgroups or type of incident. NAPALC argues that more detailed information is necessary to better determine patterns of hate violence toward a particular group or groups. As a result of weak record keeping, there is a probable undercount of actual hate crime incidents by both the FBI and NAPALC itself. Second, the mere utterance of racial slurs in and of itself is not a crime and, thus, is not reported by the FBI. A hate crime requires additional evidence that indicates bias motivation. NAPALC broadens this narrow definition and reports on anti-Asian *hate incidents* as those motivated by racial animus. NAPALC and its affiliates define racial animus as the presence of the following factors: (1) racial slurs or racist graffiti; (2) the perpetrator is a known or affiliated member of a hate group; (3) the timing of the incident coincides with key dates in U.S. history that create an anti-Asian bias

Table 5-1 Anti-Asian Incidents 1993–1998

Year	1995	1996	1997	1998	1999	2000	2001	2002
Incidents								
NAPALC	458	534	481	429	486	411	507	275
FBI	355	355	347	293	298	281	280	217

Source: National Asian Pacific American Legal Consortium, *2002 Audit of Violence Against Asian Pacific Americans* at http://www.advancingequality.org/dcm.asp?id=50; and Federal Bureau of Investigation, *Uniform Crime Report,* 1995–2002 at http://www.fbi.gov/ucr/ucr.htm.

(e.g., December 7, the anniversary of the bombing of Pearl Harbor); (4) a reported gang-related incident with strong indications of racial bias or targeting; (5) instances where Asian Americans or Pacific Islanders appear to be the sole and deliberate targets for the crimes; (6) e-mail messages specifically sent to harass or intimidate members of one ethnic group; or (7) incidents of police abuse where racial animus, bias, or insensitivity is evident. The NAPALC definition is much more expansive, and is used to show that hate violence is far more common than what the FBI narrowly calls hate crimes. NAPALC's numbers tend to be higher than government figures, as seen in Table 5-1.[6]

Verbal Assaults

One high-profile example of what NAPALC would consider an anti-Asian hate incident that cannot be classified as a hate crime occurred in January 2005 when the New York radio station WQHT-FM morning show repeatedly aired an appalling song mocking the victims of the South Asian tsunami, referring to them as "screaming chinks" and "little Chinamen swept away," and saying, "You can hear God laughing, 'swim you bitches swim.'"[7] WQHT-FM morning host Tarsha Nicole Jones (a.k.a. Miss Jones) continued playing the song for more than a week despite calls to stop broadcasting the tasteless song because hundreds of thousands of people were killed and missing after the tsunami tragedy and because of the song's obvious racial overtones. When the show's newscaster, who happened to be Asian American, complained about the song Miss Jones went on the attack. "I know you feel superior because you're Asian," snapped Jones, "but you're not." The morning show's co-host Todd Lynn added more fuel to the fire saying, "I'm gonna start shooting Asians."[8] It took two weeks before the station finally stopped airing the song and suspended Miss Jones, Todd Lynn, and morning show producer Rick Delgado indefinitely. "What happened is morally and socially indefensible," said Rick Cummings, president of WQHT-FM's parent company, Emmis Radio. "All involved, myself included are ashamed and deeply sorry. I know the members of the morning team are contrite. They know their actions here are inexcusable." Miss Jones was returned to the airwaves a month after airing the racist musical parody, but Lynn and Delgado were fired.[9]

Today Asian American activists, civil rights organizations, and media watchdog groups like Asian Media Watch (http://www.asianmediawatch.net/)

respond aggressively to anti-Asian verbal assaults. These statements of ignorance and stereotypes are often reflections of deeply held popular sentiments. In 2004 pro-football coach Bill Parcells of the Dallas Cowboys praised quarterback coach Sean Payton, telling a press conference the coach is "going to have a few [pause] no disrespect for the Orientals, but what we call Jap plays. Okay? Surprise things." After a few moments of awkward silence from the audience of journalists, Parcells tried to recoup. "No disrespect to anyone," he added.[10]

Parcells' comments were met with a firm response from the Asian American community, and the Japanese American Citizen's League issued a strongly worded statement: "We are deeply disappointed and highly offended by Coach Bill Parcells' use of the word 'Jap' during a press appearance yesterday. In this day and age, we find it reprehensible that any organization—be it amateur or professional—would tolerate, let alone invoke, racial epithets in any context and use them as standard designations in their operations. . . . We will be contacting the Dallas Cowboys franchise to discuss this specific incident and to encourage them to develop policies that enhance racial sensitivity throughout the organization. Further, we welcome the opportunity to educate Mr. Parcells and the Dallas Cowboys organization about racial slurs such as 'Jap' and offensively outmoded language such as 'Oriental.'"[11] Although Parcells and the Dallas Cowboys organization issued apologies, many felt the incident was much more than just a slip of the tongue. *AsianWeek* columnist Emil Guillermo was particularly perturbed, arguing that in one statement Parcells showed (1) his ignorance, (2) his recognition that what he was about to say was wrong and didn't care, and (3) he thought he could get away with it without any repercussions. Guillermo wrote: "He used the word Orientals. Bad. That's like calling your best players Negroes. It's outdated, but it shows where his thinking is on APAs. Back in World War II . . . Then, after the pre-offense apology, Parcells delivered the slur with full gusto . . . What bothers me the most is that his pre-offense apology showed he knew it was wrong. In essence he said, I'm going to do it anyway, even if you don't like it."[12]

These incidents may seem rather innocuous and most certainly would not have been reported except that public figures made the slurs. Many other incidents may be less publicized but can be far more vicious, threatening, and unforgiving. During the spring 1999 semester, Lane Hirabayashi, professor of Ethnic Studies and Anthropology at the University of Colorado, Boulder, received an anonymous death threat on his campus voice mail. Stating "you're dead meat," the caller told Hirabayashi he was going to "trigger your mother fucking ass" and declared "white people rule." Hirabayashi could also hear other people laughing in the background as the caller threatened him. In almost twenty years of college instruction, he had never received any kind of call or threat like this. Hirabayashi's shock, sadness, and outrage over the incident was only compounded when the first campus police officer on the scene belittled the threat and wanted to treat it as simply a prank. "I was frustrated," Hirabayashi recalls. "I found myself having to explain to him what hate violence was, just as if he was one of my lower-division students. It seem awkward and silly to me. It took a week before a senior member of the campus police was assigned the case and the threatening call was taken seriously."[13]

The caller was never apprehended, but Hirabayashi was able to find some satisfaction when he took this incident and turned it into "a teaching moment." He dubbed the hateful voice mail message, transcribed the call word for word, and copied it onto an overhead transparency. He then prepared a lecture on hate violence, played the tape several times in all of his classes, and let the students read the transcription. He then led an open-ended discussion to get student reactions. Reliving the incident was painful for him, but Hirabayashi was glad he was able to draw from the experience. "Giving the lecture was a catharsis for me, and I daresay my students found it both thought-provoking and informative."[14]

No one is calling for a censorship of speech, even if it is hate speech. However, it is important to recognize the line between the expression of unpopular views and views that rise to the level of harassment and violence. Asian Americans know too well verbalized assaults often escalate to physical assaults. This line was most notably crossed during what law enforcement authorities and the media came to call the "Summer of Hate." During this three-month period three synagogues in Sacramento, California, were set aflame. Two brothers were arrested for the arson and were later charged with the murders of two gay men. In a separate incident, a lone white supremacist shot and killed an African American man and a Korean American man during a three-day shooting spree in the Midwest. The following month another white supremacist opened fire on a Jewish day-care center and later killed a Filipino American in Los Angeles. Each of these incidents were ideologically influenced by the thousands of Web sites intended to incite the gullible and disturbed "lone wolves" of the hate movement to commit violence.[15] Unfortunately, the hate-related killings did not end that summer. On April 28, 2000, gunman toting a .357 caliber revolver and a box of bullets went on a murderous rampage in Pennsylvania. When he was done, five people lay dead including three Asian Americans. The incident followed another Pennsylvania shooting spree in which an African American man allegedly killed three white men and wounded two others.[16]

Physical Violence

As stated above, the overall number of incidents of anti-Asian violence has decreased, but the "deadly nature" of these crimes has increased. NAPALC found the high percentages of physical violence particularly alarming, especially compared with FBI figures that show only about 12 percent of reported crimes are against individuals, while 88 percent are aimed at property.[17] NAPALC cites studies that show hate-motivated assaults tend to result in greater numbers of deaths and personal injuries than other non-hate-motivated assaults. Indeed, hospitalization is required in 30 percent of bias-based assaults, while assaults in general had only a 7 percent hospitalization rate.[18] In short, hate violence is more dangerous than similar acts not motivated by hate. *The 2002 Audit of Violence Against Asian Pacific Americans* reported 29 percent of incidents were assault and/or battery, 27 percent were vandalism, 21 percent were harassment, and 16 percent were threats.[19] The following are notable cases of recent hate-motivated violence, and the efforts made to publicize and monitor individual cases.

The vicious murder of 17-year-old Kenneth Chiu by a neighbor shocked the small middle-class suburb of Laguna Hills, California, and caused an outpouring of grief from Asian American communities across the nation. Chiu was stabbed twenty-five times by Christopher Hearn, 20, with whom Chiu played video games growing up and knew well. On the night of July 30, 2001, Hearn saw Chiu outside his house saying goodbye to a friend. Hearn went to his kitchen, pulled out a knife, and waited for Chiu's friend to leave. He then went out to meet Chiu and within a few minutes began his senseless attack. Chiu's father later found his son outside in a pool of blood and desperately called 911 for help. Before he died Chiu identified Hearn, who had a history of erratic and violent behavior, as his assailant. When the police arrested Hearn in his house they found the murder weapon and anti-Asian hate literature. Hearn is a deaf mute, but he was able to communicate through sign language. Through an interpreter Hearn confessed to the attack and told investigators he was proud of what he had done, that he "just hated seeing" Chiu because "Chinese and blacks have weapons," and that he was acting "like a Marine, like a KKK [Ku Klux Klan] person."[20] In the months prior to the slaying, the Chiu family endured several incidents of vandalism to their home and a racial slur scratched into the family car. "Personally, I feel like there is racial discrimination in this community," said a distraught Christopher Chiu, father of the victim. "We always knew something bad was going to happen. We just never thought it would be something this bad."[21]

More than two years past between Chiu's killing and the court trial. The defense attorney argued that Hearn had the mentality of a third grader, suffered from schizophrenia, and believed he had government orders to kill people whom he considered dangerous. The defense also argued that the police interpreter did not properly inform Hearn of his rights before he was formally interrogated. On September 26, 2003, Superior Court Judge Kazuharu Makino finally ruled that Hearn was not guilty by reason of insanity for the killing of Kenneth Chiu. Recognizing the gravity of his ruling, Judge Makino told the courtroom: "I don't want anyone thinking this is absolving anyone. The question is, was he sane or insane based on the legal standards we use." The outraged Chiu family reacted bitterly to the ruling and vowed to find a way to overturn the judge's decision and find justice for their son. Unfortunately, there was no legal standing for the family in a criminal case and no venue for an appeal. Rather than a prison sentence, Hearn will receive treatment and, if eventually declared sane and no longer a danger to society, he will be released. "The trial is over, but the outcome sent out the wrong message," said Christopher Chiu. "[I]f you're a racist and mentally ill, it's O.K. to kill."[22]

It was the Kenneth Chiu case that prompted California State Assembly member Judy Chu to sponsor Assembly Bill 2428, known as "Kenny's Law," which would among other things require that the families of violent hate-crime victims be informed where and when their attackers are released, either from prison or mental institutions. The Chiu family was actively involved with crafting the law, lobbying the state legislature in its favor and speaking out about their personal experience with hate violence. On September 27, 2004, a year after Hearn was sentenced and three years since the murder of Kenneth Chiu, California Governor Arnold Schwarzenegger signed AB 2428 into law.[23]

Violent hate crimes are overwhelmingly single-bias incidents. That is, one person committing one act against one person. For example, FBI statistics from 2002 showed that out of 7,462 hate crime incidents, only 3 cases were classified as multiple-bias incidents.[24] This information makes the case involving Richard Baumhammers especially dramatic. On April 28, 2000, Baumhammers, 34, an immigration and import lawyer from a prominent upper-middle-class family went on a shooting spree, killing five individuals in less than two hours. After his arrest, law enforcement authorities carefully combed through Baumhammers' home and personal computer and found racially tinged writings that may explain what drove him to leave a trail of carnage throughout the suburbs west of Pittsburgh, Pennsylvania. County Coroner Cyril Wecht said that anyone who would doubt that the attacks were driven by racial and religious hatred is also still "looking at the Empire State Building to see if we'll classify it as a skyscraper."[25] The rampage began after Baumhammers allegedly shot to death his next-door neighbor, Anita (Nikki) Gordon, 63, whom he had known since childhood. He apparently set fire to Gordon's house and may be responsible for spray-painting a swastika and the word "Jew" at the synagogue Gordon regularly attended. Baumhammers allegedly fired shots into this and one other synagogue in the area. He then drove to a nearby Indian grocery store where he allegedly shot and killed Anil Thakur, 31, and severely wounded Sandip Patel, 24. He next drove to a Chinese restaurant where police say Baumhammers asked for the manager Ji-Ye Sun, 34, and the deliveryman Thao "Tony" Pham, 30, by name before opening fire and killing both of them. A short time later, police received a call from the C. S. Kim Karate School where they found the last victim, 22-year-old Gary Lee, an African American.

It was reported that Baumhammers had briefly maintained a Web page calling for increased immigration of Europeans and decried the influx of non-Europeans to the United States. The Web page was not as racist and extreme as others, according to Jerry Tapolci, president of the company that hosted the site. "I've seen worse," Tapolci recalled. "It seemed like his actions were a lot more extreme than his Web page."[26] Baumhammers smirked at onlookers during his arraignment, but his lawyer said the look was caused more by mental illness rather than any racial and religious animus. Shortly after the killings, NAPALC issued a press release expressing grief for all the victims and decrying the violence. The statement also called to attention the fact that eight Asian Americans had been killed in hate-related violence since 1998. "Our nation's leaders must act to send a clear message to the purveyors of hate before another Asian Pacific American life is lost," the statement said.[27]

Baumhammers's trial the following year received a great deal of media attention, as the defense attorney claimed his client was a paranoid schizophrenic with delusions that he was being ordered to kill his victims. Unlike the Kenneth Chiu case, however, Baumhammers was convicted of five counts of murder and twenty-three other charges including ethnic intimidation, institutional vandalism, attempted homicide, aggravated assault, reckless endangerment, and weapons violations. He received the death sentence for the murders and essentially life imprisonment (112 to 225 years) for the other charges. The life imprisonment would only occur should the death penalty be commuted.[28] Shortly after the conviction a rally was held in support of a proposed Local Law Enforcement Enhancement Act, which would allow for harsher penalties for crimes motivated by hate. The first speaker at the rally was shooting survivor Sandip Patel, who was in a wheelchair, paralyzed from the neck down. "I am a victim of a hate crime, along with others," Patel told the audience. "Please support today's cause. I feel that God created a variety of people on this planet and all of them should live in harmony in peace."[29] While the community where the killings took place found a way to cope, family members of the individual victims also had to find a way to carry on with the sudden tragedy and loss. On Father's Day 2001, 7-year-old Chris Pham and Chris's mother Bonnie Ngo set a place at the dinner table in memory of Thao Pham. In Pham's honor his son burned a portion of his meal as an offering. "That's how they handled it and helped Chris deal with another Father's Day with out Tony [Thao]," explained the family's attorney, Charles A. Knoll, Jr.[30]

Another incident took place on August 10, 1999, when Filipino American postal worker Joseph Ileto, 39, was shot nine times and killed in broad daylight on the streets of Los Angeles. Several of the bullet wounds were in the back of Ileto's head, as he was shot execution-style. According to an affidavit filed days after the shootings, Buford O. Furrow, 37, admitted he killed Ileto because he was nonwhite, worked for the federal government, and was a good "target of opportunity." Furrow, who earlier had burst into a Jewish community-center day camp and fired more than seventy shots, wounding five people, had long been involved with the neo-Nazi group Aryan Nations and had dreams of killing Jews and minorities.[31]

At Ileto's funeral, family members and uniformed postal workers mourned his loss. Condolences from President Clinton, Vice President Al Gore, and U.S. Senators Dianne Feinstein and Barbara Boxer were read. That same day, Richard Butler, head of the Idaho-based Aryan Nations, praised Furrow as "a good soldier."[32] For days after the shootings Internet chat rooms that serve white supremacist groups received a flurry of messages. The messages offered both praise and damnation for Furrow's actions, and debated future strategies. "What you don't hear is any shred of regret, guilt, or shame," said Jordan Kessler, an Internet monitor for the Anti-Defamation League of B'nai B'rith.[33]

Furrow eventually turned himself in to authorities after fleeing to Las Vegas, confessed to his crimes, and later pled guilty in court in exchange for a mandatory life-in-prison sentence. Federal prosecutors decided to drop plans to seek the death penalty for Furrow after learning he had tried for ten years to get help for his violent behavior. In fact, in 1998 Furrow tried to commit himself to a private psychiatric facility in Washington State, but when he was not accepted he became violent and threatened the staff with a knife. It was only then he was arrested and sent to a mental institution for treatment. He was released on May 1999 for good behavior, just three months before his shooting rampage in Los Angeles.[34] On March 26, 2001, a Los Angeles federal judge formally sentenced Furrow to five life terms in prison. "I hold myself responsible for what happened," Furrow said in a statement at his sentencing hearing. "I wish I had been kept in the [mental] hospital I was previously in. I think about what happened every day and I will grieve for it every day for the rest of my life." Joseph Ileto's mother and siblings were also at the hearing and they, too, had their say in court. "When he killed my son, he killed part of me," explained Lilian Ileto to the hushed courtroom audience. "I was brought up to always forgive. We will never go down to that level of hate. . . . I pity Buford. He has to wake up every day and see his reflection in the mirror." Furrow acknowledged the strength of her words as he nodded his head in agreement.[35]

The Asian Pacific American Legal Center in Los Angeles (APALC), a partner organization of NAPALC, has been working closely with the Ileto family in rallying community-based efforts around passing tougher hate crimes and gun control legislation, as well as expanding national resources to address race relations. The Ileto family and APALC also established the Joseph Ileto Hate Crime Prevention Fellowship with a goal of establishing a permanent staff focused on aiding victims of hate crimes, educating the public about hate crimes, and supporting legislation and policy changes aimed at hate crime prevention. Another tribute to Joseph Ileto was the renaming in his honor of the post office where he worked in Chino Hills.[36]

There was still another recent multiple–bias incident occurring over the Fourth of July weekend that killed two people and wounded nine. On Friday evening, July 2, 1999, a man shot wildly at worshipers as they were leaving their synagogue in Chicago, Illinois. Seven people were wounded in this incident. About a half-hour later an African American man, Ricky Birdsong, 43, was shot twice in the back as he was walking with his children. Birdsong died the next day. That same evening an Asian American couple were fired at, but neither was injured. The following morning three African American men were fired upon; one was wounded. Just one half-hour later a group of six Asian American men were shot at near the University of Illinois campus. One person was hit in the leg. On Sunday, July 4, four shots were fired at a crowd in front of the Korean United Methodist Church in Bloomington, Indiana. Won Joon Yoon, a 26-year-old student at Indiana University was killed. That evening the suspect, 21-year-old Benjamin Nathaniel Smith shot himself during a high-speed chase with Illinois State police and later died.[37]

Smith was a known white supremacist member of the World Church of the Creator. Smith wrote about the beginnings of his racist and anti-Semitic attitudes in the church's newsletter, dismissing the history lessons he learned in school. "The Jew teacher began with the 'slaughtering' of the Indians by white pioneers and settlers," Smith wrote. "He then moved to the 'evils' of black slavery, and ended with the 'murder of 6 million Jews.' . . . The entire class was mind-manipulation, pure and simple . . . ." When a student at Indiana University,

Smith frequently wrote racially biased letters to the school newspaper editor, and distributed anti-Semitic and racist leaflets on campus and around town.[38]

The Indiana University college town of Bloomington reacted strongly to the senseless murder of the student Yoon and especially to the fact that Smith was a former Indiana University student. Signs reading "Hate: Not Here" were posted in town and a scholarship in memory of Yoon was established, specifically for students who "exemplify tolerance and understanding across racial and religious lines."[39] Nonetheless racial and religious hatred has not been easily erased in the community. Indiana University's Student Ethics and Anti-Harassment Programs office annually reports dozens of bias-related incidents on campus. In July 2005, there was an attempted arson attack against a mosque next door to the Korean United Methodist Church where Yoon was gunned down. "It was sad news to see what happened," said Paster Gi-Chae Lee. "I know Bloomington is a peaceful place to live and I hope this sort of thing will never happen again." Indiana University student Alice Feng agreed with Paster Lee that Bloomington is generally tolerant and accepting, but added: "From an Asian American viewpoint I think Bloomington still has a lot of room to expand itself."[40]

CONTRIBUTING FACTORS TO ANTI-ASIAN VIOLENCE

What are the reasons behind anti-Asian sentiment and violence? Is it merely intolerance toward individuals who are physically distinct? Those who focus on these types of incidents point to much broader issues. NAPALC and the U.S. Commission on Civil Rights have identified a number of factors that contribute to anti-Asian violence and hate crimes. Among the most important are (1) increase in anti-immigrant sentiment, (2) economic competition between racial and ethnic groups, (3) "move-in" violence, and (4) poor police–community relations. All of these factors play an important role in hate-related activities against Asian Americans, and they are frequently interrelated.

Anti-Immigrant and Perpetual Foreigner Sentiment

Chapter 1 described the increase in anti-immigrant sentiment in the United States in recent years. Federal, state, and local politicians have used immigration—and the fact that most immigrants to the United States today are from Asia and Latin America—as hot-button issues to excite voters. In addition, Congress has made a number of recent proposals intended to halt, or at least reduce, the number of legal immigrants to the United States. Immigrants have also been targeted for deep cuts and even elimination from programs such as welfare, free school lunches, and health care. These sentiments go far beyond political rhetoric and public policy debates. Racial slurs against Asian Americans are quite often coupled with anti-immigrant insults such as "go home" and other obvious phrases that show animosity against others who are not considered "Americans." The backlash against certain groups after the terrorist attacks of September 11, 2001, and how immigrant communities have been negatively and violently impacted have been well documented. The *2001 Audit of Violence Against Asian Pacific Americans* focused on bias-related incidents following 9/11. The American Civil Liberties Union (ACLU) of Northern California and Human Rights Watch (HRW) both published reports also calling attention to cases of hate-related violence and concerns about human rights. In addition, the anthology *Asian Americans On War & Peace* (2002), edited by Russell C. Leong and Don T. Nakanish, looks at the events following 9/11 from an Asian American perspective.[41]

The case of Balbir Singh Sodhi described at the beginning of this chapter is a jarring reminder of the post-9/11 backlash. Sodhi was a victim of a multiple-bias hate incident, which took place on September 15, 2001, that included shots being fired into the home of an Afghan American family, as well as a Lebanese American gas attendant. Assailant Frank Roque went on a drunken rage ranting how he wanted to kill those responsible for the 9/11 attacks, according to police reports in Mesa, Arizona, where the shooting spree took place. His first victim was Sodhi who was tending flowers in front of the gas station he owned. Over the next several weeks the news media reported several other individuals who may have been murder victims simply because of their ethnic background. They include Waqar Hasan, 46, a Pakistani American who was shot in his grocery store; Abodo Ali Ahmed, 50, a naturalized American citizen from Yemen who was shot at a gas station; and Abdullah Nimer, 53, a Palestinian American salesman who was shot and killed at work. In all three cases friends and family members strongly suspect they were hate crimes because neither cash nor goods were stolen. However, police authorities reported them all as botched robberies.[42] Across the United States, more than two hundred incidents of anti-Sikh violence were reported within a month of 9/11, causing alarmed Sikh Americans, as well as others who believed they may become victims of the violent backlash, to prominently display American flags outside their homes, their workplaces, and places of worship as an act of both patriotism and protection. Some newly created Sikh Web sites even recommended people wear "I am Sikh (Not A Muslim)" placards.[43]

Two years after the murder of Sodhi the criminal trial began, with the prosecution emphasizing hate as the primary motivator in the killing. Frank Roque's defense claimed he had a long history of mental illness and the events of September 11, 2001, caused him to hear voices telling him to commit the crimes. The prosecution was able to counter this mental illness argument with psychologists who said Roque could distinguish between right and wrong and that he had never sought treatment for his psychological problems before the shooting. On October 9, 2003, a jury convicted Roque and sentenced him to death. "This jury came with a verdict of the truth," said Lakhwinder Singh Sodhi, brother of the murder victim. "We showed a whole world this is a country of justice." Sikhs across the United States and around the world closely followed the trial. Dr. Rajwant Singh, the leader of the Sikh Council on Religion, said he believed the verdict was a strong statement against violent hate crimes, which has created an increased amount of fear among Sikh Americans. "We regret the ignorance which prompted Frank Roque to this senseless killing as it has also caused deep suffering in his family." Singh told reporters. "We pray for his family and even the man himself."[44]

Despite the conviction and harsh penalty against Frank Roque, antagonism and ignorance against Sikh Americans continues. In the summer of 2004, five drunken men in Queens, New York, began harassing 55-year-old Rajinder Singh Khalas outside of a restaurant. The verbal assault escalated when the men demanded Khalas give them his turban, which they referred to as "a dirty curtain." Khalas refused and tried to explain the religious significance of his turban. The men then attacked him and beat him unconscious. Khalas suffered a broken nose and a fractured left eye socket, and could not work for several months. Despite his injuries and emotional distress, Khalas decided to file a civil lawsuit against his attackers and the restaurant that served the men alcohol. According to Khalas's attorney, this is the first time since 9/11 that a Sikh American has filed such a suit, despite more than four hundred hate crimes against Sikh victims. "People should know that Sikhs will not suffer in silence," said Khalas. "I hope for justice not only for myself, but all hate-crime victims."[45]

Economic Competition

Anti-Asian sentiment and violence is also fueled by economic competition between racial and ethnic groups. This competition manifests itself in two ways. One way is the result of animosity and jealousy of Asian Americans who many perceive as having achieved status as the "model minority" at the expense of others. One notable example took place in November 1995, when Robert Page, a 25-year-old unemployed meat cutter in Novato, California, wrote a note to himself declaring, "What the fuck, I'm going to kill a Chinaman!" Later that morning Page attacked a Chinese American male with an eight-inch knife in a grocery store parking lot, chased him into the store, and then began stabbing him again in front of shocked patrons. Page hated Chinese because in his mind they "got all the good jobs."[46]

A second effect of this competition is related to the economic and political relationship between the U.S. and Asian nations. The most obvious example of this type of economic competition and misplaced hostility was seen in what was popularly referred to in the early 1990s as "Japan-bashing." Trade imbalance conflicts with Japan, continued high unemployment rates in the United States, along with a growth in well-recognized Japanese name brand products such as Honda, Toyota, Mitsubishi, Sony, Nikon, Nintendo, and Toshiba have all led to a blind backlash against Asian Americans. The U.S. Commission on Civil Rights 1992 report on Asian Americans specifically addressed the problems created by the model minority stereotype and Japan-bashing.[47] However, at the New York press conference to announce the report, concerns over Japan-bashing took center stage. According to Commission Chairman Arthur A. Fletcher, "Japan-bashing is on the rise across this nation, and there are signs that racial animosities toward Japanese Americans and other U.S. residents who trace their origin to many different Asian lands are increasing as well."[48] The commission's report cited the 1982 killing of Vincent Chin by two autoworkers in Detroit as the most obvious example of how Japan-bashing and anti-Asian feelings can lead to deadly consequences, and recommended that political leaders stop using Japan as a scapegoat for all of the economic woes in the United States.

In the early 1990s the growth of the "buy-American" movement reflected the popular sense of unease that the United States was losing its independence, identity, and economy to Japan.[49] This buy-American campaign was reportedly started in 1991 by an Ohio ear surgeon, Dr. William Lippy, who offered a $400 bonus to his employees who purchased a new or used American automobile by July 4. In less than one year, the movement had spread and escalated across the nation. In Edwardsville, Illinois, Bill Chartrand offered a 2-cent-a-gallon discount to customers who drove American cars. In Greece, New York, the small upstate suburban community voted against buying a $40,000 excavating machine that was made in Japan in favor of a similar piece of equipment made by an American company that cost $15,000 more. The Los Angeles County Transportation Commission rescinded a $122 million contract for new railcars it had just issued following heavy protests by union workers and local politicians. Probably the most publicized example of the buy-American crusade took place in 1992, when the Seattle Mariners baseball franchise announced that a group of investors led by Minoru Arakawa, president of Nintendo of America, was interested in purchasing the team. Local residents and baseball fans rejoiced because Minoru, a fifteen-year resident of Seattle, offered to keep the financially ailing team in town. At the same time, the competing bidder for the franchise wanted to relocate the team to a more lucrative market. Baseball owners balked at Arakawa's offer, saying they didn't want any "non-North American" ownership of America's national sport. The Japanese American Citizen's League immediately wrote to baseball commissioner Fay Vincent, objecting to the spirit and tenor of the owners' rationale. "What is at issue here," the letter stated, "is the underlying sense of racial xenophobia which permeates the dialogue of U.S.–Japan relations."[50]

Without denying problematic elements with Japanese trade and economic policies, most economists and trade experts are dubious about the merits and long-term wisdom of the buy-American efforts. There is a great deal of attention placed on the American auto industry, but there is concern that U.S. protectionist policies in one area would harm the motion picture, music, apparel, and food industries that enjoy a lucrative market share in Japan. In his book, *The Work of Nations* (1991), economist and former U.S. labor secretary Robert Reich argues that the answer to improving the overall American economy boils down to (1) a willingness of industries to retool and educate or retrain workers to compete effectively in a rapidly changing global economy and (2) a commitment by the nation to educate and prepare young people for the jobs in the future. In essence, make the U.S. more competitive, rather than wallow in self-pity and finger-pointing. A similar theme comes from journalist James Fallows in his book *More Like Us: Making America Great Again* (1989). Fallows is a harsher critic of Japan and its economic policies than Reich, but he nonetheless agrees that reinforcing America's strengths in innovation, entrepreneurship, pioneering spirit, and freedom goes a lot farther than complaining about Japan.[51] So why is there fear and hate mongering against Japan?

Asian American and civil rights leaders believe racism is at the core of this matter. Would Americans be upset if Canadians purchased the Seattle Mariners and moved them to Vancouver? Does anyone complain that Rupert Murdoch, an Australian, owns the Fox Television Network and is one of the largest media moguls in the nation? In contrast to Arakawa's attempt to buy the Seattle Mariners, very little was said when Murdoch purchased the Los Angeles Dodgers in 1997. Where are the demonstrations that feature protesters taking sledgehammers to Volkswagen automobiles because Germans don't buy American cars? Was anything said when Mobil Oil and Arco were bought out by BP (British Petroleum)? Dennis Hayashi, then national director of the Japanese American Citizen's League in San Francisco, praised the strong stand by the U.S. Commission on Civil Rights against Japan-bashing. "(W)e feel this 'Buy American' campaign that's spreading across the nation is the cutting edge of anti-Asian prejudice that leads to anti-Asian violence."[52]

The Asian economic crisis, coupled with the boom in the U.S. economy throughout the mid-1990s, has reduced the intensity of Japan-bashing and buy-American activism. However, the recent decline in the U.S. economy has raised tensions once again. On January 2004, NASCAR (National Association of Stock Car Auto Racing) driver Jimmy Spencer complained about the introduction of Toyota trucks in the Craftsman Truck competition, saying: "Those sons of bitches bombed Pearl Harbor, don't forget," and added, "I hope Ford, Chevrolet, and Dodge kick their ass." Spencer's comments were reported in the media, but in this case Asian American groups did not organize a protest, and NASCAR officials merely shrugged off the incident. "Jimmy's going to be Jimmy, and he's going to be Jimmy," said NASCAR spokesman Jim Hunter. "He's old-school."[53]

Unfortunately, Spencer's comments are far from isolated. According to sports columnist Scott Rabalais of the *State-Times/Morning Advocate* (Baton Rouge, Louisiana): "If not for the fact it would create too much wind resistance, NASCAR teams would probably fly an American flag from every car and truck that takes the track . . . Rampant patriotism is as much a part of every race as gas and tires. . . . And all that sits quite well with most people in the seats at the race track, which tells you why for many of them the sight of Toyota fielding entries in NASCAR's Craftsman Truck Series this year is about as popular as higher prices at the pump. . . . It was a historic race considering that it marked the first time a non-U.S.-based automaker ran a NASCAR race, but that didn't make it popular."[54] Since 1954, NASCAR has banned "foreign cars" from its national races. But at the 2004 Craftsman Truck Series—sponsored by Florida's Dodge dealers—held at the Daytona International Speedway, seven Toyota Tundras qualified in the 36-truck field. The loophole in the rule is that all vehicles in NASCAR races must be "American-made." What many critics failed to recognize is that the only place in the world that makes Toyota Tundras is Princeton, Indiana, with another plant soon to open in San Antonio, Texas. That fact still does not satisfy racing team owner Jack Roush. "Even though Toyota has factories in the United States that use American workers, it's Japanese capital, and the returns on the investment and all those things that wind up building the economy and building the country go over there," Roush said. "I think there will be a significant backlash from fans who say Toyota shouldn't be here because it's bad for our economy and people like myself, who are more nationalistic than some of our population and some of our fans."[55] Roush, Spencer, and others who think like them conveniently forget that Dodge, which sponsors the 2004 Craftsman Truck Series, is owned by Daimler-Chrysler, a company based in Germany. There is far more interdependence in the world economy than most people assume.

Most recently, another Asian threat besides Japan has emerged—China. The U.S. and China governments have a favorable trade relationship, as recognized by Congress giving China Most-Favored-Nation trade status in 2000, but the political tensions between the U.S. and China are still apparent. These tensions are seen in the 1996 investigations into illegal campaign contributions from Asian governments, corporations, and individuals described in the introduction of this book. The arrest of Dr. Wen Ho Lee in 1999 and allegations of Chinese spies stealing U.S. nuclear weapons secrets described at the beginning of this book also serve to maintain the generalized image of Asian Americans as disloyal foreigners.[56] The fear of China is also manifested in the publication of two provocative books. In *The Coming Conflict With China* (1998), authors Richard Bernstein and Ross Munro argue that the U.S. will face direct competition from China for global economic control, military superiority, and diplomatic influence in the twenty-first century. *A Firing Offense* (1998) by David Ignatius is a fictional account of conniving Chinese officials conspiring with French businessmen to accumulate wealth and weapons of mass destruction to defeat the unsuspecting and overcomplacent United States.[57]

The fears expressed in these books notwithstanding, the reality is that China has already emerged as a maturing player in the global economy and has increased its share of the global market for goods ranging from textiles to computers. In 2004, the Lenovo Group, China's top maker of personal computers, paid $1.75 billion to acquire a majority stake in IBM's PC business, a move that makes it the third largest computer maker after Dell and Hewlett-Packard. China government-controlled businesses made unsuccessful bids to purchase appliance giant Maytag, as well as oil giant Unocal, both of which created a major outcry against what critics saw as an economic invasion.[58] The Chinese oil company CNOOC Ltd. eventually withdrew its offer to buy Unocal after Congress passed legislation to delay the deal. In frustration, CNOOC Ltd. backed off and offered a terse statement. "The unprecedented political opposition that followed the announcement of our proposed transaction . . . was regrettable and unjustified," the statement read. "The political environment has made it very difficult for us to accurately assess our chance of success, creating a level of uncertainty that presents an unacceptable risk to our ability to secure this transaction." CNOOC Ltd. also said it would have raised its $18.4 billion offer to Unocal if not for the opposition in Congress.[59] Even more confrontation is on the horizon as it is expected that China will begin exporting economy cars to the United States by 2006, introducing itself to the market. By 2007 China will be selling midsize four-door sedans, sports utility vehicles, and sports cars. According to *BusinessWeek*, the Chinese-made SUV of the near future will sell for $15,000 and will be marketed as being comparable in quality to the BMW X3, which sells for $31,000.[60] The extent of the backlash against continued economic competition with China on Asian Americans remains to be seen.

Move-in Violence

Harassment and vandalism were the most common forms of what NAPALC and the U.S. Commission on Civil Rights both call "move-in violence." This form of violence is intended to intimidate individuals and families from living in certain neighborhoods or housing projects. The report, *Civil Rights Issues Facing Asian Americans in the 1990s*, cited several examples of racist literature being distributed in neighborhoods across the country where Asian Americans had recently taken up residence. These neighborhoods ranged from suburban communities favored by middle-class and professional Asian Americans to low-income areas that recent Southeast Asian refugees have found affordable. From there, incidents escalate to verbal taunts, egg throwing, shattering windows with rocks or BB guns, and to more serious acts of vandalism, fire bombings, physical assaults, and murder.

Palisades Park, New Jersey, is a small community located just a few miles from New York City that has recently seen an influx of Korean Americans. Indeed, it is estimated 90 percent of the businesses in the city's main commercial thoroughfare are owned and operated by Korean Americans. Korean-language business signs came under attack in 1996 when the Palisades Park city council passed a law requiring all business signs written in a foreign language to also have equal-sized translations in English. The city council targeted Korean businesses that stayed open all night by passing an ordinance requiring all businesses to close at 3 A.M., but allowed one "American-style" restaurant to remain open twenty-four hours. Korean American merchants fought back against these actions and eventually both were overturned in court. Since that time Korean-owned and -operated businesses have confronted numerous cases of graffiti and other forms of vandalism. In October 1999, the Asian American Legal Defense and Education Fund (AALDEF) held a press conference to denounce the graffiti. "This kind of tension is such that it's moved beyond bad feeling and into action," said Stanley Mark, AALDEF program director. "We're worried it's going to more of a higher level."[61]

The antagonism against the increased number of Korean Americans moving in to New Jersey continues to percolate. Craig Carton and Ray Rossi, two "shock jocks" on radio station WKXW-FM in New Jersey began a diatribe against a Korean American mayoral candidate from Edison, New Jersey, a suburban community where Asian Americans represent 30 percent of the population. The April 25, 2005, episode began with Carton asking the listening audience, "Would you really vote for someone named Jun Choi?" and quickly escalated to complaints about too many Asians moving to New Jersey, punctuated with mimicking Asian accents and stereotypes of Asian Americans as perpetual foreigners. "And here's the bottom line," Carton explained. "No specific minority group or foreign group should ever dictate the outcome of an American election. I don't care if the Chinese population in Edison has quadrupled in the last year, Chinese should never dictate the outcome of an American election." Carton's anger coupled with his ignorance encouraged listeners to call in and share similar opinions including this exchange:

> Caller: I just moved out of Edison because of what has happened in the past 10 years . . . Orientals are all along, the whole complete route 27. And Indians have taken over Edison in the north and all over.
>
> Carton: Damn Orientals and Indians.
>
> Caller: I can't handle them! There's no American people anymore . . . [They are] shoving us the hell out!
>
> Carton: It's like you're a foreigner in your own country isn't it?
>
> Caller: You go to [a] store and you can't even see American people, you don't see our own kids, American kids, working in the store anymore . . .

Just before the commercial break "America, the Beautiful" was played.[62]

From this event emerged the New Jersey/National Task Force Against Hate Media, a coalition of more than one hundred organizations formed to call for the station to fire the two offending show hosts. "We are outraged by these bigoted comments," said Jason Kim, a councilman from Palisades Park, New Jersey. "101.5's message is offensive to all Americans regardless of race or ethnic background, and violates the American spirit of diversity and inclusion." WKXW-FM's station manager Eric Johnson said that the show's hosts would not be fired nor suspended and made excuses for their comments and behavior. "They were making light of old-fashioned ethnic stereotypes," Johnson explained. "If in the course that anyone was offended, we're sorry."[63] This half-hearted apology did not satisfy Asian American protesters and they pressured the station's advertisers to boycott the show. The intensity of the protest took the station by surprise and within a month Carton and Rossi made a live on-air apology directly to Choi for their comments. "Man to man, I'm sorry," Carton said. "The intent was never to hurt you personally or hurt your mayoral campaign." Choi graciously accepted the apology, telling radio listeners: "It wasn't that I was offended personally or found your comments hurtful, (but) I believe it crossed a line. By saying these groups were un-American, that was what hurt me."[64]

Palisades Park and Edison are beginning to look like a contemporary version of events in Monterey Park, California, commonly known as, "The First Suburban Chinatown" throughout the 1980s. Monterey Park is located just eight miles east of downtown Los Angeles and was a major migration point for many immigrants from Taiwan and Hong Kong. Ethnic-oriented businesses sprang up to accommodate the newcomers and the city's main commercial street conspicuously displayed Chinese characters with little English translation. In 1985, some three thousand residents signed a petition attempting to get an "Official

English" initiative on the municipal ballot. In addition, a local newspaper printed an article accusing the Chinese of being bad drivers, and bumper stickers began appearing asking, "Will the Last American to Leave Monterey Park Please Bring the Flag?" By 1986 the Monterey Park city council passed a broad moratorium on new construction that many believed was aimed at stopping the growth of the Chinese immigrant population and Chinese-financed developments. But it was the rejection of plans proposed by a Taiwanese group to build a senior housing project that prompted a rare display of public protest. Four hundred people, mostly elderly Chinese, marched to City Hall carrying American flags and signs reading, "Stop Racism," "We Are Americans Too," and "End Monterey Park Apartheid."[65]

The deadly nature of move-in violence was seen in the shooting of 18-year-old Xuyen Nguyen in front of his home on September 18, 1992. This incident demonstrated the ongoing dangers faced by many Southeast Asian refugee families in several of San Francisco's low-income housing projects. "I saw it coming," Nguyen's mother told a reporter from the *San Francisco Examiner.* "I think we were attacked because we are Vietnamese." She went on to describe several other incidents of violence and hostility the family quietly endured, including one youth who came to their front door and screamed, "Move! Move! Move!" Other Southeast Asian refugee tenants reported their children were repeatedly harassed and attacked on their way to and from school. Despite these incidents, the San Francisco Housing Authority (SFHA) denied that refugees were victims of racially-motivated intimidation. "We're concerned about the possibility of Asian families being targeted, but in fact that's not what we have in front of us right now," explained one housing authority official. "The problem, as I see it, is increasing crime." Housing and police officials also admitted that Southeast Asians were repeatedly victimized because they had a reputation of not reporting crimes.[66]

The Asian Law Caucus (ALC) of San Francisco viewed the issues and sequence of events very differently. First, it is important to note that SFHA began randomly assigning Southeast Asian families into predominantly African American housing projects as part of a "Voluntary Compliance Agreement" following allegations of racial segregation raised by the federal department of Housing and Urban Development (HUD). Second, this response to "integrate" the projects was done without any explanation to the established residents who saw Southeast Asians as "intruders" and interpreted their sudden arrival as simply a displacement of needy African Americans. Third, Southeast Asian tenants who were limited-English speakers found the lack of bilingual housing staff only reinforced an environment of isolation and alienation within the projects. Fourth, ALC began receiving complaints from Southeast Asian tenants in the projects, and took about a year to gather enough information to show a distinct pattern of racially motivated harassment and violence. Fifth, even when Southeast Asian tenants did come forth to complain to the housing authority about their situation and conditions, their needs were ignored. For example, immediately after their son was killed, the Nguyens requested a transfer out of their housing unit, but they received no response. Even a letter from the San

Francisco Police Department's Hate Crime unit on the Nguyen's behalf sent to the director of the San Francisco Housing Authority failed to elicit a response. As a result, the Nguyen family was forced to find more expensive housing on their own. Lastly, ALC realized the institutional roots and policy blunders, along with individual ignorance and prejudice, all worked together to create a highly volatile situation. The latent effect of this attempt to integrate public housing actually resulted in fewer needy Southeast Asian families in the projects because so many moved away in fear of their lives.[67]

ALC filed a class-action lawsuit on behalf of the Southeast Asian tenants who sought increased security, staff training, and improved assignment and emergency transfer policies that would benefit all residents. In addition, the suit sought language assistance and increased support services for new residents. A settlement in the case with the SFHA and HUD was reached in early 1995, which included public hearings on integration strategies and race relations in public housing. Unfortunately, the SFHA failed to enforce the settlement agreement and the percentage of Asian Americans in the city's largest public housing developments fell dramatically because of continued harassment and violence. In 1997 Tem Le was attacked in broad daylight with rocks and bottles and beaten unconscious. The ALC, along with the Vietnamese American Civil Rights Coalition, filed separate federal complaints against the SFHA alleging the agency was unresponsive to racial violence against Asian Americans, which denies them equal access to federally assisted housing in the city. In July 1999 the SFHA agreed to a consent decree that calls for two community-based programs to address tenant complaints about racial discrimination and assist families on the waiting list for public housing. The programs are overseen by an outside monitor and cost up to $350,000 a year to run. The monitor is responsible for establishing standards of conduct and service that the SFHA must maintain. If the standards are not met, the result would be the return of the original lawsuit and the possibility of an expensive and lengthy court trial.[68]

Poor Police–Community Relations

Both NAPALC and the U.S. Commission on Civil Rights recognize relations between the various Asian American communities and local police is critical in addressing anti-Asian violence and crime. In recent years, police departments have attempted to reach out to the growing Asian American population, but sustained efforts are rare. Confronting police misconduct against Asian Americans is one area in need of improvement. Harassment and abuse by police is commonly seen as an issue faced by African Americans and Latinos, but this is also a concern for Asian Americans. The most notable case in this area involves the fatal shooting of Kuan Chung Kao, a 33-year-old computer engineer in Rohnert Park, California, on April 29, 1997. Rohnert Park is located in California's world famous Sonoma County wine country and would seem to be the last place one would expect deadly violence. At approximately 2 A.M. that day police responded to several 911 calls that a man was yelling in his driveway. Two officers arrived on the scene and found Kao, who was drunk at the time, waving a broomstick in what they said was a "martial arts fashion." Officers Jack Shields and Mike Lynch drew their guns and instructed Kao to drop the stick. Kao refused and began striking the police cars with the stick. By this time Kao's wife was outside and offered to talk to her husband and take the stick from him. The officers ordered her to stay back. Shields felt his safety was in jeopardy and fired one shot striking Kao in the chest. Kao's wife, a registered nurse, tried to help her husband but was physically kept away by the officers. Kao was handcuffed and left face down and bleeding for about ten minutes before help arrive. He died at the scene.[69]

Asian American civil rights activists called for an immediate investigation into the case. Kao had no martial arts training, but officers perceived Kao as more of a threat than the average intoxicated man and may have acted with excessive force. An administrative review by the Rohnert Park Police Department later cleared Shields and Lynch of any wrongdoing, saying the two officers complied with department policy and procedures in the use of deadly force. However, Victor Hwang, a staff attorney at the ALC examined the report and found several inconsistencies. For example, Hwang found that the police officers sped toward Kao in their patrol cars pretending to try to run him over when they first arrived. This may have provoked the dazed and agitated Kao into striking the vehicles. In addition, officer Shields claimed that Kao was only about three feet away with the stick raised when the fatal shot was fired. Hwang could not find a witness who could testify how far Kao was from the officer when he was shot, but there were witnesses who said Kao was holding the stick parallel to the ground and not over his head ready to strike. "Kao didn't have to die," Hwang said. "We have to stay committed to ensure that justice will be done for his family." One thing that was agreed upon was that only thirty seconds passed between the time the police arrived and the time Kao was shot.[70]

It should be noted why Kao was drunk and screaming outside his home on that fateful morning. According to news accounts, Kao was celebrating a new job at his favorite bar the night before his death. The celebration was spoiled, however, when another customer referred to Kao as Japanese. When Kao said that he was Chinese, the customer responded: "You all look alike to me." The bartender quickly intervened and separated the two men. After a couple of hours and several drinks later, the customer apparently confronted Kao again. Witnesses said Kao shouted, "I'm sick and tired of being put down because I'm Chinese. If you want to challenge me, now's the time to do it." A scuffle broke out and the police were called. The bartender was able to stop the fight and talked police out of taking Kao into custody. Kao was livid over the incident.[71]

In February 1998, Kao's widow, Ayling Wu, filed a $50 million federal law suit charging Rohnert Park, its police department, and the two officers with wrongful death, negligence, and violating the civil rights of Kuan Chung Kao. "I will fight all the way through to make sure people know that my husband was wrongfully killed," Wu said. "It shouldn't have happened." She also described how her 6-year-old daughter was traumatized seeing her father dead in their driveway. Wu also had 1-year-old twins. "It's been a lonely New Year for myself and my kids," Wu said. The civil lawsuit was filed days after the U.S. Department of Justice found insufficient evidence to prosecute the officers on criminal charges.[72] Wu's case was eventually settled for $1 million. According to the attorney for Rohnert Park, the city settled the case for economic reasons and there was no admission of liability or guilt.[73]

Asian American civil rights activist were shocked and dismayed by the Kuan Chung Kao incident, and they continued to press for justice. The publicity around the case drew attention from the California Advisory Committee to the United States Commission on Civil Rights, which initiated an investigation. The investigation offered a damning assessment of the police practices in Sonoma County. In particular, the Advisory Committee found eight cases of the use of deadly force by law enforcement in Sonoma County. In every case the killings were ruled as justified and no law enforcement officer was disciplined. "The Advisory Committee is appalled at the number of deadly incidents, justified or not, that have occurred within 25 months," the report stated. "At minimum, the departments must adopt policies and train officers to have the attitude that deadly force is the option of last resort. If they do not, the community is obliged to continue its efforts for reform of a system they believe requires drastic change."[74] The advisory committee highlighted several areas in need of reform including increasing diversity among the police forces, better training of officers in terms of cultural diversity and the handling of potentially violent situations, the need for independent and critical incident investigations, an improved process for handling complaints, and the institution of community review boards. Kao's killing at the hands of the police shows the importance of exposing such abuses and also provides context for other high profile incidents against Asian Americans.

A great deal of negative attention regarding police brutality and excessive force has been focused on New York. In February 2000, four police officers were acquitted in the shooting death of Amadou Diallo, an immigrant from Guinea. Officers fired forty-one shots at Diallo and he was struck nineteen times. In 1999 one police officer confessed to the savage torture of Abner Louima, a Haitian immigrant, in a police station bathroom. Later another officer was convicted of the same crime, but three others were found not guilty. In this case, Louima was so viciously sodomized with a wooden stick that he suffered severe internal injuries.[75] At the same time, there have been examples of police misconduct against Asian Americans that have not been as widely publicized. Since 1986 the Coalition Against Anti-Asian Violence (CAAAV) has been in the forefront of highlighting police brutality cases against Asian Americans. CAAAV's activities have been confrontational, as seen in its joint effort with the National Congress for Puerto Rican Rights to close down the Manhattan Bridge in April 1995, protesting racial violence and police brutality. The demonstration brought attention to the killing of Young Xin Huang, a 16-year-old high school student who was shot in the back of the head by police. Huang's family later agreed to a $400,000 settlement with the city.[76]

Despite CAAAV's efforts, outrageous acts continue. For example, Dr. Henry Huang, a retired college professor, charged that a police officer choked him and threw him to the ground after entering his apartment. Huang suffered a stroke two days after the incident. In September 1998, the Manhattan district attorney's office dropped its investigation into charges of police brutality due to insufficient evidence. The district attorney also stated that it could not be established that Huang's stroke was a result of the encounter with the officer. Jack Litman, one of Huang's attorneys promised to continue with a lawsuit against the NYPD. "We are sadden by the D.A.'s decision," Litman said. "It really is not right when a police officer chokes a 78-year-old man."[77] Another New York case involved Korean American grocery store owners who called the police after a dispute with a customer, but wound up being the ones who got arrested. The two brothers, Kevin and Scott Yu, are suing the NYPD for false arrest and allege that their apartment above the store was burglarized because officers failed to lock the door after taking them into custody. "We were the ones who called 911," explained Scott Yu. "But . . . my brother and I were arrested and our home was burglarized. What kind of justice is that?" Elizabeth OuYang, an attorney with the Asian American Legal Defense and Education Fund, complained that this was not the first time Asian American business owners have been victimized by police. "This case underscores how New York City police do not treat Asian American store owners seriously or fairly," she said.[78] The incident with the Yus is similar to a case where an NYPD officer was convicted of attempted assault on a Korean American store owner and his brother. During the incident, the officer allegedly called the two brothers "fucking Orientals" and then accused them of resisting arrest. In this case there were witnesses who saw the police officer brutalize the two Korean Americans and contradicted the officer's story.[79] In still another incident, an Asian American off-duty police officer approached a driver who had been sitting in his car for a long while. The driver screamed, "I'm a fucking cop. I'll blow your fucking head off, gook!" When the driver learned that the man who approached him was also a cop, he apologized but complained that the Asian American should have identified himself first.[80]

A recent incident of violence against Asian Americans at the hands of the police occurred on July 13, 2003, when police officers in San Jose, California, shot and killed Bich Cau Thi Tran, 25, a Vietnamese immigrant and the mother of two young children. The police were responding to a domestic violence call and when they arrived they heard a woman screaming. Police say the five-foot, ninety-pound woman threatened them with a ten-inch knife and one of the officers responded by shooting her once in the chest. Tran had a history of mental illness and her boyfriend, Dang Bui, who was a witness to the shooting, told police that she was acting "crazy." However, Bui said she pulled out a vegetable peeler and not a knife or cleaver as the police reported. The police officers said they ordered Tran to drop the weapon, but Bui heard them say only, "Hey! Hey! Hey!"[81]

Within days Vietnamese American community leaders organized a rally outside the San Jose City Hall and Police Department to protest the killing. Some participants carried signs reading, "SJPD: Stop Killing Innocent Women" and "Police/DA Whitewash." They also demanded to know why one of the twenty-eight Vietnamese-speaking officers was not called to the scene. In response, Police Chief William Lansdowne addressed the crowed but could only promise "a full and thorough investigation." At a San Jose City Council meeting the following month, several speakers expressed their anger at the incident and accused officials of withholding information on the case. Others said the Vietnamese American community was now afraid and mistrusted the police. In an attempt to ease the tension and quell the fears, a grand jury hearing about the case was held in open court rather than behind typically closed doors in order "to let the public know the truth," said District Attorney Karyn Siunu.[82] The grand jury hearing was held in October 2003 and it took a week to present all the evidence and testimony. In the end the grand jury cleared the officer who shot and killed Bich Cau Thi Tran of any wrongdoing. The attorneys, jury, and court spectators left the courtroom in eerie silence. While there was no immediate demonstration of anger or protest, this was marked as a crucial event for many in the Vietnamese American community and would be seen as the beginning of a new political activism, particularly among younger Vietnamese Americans. "A dialogue started circulating in the community about the protection of our community and the need for a strong political voice," explained Madison Nguyen, a local San Jose school district board member and the first Vietnamese American woman to hold elective office in California.[83] The shooting also was a bridge to other communities as San Jose's African American, Asian American, and Muslim American citizens formed the Coalition for Justice and Accountability. The San Jose Police Department worked with this organization to rebuild credibility in the community and to initiate new reforms.

Within a year of Tran's death, new San Jose Police Chief Rob Davis had met with Vietnamese community leaders more than forty times and the department had organized citizen's police academies for the Vietnamese community in Vietnamese, equipped and trained officers in the use of nonlethal Tasers, and made plans to hire more Vietnamese American officers, among many other reforms. "We clearly have learned more about the Vietnamese American community than we may have understood a year ago," Davis said. "But I also believe the reverse is true; they understand more about us."[84] Davis also believes the department's efforts have helped to recapture the Vietnamese American community's trust and the process is ongoing.

Taken together, these examples show the need for better law enforcement and Asian American community relations. Strategies for outreach and networking directly with the Asian American communities, along with important institutional changes and legal reforms, must be implemented and supported. The specific issue of anti-Asian violence cannot be directly addressed unless comprehensive statistical data are gathered and assessed. As stated in the beginning of this chapter, the 1990 Federal Hate Crime Statistics Act passed by Congress was intended to serve this purpose, but it is heavily reliant on state and local law enforcement agencies to provide the necessary raw data. Relatively few police departments have special units that deal specifically with identifying, investigating, and reporting hate crimes. This leaves tremendous discretion to the beat officer who most likely has no training in or sensitivity to this issue. "Incidents of anti-Asian violence cannot be fully addressed unless every crime is documented and complete information is available from every state," writes NAPALC in their 2002 audit. "In sum, state uniform crime reports provide an inaccurate picture of hate violence against Asian pacific Americans because of large gaps in the information provided. Even by piecing together information for the state UCR's, local law enforcement agencies, and community-based organizations (CBOs), we can only produce a snapshot of hate crimes against APA's."[85]

The four factors described in this section highlight the extent of anti-Asian sentiment and hate-related violence. The U.S. Commission on Civil Rights and NAPALC have called this a "national problem," and both agree that the greater awareness is the first step to improving the environment of misconception, mistrust, and misplaced hostility against Asian Americans. The Commission and NAPALC also chastised the statements and actions of public officials who consciously play on the politics of division and help to create the environment of hostility against immigrant and native-born Asian Americans. Improving the limited data collecting system on incidents of anti-Asian hate violence and hate crimes is another high priority. Data collecting has improved in recent years, but information is difficult to obtain, often incomplete, and severely limited by widespread underreporting. Because of this, anti-Asian violence will continue to be a major issue confronting Asian Americans for some time.

ASIAN AMERICAN AND AFRICAN AMERICAN RELATIONS

It is important to understand anti-Asian violence as part of what many see as a broader trend toward greater verbal, physical, and legislative attacks against many other minority groups in the United States. These groups include immigrants, people of color, religious minorities, women, gays and lesbians, the homeless, the poor, and others. It is these groups who are the targets in the politics of division and the victims of a backlash against those who are considered marginalized "outsiders" from the "mainstream." At the same time, it must be acknowledged that hate sentiment and hate violence are not limited to just whites on nonwhites. Indeed, in recent years there has been a great deal of tensions among various minority groups, including Asian Americans and African Americans in inner-city communities nationwide. These tensions exploded into the public consciousness during the 1992 urban unrest in Los Angeles immediately after a jury acquitted four white Los Angeles police officers in the beating of black motorist Rodney King.

The chaos in Los Angeles began on April 29 and lasted four days. Some 30,000 uniformed personnel (including police officers, sheriff's deputies, the California National Guard, U.S. Army soldiers, and specially trained Marines) were eventually sent to the scene to enforce a dawn-to-dusk curfew. Bus service was halted and schools were closed in many parts of the city for several days. Very real fears that the rioting would spread across the city forced the postponement of L.A. Dodger baseball games and the relocation of the L.A. Lakers

National Basketball League playoff games. According to various news reports, 58 people were killed, over 2,000 were injured, more than 12,000 were arrested; property damage estimates from the riot ran close to the $1 billion mark. An estimated 10,000 stores in Los Angeles were at least partially damaged or burned. Particularly hard hit were the more than 2,000 businesses owned by Korean Americans, whose combined property losses alone added up to nearly half of the city's total. Some Korean merchants armed themselves and stayed in their shops for days to prevent looters from coming into their stores. Most of these merchants complained they were forced to defend their own businesses because the police did not respond to their calls for help.

On a national level, the unrest triggered smaller upheavals in several other cities including San Francisco, Atlanta, Seattle, Las Vegas, and Miami. The days of rage in 1992 focused the nation's attention on the economic, social, and political inequities that divided blacks, whites, and other people of color. Edward T. Chang, professor of Ethnic Studies at the University of California, Riverside, has written extensively on black–Korean American relations and argued that the 1992 riot in Los Angeles was a clear sign of the future of race relations in America. At the same time, Chang's essay, "America's First Multiethnic 'Riots'" (1994), looks beyond the highly sensationalized stories of conflicts between African Americans and Korean Americans, and recognizes the structural roots of inequality. Chang makes important comparisons and distinctions between the 1992 Los Angeles riots and the 1965 Watts riots. The uprising in the Watts section of Los Angeles also began with a police incident against a black motorist, and resulted in several days of violence, arson, and vandalism that left 34 people dead, more than 1,000 injured, and 3,800 arrested. Beyond these basic facts, Chang asserts, the similarities between the two largest incidents of urban unrest end.[86]

First of all, the 1965 Watts riot was contained in the low-income areas of South Central Los Angeles, in which 81 percent of the residents were African American at the time. The 1992 Los Angeles riot was also centered in South Central, but the population had shifted to about 52 percent African American and more than 40 percent Latino. The African American population in South Central has been declining precipitously since 1965, including a 20 percent drop between 1980 and 1990. The 1992 riot was more widespread than the 1965 Watts riot. The civil disorder in 1992 quickly spread to other parts of the city, including middle-class neighborhoods. Journalists may have played up the black-versus-white, along with the black-versus-Korean, angle, but television cameras showed just as many Latino faces as black faces looting Korean stores. Chang cites police records showing Latinos made up 45.2 percent of the arrests during the 1992 riot, compared with 41 percent blacks and 11.5 percent whites. The 1965 Watts riot sparked a series of upheavals in cities across the nation during the next two years, all of which were eventually studied in the 1968 Kerner Commission report. The commission concluded that the United States was separated into two nations, one black and one white. Chang's analysis of the 1992 Los Angeles riot found the implications went far beyond black and white, and beyond individual race relations and antagonism.[87]

Second, Chang looked at the broader factors behind the 1992 urban unrest. He describes pressures created by the economic downsizing, or deindustrialization, of South Central Los Angeles that saw hundreds of businesses closing, manufacturing leaving the area, and thousands of jobs being lost. Chang also asserts that the structurally created economic depression in the area is further heightened with the emergence of a popular "neoconservative" ideology throughout the 1980s and into the 1990s. This ideology assumes that all groups have been, or will eventually be, accepted into the American mainstream and will enjoy the fruits of equal opportunity. But this will happen only if they are willing to work hard and pull themselves up by their own bootstraps. In other words, this view sees the persistence of joblessness and poverty found among certain groups as evidence of a lack of individual character and initiative rather than critical social problems often beyond individual control. The shifting of blame solely on the victims of structurally created inequality leads only to greater frustration and anger among the most disenfranchised people of the nation. At the same time, Korean immigrants, like other Asian Americans, are often held up as examples of the "model minority" and are used to show that the "American Dream" of economic prosperity can be achieved through hard work and sacrifice. The question is often asked, if Korean Americans can succeed, why can't other groups? Inner-city residents both resent and envy Korean immigrant entrepreneurs because of their "success." But as discussed in Chapter 1, Korean Americans often see themselves as mere economic "survivors." Indeed, for many Korean immigrants, owning a small business is a major step down in social and economic status.[88]

Lastly, Chang acknowledges police department abuses and mistrust in the judicial system as two more areas of brewing discontent, especially within the Los Angeles African American community. The savage beating of Rodney King by four white police officers, which took place on the evening of March 3, 1991, was captured on videotape and shown on national television. Just two weeks later, on March 16, 1991, a store security camera recorded the fatal shooting of 15-year-old Latasha Harlins by a Korean American grocer after a dispute over a $1.79 bottle of orange juice. This videotape was also widely broadcast across the country—sometimes in tandem with the Rodney King beating—and appeared to be yet another piece of clear evidence of the violence inflicted against African Americans. "Well, at last they see we're not lying," said South Central merchant Art Washington. "Now the world sees . . . that this stuff actually happens."[89] Unfortunately, African American hopes for justice based on seemingly irrefutable evidence were quickly and unceremoniously dashed. On November 15, 1991, Korean American storeowner, Soon Ja Du, was convicted of voluntary manslaughter, and sentenced to five years of probation for killing Latasha Harlins.[90] African American leaders were shocked by what they considered a lenient sentence, and demanded the resignation of the presiding superior court judge, Joyce A. Karlin. Their anger had barely enough time to cool when on April 29, 1992, a jury came out with the not guilty verdicts against the four police officers accused of beating Rodney King. It was then that the bubbling cauldron finally exploded.

In light of these multiethnic and structural factors, Chang is particularly critical of the media for continuing to portray the 1992 Los Angeles riot as "an extension of the ongoing conflict between Korean merchants and African American residents. . . ." He argues that interethnic tensions within the African American community had long historical roots, and that Koreans are certainly not the first group to operate stores in black neighborhoods. Prior to the 1965 Watts riot, many of the businesses in the then predominantly African American South Central area were owned by Jews. Many of these Jewish-owned stores were also destroyed during the 1965 Watts riot. After 1965, Chinese, Japanese, and finally Koreans and Latinos became major small business owners in and around South Central Los Angeles. "Although over the years the conflicts in Los Angeles have shifted from one racial group to another, the class-based nature of the struggle has remained consistent," Chang contends. "It is not, therefore, a racial issue, but a class issue involving small businesses and residents."[91] Chang does not deny individual conflict and racial antagonism, but his broader analysis was seldom addressed in the mainstream media. A brief look at black–Korean relations prior to the 1992 Los Angeles uprising shows why it was easy to focus on the more sensationalized individual, racial, and cultural differences that exist between the two groups.

History of Korean–Black Tensions

Beginning in the early 1980s, Asian American-owned businesses began opening in predominantly black neighborhoods in large numbers across the country, and it was not long before isolated incidents of hostility were reported. Although most of the media attention has focused on black–Korean conflicts, one of the first widely reported incidents took place in 1986 when Sarah Carter got into an argument with Cheung Hung Chan, the owner of a Chinese take-out restaurant in the predominantly black Anacostia neighborhood of Washington, DC. The dispute was minor—a mix-up over a food order—but it ended with Chan chasing Carter out of his restaurant while waving a .38-caliber revolver. Carter returned in less than an hour, but this time she came with Rev. Willie Williams and other residents who set up a picket line outside the restaurant, vowing to drive Chan and other Asian American-owned businesses out of the area. Rev. Wilson railed against Asian Americans as "the latest of a series of ethnic groups that have come into our community, disrespected us, raped us economically, and moved out at our expense." The boycott was also a call to residents to "support our own" and pointed to the need for more black-owned businesses in the area. The episode was a prominent news item and seemed to strike a responsive chord in other African American communities as well.[92]

Relations between Korean Americans and African Americans were especially tense in New York throughout the 1980s, where one observer counted at least five organized boycott efforts, each lasting eight weeks or more.[93] By far the most notable and longest boycott effort began in January 1990 in the Flatbush section of Brooklyn, New York. In this case, a scene erupted in the Red Apple Market when customer Ghislaine Felissaint, a Haitian American, said she was grabbed around the neck by a store employee, knocked to the ground, slapped, kicked, and verbally abused. The store employees, however, denied Felissaint's claims and told a very different story. According to their accounts, Felissaint was searching through her purse for an extra dollar to pay for her food, and then became belligerent and disruptive when the cashier began helping another customer. The store manager then came out to try and calm Felissaint down. The manager admitted he put his hands on Felissaint's shoulders as he tried to escort her out. When he did so, Felissaint fell to the ground and refused to move. The police and an ambulance were called to the store and Felissaint demanded that store owner, Bong Jae Jang, be arrested. By this time, an agitated crowd had gathered and the employees quickly closed the store. When one of the employees attempted to leave the store, he was pelted with rocks, bottles, and fruits. The employee ran for safety across the street to the Church Street Fruit and Vegetable Store, which happened to be another Korean American-owned business.[94]

A rally began early the following morning in front of both the Red Apple and the Church Street Fruit and Vegetable stores. The protesters called for a boycott of the two stores and demanded they be closed permanently. The crowd quickly grew larger and more hostile. Protesters shouted at customers as they entered the stores and handed out leaflets with racist rhetoric to passersby; the pregnant wife of one of the store owners reportedly had to undergo a medical abortion after she was attacked by demonstrators.[95] The store owners vowed to stay open and then went to court and obtained a restraining order on May 10, 1990, to keep protesters at least fifty feet away from the business entrances. The New York City Police initially refused to enforce the order, claiming that resentment from the community would create an even greater public safety concern. Tensions from the boycott were by now extremely intense and spreading. On May 13, three Vietnamese American men in Flatbush were attacked by a group of African American youths who allegedly shouted, "Korean Motherfuckers," and "Koreans, what are you doing here?" One of the Vietnamese Americans was in critical condition with a fractured skull after he was beaten with a claw hammer.[96] Finally, on September 17, the New York State appellate court ruled that the police had no discretion in this matter and that they were not entitled to make arbitrary decisions whether or not to obey the county court's authority. As soon as the police began enforcing the court order, thirteen demonstrators were arrested for disorderly conduct. New York Mayor David Dinkins made a highly publicized visit to both stores a few days later, and it was not long before customers began returning to the markets. Calls for continuing the boycott became more and more muted, although they did continue for several more months until one of the storeowners sold to another Korean American.[97]

In Los Angeles, there were tense relations between African American customers and Korean American shopkeepers throughout the 1980s. Unlike New York, lines of communication between African Americans and Korean Americans were kept open thanks to the work of the Los Angeles County Human Relations Commission, which was instrumental in helping to establish the Black–Korean Alliance (BKA) in 1985. All efforts to keep the peace were shattered by the fatal shooting of Latasha Harlins in April 1991. Two months later, a boycott effort began to grow after another African American, Lee Arthur Mitchell, was shot to death by a Korean American during a robbery attempt. The boycott was led by Danny Bakewell and his group, the Brotherhood Crusade. "The basis on which we take issue with Korean Americans . . . is what has been a blatant disregard for African American life as evidenced by some Koreans," said Bakewell.[98] He also complained that Korean American store owners sold inferior goods, suspiciously followed customers around the store, treated customers rudely at the checkout counter, and charged excessively high prices. Bakewell also continued to propagate the commonly held belief that Korean Americans succeed because they received unfair advantages in obtaining bank loans that were unavailable to African Americans.

Korean American merchants responded to Bakewell's charges by saying that they, in fact, were the ones in most danger and pointed to numerous incidents in which the Korean store owners were robbed, assaulted, and killed. In the eighteen months prior to the 1992 L.A. riot, twelve Korean merchants had been killed while working in their stores. "But who cries for these victims?" asked Tae Sam Park, the liquor store owner who shot Mitchell. Park, who suffered three broken ribs in his scuffle with Mitchell during the robbery attempt, added sharply, "I have done nothing other than defend my wife and my business."[99] Korean Americans also argue they are not rude people but are aware that cultural differences may present themselves as rudeness to customers. Polite behavior among Koreans includes maintaining a reserved demeanor, not looking people in the eyes, and placing change on the counter rather than in the customer's hand. In addition, Korean Americans acknowledge that their lack of fluency in English can cause miscommunications and unintentional problems. Most importantly, Korean American merchants do not see themselves as exploiters of the community, but as hardworking immigrants trying to run a small family business. They charge high prices relative to supermarkets, they say, because they cannot buy items in the volume needed to keep prices lower. Finally, there is very little evidence that Korean small business owners receive special treatment from government or corporations to start their stores in low-income neighborhoods. Several studies have mentioned, however, that Korean Americans do save large amounts of capital by borrowing from friends or relatives, which does give them a significant advantage when applying for a government or commercial small business loan (see Chapter 2).

In this environment of violence and mistrust, relations between African Americans and Korean Americans quickly went from bad to worse. Tensions became especially high following the release of the song "Black Korea" by popular rap artist Ice Cube that included incendiary lyrics and a tacit warning to Korean American shop owners: "Pay respect to the Black fist, or we'll burn your store right down to a crisp." The light sentence given to Soon Ja Du for killing Latasha Harlins served only to raise animosities between the two groups to even greater heights. On the afternoon of April 29, 1992, the riot in Los Angeles began. It became immediately clear that Asian American businesses, particularly Korean American businesses, were the targets of much of the mob anger and violence. The Asian Pacific Legal Center, a Los Angeles-based civil rights organization, quickly organized a press conference to denounce the acquittals of four LAPD officers in the Rodney King beating. The press conference included members of the Black–Korean Alliance, who called for citywide unity and downplayed the racial antagonism between the two groups. "I think that's overblown," said Eui-Young Yu, director of the Korean American Studies Center at California State University, Los Angeles.[100]

But on the streets of South Central Los Angeles, a different story was being told. "We went after the Oriental stores. . . . Those were the only ones really burned at first," explained Vernon Leggins, a 35-year-old local resident. "I helped, out of anger, not need. This should have happened a long time ago after they killed that little girl (Harlins) . . . over orange juice." Another local resident, Torrey Payne, added: "They burned the Koreans out because of the way the Korean merchants treated people. . . . That's who they're burning, because of that 15-year-old girl." The looting and destruction, of course, were not limited to African Americans. One Latino was asked why Korean stores were being targeted, and he bluntly stated: "Because we hate 'em. Everybody hates them."[101] Over the course of the next few days, Korean Americans were never so alone, so isolated, and so lost. Not only were they victims of a fury they did not understand, but desperate calls to the police and fire departments to help save their businesses went unheeded. Many began to believe they were being sacrificed while emergency services were directed to protect the more affluent—and predominantly white—parts of the city. "Korean American newcomers must feel utterly betrayed by what they had believed was a democratic system that would protect life, liberty and property," wrote Elaine Kim, professor of Asian American studies at the University of California, Berkeley. Kim gave eloquent voice to what she knew many Korean Americans were feeling in a moving personal editorial published in *Newsweek* shortly after the riot. "The shopkeepers who trusted the government to protect them lost everything. In a sense, they may have finally come to know what my parents knew more than a half century ago: that the American Dream is only an empty promise."[102]

The Aftermath

Days after the riot came an uneasy calm, but residents of South Central Los Angeles began to realize they were unable to get even the most basic of necessities, such as diapers for babies and food for their children. These were items that had been provided by the Korean American-owned stores. People failed to realize that the relative success of Korean merchants was because they filled an empty commercial gap in the community. Ironically, the vast majority of Asian business owners in South Central Los Angeles came to the United States following the passage of the 1965 Immigration Reform Act. It was the black-led civil rights movement that helped create this landmark legislation that directly opened the doors for large numbers of Asian immigrants to enter this country. One of the consequences of the riot is that many in the Korean American community now realize they can no longer survive by isolating themselves from the broader community. "The riots taught us it is not enough to work hard," said Ky Chuoen Kim, an economist and president of the Korean American Management Association. The unexpected result of this realization has been an increase of interest among Korean Americans, especially small business owners, to take organized cultural sensitivity classes.[103]

Although Professor Edward Chang has argued that there are much broader structural concerns that need to be addressed, in the meantime, he agrees that Korean immigrants need to know they are living in a multicultural United States and not monocultural Korea. Indeed, Chang has taught African American and Latino history in the United States in sensitivity seminars. He has also published a book on African American history written in Korean that has been widely read in the United States and in Korea. At the same time, Chang adds, cross-cultural understanding goes both ways. Noting that there are more than 800,000 Korean Americans in the United States today, Chang believes it is imperative that people understand who they are. "In the American context, Asian Americans have always been defined primarily as Chinese and Japanese," he explains. "The [L.A.] riots put Koreans officially on the map. It has since become our task to inform the American public who we are, where we stand, and what is our place."[104]

Through education, many have found important similarities especially between Korean and African Americans. Los Angeles writer Itabari Njeri described how Koreans have faced subjugation under Japanese colonial rule, along with the "day-to-day realities of anti-Asian prejudice," while African Americans not only carry the historic memory of slavery but also the status of "America's most stigmatized minority."[105] Another similarity that many were unaware of was the fact that both Koreans and African Americans are overwhelmingly Christian, and that both are strongly faith-based communities. As a result, many attempts have been made by church leaders to bridge the gaps between the two groups. For example, Kaia Niambi Shivers was selected to represent African American Catholic youth during a two-week trip to Korea in the spring of 1992 as part of a Korean/African American Dialogue program. The visit "altered" her life and she wrote a prize-winning essay about her positive experiences in Korea. "I can admit that I wasn't too fond of Korean Americans in my community," wrote Shivers, a resident of Los Angeles. "I now understand that it was lack of communication and cultural ignorance. Koreans are not mean and nasty, and African Americans are not criminals. It was misunderstanding of both groups that widened the gaps between us."[106] Lastly, Korean American organizations have sponsored programs intended to provide cultural exchange and improve race relations. In 1994, five African American college students were awarded scholarships to attend Yonsei University in Seoul, South Korea. "I'm looking forward to involving myself in the culture," said Angela Rene Crawford, a senior majoring in economics at UC–Berkeley, who stated she plans to create workshops on cultural tolerance in the future. "(T)his is just the beginning of a long, long drive."[107]

These goodwill gestures may be paying dividends as Korean American-owned businesses are slowly returning to South Central Los Angeles. In the past several years, the number of Korean American businesses has been edging close to the pre-1992 level. Not all of the same Korean American merchants have returned, as many are newcomers to the area. Still, there are some that have rebuilt from the ashes. Frank Yim is one example. His store was looted during the riots but he has returned and is making efforts to reach out to customers. He remembers birthdays, weddings, and family funerals of regular patrons by sending flowers and food. Yim correlates improved business with his extra attentiveness. Shopkeepers are also conversing more in Spanish because of the increasing number of Spanish-speaking customers. "My customers appreciate the fact that I speak Spanish to them," said Elizabeth Kim. She and her husband already owned a market in another part of Southern California before starting a new venture in South Central Los Angeles. The major reason why Korean Americans are returning to South Central is the same reason why they arrived initially—property leases and rents are cheaper. For Korean Americans with limited capital who want to start businesses, South Central is still a viable opportunity. The lessons learned from the riots have rubbed off on the Korean American merchants, as well as those who live in the community. According to Joe R. Hicks, executive director of the Los Angeles Human Relations Commission, Korean Americans are doing more to "sink into the community" and residents are more aware that the merchants serve a "vital function" in their lives. He explains that what has been happening in recent years is "one of the better stories of improving human relations that hasn't been told."[108]

CONCLUSION

This chapter describes the serious problem of violence against Asian Americans in the United States. The root causes for these anti-Asian sentiments and violent acts are both structural and individual in nature. At the same time, there are four easily identifiable factors highlighted in this chapter that are lightening rods that serve to exacerbate tensions between Asian Americans and other groups. These four factors are (1) increased anti-immigrant sentiment, (2) economic competition between racial and ethnic groups, (3) "move-in" violence, and (4) poor police–community relations. As seen throughout this chapter, all these factors play an important role in hate-related activities against Asian Americans, and they are frequently interrelated.

On numerous occasions, political and community leaders have spoken out mindlessly—or sometimes even consciously—using overgeneralizations and racially tinged rhetoric to fan the fires of anti-Asian hostility. Those who promote disharmony and racial divisiveness must be challenged, and the public must be educated to think beyond the simplistic statements intended solely to incite and scapegoat. Organizations such as the National Asian Pacific American Legal Consortium have done an excellent job in drawing attention to the problem of anti-Asian violence and helping bring communities together to change the climate of hate, ignorance, and indifference. Unfortunately, if these attitudes are left unchecked for too long, they will only fester and explode in ways that cannot be controlled. This was the case in the

1990 boycott of Korean stores in New York, as well as in the devastating civil unrest in Los Angeles in 1992. Anti-Asian sentiment and hate violence cannot be viewed in isolation; complex issues lay at the root of anti-Asian sentiment. It will take far more effort and political will than is currently being shown by local and national leaders to solve this important social problem.

One of the most unusual examples of anti-Asian violence has not come from the recent slayings of Asian Americans, but from the fatal stabbing of a white man by an Asian American man. At 2 A.M. on July 4, 2000, twin brothers Hung Duc Hong and Minh Duc Hong, along with a friend, went to get some food at a convenience store in Ocean Shores, Washington, a popular tourist location. Outside of the store about ten young white males gathered and began yelling racial slurs and made throat-slashing gestures. The two brothers and their friend believed they would be attacked on their way back to their car and so Minh Hong stole two small knives from the store to protect himself. As the trio walked out of the store, they were met with a barrage of taunts and were spat upon. Hung Hong turned and confronted the apparent leader of the group, Christopher Kinison, who immediately punched Hong in the face. Minh Hong went to help his brother, but was also struck by Kinison. Minh Hong then pulled out a knife and attacked Kinison, stabbing him 22 times including once in the heart. Minh Hong was later arrested and charged with first-degree manslaughter. If convicted, Hong could have faced up to eight years in prison. At Hong's trial the prosecution acknowledged that Kinison's actions were racist and reprehensible, but he didn't deserve to die. Hong's lawyer argued that his client feared for his life and was acting in self-defense. The jury was not allowed to hear evidence of Kinison's prior racist activities, which included taunting a Filipino American couple visiting Ocean Shores. The Asian Bar Association of Washington State, the Japanese American Citizen's League, and the Organization of Chinese Americans closely followed the case to highlight the recent rise in anti-Asian violence. Also following the case was David Jensen, president of the National Organization for European American Rights (NOFEAR), who wanted Hong prosecuted for a hate crime against a white person. "Our organization has been very concerned about hate crimes and whether it has been properly recognized," Jensen said.[109] On December 13, 2000, an all-white jury of six men and six women declared they were hopelessly deadlocked and could not come to a decision after two days of deliberation. Superior Court Judge David Foscue declared a mistrial in this highly charged case and Minh Hong was released from jail pending a decision by the district attorney's office to pursue a retrial.[110] The case was retried but a jury eventually acquitted Hong, finding he acted in self-defense. A book that provides depth and detail on this incident has been published, titled *Death on the Fourth of July* (2004), by journalist David Neiwert.[111]

What makes the Hong case even more striking is its similarity to a case in Wisconsin involving a Hmong American man who, in this case, was convicted of six counts of first degree murder. The incident took place in November 2004 when Chai Vang was on a deer hunting trip. Vang claimed he was lost when another hunter told him he was on private property and had to leave.

Vang said he began walking away when the hunter called on his walkie-talkie for other hunters to join him. When a group of five or six hunters arrived, they began threatening Vang with racial taunts like "Chink" and "Gook." According to Vang's account, one of the hunters shot at him as he was trying to leave the confrontation. What happened after that became a chaotic melee in which Vang, a U.S. Army veteran, shot and killed six men and wounded another two. Some of the men who were shot were unarmed and at least one was shot in the back. When asked why he kept shooting after the hunters scattered and ran, Vang said he thought they would get guns and come after him. Survivors of the shooting spree testified that the attack was unprovoked and that Vang fired first.[112]

Conflicts between white hunters and Hmong American hunters were not uncommon in the area, and many blame Hmong Americans for ignoring the local customs and laws of hunting. The tragic incident created tremendous polarization throughout the state even after Vang's conviction. Many of those who consider themselves true hunters see the Hmong Americans only as outsiders who don't know their place. "If Vang had not trespassed, none of this would have happened," wrote Nathan Weber in a letter to the *Wisconsin State Journal.* "Stick together, hunters—we can save our sport. Now that justice has been served, let it rest." Another hunter contended that the victims were in the right to harass Vang when he was caught trespassing. "Deer hunting land becomes somehow sacred, and only people who have been out there know," wrote Don Ward. "The whole thing could have been avoided if the simple rules of hunting had been observed."[113] These tensions are representative of the broader marginalization felt by many Hmong Americans who are newcomers to the area and have never felt welcomed despite the fact their population has increased dramatically over the past decade. In 1990, Wisconsin was home for just over 16,000 Hmong Americans. By 2000, that number more than doubled to almost 37,000. Other letters to the *Wisconsin State Journal* were sympathetic to the plight of the Hmong Americans in the state. "I'm not surprised by the verdict in Chai Vang's trial in the deaths of six hunters in northern Wisconsin. I'm not surprised, either, that the incident took place," wrote Tammy Bieberstein. "I've witnessed the harassment of and prejudice toward Hmong people in northern Wisconsin. The ignorance of my fellow human beings breaks my heart sometimes. I can imagine the fear Vang felt when he was surrounded by a mob of angry white people who were threatening him with derogatory names, in a land where most of the white people are ignorant of why the Hmong are here in the first place." A letter by Irving Chung directly challenged the antagonism faced by many Hmong Americans: "It is likely that Vang has dealt with racial prejudice for much of his life. That day he was provoked by an angry group of eight white, gun-toting hunters who surrounded him, screamed racial slurs and made threatening gestures to do physical harm. This may have forced him to react the way he did. Had he not reacted in self-defense, would he have been badly beaten or even killed? Or were these just idle threats that minorities are expected to tolerate and ignore?"[114]

NOTES

1. Ebens's conviction was overturned by the Sixth Circuit Court of Appeals in September 1986. A new trial was ordered in part because of prosecutorial misconduct. Evidence of prosecutorial misconduct included references by the prosecutor to impermissible hearsay statements in the closing argument. A new trial was also ordered because critical evidence had not been admitted at the trial court. The critical evidence included tapes of the main witnesses being questioned and potentially coached in their responses. See *United States v. Ronald Ebens* 800 F.2d.1422 (1986 6th Cir.).
2. In October 2005, the National Asian Pacific American Legal Consortium changed their name to the Asian American Justice Center. Their new Web site is www.advancingequality.org. However, at the time of this writing the www.napalc.org Web site used throughout this book is still functional.
3. National Asian Pacific American Legal Consortium, *2001 Audit of Violence Against Asian Pacific Americans*, p. 17 at http://www.napalc.org/files/2001_Audit.pdf.
4. Quoted in National Asian Pacific American Legal Consortium, "2002 Audit of Violence Against Asian Pacific Americans Released," *Press Release*, May 28, 2004, and National Asian Pacific American Legal Consortium, *2002 Audit of Violence Against Asian Pacific Americans*, pp. 2–3, see http://www.napalc.org/files/2002_Audit.pdf.
5. Council of Islamic American Relations (CAIR), *The Status of Muslim Civil Rights in the United States, 2002 Executive Summary*, see http://www.cair-net.org/asp/execsum2001.asp and Federal Bureau of Investigation, *Uniform Crime Report*, 2002, see http://www.fbi.gov/ucr/hatecrime2002.pdf.
6. National Asian Pacific American Legal Consortium, *2002 Audit of Violence Against Asian Pacific Americans*, pp. 6–7 at http://www.napalc.org/files/2002_Audit.pdf.
7. See song lyrics at http://www.asianmediawatch.net/missjones/.
8. Quotes in Emil Guillermo, "Condemning the Devil in Jones," *AsianWeek*, February 3, 2005.
9. Quote in "Radio Show's Staff Pulled Over Tsunami Parody Song," *San Francisco Chronicle*, January 27, 2005.
10. Sam Chu Lin, "Parcells Apologizes for 'Jap Remark,'" *AsianWeek*, June 10, 2004.
11. Japanese American Citizen's League, "JACL Bitterly Disappointed and Deeply Offended by Parcells' Use of 'Jap' and 'Orientals,' *Press Release*, June 8, 2004 at http://www.jacl.org/current_prs/040608.html.
12. Emil Guillermo, "Slur Away, Parcells," *AsianWeek*, June 17, 2004.
13. Lane Hirabayashi, "How a Death Threat Became an Opportunity to Connect With My Students," *Chronicle of Higher Education*, May 12, 2000, p. B10.
14. *Ibid.*
15. Sam Stanton and Gary Delsohn, "Violent Ideology Spred on Web," *Sacramento Bee*, June 11, 2000.
16. Eric Bailey and Eric Slater, "'Racial' Shooting Rampage Kills Five," *Sacramento Bee*, April 29, 2000.
17. Federal Bureau of Investigation, *2002 Crimes in the United States*, p. 9, see http://www.fbi.gov/ucr/02cius.htm.
18. National Asian Pacific American Legal Consortium, *1993 Audit of Violence Against Asian Pacific Americans*, p. 16.
19. National Asian Pacific American Legal Consortium, *2002 Audit of Violence Against Asian Pacific Americans*, p. 3.
20. Quoted in "Deaf Killer's Fate Rests on Mental Health," *Los Angeles Times*, September 21, 2003.
21. Quoted in "A Knife Honed by Hate?" *Los Angeles Times*, August 1, 2001.
22. Quoted in "Man in Racial Killing Ruled Insane, *Los Angeles Times*, September 26, 2003.
23. See Jason Kosareff, "Chu Bill Aims to Protect Victims," *San Gabriel Valley Tribune*, May 21, 2004, and Assembly Member Judy Chu, " 'Kenny's Law Signed by Governor Schwarzenegger; New Law Will Provide Additional Rights for Hate Crime Victims," Press Release, September 29, 2004.
24. Federal Bureau of Investigation, *2002 Crimes in the United States*, p. 5, see http://www.fbi.gov/ucr/02cius.htm.
25. Quoted in Eric Lichtblau, "Racial Writings Linked to Rampage," *Los Angeles Times*, April 30, 2000, and "Writings May Indicate Hate Motive in Spree," *Seattle Times*, April 30, 2000.
26. Quoted in Janet Kornblum, " 'Rational Rantings Return After Rampage," *U.S.A. Today*, May 4, 2000.

27. National Asian Pacific American Legal Consortium, "Civil Rights Groups Horrified by Another Wave of Hate Crimes Against Asian Pacific Americans in Pittsburgh," *Press Release,* May 2, 2000.

28. Jim McKinnon, "Death for Baumhammers: Jury Verdict Brings Tears and Cheers," *Pittsburgh Post-Gazette,* May 12, 2001.

29. Quoted in Carmen J. Lee, "Bethel Rally Puts Hatred on Hit List," *Pittsburgh Post-Gazette,* August 13, 2001.

30. Quoted in Jim McKinnon "Baumhammers To Be Sentenced: Judge to Affirm Jury's May Decree of Death," *Pittsburgh Post-Gazette,* September 6, 2001.

31. Matt Lait and Norma Zamichow, "Valley Shooting Suspect Surrenders, Confesses," *Los Angeles Times,* August 12, 1999.

32. "Racist Leader Credits Furrow as Mourners Gather," *Oakland Tribune,* August 15, 1999.

33. Stephen Braun and John Beckham, "On Hate-Filled Web Sites, 'Wake-Up' Call Gets a Volatile, Divided Reaction," *Los Angeles Times,* August 15, 1999.

34. "Furrow Spared by His Mental Illness," *Los Angeles Times,* January 25, 2001.

35. Quoted in "Furrow Gets 5 Life Terms for Racial Rampage," *Los Angeles Times,* March 27, 2001.

36. National Asian Pacific American Legal Consortium, *2002 Audit of Violence Against Asian Pacific Americans,* pp. 35–36.

37. Ed Walsh, "Racial Slayer Killed Himself in Struggle," *Washington Post,* July 6, 1999, and Ed Walsh, "Midwest Gun Spree Suspect Is Dead; Man Shot Himself, Pursuing Police Say," *Washington Post,* July 5, 1999.

38. Eric Slater and John Beckham, "Shooter Cultivated His Racist Views in College," *Los Angeles Times,* July 6, 1999.

39. See http://www.indiana.edu/~global/yoonscholarship.htm.

40. Rami Chami, "Indiana U. Students, Community Responds to Hate Crimes," *Indi-ana Daily Student,* July 11, 2005.

41. National Asian Pacific American Legal Consortium, *2001 Audit of Violence Against Asian Pacific Americans;* American Civil Liberties Union of Northern California, *Caught in the Backlash: Stories from Northern California* (San Francisco, CA, 2002) at http://www.aclunc.org/911/backlash .pdf; Human Rights Watch, *We Are Not the Enemy* (Washington, DC, 2002) at http://www .hrw.org/reports/2002/usahate/ usa1102.pdf; and Russell C. Leong and Don T. Nakanishi, *Asian Americans On War & Peace* (Los Angeles, CA: UCLA Asian American Studies Center Press, 2002).

42. Alan Cooperman, "Sept. 11 Backlash Murders and the State of Hate," *Washington Post,* January 20, 2002.

43. Larry Stammer, "Turbans Make Sikhs Easy Targets," *Los Angeles Times,* September 20, 2001, and Jo Becker and Phuong Ly, "Sikhs Campaign Against Hate," *Washington Post,* September 24, 2001.

44. Quotes in Sandy Yang, "Man Sentenced to Death for Killing Sikh Immigrant," *Associated Press,* October 10, 2003, and Julian Borger, "September 11 Revenge Killer to Die for Shooting Sikh," *The Guardian,* October 11, 2003.

45. Tamer El-Ghobashi, "Sikh Files Suit vs. 5 in Bias Attack," *New York Daily News,* July 13, 2005. More information about this case and other bias-related incidents against Sikh Americans since 9/11 at http://www.sikhcoalition.org/.

46. National Asian Pacific American Legal Consortium, *1995 Audit of Violence Against Asian Pacific Americans,* p. 32 at http://www.advancingequality.org/dcm.asp? id=50; and Torri Minton, "Quiet Marin Confronts Hate Crimes," *San Francisco Chronicle,* November 29, 1995.

47. U.S. Commission on Civil Rights, *Civil Rights Issues Facing Asian Americans in the 1990s,* pp. 18–24.

48. Quoted in Lynne Duke, "Panel Links Japan-Bashing, Violence," *Washington Post,* February 29, 1992.

49. Walter Schapiro, "Japan Bashing on the Campaign Trail," *Time,* February 10, 1992, pp. 23–24.

50. Robert Reinhold, "Buying American Is No Cure-All, U.S. Economists Say," *New York Times,* January 27, 1992; "The Push to 'Buy American,'" *Newsweek,* February 3, 1992, pp. 32–35; Lance Morrow, "Japan in the Mind of America," *Time,* February 10, 1992, pp. 17–21; and Carl Nolte, "Racism Charge Over Mariners Sale," *San Francisco Chronicle,* February 7, 1992.

51. Robert B. Reich, *The Work of Nations* (New York: Alfred A. Knopf, 1991); and James M. Fallows, *More Like Us: Making America Great Again* (Boston: Houghton Mifflin, 1989).

52. Quoted in Sam Fulwood III, "Japan-Bashing Condemned by Rights Panel," *Los Angeles Times,* February 29, 1992.

53. Quoted in Richard Oliver, "Spencer Slams Toyota Entry; Veteran Driver Uses Pearl Harbor Reference In His Remarks," *San Antonio Express-News,* January 29, 2004.
54. Scott Rabalais, "Toyota Takes On American Sport," *State-Times/Morning Advocate* (Baton Rouge, Louisiana), February 14, 2004.
55. Quoted in Lindsey Young, "NASCAR Stirred by Toyota's Entry," *Chattanooga Times Free Press,* February 13, 2004.
56. See Frank Wu, "China: The New Scapegoat," *AsianWeek,* May 6, 1999, and Helen Zia, "I Am Not a Spy—Are You?," *AsianWeek,* June 10, 1999.
57. Richard Bernstein and Ross H. Munro, *The Coming Conflict With China* (New York: Vintage Books, 1998), and David Ignatius, *A Firing Offense* (New York: Random House, 1998).
58. Evelyn Iritani, "China Showing Bigger Interest in U.S.," *Los Angeles Times,* June 22, 2005.
59. David R. Baker, "China Walks Away." *San Francisco Chronicle.* August 3, 2005.
60. Brian Bremmer and Kathleen Kerwin, "Here Come Chinese Cars," *BusinessWeek,* June 6, 2005.
61. Jason Ma, "Hate 'Was There All The Time,'" *AsianWeek,* November 11, 1999, p. 8.
62. Transcripts from the program can be found at http://www.asianmediawatch.net/ jerseyguys/.
63. David Porter, "Asian American Groups Call for Boycott over 'Bigoted' Remarks," *Associated Press,* April 28, 2005.
64. Quoted in "Radio Hosts Apologize for Remarks about Asian American Candidate," *Associated Press,*" May 26, 2005.
65. Timothy P. Fong, *The First Suburban Chinatown: The Remaking of Monterey Park, California* (Philadelphia: Temple University Press, 1994).
66. Quoted in Steven A. Chin, "Asians Terrorized in Housing Projects," *San Francisco Chronicle,* January 17, 1993.
67. National Asian Pacific American Legal Consortium, *1993 Audit of Violence Against Asian Pacific Americans,* pp. 10–11; Chin, "Asians Terrorized," January 17, 1993.
68. See Eric Brazil, "SF Housing Agency Settles Asian Bias Suit," *San Francisco Examiner,* July 19, 1999; Yumi Wilson, "Consent Decree Ends Asians' Housing Bias," *San Francisco Chronicle,* July 19, 1999; and Janet Dang, "Asian Law Caucus Settles Housing Suit," *AsianWeek,* July 22, 1999.
69. "Rohnert Park Man Fatally Shot by Cops," *San Francisco Chronicle,* April 30, 1997, and Julie Chao, "Outrage at Killing by Cop in North Bay," *San Francisco Examiner,* May 21, 1997.
70. Quoted in Bert Eljera, "Police Clear Officer in Kao Shooting," *AsianWeek,* August 15, 1997.
71. Quoted in Julie Chao, "Asian Man's Shooting by Police Spurs Three Probes," *San Francisco Examiner,* May 21, 1997.
72. Emelyn Cruz Lat, "Widow Files Lawsuit in Rohnert Park Death," *San Francisco Examiner,* February 3, 1998.
73. Ryan Kim, "$1 Million Settlement in Slaying by Rohnert Park Police," *San Francisco Chronicle,* August 16, 2001.
74. California Advisory Committee for the United States Commission on Civil Rights, "Community Concerns About Law Enforcement in Sonoma County" (December 1999), p. 54. See the full report at http://www.pressdemo.com/evergreen/review/commission.html.
75. See Henri E. Cauvin and Bill Hutchinson, "Disappointed Louima Hopes His Case Will Change System," *New York Daily News,* June 9, 1999, and William K. Rashbaum, "Marchers Protest Diallo Verdict, Taunting Police Along the Way," *New York Times,* February 26, 2000.
76. Tomio Geron, "APA Activism, New York Style," *AsianWeek,* April 5, 1996.
77. Quoted in Heather Harlin, "NYC Prosecutor Drops Charges Against Cop," *AsianWeek,* September 10, 1998.
78. Quoted in Heather Harlin, "Storeowners Sue NYPD Over Arrest," *AsianWeek,* June 4, 1998.
79. Tomio Geron, "N.Y.P.D. Settles APA Complaints," *AsianWeek,* March 1, 1996.
80. National Asian Pacific American Legal Consortium, *2002 Audit of Violence Against Asian Pacific Americans,* p. 4.
81. Truong Phuoc Khanh, "In Shooting, Probes to Deal in the Details," *San Jose Mercury News,* July 27, 2003.
82. Alan Gathright, Vietnamese Community Rallies," *San Francisco Chronicle,* July 17, 2003.
83. Quoted in Rodney Foo, "Vietnamese Find Unity, Voice in Wake of Fatal S.J. Shooting, *San Jose Mercury News,* July 12, 2004.
84. *Ibid.*
85. National Asian Pacific American Legal Consortium, *1998 Audit of Violence Against Asian Pacific Americans,* pp. 19–22.
86. Edward T. Chang, "America's First Multiethnic 'Riots,'" in Karin Aguilar-San Juan (ed.), *The State of Asian America: Activism and Resistance* (Boston: South End Press, 1994), pp. 101–118.

87. For more details see Robert Gooding-Williams, ed., *Reading Rodney King: Reading Urban Uprising* (New York: Routledge, 1993);. Nancy Abelmann and John Lie, *Blue Dreams: Korean Americans and the Los Angeles Riots* (Cambridge, MA: Harvard University Press, 1995); Elaine H. Kim and Eui-young Yu, *East to America: Korean-American Life Stories* (New York: New Press, 1996); Edward T. Chang and Jeannette Diaz-Veizades, *Ethnic Peace in the American City: Building Community in Los Angeles and Beyond* (New York: New York University Press, 1999).

88. Chang, "America's First Multiethnic 'Riots,'" pp. 108–109. Also see Edward T. Chang, "New Urban Crisis: Intra-Third World Conflict," in Shirley Hune et al. (eds.), *Comparative and Global Perspectives* (Pullman, WA: Washington State University Press, 1991), pp. 169–178.

89. Quoted in "How Los Angeles Reached the Crisis Point Again, Chapter 5," a *Los Angeles Times* special report, May 11, 1992, p. T10.

90. For details on the shooting and profiles on Latasha Harlins and Soon Ja Du, see Jesse Katz and John H. Lee, "Conflict Brings Tragic End to Similar Dreams of Life," *Los Angeles Times*, April 8, 1991. For an excellent analysis of the sentence given to Du, see Neil Gotanda, "Re-Producing the Model Minority Stereotype: Judge Joyce Karlin's Sentencing Colloquy in *People v. Soon Ja Du*," in Wendy L. Ng et al. (eds.), *Reviewing Asian America: Locating Diversity* (Pullman, WA: Washington State University Press, 1995), pp. 87–106.

91. Chang, "America's First Multiethnic 'Riots,'" pp. 110–111.

92. Karl Zinsmeister, "Asians and Blacks: Bittersweet Success," *Current*, February 1988, pp. 9–15; quoted in Susanna McBee, "Asian Merchants Find Ghettos Full of Peril," *U.S. News and World Report*, November 24, 1986.

93. Pyong Gap Min, "Problems of Korean Immigrant Entrepreneurs," *International Migration Review* 24 (1990): 436–455.

94. U.S. Commission on Civil Rights, *Civil Rights Issues Facing Asian Americans*, pp. 34–40.

95. Pete Hamill, "New Race Hustle," *Esquire*, September 1990, pp. 77–80 and *Ibid.*, p. 36.

96. Hamill, "New Race Hustle," p. 77, and Robert D. McFadden, "Blacks Attack Vietnamese; One Hurt Badly," *New York Times*, May 14, 1990.

97. U.S. Commission on Civil Rights, *Civil Rights Issues Facing Asian Americans*, p. 39; Pyong Gap Min, "Cultural and Economic Boundaries of Korean Ethnicity: A Comparative Analysis," *Ethnic and Racial Studies* 14 (1991): 225–241.

98. Quoted in Solomon J. Herbert, "Why African-Americans Vented Anger at the Korean Community During the LA Riots," *Crisis*, August–September, 1992, pp. 5, 38.

99. Quoted in Rick Holguin and John Lee, "Boycott of Store Where Man Was Killed Is Urged," *Los Angeles Times*, June 18, 1991.

100. Quoted in Lisa Pope, "Asian American Businesses Targeted," *Los Angeles Daily News*, May 1, 1992.

101. Quoted in *Ibid.*, and in Sumi Cho, "Conflict and Construction," in Robert Gooding-Williams (ed.), *Reading Rodney King: Reading Urban Uprising* (New York and London: Routledge, 1993), p. 199.

102. Kim, "They Armed in Self-Defense," *Newsweek*, May 18, 1992.

103. Quoted in K. Connie Kang, "No Longer 'Work, Work, Work,'" *Los Angeles Times*, October 22, 1994.

104. Quoted in Daniel B. Wood, "As Korean Americans Become Visible, They Seek Understanding," *Christian Science Monitor*, July 27, 1993.

105. Itabari Njeri, "Power Elite Turns Out a Bitter Brew," *Los Angeles Times*, November 29, 1991.

106. Quoted in Wood, "As Korean Americans Become Visible" (1993).

107. Quoted in Elisa Lee, "Martin Luther King, Jr. Scholarship Recipients Depart for Seoul," *AsianWeek*, June 17, 1994.

108. Quoted in K. Connie Kang, "Korean Americans Return to District Torn By Riots," *Los Angeles Times*, April 29, 2000.

109. "Was Stabbing a Racist Attack or Merely Self-Defense?" *Seattle Post-Intelligencer*, December 13, 2000.

110. "Hung Jury in Ocean Shores Stabbing," *Seattle Post-Intelligencer*, December 14, 2000.

111. See David Neiwert, *Death on the Fourth of July* (New York: Palgrave McMillian, 2004).

112. Lisa Schuetz, "Accused Killer: Victim Shot First," *Wisconsin State Journal*, November 24, 2004; Tom Kenworthy, "Wis. Suspect Says He Was Taunted," *USA Today*, November 24, 2005; and Larry Oaks, "Vang Tells of Confrontation in the Woods," *Star Tribune* (Minneapolis, Minnesota), June 10, 2005.

113. Quoted in "After the Guilty Verdict," *Wisconsin State Journal*, Spectrum Section, September 22, 2005.

114. Quoted in "Asian Americans: Be Assertive," *Wisconsin State Journal*, Opinion Section, September 20, 2005.

6

Charlie Chan No More:
Asian Americans and
Media Images

VISIBILITY AND INVISIBILITY

The door of opportunity is beginning to break open for Asian Americans in the mainstream media and they are gathering a wider and more appreciative audience. Among the best known major market "cross-over" breakthroughs include George Takei's portrayal of Lt. Sulu on the original *Star Trek* television series (1966–1969) and Bruce Lee's kung fu classic *Enter the Dragon* (1972), along with Maxine Hong Kingston's novel *Woman Warrior* (1976). Amy Tam's novel *Joy Luck Club* (1989) was later produced as a major motion picture (1993) and B. D. Wong's Tony award-winning performance in the Broadway play *M. Butterfly* (1988) also served to open the door for Asian Americans in the media. Other well-known examples include Margret Cho's short-lived television sitcom *All-American Girl* (1994), Lucy Liu's regular television role on *Ally McBeal* (1997–2002), and Ming-Na's (aka Ming-Na Wen) major roles on *ER* (1994–2004) and *Inconceivable* (2005). There is the pioneering work of Anna May Wong, Sessue Hayakawa, and James Shigeta in major Hollywood motion pictures, and there are the contemporary U.S.-made films featuring Jackie Chan, Jet Li, and Chow Yun-Fat. In addition, there are some lesser-known films with Asian Americans in lead roles such as *Better Luck Tomorrow* (2003) and *Harold and Kumar Go to White Castle* (2004).

Today's images of Asian Americans in popular culture have improved and provide more breadth than in the past. This is a contrast from earlier days when popular images of Asians and Asian Americans were predominantly mediated by non-Asian studio executives and writers. The earlier characterizations were often quite negative and demeaning. Unfortunately, some of these images are still perpetuated today. Asian American media watchers and critics continue to complain about racist stereotypes that emerge in popular culture. Several Asian American organizations recently expressed outrage at the Internet entertainment site Icebox.com for its promotion of the cartoon series *Mr. Wong,* which premiered in 2001. The cartoon features an aged and buck-toothed Chinese "houseboy" who serves a wealthy white socialite, Ms. Pam. Along with episodes of *Mr. Wong* on Icebox.com, there are comments from viewers, the vast majority of which crudely chastise those who complained that the cartoon is racist. "All you Chinese Americans mellow out," wrote DonDon (1/19/01). "This is true art and Wong is no offence [sic] to anyone. Just because you have dirty little secrets doesn't mean you have to spoil it for everyone." Another writer, Your Mother (1/18/01), wrote: "People who like to curtail free speech scare me. . . . I thought we taught them a lesson in 1945, but it seems the viewpoint must always continue." Another commentator was similarly direct. "If you don't like Mr. Wong then don't watch it you dumb ass!" wrote T-Man (1/18/01). "Your [sic] the idiot that gets on the web and spends 5 minutes watching a cartoon you hate. Mr. Wong is a humorous (sometimes sick) cartoon that makes people (including myself) laugh."[1]

In February 2004, the *National Lampoon* and Maverick Entertainment released a DVD compilation of *Mr. Wong* cartoons. It is no coincidence that the renewed interest in *Mr. Wong* immediately followed the humiliating January 27, 2004, appearance by William Hung, the 21-year-old engineering student from UC–Berkeley who sang the Ricky Martin song, "She Bangs," to a national audience on the television program *American Idol.* Hung got only as far as the first chorus before the judge Simon Cowell ordered him to stop. "You can't sing, you can't dance, so what do you want me to say?" asked Cowell in disgust. The Hong Kong-born Hung, who looks and sounds like a younger version of Mr. Wong, replied in all sincerity that he tried his best despite no professional training and had "no regrets at all." Perhaps it was his grace in the face of ugly rejection that captured attention, but Hung immediately became a most unusual comic pop star. Hung was featured in numerous television talk shows, news programs, commercials, music videos, and print articles; he has his own fan Web site, has given concerts across the United States and Asia, and has released three CDs. Hung's first CD, *Inspiration,* sold more than 3,000 its first day and has since sold tens of thousands more.[2]

Many Asian Americans took the Hung phenomenon lightly, assuming his novelty act would fade out rather quickly. However, Hung has persisted much to the chagrin of many observers who saw him as negative racialized caricature of Asian American males propagated by the mass media similar to Mr. Wong. "Asian Pacific Americans have been so quiet on William Hung's rise to fame, it's puzzling," wrote *AsianWeek* columnist Emil Guillermo. "Or is the community really blinded by the infantilization of the APA male in our pop culture, looking the other way because, after all, Hung appears to be successful. . . . Perfect for a white mainstream culture."[3] Asian American men, in particular, and especially those involved in acting and the music industry, were appalled by Hung's accidental success. "I am disgusted at what is going on," wrote struggling Asian American actor Dennis Takeda. "The entertainment industry is still using this stereotype of the Asian American male for their pocketbooks, and William is perpetuating it." He added, "I guess if we want to work in this industry, we should have ourselves made over like him!"[4] While these comments may come off as sour grapes, one needs only look at Harlemm Lee, who won the national television talent show *FAME* in summer 2003, only to fall into instant obscurity. As the winner of the summer-long competition, Lee received a management deal from a top music manager, one year of training at the Debbie Allen Dance Academy, and free accommodations at the W Hotel in Los Angeles for one year to help him launch his career. Lee's story could not be more different than William Hung's. Lee struggled for years to break into the music industry, and he was 35 when he finally got his break winning the *FAME* talent contest, besting much younger competition on the show. His shaved head, alto soprano voice, and high-energy dancing made him appear at least ten years younger; neither his real age nor ethnicity seemed to matter to the prime-time audience who week after week voted for him as the most talented performer.

Lee released a CD titled *Introducing Harlemm Lee* in November 2003, but despite positive reviews the CD sold just five hundred copies and was pulled from the shelves because of low sales. In June 2004, Lee posted a message on his Web site thanking his fans for their support, but admitted he was "disappointed" at how things have turned out since *FAME*. "I have been completely invisible since winning *FAME*, and unable to capitalize from all my hard work and national exposure gained from the show," Lee wrote. "If it weren't for my unemployment checks and my year-long stay at the W Hotel, I would be completely penniless and homeless." Lee stated that he was denied the most basic promotion and marketing resources, and the justification given to him was that his story was not "compelling enough." He added, "without their machinery behind you, you will definitely not be seen nor heard."[5] Lee's experience comes as no surprise to Chi-hui Yang, director of the San Francisco International Asian American Film Festival. According to Yang, William Hung became popular precisely because he was seen as a comical figure with no talent who sings with a thick accent: "What informs that kind of humor is something that is deeply rooted in the American depiction of Asian men as ineffective, effeminate or wimpy, and I think William Hung fits right into it. On the other hand, someone like Harlemm who is talented hasn't gone very far. It feeds back into the people with the marketing dollars and knowing what the American public wants to see or what is familiar."[6]

This chapter focuses on how dominant media images have impacted how others see Asian Americans and how Asian Americans see themselves. Particular emphasis in this chapter will be on film, television, and theater. In addition, this chapter examines the relatively recent influx of Asian and Asian American professional athletes and its impact on popular culture. Although there has been a great surge of important and highly acclaimed literary works written by Asian Americans, it is far beyond the scope of this chapter to cover this area. This chapter first provides an overview of popular images of Asians and Asian

Americans in motion pictures, highlighting important gender differences, how they've changed over time, and how they emerged again in the heavily protested film premiere of *Rising Sun* (1993). This section also examines two high-profile feature films, *Better Luck Tomorrow* (2003) and *Harold and Kumar Go to White Castle* (2004), to discuss the future of Asian Americans on the big screen. Next, this chapter looks at Asian Americans on television with emphasis on dominant Asian American characters in recent shows. Third, this chapter details the controversies generated by two major theater productions, *M. Butterfly* (1988) and *Miss Saigon* (1990), in their long-term impact on theatrical casting and production leading to the updated revival of the stage musical *Flower Drum Song* (2002). Lastly, in recognition that sports is a major part of both the television and print media, this chapter examines the recent surge in Asian Americans in sports and the media attention it has garnered.

HISTORY OF ASIAN AMERICANS IN MOTION PICTURES

The depictions of Asians and Asian Americans in motion pictures can be categorized in two general ways. The first focuses on Hollywood films that include roles for Asian Americans. Most of these films do not explore Asian American themes but rather are highly influenced by dominant society's image of Asian Americans here in the United States and Asians abroad, most of which have been negative. The second category focuses on films that are written, produced, and/or directed by Asian Americans. These films include documentaries and independent feature films often, but not exclusively, about the Asian American experience. Most of these films are in English. While I do not focus on foreign films from Asia, it is important to mention them because many of the most prominent Asian actors and directors working in Hollywood today reached international acclaim through their work in Asian films. This section does not judge Asian Americans in motion pictures exclusively in terms of "positive" versus "negative" portrayals; instead the intention is to provide a critical examination of the historical and social trends with an understanding of how and why certain images are perpetuated and others are not. Attention is also given to the diverse perspectives and identity formations that make up the ever-changing Asian American experience that, in turn, creates broader social change.

Negative images of Asians in mainstream Hollywood motion pictures can easily be traced back to the mid- to late 1800s when Asian migrants first arrived in large numbers in the United States. The common theme was of the "Yellow Peril," or an invasion of faceless and destructive Asiatics, who would eventually overtake the nation and wreak social and economic havoc. There are a number of recent books focusing on Asian Americans in motion pictures including Russell Leong (ed.), *Moving the Image: Independent Asian Pacific American Media Arts* (1991); Robert G. Lee, *Orientals: Asian Americans in Popular Culture* (1999); Gina Marchetti, *Romance and the "Yellow Peril"* (1993); Jun Xing, *Asian America Through the Lens* (1998); Darrell Hamamoto and Sandra Liu (eds.), *Countervisions: Asian American Film Criticism* (2000); and Peter Feng, *Identities in Motion: Asian American Film & Video* (2002). All argue that Hollywood films are not merely harmless entertainment, but are reflective of race, class, and gender ideologies and pressing social and political concerns."[7] Edward Said's seminal book *Orientalism* (1978) examines how the West (Occidental) views itself has traditionally and fundamentally based on its own disapproving images, descriptions, and attitudes of the East or the "other" (Oriental).[8] Thus, the dominant ideology of Western superiority versus Eastern inferiority eventually led to the passage of the 1882 Chinese Exclusion Law, as well as a multitude of other anti-Asian legislation. Among the most powerful anti-Chinese statements during this period is writer Bret Harte's poem, "The Heathen Chinee," published in 1870. The immensely popular poem was reprinted across the country. In the poem, Harte describes a "peculiar" Chinese character, Ah Sin, who is wily and sly, but gets caught cheating at a card game. Ah Sin is then attacked and beaten by his white competitor, who yells, "We are ruined by Chinese cheap labour."[9] Similarly, Atwell Whitney's novel *Almond Eyed* (1878) depicts hoards of Chinese immigrants polluting the environment, degrading American labor, debasing white women, and destroying American society. These types of images continued with the advent of silent films such as *Tsing Fu, the Yellow Devil* (1910), where the sinister Chinese wizard plots revenge against a white woman who rejects his lecherous intentions. The rise of Japan as a military and industrial power following the 1905 Russo-Japanese War was the inspiration for *The Japanese Investigation* (1909), which prominently featured the threat of U.S. involvement in an Asiatic war.[10] The theme of the "Orientals" being the "other" was a consistent theme in Hollywood films for decades.

The 1920s and 1930s saw a series of movies that provided highly stereotypical images of "good" and "bad" Asian characters. The personification of evil was seen in the infamous Fu Manchu movies. Fu Manchu was the world-threatening villain originally created in a 1911 short story by British author Sax Rohmer, but this character was soon found in novels, heard on radio programs, and eventually seen on the big screen. Fu Manchu served only to enhance the most negative images of Asians and the Yellow Peril. On one hand, he possessed superhuman intellect and ambition, and on the other, he was subhuman in his immorality and ruthlessness. Contrasting Fu Manchu is the benign and non-threatening character, Charlie Chan, the cherubic and inscrutable Chinese American detective from Honolulu. Charlie Chan began as a series of novels by Earl Derr Biggers and quickly made it into the movie houses. Nearly fifty Charlie Chan movies were released between 1926 and 1949. Chan was a super-sleuth who solved complex murders while reciting phony "Confucius say" proverbs, such as "Bad alibi like dead fish; can't stand the test of time."[11] These popular Asian characters were not only created by white writers and producers, whites usually portrayed the Asian characters as well. All the actors in the early Fu Manchu movies were whites grotesquely made up to look Asian. The first two Charlie Chan movies had Japanese American actors in the lead role, but as the films gained popularity the actors were replaced by white actors who colored their hair jet black and used scotch tape to alter the shape of their eyes. Ironically, Charlie Chan frequently worked with his bumbling number one and number two sons, both of whom were always played by Asian American actors.

Asian and Asian American roles were quite rare in Hollywood, but when one did come up, it was often "scotch tape Asian" actors who got the parts. Paul Muni and Louise Rainer, both Austrian Jews, played the lead roles in the epic *The Good Earth* (1942), the film adaptation of Pearl Buck's classic novel about heroic Chinese peasants. Some rather well-known actors were also given the opportunity to play roles that were simply not available to Asian Americans. For example, Katherine Hepburn played a feisty Chinese peasant in *Dragon Seed* (1941) and Marlon Brando played a Japanese interpreter in *Teahouse of the August Moon* (1956). Micky Rooney in *Breakfast at Tiffany's* (1961) is probably the most infamous example of a scotch tape Asian. In this romantic comedy, Rooney plays a Japanese photographer complete with thick glasses, squinty eyes, and buck teeth. Another notable example of a scotch tape Asian is in *Year of Living Dangerously* (1983), starring Mel Gibson and Sigorney Weaver. In this film, actress Linda Hunt was cast to play the part of a male Chinese photographer.

The casting of a woman actress to play an Asian male character presents yet another media image issue that is not only racist but highly gendered. Popular media images of Asian males historically have been depicted as either uncontrollably lustful or completely asexual. Fu Manchu's lasciviousness toward white women was, of course, never directly acted upon on screen, but the threat was always there. At the other end of the spectrum, Charlie Chan exemplified the completely asexual Asian male character. Although he was married and had a large family, audiences were introduced to only two of his sons. We never get to see his wife and, of course, Chan was never enticed by other women nor were any women enticed by him. In most other instances, Asian American males were depicted as domestic servants, never having a life outside of catering to whites and doing their jobs. More recently, Asian American males have been seen as nerdy and inept characters, who are clumsy rather than threatening in their attraction to white women. A good example is the Chinese exchange student in the film *Sixteen Candles* (1984) played by Gedde Watanabe. Even virile Bruce Lee in his mega-hit *Enter the Dragon* (1972) was precluded from having any interest in women, unlike his white (John Saxon) and black (Jim Kelly) co-stars. Lee may have been one of the few chaste action heroes in Hollywood. A similar example can be found in Chow Yun-Fat's first Hollywood feature film, *The Replacement Killers* (1998), where at the end he says goodbye to his female co-star, Mira Sorvino. In the theater version of the film, Chow touches Sorvino's face and then they walk away in opposite directions, assuring no sexual tension or contact. In the alternative ending that is included on the DVD release of the film, Chow passionately kisses Sorvino before the two separate. As they walk away in opposite directions they turn around and look longingly at each other, creating the image of sexual attraction, albeit unrequited. However, the Jackie Chan film *The Medallion* (2003) does end with Chan and his female co-star, Claire Forlani, running off together as a couple ready for the next fight. This was a genuine motion picture rarity for an Asian man in Hollywood.

The Ballad of Little Jo (1993) provides a typical gendered image of the Asian American male with a fascinating twist. In this Western, a young middle-class, educated woman from the East Coast bears an illegitimate child and leaves home in disgrace. She discovers that the rugged, untamed, and ruthless West during the late 1800s is no place for a woman alone. Josephine Monaghan (Suzy Amis) cuts off her hair and disguises herself as a young man named Little Jo. She conceals her true identity for years, successfully confronting the dangers and challenges the Wild West has to offer. She eventually purchases some property on the outskirts of town and builds a cabin to live in seclusion. Over time, through hard work and self-sufficiency, Little Jo becomes a respected—although distant—part of the community. The film changes direction when Little Jo saves a Chinese laborer (David Chung) from a group of harassing townsfolk by agreeing to take him home as her houseboy. In the company of another person for the first time, Little Jo cannot for a moment let her guard down for fear of giving away her secret identity. Under this pressure, she initially treats him with contempt, verbally abusing him and forcing him to sleep outside the cabin like an animal. The gender role reversal is particularly stark with the lean long-haired houseboy acting demurely toward scruffy Little Jo. He even tries to win her favor by cleaning, cooking, and baking her favorite fruit pies. Perhaps because of the injustices she has faced, Little Jo slowly begins to treat her houseboy with more civility, then with affection, then eventually with love. He is the only one with whom she shares her secret, and then the two share a secret relationship of their own. The male–female roles between the two outcast lovers become somewhat more egalitarian in the privacy of their cabin; but in public, she must maintain her dominant masculine persona while he maintains a submissive feminine one. Their secret life together lasts for many years, but eventually he dies of an unknown illness. Little Jo must suffer alone in silence over the loss of her mate, and soon she herself becomes extremely ill and dies. *The Ballad of Little Jo* was directed by Maggie Greenwald and is keenly aware of the race and gender dynamics of the era it depicts.

With a few notable exceptions, Asian men have most often been depicted as strangely asexual characters. Asian women, on the other hand, have often been depicted as almost completely sexual. The Asian woman's sexuality is based on images of being petite, exotic, and eager to please and serve men. Another extreme element of this stereotype is the "dragon lady" character who uses her exotic charms to seduce innocent, unsuspecting men for evil purposes. This type of character is best seen in the early films of Ann May Wong, produced in the 1920s and 1930s. Wong was born in Los Angeles' Chinatown and started her career as a movie extra. Her big break came playing opposite Douglas Fairbanks, Sr., in the silent classic *The Thief of Baghdad* (1924). But Wong became most famous for her dragon lady roles as Fu Manchu's daughter in *Daughter of the Dragon* (1931) and *Shanghai Express* (1932), starring opposite Marlene Dietrich. The other version of the sexual Asian woman can be seen in *Sayonara* (1957), starring Miyoshi Umeki. Umeki won an academy award for best supporting actress for her portrayal of a Japanese woman who falls in love with an American serviceman stationed in Japan after World War II. One scene from the movie has Umeki gently scrubbing her lover's back in a Japanese bathtub. Umeki is so loyal to her man, she commits suicide when she finds she is not allowed to marry the American and live with him in the United States. A similar scenario is seen in *The World of Suzie Wong* (1960), starring Nancy Kwan. Kwan plays a Hong Kong prostitute who falls in love with an American artist, played by William Holden. In the film, Suzie is willing to give herself unconditionally to the white man, but expects nothing in return.

Asian American studies professor Elaine Kim, who has written extensively on racial and sexual stereotypes in the media, argues that these types of images are deeply ingrained in American attitudes, that "it is sometimes difficult to distinguish fact from fantasy or to see members of racial minority groups as individuals." She adds: "We would be hard pressed to think of many portrayals in American popular culture of Asian men as lovers of white or Asian women, but almost every exotic Asian woman character is the devoted sexual slave of a virile white man. The image of the Asian woman as exotic sex object describes the sexual power and significance of the white man at the expense of the Asian man."[12]

Nonetheless, a few Asian American men have, in fact, distinguished themselves on the big screen in other ways. A popular dramatic actor and romantic lead in early silent films was Sessue Hayakawa. His career faded rather abruptly with the advancement of talking films and the increased anti-Japanese sentiment before, during, and after World War II. However, Hayakawa did return and gave an Academy Award-nominated performance in *The Bridge on the River Kwai* (1957). Hawaiian-born James Shigata was the best-known Asian American lead actor during the late fifties and early sixties for films like *The Crimson Kimono* (1959), *Walk Like a Dragon* (1960), *Bridge to the Sun* (1961), and *Flower Drum Song* (1961). His up-and-down career is a reflection of changing interest in Asian American characters, but through the years he has kept busy with movies, television, and cartoon voice-overs. The actor Mako was also nominated for an academy award for his bravado work in *The Sand Pebbles* (1966). One of Hollywood's most distinguished cameramen was the late James Wong Howe, who worked on 125 films during his 52-year career in Hollywood. And first-time actor Haing Ngor, a physician from Cambodia, won an Academy Award for best supporting actor in the powerful film *The Killing Fields* (1987). Two films are rather exceptional. One is *Go for Broke* (1951), about the all-Japanese American 442nd Regimental Combat Team and its heroic campaigns in Europe during World War II. The other film is the musical *Flower Drum Song* (1961) based on the 1957 novel by Chin Yang Lee. This was the first and only film that featured Asian Americans in singing and dancing roles. Although both films are heavily burdened with assimilationist sentiments, they provide a different perspective on Asian American life to mainstream audiences.

In response to the lack of quality roles in Hollywood, young independent Asian American media artists and activists began producing their own films. Filmmaker Renee Tajima has described Asian American cinema as going through two stages of development. The first stage took place in the late 1960s and early 1970s, sparked by increased ethnic awareness and social consciousness.

These early filmmakers were dedicated to highlighting the Asian American experience and changing the distorted images of the past. In 1970 the first Asian American media organization, Visual Communications, was formed in Los Angeles to provide technical and distribution assistance to a new generation of media producers. Visual Communications produced a number of documentaries including *Pieces of a Dream* (1974) and *Cruising J-Town* (1976), as well as a feature film, *Hito Hata: Raise the Banner* (1980). The second stage emerged in the 1980s and early 1990s as a period that Tajima calls "institutionalization, pragmatism, and skills attainment." During this time several other media-related organizations across the country formed and gave greater attention to art and professionalism over politics and to expanding the audience. High-quality documentaries such as Loni Ding's *Nisei Soldier* (1983) and *The Color of Honor* (1987), Arthur Dong's *Sewing Woman* (1983) and *Forbidden City, U.S.A.* (1989), Felicia Lowe's *Carved in Silence* (1987), Lisa Yasui's *Family Gathering* (1988), Rene Tajima and Christine Choy's *Who Killed Vincent Chin* (1988), and Steven Okazaki's *Unfinished Business* (1984) and *Days of Waiting* (1990) are examples of films and videos produced during the second-stage period. Feature films also started to emerge during this stage. Wayne Wang's first film, *Chan Is Missing*, opened in theaters in 1981 and received rave reviews. Other notable films during the 1980s include Peter Wang's *A Great Wall* (1984) and Steve Okazaki's *Living on Tokyo Time* (1987).[13]

Another stage can be added beyond the first two described by Tajima. This stage can be called "mainstreaming." During this period there were major gains made by Asian American actors, directors, writers, and producers in Hollywood. Joan Chen emerged as one of the most highly recognized actresses in Hollywood during this period with starring roles in two major films *The Last Emperor* (1987) and *Heaven and Earth* (1993). Neither of these films focused on Asians in the United States, but did employ large Asian casts. Since then she has appeared in a number of mediocre films such as *Golden Gate* (1994), *On Deadly Ground* (1994), *Wild Side* (1995), and *Judge Dredd* (1995). More recently Chen has taken roles in ensemble and independent films such as *What's Cooking* (2000) and *Saving Face* (2004) that offer her broader opportunities for her acting skills and maturity. Chen made her mark as the director of the critically acclaimed independent film *Xiu Xiu* (1999). The success of the film led her to direct *Autumn in New York* (2000), a big budget Hollywood film starring Richard Gere and Winona Rider. Tia Carrere was another recognized actress who is of mixed Asian Pacific (Hawaiian, Filipino, and Chinese) and Spanish ancestry. However, the roles she's played have been fairly limited and stereotypical. She played the exotic Asian female in *Wayne's World* (1992) and the dragon lady in *True Lies* (1993). But Carrere also had a major role in *Rising Sun* (1993), a controversial film that is discussed in the next section. Since then, Carrere has starred in a series of forgettable "B" movies. She has made a comeback of sorts doing voice-overs for animated films like *Lilo & Stitch* (2002) and *Aloha Scooby-Doo* (2005). Currently, the most busy and recognized Asian American actress in motion pictures is Lucy Liu. Liu has played a dominatrix in the film *Payback* (1999) with Mel Gibson, a Chinese princess in *Shanghai Noon* (2000) with Jackie

Chan, and one of the lead characters in *Charlie's Angels: The Movie* (2000) and *Charlie's Angels: Full Throttle* (2003) with Drew Barrymore and Cameron Diaz. Liu was also the female villain in *Kill Bill: Vol. I* (2003). The film *The Joy Luck Club* (1993) has generally been heralded as a major breakthrough specifically because of its Asian American theme, its mainstream appeal, and its move away from stereotypes of Asian and Asian American women. The Disney animated film *Mulan* (1998) was also a breakthrough of sorts. Although it was not specifically an Asian American theme, it did provide an important boost to Asian American actress Ming-Na, who was the speaking voice of the lead character, and a positive image of Asian women. Martial artist and actress Michelle Yeoh is best known by U.S. audiences for her role in the James Bond film *Tomorrow Never Dies* (1997) and her stunning performance in *Crouching Tiger, Hidden Dragon* (2000). Kelly Hu can be seen in recent films *The Scorpion King* (2002), *Cradle to Grave* (2003), *X-Men* (2003), and *Star Wars: The Sith Lords* (2004). Sandra Oh has had important roles in blockbuster hits *Under the Tuscan Sun* (2003) and *Sideways* (2004).

These actresses have varied backgrounds and have played a wide range of film roles, but the best-known Asian actors in Hollywood all came to the United States only following phenomenal success in Asia and are limited to martial arts/action hero roles. The most well-known are Jackie Chan, Chow Yun-Fat, and Jet Li. Chan was born in Hong Kong and was formally trained at the China Drama Academy where he learned martial arts, acrobatics, singing, and acting. His breakthrough Hong Kong martial arts movie was *The New Fist of Fury* (1976), which was a remake of the original Bruce Lee classic of the same name. For the next two decades Chan made numerous action-comedy films in Asia where he became widely popular. However, it wasn't until the Hong Kong-made *Rumble in the Bronx* (1996) that Chan caught the eye of Hollywood producers. Chan's first major U.S.-made movie was *Rush Hour* (1998); it was unique in that it combined Chan's martial arts and comedy skills with the culture clash of an African American Los Angeles cop (Chris Tucker) and a Hong Kong cop (Chan) for a cop/buddy theme. The film was a smash hit and Chan went on to star in a string of comedies with the same formula that feature his marital arts prowess including *Shanghai Noon* (2000), *Rush Hour 2* (2001), *The Tuxedo* (2002), *Shanghai Knights* (2003), *The Medallion* (2003), and *Around the World in 80 Days* (2004). Although his movies are popular and make lots of money, Chan yearns to move on beyond his typecast roles. "It's all the same, cop from Hong Kong, cop from China," Chan admits. "Jet Li, Chow Yun-Fat and I all face the same problem. Our roles are limited."[14] Chow Yun-Fat made more than seventy action films and was a cult hero in Hong Kong before making his film debut in the United States. His first two Hollywood films, *The Replacement Killers* (1998) and the *Corruptor* (1999), were full of action, but empty in plot. His third film, *Anna and the King* (2000), was a big-budget extravaganza with co-star Jodie Foster. This film provided him the opportunity to break out of the action film mold. Of course he returned to his action role with *Crouching Tiger, Hidden Dragon* (2000) and again in *Bulletproof Monk* (2003). Jet Li was a national martial arts champion in China before his film career began. After a number of successful films in China and Hong Kong, Li has had prominent martial arts related roles in *Lethal Weapon 4* (1999), *Romeo Must Die* (2000), *Kiss of the Dragon* (2001), *Cradle 2 the Grave* (2003), and *Unleashed* (2005).

Asian American men with talent but without accents seem be having a much more difficult time in Hollywood. In the early 1990s Jason Scott Lee emerged as the first Asian American actor cast as a romantic lead with broad major-market appeal since Sessue Hayakawa in the early silent screen era. Lee starred in *Map of the Human Heart* (1992), *Dragon: The Bruce Lee Story* (1993), and *Jungle Book* (1994). Lee's success waned a bit, but he recently starred in the made-for-TV movie *Arabian Nights* (2000), playing the part of Aladdin, and has kept busy with lead roles in action thrillers *Dracula II: Acension* (2003), *Timecop: The Berlin Decision* (2004), *Dracula III: Legacy* (2005), and *The Prophecy: Forsaken* (2005). He also did voice-overs for animated cartoons *Lilo & Stitch* (2002) and *Lilo & Stitch 2* (2005). Paolo Montelban, the handsome Filipino American singer and actor best known for his role as Prince Charming in Disney's *Cinderella* (1997), has also learned the limits of casting for Asian American men. Following his critically acclaimed film debut in *Cinderella*, he was cast as the lead in the short-lived television martial arts show *Mortal Kombat* (1998–1999). He was not seen on the big screen again until he appeared in the Filipino American independent film *American Adobo* (2001). He appeared next in a small role in *The Great Raid* (2005), a film based on the true story of the daring rescue of five hundred U.S. and British soldiers from a Japanese Word War II prison camp in the Philippines by an elite team of U.S. Army Rangers and Filipino guerillas.

Behind the camera, Asian Americans have made better progress. *The Joy Luck Club* provided director Wayne Wang with big-budget experience, and the film's success has opened opportunities for him to direct other Hollywood films such as *Smoke* (1995), *Blue in the Face* (1995), *The Chinese Box* (1998), *Anywhere But Here* (1999), *Maid in Manhattan* (2002), and *Because of Winn-Dixie* (2005). Other filmmakers are branching out in Hollywood and directing films not at all related to Asian or Asian American themes. Ang Lee directed the heralded film *Sense and Sensibility* (1995) based on the book by Jane Austen, although, he is best known as the director of the acclaimed films *The Wedding Banquet* (1993) and *Eat, Drink, Man, Woman* (1994), as well as *Crouching Tiger, Hidden Dragon* (2000), a Chinese-language film that was custom-made for a Western audience. Lee, however, is also the Academy Award-winning director of the recent film *Brokeback Mountain* (2005), which is considered a major mainstream breakthrough film focusing on the relationship between two gay cowboys. Meanwhile, Hong Kong action film director John Woo was behind the camera on a series of recent blockbusters. They include *Broken Arrow* (1995), *Face Off* (1997), *Mission Impossible II* (1999), *Windtalkers* (2002), *The Hire: Hostages* (2002), and *Paycheck* (2003).

Internationally acclaimed writer and director Mira Nair has done films that focus on her native India such as *Salaam Bombay!* (1988), *Kama Sutra: A Tale of Love* (1996), and *Monsoon Wedding* (2001), as well as films focusing on the United States and England. Her film *Mississippi Masala* (1991) focused on a relationship between an Asian Indian woman whose family was in the motel business and an African American man in the Deep South, while *The Perez Family* (1995) told the story of Cuban refugees in Florida. Writer and director M. Night Shyamalan's film, *Sixth Sense* (1999) received rave reviews and two Academy Award nominations, one for best picture and another for best director. Since that time he has been a sought after director specializing in dramatic thrillers like *Unbreakable* (2000), *Signs* (2001), and *The Village* (2004), all of which have received positive reviews from critics. Only his first film, *Praying With Anger* (1992), related to Shyamalan's Asian Indian background. An up-and-coming writer and director is Gurinder Chadha, who specifically looks at the Asian Indian experience in her films. Chadha started out directing several award-winning documentaries for the British Broadcasting Corporation (BBC) before branching off into wildly successful films on the Asian Indian experience in England such as *Bahi on the Beach* (1993) and *Bend It Like Beckham* (2002). Her film *Bride and Prejudice* (2004) is a musical comedy based in Los Angeles. Another up-and-coming director is Timothy Linh Bui, whose most notable film, *Green Dragon* (2003), was not well received by critics but was acknowledged as a breakthrough in that it focused on the early post-war experiences of Vietnamese refugees in the United States and not the U.S. Armed Forces' experience in Vietnam.

The rapid ascent of Asian Americans behind the camera may be attributed to the increase of Asian Americans gaining powerful positions with major studios and production companies. Top executives include Janet Yang, president at Oliver Stone's Ixtlan Productions; Fritz Friedman (of Filipino and Jewish descent), vice president at Columbia TriStar Home Video; Teddy Zee, executive vice president at Columbia Pictures; and Chris Lee, senior vice president of production at Tri-Star. In 1992 Friedman and independent producer Wenda Fong formed the Coalition of Asian Pacifics in Entertainment, with the intention of creating a network for Asian Americans in the film, television, and music industries. "People are so intimidated by Hollywood," says Janet Yang. "It's important to help each other out because it's such a tough business."[15]

Outside the Hollywood mainstream, Asian American independent filmmakers are making their mark, addressing love and relationship themes not commonly portrayed on the screen. Less well known but critically acclaimed independent films include Eric Koyanagi's *One Hundred Percent* (1999), which focuses on the lives of three Asian Americans as they grapple with love, success, and identity. There is also Chi Muoi Lo's *Catfish in Black Bean Sauce* (2000), a comedy featuring a Vietnamese American and his African American girlfriend. Bertha Bay-Sa Pan's *Face* (2002) also features an Asian American and African American romance, this time with an Asian American woman and an African American man. Eric Byler's film *Charlotte Sometimes* (2003) is an unconventional romantic drama featuring two Asian American couples. Alice Wu's *Saving Face* (2005) is a unique romantic comedy about a 28-year-old Chinese American lesbian, who is shocked when her 48-year-old mother comes to her doorstep pregnant. Both have secrets to hide from each other about unspoken loves, cultural taboos, and how best to confront life honestly.

In addition to independent feature films, Asian Americans are making their mark in documentary films as well. For example, Jessica Yu won an Academy Award in 1997 for her documentary *Breathing Lessons: The Life and Work of Mark O'Brien,* about a remarkable journalist and poet living with severe physical disabilities as a result of childhood polio. She also received acclaim for her latest documentary, *Realms of the Unreal* (2004), focusing on the life of visionary artist and novelist Henry Darger, who lived in obscurity and worked most of his life as a janitor. The National Asian American Telecommunications Association is the clearinghouse for documentaries, feature, and experimental films and their program list can be found at http://www.naatanet.org.

From *Rising Sun* and *Pearl Harbor* to *Better Luck Tomorrow* and *Harold* and *Kumar*

Despite these recent advances, many Asian American media artists and activists contend they still need to be vigilant. This vigilance is best seen with the release of two controversial motion pictures, *Rising Sun* (1993) and *Pearl Harbor* (2001). The big-budget thriller *Rising Sun,* starring Sean Connery, Wesley Snipes, and Harvey Keitel, is based on a 1992 book by Michael Crichton that told the story about a beautiful blonde woman murdered by a Japanese businessman. The book was released during a period of sharp tensions between the United States and Japan over trade issues and around the fiftieth anniversary of the bombing of Pearl Harbor; it was very reminiscent of the Yellow Peril books written one hundred years earlier. In Crichton's book, the inscrutable Japanese were described as superior in terms of their technology, discipline, and efficiency. But at the same time the Japanese were seen as morally inferior because of their ruthless ambition to take over the U.S. economy, corrupt nature and predatory business practices, manipulation of trade laws, and lustful behavior toward white women. Although Crichton had never spent more than forty-eight hours in Japan, he was heavily influenced by the work of writers like Pat Choate, Clyde V. Prestowitz, Jr., Karl van Wolferen, and others who have argued that Japan is plotting to take over America. It is clear that Crichton wanted his book to be more than a mere murder mystery, as evidenced by the inclusion of an afterword and bibliography at the end of *Rising Sun.* Japanese economic success has not been accomplished "by doing things our way," Crichton writes. "(T)he Japanese have invented a new kind of trade—adversarial trade, trade like war, trade intended to wipe out the competition—which America has failed to understand for several years."[16]

Within this context, Asian American activist groups began organizing and expressing their concerns when plans for a major motion picture based on Crichton's novel were released. Representatives from the group Media Action Network for Asian Americans (MANAA), met with the film's production team in early 1993 and requested that they be allowed to view a rough cut of the film. MANAA also wanted the film to begin with a disclaimer stating that it is a work of fiction and "not meant to imply that all Japanese people are trying to take over America." MANAA was seeking a similar disclaimer to be added to director Michael Camino's film *Year of the Dragon* (1984), which depicted criminal activity in New York's Chinatown. MANAA emphasized it was neither trying to serve as censor nor attempting to defend Japanese trade, corporate, or government practices. At the same time, MANAA was fearful about a possible rise in anti-Asian violence because the portrayals in *Rising Sun* could "fuel racial paranoia, resentment and violence against Asian Americans because of the confusion many Americans have with differentiating between Asian Americans and the fictional images in the media."[17] When the talks broke down, MANAA sent a letter of protest directly to Strauss Zelnick, president and chief operating officer of Twentieth Century Fox, the studio producing the film. In its letter, MANAA reiterated its demands and this time threatened a high-profile protest upon the release of *Rising Sun* if their demands were not met. Zelnick rejected MANAA's demands, citing both free speech rights and damage to the film's "commercial potential."[18]

Although the studio and the film's producers did not concede to MANAA's demands, the group's demands did not go completely unheard. The revised movie script did blunt some of the more strident anti-Japanese attacks and the murderer in film was changed from the original book's version. These changes so irked Crichton and co-screenwriter Mike Backes, they walked off the project after just seven weeks. *Rising Sun* director Philip Kaufman denied he was influenced by Asian American protests. In a *Los Angeles Times* profile he stated, "I don't think the movie softsells any of the [political] issues at all. In fact, if anything, it opens up discussion." In terms of the movie script that differed significantly from the original book, Kaufman added bluntly, "(Y)ou can't make a movie that lectures or has a bibliography of sources the way the novel does."[19] Despite these changes, MANAA made good on its threat and organized demonstrations in Los Angeles, San Francisco, New York, Chicago, and Washington, DC. In a news conference, MANAA president Guy Aoki complained that Japanese characters in the film were depicted as "ruthless, aggressive people intent on getting their way in business through blackmail, extortion and even murder."[20] These types of portrayals, he added, could contribute to escalating hate crimes against Asian Americans. Even actors in the film were uneasy about the final results. Veteran actor Mako, who played a Japanese executive in the film, had his concerns. "There aren't enough Japanese elements in *Rising Sun*," he said. "What you see is a superficial glimpse." Actor Cary-Hiroyuki Tagawa, who played the film's primary murder suspect, "Fast" Eddie Sakamura, admits there were parts of the film he would liked to have changed. "I think so, only because I've played a lot of stereotypes."[21]

The tangible results of the *Rising Sun* protest are subtle. MANAA never called for a boycott of *Rising Sun*, nor criticized the actors for accepting roles in the film. Instead, MANAA worked to educate both the studio and the movie audience on issues important to Asian Americans, especially increased concern about anti-Asian violence. In this way MANAA has earned respect and credibility in Hollywood. MANAA has shifted its emphasis from reacting to negative depictions of Asians in film. They now focus on working with studios to discuss the need for greater representation of Asian Americans in all areas of the entertainment business and to help producers develop more positive Asian American-themed projects for the mainstream audience. Asian American actors and actresses appreciate MANAA's efforts and hope they will eventually lead to the creation of more roles for them to play. Actor Cary-Hiroyuki Tagawa found the protests of the film he starred in to be refreshing. "This was the first nationwide Asian American mobilization since *Year of the Dragon*," he explained. "And in America . . . if you're not rebellious you don't get noticed."[22]

Years after the *Rising Sun* controversy died down, another controversy erupted. When John Tateishi, national executive director of the Japanese American Citizen's League (JACL), read that Walt Disney Studios was planning to make *Pearl Harbor* (2001), a film about the 1941 Japanese attack on U.S. forces in Hawaii, he knew he had to respond. In this case it appeared that both sides learned important lessons from the fight over *Rising Sun*. The first thing Tateishi did was request a meeting with executives at the Walt Disney Company, which he received. He was assured that the film would be sensitive to Japanese Americans. Next, Tateishi asked for a meeting with the film's producer Jerry Bruckheimer. "When I saw it was a Bruckheimer production, my immediate reaction was, 'Oh my God,'" Tateishi said. Bruckheimer is one of the most successful contemporary Hollywood producers with a long track record of making blockbuster action films such as *March or Die* (1977), *Top Gun* (1986), *Crimson Tide* (1995), *The Rock* (1996), and *Con Air* (1997). Bruckheimer agreed to meet with Tateishi and even gave a copy of the script to Tateishi to review. According to Bruckheimer, "[Tateishi] had very legitimate concerns and we wanted to honor them. If we feel suggestions don't hurt us artistically, then we try to make changes."[23]

These meetings demonstrate the growing influence of groups confronting media stereotypes in film and television. Despite the congeniality between the movie studio and Asian American community leaders, precautions were still taken. Prior to the Memorial Day weekend premiere of *Pearl Harbor*, U.S. Senator Daniel K. Inouye (D–Hawaii), a decorated World War II veteran and a Congressional Medal of Honor recipient for battle-wounds he suffered, issued the following statement: "The movie 'Pearl Harbor' may well revive the emotion of 60 years ago and cause some people to reflect negatively upon the Japanese residents of our nation. . . . However, we hope that those who may be so inclined will recall that, notwithstanding the incarceration of [Japanese Americans], thousands of Japanese Americans volunteered to stand in harm's way for our nation." John Tateishi was equally cautious when the film was first being released. "I've ordered the security in this building stepped up," he said from the JACL national headquarters in Washington, DC. "I've talked to the directors of my organization around the country and sent out an alert action plan to chapters around the country."[24] While there were reports of hate messages sent to individual JACL offices, there were no specific incidents of physical hate violence or hate crimes related to the release of *Pearl Harbor*.

Just two years after *Pearl Harbor* hit the big screen, a new film created a major stir and a different type of controversy. Justin Lin's independent work *Better Luck Tomorrow* (2003) is the story of four high school overachievers in upper-middle class Orange County, California, who are the stereotypes of the "model minority" in terms of their academic prowess and, at the same time, the Yellow Peril for their violent criminal behavior. The film was initially shown at the Sundance Film Festival in 2002, where the audience was perplexed about how to categorize it. Some criticized *Better Luck Tomorrow* (*BLT*) for its share of sex and graphic violence, and accused the filmmaker of perpetuating Asian stereotypes. Some commented on the characters' moral corruption and found the lack of positive Asian American role models in the film offensive. Others, including film critic Roger Ebert, spoke in favor of *BLT*, arguing that it was condescending to think that movie depictions of Asian Americans only have to be good. "This film has the right to be about these people and Asian American characters have a right to be whoever the hell they want to be," Ebert told the crowd. "They do not have to 'represent their people.'" *BLT*, with its all-Asian American cast, was made for only $250,000, but the exposure at the Sundance Film Festival encouraged MTV Films to pay $500,000 for the rights to the film and invest $1 million to market it nationwide. In April 2003, *BLT* opened in thirteen theaters and, to the surprise of many, earned more than $360,000 its opening weekend. By the third week, BLT was showing in 380 theaters and earned over $1 million. After six weeks in the theater, BLT made just under $3.7 million.[25]

On the heels of *BLT* came *Harold and Kumar Go to White Castle* (2004), a comedy adventure that is nonetheless notable in that it was the first mainstream Hollywood film that featured two Asian American male leads whose characters weren't foreign-born, didn't have accents, weren't martial arts fighters, and weren't high achievers. Marketed as a movie "starring that Asian guy" from the film *American Pie* (1999) and *American Pie 2* (2001) "and that Indian guy" from the film *Van Wilder* (2002), the film uses a lot of low-grade adolescent humor to tell the story of two twenty-something potheads whose search for White Castle hamburgers leads them into a series of misadventures. "A Hollywood movie with two Asian American male leads? I didn't think the film would ever get made," said John Cho, who plays Harold Lee in the film. "Even while it was being made, I couldn't believe it." Cho was also in *BLT*, playing a very different type of role as the eventual murder victim. Cho adds: "This is our big at bat fiscally. Hollywood has put out a product with two [Asian American] leads and the question is, will audiences vote for it?" *Harold and Kumar* ranked seventh in the box office the first week of its release, earning almost $5.5 million in just over 2,100 theaters. Reviews of the film were mixed at best, and after eight weeks it was pretty much out of the theaters. By that time, however, it had earned more than $18 million. *Harold and Kumar* was listed in the top ten home videos sold the first two weeks it was available, earning an additional $1 million. The financial figures are not bad, but it remains to be seen if major Hollywood studios will take another chance on Asian American actors to carry a film or if this is just another trend that will come and go. Those who have been involved in the motion picture industry for a while have seen this before and even the newcomers understand that all the attention to *BLT* and *Harold and Kumar* might be temporary. "I know something like this may not come around again," admits Cho.[26]

This realization increasingly has led Asian American actors frustrated in their media careers to leave the United States all together. This was the case for Allan Wu, an aspiring actor, who despite his good looks and flawless English could get auditions in Hollywood only for bit parts or stereotypical negative Asian male roles. Wu decided it was better to move to Asia rather than give up completely. Since moving to Singapore, Wu has starred in two television dramas, appeared in several movies, and done numerous commercials throughout Asia. Although he is not a superstar, he is making a living, which is something he could not do in the United States. "You come to Asia and realize there's a huge market," Wu said. "I'd like to stay in entertainment, maybe go behind the camera, directing and producing—which I can learn out here, too." Wu was born and raised in California and worked in the biotechnical field for a short time before going to Asia to launch his new career. Because he did not speak much Chinese while growing up, he had to work intensely with private language tutors in both Cantonese and Mandarin before his career could take off.[27]

ASIAN AMERICANS ON TELEVISION

The Asian American experience on television parallels what has happened in the movie theaters. Like the movies, network television mirrors the ideology and events of its times. Asian Americans have for the most part been portrayed in predictable stereotypical fashion. The best analytical work on this subject is Darrell Hamamoto's book *Monitored Peril: Asian Americans and the Politics of TV Representation* (1994). Hamamoto writes, "In the postwar era, television has been the principal medium by which rituals of psychosocial dominance are reenacted daily. . . . Even the most seemingly benign TV programs articulate the relationship between race and power, either explicitly or through implication."[28] Hamamoto found one of the most common roles for Asian American males on television until recently was as a domestic servant to whites. Three early television programs of this kind were *Bachelor Father* (1957–1960), starring John Forsythe as a single man caring for his orphaned niece with the help of his "houseboy," played by Sammee Tong. In *Have Gun Will Travel* (1957–1960, 1961–1963), gunfighter Paladin (Richard Boone) had a personal valet, "Hey Boy," played by Kam Tong. Tong was replaced on the show after the 1960 season. His replacement was Lisa Lu, who was known as "Hey Girl." Easily the most famous Chinese domestic servant was Victor Sen Yung, who was the character Hop Sing in the *Bonanza* series that ran for fourteen years (1959–1973). Even Bruce Lee got his start on television as the faithful houseboy Kato in the show *The Green Hornet* (1966–1967). A Chinese domestic, played by actor Chao-Li Chi, was also seen in the nighttime soap opera *Falcon Crest* (1981–1990).

Roles for Asian American men have been extremely narrow on television. Indeed, television has consistently insulted Asian American men, as witnessed by its own version of a scotchtape Asian in the series *Kung Fu* (1972–1975). This was the show originally conceived by Bruce Lee, who desperately wanted to play the lead role. The story line involved a Shaolin priest who escapes China in the late nineteenth century after avenging the death of his mentor, and finds adventure wandering around the American West. It would have been the perfect vehicle for Lee to demonstrate his martial arts prowess to a national audience that wanted more after his debut in *The Green Hornet*. Lee seemed primed for network stardom, especially after his well-received guest appearance on the detective show *Longstreet* (1971–1972) where he played a martial arts instructor. When *Kung Fu* premiered on television, the starring role was played by David Carradine. The character was changed from Chinese to half-Chinese, half-white. Lee was terribly embittered by this rejection and he left the United States to make his mark in Hong Kong martial arts films. Although *Kung Fu* was a personal disappointment for Lee, it did provide an opportunity for a number of Asian American actors in co-starring roles and guest appearances, which had been extremely rare.

Drawing from the Charlie Chan stereotype in motion pictures, Hamamoto cites police detectives as another common role for Asian American males on television. A recent example is seen in the San Francisco-based show *Nash Bridges* (1996–2001), starring Don Johnson, where Cary-Hiroyuki Tagawa had a recurring role as Lt. A. J. Shimamura. Except for Sammo Hung in *Martial Law* (1998–2000) and Pat Morita starring in his own short-lived series *Ohara* (1987–1988), all Asian American detectives have played backup roles to white males. For example, Jack Soo as Sergeant Nick Yemana had a secondary role in the program *Barney Miller* (1975–1982). In the popular television show *Hawaii Five-0* (1968–1980), actors Jack Lord and James MacArthur led a group of Asian American detectives to solve crimes in the aloha state. Actors Kam Fong and Zulu, among others, played the silent background roles, rushing off when orders were given. Steve McGarrett (Lord) and Danny Williams (MacArthur) did all the talking and thinking while their subordinates did the running around. After the criminals were captured, the Asian American detectives received none of the credit or glory for making the arrest—that was saved for the white men in charge. "Book 'em, Danno" were the famous last words at the end of each *Hawaii Five-0* episode. In the series *Midnight Caller* (1988–1991), actor Dennis Dun played Billy Po, the assistant to the show's lead star, Jack Killian (Gary Cole), a radio talk-show host who solved crimes in his spare time. Although Dun is a talented and established stage actor, and his character was much more developed than the standard Asian detective sidekick, his role was clearly the helper to the hero.

The teen-oriented show *21 Jump Street* (1987–1990) featured four hip undercover officers, among them Dustin Nguyen, who played the character H. T. Ioki. The dashing and handsome Nguyen quickly became the heartthrob of thousands of teenage girls, but the studio highlighted lead actors Johnny Depp, and later Richard Grieco, to carry the show. Both Depp and Grieco quickly moved on to bigger and better acting roles, while Nguyen faded out of the show. Nguyen did reemerge in the made-for-television movie *Earth Angel* (1991), but he played a stereotypical nerdy Asian American honor student who worked as pet shop cleanup boy. The movie was a breakthrough of sorts because Nguyen's character, Peter Joy, did win the affections of a popular all-American girl (Rainbow Harvest), but only after he helped her with her homework and was beaten up by the school bully. Television did not know what to do with an atypical Asian American male except to relegate him to a typical Asian American role.[29]

Except for the one role in *Earth Angel*, Asian American males have been basically asexual characters. Even the most famous Asian American on television, Lt. Sulu (George Takei) in the original *Star Trek* series (1966–1969), was a sexless character. While all the primary male members on the starship *Enterprise* had intergalactic encounters with women—human and alien—Lt. Sulu was always left alone. On the other hand, Hamamoto found several examples of Asian American women who were sexually involved with white men. An early example of this is a 1966 episode of the long-running western program *Gunsmoke* (1955–1975) entitled "Gunfighter, R.I.P." In it gunfighter Joe Bascome (Darren McGavin) is seriously wounded helping to protect a Chinese laundryman, Ching Fa (H. T. Tsaing), and his daughter, Ching Lee (France Nuyen), from harassing thugs. The father is killed, but his daughter takes the gunfighter to her home and nurses him back to health. They fall in love and the gunfighter stays to help out the family business. Before too long, however, he is discovered and is reminded that he has already been paid to kill Matt Dillon (James Arness), the marshal of Dodge City. Bascome does not want his Chinese lover to know about his notorious past as a gunfighter, so he verbally abuses her and pretends to reject her in hopes she will forget him. The episode concludes when Ching Lee finds $500 left for her by Bascome. She realizes he loves her after all, and she goes to find him. Ching Lee manages to find Bascome but is shot trying to protect him and dies at the end of the show.[30]

Hamamoto also describes a 1979 episode from the series *How the West Was Won* (1978–1979) entitled "China Girl." The rather twisted storyline focuses on a family who sails from China to settle in the United States in 1869. During the long voyage, the daughter, Li Sin, played by Rosalind Chao, is raped by the ship's captain and becomes pregnant. Rather than expressing anger and horror at her debasement, Li Sin is instead rather pleased with the idea that her child is half-white and will be an American citizen when it is born. The story then shows the conflict between Li Sin who wants to keep the child and raise it as an American, and her evil Chinese father, who wants the child killed. In the end, Li Sin marries a Chinese man who agrees to adopt the child as his own, and the family moves to Montana to live happily ever after. "In both *Gunsmoke* and *How the West Was Won*, the theme of Asian female sexual possession by the white male Westerner was clearly articulated," Hamamoto writes. "Whether for the purposes of sexual gratification, as in the instance of 'Gunfighter R.I.P.,' or to exert power and assert authority, as seen in the rape of Li Sin by the ship's captain in 'China Girl,' white males are afforded such license as part of their social endowment as the master race."[31]

At the same time, the Asian woman's sexual prowess and uncontrollable attractiveness to white males is often quite blatant, as witnessed in the made-for-television movie epic *Tai-Pan* (1986), based on the book by James Michener and produced by movie mogul Dino de Laurentis. In this miniseries, Joan

Chen plays the China-doll harlot to a British sea trader, played by Brian Brown. Chen also played a similar sexually insatiable role in a 1989 episode from the show *Wiseguy* (1987–1990). In that episode Chen portrays a labor organizer who transforms from a teary-eyed political idealist into a kinky sex kitten while seducing the show's lead character, an undercover FBI agent, played by Ken Wahl.[32]

Asian American women have more recently played wider variety of television roles than Asian American men. For example, on the hospital drama *St. Elsewhere* (1982–1988), France Nuyen played surgeon Dr. Paulette Keim, and Kim Miyori played a doctor named Wendy Armstrong. Joan Chen was a regular on *Twin Peaks* (1990–1991), playing the character Jocelyn "Josie" Packard. It is interesting to note that there have also been Asian American actresses on television who are married to white men. For example, in the last year of the hit program *M*A*S*H* (1972–1983), an Asian character finally was featured. It was a woman, Soon-Lee (Rosalind Chao), who eventually married the cross-dressing corporal Max Klinger (Jamie Farr). Their marriage continued into a post-*M*A*S*H* spinoff, *AfterM*A*S*H* (1983–1984). Chao was also a regular on *Star Trek: The Next Generation* (1987–1994) and its spinoff *Star Trek: Deep Space Nine* (1993–1999). In these shows, Chao plays botanist Keiko Ishikawa, wife of Transporter Chief Miles O'Brien (Colm Meaney). Stand-up comic Margaret Cho starred in her own short-lived situation comedy, *All-American Girl* (1994). In the hit comedy series *Friends* (1995–2000), Lauren Tom had a temporary recurring role as the girlfriend of one of the show's main characters. And Ming-Na played a sharp-talking gallery owner, social butterfly, and love interest in the show *The Single Guy* (1995–1997). Ming-Na is also Dr. "Deb" Chen in the popular series *ER* (1994–2004) and stars on her own short-lived show, *Inconceivable* (2005), where she also plays a medical doctor. Actress Kelly Hu has played a police detective in *Martial Law, Nash Bridges,* and *CSI: NY* (2004–present). Another actress, Lindsay Price, who is half–Korean American, had regular roles on *Beverly Hills 90210* (1990–2000) during the last two years of the show and in the short-lived program *Coupling* (2003). Lauren Tom has a regular role in the new comedy show *DAG* (2000–present) and on *Barbershop* (2005–present), and Tia Carrere played an archaeology professor who searches the globe for artifacts and adventure on *Relic Hunter* (1999–2002). The most notable Asian American woman is Lucy Liu, who played the contentious and cool lawyer Ling Woo, on *Ally McBeal* (1997–2002).

Television Highlights and Lowlights for Asian Americans

The television breakthrough for Asian Americans was not a series, but the prime-time made-for-television movie *Farewell to Manzanar* (1976). The movie, based on the book co-written by Jeanne Wakatsuki Houston and her husband, James Houston, was about the experiences of a Japanese American family after the bombing of Pearl Harbor in 1941. The movie followed the Wakatsuki family into the internment camp at Manzanar, focusing on the destruction and divisions wrought by this event. The father, Ko Wakatsuki (Yuki Shimoda), was temporarily separated from his family and was unfairly detained by government agents who accused him of being subversive and disloyal to the United States. Wakatsuki was eventually allowed to rejoin his family in Manzanar, but was a broken man who drank bootleg sake to forget his humiliation and misery. In this way *Farewell to Manzanar* did not shy away from showing the hardships created by the forceful relocation of more than 110,000 Japanese Americans. The movie also showed the controversy that erupted within the camps over the War Relocation Authority's (WRA) questionnaire asking respondents to state their loyalty to the United States. Specifically, question 27 of the WRA questionnaire asked Japanese Americans if they would be willing to serve in the United States armed services whenever ordered, and question 28 asked them to foreswear any form of allegiance to the Japanese emperor. There was a group of Japanese American dissidents who either refused to answer both questions or responded "no" to both for political reasons. In the movie, however, Ko Wakatsuki pleads to fellow internees to answer "yes" to both answers, arguing that life was still better in the United States than in Japan despite their present situation. Wakatsuki's two sons Richard (James Saito) and Teddy (Clyde Kusatsu) both answer "yes-yes" to the two questions and quickly enlist in the U.S. Army. An interesting subplot in the movie is a love affair between Richard Wakatsuki and a white nurse (Gretchen Corbett). This was the first instance of a consental Asian American male–white female sexual liaison, but it was short-lived because Richard was soon killed serving with the famous 442nd Regimental Combat Team in Europe. *Farewell to Manzanar* was criticized by some Asian American activists who found that the story glorified assimilationist ideals, made internment seem like an uncharacteristic accident of U.S. history, and did not focus enough on the dominant role of anti-Japanese racism in the creation of the wartime relocation policy.[33] Nonetheless, *Farewell to Manzanar* received favorable reviews in the mainstream press and provided a showcase for some superb performances, especially by Nobu McCarthy, who was the movie's narrator and played the role of the mother, Misa Wakatsuki.

Despite the success and attention given to *Farewell to Manzanar*, it was nearly twenty years before a major prime-time event with a largely Asian American cast would again be on television. In the fall 1994 season, ABC premiered the situation comedy *All-American Girl*, starring comedienne Margaret Cho. The show was produced by Disney Studios and was loosely based on Cho's stand-up comedy material focusing on her Korean American family living in San Francisco. Cho and the veteran Asian American cast, which included a mother (Jodi Long), father (Clyde Kusatsu), grandmother (Amy Hill), older brother (Tony Award-winning actor B. D. Wong), and younger brother (J. B. Quon), created a great deal of excitement among Asian Americans who wanted to see the show succeed. "For there to be an all-Asian family in prime time was not even conceivable to the networks a few years ago," gushed co-star B. D. Wong during an Asian Pacific Heritage Month event at Stanford University. "When I grew up and watched TV, I saw no Asians. . . . We weren't thought of as Americans, but as exotics. The existence of this show is really major and an indication of the change in sensibilities to how we're viewed as people."[34] Along with the excitement also came pressure and extremely high expectations. Because only two of the show's writers were Asian Americans, there was tremendous concern whether or not *All-American Girl* would perpetuate or shatter many of the stereotypes about Asians. Many Asian American groups scrutinized the pilot, read scripts, and attended tapings for weeks before the show even reached the airwaves. Aside from the external pressures, there were also internal problems with *All-American Girl*. The original pilot for the show was so bad that critics dubbed it "The Joy Less Club," and Disney sent it back for revisions. The premiere program that was aired on September 14, 1994, was actually the show's second segment, and it received only lukewarm reviews.[35]

There was also a great deal of disagreement about the show among Asian Americans themselves. Organized Asian American media advocacy groups, such as MANAA, praised the program primarily because it highlighted and validated the existence of Americans of Asian ancestry. "It's basically an affirmation of our existence," said Guy Aoki, president of MANAA. "That's so important, because we've usually been invisible. We've waited so long for an Asian American sitcom."[36] MANAA later honored Cho and the producers of *All-American Girl* at its second annual Media Achievement Awards banquet in late 1994. Asian American viewers, however, were much less enamored. The first major criticism of the show was the poor quality of writing that produced a situation comedy indistinguishable from anything else on television. *"All-American Girl* is a disappointment and commits the biggest show-business sin: it isn't funny," wrote columnist William Wong. "That it is very much in the mold of other TV comedies starring white and black actors means it is banal entertainment, a specialty of commercial television. If Asian Americans were hoping for a TV show that genuinely reflects Asian cultural sensibilities, they'll have to wait for some future show."[37]

Another major criticism was the show's treatment of Asian American men. While the spunky Cho character was a definite change from the meek and exotic Asian woman so often seen in the media, many were aghast that the show perpetuated the negative images of Asian American males. "My main criticism, frankly, was the way Asian men were portrayed," said Deann Borshay Liem, the executive director of the National Asian American Telecommunications Association.[38] Neither the father nor the older brother was very developed as characters. In several episodes Cho's attraction to white males over Asian American males was the central theme. In the opening program, for example, the mother tries to dissuade Cho from dating a white auto mechanic by introducing her to two Asian American men: one was a wimpy-looking graduate student from MIT and the other an accountant with a speech impediment. In a subsequent episode, Cho becomes interested in a handsome Asian American male, but in the end rejects him because she is too "American," while he is too "Asian." Still another source of criticism came directly from many in the Korean American community. They complained that the cast (except for Cho) wasn't Korean, the mother's accent is more Chinese than Korean, and when the Korean language was spoken it was so badly garbled that native-Korean speakers couldn't understand it. "I felt sort of awkward watching it," explained Wes Kim, a Korean American from Chicago. "It's sort of strange to see this Hollywood conception of what a Korean family is supposed to be like."[39] At best, Korean Americans seemed moderately enthused about the show. Professor Elaine Kim also expressed "misgivings" about *All-American Girl*, but hoped it might improve with time.[40]

By midseason, however, *All-American Girl* went from bad to worse. The show's producer and writers were fired, and major changes were made. One of the changes was to move the Cho character out of the family house and into an apartment with roommates. The experiment was intended to target a younger audience of viewers but, if successful, would have reduced roles for the rest of the family members. If the experiment didn't work, there was concern the show would be on its way out completely. MANAA and other Asian American groups organized a furious letter-writing campaign to the studio and the network calling for *All-American Girl* to be renewed for another season. These last-ditch efforts proved unsuccessful and the show was canceled after just one season.

At the same time so much attention was paid to *All-American Girl*, the syndicated miniseries *Vanishing Son* (1994) premiered on the Fox Television network. *Vanishing Son* featured Russell Wong as Jian-Wa Chang, a human rights activist forced to flee Mainland China with his brother after the 1989 Tiananmen Square massacre because of their political beliefs. But once in the United States, the brother is killed and Chang is framed for the murder of two federal agents. The show focuses on Chang trying to clear himself while evading capture and deportation by the U.S. government. *Vanishing Son* was somewhat like a modern-day "Kung-Fu, except the Jian-Wa character was written to be intense, virile, and sexual. This was a major leap for Asian American men in the media, who have been relegated to less than appealing assistant roles up to this point. Being a representative of the Asian community, I'm mindful of the dialogue and care what kind of image is put out there—the quality and integrity," Wong explains. "Jian-Wa's got a lot of energy and sex appeal. He's a passionate guy. It would be unrealistic not to show it."[41]

The miniseries gathered very positive reviews along with a small but dedicated following, and *Vanishing Son* was turned into a midseason weekly series in 1995. While the weekly series was met with great anticipation and high expectations just like *All-American Girl*, two major questions were also raised. The first question was whether or not a strong Asian male character in a serious role would be acceptable to a large mainstream audience. The second question was whether *Vanishing Son* could smoothly adjust from a well-crafted and well-planned miniseries to the rigorous pace of a weekly series and maintain its production quality and audience appeal. This would be difficult for any show, especially since the per-episode budget for a weekly program was 30 percent less than the per-episode costs for the original miniseries.[42] Despite the production company's best efforts to keep the show together, it soon became clear that the weekly series could not maintain either the quality or audience it gained from the miniseries. *Vanishing Son* was quietly dropped from the network's program list.

The rapid rise and fall of *All-American Girl* and *Vanishing Son* indicates that Asian Americans still lack a solid presence in the television mainstream.

According to a report by the National Asian Pacific American Legal Consortium (NAPALC), Asian American representation on TV peaked at 2.3 percent in 1994. This figure fell to 1.9 percent in 1998. This reduction took place despite the high profile programs featuring Sammo Hung and Lucy Liu. Since August 1999 NAPALC has led the Asian Pacific American Media Coalition, a group of nineteen organizations, in a campaign against the lack of diversity in television programming. The Coalition joined forces with the National Association for the Advancement of Colored People (NAACP), the national Latino Media Council, and American Indians in Film and Television after the fall 1999 schedule of the four major television networks revealed a virtually all-white slate of new programming. After months of confrontation and negotiation, the Coalition eagerly awaited the fall 2000 lineup of programs. While there was some improvement, the Coalition was very disappointed with the overall results. Of the thirty new shows, seven Asian Americans were cast and all had only minor supporting roles. In addition, CBS announced it would be canceling *Martial Law* after the 2000 season.[43]

The most recent analysis of Asian Americans on television from NAPALC, titled "Asian Pacific Americans in Prime Time: Lights, Camera, and No Action" (2005), shows 2.5 percent Asian Pacific Islander American (APIA) representation on television—only slightly more than the representation a decade ago. In total, there were eighteen APIA actors on prime-time television (see Table 6-1 on p. 216). There were several other key findings from the report:

- Out of 113 prime-time programs, only thirteen featured at least one recurring Asian American, Pacific Islander, or multiracial Asian American/ Pacific Islander character. Only three programs on television in fall 2004 had more than one APIA character (*ER, Hawaii,* and *Lost*).
- Of the thirteen television programs, APIA actors were featured far less than non-APIA actors. White actors had 83.3 percent of the screen time on these programs, while APIA characters consistently had the lowest screen time. It is interesting to note that the multiracial APIA actors, some of whom played white characters, received significantly more screen time than non-multiracial APIA actors.
- In this study, male APIA actors (11) outnumbered female APIA actors (7).
- There were a number of television programs that were located in cities such as Honolulu, San Francisco, Queens (New York), Seattle, and New York City that have large APIA populations, but had no regular APIA cast member. For example, the programs *Half and Half* on UPN and *Charmed* on WB were set in San Francisco but had no APIA cast members. There were seven television programs set in Los Angeles that had no regular APIA cast member. Two shows set in Honolulu, *Hawaii* on NBC and *North Shore* on FOX, had relatively high APIA representation on the cast (27 percent), although APIA's represent 63 percent of the city's population.
- The characterizations of APIA's on television are not as stereotypical and limited as in the past. Of the eighteen APIA characters on television, five were in the medical field (two doctors, one medical examiner, one

Table 6-1 Names and Ethnicities of Actors and Characters in the Fall 2004 Prime-time Television Lineup

Actor/Show	Character	Actor Ethnicity	Character Ethnicity
Rhona Mitra/ *Boston Legal*	Tara Wilson	Multiracial APIA	White
Ravi Kapoor/ *Crossing Jordan*	"Bug"	South Asian	South Asian
Linda Park/*Enterprise* (Will be cancelled at the end of the 2004–05 season.)	Hoshi Sato	Korean	Japanese
Ming-Na/*ER*	Jing-Mei/ "Deb" Chen	Chinese	Chinese
Parminder Nagra/*ER*	Neela Rasgotra	South Asian	South Asian
Keiko Agena/*Gilmore Girls*	Lane Kim	APIA	Korean
Aya Sumika/*Hawaii* (Cancelled October 2004)	Linh Tamiya	Multiracial APIA	APIA
Cary-Hiroyuki Tagawa/ *Hawaii* (Cancelled October 2004)	Terry Harada	Japanese	Japanese
Peter Navy Tuiasosopo/ *Hawaii* (Cancelled October 2004)	Kaleo	Samoan	Pacific Islander
B. D. Wong/*Law & Order*	George Huang	Chinese	Chinese
Daniel Dae Kim/*Lost*	Jin	Korean	Korean
Naveen Andrews/*Lost*	Sayid	South Asian	Iraqi
Yunjin Kim/*Lost*	Sun	Korean	Korean
Bobby Lee/*MADtv*	(various)	Korean	Korean
Jason Momoa/*North Shore*	Frankie Seau	Multiracial APIA	Ambiguous
Mark-Paul Gosselaar/ *NYPD Blue*	John Clark, Jr.	Multiracial APIA	White
Kristin Kreuk/*Smallville*	Lana Lang	Multiracial APIA	White
Anthony Ruiviar/*Third Watch*	Carlos Nieto	Multiracial APIA	Ambiguous

Source: National Asian Pacific American Legal Consortium, "Asian Pacific Americans in Prime Time: Lights, Camera, No Action" (2005), Table 4, p. 11 at http://www.advancingequality.org/files/NAPALC_report_final.pdf.

forensic psychologist, and one paramedic), and three were in law enforcement (one captain and two officers). There was one linguistic specialist, one bartender/nightclub owner, one "brainy student," and two whose occupation is unknown because they are survivors of a plane crash forced to live on a remote island (*Lost*).[44]

The challenges of racist, gendered, and stereotypical images facing Asian American men and women described in this chapter are not unique to the movies or television sitcoms and dramas. Indeed, they carry over onto the stage as well.

ASIAN AMERICANS IN THE THEATER

Compared with movies and television, Asian Americans have been practically invisible in mainstream theater. Nonetheless, Asian American actors and playwrights have made remarkable strides in a relatively short time both in large Broadway productions as well as in small local theater houses across the nation. According to James S. Moy, author of *Marginal Sights: Staging the Chinese in America* (1993), among the earliest depictions of Chinese in America were in circus performances as exotics, comic relief, or sideshow freaks. During the intense anti-Chinese period in the late nineteenth century, decidedly negative portrayals of the Chinese were seen in theatrical works such as *Ah Sin!* (1877), written by Mark Twain and Bret Harte, and *The Chinese Must Go* (1879), written by Henry Grimm. Whites frequently played the Chinese characters in these theatrical productions. This continued throughout the first half of the twentieth century. For example, whites were cast in all the main roles in Eugene O'Neill's play about the adventures of Marco Polo in China, *Marco Millions* (1927). It wasn't until the late 1950s that the first big Broadway play with a large Asian American cast was produced. This was *Flower Drum Song* (1958), which served as the basis for the movie musical by the same name. It took nearly twenty years before another Asian-themed musical, *Pacific Overtures* (1976), was brought to the Broadway stage. *Pacific Overtures* made a successful run in New York and later toured across the United States.[45]

These mainstream theatrical breakthroughs were few and far in-between, and by the mid-1970s Asian American actors and writers became understandably impatient. As a result, four independent full-time Asian American theater groups were formed: The Asian American Theater Company (San Francisco), The Pan Asian Repertory Theater (New York), The Northwest Asian American Theater (Seattle), and The East-West Players (Los Angeles). Many Asian American performers and writers working in theater and Hollywood today received their early training in one or more of these groups. Their emergence in the previously closed world of theater has had a major impact. The controversies surrounding two of the most highly acclaimed plays involving Asian Americans is evidence of this fact. The two plays, *M. Butterfly* (1988) and *Miss Saigon* (1990), caused an unparalleled firestorm among many Asian Americans both in and out of the theater community.

M. Butterfly won the prestigious Tony Award for best play in 1988 and was the runaway theater event of the season. Another Tony Award went to the play's star, B. D. Wong, for "Best Featured Actor." With all this attention, playwright David Henry Hwang suddenly became the toast of Broadway. *M. Butterfly* was based on the true story of a French diplomat who carried on a twenty-year love-affair with a person he thought was a female Chinese opera singer, who instead turned out to be a male Chinese government spy. The title of the play was drawn from Puccini's famous opera, *Madame Butterfly* (1904), about a tragic love story between Pinkerton, an American naval officer stationed in Japan, and Cho-Cho-San, a local Japanese woman. Pinkerton returns to the United States shortly after initiating the affair and leaving Cho-Cho-San pregnant with his child. While he is away, she pines for his return and rejects all other Japanese suitors to remain faithful for her lover's eventual return. Pinkerton does return to Japan three years later, but this time with his white wife. Pinkerton's mission was not to reunite with Cho-Cho-San but to retrieve the child he had abandoned three years earlier. His traumatic arrival and unceremonious rejection is such a humiliating blow to Cho-Cho-San that she commits ritualistic suicide. The opera *Madame Butterfly* articulates the white male fantasy stereotype about dominance over the submissive Asian woman. It is also a metaphor of the traditional colonial and neocolonial attitude demonstrating Western superiority over the East. Playwright David Henry Hwang, who wrote a number of plays produced by several local Asian American theater companies, was well aware of these themes and in *M. Butterfly* sought to subvert the imagery in no uncertain terms.

Early in the play, the French diplomat, Gallimard (John Lithgow), tells the Chinese opera singer/male spy, Song Liling (B. D. Wong), how much he enjoyed the beauty of love and the purity of sacrifice seen in Puccini's opera *Madame Butterfly*. Song chides the diplomat, telling him, "It's one of your favorite fantasies, isn't it? The submissive Oriental woman and the cruel white man." Gallimard is taken aback by the blunt remark and does not know how to respond. Song presses the point and asks the diplomat to reverse the roles. What if a blond homecoming queen falls madly in love with a Japanese businessman who treats her with contempt? What if the Japanese businessman leaves for three years, and the homecoming queen spends the entire time praying for his return, only to kill herself when she learns he has remarried? "Now, I believe you would consider this girl to be a deranged idiot, correct?" states Song flatly. "But because it's an Oriental who kills herself for a Westerner—Ah!—you find it beautiful."[46] This was one of many twists in the *M. Butterfly* story line that differ from *Madame Butterfly*. Another comes at the end of the play when Gallimard discovers Song's true identity. This time it is Gallimard who is crushed and humiliated, and it is he who eventually commits suicide. Just before his death, the diplomat cries out in anguish, "Tonight, I've finally learned to tell fantasy from reality. And, knowing the difference, I choose fantasy."[47]

Despite Hwang's complex intentions and clever juxtapositions, the play generated both praise and scorn from many Asian American viewers. The positive and negative reviews generally seemed to fall along gender lines. A forum held at the 1989 National Conference of the Association for Asian American Studies in New York City displayed these divergent perspectives. Chalsa Loo, professor of psychology at the University of Hawaii at Manoa, stated that if Puccini's opera *Madame Butterfly* reinforces the white male fantasy of superior race power and domination, Hwang's play *M. Butterfly* shows that perpetuation of this white male fantasy will eventually serve as the vehicle for his own destruction. Loo lauded the play as a "revenge fantasy" for Asian American women: "Hwang touched a fantasy and desire for Asian American women to throw the sexist, racist stereotype back in his face."[48] Others, like Williamson Chang, professor of law also at the University of Hawaii at Manoa, were clearly upset with *M. Butterfly*. Chang argued that although the play may have challenged some stereotypes, it also perpetuated may others. "Asians, particularly Asian women, are portrayed as cunning, shrewd, manipulative, and deceptive," he said. "The plot of 'M. Butterfly' is much like that of Pearl Harbor—Asians succeed through deception." Chang also complained that the Song Liling character was yet another media insult to Asian men whose image has historically been invisible and emasculated. "Asian males had a lot to lose," he emphasized. "Was this 'he-woman' Song going to be representative of us in years to come? Will colleagues at the office look at you differently when you show up on Monday morning?" Chang concluded his talk by firmly stating: "Give me Bruce Lee or give me death."[49] At the end of this forum, David Henry Hwang spoke. He stated that he wanted *M. Butterfly* to create confusion among many people and he wanted them to confront a multitude of stereotypes. When asked by an audience member if he was taking a chance that people might get the wrong message, or perceive a message he did not intend, Hwang responded: "(Y)ou try and reach the greatest number of people you can with whatever you feel is important to say, and if people choose to misinterpret that work, then that's that. But at least they're being exposed to it which is better than if they had gone to something which only reinforced their reactionary thinking."[50]

The debate over *M. Butterfly* did not settle before issues of the oppression of Asian women, the renewal of the *Madame Butterfly* fantasy, and the invisibility of Asian American males were again raised on Broadway with the musical extravaganza *Miss Saigon*. The production created an even bigger stir among Asian Americans, and the criticisms were far more unified and heated. In 1990, Broadway was buzzing about the planned arrival of the hit musical from London, *Miss Saigon*. The musical was expected be a smash in New York and then stop at several other cities as part of its U.S. tour. The plot for *Miss Saigon* was simple and familiar: A Vietnamese prostitute (Kim) falls in love with a white American soldier (Chris). She becomes pregnant, but the two are separated after the fall of Saigon. Kim faithfully waits for Chris to return and take her and their child away. Chris returns to Southeast Asia three years later with his white wife (Ellen) to look for his abandoned child. Kim kills herself after finding out that Chris has remarried.

The publicity around the *Miss Saigon* tour and its reuse of the *Madame Butterfly* scenario created tremendous protest by Asian American media activists, who vowed to organize demonstrations wherever the musical is performed. Even more complaints were heard when it was announced that the prominent role of the Vietnamese pimp (Engineer) was going to be performed by a white actor. This role belonged to Jonathan Pryce who played the part in London using heavy makeup to make him "look Asian." David Henry Hwang and B. D. Wong, among many others, bitterly criticized the use of a scotch tape Asian, or a white man in "yellow face," as an insult to every Asian American performer whose choices for roles are already severely limited. As pressure mounted, the Actor's Equity Union tried to bar Pryce from playing the character, but the union quickly backed down when *Miss Saigon* producer, Cameron Mackintosh, claimed his right of artistic freedom and also threatened to cancel the show's U.S. tour.

The controversy escalated even further and Asian American activists were stung by accusations that they were trying to censor the arts. According to B. D. Wong, nothing could be further from the truth. "I resent being labeled a person who somehow thought that artistic freedom was not important," he said in a magazine interview.[51] Although the Actor's Equity Union reversed its decision and allowed Jonathan Pryce to play the role of Engineer, Wong and other Asian American artists felt their high-profile protests were worth the effort for a number of reasons. First, it brought attention to the limited number of prominent roles for Asian American actors, and highlighted the blatant contradictions found in "color-blind" or "nontraditional" casting. In its ideal form, color-blind casting recognizes that there are relatively few roles written for actors and actresses of color to play on the mainstream stage. The informal policy of color-blind casting serves to encourage directors and producers to cast qualified Asian American actors in roles they ordinarily would not be allowed to play. In reality, however, color-blind casting has only helped Asian Americans land secondary roles as non-Asian characters but has also continued to allow whites to take major roles as Asian characters. "Parts playable by any actor are not open to people of color, but to white actors who move easily from role to role, ethnicity to ethnicity," wrote Dom Magwili, former director of the Asian American Theater Project of the Los Angeles Theater Center in a guest editorial published in the *Los Angeles Times*. He cited the casting of African American actor and singer Robert Guillaume as the Phantom in *Phantom of the Opera* to be an excellent, though rare, example of color-blind casting. Magwili then asks wryly: "How about the novel idea for 'Miss Saigon' that Asians play themselves? Not a chance."[52]

Second, media activists also said their protests against *Miss Saigon* helped those both inside and outside the theater world to realize that the use of scotch tape Asians should be seen as unthinkable as casting a white actor in blackface. The musical *Miss Saigon* opened as planned in 1991, but Pryce performed without yellow face makeup. In addition, after Pryce left the show and *Miss Saigon* began its U.S. tour, an Asian American actor was eventually cast in his place. Third, and most important, was the fact that the Asian American performing community was willing this time to stand up and make noise, when in the past they had not. "It is no wonder that these artists become restless and active," wrote playwright Velina Hasu Houston, in another guest editorial published in the *Los Angeles Times*. "They have to be. They're mad and they won't be silent anymore."[53] George Takei also believes increased activism among Asian American writers and performers, along with greater participation and criticism by the Asian American audience, are two essential ingredients for change. "The other part of my soapbox to the community is that we need to be visible in the audiences as well. . . . (T)here's no reason why we shouldn't be supporting the arts."[54]

The enormous success of *M. Butterfly* and the controversies surrounding *Miss Saigon* have brought greater attention to Asian Americans in the theater world. Since the 1970s Asian American writers and performers had been working tirelessly, but in almost total obscurity. Today, many of their efforts have begun to bear fruit and this is exemplified by the quantity and quality of plays that have been produced in recent years. Among the more notable Asian Americans that have emerged in the theater is prolific Philip Kan Gotanda, who has written a number of plays including *Yankee Dawg You Die, Fish Head Soup, The Wash, Day Standing on Its Head*, and *The Ballad of Yachiyo*. Another prolific playwright is Velina Hasu Houston, whose works include *Asa Ga Kimishita* (Morning Has Broken), *American Dreams, Tea*, and *Basic Necessities*. Small venue one-person plays by Jude Narita ("Coming into Passion/Song for a Sansei" and "Stories Waiting to Be Told/The Wilderness Within"), Amy Hill ("Tokyo Bound" and "Beside Myself"), and Lane Nishikawa ("Life in the Fast Lane," "I'm on a Mission from Buddha," and "Mifune and Me") have inspired audiences in tours across the country.

Interest in Asian American themes in theater is also seen in David Henry Hwang's reworked version of the musical *Flower Drum Song*. The original *Flower Drum Song* opened on Broadway on December 1, 1958, and ran for six hundred performances, closing on May 7, 1960. As described earlier in this chapter, the Hollywood film version of the musical premiered in 1961. On October 17, 2002, the new *Flower Drum Song* opened at the Mark Taper Forum in Los Angeles, California, forty years after the original production. The revised musical became a hit and extended its original run for an additional six weeks. The following year the revival was being performed on Broadway. Hwang's initial interest in reworking *Flow Drum Song* was to challenge early Hollywood stereotypes about Asian Americans. "I began writing plays as a college student in the late 1970s," Hwang recalled for an article in the *New York Times*. "As part of this movement, we rather simplistically condemned virtually all portrayals of Asian Americans created by non-Asians. So I ended up protesting 'Flower Drum Song' as 'inauthentic,' though the show remained a guilty pleasure for many of us."[55] Much of the dialogue from the 1961 movie version was changed, as was some of the storyline. While the conflict over Chinese Americans assimilating into mainstream society in the United States is still a major theme, the characters confront their identity issues more assertively and grapple with their reality rather than passively being victims of the cultural clash.

The critical reviews of the new *Flower Drum Song* were generally good, although there were some critics who felt Hwang's work smacked of "political correctness" superseding "art." This prompted historian John Kuo Wei Tchen of New York University to accuse the most strident critics of Hwang as being stuck in time and ignorant of changes in Asian American sensibilities since the 1958 and 1961 versions of *Flower Drum Song*. Tchen argued that the best way to preserve and perpetuate the important essence of the original book and subsequent musicals of *Flower Drum Song*, requires shaking up, and shaking off, the social baggage of the past.[56] Hwang acknowledged this fact and admitted the research and script variations for the remake of *Flower Drum Song* became a personal catharsis for him. He wrote: "Perhaps the riddle of identity is not one that we are ever meant to answer definitively. Rather it is by asking the questions throughout our lives, and over the course of generations, that we give meaning to our existence, and assert our common humanity."[57] The maturation of writers and performers and the emergence of a more appreciative audience are hopeful signs for the future of Asian Americans on the theatrical stage. Asian American involvement in the theater is far more than mere entertainment; it is also a political act. Josephine Lee's groundbreaking book *Performing Asian America* (1999) considers how various Asian American playwrights bring together the issues of performance, race, and ethnicity that help inform our understanding of Asian American identity. "We can no longer assume that the canonical classics can be evaluated according to supposedly universal or objective aesthetic standards," Lee writes. "The old theories of genre, form, and response that erase racial difference and that separate art neatly into either political or aesthetic dimensions are inadequate to the demands of new works: to their immediate topical concerns, the complexity of their artistic presentation, the difficult questions of art and political representation they raise."[58]

ASIAN AMERICANS IN SPORTS

The media and sports have become closely interconnected in our society. Sporting events have become a major part of media content and advertising. The commercialization of sports and the media has created a symbiotic relationship, as each has grown dependent on the other for their popularity and revenues. The emergence of Asian and Asian American athletes in high profile sports in the United States is a growing phenomenon.[59] While there has been a great deal of scholarly literature on race and sports, as well as on the media and sports, only recently has work been written on Asian Americans in sports.[60] Asian Americans in sports has not been considered an appropriate subject for scholarly inquiry due to the relatively few Asian Americans who participate in commercial sports. For example, African Americans represent about 13 percent of the U.S. population, but they are the vast majority of professional basketball players. African Americans are also highly prominent in football, while Latinos are increasingly prominent in baseball. Asian Americans have been stereotyped historically as hard working but not physically strong, as intelligent but not athletic.

This is all changing and changing rapidly. The most successful and well-known U.S.-born Asian American athletes include ice skaters Kristi Yamaguchi and Michelle Kwan; tennis pro Michael Chang; golf superstars Tiger Woods, Michelle Wei, and Christina Kim; and Olympic gold medal winners Amy Chow (gymnastics) and Apolo Ohno (speed skating). The first person of Asian descent in major league baseball was Japan-born pitcher Masanori Murakami, who played for the San Francisco Giants from 1964 to 1965. During the next several decades there were a few U.S.-born players of Asian descent including outfielder and first basement Mike Lum (1967–1981), infielder Len Sakata (1977–1987), pitchers Atlee Hammaker (1981–1995) and Ron Darling (1983–1995), and outfielder Benny Agbayani (1998–2002). Wendell Kim was never a major league player, but he has been a successful coach for the San Francisco Giants, the Boston Red Sox, the Montreal Expos, and the Chicago Cubs. Attention to Asian Americans in baseball really began in 1995 with the arrival of pitcher Hideo Nomo who left the Japanese major leagues and joined the Los Angeles Dodgers. Nomo, nicknamed "The Tornado" for his unusual delivery, possessed a blazing fastball along with a variety of other pitches. In his first season he struck out 236 batters in just 191 innings and posted an impressive 2.54 earned run average on his way to winning the National League Rookie of the Year award. At 6-foot-2 and 210 pounds, Nomo defied the image of the small-framed Asian and redefined the meaning of "power pitching."

Since that time professional baseball players from Asia have been well represented. Most of the Asian players in major league baseball are from Japan, although there are others from Korea, Taiwan, and one from Panama (Bruce Chen). Ichiro Suzuki of the Seattle Mariners is the best-known baseball player from Asia. Suzuki broke in to the major leagues in 2001 and was the first major league position player born in Japan. In his first season Suzuki led the American League in batting (.350) and earned both Rookie of the Year and Most Valuable Player awards. In 2004, Suzuki broke an 84-year-old record for most hits in a season with 262. In 2005 Suzuki became one of only five players in major league history to have 200 or more hits in five consecutive seasons. Suzuki was elected by fans to start in baseball's All-Star game four times and he has won three coveted "Golden Glove" awards for his solid defense and strong throwing arm in the outfield. Another Japan-born player is power-hitting outfielder Hideki Matsui, who was signed by the New York Yankees before the 2003 season. In three seasons with the Yankees Matsui has fulfilled the high expectations by averaging more than 100 runs batted in (RBIs) and 23 home runs per season.

A growing number Asian Americans and Pacific Islander Americans also have entered the ranks of professional football. Many will be surprised to learn about Filipino American quarterback Roman Gabriel, who played from 1962 to 1977. Gabriel was an all-pro four times (1968, 1969, 1970, and 1974) and was the league's most valuable player in 1969. A number of Pacific Islanders also have been quite successful in football. The most famous is all-pro linebacker Junior Seau, who was the number one draft choice of the San Diego Chargers in 1990. Seau is considered to be one of the best linebackers in the history of the game. Other Asian Americans have made inroads into the sport, such as offensive lineman Eugene Chung, a first-round draft pick with the New England Patriots in 1992. Linebacker Dat Nguyen of the Dallas Cowboys started his National Football League (NFL) career in 1999 after having starred in college at Texas A&M. The son of Vietnamese refugees, Nguyen has had to confront the perception of professional scouts that he is "undersize" to play football. Nonetheless, at only 5-foot-11 and 238 pounds, Nguyen became the starting middle linebacker in his second season with the Cowboys. Nguyen was later selected defensive team captain for his work ethic and leadership skills. In 2004, University of Hawaii quarterback Timmy Chang capped a career setting records for most passing yards (17,072), attempts (2,346), completions (1,388) and total offense (16, 910). In addition, Chang threw 117 touchdowns, which is the second most of any major college quarterback. Despite his impressive statistics, Chang was not well regarded by professional scouts because he is undersize (6-foot-2 and 195 pounds) and did not play in a pro-style offense in college. He was not drafted by any NFL team, although he was signed as a free-agent by the Arizona Cardinals. Chang was cut before the 2005 season and was later signed by the Detroit Lions. Chang is considering a career with the Canadian Football League or the Arena League, both of which play offensive styles better suited for his skills and college experience.[61]

The first and only Asian American coach in the NFL is Tennessee Titans' offensive coordinator, Norm Chow, who joined the team in 2005 after a long and successful career as an assistant coach at Brigham Young University (BYU), North Carolina State, and the University of Southern California (USC). Chow won the 2002 "Broyles Award" as the nation's top assistant coach and was also named the 2002 NCAA Division I-A "Offensive Coordinator of the Year" by American Football Monthly. Chow has made no secret of his desire to become a head coach of a Division 1-A football team, and to be the first Asian American ever to hold such a position. "There are not many of us that are in this profession," admitted Chow. "As a young person you always looked up and admired and tried to follow someone. If we're doing something that others aspire to and want to do and can maybe follow through with, than it's all worthwhile." Chow has seen the "glass ceiling" in action in his football-coaching career. After spending twenty-seven years as an assistant coach at BYU, Chow saw there was no opportunity for advancement. What finally motivated Chow to leave was an incident when BYU's vice president used a racial slur during a public address. "This was not a minor incident," Chow explained. "It made me realize how important it was to work in the proper environment. I went home and told my wife it was time to go. Chow spent one year coaching at North Carolina State (2000) and then moved on to become the offensive coordinator for USC, where he flourished. The USC Trojans won two national championships while Chow was in charge of the offense, and his name finally was mentioned as a head-coaching candidate. Chow was one of the top candidates for the head-coaching position at Stanford University in 2004, but he was not chosen. At the age of 58, Chow knew his opportunities for becoming the first Asian American head coach of a major college football team were fading. He then decided to leave college coaching and was hired as the offensive coordinator by the Tennessee Titans.[62]

It was believed that an Asian would never stand out in the National Basketball Association (NBA). This is why there was phenomenal attention and excitement when the Houston Rockets made Yao Ming their first pick in the 2002 NBA draft. At 7-foot-5 and 295 pounds, Yao was only 21, but was already known as one of the top amateur basketball players in the world. The official NBA scouting report about Yao was glowing: "At 7-5 has very good agility and athleticism. Can knock down jumpshots all the way out to NBA 3 point range with consistency. . . . Runs the floor with fluidity, and good quickness. Has good aggressiveness, loves to dunk, and does so with authority. Has the motivation to become better, and has expressed a strong interest in playing in the USA against the best in the world."[63] Yao was not the first player from China to play in the NBA. Centers Wang Zhizhi (Miami Heat) and Mengke Bateer (Denver Nuggets) came before Yao in 2001, but they were seen more as novelties that have not made much of a mark on the game or the fans. However, "Yaomania" started as soon as he was drafted and he has become larger than life in more ways than one. In China, Yao has become a star who has transcended borders. In Houston the Rockets play to sellout crowds of fans just wanting to watch Yao play. Throughout the NBA, teams market special "Asian American" game-day specials whenever the Rockets come to town. In Houston and on the road, the number of Asian faces in the crowd of NBA games has increased precipitously. On top of everything else, Yao has proved to be a very good player. As a rookie in 2002–2003, Yao averaged a respectable 13.5 points a game and led the Rockets in both rebounds and block shots per game. He earned unanimous All-Rookie First Team honors and was voted by fans to be the starting center in the 2003 NBA All-Star game. His statistics have improved every year since. Yao averaged 17.5 points per game in 2003–2004 and 18.3 points per game in 2004–2005. Yao has been voted to the All-Star game every year he has been in the league and in 2005 he received the most All-Star fan votes (2,588,278) of any player in NBA history.

Yao's entrance into the NBA and the media spotlight were not without controversy. On December 16, 2002, Shaquille O'Neal, then–Los Angeles Lakers superstar center, taunted Yao in a national radio interview and spouted off gibberish that was supposed to be mock Chinese language: "Go tell Yao Ming 'Ching-chong-yang-wah-ah-soh. . . .'" The comment got some laughs but greatly offended many Asian American listeners. Irvin Tang heard the interview and was so incensed he began a campaign calling for O'Neal to apologize. "Forgive my bitterness," Tang wrote in an *AsianWeek* article. "I grew up in Texas, facing those 'ching-chong' taunts daily while teachers averted their ears. . . . I am calling Shaq out. Come on down to Chinatown, Shaq. You disrespected Asian Pacific America, and we will break you down. Perhaps when you and the Lakers come to Houston on Jan. 17 to play Yao Ming and the Rockets, the APA community will have a press conference waiting for you. Perhaps there, before a national audience, you can apologize to Yao Ming."[64] As pressure from Asian American groups began to mount, Shaquille O'Neal came out with a statement: "To say I'm a racist against Asians is crazy. I'm an idiot prankster. I said a joke. It was a 70–30 joke. Seventy percent of the people thought it was funny. Thirty didn't. I don't have to have a response to (charges of racism) because the people who know me know I'm not. . . . But if I offended anybody, I apologize."[65] On January 17, 2003, O'Neal and the Lakers arrived in Houston to play Yao and the Rockets, and the atmosphere in the area was electric. O'Neal offered a short comment upon his arrival: "All I am going to say is Yao Ming is my brother. All Asian people are my brothers. . . . I'm disappointed in the media making a big deal about my words."[66] O'Neal whispered something in Yao's ear before the opening tip-off. The Rockets won the hard-fought game,

108–104 in overtime. Yao Ming sealed the game with a slam dunk and the crowd went wild.

Professional golf is one sport where both U.S.-born and foreign-born Asian men and women have come to dominate. The most recognizable player is Tiger Woods, whose mother is from Thailand. Woods turned pro in 1996 at the age of 20, dropping out of school at Stanford University. As soon as he turned pro, he signed endorsement contracts worth $40 million from *Nike* and $20 million from *Titleist*, among others. He has since won numerous major tournaments and championships including the Masters (1997, 2001, 2002, and 2005), the U.S. Open (2000 and 2002), the British Open (2000 and 2005), and the PGA Championship (1999 and 2000). In 2004, Woods became the first golfer to earn $40 million in prize money. Another well-known golfer is Vijay Singh, who is Asian Indian from Fiji. He has three major championship victories, the Masters (2000) and the PGA Championship (1998 and 2004), and he was ranked the number one golfer in the world in 2004. In the Ladies Professional Golf Association (LPGA) foreign-born Asians are making a strong impact as well. Though many are not household names, five out of the top ten money-earners on the 2005 LPGA tour were Asian women, and eleven Asian women were in the top thirty (see Table 6-2). By far the most well-known Asian American female golfer is Hawaii-born Michelle Wie, who announced she was turning pro on October 5, 2005, just after her sixteenth birthday. Wei had competed in many men's and women's tournaments, but was unable to claim any prize money because of her amateur status. Wie first gained notoriety at 13 when she won the U.S. Women's Amateur Public Links. Wie was just 14 when she shot a 68 at the Sony Open, the lowest score ever by a female competing on a men's tour. On the women's circuit she would have earned over $640,000 on the 2005 LPGA Tour had she been a pro.

It was the conspicuousness of women golfers from Asia that created an early backlash, much of which was rooted in some of the same contributing factors to anti-Asian sentiment described in Chapter 5. In an October 2003 question-and-answer session with *Golf Magazine*, veteran LPGA player Jan Stephenson told writer Peter Kessler: "This is probably going to get me in trouble, but the Asians are killing our tour. Absolutely killing it. Their lack of emotion, their refusal to speak English when they can speak English. . . . Our tour is predominantly international and the majority of them are Asian. They've taken over." Stephenson, an Australian, also remarked that women Asian golfers are taking "American money" and if she were the LPGA commissioner she would put a quota on Asian players.[67] Stephenson apologized a day later for comments, but a flurry of letters was sent to WorldGolf.com, with many supporting Stephenson's position and right to speak out:

> In regards to Stephenson's remarks, I could not agree more. I belong to a Private Country Club where competition and friendship are normal. Unfortunately, the Asian members do not want to be a part of the club competitions or social events. It is like two [separate] clubs with one group being very active in the club and the Asians refuse to be a part of

Table 6-2 LPGA Top Money Winners as of November 28, 2005

1	Annika Sorenstam	$2,588,240
2	Paula Creamer	$1,531,780
3	Cristie Kerr	$1,360,941
4	Lorena Ochoa	$1,201,786
5	Jeong Jang	$1,131,986
6	Natalie Gulbis	$1,010,154
7	Meena Lee	$870,182
8	Hee-Won Han	$856,364
9	Gloria Park	$842,349
10	Catriona Matthew	$776,924
11	Candie Kung	$753,959
12	Marisa Baena	$744,679
13	Birdie Kim	$715,006
14	Soo-Yun Kang	$710,710
15	Lorie Kane	$698,763
16	Heather Bowie	$677,425
17	Wendy Ward	$675,129
18	Pat Hurst	$634,389
19	Christina Kim	$621,149
20	Rosie Jones	$615,499
21	Carin Koch	$612,036
22	Liselotte Neumann	$607,474
23	Mi Hyun Kim	$584,367
24	Juli Inkster	$579,240
25	Michele Redman	$540,167
26	Jennifer Rosales	$514,279
27	Karrie Webb	$500,268
28	Sophie Gustafson	$484,839
29	Young Kim	$470,926
30	Karine Icher	$451,981

Source: www.lpga.com.

that. We have tried to change that but were met with resistance. Out of 150 Asian members 6–10 are involved in the Clubs activities. Very sad.

Brian Baumgardner, via email

Sorry but I feel Jan Stephenson is right. The LPGA is an American tour. They should have the right to limit the percentage of international players.

Janet Moore, via email

I totally agree with Jan Stephenson, although I do enjoy watching excellent golf.

Frank Lisk, via email

Jan hit it on the head. Asians are taking the LPGA tour down. They do not relate to the fans [who] eventually will go away as I did.

Nick, via email

[H]ooray for Jan Stephenson. . . . She [has] done more for golf than the dykes and Asians, by far.

Ron Fogarty, via email

Jan just told the truth. Are we so racially divided that we cannot do this? The fact that this has become an issue proves failure is certain. Ignorance is always alleged but true ignorance is ignoring the truth of a matter. Jan didn't.

Lawrence Klotz, via email[68]

Stephenson's comments hit a raw nerve among many LPGA fans and the feeling lingers. In an August 26, 2005, article in *Golf World*, "On Asians and Racism," writer Ron Sirak quoted an email message from a reader: "The plain and simple truth is Americans want to see Americans playing or Europeans [who] look like Americans. Most have nothing against Asians, they just don't want to watch events totally dominated by Asians. I see this as a BIG problem for the LPGA."[69] This explains why there haven't been any complaints about Swede Annika Sorenstam being the top ranked female golfer and highest money winner on the LPGA tour in recent years (2001–2005). The anti-Asian sentiment is sure to percolate even more now that Michelle Wie has joined the competition.

The recent success of Asian Americans in sports today should not overshadow the history of Asian American involvement in athletic competition. During the 1920s and 1930s there were about hundred Japanese American baseball teams throughout Hawaii and the states of California, Washington, Colorado, Utah, Nebraska, and Wyoming. Japanese American passion for baseball was threatened by the onset of World War II and Japanese internment, but it did not die. Organized baseball teams sprouted in internment camps and there were even games played with teams from different camps.[70] In 1939 and 1940 the first all-Chinese American professional basketball team, the Hong Wah Kues, was formed and played local teams across the nation. Like the Harlem Globetrotters basketball team, the Hong Wah Kues were a traveling novelty act that generated a great following. In fact, the Hong Wah Kues once played the Globetrotters, but lost.[71] The first Asian American to win an Olympic gold medal for the United States was diver Dr. Sammy Lee. He was awarded the gold medal for the 10-meter platform at the 1948 London Olympics and another gold medal for the 10-meter springboard at the 1952 Helsinki games. Lee, a Korean American born in Fresno, California, was a student athlete at the University of Southern California School of Medicine and earned his medical degree in 1947. Following his success at the Olympics, Lee continued his medical career and coached the U.S. diving teams in the 1960 and 1964 Olympics.[72] In recent years a number of athletes of Asian decent have competed for the United States in both the Summer and Winter Olympics, and have won metals in various individual and team sports. In the 2004 Summer Olympics in Athens, Hawaiian-born Bryan Clay won the Silver Medal in the decathlon. The decathlon is a two-day competition in involving the following ten events: 100-meter dash, long jump, shot put, high jump, 400-meter dash, 110-meter hurdles, discus throw, pole vault, javelin throw, and 1500-meter run. Because this competition requires a combination of strength, speed, and stamina, decathletes are generally considered to be the "world's greatest athletes."[73]

Theories on Asian Americans and Sports

To examine the emergence of Asian Americans as sports media stars we must ask the question, "Why has it taken Asian Americans so long to emerge in major sports?" Three explanations have been used—genetic, cultural, and social. The common explanation for the overrepresentation of African Americans in certain sports and the underrepresentation of Asian Americans is that African Americans are naturally better athletes, while Asian Americans are not as naturally gifted. This biological determinism explanation assumes innate physical differences exist within artificially created racial categories and fails to recognize that African Americans, like Asian Americans, exhibit a wide range of physical builds and other physiological features. While big and tall might be desirable for most professional athletes, these physical attributes alone do not determine success. For example, 5-foot-3 basketball player Muggsy Bogues was the number one draft pick of the Washington Bullets in 1987. He is 16 inches shorter and about 80 pounds lighter than the average NBA player today, but has had a long and successful career in basketball. Second baseman Joe Morgan played professional baseball for twenty-two years and was elected to the Hall of Fame in 1990. Morgan was just 5-foot-7 and 150 pounds, yet he once led the National League in slugging percentage and has 268 career home runs. He was also awarded as the National League Most Valuable Player in 1975 and 1976. At 5-foot-8, National Football League all-pro cornerback Darrell Green is considered "undersized" for the game. Green nonetheless played football for nineteen seasons (1983–2002) and intercepted 54 passes during his long career. At the same time many Asian American athletes are more than adequate in size and weight compared to others in their respective sports. Roman Gabriel stood at 6-foot-4 and weighed 235 pounds in his prime and was considered the first "big" quarterback of the modern era. At 6-foot-5 and 300 pounds, Eugene Chung measures up pretty well with other offensive linemen. Baseball slugger Hideki Matsui's nickname is "Godzilla" for being 6-foot-2 and weighing 230 pounds. Even more impressive is major league first baseman Hee-Seop Choi who is 6-foot-5 and weighs 240 pounds. China-born basketball players Yao Ming and Haixia Zheng (WNBA) are above the competition in their leagues. In sum, whatever differences there are among African Americans and Asian Americans in sports cannot simply be explained by genetic advantage. The genetic argument is never used to explain why skiers from Switzerland and other Scandinavian countries consistently win world championships compared to skiers from other countries.[74]

With this in mind, another explanation for the overrepresentation of African Americans in sports is their positive emphasis on sports as life chances within African American subculture. Both male and female athletes achieve a level of status and recognition, but only in certain high-profile sports. African

Americans are virtually absent in a number of sports including bicycling, rodeo, auto racing, swimming, bowling, skiing, kayaking, etc. In addition, we find great variances between African and African American athletes. In track events Africans excel in long distance running, while African American participation in distance running (particularly among males) is not nearly as pronounced.[75] Chapter 3 discussed Asian American emphasis on education over other avenues for social and economic upward mobility. In Asia, baseball is very popular and this may explain why there are more overseas Asian players in professional baseball compared to U.S.-born Asians. Since football is not played in Asia, only U.S.-born Asians play that game.

While the pseudo-cultural argument may have some explanatory power, it must be related to some of the social structure constraints that affect both African Americans and Asian Americans. Noted sports sociologist Harry Edwards is keenly aware of socioeconomic discrimination against African Americans, particularly males, and how it influences occupational choices and aspirations. "In high-prestige occupational positions outside of the sports realm, black role models are in all but an insignificant few," Edwards writes. "Whites, on the other hand, because they have visible alternative role models and greater potential access to alternative high-prestige positions, distribute their talents over a broader range of endeavors. Thus the concentration of highly gifted whites in sports is proportionately less than the number of blacks."[76] This argument can help to explain why relatively few Asian Americans participate in sports, but can also be extended to point out insidious discrimination that can affect even the most successful Asian American athletes. U.S. figure skating champion Kristi Yamaguchi's capture of a gold medal during the 1992 Winter Olympics is an interesting case in point. Many observers of her spectacular performances at the Olympics assumed she would reap huge benefits in the form of major endorsement contracts. However, Yamaguchi was never able to cash in on the endorsements. It was her misfortune to compete in the Olympics during a period of intense anti-Japanese sentiment in the United States, and to win a gold medal exactly on the fiftieth anniversary of President Franklin D. Roosevelt's signing of Executive Order 9066 (February 19). The executive order authorized the mass removal of more than 110,000 people of Japanese ancestry into internment camps. This historical coincidence was an uncanny reminder of the persistent image of Asian Americans as perpetual foreigners. This despite the fact that Yamaguchi's family has lived in the United States for generations, and even though Yamaguchi gave a rousing free-skate performance to the music of "Yankee Doodle Dandy" while dressed in a red, white, and blue costume.[77]

The March 9, 1992, issue of *BusinessWeek* confirmed corporate sponsors' unease with her Japanese heritage in an article entitled, "To Marketers, Kristi Yamaguchi Isn't as Good as Gold."[78] Advertisers simply didn't know what to do with Yamaguchi. The Olympic skater who really brought home the gold was third place skater, Nancy Kerrigan, whose endorsement contracts far exceeded Yamaguchi's. A 1993 *People Magazine* article succinctly described the popular sentiment of the time. "Kristi Yamaguchi may have won the Olympic gold last year, but bronze-medal winner Nancy Kerrigan got the gasps for her Grace Kelly gleam. . . . Pal Paul Wylie, though, an Olympic Silver medalist, cuts right to her charm: 'Nancy's the girl next door.'"[79] Yamaguchi did not quite fit the ideal wholesome fresh-faced "All American" girl-next-door type sponsors looked for to sell their products. Ironically, one of her earliest and most lucrative contracts was with an optical company that promised to change one's looks and self-image with colored contact lenses. Yamaguchi has never publicly complained about her endorsement situation and has earned good money as a professional ice skater. Nonetheless, many agree that her ability to profit even more handsomely from her hard work and achievements was considerably diminished primarily because of conflicting images of her by others.

The Yamaguchi-Kerrigan example was no fluke. After Tara Lipinski beat Michelle Kwan for the 1998 Olympic gold medal in women's figure skating, MSNBC flashed the Internet headline: "American Beats Kwan." The message was clear: Lipinski is an American, while Kwan is a foreigner.[80] Similar treatment has been given to U.S. tennis star Michael Chang, whose most lucrative advertising contracts were in Asia and Australia, not in the United States. Chang was featured in advertising campaigns with Proctor & Gamble and Eveready Energizer batteries that were shown only in Asia, and he was purported to be the highest paid pitchman in Hong Kong. It is interesting to note that Tiger Woods' multiracial background has not affected his endorsement prowess. Indeed, his perceived "blackness" has given him the status as an "American" rather than a foreigner, and he has successfully captured loyal fans in both the United States and Asia.[81] Tiger Woods notwithstanding, the overall perception is that Asian Americans have simply not been accorded the media attention or advertisement dollars relative to other athletes at or near the top of their respective sports. According to media researchers Charles R. Taylor and Barbara B. Stern (1997), there is a pattern in media advertisement to include Asian Americans, but most likely in background roles. "Asian Americans are victims of tokenism, for they are the minority most likely to be depicted as anonymous figures in the background," the authors write. "Their presence as token faces in a crowd has negative consequences for both first-generation immigrants and the U.S.-born."[82] While it can be argued that Asian Americans have avoided sports because they have other career options, there are relatively few role models to emulate, and those who have excelled in sports have not been treated well in the media. But this, too, seems to be changing, at least for those athletes advertisers deem most deserving of top dollar for their endorsements. After turning pro Michelle Wie signed endorsement contracts making her the highest-paid female golfer, surpassing the endorsement earnings of Annika Sorenstam.[83]

In addition, the more successful and high profile Asian Americans in sports may help to change people's perceptions and serve as inspiration. For non-Asian Americans, seeing and perhaps admiring Asian American sports heroes may, over time, provide a more positive image of Asian Americans. Seeing Asian Americans in sports may serve to replace the "foreign" image. Anthropologist Mark Grey (1992) found that because Southeast Asian refugees in a Kansas City High school did not actively participate in sports, they were perceived as not wanting to be "true Americans."[84] Studies have found that assimilation may occur more readily when members of a team come from diverse ethnic backgrounds, while athletic participation exclusively with people of the same ethnic group serves to inhibit assimilation.[85] On the other hand, in a study of Japanese American basketball leagues Haruo Nogawa and Sandra J. Suttie (1984) found mixed, but ultimately positive, results. In comparing fifty Japanese American basketball players to thirty-six non-players, the researchers did not find significant differences in assimilation to mainstream society, but did find an improved sense of ethnic solidarity and self-image among the athletes.[86] Although the conclusions in these studies are contradictory, they both point to the importance of sports participation for Asian Americans. Other studies of Korean American, Japanese American, and Chinese American youth found they were more likely to have lower scores on physical self-esteem measures.[87] Thus, it is all the more encouraging to see a new generation of up-and-coming Asian Americans in sports who are not household names as yet, but may well be on their way.

CONCLUSION

This chapter shows how stereotypes about Asians and Asian Americans have made their way into various formats of media. These stereotypes and negative images have historic roots and reflect the racialized and gendered attitudes in the mainstream society. This chapter focuses on the broad trends of how the popular media thinks of and sees Asians and Asian Americans, and how Asian Americans see themselves. These images are constantly in flux and they can change rapidly. An understanding of the context for how and why Asian Americans have been portrayed in the media serves to explain why there is a need for constant vigilance. Asian Americans, of course, are not merely victims of media ignorance and manipulation. They continue to struggle against stereotypical and negative images and have worked to recapture and recreate their own self-images and identities. This chapter shows that media depictions of Asian Americans in film, television, theater, and sports are an important part of the highly complex process of identity formation. Chapter 7 focuses on other important elements that work to influence and help create identity.

NOTES

1. See: http://www.icebox.com/icebox/shows/show_54/show_frameset.html.
2. See: http://www.williamhung.net.
3. Emil Guillermo, "The William Hung Joke," *AsianWeek*, April 15, 2005.
4. Quoted in Emil Guillermo, "Hung As Buckwheat," Special to SF Gate.com, April 20, 2005, at http://www.sfgate.com.
5. See comments at http://www.harlemmlee.com. Also see a contrasting early interview with Lee at http://www.aarising.com/aprofiler/harlemm.htm.
6. Quoted in Erin Chan, "A Loser's Success and a Winner's Failure," *Detroit Free Press*, May 7, 2004.
7. Russell Leong (ed.) *Moving the Image: Independent Asian Pacific American Media Arts* (Los Angeles: UCLA Asian American Studies Center, 1991); Robert G. Lee, *Orientals: Asian Americans in Popular Culture* (Philadelphia: Temple University Press, 1999); Gina Marchetti, *Romance and the*

"Yellow Peril": Race, Sex, and Discursive Strategies in Hollywood Films (Berkeley and Los Angeles: University of California Press, 1993); June Xing, *Asian America Through The Lens* (Walnut Creek, CA: AltaMira Press, 1998), Darrell Hamamoto and Sandra Liu (eds.), *Countervisions: Asian American Film Criticism* (Philadelphia: Temple University Press, 2000); and Peter Feng, *Identities in Motion: Asian American Film & Video* (Durham, NC: Duke University Press, 2002).

8. Edward Said, *Orientalism* (New York: Pantheon Books, 1978).

9. Cited in Ronald Takaki, *Strangers from a Different Shore* (Boston: Little, Brown and Company, 1989), p. 105.

10. Kidotj Farquhar and Mary L. Doi, "Bruce Lee vs. Fu Manchu: Kung Fu Films and Asian American Stereotypes in America," *Bridge: An Asian American Perspective* 6:3 (Fall 1978): 23–40.

11. *Ibid.*

12. Elaine Kim, "Asian Americans and American Popular Culture," *Dictionary of Asian American History* (Chicago: University of Chicago Press, 1986), pp. 99–114.

13. Renee Tajima, "Moving the Image: Asian American Independent Filmmaking 1970–1980," in Russell Leong (ed.) *Moving the Image: Independent Asian Pacific American Media Arts* (Los Angeles: UCLA Asian American Studies Center, 1991), pp. 10–33.

14. "Chan Complains of Limited Roles," *AsianWeek*, October 7, 2004.

15. Philip W. Chung, "Beyond Asian Chic," *A Magazine*, Summer 1994, p. 22.

16. Michael Crichton, *Rising Sun* (New York: Ballantine Books, 1992), p. 93; also see Pat Choate, *Agents of Influence* (New York: Alfred A. Knopf, 1990), Clyde V. Prestonowitz, *Trading Places: How We Are Giving Our Future to Japan and How to Reclaim It* (New York: Basic Books, 1989), and Karl van Wolfen, *The Enigma of Japanese Power* (New York: Alfred A. Knopf, 1989).

17. "MANAA's Official Statement on the Movie 'Rising Sun,'" March 1993. Also see Jane Galbraith, "Group Takes 'Rising Sun' Protest Public," *Los Angeles Times*, April 7, 1993; and Guy Aoki and Philip W. Chung, "'Rising Sun,' Hollywood and Asian Stereotypes," *Los Angeles Times*, May 3, 1993.

18. Letter from Straus Zelnick to Guy Aoki, March 23, 1993.

19. Quoted in Gene Seymour, "When Simple Isn't Good Enough," *Los Angeles Times*, July 25, 1993.

20. Quoted in David Ferrell and K. Connie Kang, "'Rising Sun' Opens to Charges of Racism," *Los Angeles Times*, July 31, 1993.

21. Quoted in "The Dark Side of the Sun," *Entertainment Weekly*, August 6, 1993, pp. 26, 29.

22. Quoted in Elaine Dutka, "Asian Americans: Rising Furor Over 'Rising Sun,'" *Los Angeles Times*, July 28, 1993.

23. Quoted in Lorenzo Munoz, "60 Years Later, It's a Sensitive Topic," *Los Angeles Times*, May 22, 2001.

24. *Ibid.*

25. Quoted in Justin Lowe, "All or Nothing," *AsianWeek*, April 10, 2003. Also see Roger Ebert, "No Place For Political Correctness in Films," *Chicago Sun-Times*, January 18, 2002; Jay A. Fernandez, "Controversy Gives A Push," *USA Today*, April 14, 2003; Justin Lowe, "'Better Luck Tomorrow' Makes Box Office History," *AsianWeek*, April 17, 2003; Philip W. Chung, "Better Luck Today," *AsianWeek*, April 24, 2003.

26. Quoted in Philip W. Chung, "Asiandudes to Hollywood," *AsianWeek*, July 29, 2004.

27. Vanessa Hua, "Asian American Entertainers Find Demand For Their Talent Overseas Very Rewarding," *San Francisco Chronicle*, November 27, 2005.

28. Darrell Y. Hamamoto, *Monitored Peril: Asian Americans and the Politics of TV Representation* (Minneapolis: University of Minnesota Press, 1994), p. 3.

29. *Ibid.*, pp. 28–29.

30. *Ibid.*, pp. 39–42.

31. *Ibid.*, p. 46.

32. *Ibid.*, pp. 191–193.

33. Raymond Okamura, "Farewell to Manzanar: A Case of Subliminal Racism," in Emma Gee (ed.), *Counterpoint: Perspectives on Asian America* (Los Angeles: UCLA Asian American Studies Center, 1976), pp. 280–283.

34. Quoted in Jefferson Graham, "Actor's Chance to Part a Racial and Cultural Curtain," *USA Today*, September 13, 1994.

35. Raymond Okamura, "Farewell to Manzanar: A Case of Subliminal Racism," in Emma Gee (ed.), *Counterpoint: Perspectives on Asian America* (Los Angeles: UCLA Asian American Studies Center, 1976), pp. 280–283.

36. Quoted in Benjamin Pimentel, "'All-American Girl' Stirs Debate Among Asians," *San Francisco Chronicle*, November 1, 1994.

37. William Wong, "A Disappointing 'All-American Girl,'" *Oakland Tribune,* October 9, 1994.
38. Quoted in J. K. Yamamoto, "Cho Watch," *San Francisco Bay Guardian,* December 7, 1994.
39. Quoted in Pimentel, "'All-American Girl'" (1994).
40. *Ibid.*
41. Quoted in Jeff Yip, "A Heroic Leading Role for One Asian 'Son,'" *Los Angeles Times,* March 25, 1995.
42. Carlos Mendez, "'Vanishing Son': No Plans to Disappear," *AsianWeek,* February 3, 1995.
43. Jennifer Lee, "NAPALC Leads Effort to Diversify Television," and Chong-Ho Chung, "Striking a Deal for Diversity," both in *The NAPALC Review* 6:1 (Spring 2000).
44. For details see the report at http://www.advancingequality.org/files/NAPALC_report_final.pdf.
45. James S. Moy, *Marginal Sights: Staging the Chinese in America* (Iowa City: University of Iowa Press, 1993), pp. 7–48, 94–103.
46. Henry David Hwang, *M. Butterfly* (New York: Penguin Books, 1988), Act 1, Scene 6, p. 17.
47. *Ibid.,* Act 3, Scene 2, p. 90.
48. Chalsa Loo, "M. Butterfly: A Feminist Perspective," in Linda A. Revilla et al. (eds.), *Bearing Dreams, Shaping Visions: Asian Pacific American Perspectives* (Pullman, WA: Washington State University Press, 1993), pp. 177–180.
49. B. C. Chang Williamson, "M. Butterfly: Passivity, Deviousness, and the Invisibility of the Asian American Male," in *Ibid.,* pp. 181–184.
50. "A Conversation with David Henry Hwang," in *Ibid.,* pp. 185–191.
51. Quoted in Steven A. Chin, "The World of B. D. Wong," *Image,* September 5, 1993, pp. 6–10, 31.
52. Dom Magwili, "Makibaka! Asian-American Artists Should Struggle—and Not Be Afraid," *Los Angeles Times,* August 13, 1990.
53. Velina Hasu Houston, "It's Time to Overcome the Legacy of Racism in Theater," *Los Angeles Times,* August 18, 1990.
54. Quoted in Jan Breslauer, "After the Fall," *Los Angeles Times,* January 13, 1991, Calendar Section.
55. David Henry Hwang, "A New Musical by Rogers and Hwang," *New York Times,* October 13, 2002.
56. John Kuo Wei Tchen, "Critics Clueless About Emergent American Sensibility," *AsianWeek,* December 12, 2002.
57. Hwang, *op cit.,* October 13, 2002.
58. Josephine Lee, *Performing Asian America: Race and Ethnicity on the Contemporary Stage* (Philadephia: Temple University Press, 1999), p. 5.
59. See http://www.asianathlete.com and http://www.asiansportsnet.com.
60. See Joel S. Franks, *Crossing Sidelines, Crossing Cultures: Sport and Asian Pacific American Cultural Citizenship* (New York: University Press of America, Inc., 2000), and Brian Niiya, ed., *More Than a Game: Sport in the Japanese American Community* (Los Angeles: Japanese American National Museum, 2000).
61. See NFL scouting report of Chang at http://www.nfl.com/draft/profiles/2005/chang_timmy.
62. Quoted in Sam Chu Lin, "Norm Chow Leads USC's National Football Title," *AsianWeek,* January 8, 2004.
63. See NBA scouting report of Yao Ming at http://nbadraft.net/profiles/yaoming.htm.
64. Irwin Tang, "APA Community Should Tell Shaquille O'Neal to 'Come down to Chinatown,'" *AsianWeek,* January 2, 2003.
65. Quoted in Annie Nakano, "Forgiving Shaq is a Tall Order to Fill," *San Francisco Chronicle,* January 21, 2003.
66. Quoted in Jonathan Feigen, "Rockets Summary," *Houston Chronicle,* January 19, 2003.
67. Quoted in Peter Kessler (interview), "Jan Stephenson: LPGA's Original Siren Still Making Waves," *Golf Magazine,* November 1, 2003, p. 120. Also see Clifton Brown, "Stephenson Apologizes For Remarks on Asians," *New York Times,* October 12, 2003, and Susan K. Sim, "Why No Outrage Over Slur of Asians?" *Atlanta Journal-Constitution,* November 5, 2003.
68. See http://www.worldgolf.com/features/stephenson-letters.htm.
69. Quoted in Ron Sirak, "On Asians and Racism," *Golf World,* August 26, 2005 at http://www.golfdigest.co.za/stories/df_On_Asians_and_racism541.php.
70. "Diamond in the Rough," *AsianWeek,* October 30, 1997, p. 8; also see "Japanese American Baseball History Project" online at http://www.nikkeiheritage.org/ research/bbhist.html.
71. Carl Nolte, "Slam-Dunk Memories," *San Francisco Chronicle,* May 28, 1999.

72. See "Dr. Sammy Lee" online at http://www.ishof.org/68slee.html.
73. Nick Peters, "A Silver Star Emerges," *Sacramento Bee,* August 25, 2004.
74. Jay J. Coakley, *Sport in Society: Issues and Controversies,* Fifth Edition (St. Louis: Mosby, 1994), pp. 245–247.
75. D. Stanley Eitzen and George H. Sage, *The Sociology of North American Sport,* Fifth Edition (Madison, WI: Brown & Benchmark, 1993), pp. 329–330.
76. Harry Edwards, *Sociology of Sport* (Homewood, Ill: The Dorsey Press, 1973), pp. 200–301.
77. Tim Fong, "Yamaguchi's Gold Won't Deter Hate Crimes," *San Jose Mercury News,* February 25, 1992.
78. Laura Zinn, "To Marketers, Kristi Yamaguchi Isn't as Good as Gold," *BusinessWeek,* March 9, 1992, p. 40.
79. "The 50 Most Beautiful," *People Magazine,* April, 1993, p. 62.
80. Mai Tuan, "On Asian American Ice Queens and Multigeneration Asian Ethnics," *Amerasia Journal* 25:1 (1999): 181–186.
81. Andrew Tanzer, "Tiger Woods Played Here," *Forbes,* March 10, 1997, pp. 96–98.
82. Charles R. Taylor and Barbara B. Stern, "Asian Americans: Television Advertising and the Model Minority Stereotype," *Journal of Advertising* 26:2 (Summer 1997): 47–62.
83. Jerry Crowe, "Wie Starts Life as a Money Player," *Los Angeles Times,* October 13, 2005.
84. Mark Grey, "Sports and Immigrant, Minority, and Anglo Relations in Garden City High School," *Sociology of Sport Journal* 9:3 (1992): 255–270.
85. Barry D. McPherson, James E. Curtis, and John W. Loy, *The Social Significance of Sport* (Champaign, IL: Human Kinetics Books, 1989), pp. 211–212.
86. Haruo Nogawa and Sandra J. Suttie, "A Japanese-American Basketball League and the Assimilation of Its Members Into the Mainstream of United States Society," *Review for the Sociology of Sport* 19 (1984): 259–271.
87. Lee C. Lee and Ginny Zhan, "Psychosocial Status of Children and Youths," in Lee C. Lee and Nolan W. S. Zane, eds., *Handbook of Asian American Psychology* (Thousand Oaks, CA: Sage Publications, 1998), pp. 137–164.

7

More Than "Family Values":
Asian American Families
and Identities

VISIBILITY AND INVISIBILITY

The diversity of Asian Americans makes it extremely difficult to speak about any one generalized Asian American "family" or "identity." Yet it is not uncommon to hear that the success of Asian Americans has everything to do with their "family values" so deeply rooted in the rich cultural resources brought from their Asian homelands. Asian family values, it is said, work to enhance Asian American self and ethnic identity and group cohesion in the United States. This is especially true with regard to Asian American educational and economic achievements, even when referring to second- and third-generation Asian American families. The strength of the Asian American family, self and ethnic identity, and group cohesion is often held up for other minority groups to envy and emulate, and is closely related to the model minority stereotype. This implies that the lack of success among other racial minority groups is directly attributed to a weakness in their family values and cultures.

The favorable comparison of Asian American family values with other groups persists despite the relatively little solid research on Asian American families. Sociologists interested in Asian Americans have tended to focus on race relations issues and broader sociohistorical experiences, but have given only cursory attention to Asian American families. At the same time, sociologists interested in families have failed to conduct much research on Asian Americans. In this area of specialization, sociological research historically has suffered from weak methodologies, been heavily biased toward white and middle-class norms, and maintained myths, stereotypes, and oversimplifications about racial minority families.[1]

Similarly, most psychological studies on Asian American families and cultural identity are also lacking. Most of the studies that do exist focus on Chinese and Japanese Americans, and cannot be considered reliable nor generalizable due to small sample sizes and a lack of replication. "There has never been a time when many researchers systematically examined the structure, function, and variety of Asian American families," writes psychologist Laura Uba (1994). "Consequently, the empirically based picture of Asian American families is fragmented and incomplete."[2] Because of these limitations, the purpose of this chapter is to look beyond the superficial and static model minority image of the Asian American family and identity type. It is much more realistic to examine the more dynamic nature of contemporary Asian American families and identities.

With this in mind, this chapter first examines contemporary Asian American families as fluid and adaptive, rather than rigid and imbedded cultural phenomena. It is important to note that Asian American families have, in fact, not shown any one consistent pattern throughout their history in the United States. Instead, Asian American families have experienced continuous change in response to the social and structural challenges they've faced. The experiences of the post-1965 Asian Americans are no exception. Second, this chapter focuses on Asian American identities and mental health issues. There is a popular image that Asian Americans are generally well adjusted and do not face significant mental health problems. But as increasingly large numbers of Asian American immigrants and refugees enter the United States, they are challenged to cope in a new social and cultural environment. Pressures to make a living, to conform, to adjust to dramatically changing family roles, and to raise children can and do lead to increased identity and mental health problems. Lastly, this chapter examines new and emerging Asian American families and identities. Emphasis in this section is placed on interracial marriages and the natural results of these unions—biracial Asian Americans. This section also looks at family and identity creation, and/or recreation, among Asian American gays and lesbians. Another emerging area focuses around young orphans from Asia who were brought to the United States at an early age and raised by non-Asian parents.

ASIAN AMERICAN FAMILIES

Assimilation has been the key sociological concept in explaining the experiences of racial minority families. In his book *Assimilation in American Life* (1964), sociologist Milton Gordon describes Anglo-conformity as the historical pattern of assimilation of ethnic and racial minorities in the United States. This means every effort has been made to "Americanize" both minority groups and immigrants by demanding that they surrender all aspects of their culture and adopt the values of the dominant society. Ideally, of course, this should also be the long-term goal of all minorities. The Anglo-conformity perspective has been challenged by more contemporary social scientists, but it still serves as the foundation for many academic and popular beliefs about minority group status, upward mobility, and family values. This can be seen in a brief review of research on African American, Chicano (Mexican American), and Asian American families.

It is not surprising to find the largest body of literature on racial minority families centers on African Americans, given the black-white focus on race relations in the United States. Although the numbers of studies and types of research on African Americans is significant compared with other groups, sociologist Walter Allen (1978) identified three basic ideological perspectives in a survey of studies conducted on this group. They are (1) the culturally deviant approach, which views African American families as dysfunctional and pathological compared to white, middle-class norms; (2) the culturally equivalent approach, which maintains the success of African American families only in relation to white, middle-class norms; and (3) the culturally variant approach, which views the African American family as different, but legitimate and functional.[3] The first two perspectives are rooted in Anglo-conformity, while the third perspective is an attempt to challenge this basic ideology. The culturally deviant approach, rooted in the thesis that the experience of slavery destroyed African American culture and family life, has been the most dominant perspective in social science literature. Two issues make this thesis highly controversial. First is its tendency to place attention on low-income inner-city African Americans and generalize these descriptions for the entire group. Second is its assumption that the passage of sweeping laws ending racial discrimination in employment and housing passed during the 1960s is ample evidence of equal opportunity for everyone in the United States today. According to this perspective, it is the historical legacy of slavery that continues to haunt African Americans rather than any de facto racism or economic inequality existing today. In the past twenty years, however, important research has emerged taking the culturally variant approach. From this perspective, researchers have sought to show the development of a rich and vital African American family life despite the abuses of slavery. At the same time, new research also highlights the continued existence of race and class inequality and discrimination in the United States that serves to perpetuate socioeconomic differences between black and white families.[4]

Research on Chicano families has witnessed similar treatment. The early social science literature on Chicano families has also taken a culturally deviant approach, and found "traditional" ways of Mexican American culture as a serious problem. From this perspective, *machismo,* or rigid male dominance, was viewed as the most dysfunctional cultural tradition in the Chicano family. Chicano men were seen as irresponsible, preoccupied with sex and alcohol, and violent, compared with Chicanas who were viewed as helpless, submissive to a fault, and hopelessly abused. Since the 1970s, scholars have taken a more critical approach to examining Chicano culture and families, and have expanded their focus to look at external structural factors and their impacts on the Chicano family. "What was once labeled culturally deficient family patterns may now be viewed as family strategies that serve as solutions to constraints imposed by economic and social structures in the wider society," writes sociologist Maxine Baca Zinn. "Although themes of patriarchy remain, the nature of male dominance is different from that described in earlier studies."[5] More contemporary research on Chicano families has found greater range of experiences and more sharing of power than previously assumed.

Compared with African American and Chicano families, relatively little research has been done on Asian American families. The two primary reasons for the dearth of research on Asian American families has to do with their historically small population and their more contemporary image of not being a "problem" group.[6] Early research on Asian Americans (primarily Chinese and Japanese Americans) has complimented the group for its ability to preserve its "positive" traditions and values, despite its long history of prejudice and discrimination. Traditional Asian culture has been positively associated with the middle-class Protestant ethic, which encourages self-discipline, sexual conservatism, achievement orientation, thrift, as well as a high level of respect for authority and social control. Asian culture is seen as perhaps being overly strict, but over time it can acceptably blend with more liberal Anglo American patterns. In this regard, a culturally equivalent approach has been the most common explanation for why Asian Americans enjoy success compared to other racial minorities.[7]

Researchers have also pointed to several specific features of Asian American families as evidence of their cultural strength and continuity. Chief among them is the strong nuclear family unit. Sixty percent of all Asian Americans over the age of 15 are married, compared with 54 percent of the total population. Asian Americans also have a low divorce rate of 4.2 percent compared to the 9.7 percent divorce rate of the total U. S. population. For Native Hawaiians and Pacific Islanders, the marriage rate is lower and the divorce rate is higher than the total population (see Table 7-1). More than 60 percent of Asian American

Table 7-1 Marital Status, 2000: Percent Distribution of Population 15 and Older

Group	Never Married	Married	Divorced
Total Population	27.1	54.4	9.7
Asian American	30.0	60.2	4.2
Native Hawaiian/ Pacific Islander	34.9	51.2	7.6
Chinese	28.7	62.2	3.8
Filipino	29.0	58.8	5.2
Asian Indian	26.7	67.4	2.4
Vietnamese	35.6	54.9	4.1
Korean	30.5	59.6	4.6
Japanese	27.1	58.1	6.7
Cambodian	38.9	48.7	3.8
Hmong	36.4	55.2	2.3
Laotian	36.5	53.1	4.4

Source: U.S. Census Bureau, *We the People: Asians in the United States* (December 2004), Figure 4, p. 7 at http://www.census.gov/prod/2004pubs/censr-17.pdf and U.S. Census Bureau, *We the People: Pacific Islanders in the United States* (August 2005), Figure 4, p. 7 at http://www.census.gov/prod/2005pubs/censr-26.pdf.

Table 7-2 Household Type and Average Size, 2000: Percent Distribution of Households

	Married Couple	Female House- holder No Spouse Present	Non-family Households	Average Household Size
Total Households	52.5	11.8	31.5	2.59
Asian American	61.8	8.8	24.9	3.08
Native Hawaiian/ Pacific Islander	56.4	15.4	20.9	3.60
Chinese	61.8	7.7	26.6	2.90
Filipino	61.7	13.6	20.0	3.41
Asian Indian	70.7	3.8	22.1	3.06
Vietnamese	64.0	11.9	16.0	3.70
Korean	59.4	9.2	27.9	2.76
Japanese	48.7	7.5	40.9	2.25
Cambodian	61.4	21.5	9.4	4.41
Hmong	78.1	10.5	6.0	6.14
Laotian	66.6	12.2	11.4	4.23

Source: U.S. Census Bureau, *We the People: Asians in the United States* (December 2004), Figure 5, p. 8 at http://www.census.gov/prod/2004pubs/censr-17.pdf, and U.S. Census Bureau, *We the People: Pacific Islanders in the United States* (August 2005), Figure 5, p. 8 at http://www.census.gov/prod/2005pubs/censr-26.pdf.

households were maintained by married couples, compared with 53 percent of households in the total population. The high percentage of married households is related to the low 8.8 percent of female-headed Asian American households. Female-headed households were 11.8 percent in the total population. Pacific Islanders also have a higher percentage of married households, but also a higher percentage of female-headed households (see Table 7-2). The average household size for Asian Americans and Pacific Islanders is larger than the total population, and both groups have a higher percentage of five-member house- holds compared to the total population. Figures from the 2000 census show 12.6 percent of Asian American households and 16 percent of Pacific Islander house- holds have at least five members, compared with 9.6 percent of the total popula- tion with the same number of household members. Japanese Americans have the lowest percentage of five-member households among all Asian American groups (see Table 7-3). The large and extended Asian American households are a reflection of three factors. First, there is the tendency of these households to have more adult children living at home while they are completing their educa- tion. Second, there are also more elderly relatives living with their families. Third, there are more established families that often host newly arrived immi- grant relatives for some time. It is no surprise to find an even higher percentage of Southeast Asian families living in large and extended households. This is due to a combination of the factors just stated as well as their economic conditions, recent migration to the United States, refugee status, and high fertility rates.

Table 7-3 Family Household Type by Household Size

	5 Members Percent	4 Members Percent	3 Members Percent	2 Members Percent
Total Population	9.6	20.3	22.9	27.8
Asian American	12.6	25.2	23.1	26.6
Native Hawaiian/ Pacific Islander	16.0	21.1	20.2	20.9
Chinese	11.1	24.8	26.2	29.3
Filipino	15.3	24.0	23.2	22.5
Asian Indian	11.8	27.6	25.0	27.1
Vietnamese	17.5	25.3	21.6	16.7
Korean	9.8	30.4	25.9	29.6
Japanese	6.7	20.0	24.9	45.5
Cambodian	20.3	21.4	15.5	10.2
Hmong*	12.0	10.1	7.2	5.8
Laotian	19.5	23.9	17.7	11.2

* The percentage of Hmong family households with 7 or more members is 51.6.
Source: U.S. Census Bureau, Summary File 4, PCT 17.

Another possible indicator of the strength of Asian American extended family structures is the generally low rate of poverty found among single-female-headed households with children under 18. Asian American women who find themselves divorced, widowed, or separated from husbands often can rely on their parents or other relatives for support. This was highlighted in the 2000 U.S. census, which provides the most comprehensive data on poverty rates for different Asian ethnic groups. In 2000, more than 34.3 percent of all female-headed households with children under 18 lived below the poverty level. For Asian Americans, 27.9 percent of female-headed households with children under 18 lived below poverty level. A breakdown by individual Asian American group provides some intriguing information. For example, only 17.8 percent of Japanese American female-headed households with children under 18 lived below the poverty level. Among Filipino American female-headed households with children under 18, only 15.9 percent lived below poverty level. At the same time, note that recent Southeast Asian refugee groups, whose extended family structures have often been fractured due to their migration experiences, had extremely high rates of poverty among female-headed households with children under 18. Within this category, the 2000 census figures show the poverty rates for Vietnamese, Cambodian, Laotian, and Hmong Americans in this category were 37.4 percent, 56.2 percent, 37.5 percent, and 62.4 percent, respectively (see Table 7-4). Another indicator of Asian American family strength can be seen in statistics showing 32 percent of Asian Pacific Islander female-headed households earn less than $25,000 compared with 41.1 percent for non-Hispanic white female-headed households. At the same time, however, 14.2 Asian and Pacific Islander married couples have family incomes below $25,000 compared to 11.8 percent of non-Hispanic white families (see Table 7-5).

Table 7-4 Asian American Female-Headed
Households and Poverty Rates, 2000

Group	% of Female-Headed Households Below Poverty
All	34.3
Pacific Islanders	37.1
Asian Americans	27.9
Chinese	26.4
Filipino	15.9
Japanese	17.8
Asian Indian	27.8
Korean	32.2
Vietnamese	37.4
Cambodian	56.2
Laotian	37.5
Hmong	62.4

Source: U.S. Bureau of the Census, 2000 Summary File 4, DP-3.

Table 7-5 Total Family Income by Family Type by Race 2001

Family Type Race	Percent $75,000+	Percent $50,000– $74,999	Percent $35,000– $49,999	Percent $25,000– $34,999	Percent Less than $25,000
Married-Couple Family					
Asian and Pacific Islander	44.2	20.6	13.5	7.4	14.3
Non-Hispanic White	40.1	23.5	15.0	9.6	11.8
Female Householder, No Spouse Present					
Asian and Pacific Islander	17.1	14.0	16.5	20.4	32.0
Non-Hispanic White	10.5	13.5	17.6	17.2	41.2

The percentages may not add to 100.0 percent because of rounding.
Source: U.S. Census Bureau, *The Asian and Pacific Islander Population in the United States: March 2002,*
Figure 5, p. 6 at http://www.census.gov/prod/2003pubs/p20-540.pdf.

Any examination of contemporary changes in Asian American families must first and foremost look at the diverse immigrant population among Asian Americans and the changing roles of Asian American women since 1965. Only after the passage of the 1965 Immigration Reform Act has the gender balance between Asian American men and women reached parity. The earliest immigration laws in the late eighteenth and early nineteenth centuries described in Chapter 1 worked to perpetuate a distinct gender imbalance among Asian Americans—especially Chinese, Filipino, and Asian Indian Americans. This did not begin to change until the end of World War II. Along with their dramatic increase in numbers, a high percentage of Asian American women also work outside the home. The 2000 U.S. census figures show that labor force participation among Asian American women 16 years and older is 62.7 percent, slightly higher than the 62.5 percent for all women, and lower than the 64.6 percent for Pacific Islander women. A detailed look at Asian Americans shows a considerable range of labor force participation among Asian American women. For example, a remarkable 73.1 percent of Filipinas work outside the home compared with 52.2 percent labor force participation among Hmong women. The percentage of Korean American women may be artificially low because the census does not count Korean American women who work in their family business; they are usually unpaid labor. A survey conducted by sociologist Pyong Gap Min (1992) found 70 percent of Korean American women in New York worked outside the home.[8]

The general figures on labor force participation include full-time as well as part-time workers; however, there is a separate breakdown for women who work 35 hours or more. These data are important to examine because they show that a higher percentage of Asian American women work more hours. The 2000 census found 74.8 percent of Asian American women and 74.6 percent of Pacific Islander women work 35 hours or more, compared to 71.0 percent of all women in the United States. Filipino Americans again top this category with 79.5 percent of the women working 35 hours or more. It is interesting to find that women in three out of the four Southeast Asian groups (Cambodians, Laotians, and Vietnamese) also have a higher-than-average full-time employment record compared to the national average (see Table 7-6).

Labor force participation and full-time employment have both positive and negative consequences for working women. On the positive side, women without husbands must work to earn a living and those who are married can

Table 7-6 Percentage of Asian American Women 16 Years and Older in the Labor Force, 2000

Group	% of Women in Labor Force	% at Work 35 or More Hours
All	62.5	71.0
Pacific Islanders	64.6	74.6
Asian Americans	62.7	74.8
Chinese	62.5	75.2
Filipino	73.1	79.5
Japanese	53.1	70.6
Asian Indian	59.1	74.2
Korean	58.5	70.8
Vietnamese	64.0	74.5
Cambodian	54.8	73.6
Laotian	64.3	78.9
Hmong	52.2	66.7

Source: U.S. Census Bureau, Summary File 4, PCT 82.

enjoy the benefits of a two-paycheck household. In addition, the challenge of the job and the social contacts with other workers are as important for women's attachment to paid work as it is for men. The fact that a woman is earning a significant income can, in some cases, create a more egalitarian marital relationship over the traditional or authoritarian family structure. This tends to be the case for the more educated, second- and third-generation Asian American professionals.[9] On the other hand, as with all other dual-earner families, conflicts can, and often do, arise. When both the wife and husband work, there is precious little time for each other, their children, or household tasks. This is particularly true for working-class families in which one or both the parents may be working more than one job or irregular hours. In a survey of Chinese American high school students in New York, Betty Lee Sung (1987) found 32 percent of the students did not see their fathers for days at a time, and 21 percent of the respondents experienced the same situation with their mothers. Sung also found that 21 percent of the respondents did not see their fathers all week, while 17 percent did not see their mothers all week. Not surprisingly, a common complaint among parents Sung heard in her research was that they did not have any time to spend with their children. Many of her respondents worked in garment factories or restaurants that are open seven days a week and late into the evening.[10] As with all other groups, Asian American women still bear most of the responsibility for cooking, domestic chores, and child rearing even in dual-earner families. Min's New York study found high levels of stress and marital conflict among Korean American wives who spent 75.5 hours a week working a job and doing housework, which was 12 more hours a week than their husbands worked.[11] Within these types of families, domestic violence may erupt.

Domestic Violence

Attention to domestic violence within the Asian American and Pacific Islander communities is increasing. A leading organization in this effort is the Asian and Pacific Islander Institute on Domestic Violence. The Institute serves as a clearinghouse on information, research, and resources on critical issues about violence against women in Asian and Pacific Islander communities. According to the Institute, domestic or intimate partner violence is described as "a pattern of behaviors that includes physical, sexual, verbal, emotional economic, and/or psychological abuse."[12] Domestic violence against women and men exists in all social classes and among all ethnic groups. In one national survey, 12 percent of Asian and Pacific Islander women reported physical assault by a spouse or partner and 3.8 percent reported having been raped.[13] A National Asian Women's Health Organization (NAWHO) telephone interview of 336 women ages 18–34 found 27 percent of those who responded experienced emotional abuse from a spouse or intimate partner.[14] Several studies in the Boston area found more than 40 percent of Cambodian, South Asian, and Vietnamese women acknowledged or experienced domestic violence.[15] A study of Korean American men in Chicago and in Queens, New York, reported 18 percent said they committed acts of physical violence against a spouse within the past year (e.g., slapping, shoving, grabbing, throwing something, etc.) and 6.3 percent admitted to having committed what the researcher called "severe violence" (e.g., kicking, biting, hitting with a fist, threatening with a gun or knife, or actually shooting or stabbing).[16] Similarly, another study of Chinese in Los Angeles found 18.1 percent of those surveyed experienced "minor physical violence" and 8 percent experienced "severe physical violence."[17]

In an online report, *Innovative Strategies to Address Domestic Violence in Asian and Pacific Islander Communities: Examining Themes, Models, and Interventions* (2002), the Institute was critical of what they call the "mainstream" model of how to respond to domestic violence and offered alternative approaches. One mainstream model characteristic focuses on the individual as the unit of intervention rather than examine abuse within a broader family, community, and social context. According to the Institute, "API women do not necessarily experience domestic violence as an individual survivor abused by an individual batterer. Immediate and extended family members are often actively involved in the pattern of abuse."[18] This was the case for Jin Sook Hong, a Korean American who withstood torturous abuse in her eleven-year marriage. Like many Korean American women, Hong did not admit she was a victim of domestic violence because she was afraid people in her close-knit Korean American community would gossip and ostracize her. She also thought her family and community would consider her a bad wife. The situation was especially difficult for Hong because her husband was a young assistant pastor in her father's church. "I thought that nobody would believe this because he was so good on the outside," Hong said of her former husband. "It was a dungeon for 11 years." Eventually she confided in her sister-in-law about the violence and pleaded for help. Unfortunately the sister-in-law was more interested in protecting her brother and offered no assistance.[19] Often it isn't until the violence becomes extreme that most Asian and Pacific Islander women come forward and admit to being abused. Only after Abraham Abraham, an immigrant from India, who went on a rampage stabbing his wife with a butcher's knife in front of the couple's three children, did their history of domestic violence become public. During the court trial Abraham's wife testified that she had been attacked many times by her husband. He was eventually convicted of attempted murder and later deported back to India. "The biggest problem in our community is the fear from the community itself," explains Mehru Master, from the South Asian Network. "Our community is in denial. Sometimes when a woman is brave enough to come out, the community brands her, 'Oh there must be something wrong with her.'"[20]

It is for this reason the Institute highlights the importance of raising awareness of the prevalence of domestic violence and encourages ending the silence. National attention to domestic violence against Asian women began after the March 1995 murder of Susana Remerata, her 7-month-old fetus, and two friends by her estranged husband in Seattle, Washington. Remerata was a 27-year-old mail-order bride and former beauty queen from the Philippines who was seeking a divorce from her husband, 47-year-old Timothy Blackwell.

During the bitter court proceedings, Remerata alleged he violently abused her, while Blackwell claimed he entered the marriage fraudulently, which would be grounds for her deportation. The trial was about to enter closing arguments when Blackwell walked up to the three women and shot them at point-blank range. Blackwell was convicted of aggravated first-degree murder, but the incident resonated far beyond this one tragedy. A year after the shootings, fifteen groups organized a vigil and remembrance to the murder victims. "We have come together to remember the lives of Susana, Phoebe [Dizon] and Veronica [Laureta Johnson] because we need to draw attention to their deaths," said Emma Catague, who helped plan the event. "We need to convince battered women there is hope and a way for them to find safety."[21] Efforts to remember what happened to the victims in this case have continued in Seattle. One example is the recent exhibit at the Wing Luke Asian Museum titled "Women and Violence." As part of the exhibit, empty jars were placed throughout the museum with a note asking: "Have you ever known someone who is a victim of domestic violence?" along with a pile of rocks. Visitors are encouraged to place a rock in a jar if their answer to the question is yes. "Domestic violence is still a taboo issue in the community," said Emma Catague, program manager for the Asian and Pacific Islander Women and Safety Center, which was one of the exhibit's community partners. "The community has a role to prevent it. The more education we do, the better."[22]

The Institute's most recent report (2005) highlights a "community engagement continuum" and successful model programs that focus on domestic violence in the Asian and Pacific Islander communities.[23] The first part of the continuum is community outreach and education, which raises community awareness about the issues of violence against women and children and antiviolence resources. The report featured the work of the Cambodian Association of America based in Long Beach, California, which started a labor intensive "Door-Knocking Campaign" as part of its Stand Against Violence Effectively (SAVE) program. This program is unique in that it goes directly to the homes of families to talk about a variety of family concerns including domestic violence, rather than wait for the victims of violence to come to the program. This program has led women to come forward when, if left alone, they would not have sought help. Once formal contact has been made individuals can meet with a program advocate individually or be referred to other resources. Project SAVE also has a batter's treatment and counseling component.[24]

The second part of the continuum is community mobilization, which aims for active community participation and engagement supporting the antiviolence organization or addressing the problem of violence against women and children. The model organization in this area is Shimtuh ("Resting Place" in Korean), a program that started as a collaborative effort between Asian Women's Shelter in San Francisco, the Korean Community Center of the East Bay, and the Korean American Coalition to End Domestic Violence. The first activity of Shimtuh was to create a needs assessment report to find out the extent of domestic violence in the Korean American community and then create a forum for discussion. The assessment was based on interviews with more than three hundred women and men of various ages and backgrounds, as well as six focus groups. The research found 42 percent of the respondents reported they knew a woman who had been hit, kicked, or otherwise physically abused by a husband or boyfriend. A third of the respondents had witnessed their father physically abusing their mother while growing up. These figures showed the prevalence of domestic violence in the Korean American community and how great the need is for awareness, intervention, and prevention programs. The assessment survey and the dissemination of results were developed with the intention of maximizing community involvement. The results were alarming, but highly insightful, and were an important beginning for mobilizing the community around the issue.[25]

The third part of the continuum is community organizing, which involves longer-term strategies to increase sustained community-based capacities to address violence against women and children. The Asian and Pacific Islander Women and Family Safety Center (API Safety Center) in Seattle, Washington, was singled out for its exclusive focus on community organizing and the creation of partnership programs rather than its own direct services. API Safety Center has long been involved with addressing domestic violence, from the Susana Remerata murder case to the "Women and Violence" exhibit at the Wing Luke Asian Museum. Another project API Safety Center helped initiate is the Natural Helper Program with the Samoan Parenting Group of the Samoan Christian Congregational Church. Led by the church's minister and his wife, this program started as a gathering of families to talk about communication issues that became a discussion of domestic violence and child abuse. The group offers education on domestic violence for Samoan families and opportunities to learn nonviolent alternatives for conflict resolution.[26]

The last part of the continuum is community accountability, which develops the capacity of community members to support survivors and hold abusers accountable for their violence. This is the farthest end of the continuum and is highly controversial. A notable example is the work of Sakhi, a community-based organization in New York dedicated to ending violence against South Asian women. Like the API Safety Center, Sakhi prioritizes organizing efforts; demonstrations by staff, volunteers, community supporters, and domestic violence survivors are common practices. This includes gathering at the home of an abuser, distributing flyers to neighbors documenting the abuse, and shouting their outrage at the acts of violence. This type of "public naming" protest occurs only at the request of the victim, is thoroughly researched in terms of legal concerns, and is announced to the police and media well ahead of time. Community accountability activities such as this emerged from of the ambivalence toward the criminal justice system often felt in immigrant communities, and especially by immigrant female victims of domestic violence. There are some well intended laws that make it easier to deport those who are convicted of crimes related to domestic violence crimes. However, these laws may discourage the reporting of domestic violence because victims want the abuse to stop, but not necessarily want the spouse or intimate partner deported. On the other hand, some argue that these laws have helped victims because it gives them a threat that stops the abuse. Community accountability intervention strategies are often called "extra-legal" or alternative approaches to the criminal justice system.[27]

The issue of domestic violence is not merely an individual concern for Asian Americans and Pacific Islanders. Community engagement is fundamental in acknowledging, addressing, and confronting abusive relationships. The studies and reports of the Asian and Pacific Islander Institute on Domestic Violence have raised the profile of this important issue, critiqued mainstream theories and approaches on what can be done to stop and prevent violence in the home, and examined a conceptual framework and model programs aimed at finding a more strategic approach unique to the experiences and perspectives of Asian Americans and Pacific Islanders across the country.

NEW GENERATIONS AND IDENTITY FORMATION OF ASIAN AMERICANS

Another area of stress for Asian American families is the changes that happen between generations and new identity formations. As discussed in Chapter 1, the passage of the Immigration Reform Act of 1965, global economic restructuring, and the end of the Vietnam War in 1975 have had a dramatic impact on the number and type of immigrants from Asia entering the United States. Since 1971, more than 8.6 million people from Asia have come to this country either as immigrants or refugees. The large influx of people from Asia is a relatively new phenomenon. Early research on Asian immigrants focused almost exclusively on the experiences of the first generation, or the foreign-born, with relatively little attention to the children of immigrants, or second generation, born in the United States. Until recently only the experience of second generation (Nisei) Japanese Americans were researched in great detail, as seen in Bill Hosokawa's book *Nisei: The Quiet Americans* (1969).[28] Most of the books on the Nisei experience have centered on Japanese American internment during and after World War II. Attention to first-generation Asian American immigrants and refugees is understandable as 68.9 percent of all Asians living in the U.S. are foreign-born, according to the 2000 census. At the same time, the 2000 census found 74.2 percent of Asian males under 18 and 72.2 percent of Asian females under 18 are born in the United States.[29]

Among the most important books on U.S.-born Asian American experiences are Margaret Gibson's *Accomodation Without Assimilation: Sikh Immigrants in an American High School* (1988), Nathan Caplan, Marcella Choy, and John Witmore's (eds.) *Children of the Boat People: A Study of Educational Success* (1991), Donna Nagata's, *Legacy of Injustice: Exploring the Cross-Generational Impact of the Japanese American Internment* (1993), Nazli Kibria's, *Family Tightrope: The Changing Lives of Vietnamese Americans* (1993) and *Becoming Asian American: Second Generation Chinese and Korean American Identities* (2002), Stacey J. Lee's, *Unraveling the Model Minority Stereotype: Listening to Asian American Youth* (1996), Min Zhou and Carl Bankston III's *How Vietnamese Children Adapt to Life in the United States* (1998), Pyong Gap Min and Rose Kim's (eds.) *Struggle for Identity: Narratives by*

Asian American Professionals (1999), Pyong Gap Min and Kyeyoung Park's (eds.) *Amerasia Journal: Second Generation Asian Americans' Ethnic Identity* (1999), Mai Tuan's, *Forever Foreigners or Honorary Whites? The Asian American Experience Today* (1998), and Jennifer Lee and Min Zhou's (eds.) *Asian American Youth: Culture, Identity, and Ethnicity* (2004).[30] Research cited above has generally used a redefinition in describing the various generations. In the past, first generation strictly meant foreign-born, second generation strictly meant children of immigrants born in the United States, and third generation referred to grandchildren of immigrants, etc. However, these rigid definitions are not appropriate to the broad diversity of the Asian American experience. For example, what "generation" are you if one parent is an immigrant and the other parent is U.S.-born? Similarly, does it make sense to call someone first generation if they were born in another country but came to the United States as an infant? As a result, many scholars use definitions outlined by Zhou (1999). The first generation includes foreign-born individuals and arrived to the U.S. after the age of 13. The 1.5 generation is made up of those born abroad but entered the United States between the ages of 5 and 13. The second generation population consists of those born in the United States *and* those foreign-born who came to the United States before the age of 5. The third generation and beyond are presumed to be born in this country. These definitions are more realistic in terms of identity formation based on experience rather than just birthplace.[31]

Asian American Identity Formation

Identity generally refers to a person's sense of belonging in society based on his or her social experience. In today's rapidly changing, increasingly diverse, and highly technological world, many people feel isolated and find it difficult to establish any solid sense of identity. One way of maintaining a sense of identity is to define oneself based on ethnic characteristics. Ethnic identity not only impacts thoughts, beliefs, and behavior, but it also serves as the basis of how a person is viewed by others. In 1971, psychologists Stanley Sue and Derald Sue developed a personality structure for interpreting Asian American identity. Drawing from ethnic culture and American racism, and highly influenced by assimilation theory, their four classifications were labeled traditionalist, assimilationist, bicultural, and marginal. The traditionalist usually represented recent immigrants who held close to their Asian cultural heritage. On the other side, assimilationists were those who chose to fully adopt American values and behavioral norms as their own. Those in this category tend to have little ethnic identity and generally associate with people outside of their own ethnic group. Bicultural Asian Americans are those who maintain, and move freely in, both Asian and American cultural spheres and tend to be the most successful. Ethnic identity for these individuals is high, yet they also participate well within the broader American cultural milieu. Lastly, those who are marginal reject both Asian and American cultures and are left isolated, alienated, and alone.

This model is very simple and easy to understand, but it has also been criticized for being a somewhat static one-size-fits-all framework that lacks the ability to explain how ethnic identity by different generations is developed. Uba (1994) points out that the development of ethnic identity is a highly complex phenomenon and can vary greatly from one individual to another. Consciousness, adoption, and adhibition (application) of ethnic identity will often ebb and flow within an individual over time depending on his or her situation and environment. Uba highlighted a number of factors that can account for individual differences in ethnic identity. These factors are formulated externally and are considered contextual; at the same time, these factors are often subject to internal interpretations. First of all, Uba recognizes that experiences with racism are the "root" of individual differences in ethnic identity. Confronting the harsh realities of racism may cause a person to enhance ethnic identity, or it may cause him or her to reject and deny any ethnic affiliation. Second, Uba identified nativity (foreign-born vs. American-born) and generation differences as important factors in creating and maintaining ethnic identity. It is generally expected in the assimilationist model that the first generation of Asian immigrants would have a greater sense of ethnic identity, while subsequent generations would become much more assimilated into the dominant society, and have less and less ethnic identification.[32]

A newer and more complex explanation of second-generation identity formation as well as social and economic mobility comes from the work of Alejandro Portes and Rubén Rumbaut (1996). Similar to the Sue and Sue model, Portes and Rumbaut describe what they call four types of acculturation. The first type is "Consonant Resistance to Acculturation," which means the immigrant family, both the parents and the children, are separated and isolated within the ethnic or immigrant community. For Sue and Sue, this could be considered traditional. The second type is "Consonant Acculturation," or the immigrant family's search for acceptance into the mainstream society. This is akin to assimilationist for Sue and Sue. The third type is "Dissonant Acculturation," which takes place when the first-generation immigrant parents want to maintain ethnic ties primarily by maintaining their culture, not learning English, and often living in an ethnic enclave, but the children seek to abandon the ethnic community culturally, linguistically, and geographically. The outcome of this scenario could be the children feeling marginal, especially if the family lives in a strong ethnic community. However, if the family lives in a more integrated community, the outcome for the children may be more assimilationist. Regardless, this type most certainly leads to a rupture of family ties, as well as a loss of parental authority. The fourth type is "Selective Acculturation," when both the first-generation immigrant parents and the children learn the culture and the language of the dominant society but still have close ties and respect for the ethnic community. This type is very much like being bicultural in the Sue and Sue model.[33]

Along with the types of acculturation, Portes and Rumbaut also focus on the social context that the immigrant family confronts. One possible social context is a high level of discrimination from the host society coupled with little support from an ethnic community. The other possible social context is a low level of discrimination from the host society and a great deal of community resources, or support from an ethnic community. The last element of the Portes and Rumbaut model is what they call "segmented assimilation outcomes," based on the type of acculturation and social context experienced by the individual and family for at least one generation. For Portes and Rumbaut, positive or upward outcomes are primarily educational and economic mobility. Figure 7-1 (p. 252) provides a graphic explanation of this model. It should be noted that Portes and Rumbaut emphasize that the outcomes listed below "should not be seen as exhaustive of all possible forms."[34]

The Portes and Rumbaut model provides important explanatory power into the generational changes experienced by immigrant groups, both historically and contemporarily. The model is also useful in understanding different outcomes within a specific ethnic community. The work of Zhou and Bankston, *How Vietnamese Children Adapt to Life in the United States,* focuses on a Vietnamese community in New Orleans and argues the 1.5- and second-generation Vietnamese children excelled in school primarily because the immigrant families were strong on traditional culture with selective acculturation to the new culture. The Vietnamese Americans in New Orleans fit somewhere between Cell G and Cell H in the Portes and Rumbaut model. At the same time, Zhou and Bankston highlight young Vietnamese delinquents, who are described as young people who have lost the positive relationship with their parents and culture. These youngsters would be placed in Cell E in the Portes and Rumbaut model.

Simlarly, Kibria's *Family Tightrope: The Changing Lives of Vietnamese Americans* provides excellent insight into these role shifts and challenges faced by Vietnamese American families she studied in Philadelphia, a city without a sizable or strong Vietnamese community. She describes the traditional Vietnamese family as an extended structure that is based on hierarchical Confucian principles of the dominance of males over females, and elders over the young. This kind of organizational form works to instill a strong sense of individual dependence on the larger family unit. Clinging to the safety and security of traditional values is one way Vietnamese American families try to endure the dramatic relocation away from their homelands. At the same time, Kibria found that patterns of family roles and authority are constantly being challenged in the United States. She describes older women often exercising considerable power in their households, especially when they work outside the home. In some cases, Vietnamese American refugee women assume the primary role as family "breadwinner" because female-dominated service sector jobs are more easily available for Vietnamese American women than low-skill jobs sought by Vietnamese American men.

It should be noted that this gender-reversal situation may be temporary, as the husband takes the time to obtain educational or technical training that eventually enables him to gain more skilled employment. Nonetheless, tensions arise as the traditional role of the male as the primary breadwinner for the family is often undermined in the United States by economic necessity. Although the economic well-being of Vietnamese American families has risen over time, this is often due to a pulling together of resources between the husband, wife, and perhaps other wage earners in the family. Along with changing

FIGURE 7-1

Type of Acculturation	Social Context: Discrimination High; Family/Community Resources High	Social Context: Discrimination Low; Family/Community Resources Low	Segmented Assimilation Outcomes
Consonant Resistance To Acculturation/Family isolation within the ethnic community. (Traditionalist)	Cell A X−	Cell B X+/−	Downward: probable return to home country (−) Stagnant: perpetuation of distinct ethnic subculture (−/+)
Consonant Acculturation/Family Integrates and is accepted into the mainstream. (Assimilationist)	Cell C X−	Cell D X+	Downward: blocked entry into American mainstream; Reactive ethnicity (−) Upward: integration into mainstream and gradual Abandonment of parental culture (+)
Dissonant Acculturation/First generation resists acculturation, second generation accepts acculturation (Marginal or Assimilationist or Traditionalist)	Cell E X−	Cell F X?	Downward: socialization into urban underclass roles; Adoption of adversarial stance toward the mainstream (−) Uncertain: contingent on individual traits and resources (?)
Selective Acculturation/First generation and children learn the culture and language of the dominant society but still have close ties and respect for the ethnic community. (Bicultural)	Cell G X+	Cell H X+	Upward: slow mobility into white-collar occupations (+) Upward: rapid mobility into professional and managerial Occupations (+)

Source: Adapted from Alejandro Portes and Rubén Rumbaut, *Immigrant America: A Portrait*, 2nd Edition (Berkeley and Los Angeles: University of California Press, 1996), pp. 249 and 252, Figures 9 and 10.

gender relations, Vietnamese families confront major shifts in authority roles between old and young. Kibria described many Vietnamese families in which the children and younger adults have grown up in the United States and today possess greater language skills, educational opportunities, and job training skills than their parents. In the case of Vietnamese families in Philadelphia, they would oscillate between Cell F and Cell G.

Additional Factors for Identity Formation

Of course, this model does have its weaknesses. First, as mentioned above, positive outcomes are primarily seen as educational and economic mobility. But as we learned in Chapters 3 and 4, does a high level of education and a reasonably well paying job equate to happiness and social acceptance? Portes and Rumbaut cite the work of Gibson (1988) as a positive example of "selective acculturation," somewhere between Cells G and H.[35] However, in their article "Invisible Americans: An Exploration of Indo-American Quality of Life" (1995–1996), Snehendu B. Kar et al. surveyed 264 Asian Indian parents and 224 Asian Indian college students. They measured a number of attitudes and experiences including intergenerational dynamics and areas of conflict and congruence. The researchers found 39 percent of Asian Indian parents reported that the behavior of their children was a major cause of conflict in the family. The greatest source of intergenerational tension within Asian Indian families was around dating and marital preferences of the younger generation. Traditional Asian Indian parents believe dating and marriage concern the whole family and are not matters of individual choice. Among the college-aged children, 52.6 percent of Asian Indian women and 40.9 of Asian Indian men responded that dating preferences were the major conflict issue with their parents. Other major conflict areas highlighted in the survey were also interesting. More Asian Indian women (13.2 percent) had conflicts over education compared to Asian Indian men (6.8 percent). This may be an indicator that the women are unhappy about not being given the same opportunities as men. Conversely, more Asian Indian men (15.9 percent) expressed dissatisfaction with their careers, compared with women (7.9 percent). This may be an indicator that the men were pushed into careers that were not of their own personal choosing. One of the most significant findings of the survey was that nearly twice as many younger generation Asian Indians reported depression and suicidal tendencies, compared with the Asian Indian parents (12 percent to 6.5 percent). These findings were confirmed in a follow-up study (1998).[36]

Similarly, as the titles of the books by Tuan, *Forever Foreigners or Honorary Whites* (1999), as well as Min and Kim, *Struggle for Identity: Narratives by Asian American Professionals* (1998), imply, economic and professional success does *not* necessarily mean freedom from conflict within the family or translate into social acceptance. In particular, Tuan argues that a new generation of Asian Americans has greater flexibility to choose their own ethnic identity but still has to confront the contradictions of how others identify Asian Americans.

Although African Americans may be economically marginalized, they are not considered foreign; Asian Americans are much better integrated economically, yet they face "an assumption of foreignness" and ultimately are not fully accepted as "American."[37] Kibria (2002) picks up on this same theme in looking at the "puzzle" of integration by new generations of Asian Americans. She coined a new term *ethnicization* to describe Asian Americans who have a "double-edged position of Asian Americans . . . straddling both integration into and marginalization from the dominant society."[38]

Along with external factors, there are internal factors that add to the development of ethnic identity. Uba describes how Asian American ethnic identity is affected by differences in cognitive development. Some of these cognitive differences are age specific; that is, younger children are simply too immature to understand the complexities of ethnicity. More common differences, however, have much more to do with the sophistication of a person's thinking processes and his or her abilities to integrate divergent experiences and information. Another internal factor she describes is the individual's selective attitude toward different aspects of ethnicity. For example, someone may reject notions of male dominance within Asian American culture, yet maintain language and ceremonial traditions. One more internal factor Uba describes is one's ability to appropriately evaluate the salience of ethnicity. This means individuals can consciously invoke ethnic identity on a selective basis. At home one may have strong ethnic affiliation, but at work or at school one's ethnicity is kept much more subdued.[39]

Cultural and generational conflicts are additional stressors on Asian Americans identified by researchers. Although some social scientists have argued there are some important culturally equivalent elements between middle-class Western and Asian culture, Asian American scholars also point to important differences. The most common cultural and generational conflict among Asian Americans centers on individualism. In the United States the notion of the independent, spontaneous, outspoken, and aggressive individual is highly valued, whereas in Asian cultures filial piety (obligation to one's parents), modesty, and respect for others are highly regarded. The uncritical adoption of American values can become a mixed blessing for a new generation of Asian Americans, especially when it creates a schism in terms of customs and attitudes on individualism between the different generations in the family as well as internalized oppression. Asian American women are doubly hampered by the conflict of their family's and dominant society's expectations of what it means to be an Asian woman.

Sociologists Karen Pyke and Denise Johnson (2003) interviewed hundred daughters of Korean and Vietnamese immigrants and provide many quotes from the women in their study. Elizabeth, a 19-year-old Vietnamese American told researchers, "I feel like when I'm with other Asians that I'm the *typical* passive [Asian] person and I feel that's what's expected of me and if I do say something and if I am the *normal* person that I am, I'd stick out like a sore thumb." (emphasis added by the researchers) Similarly, Lisa, an 18-year-old Korean American, talks about being among non-Asians saying: "They think

I'm really different from other Asian girls because I'm so outgoing. They feel that Asian girls have to be the shy type who is very passive and sometimes I'm not like that so they think, 'Lisa, are you Asian?'" According to Pyke and Johnson, the words of these high achieving university students are filled with ambiguity that is not easily solved, and far from an optimistic selective acculturation based on free choice. "Our findings illustrate the powerful interplay of controlling images and hegemonic femininity in promoting internalized oppression," the authors write in their conclusion. "Respondents draw on racial images and assumptions in their narrative construction of Asian cultures as innately oppressive of women and fully resistant to change against which the white-dominated mainstream is framed as a paradigm of gender equality. This serves as a proassimilation function by suggesting that Asian American women will find gender equality in exchange for rejecting their ethnicity and adopting white standards of gender. . . . This marking of ethnic culture as a symbolic repository of patriarchy obscures variations in ethnic gender practices as well as gender inequality in the mainstream. Thus compliance with the dominant society is secured."[40]

Ethnic identity for Asian American women and men is even further complicated by the multiplicity of ethnic identities possible. For example, a Filipino American whose parents are immigrants from the Philippines can be identified as a Filipino, a Filipino American, an Asian American, perhaps even Hispanic, or simply as an American, along with many other nonethnic choices. Uba points out that the degree to which an individual Asian American identifies with other Asian American groups has a great deal to do with how the other Asian Americans are perceived.[41] During World War II, many Asian American groups made a point not to be identified with Japanese or Japanese Americans. This was especially true when Japanese Americans were removed to internment camps. Similarly, many Asian Americans did not want to be identified with Koreans or Korean Americans during the L.A. riot in 1992.

Some studies have found a reawakening of ethnic identification within some third-generation Asian American groups. This variation of the standard assimilation pattern is not unique and has been observed among European groups by historian Marcus L. Hansen. From his book *The Problems of the Third Generation* (1938) emerged "Hansen's Rule" that says, in essence: What the second generation tries to forget, the third generation tries to remember.[42] A very good example of how racism, nativity, and generational difference have affected ethnic identity among one Asian American group can be found in the book by psychologist Nagata (1993). In it, she describes how the forced relocation during World War II continues to haunt Japanese Americans generations later. The most striking finding from Nagata's work is the legacy of silence between the second-generation Japanese Americans (Nisei) who wanted to forget the internment camp experience, and the third-generation Japanese Americans (Sansei) who wanted to remember and learn from the internment experience. Nisei parents interned during the war wanted to be seen as Americanized and wanted to separate themselves from their first-generation immigrant (Issei) parents. After the war, the Nisei hoped to protect their children from any further racial humiliation and tended de-emphasize anything distinctly Japanese, while encouraging their children to Americanize to the greatest extent possible. It was not unusual for the Japanese American Sansei, who were coming of age in the 1960s and 1970s, to first learn the details of the internment camp experience in college and only then begin to develop their own sense of ethnic identity and ethnic pride. Nagata sent out a twenty-page survey to some seven hundred Sansei across the United States as part of her research and asked them a number of questions about their family histories. She learned that in most cases any conversations about the camps among the different generations of Japanese Americans were very rare, lasting no more than fifteen minutes. Despite this pattern of denial, the children of these Nisei were more likely to develop a stronger ethnic identity, associated more with other Japanese Americans, and have distinct feelings about their vulnerable minority status than those Sansei whose parents were not interned.[43]

NEW ASIAN AMERICAN FAMILIES AND IDENTITIES

So far this chapter has focused on the diverse and changing Asian American families and identities. Other important areas of research in Asian American studies focus on Asian Americans who are interracially married, biracial and multiracial, and gay and lesbian. They are all part of the ever-expanding Asian American experience, and much of the recent research done on these populations have concentrated on the creation and recreation of new family and identity structures.

Interracial Marriage

Interracial marriage (the marriage between people of different races) is a growing but still small percentage of all marriages in the United States. The latest 2003 census figures counted more than 2 million interracial couples, representing about 3.6 percent of all marriages. The numbers in Table 7-7 show the upward trajectory of interracial marriage from 1980 to 2003. In this table, the Census Bureau placed Asian Americans into the "other race" group. Although many people view interracial marriage as a phenomenon involving black-white couples, interracial marriages more commonly involve a wide range of combinations. Indeed black-white marriages represent less than 20 percent of interracial marriages. Interracial marriages among whites and "others" and blacks and "others" make up more than 80 percent of the interracial marriages in the United States. The U.S. Census Bureau does not break down interracial marriage beyond the broad white, black, and other categories. Experts generally agree, however, that Asian Americans make up a significant portion of this "other" category.

C. N. Le published statistics based on the 2000 census on Asian American marriage partners on his Web site, Asian-Nation.org. According to Le's

Table 7-7 Married Couples by Race 1980–2003 (in thousands)

Race	1980	1990	2000	2003
Total (1)	49,714	53,256	56,497	58,586
Interracial Married Couples, Total	651	964	1,464	2,094
White (2)/Black(2)	167	211	363	416
White(2)/Other race(3)	450	720	1,051	1,546
Black(2)/Other race(3)	34	33	50	132

(1) Includes other married couples not shown.
(2) The 2003 Current Population Survey (CPS) allowed respondents to choose more than one race. Beginning 2003 data represent persons who selected this race group only and exclude persons reporting only one race. The CPS in prior years only allowed respondents to report one race group.
(3) "Other race" is any race other than white or black, such as American Indian, Asian Americans, etc. This total excludes combinations of other races.
Source: U.S. Census Bureau, *Statistical Abstract of the United States: 2004–2005*, Table 52, p. 48.

calculations shown in Table 7-8 (p. 258), Japanese American men and women have the highest rates of *exogamy*, marriage to someone outside of their own racial or ethnic group. This has been consistent for decades. Korean American men and Asian Indian women, conversely, have the highest rates of *endogamy*, marriage to someone within their own specific ethnic group. Le has separate statistics for Asian Americans who are born in the United States or are 1.5 generation. In Table 7-9 (p. 260), we see the numbers change rather dramatically. In this case Filipino American men and women have rates of *exogamy* that exceed 50 percent. We also see a very high rate of exogamy among Korean American women. On the other hand, Vietnamese American men (72.7 percent) and Asian Indian women (69.9 percent) have the highest rates of endogamy. Two trends are important to note. First, we also see in all Asian American groups, except for Asian Indians, that women have a much higher rate of exogamy than men. Second, those involved in exogamous marriages typically interracially marry whites more than any other racial or ethnic group. Both have been consistent for decades, and both need further explanation.

Prior to the 1965 Immigration Reform Act, Asian American interracial marriage was a rare, although not unheard of, phenomenon. For example, the earliest recorded interracial marriages included Yung Wing, the first Chinese national to graduate from Yale University, who married a white woman, Louise Kelloge, in 1877. Chinese pioneer woman Lalu Nathoy arrived in the United States in 1872 and after years of struggle married Charlie Bemis in 1898. She became better known as frontier woman Polly Bemis. Interracial marriages between Chinese and blacks were recorded in Mississippi in the late nineteenth and early twentieth centuries. There were also small communities of Filipino men married to white women in urban Chicago, as well as Asian Indian men married to Mexican American women in rural California during the early part of the twentieth century.[44]

Table 7-8 Percentage of Marriage Partners Six Largest Asian American Groups, 2000

Group	Marriage Partner	Percentage	Group	Marriage Partner	Percentage
Asian Indian Men	Asian Indian	89.7	Asian Indian Women	Asian Indian	92.0
	Other Asian	1.5		Other Asian	1.2
	White	6.3		White	4.1
	Black	0.6		Black	0.6
	Hispanic/Latino	1.4		Hispanic/Latino	0.8
Chinese American Men	Chinese	89.5	Chinese American Women	Chinese	83.0
	Other Asian	4.1		Other Asian	3.3
	White	5.1		White	12.0
	Black	0.1		Black	0.6
	Hispanic/Latino	1.4		Hispanic/Latino	1.1
Filipino American Men	Filipino	83.1	Filipino American Women	Filipino	62.7
	Other Asian	2.5		Other Asian	2.7
	White	10.1		White	27.3
	Black	0.2		Black	2.8
	Hispanic/Latino	3.3		Hispanic/Latino	3.9

	Men	Women
Japanese American		
Japanese	69.2	50.9
Other Asian	8.8	5.4
White	17.5	37.1
Black	0.3	1.7
Hispanic/Latino	2.7	2.4
Korean American		
Korean	93.1	69.4
Other Asian	1.9	2.8
White	3.9	24.3
Black	0.0	1.7
Hispanic/Latino	0.9	1.4
Vietnamese American		
Vietnamese	92.4	86.4
Other Asian	3.7	3.3
White	2.7	9.0
Black	0.1	0.3
Hispanic/Latino	1.1	1.0

Totals do not add up to 100 due to rounding.

Source: C. N. Lee at http://www.asian-nation.org/interracial.shtml. © 2004–2006 by C. N. Lee. Used by permission.

Table 7-9 Percentage of Marriage Partners Six Largest Asian American Groups Second and 1.5 Generation, 2000

Group	Marriage Partner	Percentage	Group	Marriage Partner	Percentage
Asian Indian			Asian Indian		
Men	Asian Indian	69.2	Women	Asian Indian	69.9
	Other Asian	3.7		Other Asian	4.1
	White	20.5		White	21.1
	Black	1.7		Black	2.5
	Hispanic/Latino	4.3		Hispanic/Latino	1.6
Chinese American			Chinese American		
Men	Chinese	65.5	Women	Chinese	55.0
	Other Asian	12.7		Other Asian	10.8
	White	19.3		White	29.9
	Black	0.2		Black	0.7
	Hispanic/Latino	2.6		Hispanic/Latino	2.9
Filipino American			Filipino American		
Men	Filipino	49.6	Women	Filipino	37.0
	Other Asian	12.6		Other Asian	9.2
	White	28.1		White	40.5
	Black	0.6		Black	4.0
	Hispanic/Latino	7.7		Hispanic/Latino	7.6

Japanese American Men		Japanese American Women	
Japanese	62.7	Japanese	56.2
Other Asian	13.9	Other Asian	11.2
White	19.7	White	28.1
Black	0.3	Black	0.9
Hispanic/Latino	2.8	Hispanic/Latino	2.6
Korean American Men		Korean American Women	
Korean	63.2	Korean	40.0
Other Asian	9.2	Other Asian	7.5
White	23.9	White	48.0
Black	0.1	Black	1.4
Hispanic/Latino	3.4	Hispanic/Latino	2.5
Vietnamese American Men		Vietnamese American Women	
Vietnamese	72.7	Vietnamese	66.8
Other Asian	11.7	Other Asian	7.1
White	11.3	White	22.7
Black	0.7	Black	0.7
Hispanic/Latino	2.9	Hispanic/Latino	2.4

Totals do not add up to 100 due to rounding.
Source: C. N. Lee at http://www.asian-nation.org/interracial.shtml. © 2004–2006 by C. N. Lee. Used by permission.

Asian interracial marriages took prominence after World War II. This time the vast majority of these marriages involved U.S. armed services personnel stationed in Asia and native Japanese and Korean "war brides." According to researcher Bok-Lim Kim (1972, 1977), these marriages tended to be happy and successful because the wives lived on U.S. military bases that served to insulate them from the poverty and strife in their home country. These war bride marriages also remained stable because the wives were able to maintain their own social networks outside of the base. However, Kim found that troubles began when these interracial couples relocated to the United States. Between the mid-1940s and the mid-1970s, approximately 100,000 women from Japan and Korea entered the United States as wives of U.S. servicemen. Cultural differences between the couples and adjustment difficulties for the immigrating women were two of the most common issues to arise between couples in these marriages. Frequent antagonism from both sides of the family, and scorn from some outsiders who objected to interracial marriages, were two common external factors that created a great deal of tension for the couple. Two thirds of the couples in Kim's study had either separated or divorced within three years of their arrival to the United States.[45]

At the same time, other studies showed that if these couples survive the initial pressures placed on their marriages, they will be successful, well-adjusted, and generally no different from any other married couples.[46] Research on the relative failure and/or success of these war-bride marriages of the 1940s through the 1960s is mixed because the available studies tend to be anecdotal and have sample sizes too small to be definitive. Despite these limitations, the war-bride experience is very important to examine with regard to the increased attention on Asian American interracial marriages in recent years.

Interest in Asian American interracial marriage reached a peak in the 1980s and early 1990s, especially in the popular media. The realities of Asian and Asian American women dating and marrying usually white males no longer seemed odd, but rather common and acceptable. By this time thousands of American servicemen were bringing home more war brides from the Philippines and Vietnam to join the mix of earlier war brides from Japan and Korea. What few television and movie images offered about Asians at the time generally depicted Asian women as spoils of war, docile, petite, and ever-eager to please men. In response to the Asian-white interracial marriage trend, and the images accompanying it, businesses began to emerge specializing in matching "mail-order" or "correspondence" brides from Asia (usually from the Philippines) with white males in the United States, Canada, and Australia.[47] Attention to this "new" trend of Asian-white interracial dating and marriage was raised to an even higher level when the *San Francisco Chronicle/Examiner* Sunday magazine printed a feature story entitled, "Asian Women, Caucasian Men" (1990), that sparked tremendous debate and inspired the greatest number of letters in the magazine's history. Writer Joan Walsh was heavily criticized for what many felt was an article laced with stereotypical images. The magazine's editors certainly contributed to the titillating nature of the story by providing an illustration of an Asian woman with long black hair whose arms are wrapped around a blond man, her head resting submissively on his broad shoulders.[48]

Amid all this mainstream media attention, several studies by Asian American scholars were published that attempted to describe and explain the high rate of Asian-white interracial marriages. Among the earliest research efforts was conducted by psychologist Harry Kitano and his colleagues. In his article, "Asian-American Interracial Marriage" (1984), Kitano counted 1,979 marriage licenses of Japanese, Chinese, and Korean Americans in Los Angeles County, and tabulated how many of them married individuals outside their own ethnic group. The research found that 49.9 percent of Japanese Americans, 30.2 percent of Chinese Americans, and 19.2 percent of Korean Americans married outside their own group. Kitano's research also found that women in all three Asian American groups *intermarried* (marriage between two people either from a different race or a different ethnic group) significantly more then Asian American men. In 1979, for example, 79.6 percent of the Korean American women counted married outside their own group. By contrast, 52.7 percent of the Japanese American women counted married outside their own group, while 56.3 percent of the Chinese American women counted married outside their own group. It should be noted that these figures on Asian American men and women do not separate Asian interracial marriage from interethnic marriages, although it is clear from Kitano's research that most of these marriages were to non-Asians.[49]

Kitano and his colleagues' work was highly provocative, but was also criticized for its rather crude methodology and limited scope. With this in mind, sociologists Sharon M. Lee and Keiko Yamanaka (1990) conducted research similar to Kitano's, but looked at the entire United States, and added Filipino, Asian Indian, and Vietnamese Americans. Lee and Yamanaka used a 5 percent sampling of 1980 U.S. census data to confirm many of Kitano's findings. For example, Lee and Yamanaka found that 92 percent of all Asian American intermarriages were in fact interracial. The researchers also confirmed that more Asian American women than men interracially married. This was due to the high number of foreign-born Asian American women who interracially married compared to the relatively low number of foreign-born Asian American men who interracially married, although the interracial gender gap between U.S.-born Asian men and women was not nearly as pronounced. Based on their detailed research, Lee and Yamanaka also found interracial marriage occurs most often among well-educated and professional Asian Americans.[50]

Why Do Asian Americans Interracially Marry?

The two studies above show the high rate of Asian American interracial marriage. Three perspectives on interracial marriage are commonly raised to explain the reasons for this phenomenon. The most simple and basic explanation for Asian American interracial marriage is a matter of individual choice. Asian Americans just happen to meet many people of different races, fall in love, and get married. Race is not a factor in these intimate personal decisions. In their book *Adjustment in Intercultural Marriage* (1977), Wen-Shing Tseng et al. explain intermarriage in general by the fact that some people have the need to be different; that is, they are more adventuresome than others and are always interested in trying and liking something different than the usual choice. Similarly, there are some people who marry someone of another race or ethnic group because that other person possesses a valued attribute that their own culture is not as likely to supply.[51] The problem with this perspective is that it doesn't explain variations in interracial marriages among racial minority groups. If love is indeed color-blind, and individuals exercise free choice in personal decisions, why is the interracial marriage rate for African Americans so low?

Another common explanation of Asian American interracial marriage is closely related to the assimilation theory and the work of Milton Gordon (1964). Gordon argues that marital assimilation, or intermarriage, between members of a minority group to members of the majority group is a positive sign of acceptance by the larger society. Compared to the individual free choice perspective, assimilation theory understands that interracial marriage between Asians and whites would not be taking place in any significant scale unless the larger society was willing to accept it. Sociologist Betty Lee Sung calls marriage between an Asian American and a non-Asian "the ultimate assimilation" and has dedicated a book, *Chinese American Intermarriage* (1990), to the subject.[52] The assimilation perspective offers a broad insight into interracial marriage, but it fails to answer some very important questions. If Asian Americans are so well accepted by the American mainstream, why is it that their interracial marriage patterns are mainly characterized by well-educated Asian Americans with high incomes, and not distributed equally throughout the Asian American population? More importantly, why is it that more Asian American women interracially marry than Asian American men?

An attempt to answer these questions produced by far the most controversial perspective on Asian American interracial marriage. In their article "Marriage Patterns of Asian Americans in California, 1980" (1990), sociologists Larry H. Shinagawa and Gin Y. Pang reinterpreted the statistical data on Asian American interracial marriage and offered a sophisticated analysis that challenged the individual choice and assimilation perspectives.[53] Shinagawa and Pang focused their attention on hypergamy theory, which tries to explain why in most cultures, women generally marry men of higher social and economic status rather than men of lower status (hypogamy). Shinagawa and Pang then added to the mix the fact that in a class and racially stratified society like the United States men and women often enter into romantic relationships depending on whether the other person possesses certain tangible and/or intangible resources. Tangible resources include money and a good job; intangible resources include physical appearance (i.e., race) and social status.

Shinagawa and Pang concluded that privileged Asian American women "maximize their status" by marrying the "most advantaged individuals with the highest racial position." In other words, well-educated Asian American women in a professional job can generally choose from one of two marital choices: (1) an Asian American man who has the same or higher economic status, but same racial status; or (2) a white male with the same or higher economic status and higher racial status. Interracially married men, on the other hand, tend to have spouses who "have lower educational and socioeconomic status although they are higher in racial position." This means that the choices for well-educated, professional Asian American men are generally equal: (1) an Asian American woman with lower or the same economic status and the same racial status; or (2) a white woman with lower economic status but higher racial status. These types of choices help to explain why Asian American women interracially marry more than Asian American men.[54]

The problem with the above studies on Asian American interracial marriage stems from the collection and generalized interpretation of statistical data on a subject that is deeply personal and subjective. It is with this in mind that researchers Colleen Fong and Judy Yung (1995) conducted a number of in-depth interviews with Asian American men and women in the San Francisco Bay Area and asked them about their marital choices. The researchers found that interracial marriage involved a multitude of complex issues, some of which have been described above. A few respondents admitted they married whites for some measure of upward mobility and social status, which is evidence of hypergamy. More commonly, respondents focused on elements of free choice. Both Asian American women and men frequently stated they married interracially because they wanted to avoid traditional Asian patriarchy, and were seeking more egalitarian family relationships.

At the same time, Fong and Yung also found that the marital choices of Asian American women and men were not completely free. For example, both Asian American men and women were very much affected by stereotypical sexist and racist media images that surrounded them as they were growing up. This is discussed in detail in Chapter 6. Asian American women admitted negative media images of Asian men were a factor in why they viewed white males as more "attractive" and "exciting." Asian American men said they were not affected by erotic media images of Asian women because they saw Asian women more like sisters, rather than sex objects. Asian American men, on the other hand, thought media images depicted white women as more "vivacious," compared to the Asian women they knew who were "too introverted." According to Fong and Yung, "both women and men faulted the opposite sex for the same weaknesses: being overly serious, having pragmatic occupations or narrow interests, being rather lackluster and not a part of the dominant or counter culture." It is interesting to note that interviewees in this study realized the media stereotypes of others, but did not believe they themselves were affected. Most of the interviewees in this study were comfortable with their marital choices because they felt their spouses better reflected their own self-concept, rather than any family or socially imposed image. The work of Fong and Yung shows the complex factors involved in interracial marriage.[55]

This issue becomes even more complex as Shinagawa and Pang expand their research in their article "Asian American Pan-Ethnicity and Intermarriage" (1996). They found that between 1980 and 1990 the number of *interethnic* marriages of Asian and Pacific Islander Americans in the United States (e.g., a Chinese American marrying a Korean American, or a Japanese American marrying a Vietnamese American) approached or exceeded interracial marriages. Indeed, increase in interethnic marriages rose from 200 to 500 percent in just ten years. Some of the reasons for this increase in interethnic marriages are: (1) a rise in the number of recent foreign-born Asian Americans who are generally *intraethnically* (marriage between two people of the same ethnic group) or interethnically married; and (2) the counting of Pacific Islander groups such as Hawaiians, Samoans, Tongan, and Chamorran who, because of their geographic location and limited contact with whites, naturally tend to marry intraethnically and interethnically. Given these factors, assimilation theory would still assume that the more assimilated U.S.-born Asian Americans would maintain a high interracial marriage rate. Shinagawa and Pang were aware of this, and focused their attention on select U.S.-born Asian American groups in California to see if the above interethnic versus interracial marriage patterns continued. Table 7-10 shows that at least with Chinese, Filipino, and Japanese Americans, there is still a significant rise in the number of interethnic marriages.[56]

Shinagawa and Pang also looked at five specific Asian American "cohorts" in California that represent various age groupings, as well as their major social and historical influences. The researchers found distinct marriage patterns in the various cohorts. The pre–World War II and World War II cohort (prior to 1946) was a period of high levels of racial hostility and antimiscegenation laws in many parts of the United States. This was also a period when there were very few interracial marriages. The post–World War II cohort (1946–1962) and the civil rights era cohort (1963–1974) were times when race relations were liberalized and, of course, the war bride era. These were the periods when Asian American interracial marriages began to increase steadily. The post-1960s cohort (1975–1981) and the Vincent Chin cohort (1982–1990) were periods of higher interethnic marriage. Shinagawa and Pang attributed this current trend to a number of factors. They include (1) the increased population size and concentration of Asian American communities in California; (2) the growing similarities in socioeconomic attainment and middle-class status among Asian Americans; (3) the bridging of Asian ethnic differences due to a common language and common experiences in the United States together with an increased feeling of Asian ethnic cultural affinity among young Asian Americans; and most importantly (4) an increased sense of racial consciousness and unity. "This racial consciousness and awareness is especially acute in California," the researchers write. "Race, increasingly more than ethnicity, powerfully shapes the experiences and development of identity among Asian Americans." They conclude that, like whites, who marry other whites of different ethnic groups (e.g., an Irish American marrying a German American), Asian American interethnic marriage may soon become the more common phenomenon. If true, this will serve to forge the creation of a more generalized Asian American identity, rather than maintain distinct Asian ethnic identities.[57]

Shinagawa and Pang's findings were verified on a national level by Sharon Lee and Marilyn Fernandez (1998), who compared 1990 and 1980 U.S. census

Table 7-10   Marriage Patterns for Select Asian American Groups by Nativity in California, 1980 and 1990

Group	Total			U.S.-born		
	1980	1990	Change	1980	1990	Change
Chinese/men						
Intraethnic	88.9	75.8	14.7	74.3	57.1	−23.1
Interethnic	4.3	16.7	288.4	8.8	23.9	171.6
Interracial (white)	5.4	6.0	11.1	14.3	15.4	7.7
Interracial (non-white)	1.4	1.5	7.1	2.6	3.6	38.5
Chinese/women						
Intraethnic	86.1	74.3	13.7	71.7	51.4	−27.9
Interethnic	2.5	13.9	456.0	6.4	24.4	281.3
Interracial (white)	9.9	10.4	5.1	18.3	20.9	14.2
Interracial (non-white)	1.5	1.4	6.7	3.6	3.0	16.7
Filipino/men						
Intraethnic	79.3	3.8	6.9	38.4	43.3	12.8
Interethnic	2.5	13.9	456.0	5.9	19.4	228.8
Interracial (white)	11.0	8.0	27.3	36.3	26.4	27.3
Interracial (non-white)	7.2	4.3	40.3	19.4	10.9	43.8
Filipino/women						
Intraethnic	73.4	59.8	18.5	42.3	35.2	16.8
Interethnic	2.5	15.0	500.0	4.7	23.2	393.6
Interracial (white)	5.8	5.5	5.2	19.7	12.0	39.1
Interracial (non-white)	18.3	19.7	7.7	33.3	29.6	11.1
Japanese/men						
Intraethnic	82.9	62.1	25.1	80.5	60.5	−24.7
Interethnic	3.8	21.2	457.9	4.5	20.6	357.8
Interracial (white)	10.7	13.9	29.9	11.8	14.6	23.7
Interracial (non-white)	2.6	3.6	38.5	3.3	4.2	27.3
Japanese/women						
Intraethnic	64.2	48.1	25.1	76.8	50.3	34.5
Interethnic	4.2	20.0	376.2	5.0	22.4	348.0
Interracial (white)	27.5	27.5	0.0	15.6	23.1	48.1
Interracial (non-white)	4.1	4.4	7.3	2.6	4.2	61.5

Source: Calculations by Larry Haijime Shinagawa, Ph.D., based on 5 percent Public Use Microdata Sample (PUMS), U.S. Bureau of the Census, 1990. Copyright 1996, Larry Haijime Shinagawa, Ph.D., Assistant Professor, Department of American Multicultural Studies, Sonoma State University. Used with permission.

data. Lee and Fernandez found the overall intermarriage rate for Asian Americans decreased from 25.4 percent in 1980 to 14.5 percent in 1990. At the same time, interethnic marriages increased from just 10.7 percent in 1980 to 21.2 percent in 1990. This finding was surprising given the fact that intermarriage among non-Hispanic whites increased from 1 percent to 2.6 percent, and African American intermarriage rates increased from 2.2 percent to 5.8 percent.

Table 7-11 Percent Exogamous, Married Couples, by Race/Ethnicity of Householder, 1990 and 1980

Race/ Ethnicity	1990			1980		
	% Total Exogamous	% Interethnic	% Interracial	% Total Exogamous	% Interethnic	% Interracial
Non-Hispanic White	2.6	n/a	n/a	1.0	n/a	n/a
Hispanic	18.6	n/a	n/a	12.7	n/a	n/a
African American	5.8	n/a	n/a	2.2	n/a	n/a
Asian American	14.5	21.2	78.8	25.4	10.7	89.3
Chinese	12.1	32.7	67.3	15.7	22.2	77.8
Filipino	18.9	12.2	87.8	30.0	6.9	93.1
Indian	12.1	11.4	88.6	15.5	3.2	96.8
Japanese	25.6	20.3	79.7	34.2	11.9	88.1
Vietnamese	8.0	39.1	60.9	19.8	6.7	93.3

Source: Sharon M. Lee and Marilyn Fernandez, "Trends in Asian American Racial/Ethnic Intermarriage: A Comparison of 1980 and 1990 Census Data," in *Sociological Perspectives* 41:2 (1998):323–342, Table 1.

Table 7-12 Ethnicity of Spouses of Intermarried Couples 1990 / 1980

Ethnicity	White 1990/1980	Hispanic 1990/1980	African American 1990/1980	Other Asian 1990/1980
Non-Hispanic White	—	54.1/18.5	5.2/4.8	25.1/30.7
Hispanic	89.6/82.6	—	3.9/4.8	3.3/4.8
African American	64.6/69.0	19.0/7.8	—	10.8/12.8
Asian American	61.4/76.6	11.2/2.5	2.2/5.2	21.2/10.7
Chinese	53.7/66.5	8.6/2.3	1.8/2.8	32.7/22.2
Filipino	61.0/74.8	18.7/4.8	1.6/6.3	12.2/6.9
Indian	69.3/86.8	11.5/1.4	5.7/5.5	11.4/3.2
Japanese	64.9/77.7	8.7/1.9	1.2/3.9	20.3/11.9
Korean	67.9/79.3	6.1/1.5	1.1/8.3	23.1/8.7
Vietnamese	47.2/84.9	10.4/1.1	1.5/4.4	39.1/6.8

Source: Sharon M. Lee and Marilyn Fernandez, "Trends in Asian American Racial/Ethnic Intermarriage: A Comparison of 1980 and 1990 Census Data," in *Sociological Perspectives* 41:2 (1998):323–342, Tables 2 and 3.

Intermarriage rates among Hispanics also increased but only slightly from 12.7 percent to 18.6 percent (see Table 7-11). The analysis of the 1990 census revealed that the percentage of interracial marriage between Asian Americans and non-Hispanic whites dropped from 76.6 percent in 1980 to 61.6 percent in 1990. In contrast, interracial marriage between Asian Americans and Hispanics increased from just 2.5 percent in 1980 to 11.2 percent in 1990 (see Table 7-12).

The researchers did find some consistent trends as well. U.S.-born Asian Americans were more likely to be involved in an interracial or interethnic marriage than foreign-born Asian Americans. Overall, Asian American women were almost twice as likely to intermarry (27.1 percent) compared to Asian American men (14.1 percent). The only exception in this case was for Asian Indian men who intermarried at a higher rate than Asian Indian women. U.S.-born Asian American men were found to be four times as likely to intermarry compared with foreign-born Asian American men (see Table 7-13).[58]

Does the direction toward declining exogamous marriages seen in the studies above still hold true in the 2000 census data? The answer is yes and no. Drawing from the numbers in Tables 7-8 and 7-9, and comparing them with

Table 7-13 Percent Exogamous by Nativity, Ethnic Group, and Gender, 1990 and 1980

	1990		1980	
	Men	Women	Men	Women
Asian				
American	14.1	27.1	16.6	31.5
(NB)	37.7	42.5	33.1	35.9
(FB)	9.1	24.3	10.5	30.1
Chinese	11.9	16.3	14.4	16.8
(NB)	44.5	48.2	37.6	36.8
(FB)	6.7	11.3	8.2	11.9
Filipino	18.2	37.4	22.2	35.5
(NB)	64.0	65.5	60.4	56.9
(FB)	11.9	34.4	12.9	31.4
Asian Indian	12.7	5.7	*	*
(NB)	45.1	32.2	*	*
(FB)	12.4	5.2	14.1	5.2
Japanese	24.8	43.9	21.3	41.6
(NB)	28.2	34.2	23.0	24.8
(FB)	17.3	54.3	16.2	62.1
Korean	5.4	34.0	7.5	44.5
(NB)	69.7	73.3	69.4	66.9
(FB)	3.5	33.3	4.2	43.8
Vietnamese	7.3	18.3	7.5	44.5
(NB)	18.1	27.4	*	*
(FB)	7.2	18.2	4.2	43.8

* The researchers excluded some 1980 data for Asian Indians and Vietnamese because of problems with the native-born Asian Indian group and small sample sizes for native-born Vietnamese. They omitted the total figures for Asian Indians in 1980 because these would be misleading since there was a sizable native-born sample. The 1980 total for Vietnamese is shown, and includes both native- and foreign-born. Given the small number of native-born Vietnamese, findings for Vietnamese essentially refer to foreign-born.

Source: Sharon M. Lee and Marilyn Fernandez, "Trends in Asian American Racial/Ethnic Intermarriage: A Comparison of 1980 and 1990 Census Data," in Sociological Perspectives 41:2 (1998): 323–342, Table 4.

Table 7-13, the overall rates for exogamous marriages were *lower* among Chinese American men, Filipino American men and women, Asian Indian American men, Korean American women, and Vietnamese American women in 2000 compared to 1990. On the other hand, exogamous marriage rates for Chinese American women, Asian Indian American women, Japanese American men and women, Korean American men, and Vietnamese American men were *higher* in 2000 compared to 1990. Interestingly, the exogamous marriage rates for second- and 1.5-generation Asian Americans were lower for every group except for Japanese American men and women and Vietnamese American men and women. The 2000 census data still shows that Asian American women are more than twice as likely to be involved in exogamous (interethnic and interracial) marriages compared to Asian American men. The data also continues to show that more than 80 percent of the exogamous marriages among Asian Americans are, in fact, interracial marriages primarily to whites. Relatively few Asian Americans marry Latino Americans and even fewer marry African Americans. Today, the research on interracial and interethnic marriage among Asian Americans has probably reached its peak. There seems to be much less attention, as seen in the few studies published on this topic in academic books and articles in recent years. More recent attention has been focused on biracial Asian Americans who are now coming of age and are speaking from their own unique perspectives.

Biracial and Multiracial Asian Americans

The interracial marriage patterns among Asian Americans provide ample evidence of the creation and recreation of new types of families and identities. Whatever the causes behind these marital trends, they mark tremendous change in the Asian American population. With this in mind, a distinct and growing part of the diverse contemporary Asian American experience are the offspring of Asian and non-Asian interracial unions. Many already know that professional golfer Tiger Woods is of mixed-race heritage (one-eighth Native American, one-eighth African American, one-quarter white, one-quarter Thai, and one-quarter Chinese). Other famous mixed-race Asian Americans include baseball player Johnny Damon (Thai and white), actor Keanu Reeves (Chinese, Hawaiian, and white), news anchor Ann Curry (Japanese and white), and singer Nora Jones (Asian Indian and white).[59] The 2000 census allowed respondents to mark more than one race and ethnicity box on the census form and more than 7.2 million people, or 2.6 percent, reported to be more than one race. Table 7-14 shows there were 10.2 million Asian Americans alone counted in the 2000 census with an additional 1.6 million Asian Americans in combination with other races. A very high percentage of Native Hawaiian and Pacific Islanders (NHPI) were listed in combination with one or more races. There were 398,835 NHPI alone counted in 2000, but the number went up to 874,414 for NHPI in combination with one or more races. Among Asian American groups, Japanese Americans reported the highest percentage of mixed heritage, at 30.7 percent. This percentage may seem high, but it is

Table 7-14 Asian, Native Hawaiian, and Pacific Islander Population, 2000

Race	Number
Total Population	281,421,906
Asian Alone or in combination with one or more other races	11,898,828
Asian Alone	10,242,998
Asian in combination with one or more other races	1,655,830
Asian/White	863,395
Asian/Some other race	249,108
Asian/Native Hawaiian and other Pacific Islander	138,802
Asian/Black	106,782
All other combinations including Asian	292,743
Native Hawaii and Other Pacific Islander (NHPI) Alone or in combination with one or more races	874,414
NHPI alone	398,835
NHPI in combination with one or more other races	475,579
NHPI/Asian	138,802
NHPI/White	112,964
NHPI/White/Asian	89,611
NHPI/Some other race	35,108
All other combinations including NHPI	99,094

Sources: U.S. Census Bureau, *The Asian Population: 2000* (February 2002), Table 1, p. 3 at http://www.census .gov/prod/2002pubs/c2kbr01-16.pdf; U.S. Census Bureau, *The Native Hawaiian and Other Pacific Islander Population: 2000* (January 2002), Table 1, p. 3 at http://www.census.gov/prod/ 2001pubs/c2kbr01-14.pdf; U.S. Census Bureau, *We the People of More Than One Race in the United States* (April 2005), Table 1. p. 1 at http://www.census.gov/prod/2005pubs/censr-22.pdf.

about average for Pacific Islander groups and quite low compared to Native Hawaiians (see Table 7-15).

The Census Bureau conducted a study to find how mixed-race couples chose to identify their children for census purposes. In the 1980 census, it was found that 66 percent of children with one black parent and one white parent were counted as black. For children born to white and Asian parents, just 35 percent were listed as Asian. Other sources of demographic information have also proven to be of little practical use for counting biracial or multiracial individuals. Prior to 1989, for example, the National Center for Health Statistics tabulated the races of children born in the United States from data about the parents' races on birth certificates. A child born to one white parent and one nonwhite parent was generally classified as nonwhite. If neither parent were white, the child was classified based on the race of the father. This became problematic because in 13 to 15 percent of the cases, there was no data about the fathers.[60]

Individuals of mixed-race backgrounds continue to confront and confound American society's rigid racial boundaries. Those who don't fit in to a

Table 7-15 Percent Distribution Alone or in Combination Populations of Detailed Asian, Native Hawaiian, and Pacific Islander Population Groups, 2000

Group	Alone	In combination with one or more other races and/or detailed Asian groups
Asian		
Asian Indian	88.4	11.6
Chinese	84.6	15.4
Filipino	78.2	21.8
Japanese	69.3	30.7
Korean	87.7	12.3
Vietnamese	91.7	8.3
NHPI		
Native Hawaiian	35.1	64.9
Samoan	68.3	31.7
Tongan	75.2	24.8
Guamanian or Chamorro	62.9	37.1
Fijian	72.1	27.9

Sources: U.S. Census Bureau, *The Asian Population: 2000* (February 2002), Figure 5, p. 10 at http:// www.census .gov/prod/2002pubs/c2kbr01-16.pdf; U.S. Census Bureau, *The Native Hawaiian and Other Pacific Islander Population: 2000* (January 2002), Figure 5, p. 10 at http://www.census.gov/prod/2001pubs/c2kbr01-14.pdf.

specific category are considered an aberration. This is clear when looking at the negative social and historical mythologies that have evolved to maintain a marginal status for mixed-race people. Ethnic studies scholar Cynthia Nakashima (1992), herself a biracial Asian American, vividly describes several biological arguments that viewed mixed-race people as "genetically inferior to both (or all) of their parent races." Nakashima also found sociocultural stereotypes that maintained mixed-race people have severe inferiority complexes and were in a constant state of restlessness and discontentedness.[61] Despite official U.S. census recognition of people of mixed race heritage, there are still attempts to deny the existence of mixed-raced people and to categorize them into rigid racial categories. A major issue for biracial and multiracial Asian Americans, along with mixed race people in general, is the social pressure to have to "choose" what group they belong to.

According to Nakashima, biracial and multiracial people who are part white are sometimes seen as "whitewashed," are not allowed to discuss their multiraciality, and are not truly seen as a "person of color." Nakashima cites the Japanese Cherry Blossom Festival that prohibits participation from people who are below one-half Japanese American, or if they don't "look" Japanese.[62] This sentiment is confirmed by research on Asian/white college students on the East Coast conducted by Kwai Julienne Grove (1991). Grove quotes one young woman saying, "A lot of times I talk with Asians, I am not a 'real Asian' because I don't look Asian so I don't get discriminated against as an Asian does." Many of the Asian/white respondents in Grove's survey did admit they were able to "float" across racial boundaries and felt relatively free to choose their identity rather than have it chosen for them. "You can't be quite identified," reported one of Grove's male Asian/white respondents. "I like that because no one else is like you and it frees you to make your own identity. . . . People do not look at you and say, 'Oh, you're Asian, so you must be good at math and science.'"[63] However, conflicts over issues of identity and isolation can be especially strong for individuals of Asian and African American descent who often face racism not only from whites but from other Asians as well. The words of Song Richardson are particularly telling: "I can see them look at me and some don't think I can understand Korean. I hear them making derogatory remarks about the fact that I'm mixed. . . . I'll walk into a market and see someone behind the counter who looks like my Mom, and I'll feel a certain affection. But then she'll treat me with complete lack of respect and cordiality. Differently than she would treat a white person who comes into the market."[64]

Attitudes and policies that continue to marginalize mixed-race people are being challenged in a variety of ways. One way is through organizing. This is seen in the growing number of multiracial or multiethnic organizations emerging across the country, as well as student groups formed on many college campuses. Together these organizations and groups were successful at pressuring the federal government to create a multiracial category on the 2000 census. This effort did not come about with out a great deal of struggle, as highlighted by sociologist Rebecca Chiyoko King's recent article "Racialization, Recognition, and Rights: Lumping and Splitting Multiracial Asian Americans in the 2000 Census" (2000). King described how activists faced the dilemma of supporting mixed-race people to identify themselves in the census (politics of individual recognition), while addressing the concerns of traditional civil rights groups wanting to maintain monoracial categories to protect their political and economic interests (politics of group rights). It should be noted that racial categories in the census and the statistics that are gathered are useful data for many federal agencies. For example, the Department of Justice and the Equal Employment Opportunity Commission use race statistics to ensure that states comply with civil rights laws. In addition, census data are used to determine the number of representatives each state is entitled to send to the U.S. House of Representatives and to draw the boundaries of each congressional district. Equal representation at state and local levels is also based on the census, as are boundaries of local political districts.

Most Asian American civil rights groups opposed multiracial counting for fear it would diminish the overall numbers of Asian Americans and thus diminish their political clout. A 1996 Racial and Ethnic Target Test (RAETT) conducted by the Census Bureau did show that Asian Americans lost more of their population than any other group when multiple responses were allowed. The only group that supported the need for a multiracial category was the Japanese American Citizen's League. Some multiracial groups, such as Happa Issues Forum, have supported one initiative to ease the conflict. It involves counting a biracial or multiracial person in several appropriate racial categories. For example, a person who is Japanese and African American would be fully counted in both categories as well as in a general multiracial category. Using this tabulation method would not take away from the overall number of who is counted as Asian American as demonstrated by the RAETT trial. Purists oppose this type of counting because the totals will not add up to 100 percent and would make any comparison with previous census counts impossible. According to King, objections to this "all inclusive" counting strategy are based on old ideologies that an individual can only be one of "race" and this is somehow immutable. "To change this assumption and allow for multiplicity and flexibility across social contexts," she writes, "would be a truly radical change and would constitute a major rethinking of legal understandings of race." At this point it remains to be seen exactly how mixed-race people will be counted and how the data will be used.[65]

King's analysis of the 2000 census is very much in keeping with what Nakashima has described as the trajectory of the multiracial movement (1996). Her article "Voices From the Movement: Approaches to Multiraciality" points to three approaches to advocating the multiracial experiences and interests. The first approach was the struggle of mixed-race people for inclusion and legitimacy in the traditional raciall and ethnic communities. Nakashima describes how glad she was that her Japanese American grandmother accompanied her to a meeting of Japanese American scholarship sponsors to help validate her genuine "Japaneseness." The second approach is the shaping of a shared identity and common agenda among racially mixed people into a new multiracial community. This approach involves the creation of organizations that support the interests of interracially married couples and their children. From this came the increased interest in multiraciality in scholarly research, as well as regular courses within a college curriculum. The third approach that relates to the King article is the struggle to dismantle dominant racial ideology and group boundaries and to create connections across communities. According to Nakashima, "we need to take 'multiracial' in the direction of *supraracial,* without jeopardizing our communities of color and without giving up the connections that add value to our lives".[66] This theme is continued in the book *Sum of Our Parts: Mixed Heritage Asian Americans* (2001), edited by Teresa Williams- Leon and Cynthia Nakashima. This book is the first collection of essays focusing exclusively on the Asian American multiracial experience.[67]

Another prominent scholar of the multiracial experience is Maria P. P. Root. She has written and edited a number of books in this area including *Mixed Race People in America* (1992), *The Multiracial Experience: Racial Borders as the New Frontier* (1996), and *Love's Revolution: Interracial Marriage* (2001). She has also written "The Bill of Rights for Mixed Race People," often cited in books, articles, and reprinted on various Web sites. Among the rights listed are "Not to keep the races separate within me; To identify myself differently than strangers expect me to identify; and To have loyalties and identification with more than one group of people."[68] The search for identity for mixed-race people is a continuing struggle. However, the works of individuals like Nakashima, King, Williams-Leon, and Root, along with many others, are making real progress not only for themselves but for society as well.

Amerasians

Most biracial and multiracial Asian Americans were born in, or have spent a great deal of their lives in, the United States. They are, for the most part, culturally "American." But there is another group of mixed-race Asians who have their own set of distinctive circumstances. Known as "Amerasians" they are also of mixed-racial heritage, but they were born in Asia. When Amerasians come to the United States, they have sharp cultural and linguistic issues not faced by other biracial and multiracial Asian Americans. It has been estimated that between 30,000 and 50,000 Amerasian children were left behind in Vietnam following the U.S. military evacuation from Saigon in 1975. The Amerasian experience in postwar Vietnam was extremely difficult. They were known as "dust children," or half-breeds, harassed by the Vietnamese government because they were seen as offspring of the enemy, and because of their obvious physical differences in a largely homogeneous society.

The photographs of Amerasians begging or selling cigarettes on the streets of Vietnam in the late 1970s brought international attention to their plight. In addition, there were increasing complaints by American fathers who faced tremendous obstacles trying to bring their children to the United States. The Orderly Departure Program in 1980 created the first opportunity for separated families to reunite. Unfortunately, only about 4,500 Amerasians were able to leave Vietnam under this program, and this was through a provision that was established in 1982. It wasn't until the passage of the Amerasian Homecoming Act of 1987 that large numbers of Americans and their accompanying relatives were able to leave Vietnam. Since the early 1980s, 81,500 Amerasians and their family members have immigrated to the United States. Some Amerasians hope to find their fathers once they arrive in the United States, but they are usually disappointed.

Tanisha Terry was one of the lucky ones. She was born in Vietnam and was just a baby when her father, George Terry, left for the United States with plans to send for his daughter and her mother. This proved more difficult than expected as the Vietnam conflict escalated and the situation became even more complicated. Tanisha's mother married another American serviceman and sent Tanisha to live with her grandmother. Then Tanisha's mother left Vietnam just before the fall of Saigon in 1975. It was ten years before her mother could sponsor Tanisha and her grandmother to come to the United States. As Tanisha grew older she became more and more determined to find her father. She fortunately discovered a copy of her father's birth certificate and a partial Social Security number. She hired a private investigator in 1994 and relatives of George Terry were soon found in Alabama. Tanisha learned that her father moved to Germany, and sent him a letter in early December. "Dear Mr. Terry," the letter began, "While you were in Vietnam, you met a woman and together produced a baby girl you named Tanisha. After the war you never had contact with her again. If possible I'd like that to change. I am Tanisha." Terry returned to the United States just before Christmas to meet the daughter he hadn't seen in more than twenty-two years. "I never forgot her," Terry said tearfully. He was particularly thankful to be reunited with his daughter because he suffers from serious heart condition. "I'm just glad I've lived long enough to see this day. I never want to lose her again."[69]

Tanisha's story is heartwarming but, unfortunately, all too rare. Unlike other biracial and multiracial Asian Americans in the United States, Amerasians do not often have family support systems. Kieu-Linh Caroline Valverde's article "From Dust to Gold: The Vietnamese Amerasian Experience" (1992) describes how Amerasians have a double-double burden when they come to the United States. Their first double burden comes from being both refugees and biracial. Amerasians faced the same hardships encountered by refugees suddenly reset-tled into a new environment, but their needs—particularly around mental health issues—are different from those of "standard" refugees. The second double burden is the negative reaction against Amerasians by both the Vietnamese and non-Vietnamese American communities. Amerasians confront a particular type of hostility from members of the Vietnamese community in the United States. Many Vietnamese Americans assume that the mothers of Amerasians were bar girls and prostitutes, and that Amerasians themselves are cheap lowlifes. The antagonism against Amerasians among Vietnamese Americans often drives them away from the community, and they try to seek relief in mainstream society. What most find instead are more stereotypes as well as adaptation problems. Valverde describes the case of one black Amerasian who was rebuffed by Vietnamese men because of her race and rejected by African American men because she was so culturally different.[70]

Amerasians started coming to the United States in the early 1980s, and media attention was given to many of them because they were children. Today, as adults, their plight has all but been ignored. Because many Amerasian children were not given any formal education in Vietnam, their educational, social, and economic adjustment to the United States has been particularly acute. Psychologist Robert S. McKelvey (1999) and journalist Thomas A. Bass (1996) have written books that provide moving portrayals of the extraordinary problems Amerasians face. Though leaving Vietnam was the opportunity of a lifetime, for many coming to the United States has meant parental rejection, bureaucratic abuse and neglect, persistent unemployment or underemploy-ment, and a prolonged crisis of personal identity.[71] "I feel so sad for them," said Sister Christine Trong My Hanh, a Catholic nun who is the founder of Good Shepard Services, which offers programs to the Vietnamese community in Atlanta, Georgia. Sister Christine worked with young Amerasians as a young nun in Vietnam and estimates there are up to eight hundred Vietnamese Amerasians in Georgia. So many that on Memorial Day she helps to organize a dinner gathering hundreds of Amerasians to bring their community together for companionship and mutual support. "They were abused as children in Vietnam, they come here with nothing, and there's nobody to help them," Sister Christine adds.[72]

Although Amerasians were allowed to enter the United States for humani-tarian reasons, they were not permitted to become U.S. citizens unless they found their fathers or went through the same lengthy citizenship process as any other immigrants who do not have U.S. citizen parents. Dr. Robert McKelvey, who has studied the Amerasian experience, is angered by what he has seen because it is so reminiscent of the U.S. involvement in Vietnam, which started with hope, continued through false promises, and eventually ended in abandonment. "These people are our children," explains McKelvey, a Vietnam War-era veteran. "(Amerasians are) intimately entwined genetically with us and our history. . . . They're part of us, but we don't treat them that way any more than the Vietnamese did."[73] This is certainly the case for Hong Lam, who came to the U.S. as a young adult in 1994. Lam was abandoned by her parents and was raised by a distant relative, a person she refers to as her grandmother. "I only remember my grandmother holding me and feeding me," she said through an interpreter. "That's the best memory I have." When Lam arrived in this country she was alone, illiterate, and had no record of who her father was. Since she immigrated, Lam has lived on the margins of the Vietnamese community in Texas, working two jobs. At 4:30 A.M. she begins work on an assembly line for a local refrigerator manufacturing company, and in the afternoon she works as a kitchen helper in a nursing home. She cannot write or speak English very well, and for this reason she has not even tried to apply for citizenship. Still, she wants to be a U.S. citizen primarily because she wants to return to Vietnam to visit the woman she knows as her grandmother. Unfortunately, without citizenship Lam cannot get a U.S. passport and, ironically, without the U.S. passport she is unable to go back to Vietnam. Nor can she sponsor her only known relative in Vietnam to come to this country.[74]

It is stories like Lam's that prompted U.S. Representative Zoe Lofgren, a former immigration law professor, to introduce the Ameriasian Naturalization Act of 2003 (HR 3360) and a similar bill in 2004 (HR 2687). This law confers automatic citizenship upon Amerasians who legally enter the United States in the future or have already entered through the *Amerasian Homecoming Act of 1988*. For those who already entered, they would become U.S. citizens upon the effective date of the *Amerasian Naturalization Act of 2003* without having to undergo any additional processes. In a press release issued by her office, Lofren said: "This legislation is about fairness and equality. Amerasians should not be treated differently than other sons and daughters born to U.S. citizen fathers. These individuals lived through devastation during the Vietnam War and have been mistreated by the Vietnamese government because of their mixed race. Now is the time to treat them as the U.S. citizens they are and give them the equality they deserve."[75] As of this writing both HR3360 and HR 2687 have failed to make it past the Immigration Subcommittee in the House of Representatives. If eventually passed, this law would allow Lam to become a citizen and to once again see the woman she calls her grandmother.

There are a few examples of Amerasians returning to Vietnam for happy reunions. Law student Sarah Williams, 29, was adopted by a family in the United States and returned to Vietnam twenty-five years later. "I don't wonder about my past," she said. "There's no question about why I was given up. It was war. My father was probably a black soldier. My mother was probably poor. I know that if I'd stayed, I'd be living on the streets. I had a wonderful childhood. I know that I'm lucky." One of Williams's goals in returning to Vietnam was to find her foster mother who cared for her before she was adopted. Two days before she was to return to the United States, Williams learned that her foster mother had been found. The emotional homecoming became even more special. Chuong Thi Chi, 72, rushed into Williams's arms the moment they met. "I recognized you immediately," wept the foster mother. "You are my daughter. All these years, I have thought about you but I never believed I would see you again."[76]

Gay and Lesbian Asian Americans

The Asian American gay and lesbian experience is not new, but has only recently been openly and thoughtfully discussed. Homosexuality has existed in Asian countries for centuries, yet sexuality is seldom, if ever, talked about in traditional Asian American families.[77] In her study "Issues of Identity Development among Asian American Lesbians and Gay Men" (1989), Connie S. Chan found only nine of thirty-five interviewees told their parents about their sexual orientation. Chan attributed "Asian cultural factors" as a major reason for this low rate of "coming out."[78] Another example of the hidden nature of homosexuality in the Asian American community can be seen in the groundbreaking feminist anthology *Making Waves* (1989). The anthology was written by, for, and about Asian American women. However, the only essay that withheld the author's full name was the one about Asian American lesbians. Ironically, the essay's author, "Pamela H.," wanted to remain anonymous even though she was arguing that Asian American lesbians were an "emerging voice" in the Asian American community.[79] Attention to Asian American gays and lesbians has increased in recent years, and is no longer a taboo subject. For example, in 1994 the Japanese American Citizens' League (JACL) national board of directors adopted a resolution supporting same-sex marriages. The issue sparked a great deal of controversy from a conservative faction of the organization. The faction tried to rescind the board's decision at the JACL national convention, but its attempt failed for lack of votes.[80] A letter to the JACL national board and members signed by a coalition of fifteen Asian Pacific American gay and lesbian groups from across the nation thanked the organization for its stand. "Recognizing that same-sex relationships are a matter of civil rights is indeed to understand the importance of expanding in today's society," the letter said. "It is encouraging efforts such as yours that give us hope that we can work together on common issues to achieve a much fairer and more tolerant world in which we will all benefit."[81]

That same year, *Amerasia Journal* dedicated an entire issue to gay, lesbian, and bisexual identities and orientations. The issue was lauded for presenting important and provocative articles on matters never openly discussed before. In Dana Y. Takagi's introduction she cautions against rigidly categorizing the Asian American gay and lesbian experiences and identities. "[O]ur search for authenticity," Takagi writes, "will be tempered by the realization that in spite of our impulse to clearly [de]limit them, there is perpetual uncertainty and flux governing the construction and expression of identities."[82] Attempts to limit, or categorize, a specific identity is a major issue for biracial Asian Americans, who are constantly asked to "choose" one identity over another. Likewise, Asian American gays and lesbians are also asked to choose between their Asian American and sexual identities and loyalties.

The issue of "choosing" was quite prominent in the roundtable discussion, "In Our Own Way," published in the same *Amerasia Journal* volume. In this discussion, four Asian American lesbians described in great detail their experiences of homophobia in Asian American communities, as well as racism and tokenism in the gay and lesbian communities. "Those of us who are gay people of color are often forced to choose between the gay culture and people of color culture," said Zoon Nguyen. "The point is that we have to choose and we just can't be who we are."[83] Increased visibility and activism of Asian American gays and lesbians since the 1970s have also served to slowly, but surely, break the barriers of the forced marginalization just described. Gil Mangaoang's autobiographical article, "From the 1970s to the 1990s: Perspective of a Gay Filipino American Activist," highlights the early "schizophrenia" he felt between his political and social identities that needed to be reconciled. "I began to understand that the discrimination and homophobia I perceived were two sides of the same coin and, that in fact, there were similarities of oppression," Mangaoang wrote. "I had to take responsibility for defining what my life was to be a gay Filipino American man and I have found that process of liberation is a continuous one." Mangaoang believes the environment for Asian American gays and lesbians is better and less isolated today than in the 1970s. This is because more Asian Americans are openly accepting their sexual orientation and established organizations have been formed to support them.[84]

For all the activism, organization, and high-profile role models, the biggest personal issue for Asian American gay and lesbians is still "coming out" to parents. This and other chapters have described the pressures, control, and expectations of Asian American parents. Conformity is highly valued in many Asian American families, while being "different" or "independent" is not. This has led many Asian and non-Asian Americans to assume that Asian American parents would be much less tolerant and homophobic than other parents; therefore many Asian Americans feel they must stay in the closet. This stereotype, however, is not necessarily true. "I don't think any group of people is more or less homophobic than the other," says Zoon Nguyen. "Mom and Dad will not disown you, though there are some who do; but then there are lots of white families who have also disowned their gay kids." What may be true is the strong sense of mutual dependency and obligation fostered in Asian American families, and this makes it extremely difficult for sons and daughters to even contemplate coming out and taking a risk at losing family relationships. "Our families are important," Nguyen explains. "I could never cut them out of my life. That's me, I am an extension of my family." Similarly, Christy Chung admits when she came out to her father, she did it with "respect" for him. "He'll love me forever and he knows . . . I would never tell anyone on his side of the family. It's out of respect for his family, his position in the family. . . . I don't feel like it's my place to upset that balance. And I don't feel I need to."[85] Like many other parents, one of the first reactions of Asian American parents when they learn about their son's or daughter's sexual orientation is to blame themselves. The other major reaction is a sadness that comes with the realization that the long-term plans and expectations they had for their child may not come to pass. "It was the thing of disbelief, horror and shame and the whole thing . . . (t)hat she didn't turn out the way we raised her," explained one Japanese American mother. "The grieving process took a long time. Especially the thing about not being a bride. Not having her be a bride was a very devastating change of plans for her life. . . . I didn't know how I could fit into her life because I didn't know how to be the mother of a lesbian."[86]

Several essays from *Dimensions of Desire* were reprinted and new essays were added for a book under the title *Asian American Sexualities: Dimensions of Gay & Lesbian Experience* (1996). Among the most compelling new additions is found in the selection "Communion: A Collaboration on AIDS," which is a collage of short first-person narratives by five gay men of color living with and around AIDS. In these accounts, Joel B. Tan writes: "These men are my family. Traditionally, families are defined as persons who are bound by blood and a common history. . . . AIDS has brought us together and kept us together. Mortality is our worst enemy and our greatest gift. Our losses and our fears have motivated us to live and love fiercely. . . . Our courage, strength, and genuine affection for each other keeps us joyful and hopeful in our darkest times."[87]

Among the most serious issues particularly facing gay men is HIV/AIDS. Researchers have acknowledged relatively low incidence of HIV/AIDS among Asian Americans, and this has led to a general sense of unconcern and even myths of genetic immunity among Asian Americans.[88] The death of Sionghuat Chua, founder of Boston Asian Gay Men and Lesbians, one of the first gay and lesbian support groups, served to bring greater attention to the realities of HIV/AIDS in the Asian American community.[89]

According to the University of California, San Francisco Center for AIDS Prevention Studies, Asian and Pacific Islander Americans (APIs) are only about 1 percent of the total cases of AIDS reported in the United States. However, the center recognizes that underreporting may mask the true nature of the spread of AIDS within these specific populations. The center cited a survey showing API men do not perceive themselves to be at risk for HIV/AIDS because relatively few are injection drug users, even though 57 percent engage in risky sexual behavior, such as drinking alcohol before sex, and 24 percent participated in unprotected anal sex. Indeed, of those gay APIs surveyed, 85 percent believed they were unlikely to contact HIV and 95 percent believed they were unlikely to transmit HIV.[90] Activist Ignatius Bau has worked on educating the community on the risks and impending dangers of this disease. He cites an estimate by San Francisco HIV Prevention Planning Council that 37 percent of the Asian American gay men are living with HIV and warns that this high rate of HIV seroprevalence indicates that there may very well be a sudden increase in AIDS in the near future. One of the most important aspects of Bau's work is to get HIV prevention materials out to specific Asian American homosexual and heterosexual target audiences. This includes translating information into the various Asian languages, and then publishing it in widely-circulated ethnic newspapers, and broadcasting it on radio stations and cable television programs that serve a predominantly Asian audience.[91]

A study by Hirokazu Yoshikawa (1999) provides even more specific HIV/AIDS prevention strategies most effective in API gay and lesbian communities. Based on the experiences of peer educators from the Asian Pacific Islander Coalition on HIV/AIDS (APICHA), it was concluded that traditional mainstream practices of short one-on-one contacts handing out brochures and/or condoms was an unsuccessful and inappropriate way to educate API communities about HIV/AIDS. This is primarily because these populations are generally uncomfortable talking with strangers about sex and are easily offended when strangers try to give them condoms. One of the recommendations for alternative approaches is the identification of, and interaction with, the social networks of specific API populations. This includes grocery stores, restaurants, clubs, and bathhouses. Another recommendation is the "diffusion of new norms" concerning safe sex and preventive practices with the help of leaders (often termed "opinion leaders"). An example cited in the report profiled the group SLAAAP (Sexually Liberated Asian Art Activist People), which brought together artists and educators to develop a campaign around the issues of gay and lesbian identity and prevention of sexually transmitted diseases.[92] Similarly, APICHA has initiated other support groups. One such group emerged in New York called Persimmon Space, which provides a social and educational forum specifically for API lesbians and bisexuals. Other support and education groups sponsored by APICHA include the Young People's Project and Young Men Having Sex with Men.[93]

Recently, there have been a number of new anthologies examining Asian American sexuality including David L. Eng and Alice Hom's *Q & A: Queer in Asian America* (1998) that further expand the identity formation among gay and lesbian Asian Americans. Eng and Hom identify two historical circumstances that have given rise to what they call queer Asian American studies. During the past several years there has been an increasing attention to issues of sexuality in Asian American scholarship published in journals, presented at academic conferences, and seen in the classroom curricula. "From a queer studies point of view, to insert questions of sexuality, sexual identification, and sexual orientation into our concept of Asian American identity would immediately help to dislodge a static, outdated, and exclusively *racial* notion of who 'we' are," Eng and Hom write in their introduction (emphasis theirs).[94] Eric Wat's *The Making of a Gay Asian Community: An Oral History of Pre-AIDS Los Angeles* (1998) provides first-hand accounts of the gay scene in Southern California and the development of a gay Asian American identity, with particular attention on the first Asian American gay and lesbian organization in the region. Another book using first-person narratives is Kevin K. Kumashiro's *Restoried Selves: Autobiographies of Queer Asian Pacific American Activists* (2004), which contains seventeen stories of individuals ranging from high school and college students, journalists, academics, and professionals discussing a wide range of topics related to cultural and generational conflicts, family and community diversity, and the difficulties and rewards of coming out. This book is highly accessible to a general audience and is a follow up to Kumashiro's earlier book *Troubling Intersections Between Race and Sexuality: Queer Students of Color and Anti-Oppressive Education* (2002), which is a mix of autobiographical accounts with academic qualitative and quantitative research on gay and lesbian students of different racial backgrounds.[95]

The Asian American and Pacific Islander gay and lesbian experience affects not only the individuals but also their families. Gay and lesbian Asian Americans and their families still face challenges in their efforts to recreate a new kind of family experience that includes a different set of expectations on all sides. San Francisco, which has a population of more than 30 percent Asian American, became the center of controversy in February 2004 when city officials began allowing gay and lesbian couples to marry in civil ceremonies. It was City Assessor Mabel Teng who officiated the very first same-sex civil marriage. "I am proud that San Francisco is leading America in the ongoing effort to breakdown institutionalized discrimination," wrote Teng in an editorial published in *AsianWeek*. "Our actions will inspire other cities and states to address discrimination and recognize same-sex marriages. . . . What the leadership in San Francisco has done is extend an existing fundamental right of American citizenship to another minority group as a matter of policy and practice."[96]

However, this new policy and practice was not uniformly accepted in San Francisco. In April 2004, a rally of more than 7,000 conservative Christians gathered in a largely Asian American neighborhood in San Francisco to protest the movement toward same-sex marriages. "God created one man and one woman—Adam and Eve," said Thomas Wang of the Great Commission Center International, a San Francisco area missionary organization. "They became husband and wife and the first human family began. . . . We believe any deviation from it will bring disastrous results." Among the "disastrous results" predicted by Wang were polygamy and incest. "It is something that is going to happen unless we do something about it," Wang emphasized.[97] In response to this anti-same-sex protest, a counter demonstration was organized several months later to counter what gay and lesbian community leaders felt was the "misrepresentation" of Asian Americans as overwhelmingly social conservatives. "It's important that the community at large understand that there are many fair-minded Asian Americans who support marriage equally," explained Andy Wong, from the group Asian Equality. Mabel Teng acknowledged that the issue of same-sex marriage has divided the Asian American community in San Francisco. "There are Asians who are very appreciative of what San Francisco has done and Asians who are not happy," she said. "It is very natural for Asians to be on all sides of the map."[98]

In late 2004 the California Supreme Court stopped and voided all same-sex marriages in San Francisco. Twelve same-sex couples—all of whom married or planned to marry in San Francisco—quickly filed a lawsuit challenging the constitutionality of the state's marriage law. The lead plaintiff in the case known as *Woo v. Lockyer* is Lacy Woo and her partner Cristy Chung, who have been together for sixteen years and have a 6-year-old daughter, Olivia. Explaining why she became the central figure in this lawsuit, Woo said: "Having Olivia and going through so much heartache in terms of adoption and just struggling to take care of my family . . . and then realizing that the rest of the population easily gets married and that all those rights naturally come to them . . . It's not fair."[99] The ban against same sex-marriages was ruled unconstitutional in a San Francisco Superior Court and the case is making its way through to the State Court of Appeals. The case may well be argued all the way back up to the California State Supreme Court, and eventually to the U.S. Supreme Court. The actions of Lacy Woo and Cristy Chung have served to inspire others to take a stand in favor of equal rights for gays and lesbians.

Most recently, actor George Takei, also known as "Mr. Sulu" from the original Star Trek television show, announced that he was gay. Although he and his partner of eighteen years had been open to friends and family for many years, it was only now he felt comfortable enough to talk about his life to the general public. "The world has really changed," Takai explained to the *Los Angeles Times*. "Now that the movement is reaching this point, something unimaginable when I was a young teenager, I think I have a responsibility to add my voice. I thought it was time." Takei, 68, was born in an internment camp during World War II and compared that experience with the discrimination felt by gays and lesbians. In camp he remembered reciting the "Pledge of Allegiance" but was too young at the time to understand the irony of saying the pledge while living inside a camp surrounded by barbed wire fences and armed guards. Living a secret gay lifestyle "is a different kind of barbed wire fence," he added. But as an adult, "the irony of the words for me and for other gay people is penetrating."[100]

Korean Adoptees in the United States

Still another new and changing part of Asian American families and identities is the relatively large number of Asian orphans adopted by mostly non-Asian American families in the United States. Table 7-16 highlights the number of immigrant orphans arriving in the United States and the top ten countries of origin. Between 2000 and 2004, more than 46,000 orphans from Asia have received U.S. immigration visas. Although China has sent the most orphans to this country every year since 2000, the U.S. Census counted 58,825 Korean-born adoptees of all ages, which is the largest portion among all foreign-born adoptees. The number of adoptees from Korea far exceeded China (22,410), Russia (20,208), and Mexico (28,090).[101] The steady flow of orphans from Korea to the United States first began during the Korean American War, and it wasn't until 1995 that the number of orphans from China to the United States began to increase dramatically. As a result, most of the scholarly research has focused on the developmental characteristics and post-adoption adjustments among Korean adoptees in white families.

Transracial and international adoption has been a highly controversial topic because of concerns over the adoptees' self-esteem and sense of belonging within their adoptive families. A comparative study of Korean, Colombian, and African American adoptees by William Feigelman and Arnold Silverman (1983) found that most Korean adoptees reported "problem- free adjustment." At the

Table 7-16 Immigrant Orphans Adopted by U.S. Citizens by Country of Birth 2000–2004

2004		2003		2002		2001		2000	
China	7,033	China	6,638	China	6,062	China	4,629	China	4,943
Russia	5,878	Russia	5,134	Russia	4,904	Russia	4,210	Russia	4,210
Guatemala	3,252	Guatemala	2,327	Guatemala	2,361	Korea	1,863	Korea	1,711
Korea	1,708	Korea	1,793	Korea	1,713	Guatemala	1,601	Guatemala	1,504
Kazakhstan	824	Kazakhstan	819	Ukraine	1,093	Ukraine	1,227	Romania	1,103
Ukraine	772	Ukraine	691	Kazakhstan	801	Romania	781	Vietnam	709
India	394	India	466	Vietnam	736	Vietnam	730	Ukraine	645
Haiti	355	Vietnam	393	India	459	Kazakhstan	664	India	491
Columbia	279	Columbia	275	Columbia	329	India	540	Kazakhstan	392
Ethiopia	277	Haiti	246	Cambodia	275	Cambodia	384	Cambodia	368

Source: U.S. Citizenship and Immigration Service, *Yearbook of Immigration Statistics: 2004*, Table 10; *Yearbook of Immigration Statistics: 2003*, Table 10; *Yearbook of Immigration Statistics: 2002*, Table 12; *Yearbook of Immigration Statistics: 2001*, Table 15; and *Yearbook of Immigration Statistics: 2000*, Table 15. All are found at http://uscis.gov/graphics/shared/statistics/yearbook/index.htm.

same time, the researchers found that the vast majority of Korean orphans lived in mostly white communities compared with 73 percent of families with African American adoptees who lived in racially integrated neighborhoods. Not surprisingly, Korean orphans placed with families of the same ethnic or racial background did have a stronger sense of their heritage than do those who are transracially adopted.[102] Hei Sook Park Wilkerson's book *Birth is More Than Once: The Inner World of Adopted Korean Children* (1985) provided a life-course development model for transracially adopted children: (1) denial of being Korean during childhood and early adolescence, (2) inner awakening, (3) acknowledgment of their being different in early adulthood, (4) identification with being Korean, and (5) acceptance achieved to varying degrees.[103]

The developmental steps highlighted by Wilkerson seem to fit well for many Korean adoptees. Yun Jin "Susanna" Carson grew up in a predominately white suburb east of San Francisco, where she admits she tried "hard not to acknowledge that I'm not white." She even remembers consciously avoiding another Korean adoptee who tried to become a friend in school.[104] However, her inner awakening stage began during the mid to late teen years and hit with full force after moving away from her adoptive family to attend college. This time commonly sparks the Korean adoptee's acknowledgment of being different. Carson attended Chico State University where she majored in music, but it was the courses in women's studies that got her most focused on how race and gender impacted her life. Like some other Korean adoptees, Carson has traveled to Korea, meeting her half-sister and reuniting with her birth mother and father. There have also been conferences specifically aimed at bringing large numbers of Korean adoptees together in one place. The first such gathering took place in Washington, DC, in September 1999; the conference attracted four hundred attendees. Paula Johnson grew up in Portland, Oregon, and had never been to such a gathering before. "I thought maybe I would find out more about myself, about who I am," she said. A turning point in her life occurred when her adoptive mother died in 1993. It was then she started to think about who she was. "I looked in the mirror and said 'I'm not white.' It was almost like a mid-life crisis. Now I'm soul-searching." Another attendee, Susan Soon-Keum Cox, shares another personal turning point that is common for adult Korean adoptees: "As we have children of our own, those questions of identity and balance become increasingly important." A survey of conference attendees found many did not connect with their Korean identities until adulthood. Fewer than a third thought of themselves as Korean American growing up and a third referred to themselves as white. Now two-thirds of those at the conference see themselves as Korean Americans and only a tenth consider themselves white.[105]

Since that time, there have been two other conferences, one in Oslo, Norway, in 2001 and the second in Seoul, Korea, in 2005. More than four hundred fifty Koreans by birth, from fifteen different countries, gathered in Seoul to recognize the fiftieth anniversary of intercountry adoption from Korea. The conference featured workshops on adoption and individual experiences, and covered issues such as racial and cultural identity, as well as successful and unsuccessful attempts to reunite with birth families.[106] Visits to Korea and conferences correspond to the increased exposure to Korean adoptee experiences. There have been a number of recent books and documentaries focusing on the Korean adoptee experience. *The Language of Blood: A Memoir* (2003) by Jane Jeong Trenka describes the author's search for her identity and essence of family growing up in a small town in Minnesota. She recalls changing her birth name, "Kyong-a," to "Jane" in an effort to become the ideal daughter in a "typical" American family. It is a story of her search to resolve the dualities of her life as a person who is born in Korea but raised in the United States, and never feeling she truly belonged in either.[107] *Seeds of a Silent Tree* (1997) is an anthology of personal narratives, fiction, and poetry written by Korean adoptees from all over the United States and some parts of Korea and Europe.[108] Editors Tonya Bishoff and Jo Rankin, themselves Korean adoptees, bring together a multitude of voices about the conflicts and triumphs growing up in a transracial family. The anthology is self-published under the name Pandal Press, in association with Aisarema, an Asian American nonprofit literary arts organization. Pandal is the westernized pronunciation of the Korean word for "half-moon," and the name has great symbolic significance for the editors. "We are all connected to the moon. It's always there even if we can't see it," Bishoff explained. "That we cannot see one side does not mean that it does not exist."[109] Two recent documentaries on the experiences of Korean adoptees have also been produced. *Crossing Chasms* (1998) by Jennifer Arndt is filled with testimonials by other Korean adoptees in the United States as well as Belgium and France. The documentary was initially planned as Arndt's journey to find her birth mother and family in Korea, but the project evolved into a broader story after she met other Korean adoptees in Korea conducting their own searches. "If this project helps just one other person and answer any questions they may have in making the journey to Korea, then my project will have been worthwhile," Arndt said.[110] Another documentary, *First Person Plural* (2000), by Deann Borshay Liem, highlights her story as a Korean orphan brought to the United States in 1966 living with her adoptive family in California. The memory of her birth family was nearly obliterated until recurring dreams led Borshay Liem to discover the truth: her Korean mother was very much alive. The documentary tells of uniting her biological and adoptive families, and the reconciling of identities.[111]

The increasing awareness of Korean adoptees has also given rise to the formation of "culture camps," support groups, and Web sites. For example, Camp Moon-Hwa located in Rochester, Minnesota, is a week-long summer camp for children established to celebrate and share Korean heritage and culture. Activities include language instruction, Korean arts and crafts, tai-kwan-do lessons, Korean folk tales and stories, and more. Attendees also get a traditional Korean lunch every day. Most of the attendees are Korean adoptees or their siblings but anyone interested in Korea is welcome.[112] There are an estimated ten thousand Korean-born children adopted in the state of Minnesota. The group Also-Known-As was started by a group of adult international adoptees and friends in the New York metropolitan area. The organization is dedicated to sharing and celebrating the experiences of international and interracial adoptions and establishing a national community of transcultural people. Their Web site is full of meeting announcements, message boards, and links to similar organizations around the world.[113]

The number of adoptees from Korea dropped following the 1988 Summer Olympics in Seoul, Korea, when one television network aired a story on "the shame" of Korea because they still were not taking care of their children. The embarrassed and angry Korean government began to reduce the international adoption flow. Shortly after, the number of adoptees from China started to increase. Because adoption from China is still a relatively new phenomenon, it will take a number of years before we know how these adoptees will develop, evolve, and identify themselves as they grow into adulthood.

CONCLUSION

Non-Asian Americans often mistakenly assume that Asian Americans are all essentially the same, that they are ruled by some rigid and omnipresent cultural or Confucian ethos that binds them together. This chapter highlights some similarities, but concentrates on the wide variety and diversity found in Asian American families and identities. In addition, these distinct family and identity structures are constantly changing, evolving, and reacting to external forces that affect them. This chapter calls for recognizing racial, ethnic, class, gender, generational, linguistic, national, and sexual differences that exist within what is known as "Asian America." This, of course, does not mean there is no basis for unity. However, unity will not happen if differences are ignored. The presumption of "sameness" is dangerous whether imposed externally by society, or perpetuated internally by a group. Unity comes only with embracing differences in the particulars, while at the same time keeping in mind the broader issues diverse people have in common. The following chapter on political empowerment focuses on how issues of unity for Asian Americans are forged and maintained.

NOTES

1. Mary Ann Schwartz and Barbara Marliene Scott, *Marriages and Families: Diversity and Change* (Englewood Cliffs, NJ: Prentice Hall, 1994), pp. 39–41.
2. Laura Uba, *Asian Americans: Personality Patterns, Identity, and Mental Health* (New York: The Guilford Press, 1994), pp. 27–28.
3. Walter R. Allen, "The Search for Applicable Theories of Black Family Life," *Journal of Marriage and the Family* 40:1 (1978): 117–129.
4. Ronald L. Taylor, "Black American Families," in Ronald L. Taylor (ed.), *Minority Families in the United States: A Multicultural Approach* (Englewood Cliffs, NJ: Prentice Hall, 1994), pp. 19–24.
5. Maxine Baca Zinn, "Adaptation and Continuity in Mexican-Origin Families," in Taylor (ed.), *Ibid.*, pp. 70, 75.
6. Robert Staples and Alfredo Mirande, "Racial and Cultural Variations Among American Families: A Decennial Review of the Literature on Minority Families," *Journal of Marriage and the Family*, 42:4 (1980): 887–903.
7. Stanley Sue and Harry Kitano, "Stereotypes as a Measure of Success," *Journal of Social Issues* 29 (1973): 83–98; and Harry Kitano, "Japanese-American Mental Illness," in Stanley Plog and

Robert Edgerton (eds.), *Changing Perspectives on Mental Illness* (New York: Holt, Rinehart & Winston, 1969), pp. 256–284.

8. Pyong Gap Min, "Korean Immigrant Wives' Overwork," *Korean Journal of Population and Development* 21 (1992): 23–36.

9. D. D. Godwin and J. Scanzoni, "Couple Consensus During Marital Joint Decision-making: A Context, Process, Outcome Model," *Journal of Marriage and the Family* 51 (1989): 943–956; Pyong Gap Min, "The Korean Family," in Charles H. Mindel, Robert W. Habenstein, and Roosevelt Wright, Jr. (eds.), *Ethnic Families in America* (New York: Elsevier, 1989), pp. 199–229; and Morrison G. Wong, "The Chinese American Family," in Mindel et al. (eds.), *Ethnic Families in America*, pp. 230–257.

10. Betty Lee Sung, *The Adjustment Experience of Chinese Immigrant Children in New York City* (New York: Center for Migration Studies, 1987), pp. 186–195.

11. Pyong Gap Min, "Korean Americans in Pyong Gap Min (ed.), *Asian Americans: Contemporary Trends and Issues* (Thousand Oaks, CA: Sage Publications, 1995), pp. 199–231.

12. See www.apiahf.org/apidvinstitute.

13. Patricia Tjaden and Nancy Thoenes, "Extent, Nature, and Consequences of Intimate Partner Violence: Research Report," Washington, DC: National Institute of Justice and the Centers for Disease Control and Prevention (July, 2000) at www.ncjrs.org/txtfilesl/nij/181867.txt.

14. Asian & Pacific Islander Institute on Domestic Violence, "Fact Sheet: Domestic Violence in Asian and Pacific Islander Communities" (December 2002) at http://www.apiahf.org/apidvinstitute/ResearchAndPolicy/factsheet.htm.

15. *Ibid.*

16. Ja Yop Kim and Kyu-taik Sung, "Conjugal Violence in Korean American Families: A Residue of the Cultural Tradition," *Journal of Family Violence* 15:4 (December 2000): 331–345.

17. Alice Yick, "Predictors of Physical Spousal/Intimate Violence in Chinese American Families" *Journal of Family Violence* 15:3 (September 2000): 246–267.

18. Mimi Kim, "The Critique: API Response to the Standardized Models of Domestic Violence Intervention," in *Innovative Strategies to Address Domestic Violence in Asian and Pacific Islander Communities: Examining Themes, Models, and Interventions* (San Francisco: Asian & Pacific Islander Institute on Domestic Violence, 2002), p. 9 at http://www.apiahf.org/apidvinstitute/GenderViolence/innovative_exec.htm.

19. Quoted in Erin Chin, "An Asian Voice Raised Against Abuse," *Detroit Free Press,* May 2, 2005.

20. Quoted in "Reality Check on Domestic Front," *Hindustan Times,* March 13, 2005.

21. Quoted in Dee Norton, "Anniversary Vigil Highlights Domestic Violence: 15 Groups Remember Those Killed in Courthouse Shootings," *Seattle Times,* March 2, 1996.

22. Quoted in Athima Chansanchai, "Shedding Light on Exploitation Exhibit Looks at Violence Against Asian Women," *Seattle Post-Intelligencer,* April 20, 2005.

23. Mimi Kim, *The Community Engagement Continuum: Outreach, Mobilization Organizing, and Accountability to Address Domestic Violence in Asian & Pacific Islander Communities* (San Francisco, Asian & Pacific Islander Institute on Domestic Violence, 2005) at http://www.apiahf.org/apidvinstitute/PDF/Community_Engagement_Report.pdf.

24. *Ibid.,* pp. 16–19.

25. *Ibid.,* pp. 20–23.

26. *Ibid.,* pp. 24–27.

27. *Ibid.,* pp. 34–38.

28. Bill Hosokawa, *Nisei: The Quiet Americans* (New York: W. Morrow, 1969).

29. U.S. Census Bureau, "Profile of Selected Social Characteristics: 2000" (Census Summary File 4, DP-2); and U.S. Census Bureau (Census Summary File 4, PCT 44).

30. Margaret Gipson, *Accomodation without Assimilation: Sikh Immigrants in an American High School* (Ithaca, NY: Cornell University Press, 1988); Nathan Caplan, Marcella Choy, and John Witmore (eds.), *Children of the Boat People: A Study of Educational Success* (Ann Arbor, MI: University of Michigan Press, 1991); Donna Nagata, *Legacy of Injustice: Exploring the Cross-Generational Impact of the Japanese American Internment* (New York: Pleneum Press, 1993); Nazli Kibria, *Family Tightrope: The Changing Lives of Vietnamese Americans* (Princeton, NJ: Princeton University Press, 1993) and *Becoming Asian American: Second Generation Chinese and Korean American Identities* (Baltimore, MD: Johns Hopkins University Press, 2002); Stacey J. Lee, *Unraveling the Model Minority Stereotype: Listening to Asian American Youth* (New York: Teachers College Press, 1996); Min Zhou and Carl Bankston III, *How Vietnamese Children Adapt to Life in the United States* (New York: Russell Sage Foundation, 1998); Pyong Gap Min and Rose Kim (eds.), *Struggle for Identity: Narratives by Asian American Professionals* (Walnut Creek, CA: AltaMira Press, 1999); Pyong Gap Min and Kyeyoung Park (eds.), *Amerasia Journal: Second*

Generation Asian Americans' Ethnic Identity 25:1 (1999); Mai Tuan, *Forever Foreigners or Honorary Whites? The Asian American Experience Today* (New Brunswick, NJ: Rutgers University Press,1998); and Jennifer Lee and Min Zhou (eds.), *Asian American Youth: Culture, Identity, and Ethnicity* (New York: Routledge, 2004).

31. Min Zhou, "Coming of Age: The Current Situation of Asian American Children," in Pyong Gap Min and Kyeyoung Park (eds.), *Amerasia Journal* 25:1 (1999): 1–27.

32. *Ibid.*, pp. 89–118.

33. Alejandro Portes and Rubén Rumbaut, *Immigrant America: A Portrait*, 2nd Edition (Berkeley and Los Angeles: University of California Press, 1996).

34. *Ibid.*, p. 251.

35. *Ibid.*, p. 244–245.

36. Snehendu B. Kar, Kevin Campbell, Armando Jimenez, and Sangeeta R. Gupta, "Invisible Americans: An Exploration of Indo-American Quality of Life," *Amerasia Journal* 21:3 (Winter 1995–1996): 25–52; and Snehendu B. Kar, Armando Jimenez, Kevin Campbell, and Felicia Sze, "Acculturation and Quality of Life: A Comparative Study of Japanese-Americans and Indo-Americans," *Amerasia Journal* 24:1 (1998): 129–142.

37. Tuan (1998), *op. cit.*, p. 18.

38. Kibria (2002), *op. cit.*, p. 157.

39. Uba, *Asian Americans*, pp. 97–107.

40. Quoted in Karen D. Pyke and Denise L. Johnson, "Asian American Women and Racialized Femininities: 'Doing' Gender Across Cultural Worlds." *Gender and Society* 17:1 (February 2003): 33–55.

41. *Ibid.*

42. Marcus Lee Hansen, *The Problems of the Third Generation* (Rock Island, IL: Augustana Historical Society, 1938).

43. Donna Nagata, *Legacy of Injustice: Exploring the Cross-Generational Impact of the Japanese American Internment* (New York: Plenum Press, 1993).

44. Bill Lann Lee, "Yung Wing and the Americanization of China," *Amerasia Journal* 1:1 (1971): 25–32; Ruthann Lum McCunn, *Thousand Pieces of Gold* (San Francisco: Design Enterprises, 1981); James W. Loewen, *The Mississippi Chinese: Between Black and White* (Cambridge, MA: Harvard University Press, 1971); Barbara M. Posadas, "Crossed Boundaries in Interracial Chicago: Pilipino American Families Since 1925," *Amerasia Journal* 8:2 (1981): 31–52; and Karen Leonard, *Ethnic Choices: California's Punjabi-Mexican Americans* (Philadelphia: Temple University Press, 1991).

45. Bok-Lim Kim, "Casework with Japanese and Korean Wives of Americans," *Social Casework* 53 (1972): 242–279; Kim, "Asian Wives of U.S. Servicemen: Women in Shadows," *Amerasia Journal* 4:1 (1977): 91–116.

46. John Conner, *A Study of the Marital Stability of Japanese War Brides* (San Francisco: R & E Research Associates, 1976); Aselm Strauss, "Strain and Harmony in American-Japanese War-Bride Marriages," *Marriage and Family Living* 16 (1954): 99–106.

47. See Raymond A. Joseph, "American Men Find Asian Brides Fill the Unliberated Bill," *Wall Street Journal*, January 25, 1984; Venny Villapando, "The Business of Selling Mail-Order Brides," in Asian Women United (eds.), *Making Waves: An Anthology of Writings By and About Asian American Women* (Boston: Beacon Press, 1989), pp. 318–326.

48. Joan Walsh, "Asian Women, Caucasian Men," *Image*, December 2, 1990, pp. 11–17.

49. Harry H. L. Kitano, Wai-Tsang Yeung, Lynn Chai, and Herbert Hatanaka, "Asian-American Interracial Marriage," *Journal of Marriage and the Family*, 46 (1984): 179–190. Also see Harry H. L. Kitano and Lynn Chai, "Korean Interracial Marriage," *Marriage and Family Review* 5 (1982): 75–89; Harry H. L. Kitano and Wai-Tsang Yeung, "Chinese Interracial Marriage," *Marriage and Family Review* 5 (1982): 35–48.

50. Sharon M. Lee and Keiko Yamanaka, "Patterns of Asian American Intermarriage and Marital Assimilation," *Journal of Comparative Family Studies* 21 (1990): 227–305.

51. Wen-Shing Tseng, John McDermott, and Thomas Maretzki, *Adjustment in Intercultural Marriage* (Hawaii: The University Press of Hawaii, 1977).

52. Quoted in Barbara Kantrowitz, "The Ultimate Assimilation," *Newsweek*, November 24, 1986, p. 80; Betty Lee Sung, *Chinese American Intermarriage* (New York: Center for Migration Studies, 1990). Note: "Intermarriage" is a generic term referring to either interracial or interethnic marriage. "Intermarriage" is often used interchangeably with "outmarriage."

53. Larry H. Shinagawa and Gin Y. Pang, "Marriage Patterns of Asian Americans in California, 1980," in Sucheng Chan (ed.), *Income and Status Differences Between White and Minority Americans* (Lewiston, NY: The Edwin Mellon Press, 1990), pp. 225–282.

54. Shinagawa and Pang, "Marriage Patterns of Asian Americans," *op. cit.*, pp. 269–270.

55. Colleen Fong and Judy Yung, "In Search of the Right Spouse: Interracial Marriage Among Chinese and Japanese Americans," *Amerasia Journal* 21:3 (1995): 77–98.

56. Larry H. Shinagawa and Gin Y. Pang, "Asian American Pan-Ethnicity and Intermarriage," *Amerasia Journal* 22:2 (1996): 127–152.

57. *Ibid.*, p. 30.

58. Sharon M. Lee and Marilyn Fernandez, "Trends in Asian American Racial/Ethnic Intermarriage: A Comparison of 1980 and 1990 Census Data," *Sociological Perspectives* 41:2 (Summer 1998): 323–343.

59. See http://www.mixedfolks.com/aothers.htm.

60. "Interracial Children Pose Challenge for Classifiers," *Wall Street Journal,* January 27, 1993.

61. Cynthia L. Nakashima, "An Invisible Monster: The Creation and Denial of Mixed-Race People in America," in Maria P. P. Root (ed.), *Racially Mixed People in America* (Newbury Park, CA: Sage Publications, 1992), pp. 162–178.

62. Nakashima, "An Invisible Monster," pp. 173–174; also see Rebecca Chiyoko King, "Multiraciality Reigns Supreme? Mixed Race Japanese Americans and the Cherry Blossom Queen Pagent," *Amerasia Journal* 23:1 (1997): 113–128.

63. Quoted in Kwai Julienne Grove, "Identity Development in Interracial, Asian/White Late Adolescents: Must It Be So Problematic?" *Journal of Youth and Adolescence* 20:6 (1991): 617–628.

64. Quoted in Angelo Ragaza, "All of the Above," *A Magazine,* 3:1 (1994): 76.

65. Rebecca Chiyoko King, "Racialization, Recognition, and Rights: Lumping and Splitting Multiracial Asian Americans in the 2000 Census," *Journal of Asian American Studies* 3:2 (June 2000): 191–217.

66. Cynthia L. Nakashima, "Voices from the Movement: Approaches to Multiraciality," in Maria P. P. Root (ed.), *The Multiracial Experience: Racial Borders as the New Frontier* (Thousand Oaks, CA: Sage Publications, 1996), pp. 79–97.

67. Teresa Williams-Leon and Cynthia Nakashima (eds.), *The Sum of Our Parts: Mixed Heritage Asian Americans* (Philadelphia: Temple University Press, 2001).

68. Maria P. P. Root, "A Bill of Rights for Mixed Race People," in Maria P. P. Root (ed.), *op. cit.,* 1996, pp. 3–15. "A Bill of Rights for Mixed Race People" can also be found at http://www.mixedfolks.com/rights.htm.

69. "Daughter Finally Finds GI Dad," *San Francisco Chronicle,* December 24, 1994.

70. Kieu-Linh Caroline Valverde, "From Dust to Gold: The Amerasian Experience," in Root (ed.), *Racially Mixed People in America,* pp. 144–161.

71. Robert S. McKelvey, *The Dust of Life: America's Children Abandoned in Vietnam* (Seattle: University of Washington Press, 1999) and Thomas A. Bass, *Vietnamerica: The War Comes Home* (New York: Soho Press, Inc, 1996).

72. Quoted in Shelia M. Poole, "Between Cultures: Vietnamese Amerasians Find a Refuge in Atlanta from Taunts that Plagued Their Childhood," *Atlanta Journal-Constitution,* May, 18, 2005.

73. Quoted in Chris Vaughn, "Vietnamese Children of U.S. Soldiers Struggle to Make New Lives in America," *Fort Worth Star-Telegram,* November 10, 2003.

74. *Ibid.*

75. Quoted in "Lofgren Introduces Citizenship Bill for Children Born in Vietnam to American Servicemen and Vietnamese Women During the Vietnam War," *Press Release,* October 22, 2003 at http://www.house.gov/lofgren/news/2003/pr_031022_Amerasian.html.

76. Tini Tran, "War Orphans Return to Vietnam 25 Years Later, *AsianWeek,* April 13, 2000.

77. Recent publications focusing on same-sex eroticism in Asia include Martin Manalansan IV, *Global Divas: Filipino Gay Men in the Diaspora* (Durham: Duke University Press, 2003); Rakesh Ratti (ed.), *A Lotus of Another Color: An Unfolding of the South Asian Gay and Lesbian Experience* (Boston: Alyson Publications, 1993); Wayne R. Dynes and Stephen Donaldson (eds.), *Asian Homosexuality* (New York and London: Garland Publishing, Inc., 1992); Bret Hinsch, *Passions of the Cut Sleeve: The Male Homosexual Traditions in China* (Berkeley: University of California Press, 1990); Tsuneo Watanabe and Jun'ichi Iwata, translated by D. R. Roberts, *The Love of the Samurai: A Thousand Years of Japanese Homosexuality* (London: Gay Men's Press, 1989); and Peter A. Jackson, *Male Homosexuality in Thailand: An Interpretation of Contemporary Thai Sources* (Elmhurst, NY: Global Academic Publishers, 1989).

78. Connie S. Chan, "Issues of Identity Development among Asian-American Lesbians and Gay Men," *Journal of Counseling and Development* 68 (September–October 1989): 16–20.

79. Pamela H., "Asian American Lesbians: An Emerging Voice in the Asian American Community," in Asian Women United (eds.), *Making Waves,* pp. 282–290.

80. Gerard Lim, "JACL Formally Adopts Same-Sex Marriages," *AsianWeek,* August 12, 1994.

81. "Support for JACL Decision," *AsianWeek*, August 12, 1994.
82. Dana Takagi, "Maiden Voyage: Excursion into Sexuality and Identity Politics in Asian America," *Amerasia Journal* 20:1 (1994): 1–18.
83. Quoted in Trinity Oronda, "In Our Own Way," *Amerasia Journal* 20:1 (1994): 137–147.
84. Gil Mangaoang, "From the 1970s to the 1990s: Perspective of a Gay Filipino American Activist, *Amerasia Journal* 20:1 (1994): 33–44.
85. Quoted in Ordona, "In Our Own Way," pp. 142–143.
86. Quoted in Alice Y. Hom, "Stories from the Homefront: Perspectives of Asian American Parents with Lesbian Daughters and Gay Sons," *Amerasia Journal* 20:1 (1994): 19–32.
87. Ric Parish, James Sakakura, Brian Green, Joel B. Tan, and Robert Vaszquez Pacheco, "Communion: A Collaboration on AIDS," in Russell Leong, *Asian American Sexualities: Dimensions of Gay & Lesbian Experience* (New York: Routledge, 1996), pp. 202–203.
88. Terry S. Gock, "Acquired Immunodeficiency Syndrome," in Nolan W. S. Zane, David T. Takeuchi, and Kathleen N. J. Young (eds.), *Confronting Critical Health Issues of Asian and Pacific Islander Americans* (Thousand Oaks, CA: Sage Publications, 1994), pp. 247–265.
89. Daniel C. Tsang, "Founder of First Gay and Lesbian Asian Group Succumbs to AIDS," *AsianWeek*, September 2, 1994.
90. University of California, San Francisco, "What Are Asian and Pacific Islander HIV Prevention Needs? at http://www.apiahf.org/programs/hivcba/resources/ facts/apifs.pdf.
91. Ignatius Bau, "APAs and AIDS: We Are Not Immune," *AsianWeek*, January 5, 1996.
92. Hirokazu Yoshikawa, "Network-, Setting-, and Community-Level HIV Prevention Strategies for Asian/Pacific Islanders: Data from Peer Educators at the Asian Pacific Islander Coalition on HIV/AIDS" at http://www.apiahf.org/programs/hivcba/resources/archives/apichareport5.pdf.
93. For more information on the Asian and Pacific Islander Coalition on HIV/AIDS see http://www.apicha.org/apicha/pages/education/index.htm.
94. David L. Eng and Alice Y. Hom, *Q&A: Queer in Asian America* (Philadelphia: Temple University Press, 1998), p. 3.
95. See Eric C. Wat, *The Making of a Gay Asian Community: An Oral History of Pre-AIDS Los Angeles* (Landham, MD: Rowman and Littlefield Publishers, Inc., 1998); Kevin K. Kumashiro, *Restoried Selves: Autobiographies of Queer Asian Pacific American Activists* (New York: Harrington Park Press, 2004); and Kevin K. Kumashiro, *Troubled Intersections Between Race and Sexuality: Queer Students of Color and Anti-Oppressive Education* (Landham, MD: Rowman and Littlefield Publishers, Inc., 2001).
96. Mabel Teng, "We Have Won Before and We Will Win Again," *AsianWeek*, March 18, 2004.
97. Quoted in Ulysses Torassa, "Thousands Protest Legalizing Same-Sex Marriages, *San Francisco Chronicle*, April 26, 2004.
98. Quoted in Rona Marech, "Asians to Rally in Favor of Same-Sex Marriage," *San Francisco Chronicle*, August 7, 2004.
99. Quoted in Bob Egelko, "S.F. Gay Marriages Head to Court," *San Francisco Chronicle*, December 21, 2005.
100. Quoted in Lynn Smith, "Time to Add His Political Voice," *Los Angeles Times*, November 4, 2004.
101. U.S. Census Bureau, *Adopted Children and Stepchildren: 2000* (October 2003), Table 5, p. 12 at http://www.census.gov/prod/2003pubs/censr-6.pdf.
102. William Feigelman and Arnold Silverman, *Chosen Children* (New York: Praeger, 1983); also see Feigelmann and Silverman, "The Long-Term Effects of Transracial Adoption," *Social Service Review* 58 (1983): 588–602.
103. Hei Sook Park Wilkinson, *Birth is More Than Once: The Inner World of Adopted Korean Children* (Detroit, MI: Harlo Press, 1985).
104. Quoted in Vanessa Hua, "Korean-Born in U.S. Return to a Home They Never Knew," *San Francisco Chronicle*, September 11, 2004.
105. Quoted in "Korean Adoptees Gather," *Baltimore Sun*, September 10, 1999.
106. Choi Soung-ah, "Korean Adoptees Gather in Seoul," *Korean Herald*, August 6, 2005.
107. Jane Jeong Trenka, *The Language of Blood: A Memoir* (St. Paul, MN: Borealis Books, 2003).
108. Tonya Bishoff and Jo Rankin (eds.), *Seeds of a Silent Tree* (Glendale, CA: Pandal Press, 1997).
109. Quoted in Chris Kwon, "'Seeds of a Silent Tree," *Korea Times*, February 28, 1998.
110. Quoted in Ann-Marie Trost, "Korean Adoptees Share Experiences Through Documentary," *Asian Pages*, April 14, 1998.
111. For more information see www.pbs.org/pov/firstpersonplural.
112. For more information see http://hometown.aol.com/Moonhwa//.
113. For more information see http://www.alsoknownas.org/.

8

The Final Frontier:
Asian American
Political Empowerment

VISIBILITY AND INVISIBILITY

Asian Americans make up the fastest growing population in the United States, and they have excelled in science, technology, education, and business. Yet for all these achievements, Asian Americans have not developed strong political influence or political power relative to other ethnic groups. While Asian Americans are a fast growing population, they are a highly immigrant population. This is abundantly clear from the U.S. Census Bureau figures in Table 8-1 that shows the low percentage of Asian American voter participation. In 2004 less than 30 percent of Asian Americans of voting age actually voted. This compares negatively to the 65.8 percent voter participation among non-Hispanic whites and 56.3 percent of voter participation among Blacks. Voter participation among Asians is much more comparable to Hispanics (28 percent), which is another largely immigrant population. Even more problematic is the low 44.1 percent voter participation in 2004 among Asian Americans who were citizens and fully able to vote. This is much lower than the 67.2 percent of non-Hispanic white citizens and 60 percent of Black citizens who exercised their right to vote. Voter participation among Hispanic U.S. citizens was relatively low at 47.2 percent, but still higher than the percentage for Asian Americans. The low voter turnout among Asian Americans is also seen in 2002 (a non-presidential election year) and 2000 (a presidential-election year); the Asian American voter turnout has been low for decades.

Asian Americans have been considered quite invisible in U.S. electoral politics. Until recently, little attention has been paid to Asian Americans because

Table 8-1 Reported Voting by Race, Hispanic Origin, and Age Groups, November 2000 to 2004

Population	2004*	2002	2000
White Non-Hispanic			
Total Population	65.8	48.0	60.4
Citizen Population	67.2	49.1	61.8
18–24			
Total Population	48.5	19.9	37.2
Citizen Population	49.8	20.4	NA
25–44			
Total Population	61.6	39.7	56.3
Citizen Population	63.5	41.0	NA
45–64			
Total Population	72.0	57.5	68.4
Citizen Population	73.2	58.5	NA
65 and older			
Total Population	72.2	64.0	78.6
Citizen Population	73.1	64.8	NA
Black			
Total Population	56.3	39.7	53.5
Citizen Population	60.0	42.3	56.8
18–24			
Total Population	44.0	19.3	33.9
Citizen Population	47.0	20.6	NA
25–44			
Total Population	54.0	36.1	52.1
Citizen Population	59.3	34.9	NA
45–64			
Total Population	62.6	50.0	62.9
Citizen Population	65.3	52.4	NA
65 and older			
Total Population	64.1	54.8	64.7
Citizen Population	65.9	56.5	NA
Asian**			
Total Population	29.8	19.4	25.4
Citizen Population	44.1	31.2	43.4
18–24			
Total Population	23.4	10.0	15.9
Citizen Population	34.2	15.9	NA
25–44			
Total Population	23.9	21.7	22.2
Citizen Population	40.2	34.5	NA
45–64			
Total Population	38.3	29.7	32.0
Citizen Population	51.1	41.6	NA
65 and older			
Total Population	38.2	29.0	37.9
Citizen Population	47.7	38.8	NA

(Continued)

Table 8-1 *continued*

Population	2004*	2002	2000
Hispanic (any race)			
Total Population	28.0	18.9	27.5
Citizen Population	47.2	30.4	45.1
18–24			
Total Population	20.4	8.1	15.4
Citizen Population	33.0	13.3	NA
25–44			
Total Population	23.0	15.3	16.1
Citizen Population	45.2	23.2	NA
45–64			
Total Population	38.5	28.7	38.3
Citizen Population	56.2	41.6	NA
65 and older			
Total Population	45.9	29.0	37.9
Citizen Population	57.0	38.8	NA

*Shows single-race population only.
**Prior to 2004, this category was "Asian and Pacific Islanders" and therefore the rates are not directly comparable.
Source: U.S. Census Bureau, http://www.census.gov/population/socdemo/voting/tabA-1.xls.

of their small numbers and apolitical image. Both public commentators and political scientists have used a cultural argument to explain why Asian Americans seem so lacking in political interest. In his book *Asian Power and Politics* (1985), Lucien W. Pye argues Confucian concepts of political power are distinct and inconsistent with Western concepts. According to Pye, Westerners search for personal identity and autonomy, whereas Asians are more accepting of benevolent authority.[1]

While culture may be a factor in determining political behavior, Asian American nonparticipation in mainstream politics can just as easily be explained by a history of institutional racism and discrimination that served to segregate Asian Americans from the center of political life in the United States. Beginning with the Naturalization Act of 1790, which stated that only "free whites" were eligible for naturalization and citizenship, Asian Americans were denied the right to vote or run for political office until after World War II. Despite a history of institutional barriers that inhibited Asian American participation in electoral politics, it would be wrong to say that Asian Americans have been apolitical. Asian Americans have not been silent in their attempts to gain equal rights that were denied them in the United States. This was done primarily in the form of organized self-help groups and legal redress.[2]

However, it is true that Asian American involvement in mainstream electoral politics has been mixed at best. Early studies on Asian American participation in electoral politics have shown low voter registration rates relative to the general population. These studies generally have concluded that the high percentage of foreign-born among the Asian American population is the primary factor for low voter registration rates and, thus, low voter participation. For example, Don Nakanishi (1985–1986, 1986) and Grant Din (1984) found that registration rates in Los Angeles County and San Francisco were both above 60 percent. However, the percentage of registered Japanese Americans in Los Angeles was 43 percent, for Chinese Americans 35.5 percent, Filipinos 27 percent, Koreans 13 percent, and Vietnamese 4.1 percent. Similarly, registration rates for Japanese Americans and Chinese Americans in San Francisco were 36.8 percent and 30.9 percent. In a more recent study of Asian American voting patterns in Oakland, California, Albert Muratsuchi (1990) found citywide voter registration rates to be 67.4 percent, while Japanese and Chinese Americans were just 41.8 and 22.6 percent, respectively.[3]

One study found that 77 percent of California Asian American citizens were registered to vote compared to 87 percent for whites. This study by Carol Uhlander, Bruce Cain, and D. Roderick Kiewiet (1989), also found that of those Asian Americans who were registered, only 69 percent actually did vote, compared to 80 percent for whites and 81 percent for African Americans.[4] In an update of his previous work, Grant Din (1993) found that the percentage of Chinese American registered voters in San Francisco increased from 30.9 percent to 40.2 percent. Din attributes this increase to two successful voter registration drives in 1991, which registered almost 6,000 new voters, 90 percent of whom were Chinese Americans. Although the voter registration drives were important, Chinese Americans, who were 34.3 percent of the voting-age population in San Francisco at the time, were still only 21 percent of the registered voters.[5]

Other studies have found that when Asian Americans do vote, they tend to vote in racial and ethnic terms. An exit poll of two thousand Asian Americans in the San Francisco Bay Area conducted by David Binder and Catherine Lew (1992) asked respondents how they would vote if they had to choose between two equally qualified candidates in an election when one is an Asian American and the other is not. The study found 74 percent said they would more likely choose the Asian American. Similar results were seen in another exit poll in the San Francisco Bay Area in 1994 conducted by Larry H. Shinagawa.[6]

These findings correspond with exit polls in Monterey Park, California, conducted by John Horton and his researchers in 1988 and 1990. Monterey Park, known as the "First Suburban Chinatown," is the only city in the continental United States with a majority Asian American population. The exit polls came up with some interesting results. First, they confirmed low voter turnout participation among Asian Americans; although Asian Americans represented more than 50 percent of Monterey Park's population, they made up barely a third of the voters. Second, the exit polls showed a strong pattern of ethnic voting among Asian Americans. The established Chinese American candidate and eventual top vote getter in each election, Judy Chu in 1988 and Sam Kiang in 1990, captured a very high percentage of the Asian American vote. Chu received 89 percent of the Chinese and 75 percent of the Japanese American vote in 1988, while Kiang received 90 percent of the Chinese and 69 percent of the Japanese American vote in 1990. Lastly, Horton found that the most inter-esting finding from the exit polls was the relatively high percentage of cross-ethnic voting. Chu received 35 percent of the Latino and 30 percent of the white vote in 1988, while Kiang received 30 percent of the Latino and 40 percent of the white vote. Horton concluded that even with the strong Asian American support, neither Chu nor Kiang could have won their respective elections without a broad-based coalition.[7]

This sentiment was echoed and expanded by political scientists Roy Christman and James Fay (1991, 1994), who surveyed all 459 cities in California looking for Asian American representation. The two came up with some intriguing conclusions. First, Christman and Fay argued that Asian Americans are not as underrepresented in electoral politics as many might think. In 1994 there were 48 Asian Americans out of 2,468 city council members in California. This represents just 2 percent of elected city officials, which is a very low figure considering Asian Americans represent nearly 10 percent of California's popu-lation. This statistic, however, tells only half the story. According to Christman and Fay, "Asian politicians tend to get elected in large and medium-sized cities with above-average Asian populations, so they represent over three million Californians, or almost ten percent of the state's residents." Second, Christman and Fay emphasize the fact that Asian Americans are elected not because of a massive voter turnout of Asian Americans, but through the support of white, African American, and Latino voters. They cite that only two Asian Americans were elected from areas in which a majority of voters were Asian Americans. Christman and Fay predicted Asian Americans would increase their numbers and clout as long as they continue to pursue coalition-building strategies.[8]

Christman and Fay's prediction is examined in this chapter, which focuses on Asian American politics through both nonelectoral and electoral empowerment efforts. The chapter begins with the history and evolution of Asian American political activism. Next, it looks at Asian American empower-ment from the 1970s to the present. Third, it focuses on empowerment strate-gies to increase Asian American political participation, with emphasis on bilingual voting rights and redistricting efforts. Lastly, this chapter discusses alternative voting strategies to further enhance Asian American political clout. The Asian American community can be, and has been, divided along many lines. What are the points of unity? How can they be sustained? What are its limits? These and other questions are addressed in this chapter.

HISTORY OF ASIAN AMERICAN
POLITICAL ACTIVISM

Asian American involvement in mainstream politics has been a continually evolving phenomenon. Social segregation and political disenfranchisement of Asian Americans prior to World War II severely limited the ability of Asian Americans to advocate for their rights. As a result, several forms of alternative political expression and empowerment were created. The early Asian American political empowerment can be divided into four generally sequential phases: (1) mutual aid societies; (2) homeland politics; (3) early civil rights organizations formed by U.S.-born Asian Americans; and (4) the Asian American movement of the late 1960s and early 1970s.

The first and most natural phase for the first Asian immigrants in the United States was the creation of mutual aid societies. These societies were primarily intended for economic survival and the maintenance of community, but were also a source of political unity. Leaders of these groups protested to federal, state, and local authorities over anti-Asian hostility and also hired attorneys to challenge discriminatory laws. The Chinese had a complex network of mutual aid societies known as *huiguan,* which included organized kinship, language, village, region, and occupational networks. The dominant force in the Chinese American community was the Chinese Consolidated Benevolent Association (CCBA), also known as the Chinese Six Companies because it was the umbrella organization for six huiguan. Japanese immigrants organized almost exclusively around the prefectural or regional association known as *kenjinkai.* The umbrella organization among Japanese immigrants was the Japanese Association of America, which was formed in 1908 and closely tied to the Japanese consulate in the United States. Unlike the Chinese and the Japanese, mutual aid societies for Koreans and Asian Indians were heavily influenced by religion. The first Korean mutual aid organization, the Friendship Society, was formed in San Francisco in 1903, and it was not long before Korean churches became the focus of Korean immigrant life. The first Sikh temple in the United States was built in Stockton, California, in 1912, and served as the center for religion and mutual aid assistance for the early Asian Indian immigrants. The earliest Filipinos to the United States, the Pensionados, were young men from elite families who were sent abroad in the early 1900s for their college education. They tended to organize themselves into fraternal organizations that maintained cultural ties and activities. Later, as the "Pinoys," or Filipino workers, arrived in large numbers to the United States, they found unity by organizing themselves around labor issues. In 1933 the Filipino Labor Union was formed, and in 1936 the American Federation of Labor granted a charter to the California Mexican-Filipino Field Workers Union Local 30326.[9]

The second phase of political empowerment for the early Asian immigrants involved appealing to their homeland governments for help. This, however, provided minimal success. During the late nineteenth and early twentieth centuries, most Asian countries were extremely weak and could do little more than lodge complaints to the U.S. State Department. For example, the government in China was facing extreme hardships created by war, famine, foreign intrusion, and economic instability. China could only watch as the anti-Chinese sentiment expanded in the United States and the 1882 Chinese Exclusion Act was passed. On the other hand, the Japanese government enjoyed relatively high international prestige following its rapid industrialization and militarism in the early 1900s. Vehement protests by the Japanese government over attempts to exclude Japanese immigrants carried a great deal of weight with the U.S. State Department. This led to the negotiation of the 1907 "Gentleman's Agreement," which served to limit—rather than eliminate—Japanese immigration. At the same time, however, the Japanese government was powerless against states and was unable to stop the passage of California's 1913 and 1920 Alien Land Acts. Korea, India, and the Philippines were all under the colonial control of foreign governments at the turn of the century, and their abilities to act on behalf of their overseas nationals were practically nonexistent.[10]

In his article, "The Politics of Ethnic Identity and Empowerment: The Asian American Community Since the 1960s," L. Ling-chi Wang writes: "Confronted by racial oppression and stripped of any political rights in the American democratic system, Asian immigrants of all classes saw their mistreatment in the United States as a direct outcome of the powerlessness of their homeland governments."[11] Not surprisingly, Asian immigrants in the United States actively supported modernization and independence movements abroad. In particular, Chinese, Korean, and Asian Indian immigrants closely followed the political events in their home countries and often raised large sums of money to support favored political leaders. Most of the Japanese and Filipinos in the United States were not particularly active in homeland politics compared with other Asian groups. Unlike other Asian groups at the beginning of the twentieth century, the Japanese American population was dominated by American-born Japanese, and the majority of them never set foot in their parents' homeland. As a result, these second-generation Nisei were far more preoccupied with being recognized as loyal Americans. In the case of Filipinos, they were officially American "nationals" and felt they belonged in the United States despite the often harsh treatments they faced. However, Filipino nationalism was demonstrated during World War II when Japanese militarism spread to the Philippines.[12]

The third phase of Asian American political empowerment emerged with the coming of age of the second generation of Asian Americans. The early Asian American civil rights organizations were primarily concerned with improving their own economic opportunities, social lives, and political influence in the United States, as well as establishing an identity separate from their parents. As early as 1895, a small group of American-born Chinese in California founded the Native Sons of the Golden State, which was intended to fight for citizenship rights. The group renamed themselves the Chinese American Citizens Alliance (CACA) in 1915, and its leaders were decidedly assimilationist-oriented, concentrating on confronting discrimination by urging Chinese Americans to engage in politics. In 1935, the organization began publishing *The Chinese Digest*, the country's first English-language Chinese American newspaper. At the same time, however, because of the war crisis in Asia, the upstart CACA worked closely with the established CCBA to support China.[13]

By far the largest cohort of second-generation Asian Americans at this time were the Japanese American Nisei, and the vast majority of young Nisei regarded themselves as Americans first. They registered as Democrats and Republicans, and founded patriotic groups like the American Loyalty League. In 1930, delegates from several of these groups formed the Japanese American Citizen's

League (JACL), to this day the community's most important organization. It should be noted that the JACL's relationship with the established first-generation (Issei) leadership was quite paradoxical. On the one hand, the first JACL leaders were only in their twenties and early thirties and were still closely aligned with the Japanese Association of America. For example, the JACL chose to remain silent on the issue of Japanese militarism in Asia. On the other hand, JACL leaders were also sensitive to discrimination and stressed that total allegiance to the United States would overcome prejudice. Indeed, one of the requirements for membership in the JACL was American citizenship. In 1940 the JACL published a statement that clearly expressed its loyalty to the United States: "I am proud that I am an American citizen of Japanese ancestry. . . . Because I believe in America, and I trust she believes in me, and because I have received innumerable benefits from her, I pledge myself to do honor to her at all times and all places; to defend her against all enemies, foreign and domestic; to actively assume my duties and obligations as a citizen, cheerfully and without any reservations whatsoever, in the hope that I may become a better American in a greater America."[14] Their loyalty was tested after the bombing of Pearl Harbor in December 1941 and President Roosevelt's Executive Order 9066 in February 1942.

Politics within Asian American communities during part of the Cold War era between World War II and the early 1960s were highly influenced by events in their home countries. In particular, there was considerable repression and suspicion against Chinese Americans following the 1949 Communist revolution in China. This antagonism increased when the People's Republic of China sent troops to support North Korean Communist forces against the U.S.-backed South Korea government in 1950. At the beginning of the Korean War (1950–1953), many Chinese Americans feared they would be forced into internment camps just as Japanese Americans had been less than a decade before. Established Chinatown leaders actively worked to assure the U.S. government that Chinese Americans were loyal allies, forming anti-Communist organizations across the nation and persecuting those who deviated or challenged their authority. Asian Americans remained extremely low-key for fear of being branded disloyal and Communist.[15]

Things changed dramatically during the tumultuous civil rights era of the 1960s and 1970s. Civil rights demonstrations, Vietnam War protests, student unrest, urban riots, and the rise of ethnic and feminist identity were all part of the cultural milieu during this important period in U.S. history. This was the broader context for the development of the fourth phase of Asian American empowerment, led by a new, post-Cold War generation commonly referred to as the Asian American movement. This phase of Asian American empowerment made a tremendous leap from the efforts that preceded it. Its defining event was the student-led "Third World Strike" at San Francisco State College (now University) from 1968 to 1969. The Asian American movement was much more critical and deliberately confrontational. The young Asian Americans were heavily influenced by the Black Power movement's forceful challenges to racial and economic inequality in the United States. In addition, these Asian American activists rejected the established community institutions for what they believed was their accommodation to the U.S. government and their self-serving attempts at social control over the Asian American community. According to L. Ling-chi Wang, "young Asian Americans challenged the dominant ideology, relentlessly attacked established organizations—such as the Chinese Six Companies and JACL—fought for community services for the poor and disadvantaged, demanded civil and political rights for all Asian Americans, and pressured major universities to establish Asian American studies programs."[16] San Francisco State student groups like the Intercollegiate Chinese for Social Action (ICSA) and the Philippine-American College Endeavor (PACE) were instrumental in starting numerous civil rights and service projects in their respective communities.[17]

The second significant distinction between the Asian American movement and previous political empowerment efforts was the call for the establishment of Asian American studies programs and the beginning of a panethnic Asian American political movement. Karen Umemoto's essay "'On Strike!' San Francisco State College Strike, 1968–1969: The Role of Asian American Students" (1991) describes the new movement's efforts to build a coalition grounded not only on individual ethnic experience but also on the common experiences and shared interests of Asians in the United States. The lead student organization in this regard was the Asian American Political Alliance (AAPA), which was formed mainly by Japanese American women. AAPA was more clearly committed to unifying the various Asian American ethnic groups than ICSA and PACE, and was more ideological rather than service-oriented. The demand for Asian American studies was not only a way to help Asian Americans learn their history but was also part of a broader strategy for social change. "The focus of the strike was a redefinition of education, which in turn was linked to a larger redefinition of American society," Umemoto writes. "These activities were rooted in and also shaped more egalitarian relationships based on mutual respect. While this doctrine was not always fully understood nor always put into practice, it was the beginning of a new set of values and beliefs, a 'New World Consciousness.'"[18]

The third significant distinction between the Asian American movement and earlier political activism is that student activists recognized they had to band together with other students of color and supportive white students if they wanted to achieve their goals. In the fall of 1968, ICSA, PACE, and AAPA joined with Black Students Union and Mexican American Students Confederation, to form a multi-ethnic coalition known as the "Third World Liberation Front" (TWLF). November 6, 1968, marks the first day of the longest sustained student strike in U.S. history. The TWLF at San Francisco State led a five-month shutdown of the campus and called for dramatic changes in the school's education policies. Among the most important student demands was for the college to institutionalize an ethnic studies program.

The intensity of the San Francisco State strike captured the attention of the entire nation, and students at other colleges began organizing and making similar demands. Asian American student organizations began to spring up on college and university campuses throughout California and across the nation. According to historian William Wei (1993), Asian American student organizations were active on college campuses in the early to mid-1970s throughout the United States. On the East Coast, Asian American Political Alliance groups were founded at Yale and Columbia. In the Midwest, Asian American student groups were formed at the University of Wisconsin–Madison, the University of Illinois–Chicago, the University of Michigan–Ann Arbor, and Oberlin College (Ohio).[19]

The Asian American movement was a turning point in Asian American history. The most obvious accomplishment of the San Francisco State strike was the establishment of the first school of ethnic studies in the United States, which included Asian American studies. But there were other outcomes as well. Umemoto states that the strike was a spark for a new generation of young Asian American political activists and many continue to make an impact after they graduated from college. Some returned to the community to start social service agencies and focus on grassroots organizing efforts. Others went on to obtain advanced degrees and move into mainstream positions of power and influence in business and government. Still others became involved in electoral politics in the belief that it is the best avenue to effect social change. After interviewing scores of individuals who were student activists during the late 1960s and early 1970s, Umemoto found that "(a)lmost without exception, those interviewed affirmed a deep commitment to the basic values and beliefs forged during their days as students active in the strike; many traced their convictions to the period of the strike itself."[20]

ASIAN AMERICAN POLITICAL EMPOWERMENT, 1970s–PRESENT

The student-led Asian American movement of the 1960s and 1970s was what seemed to be the beginning of an impressive emerging force in American politics. Asian Americans were suddenly very active on a variety of fronts. For example, the creation of the School of Ethnic Studies at San Francisco State inspired student leaders to fight for other Asian American studies programs on college campuses throughout California and the United States. More recently, Asian Americans organized around a variety of civil rights, community, and cultural rights issues. High profile, often nationwide, mobilizations supported redress and reparations for Japanese Americans interned during World War II, workers' rights, immigrant rights, welfare rights for the poor and elderly, and fairness in the media, as well as protested anti-Asian violence. Some political pundits boldly predicted that Asian Americans were finally on the verge of assuming a prominent role as a unified political interest group much like European American ethnics and African Americans. This speculation was based on recent political successes, the rapidly growing population, and the upward mobility of Asian Americans.[21]

Unfortunately, increasing numbers and upward mobility turned out to be a double-edged sword for Asian American politics. L. Ling-chi Wang argues that the rapid growth of the Asian American population brought with it great diversity, which is extremely difficult to unify. He acknowledges that the new Asian immigrants since 1965 differ considerably from the earlier waves of immigrants. Today affluent Asian immigrants are resented for bringing capital, starting businesses, and purchasing luxury cars and expensive homes in exclusive neighborhoods. They also perpetuate the image of the successful "super minority" or "model minority" that overshadows the struggles of poor Asian Americans and Asian immigrants and refugees. In addition, many of the well-to-do Asian immigrants have no understanding of the historical struggle of Asian Americans in search of political empowerment. Wang points out divided interests that make unified Asian American political empowerment "doubly difficult." Despite these events, others have insisted that Asian Americans can be mobilized into a solid political force.

In her book *Asian American Panethnicity: Bridging Institutions and Identities* (1992), Yen Le Espiritu acknowledges the great diversity within the "Asian American community," but describes the process, construction, and maintenance of panethnicity as a fundamental political process. Some scholars have examined the primordial (cultural) and instrumental (interest group) nature of ethnic unity as the reasons why various ethnic subgroups *voluntarily* form political blocks, but Espiritu concentrates on external factors that work to forge alliances between diverse peoples. One of the external factors Espiritu discusses is the role of the state in distributing resources and privileges based on ethnic and racial similarities and differences. A good example of this is seen in the decennial U.S. census. As described in Chapter 7, a variety of government agencies now rely on the U.S. census count to ensure civil rights laws are being upheld, as well as to determine political boundaries and representation. In the past, however, the census was often more effective at excluding individuals and groups than including them. "The census classification of ethno-racial groups has been problematic," Espiritu writes. "[T]he categories have been arbitrary and inconsistent—often reflecting the Census Bureau's administrative needs rather than the population's perceptions of meaningful cultural and racial differences."[22] She details attempts by the Census Bureau before the 1980 and 1990 survey counts to simply lump Asian Americans into one group, and describes calls by Asian Americans for a more accurate and detailed count. It is ironic that because the Census Bureau treated Asian Americans as a homogenous group, diverse Asian American groups had to respond as a one group to express their individual identities.

A more direct example of external factors creating the panethnicity described by Espiritu is the response to anti-Asian violence. Chapter 5 provides ample background on anti-Asian violence and briefly describes organizations such the National Asian Pacific American Legal Consortium that was formed to address the issue. Espiritu argues that Asian Americans are very aware that the general public does not usually distinguish Asian American subgroups. This reality naturally leads to what Espiritu calls "protective pan-Asian ethnicity" or "reactive solidarity." She emphasizes that anti-Asian sentiment and violence are the most significant issues unifying Asian American groups across ethnic, class, generational, and political lines, and has forged a pan-Asian consciousness.[23] Note that panethnic movements usually have a short life span because they are often circumstantially and spontaneously created. The maintenance of a panethnic movement, however, is an act of volition by a group of people dedicated to creating a condition, as well as an organization, that can sustain and revive the issue at hand. The 1982 killing of Vincent Chin in Detroit, Michigan, continues to be a seminal moment in Asian American history because a variety of organizations have emerged to keep Chin's memory and the issue of anti-Asian violence alive.[24]

Since the 1960s politicians and social critics have called for a "color-blind" society in which all people are judged by the content of their character and not by the color of their skin. This notion is certainly appealing, but it cannot be denied that the United States continues to be a highly racialized society. "The continuing importance of race and the persistence of racial lumping in American society suggest that, at present and in the immediate future, Asian Americans cannot—and perhaps should not—do away with the notion of pan-Asian ethnicity," Espiritu writes. "Pan-Asian unity is necessary if Asian Americans are to contest systems of racism and inequality in American society—systems that seek to exclude, marginalize, and homogenize them."[25] This does not mean that Asian Americans are merely victims of a racist society and can only react to the negative situations that confront them. Indeed, Espiritu argues that "bridging" the diverse elements within the Asian American community is very much a creative process, not just a reactive one. Nonetheless, the divisions within the Asian American community are significant—and most apparent—in mainstream electoral politics. Asian American involvement in electoral politics has never approached the type of success achieved by certain European ethnic groups (e.g., Irish and Italians), African Americans, and Latinos.

The political empowerment of Asian Americans has also suffered major recent setbacks. One of the most controversial and lingering issues has been the 1996 "Asian Connection" scandal that brought attention to overseas Asian governments, corporations, and individual power brokers contributing millions of dollars to political candidates, allegedly to influence U.S. policy decisions. Much of the focus has centered on John Huang, Johnny Chung, Maria Hsia, and Charlie Yah-lin Trie (among others), who raised funds for President Bill Clinton's reelection campaign and the Democratic National Committee (DNC). In response to mounting criticism, the DNC hired an auditing firm to investigate this controversy and anyone with an Asian surname suddenly became a suspect. For example, attorney Anthony Ching was told that his $5,000 contribution to President Clinton's reelection campaign would be "invalidated" if he did not cooperate with the investigation. Ching was so insulted he demanded his contribution be returned. "I don't think many people, including the Democratic Party, understand the difference between Asian American and Asian," Ching said angrily. That same day Ching received another call from the DNC inviting him to buy tickets for Clinton's reelection inauguration. "I found it ironic and humorous."[26]

The Organization of Chinese Americans and the Japanese American Citizen's League quickly organized a press conference denouncing how the audit was being handled. "They aren't going to say they are going after Asian Americans, but their process focuses on . . . the Asian American community," said Bob Sakiniwa, the Washington JACL representative. He was particularly concerned that the DNC's investigation of individuals who attended any Asian American political event and who contributed less than $2,500 would serve only to discourage any further participation by Asian Americans. Tensions over the racialization of the issue heightened even more when the March 24 cover of *National Review* magazine featured an illustration of President Clinton, Mrs. Clinton, and Vice President Al Gore all with exaggerated slanted eyes and buck teeth. This prompted U.S. Senator Daniel K. Akaka (D-Hawaii) to lash out in anger. "Some irresponsible publications, in the interest of sensationalism, are obviously more than willing to conflate racist stereotypes with modern standards of objective journalism," Akaka said on the Senate floor. "The President, Mrs. Clinton, and the Asian American community are owed an apology for this gross affront to decency and taste."[27]

The attention and legal investigations culminated in 1999 when John Huang pled guilty to minor campaign contribution charges. In exchange, Huang agreed to testify in front of the House Government Reform Committee under a grant of limited immunity. He admitted raising nearly $1 million in illegal contributions for the Democratic Party, but said that President Clinton and Vice President Al Gore were not involved. Huang vehemently denied allegations by some Republican members of Congress that he was a spy for Communist China. That same year Johnny Chung was also convicted of breaking campaign finance laws and sentenced to three thousand hours of community service and a five-year probation.[28] In February 2000, political fundraiser Maria Hsia, a longtime associate of Vice President Al Gore, was convicted of channeling more than $100,000 in illegal contributions to Democratic candidates. According to government prosecutors, Hsia was at the center of an operation in which she persuaded Asian Americans to write large campaign fundraising checks. People who wrote the checks were later reimbursed. The "real donors" could not legally contribute for a variety of reasons. Unlike Huang and Chung, Hsia did not plea-bargain and was convicted of a felony.[29]

The repercussions from the campaign scandal have gone far beyond the conviction of a few illicit political contributors. "Not surprisingly Asian Americans across the nation were stunned by the unwanted national attention and many felt outraged, betrayed, ashamed, violated, discouraged, injured or insulted," wrote Asian American scholar L. Ling-chi Wang.[30] Rumors that former University of California–Berkeley chancellor Chang Lin Tien would be appointed to a Cabinet post in 1997 were dashed because President Clinton was said to be wary of appointing an Asian American to a top position during the early days of the fundraising scandal. The formal confirmation of Bill Lann Lee as assistant attorney general for civil rights was stalled for years in the wake of the congressional fundraising probes. The zealous pursuit of Asian donors, coupled with the infamous Cox Report on Chinese spies that led to the arrest of physicist Dr. Wen Ho Lee, created a very real cause for alarm. The example of Bonnie Wong is a case in point. Wong is the founder and president of Asian Women in Business and was an active participant in Bill Clinton's 1992 and 1996 presidential campaigns. Given the recent attacks on Asian Americans by politicians and political pundits, Wong thought about simply not participating in the 2000 elections. "You start to wonder if it's worthwhile," she sighed.[31] In an effort to win back Asian American Democratic support, President Clinton appointed former Congressman Norm Mineta to his cabinet as secretary of commerce in July 2000. It was a move heralded by Asian American leaders.[32] Just one month later, Clinton gave Bill Lann Lee a "recess appointment" as assistant attorney general for civil rights. This move came three years after Clinton had named Lee as his main civil rights enforcer, and allowed Lee to hold the post without congressional approval.[33]

ASIAN AMERICANS IN ELECTORAL POLITICS

The first Asian American elected to the U.S. Congress was Dalip Singh Saund, an Asian Indian farmer from the Imperial Valley of California. He was elected in 1956 and reelected in 1958. Unfortunately, he had to resign his position in the middle of his second term because of ill health. When Hawaii was granted statehood in 1959, decorated World War II hero Daniel Inouye was elected the state's first U.S. representative, and businessman Hiram Fong was elected to the U.S. Senate (along with former governor Oren Long, who is not Asian American). No other Asian American outside of Hawaii served in Congress until Norman Mineta, the former mayor of San Jose, California, was elected in 1974. Two years later, California elected former San Francisco State University president S. I. Hayakawa to be its U.S. senator. Hayakawa served only one term in office, but remains the only Asian American elected by a mainland state to serve in the U.S. Senate. In 1978, Japanese American, Robert Matsui from Sacramento, California, was elected to Congress. Matsui passed away in 2005, but his wife, Doris, won a special election to replace him. For years the highest-ranking Asian American state official in California was Secretary of State March Fong Eu, who was elected in 1974 but resigned to serve as ambassador to Micronesia in 1994. Outside of California, in 1996 Gary Locke, a son of Chinese immigrants, became the first Asian American to be elected governor in the continental United States. Locke campaigned as a liberal Democrat who supported gay and abortion rights but was tough on crime and a fiscally moderate in a state where Asian Americans represent less than 6 percent of the population. Locke's political popularity continued and he was reelected to office by a wide margin in 2000. Locke chose not to run for a third term in 2004.

There have been many more Asian Americans elected to public office since the days of the early political pioneers. According to the *National Asian Pacific American Political Almanac* (2004), there are more than five hundred API elected officials in the United States including its territories (e.g., American Samoa and Guam), although this figure does not include elected school board members. California has the largest number of API elected officials (189) followed by Hawaii (113), Washington (26), Texas (21), and New York (15). Among the elected officials, the *Political Almanac* listed 2 U.S. senators (both from Hawaii), 5 U.S. representatives, 97 state representatives, 19 city mayors, 123 city or county council members, and 236 judges.[34] Elections since 2000 have shown a flurry of activity for Asian Americans in electoral politics. For example, Mee Moua from Minnesota became the first Hmong American elected to a state legislature in 2001. The following year another Hmong American, Cy Thao, was also elected to the Minnesota state legislature. In 2004, two Vietnamese Americans were elected to state legislatures, Van Tran from California and Hubert Vo from Texas. Also in 2004, Bobby Jindal from Louisiana became the first Asian Indian American elected to the U.S. House of Representatives since Dalip Singh Saud. Jindal's victory came just one year after his controversial failed run for governor of Louisiana. Jindal is a conservative Republican who was endorsed by President Bush and outgoing Louisiana governor Mike Foster. Preelection surveys gave Jindal a sizable lead in this heavily Republican state, and there was great optimism that he would become the second Asian American governor in the continental United States following Gary Locke. On the day of the election however, voters turned away from Jindal giving the victory to Democrat Kathleen Blanco. Political scientists Richard Skinner and Philip A. Klinkner analyzed the Louisiana election results and concluded that conservative whites voted against Jindal primarily because of his race instead of supporting him because of his position on issues.[35]

The face of the California's legislature is rapidly changing thanks to the increasing participation of Asian Americans. From 1980 to 1992 there was not a single Asian American in the state's 120-member Legislature (the 80-member Assembly and the 40-member Senate). That drought ended when Nao Takasugi was elected to California State Assembly in 1992. Takasugi retired from office in 1998, but that same year Mike Honda and George Nakano were elected; it was the first time in twenty years that there was more than one Asian American representative in the California legislature at the same time. Honda was reelected to Congress in November 2000, and that election also saw Wilma Chan and Carol Liu elected to the California Assembly. This was the first time three Asian Americans served on the Assembly at the same time. In 2005, there were eight elected officials in the California legislature, five Democrats and three Republicans, all in the State Assembly. While this growth is impressive, the number of Asian American legislators fluctuates with every new election. Plus, California has term limits for its elected officials.

Nonetheless, Asian American representatives have come together to form the Asian Pacific Islander Legislative Caucus (APILC). Special interest caucuses are not unique in the California State Assembly, which includes the Democratic Caucus, the Republican Caucus, the Women's Caucus, the Latino Caucus, the Black Caucus, the LGBT (Lesbian, Gay, Bisexual, and Transgender) Caucus, the Rural Caucus, and the Smart Growth Caucus. All were created to support legislation for their specific constituencies.[36] The stated goals of the APILC are the following:

- increase API representation in all levels of government including statewide appointments and statewide elected offices;
- ensure the API community has equal access to education, social services, health, mental health, and other government programs and services;
- preserve safety net health, mental health, and social service programs that serve the API community;
- ensure language access and culturally competent services in government programs;
- strengthen protections against hate crimes and defend the civil rights and liberties of APIs;
- fight racial stereotypes and negative portrayals of APIs in the media;
- promote greater civic participation and knowledge about major policy issues among API communities;
- build common interest and communications among the various API communities.[37]

Who Votes, Who Does Not, and Why

Despite recent advances there are still concerns over the lack of participation among Asian Americans in the electoral process. The major concerns focus on the issues of representation and empowerment. *Representation* means having Asian Americans elected to political office who are willing to serve as advocates for the Asian American interests. Note that just because an elected official is an Asian American does not necessarily mean he or she will be a voice for Asian American interests. Nonetheless, political representation is still an important goal. In contrast to representation, *empowerment* means having a unified community of interest that can formulate a political agenda, mobilize around specific issues, and pressure their Asian American or non-Asian American political representatives to act on the community's behalf. Asian American leaders are particularly concerned with the lack of involvement among Asian American voters because it only undermines the group's political empowerment.

As discussed at the beginning of this chapter, overall Asian American voter registration rates and participation in electoral politics historically has been low relative to other major ethnic groups. The main explanation for this phenomenon is the high proportion of immigrants in the Asian American population who are currently ineligible to vote. However, this situation may be changing. In their article "Becoming Citizens, Becoming Voters: The Naturalization and Political Participation of Asian Pacific Immigrants" (1996), UCLA professors Paul Ong and Don Nakanishi highlight signs that may indicate potential growth in both the numbers and activism of Asian American voters. Ong and Nakanishi acknowledge there is a high percentage of Asian American adults (55 percent) who are currently not citizens, but at the same time they note a high rate of naturalization. They cite length of residence in the United States, age when immigrated (young immigrants naturalize at a higher rate than older immigrants), education level, and English-language proficiency as key factors that positively influence immigrants to become U.S. citizens.

Although Asian immigrants have a high rate of naturalization, they continue to have a low overall rate of voter registration. Interestingly, however, Ong and Nakanishi found that Asian American naturalized citizens who immigrated to the United States *before* 1975 have among the highest voter registration rates of any group—including U.S.-born Asian Americans. Conversely, Asian American naturalized citizens who arrived to the United States *after* 1975 have among the lowest voter registration rates. In addition, Ong and Nakanishi cite 1994 figures showing the overall percentage of Asian American registered voters was low, but contrast them with figures showing the percentage of Asian American registered voters who actually voted was higher than any other group. From these data, political participation among immigrant Asian Americans may increase as they age and become more settled. "Whether Asian Pacific Americans become a major new political force in American electoral system is nearly impossible to predict with any precision," Ong and Nakanishi cautiously conclude. "This period will be important to witness and analyze because of the extraordinary challenges and opportunities . . . for Asian Pacific Americans in seeking realization of their full potential as citizens and electoral participants."[38] The figures from Table 8-1 indicate that the "potential" is still unmet.

Nonetheless, when Asian Americans do vote, what political party do they support? Unlike other racial minority groups such as African Americans and Latinos who overwhelmingly vote Democratic, Asian American party loyalty is mixed. Early works in this area done by Don Nakanishi and his researchers who studied Monterey Park, California, in 1984 found 43 percent of Asian Americans were registered Democrats, 31 percent registered Republicans, and 25 percent declined to state. In a follow-up study in 1989, 35 percent of Asian American registered voters in Monterey Park were Democrats, 37 percent were Republicans, and 26 percent declined to state (1991). Lack of group and political party unity is further evidence of the diversity in the Asian American community, but it is also a significant reason why Asian Americans have historically been ignored and lacked political clout.

In the late 1980s and early 1990s the Republican Party was aggressive in bringing Asian Americans into its ranks and, in particular, encouraging them to run for office. "We're trying to get more involvement in general activity with the Republican Party," explains Dennis See, a Republican insider who is in charge of the party's Asian American outreach efforts. "Asian Americans need to gain political experience at all levels. . . . That includes experience as candidates and voters, but also experience as campaign workers and precinct leaders."[39] In the 1988 presidential election, 54 percent of Asian American voters supported the Republican George H. W. Bush ticket compared to 44 percent who supported the Democrat Michael Dukakis ticket. In 1989 the Republican National Committee opened a special Asian American Affairs Office, and

President Bush proceeded to appoint an unprecedented number of Asian Americans to high-level management and advisory positions. Among the appointments was Elaine Chao, who was first brought in as deputy secretary at the Department of Transportation and was later asked to head the Peace Corps. In addition, Wendy Gramm (who is married to U.S. Senator Phil Gramm from Texas) was named to chair the Commodity Futures Trading Commission, Julie Chang Bloch was named ambassador to Nepal, and Patricia Saiki was asked to lead the Small Business Administration. When President Bush was preparing for his reelection campaign in 1992, he dispatched Vice President Dan Quayle to speak in support of Asian American candidates running for elected office, attend local Asian American-sponsored fundraisers, and speak out against anti-Asian violence. All these efforts had tangible results. In the summer of 1991, an Asian American-sponsored political rally in Orange County attracted an estimated 60,000 enthusiastic Asian American supporters.[40] Indeed, one of Bush's biggest fundraisers was Zachariah Zachariah, an Asian Indian physician from Florida who collected nearly $2 million from Asian Americans.

It was clear that Bush and the Republican Party had the loyalty of many Asian Americans. According to one national presidential election exit poll, Asian Americans supported Bush over Clinton by a 55 to 29 percent margin in 1992, while 16 percent voted for Ross Perot. This is in stark contrast to the overall election results in which Clinton won 43 percent of the vote, Bush 40 percent, and Perot 19 percent.[41] Despite the Republican defeat in the 1992 presidential election, many inside the party believe Asian Americans have found their home. "Asian Americans are in many ways a natural constituency for the Republican Party," beams Dennis See. He argues that the Republican pro-business and limited government intervention agendas are positions that appeal to many Asian Americans. Asian Americans, being a generally middle-class community, are attracted to the Republican Party. See believes that Southeast Asians and many Chinese Americans also voted Republican because of the party's image of being anti-Communist.[42] But several other surveys and exit polls on how Asian Americans vote provide some very interesting details and serve to further demonstrate the group's complexity and diversity.

In the voter-rich state of California, Asian American Democrats cite two other surveys suggesting that Asian American support for Republicans is soft and could go either way. One statewide poll by the Voter News Service in 1992 showed Asian Americans supporting Bill Clinton 45 percent, George Bush 40 percent, Ross Perot 15 percent.[43] A more detailed study of that same election conducted in northern California by David Binder and Catherine Lew showed Asian Americans strongly supported Clinton over Bush by a 53 to 37 percent margin, with 9 percent going to Perot. Binder and Lew also reported that 49.2 percent of Asian Americans surveyed said Democrats were the political party that cares the most about their needs, compared to just 23.1 percent who said Republicans cared the most.[44]

The trend in California beginning in 1992 continued into the 1994 (nonpresidential) election season. An exit poll by the *Los Angeles Times* found

48 percent of the Asian American respondents said they were Democrats, while 32 percent said they were Republicans, and 20 percent said they were Independents or declined to state. An exit poll in northern California conducted by Larry H. Shinagawa found that among first-generation Asian Americans who responded to the survey, 61.6 percent were Democrats, 24.0 percent were Republicans, and the rest were Independents or declined to state. The differences were even more stark among Asian American voters who were at least second generation in the United States. More than 70 percent of at least second-generation Asian Americans who responded to the poll said they were Democrats, while only 17.9 percent said were Republicans.[45]

In 1996, the National Asian Pacific American Legal Consortium sponsored a three-region exit poll to gather data on Asian American voting patterns during that presidential election year. A total of 4,650 exit polls were counted from Los Angeles County, New York City, and the San Francisco–Oakland Bay Area. In all three areas Asian Americans strongly supported Bill Clinton over Republican challenger Bob Dole. In San Francisco and Oakland, 83 percent of Asian Americans polled voted for Clinton, while 9 percent voted for Dole, and another 9 percent voted for someone else or declined to state. In Los Angeles County, 53 percent of Asian Americans voted for Clinton, 41 percent for Dole, and 4 percent for Ross Perot. New York City results showed 71 percent supported Clinton, 21 percent voted for Dole, and 2 percent went for Perot. These findings differed considerably from the widely cited Voter News Service (VNS) poll that showed 48 percent of Asian Americans voting for Dole, 43 percent for Clinton, and 8 percent for Perot. The VNS poll was sponsored by a consortium of the major television networks and print media sources, but was heavily criticized for surveying only 170 Asian Americans nationwide out of a total sample size of about 16,000 voters. VNS's poll was also conducted without bilingual workers or materials, which biased its sample toward educated, American-born, and English-proficient Asian American voters. The NAPALC exit poll was significant precisely because it offered polling forms in different languages and had multilingual polltakers available. "The primary reason we wanted to do the survey was to monitor the need for bilingual assistance," said Karen Narasaki, executive director of NAPALC. She is sure that the use of bilingual materials and surveys were the primary reasons for the stark variation in poll findings.[46]

There are several reasons why Asian American support of the Republican Party eroded in such a short amount of time. In 1994 California's Republican governor, Pete Wilson, led the effort to pass Proposition 187, which eliminated educational and social services to undocumented immigrants. Though the proposition was not aimed at legal immigrants, its general anti-immigrant tenor was loud and clear. Two years later the federal welfare reform bill that passed in the Republican-controlled Congress included specific policies limiting social services to legal immigrants. Spurred by these two events, angry Asian Americans became motivated to naturalize, register, and to vote. Many attribute the rise in Asian American support for the Democratic Party to the unease with the Republican's stand on immigration. "There's clearly a trend towards Democratic involvement," explained Don Nakanishi.[47] Second, Republican leaders completely underestimated the wide Asian American support of Bill Lann Lee as President Clinton's nominee for assistant Attorney General. Many Asian Americans viewed Republican opposition to Lee as akin to President Clinton's refusal to appoint an Asian American to his Cabinet. Yasuo Tokita, a Japanese American Republican from Utah publicly stated, "Bill Lann Lee is 'guilty' of looking like John Huang." When Tokita was asked to gauge Asian American hostility to Republicans for their opposition to Lee, he said, "intense would be an understatement." Another Asian American Republican offered his candid assessment: "Republicans have pushed Asians toward the Democrats when most of them really had been voting Republican in the past."[48] Third, a House select committee, chaired by Republican congressman Christopher Cox, issued a controversial report in May 1999 claiming that the People's Republic of China had stolen U.S. nuclear secrets with the cooperation of Chinese Americans in illegal technology and information transfers. Republican politicians quickly seized the committee's findings and accused the Clinton administration of failing to counter Chinese espionage. U.S. Senator Richard Shelby, a Republican from Alabama, remarked on NBC's *Meet the Press* that the Chinese are "very crafty people." And U.S. Senator Robert Smith, a Republican from New Hampshire, confused Bill Lann Lee with Wen Ho Lee, the Los Alamos scientist who was alleged to have passed nuclear secrets to the Chinese government. Asian Americans once again felt their loyalty was suspect and feared a racial backlash. "The problem is guilt by association," said civil rights leader and law professor Frank Wu. This gives Asian Americans insight into African American complaints about racial profiling."[49]

Disenchantment with national politics was the motivation behind the creation of the 80-20 Initiative, a political action committee started by prominent Chinese Americans.[50] The premise of the initiative was simple. Asian Americans should consolidate their political power and organize 80 percent of Asian Americans to support one presidential candidate in the 2000 election. In doing so, the group hoped to make Asian Americans a cohesive and formidable political force. S. B. Woo, a professor of molecular and atomic physics at the University of Delaware and the state's former lieutenant governor, was one of the group's founders. "We openly state we want to establish political clout for the Asian American community," Woo explained. To earn the support of 80-20, a candidate must commit to aggressive federal efforts to combat workplace discrimination and to appoint more Asian Americans to prominent policymaking roles. The group planned to organize Asian American voters via the Internet and promised to have more than 300,000 names on its e-mail list. "Some people thought it was a very foolish idea," Woo admits.[51] However, during the presidential primaries, Democratic candidate Bill Bradley was the first to endorse 80-20's agenda. Vice President Al Gore quickly followed suit. Republicans rejected the initiative and 80-20 called for Asian Americans to boycott the Republican Party. By August 2000, the 80-20 group gained sufficient momentum and held its groundbreaking convention in Los Angeles. Representatives of presidential candidates from both parties lobbied 80-20 delegates. It was the first time an Asian American political group sought to deliver an Asian American bloc vote to a presidential nominee. At the end of the three-day meeting the group chose to endorse Al Gore for president. The next challenge for 80-20 was to deliver the votes.[52]

Several exit polls that questioned Asian American voters were conducted following the 2000, presidential election. One exit poll conducted by the Asian Pacific Legal Center surveyed five thousand people in heavily Asian neighborhoods in and around Los Angeles. The results showed 62.3 percent of Asian Americans who participated in the survey voted for Al Gore, while 34.7 percent voted for George W. Bush. The exit poll found Asian Americans who identified themselves as Republican declined from 40 percent in 1996 to 29.7 percent in 2000. Similarly, Asian Americans who identified themselves as Independents dropped from 24 percent to 19.5 percent. Twenty-five percent of Asian American voters surveyed knew about the 80-20 Initiative. A separate exit poll in San Francisco, sponsored by the Chinese American Voter Education Committee and conducted by David Binder Research, showed 82 percent of Asian America voters (mostly Chinese Americans) voted for Gore and just 16 percent voted for Bush. The poll also found that 41 percent of Asian American voters knew of 80 20. Both the Los Angeles and San Francisco area polls were conducted in various Asian languages as well as in English. These finding were consistent with the *Los Angeles Times* statewide exit poll that found 63 percent of Asian American voters supported Gore while 33 percent supported Bush. The same poll found Latinos favored Gore 75 percent to 23 percent and African Americans backed Gore 85 percent to 14 percent. Whites, on the other hand, voted for Bush 49 to 47 percent.[53] The *San Francisco Chronicle* conducted its own statewide exit poll as well. In this survey, Latinos voted for Gore 68 to 29 percent, African Americans voted for Gore 86 to 11 percent, and whites supported Bush 48 to 47 percent. The *Chronicle* findings for Asian Americans were starkly different from the other studies, as it showed Asian Americans narrowly supporting Gore 48 to 47 percent. The wide discrepancy for Asian American voters cannot be easily explained, but both the *San Francisco Chronicle* and the *Los Angeles Times* agreed that Asian Americans made up 6 percent of the voters in California.[54]

New Findings: The 2004 Presidential Election

George W. Bush won the 2000 election by the narrowest of margins and amid great controversy. After he entered the White House there were renewed efforts by the Republican Party to win back Asian American voters. One of the few things the Bush administration kept from the previous Clinton administration was the White House Initiative on Asian Pacific Americans. Bush also reappointed Norm Mineta as Secretary of Transportation and added Elaine Chao as Secretary of Labor. This is the first time two Asian Americans have served on a presidential cabinet.[55] During his first term in office President Bush appointed 225 Asian and Pacific Islander Americans to federal positions, as well as the largest number of what are called PAS (Presidential Appointment–Senate Confirmed), which are the highest ranking positions in the federal government.[56] It was no coincidence that the Bush administration and the Republican Party put a lot of effort into promoting Bobby Jindal as one of its rising political stars in part to encourage more support among the growing Asian Indian population, which is well educated and highly entrepreneurial.[57] Two more gestures of good will occurred just before the November 2004 election: President Bush issued Executive Order 13339, "Increasing Economic Opportunity and Business Participation of Asian Pacific Islander Americans," and established the president's Advisory Commission on Asian Americans and Pacific Islanders. The Commission was formed to provide recommendations to the President on the mandates of the Executive Order to (1) develop, monitor, and coordinate federal efforts to improve Asian American and Pacific Islander participation in government programs; (2) foster research and data collection for Asian American and Pacific Islander businesses and communities; and (3) increase their level of participation in the national economy and their economic and community development.[58]

At the same time, the Democratic Party was making an equally strong effort to solidify its Asian American and Pacific Islander base primarily because they were seen as possible swing votes in the 2004 election. "Of the nearly six million votes counted in Florida in the 2000 presidential election, the official tally totaled a mere 537 vote advantage for Bush, thus determining the presidency," wrote Keith Umemoto, chair of the Asian Pacific Islander Caucus of the Democratic National Committee, in a column published by *AsianWeek*. "With roughly 10,000 Asian Pacific American voters in Florida, a nominal shift in the APA vote could have changed the outcome in the election and Al Gore could have been President."[59] At the July 2004 Democratic National Convention in Boston, there were more than one thousand Asian and Pacific Islander American participants including delegates, state and local elected officials, as well as business and community leaders. Throughout the five-day convention there were a number of events sponsored by various Asian American groups to highlight their presence and enthusiasm. Two of the most prominent Asian American elected officials, Washington governor Gary Locke and Congressman Mike Honda from California, were on John Kerry's national steering committee. "We're showing just how important we are and how seriously we are to be considered," exclaimed an enthusiastic Gary Locke at the convention. "We as Asian Pacific Islanders can not just sit out. . . . That's why we have to work even harder to raise money and to get our friends to register to vote and to turn out the vote."[60] In addition to the conspicuous presence of Asian and Pacific Islander Americans at the convention, John Kerry was also endorsed by the 80-20 Initiative, marking the second time in a row this organization put its weight behind a Democratic presidential candidate.

The battle for the hearts and minds of Asian and Pacific Islander Americans was in full swing and there was great anticipation as to how they would cast their votes in the 2004 presidential election. A New California Media survey of more than one thousand Asian and Pacific Islander Americans nationwide was conducted in August 2004, several months before the November election, as a way to gauge how registered voters were likely to cast their ballots. This poll was unique in that it was conducted in nine languages (Mandarin, Cantonese, Vietnamese, Korean, Tagalog, Japanese, Hindi, Hmong, and English). The results showed the API vote was still up for grabs. Democratic nominee John

Kerry had a 43 to 36 percent lead over President Bush, but there was still about 20 percent who were undecided. There was some cause for optimism among Republicans because the poll also highlighted different political choices made by various Asian American groups. For example, Kerry ran well among Chinese, Asian Indian, and Hmong American voters, while Bush had strong leads among Vietnamese and Filipino American voters. Japanese, Korean, and Pacific Islander groups were equally split between the two candidates. The ambivalence felt among API voters is highlighted by the fact that 44 percent of those surveyed could not pick between the Democratic Party and the Republican Party when asked which party best represents the issues and opinions of their national or ethnic group. In addition, only 29 percent identified strongly with the Democratic Party and only 25 percent said they were closer to the Republican Party. However, one finding was telling: 63 percent of those polled had a positive opinion of the Democratic Party, while only 48 percent had a positive opinion of the Republican Party.[61] It was this last finding that became most evident when votes were finally cast in the November 2004 election.

Through the years there have been a number of exit polls providing information on Asian American voters (less attention has been focused on Pacific Islander voters), and all have their strengths and weaknesses. The Asian American Legal Defense and Education Fund (AALDEF), a New York-based organization, conducted the only national exit poll focusing on Asian American voters in 2004. The strength of this poll is its large sample size and that questionnaires were available in nine languages. The weakness of this poll is that it concentrated its efforts in states with large Asian American populations, many of which were considered "blue" states, or states that generally favor Democrats. This tends to skew the findings. In the AALDEF exit poll, Asian Americans voted 74 percent in favor of John Kerry and only 24 percent for George Bush.[62] The Asian Pacific American Legal Center conducted an exit poll that focused exclusively on Asian American voters in southern California that had a sample size of just over four thousand and provided surveys in six languages. This poll focused on a limited geographical area and was not necessarily representative of Asian Americans nationally. In addition, although California is considered a "blue" state, this portion of the state is generally more conservative than the state as a whole. The APALC exit poll found a narrower margin of victory, but Asian Americans supported Kerry over Bush by a strong 57 to 41 percent.[63] Mainstream exit polls in California conducted by the *Los Angeles Times* and a national exit poll conducted by the *Washington Post* and CNN are less reliable indicators of the overall Asian American vote because the sample size of Asian American respondents is usually very low and questions are not asked in any of the Asian languages. Nonetheless, both polls showed 60 percent of Asian Americans in their surveys voted for Kerry and less than 40 percent voted for Bush.[64]

INCREASING POLITICAL CLOUT

The last two presidential elections have shown that Asian Americans who do vote have become a voting bloc. However, political activists and scholars studying

Asian American political participation recognize the need to get more Asian Americans into the three-step process of naturalization, registration, and voting.[65] For this, they have focused on three strategies: (1) bilingual ballots, (2) political redistricting, and (3) grooming viable Asian American candidates for political office.

Bilingual Ballots

Asian American political and civil rights leaders still acknowledge the need for bilingual ballots to ensure Asian American participation in all levels of electoral politics. Bilingual ballots are particularly important given the large Asian American immigrant population. Table 8-2 shows that merely 21 percent of Asian Americans spoke only English at home, while 79 percent spoke a language other than English at home. The figures change depending on ethnic group, as seen in the fact that 52.7 percent of Japanese Americans spoke only English at home, while just 4.4 percent of Hmong Americans and 6.9 percent of Vietnamese Americans spoke only English at home.

In the summer of 1992, Asian Americans helped lobby Congress to approve a fifteen-year extension to the bilingual provisions of the Voting Rights Act of 1965. In addition, changes in the act required bilingual ballots be provided in counties where more than 10,000 residents speak the same foreign language and are not proficient in English. This is a dramatic improvement from the previous benchmark of 5 percent of the total voting population. This earlier standard was extremely difficult to achieve for some of the Asian American ethnic groups with fewer members, especially for those in densely populated areas such as Los Angeles County. Under the prior guidelines, an ethnic group would need to have 450,000 persons speaking the same foreign language before they

Table 8-2 Language Spoken at Home, 2000

Group	English Only	Language Other than English	Speaks English Less than "Very Well"
All	82.1	17.9	8.1
Asian American	21.0	79.0	39.5
Chinese	14.6	85.4	49.6
Filipino	29.3	70.7	24.1
Asian Indian	19.3	80.7	23.1
Japanese	52.7	47.3	27.2
Korean	18.1	81.9	50.5
Vietnamese	6.9	93.1	62.4
Cambodian	8.4	91.6	53.5
Laotian	7.2	92.8	52.8
Hmong	4.4	95.6	58.6

Source: U.S. Bureau of the Census, Summary File 4, DP-2: Profile of Selected Social Characteristics: 2000.

would be eligible for bilingual ballots.[66] Another important bilingual voting rights case occurred the summer of 1994 in New York City. In this incident the Asian American Legal Defense and Education Fund (AALDEF) organized a campaign to convince the Board of Elections to provide bilingual ballots with candidates' names translated into Chinese. The New York City election officials at first refused to comply and tried to argue there was simply not enough room on the standardized ballot machines to translate candidates' names. But AALDEF's effort was backed by a U.S. Department of Justice Civil Rights Division ruling that New York City's noncompliance was in violation of the bilingual assistance provisions in the federal Voting Rights Act. The Department of Justice agreed with AALDEF that a candidate's name is one of the most important items of information sought by voters when casting a ballot. This is because voters get election information that is translated, but become confused and frustrated when the actual ballot is not translated. AALDEF executive director Margaret Fung admits the case was only a partial victory because the entire ballot will not be translated, but the decision could open the doors for other municipalities to translate candidates' names into other Asian languages. The long-term goal continues to be translation of the entire voter ballot.[67]

In a project led by the National Asian Pacific Legal Consortium and its affiliates in collaboration with local community partners, eight counties with a total of 466 polling sites were monitored to ensure compliance with Section 203 of the Voter Rights Act requiring bilingual voting materials and language assistance in areas in need of these services. The counties involved were Cook County (Illinois), Harris County (Texas), King County (Washington), and Los Angeles, Orange, San Diego, San Mateo, and Santa Clara counties (California). The poll monitors were trained to observe the quality of interactions between poll workers and voters and the requests for special language assistance. Monitors were also on hand to report any irregularities in required voting practices. The report, *Sound Barriers: Asian Americans and Language Access in Election 2004,* was issued in 2005 and highlighted numerous common problems.

First, monitors found that some poll workers treated limited English proficient (LEP) voters with hostility and disrespect and actually impeded LEP voters' ability to cast their ballots. In Los Angeles County, one poll worker sent an Asian American voter to the back of the line for "causing too much trouble" due to the voter's inability to speak English. In another case, a Los Angeles County poll worker rushed LEP voters because they were taking too long to cast their ballots. There were also cases in Cook, Harris, Orange, and Santa Clara counties where poll workers were antagonistic and uncooperative toward poll monitors, which made it difficult for monitors to make their observations.[68] Second, the report cited examples of the written multilingual materials being either inaccessible and/or poorly translated. Monitors found "serious errors, inaccuracies, and mistakes" in translated materials, and in 43 percent of the polling sites bilingual voting materials were inaccessible, according to the report. There were also cases of poll workers who did not understand the necessity for bilingual voting materials and were not helpful in making the materials available to people coming to vote.[69] The third area of concern was the lack of bilingual poll workers. In

18 percent of the polling sites, there were no bilingual poll workers, or too few bilingual poll workers, to adequately meet the demands for direct voter assistance. For example, in a diverse area such as the San Gabriel Valley, located in Los Angeles County, there were adequate numbers of Chinese language poll workers but there were not enough bilingual workers for other Asian languages.[70]

In sum, although there is a law requiring assistance to voters who are U.S. citizens who do not speak English, the implementation of this law for LEP Asian Americans, at least, has been inconsistent and inadequate. The report also provided a number of specific recommendations based on the observations of poll monitors. The recommendations are categorized in the following areas: (1) improve poll worker training; (2) remove problematic poll workers; (3) increase accessibility of multilingual materials for LEP voters; (4) increase accessibility of oral assistance for LEP voters; (5) create multilingual instruction cards, videos, or other instructional pieces in Section 203-covered languages as well as other languages; (6) improve, or maintain high quality of, translation; and (7) increase voter education in conjunction with community organizations. The report is important because it sheds light on how the commonly taken-for-granted right of voting is not readily available to portions of our society. The report also provides ample evidence that laws are ineffectual unless there is vigilance by individuals and organizations who make legislation into a meaningful reality.[71]

Political Redistricting

A second Asian American political empowerment strategy is redistricting. Redistricting is the politically charged process of redrawing, or reapportioning, state and local political districts that follows each decennial census count. The process has taken on special significance with the rapid growth of the Asian American population and its desire to influence redistricting decisions. Elected officials historically have divided geographically concentrated ethnic groups into several districts, which has served to weaken each group's political power and influence. Conversely, strength is enhanced when a community of interest is maintained in one political district because a political representative is accountable to that community. The Civil Rights Act of 1965 prohibits the fracturing of communities and the dilution of communities through the redistricting process. However, it hasn't been until recently that Asian Americans have become active in the redistricting process. According to Leland T. Saito (1993), the inspiration for these challenges came from the 1990 Federal Ninth Circuit Court of Appeals decision in the case of *Garza* v. *County of Los Angeles*. This precedent-setting class-action lawsuit proved that Latino political strength had been undermined through the systematic process of dividing Latinos into separate districts. The Los Angeles County Board of Supervisor districts were redrawn following the court's ruling and a Latina, Gloria Molina, was elected to represent a district in which the majority of the population was Latino. On the heels of the Garza decision was the formation of the Coalition of Asian Pacific

Islander Americans for Fair Reapportionment (CAPAFR), which marked the first time such a broad-based Asian American redistricting effort had been made. For logistical reasons, CAPAFR divided itself into two ad hoc groups, one from northern California and another from southern California. At the same time, the groups were unified for two main purposes: to create a network of individuals and organizations to gather and exchange information, and to collect and present demographic information at state hearings that were to begin in December 1990.[72]

Saito highlights one of CAPAFR's successful organizing efforts, which took place in the San Gabriel Valley area of southern California. Located in this eastern region of Los Angeles County are several cities with large Asian American populations. CAPAFR's goal was to keep these cities in one state assembly district and not have them divided into three districts as was done in the 1981 redistricting. CAPAFR achieved its goal by working amicably with the San Gabriel Valley Latino Redistricting Committee on a plan that would not threaten any established Latino elected officials or districts. Asian Americans and Latinos also wanted to work cooperatively on voter registration and bilingual ballot efforts, fundamental issues for both of these largely immigrant population groups. "Asian Americans and Latinos understood that the political clout of both groups supporting one set of redistricting plans for the region would increase the possibility of the legislature adopting the plan," Saito writes. "Most important, they also knew that if Asian Americans and Latinos were pitted one against another, both groups could end up losing."[73] Saito acknowledges that Asian Americans were the newcomers to the redistricting process and had much to learn. Latinos in the region were the ones with the political experience, the established organizations, and the major elected offices in the region. The newly created 49th Assembly District now has a 28 percent Asian American population, the highest concentration of Asian Americans in California. This is not a majority, but it does create recognizable constituency and a potential base for political empowerment. In the long run, as the Asian American population in the San Gabriel Valley continues to grow, they hope to benefit from the cooperation that began with this initial redistricting effort.[74] One tangible result of this redistricting was the 2001 election of Judy Chu to the California State Assembly. Saito has continued his research work with studies of redistricting efforts in New York City, which have been highly contentious and not particularly successful.[75]

The redistricting effort in the San Gabriel Valley was relatively smooth for what can be a highly contentious process. Another example is the hotly contested redistricting effort in Oakland, California. In 1993, Asian Americans successfully worked with Latinos to create two city council districts that contained an Asian American (District 2) and Latino (District 5) plurality. This effort marked a significant achievement in Oakland especially since African Americans and whites have dominated the city's political agenda for decades. Since 1980, the Asian American and Latino populations have nearly doubled while African American and white residents comprise a declining—though still predominant—portion of the city's ethnic mix. Together, Asian Americans and

Latinos made up close to 30 percent of Oakland's population. The three areas with the largest concentration of Asian Americans in Oakland were Chinatown, New Chinatown, and China Hill. Chinatown is the traditional merchant center of the Asian American community, while New Chinatown is an area populated by many less affluent Asian immigrants and refugees. China Hill, on the other hand, is the area for mostly middle-class and American-born Asians. These three areas were divided into three separate city council districts in the 1980 redistricting.

The Asian American–Latino redistricting proposal was one of seven presented to the Oakland City Council. The Niagara Democratic Club (NDC), an African American political interest group, presented its own proposal that would keep Chinatown, China Hill, and New Chinatown in three different districts. "Votes on the council mean everything in the world, especially economically," said NDC president Geoffrey Pete. "People say 'you're being divisive' but I am just looking out for our own interests. I would expect nothing less from any other group."[76] The greatest resistance against the Asian American–Latino redistricting plan came from whites in District 2. The city council member representing District 2 at the time, Mary Moore, declared she was "standing up" for Oakland's white people and warned of a white backlash if her district were tampered with.[77] Two District 2 "community leaders" also claimed that District 2 was being "nuked" and "napalmed" by the redistricting process. The use of absurdly inflammatory words by Moore and her supporters shocked Asian Americans in the city council audience. The macabre references to weapons of mass destruction used by the U.S. military against Asians only added insult to injury.[78] Weeks of tense and racially charged debate during the redistricting process eventually ended on July 20, 1993, when the Oakland City Council approved a redistricting plan that dramatically altered two of the seven city council districts. The city council adopted a plan that linked Chinatown, New Chinatown, and China Hill into a redesigned District 2. The decision climaxed a six-month organizing effort by Asian American and Latino advocates, many of whom had been untested in citywide politics, but who were driven by the belief that the city's mandatory, once-per-decade process of remapping voting lines to follow population trends provided a chance to solidify an ethnic power base.

The coalition efforts of Asian Americans in Oakland and in the San Gabriel Valley provide evidence of an increased desire to engage in mainstream electoral politics. While similarities exist between Oakland and the San Gabriel Valley cases, it is the differences that are particularly worth noting. The first difference was that Asian Americans led the coalition effort in Oakland. Asian Americans in Oakland were the ones who had the slightly larger population, relatively more political experience, and clearly demonstrated economic resources. In the San Gabriel Valley, on the other hand, the Asian American population is much smaller compared to Latinos, and they were the self-described newcomers to the political process. The second difference is that Asian Americans and Latinos are both minority groups in Oakland, each representing less than 15 percent of Oakland's population. A coalition of Asian Americans and Latinos was a genuine necessity for both groups to gain political recognition, representation, and power. In the San Gabriel Valley, though, Asian Americans and Latinos are the majority population, and their coalition appeared to be more based on ideology and practicality, rather than genuine necessity. Latinos dominate the state and federal elected offices and the number of Asian American registered voters was too low to really threaten a solid Latino candidate, but the strong record of Asian American contributions to political campaigns makes them an attractive partner in politics.[79] Third, the Asian redistricting effort in Oakland was actually more complicated than in San Gabriel Valley because of the broad demographic mix and relatively even spread of African American, white, and Asian Americans/ Latinos in Oakland. Far more conflict, struggle, and compromise erupted in Oakland because the political rights of one group are often seen as undermining the rights of another. In the San Gabriel Valley, Latinos and Asian Americans are the two dominant populations, with whites not really being a factor and African Americans being almost absent.

With experience in the redistricting process, Asian and Pacific Islander Americans came together following the 2000 Census. At this time, CAPAFR, led by the Asian Pacific American Legal Center in Los Angeles, included in its impressive network the Council of Asian Pacific Americans Together for Advocacy and Leadership (Sacramento), the Asian Law Caucus (San Francisco), the Asian Law Alliance (Santa Clara), East Bay Asian Voter Education Consortium (Alameda), the Orange County Asian Pacific Islander Community Alliance (Orange County), and the Southwest Center for Asian Pacific American Law (San Diego), along with the Asian Pacific American Legal Center and many more that were actively involved. Learning from the past, CAPAFR also worked closely with the Mexican American Legal Defense and Education Fund and the NAACP Legal Defense Fund to build a multiracial, and not just a pan-Asian, coalition to develop its own redistricting plan for California.

CAPAFR and its coalition partners provided unified testimony to state lawmakers and forwarded a plan balancing priorities of communities of interest within the coalition, while at the same time respecting geographic continuity and partisan interests. Unlike the redistricting process after the 1990 census, CAPAFR was active and visible at all the major hearings asserting its own goals and objectives, rather than merely reacting to plans put forward by others. This effort was unprecedented in California's redistricting process and was recognized as such by the state legislature. "(T)here is no individual or organization that has come forward with such an extraordinarily well done amount of research and clear obvious efforts to reach out and work out problems between different communities of interest and make maps that work for everybody," said John Longville, Assembly Committee of Elections and Reapportionment. "I want to commend you for the extraordinary effort that you've put into this."[80] This successful endeavor sparked unprecedented political recognition for Asian Americans in California and provided momentum for Asian American already-elected officials and for those elected in the following years. Another result of this successful redistricting project was the formation of the California Commission on Asian Pacific Islander American Affairs in 2002. The Commission is charged with advising the governor, the legislature, state agencies, departments and commissions on issues relating to social and economic development, rights and interests of the Asian Pacific Islander communities. When the Commission was threatened with elimination in 2004 due to the state's budget crisis, advocates and supporters came out strongly and were able to fight off the proposal. The Commission was allowed to continue.[81]

Encouraging Prospective Candidates

In recent years political pundits predicted that Asian Americans were finally on the verge of assuming a prominent role as a unified political interest group much like European American ethnics and African Americans. However, the Asian American population is extremely difficult to unify because of its diversity and largely immigrant population. Despite the efforts toward making bilingual ballots available to voters and political redistricting, the numbers from Table 8-1 show that Asian American voter participation is still very weak. It is for this reason many believe it is essential to develop and groom qualified Asian American candidates to run for political office. This means encouraging individuals who know the political process, who have demonstrated leadership abilities, and who have a history of involvement with various Asian American communities on a multitude of levels. Some European ethnic groups, along with African Americans and Latino Americans, have had political success in areas where they are the dominant population of both the residents and the voters, but this is not the case for Asian Americans. The reality is most Asian American elected officials represent areas that do not have large Asian American populations.

Maeley Tom has thirty years of political involvement, including twenty years in the California legislature as the chief administrative officer of the State Assembly and chief of staff for the state senate president pro tem. Tom has also participated in numerous local, state, and national political campaigns, and is currently the CEO of Tom and Associates, a firm specializing in government and public affairs. She is often sought out by Asian Americans who are considering running for elective office and she has important advice that she readily passes along. First, she tells them to quit thinking about themselves as an Asian American candidate. "Just focus on your being the best-qualified person for the job," she writes. "Evaluate how you can best represent all the special interest constituencies that make up your district." She also asks people to evaluate the types of leadership roles they have played and the impact that has made, as well as the volunteer base they have at their disposal. A strong volunteer base is necessary to do the core tasks of a campaign such as precinct walking, phone banking, stuffing envelopes, organizing and attending events, and so on. Next, Tom asks if the potential candidate has the "fire in the belly" it takes to forsake personal and family time for a campaign and the energy to "fundraise, fundraise and fundraise until election time." She also asks people if they are prepared to lose. She has seen too many Asian American candidates run for office only once because they cannot overcome what she calls the "loss of face" syndrome.[82]

While Tom advises people not to see themselves as Asian American candidates, she does encourage them to embrace their Asian American history because it is part of the American experience.

When Gary Locke first ran for governor of Washington, he often spoke of his "one-hundred year journey from houseboy to the governor's office" that started with his grandfather who emigrated from China in the late 1800s and who actually worked as a houseboy just one mile from the governor's mansion. Locke also talks about his grandfather's and father's hard work in restaurant and grocery store businesses, and the challenges they faced. "I believe that each of us is defined by our own background and our family experiences," Locke said in a speech. "In many ways, my family drove me to do more for my community." Locke paid his political dues by serving in the Washington State legislature for eleven years, and was the chief executive for King County for three years, before running for governor in 1996.[83]

Similarly, when Mee Moua ran for the Senate in Minnesota in 2001, she introduced herself as "this little Hmong girl from the mountains of Laos." She and her family fled Laos in 1975 when she was just 5 years old and resettled in Appleton, Wisconsin, in 1978. The family moved to St. Paul, Minnesota, in 1988 because her parents found work in factory jobs. With an undergraduate degree from Brown University, a master's degree in public policy from the University of Texas, and a law degree from the University of Minnesota, Moua had the educational qualifications to run for office. She also received special mentoring from former Congresswoman Barbara Jordan who was one of Moua's professors in Texas. Although Moua had never run for public office, she had worked in a Minneapolis law firm, where she represented small businesses in St. Paul and lobbied extensively at the Capitol. She knew the political process well and built good relationships with political, business, and neighborhood organizations. She campaigned on core issues such as adequate funding for education, improving housing, promoting small business growth, and providing a safe and civil environment. Moua ran for the open Minnesota State Senate District 67 seat, which represents a predominantly working-class area made up of 40 percent racial minorities, and has a large population of immigrants. Although there are also more than 40,000 Hmong Americans living in St. Paul, very few of them were registered or had ever voted in an election. Moua waged a door-to-door campaign and was able to organize a multiracial coalition as her core supporters, augmented by efforts to register 1,200 Hmong American citizens who were eligible to vote but had never cast a ballot. Her first hurdle was to win the primary election, which she did by beating her opponent but just 170 votes. Of the 1,200 Hmong American first-time voters targeted, only 500 came out to vote. This was a relatively low percentage, but it was enough to win. In the general election, Moua captured 51 percent of the vote while her nearest challenger received 29 percent of the vote.[84]

In 2005, Madison Nguyen became the first Vietnamese American city council member in San Jose, California, the tenth largest city in the United States with more than 80,000 Vietnamese Americans. She already made history when she won a seat on the local school district in 2002, becoming the first Vietnamese American female ever elected to political office in California. Nguyen was well known in San Jose, not only because she was a school board member, but also because she worked as an associate ombudsman with the County of Santa Clara's office of Human Relations and a part-time sociology instructor in two local community colleges. Additionally, Nguyen served as a member of the Community Advisory Board, United Way Silicon Valley, and the Asian American Community Advisory Council at San Jose State University. Most significant, Nguyen was a leading voice protesting the shooting of a young Vietnamese American mother by a San Jose police officer in 2003 (see Chapter 5). Her city council election made national headlines, not only because of her victory, but also because her chief rival for the seat was another Vietnamese American woman, Linda Nguyen. For many, the fact that two Vietnamese American women were vying for the same political office was a sign of the increasing political clout among Vietnamese Americans in the city. Madison Nguyen received 5,242 votes (62 percent) while her opponent received 3,182 votes (38 percent), and was declared a "rising star" by the local *San Jose Mercury News.* In her victory speech, Madison Nguyen said, "This accomplishment is so huge for me because it embodies for me the American Dream, Obviously, I'm overwhelmed right now." She added that the victory was "not just for the Vietnamese-American community but for the rest of District 7."[85] In an editorial the day after the election, the *Mercury News* publicly challenged her to be a representative for her entire city council district, and not only a representative for Asian Americans.[86]

Locke, Moua, and Nguyen represent what can be called the "third generation" of Asian American political activism. They are, by necessity, advocates of specific issues and not merely representatives of a narrow ethnic constituency. In law professor Lani Guinier's provocative book *The Tyranny of the Majority* (1994), she focuses on the Voting Rights Act of 1965 and the political strategies that came after it. According to Guinier, "first generation claims" were the initial lawsuits in the 1970s brought by civil rights groups that worked to eliminate barriers to voting, such as polling taxes and literacy tests. But once African Americans could vote, southern states redrew district lines so that African Americans remained in the political minority. In what Guinier calls "second generation civil rights activism," emerged strategies to redistrict political boundaries that would ideally assure the election of racial "minority" representatives.[87] For the most part, Asian Americans have followed the same path. Calls for the expansion of the bilingual provisions in the Voting Rights Act of 1965 and voter registration drives can certainly be considered "first generation claims," and they have been important elements in increasing Asian American political participation. The recent emphasis on redistricting by Asian Americans is part of "second generation civil rights activism." Third generation political activism focuses on generating greater opportunities for cooperation and empowerment of previously unrecognized viewpoints on issues, democratic fair play, and multiracial coalition building.

CONCLUSION

This chapter shows the difficult road to political participation and empowerment for Asian Americans. The increased diversity among Asian Americans has made it very challenging to maintain a strong political presence. The negative attention aimed at Asian Americans following the 1996 campaign fundraising scandal was a major setback. Nonetheless, Asian Americans are maturing as a political force on both the local and national levels. The overall effectiveness of the 80-20 Initiative is still being debated, but it did create media attention and gave notice that Asian Americans will no longer tolerate being ignored by national politicians. "After 1996, because of the scandal, people suddenly woke up and said 'Wow, Asians are in politics,'" said Christine Chen, national director of Asian Pacific Islander American Vote, a voter registration coalition. "At the time the attention was negative, but it got the concept into people's living rooms and got us to talk about it. Initially there was a collective sense of assumed shame, but the community has moved beyond that."[88]

On a local level, Asian Americans are learning political lessons necessary to be an important partner in the political process. Asian American scholars Leland Saito and Edward Park have examined multiracial collaboration and coalitions in three urban areas (Los Angeles, New York, and Houston). Their research findings provide additional lessons on how to create political cooperation among diverse groups. First, they argue that multiracial coalitions commonly emerge when groups set aside their short-term self interests to address more fundamental issues for social change. In the cities studied, individual groups merged under overarching concerns such as "quality education for all" and "maintaining jobs." Second, multiracial coalitions still understand the importance of race in a stratified society, but do not focus narrowly on race-based politics. While a candidate would be wise not to run exclusively as a "black candidate" or an "Asian American candidate," he or she should never forget the history of racial inequality. That shared memory actually serves to enhance coalition-building with other groups. Third, coalitions need to build and sustain ongoing relationships with diverse individuals and organizations, and support one another in times of need. Lastly, Saito and Park emphasize the importance of reinforcing and expanding ethnic specific and panethnic organizations as the core source of support and strength because the reality in politics is that there is power in numbers. The more people you can mobilize, the more you can accomplish. On a community level, support of ethnic specific and panethnic organizations actually does much more to bring people together than drive people apart.[89]

An excellent model of a successful Asian American panethnic organizing can be seen in Sacramento, California, where the Council of Asian Pacific Islanders Together for Advocacy and Leadership (CAPITAL) was formed. CAPITAL was conceived to be unlike any other community-based model for organizing the Asian Americans. CAPITAL considers itself a local "resource pool" for more than ninety Asian Pacific Islander organizations and professional associations, and is not an issue-specific coalition. Issue-specific coalitions are typically transient entities that exist for a limited time to deal with narrowly focused social or political issues. When new issues form, however, coalitions break apart because the interest or focus has changed. CAPITAL was envisioned as a large box of building blocks. CAPITAL member organizations can reach into this box and gather support from other interested member organizations to form a fluid yet focused subgroup to respond to specific issues. When the crisis is resolved, these "blocks" return to the box for use at a future time. In this way, CAPITAL preserves autonomy for its member organizations while sustaining a powerful sense of unity and cooperation.

CAPITAL holds bimonthly meetings to keep lines of communication open for its member organizations and the community-at-large, providing a forum where groups freely exchange opinions and ideas. CAPITAL meetings allow groups to bring forth ideas and issues to the entire Asian Pacific Islander community for review, discussion, and education. It coordinates a community calendar that is updated bi-weekly. The calendar facilitates event planning and mutual support, and helps to avoid scheduling conflicts. CAPITAL has also made efforts to reach out to other groups by attending events and fundraisers sponsored by African Americans, Latinos, Jewish, and Islamic communities, as well as the gay and lesbian communities. In addition, CAPITAL provides Asian and Pacific Islander American communities access to politicians and policy-makers, raises funds to support leadership training and student scholarships, and sponsors nonpartisan candidate forums to educate and expose the new Asian Pacific Islander voters to the electoral process.

The analysis and prediction by political scientists Christman and Fay that Asian Americans would increase their political clout as long as they continue to pursue coalition-building strategies is essentially correct, although there is still a very low number of Asian American elected officials outside of California and Hawaii. Nonetheless this chapter and previous chapters show there are many avenues to political empowerment besides electing Asian and Pacific Islander American politicians. The book *Asian Americans: The Movement and the Moment* (2001), edited by Steve Louie and Glenn K. Omatsu, focuses on the historical and present-day involvement of Asian Americans in political activism including labor organizing, legal challenges, and get-out-the-vote campaigns, as well as community-based social service and education programs. Scholars, journalists, and political pundits should be mindful of any overgeneralizations about the political success of Asian Americans based exclusively on voter participation or the number of elected officials. Any real advancement of Asian and Pacific Islander Americans in the broad realm of political empowerment must be directly linked to a larger social justice movement, rather than individual or narrow-group self-interest.

NOTES

1. Lucien Pye, *Asian Power and Politics: The Cultural Dimensions of Authority* (Cambridge, MA: Belknap Press, 1985).
2. Roger Daniels, *Asian America: Chinese and Japanese in the United States Since 1850* (Seattle: University of Washington Press, 1988); and Bill Ong Hing, *Making and Remaking Asian America Through Immigration Policy, 1850–1990* (Stanford, CA: Stanford University Press, 1993).

3. Don T. Nakanishi, "Asian American Politics: An Agenda for Research," *Amerasia Journal* 12:2 (1985–1986): 1–27; Don T. Nakanishi, "UCLA Asian Pacific American Voter Registration Study," sponsored by the Asian Pacific American Legal Center, 1986, p. 21; Grant Din, "An Analysis of Asian/Pacific American Registration and Voting Patterns in San Francisco" (Masters Thesis, Claremont Graduate School, 1984), pp. 75, 85; and Albert Y. Muratsuchi, "Voter Registration in the Oakland Pacific American Communities: An Agenda for the 1990s" (San Francisco: The Coro Foundation, 1990), p. 10.

4. Carol Uhlander, Bruce Cain, and D. Roderick Kiewiet, "Political Participation of Ethnic Minorities in the 1980's," *Political Behavior* 11:3 (1989): 195–231.

5. Grant Din, "A Comparison of Chinese American Voter Registration in 1983 and 1992," a paper presented in San Francisco at "The Repeal and Its Legacy, a Conference on the 50th Anniversary of the Repeal of the Chinese Exclusion Acts," November 13, 1993.

6. David Binder and Catherine Lew, "Asian/Pacific Vote '92: An Analysis of the Northern California Asian/Pacific Islander Vote" (Oakland, CA: Larry Tramutola & Associates, 1992); and Larry H. Shinagawa, "Asian Pacific Electoral Participation in the San Francisco Bay Area: A Study of the Exit Poll Results of the November 8, 1994 Elections for the Cities of Daly City, San Francisco, and Oakland" (San Francisco: Asian Law Caucus, 1995).

7. John Horton, *The Politics of Diversity: Immigration, Resistance, and Change in Monterey Park, California* (Philadelphia: Temple University Press, 1995), Chapters 5 and 6.

8. Roy Christman and James Fay, "Growing Clout of Asians in California," *Sacramento Bee*, June 29, 1994; and Roy Christman and James Fay, "A New Electorate Gains Power," *Los Angeles Times*, November 4, 1991.

9. Sucheng Chan, *Asian Californians* (San Francisco: MTL/Boyd & Fraser, 1991), pp. 76–91.

10. Ronald Takaki, *Strangers from a Different Shore: A History of Asian Americans* (Boston: Little, Brown and Company, 1989), pp. 197–212.

11. L. Ling-chi Wang, "The Politics of Ethnic Identity and Empowerment: The Asian American Community Since the 1960s," *Asian American Policy Review* 2 (Spring 1991): 43–56.

12. Takaki, *Strangers from a Different Shore*, pp. 357–378.

13. Harry H. L. Kitano and Roger Daniels, *Asian Americans: Emerging Minorities*, 2nd edition (Englewood Cliffs, NJ: Prentice Hall, 1995), p. 27; and Takaki, *Strangers from a Different Shore*, p. 258.

14. Cited in Kitano and Daniels, *Asian Americans: Emerging Minorities*, p. 64.

15. Takaki, *Strangers from a Different Shore*, pp. 415–416.

16. Wang, "The Politics of Ethnic Identity and Empowerment," p. 50.

17. Karen Umemoto, "On Strike! San Francisco State College Strike, 1968–1969, The Role of Asian Amerian Studies," *Amerasia Journal* 15:1 (1991): 3–41.

18. *Ibid.*, p. 4.

19. William Wei, *The Asian American Movement* (Philadelphia: Temple University Press, 1993), pp. 24–27.

20. Umemoto, "On Strike!" p. 36.

21. "An Emerging Political Force," *Los Angeles Times*, December 22, 1992; L. A. Chung, "The Year of the Asian American," *San Francisco Chronicle*, October 31, 1992; Susumu Awanohara, "Spicier Melting Pot: Asian Americans Come of Age Politically," *Far Eastern Economic Review*, November 22, 1990, pp. 30, 32–36; and Stuart Rothenberg, "The Invisible Success Story," *National Review*, September 15, 1989, pp. 43–45.

22. Yen Le Espiritu, *Asian American Panethnicity: Bridging Institutions and Identities* (Philadelphia: Temple University Press, 1992), p. 113.

23. *Ibid.*, pp. 134–160.

24. *Ibid.*, pp. 164–165.

25. *Ibid.*, p. 175.

26. Quoted from April Lynch and Marc Sandalow, "Spotlight on Asian Americans," *San Francisco Chronicle*, March 12, 1997; and Bert Eljera, "DNC Investigates APA Contributors," *AsianWeek*, January 3, 1997.

27. Quoted in Frank Wu, "Fundraising Investigation Targets APA's," *AsianWeek*, March 7, 1997; and "From the Senate Floor," Senator Daniel Akaka's statement in the U.S. Senate on March 20, 1997, *AsianWeek*, March 28, 1997.

28. Jason Ma, "Campaign-Finance Probe Fizzling Out," *AsianWeek*, August 26, 1999.

29. Bill Miller, "Fund-Raising Friend of Gore Guilty in Scam," *Sacramento Bee*, March 3, 2000.

30. L. Ling-chi Wang, "Race, Class, Citizenship, and Extraterritorality: Asian Americans and the 1996 Campaign Finance Scandal, *Amerasia Journal*, 24:1 (1998): 1–21. Also see "In the U.S.

Commission on Civil Rights: Petition for Hearing," a 23-page petition submitted by attorneys Edward M. Chen and Dale Minami on behalf of several Asian American individuals and organizations, September 10, 1997.

31. Will Van Saint, "One Step Forward, Two Steps Back," *National Journal,* May 8, 1999.

32. Harry Mok, "Tears of Sadness, Relief Over Mineta's Nomination," *San Francisco Chronicle,* July 4, 2000, p. A19.

33. Tom Lee, "Bill Lann Lee Named Assistant Attorney General," *AsianWeek,* August 10, 2000.

34. Don T. Nakanishi, James S. Lai, Daphne Kwock (eds.), *National Asian Pacific American Political Almanac* (Los Angeles: UCLA Asian American Studies Center, 2005), p. 60.

35. Richard Skinner and Philip A. Klinkner, "Black, White, Brown and Cajun: The Racial Dynamics of the 2003 Louisiana Gubernatorial Election," *The Forum* 2:1 (2004), Article 3 at http://www.bepress.com/forum/vol2/iss1/art3.

36. See http://www.assembly.ca.gov.

37. See http://democrats.assembly.ca.gov/apilegcaucus/history.htm.

38. Paul Ong and Don Nakanishi, "Becoming Citizens, Becoming Voters: The Naturalization and Political Participation of Asian Pacific Immigrants," in Bill Ong Hing and Ronald Lee (eds.), *Reframing the Immigration Debate* (Los Angeles: LEAP Asian Pacific American Policy Institute and UCLA Asian American Studies Center, 1996), pp. 292–293.

39. Quoted in John J. Miller, "Asian Americans and the Republicans: A Natural Fit or a Party in Turmoil?" *AsianWeek,* September 16, 1994.

40. Howard Hong, "Asian Americans Welcome Bush with Open Arms," *AsianWeek,* June 21, 1991.

41. John J. Miller, "Asian Americans Head for Politics: What Horse Will They Ride?" *AsianWeek,* April 7, 1995. Reprinted from the March–April 1995 issue of *The American Enterprise.*

42. *Ibid.*

43. *Ibid.*

44. Binder and Lew, "Asian/Pacific Vote '92," pp. 7–8.

45. "State Wide Exit Poll," *Los Angeles Times,* November 10, 1994; and Shinagawa, "Asian Pacific American Electoral Participation in the San Francisco Bay Area" (1995), p. 116, *op. cit.*

46. Althea Yip, "Asian Votes Shift to the Left," *AsianWeek,* November 11, 1996.

47. Quoted in Will Van Saint (1999), "One Step Forward, Two Steps Back," *op. cit.*

48. Quoted in Peter Beinart, "The Lee Route: How the GOP Lost Asian America," *The New Republic,* January 5, 1998, pp. 10–12.

49. Quoted in Annie Nakao, "Asian Americans Fear Backlash," *San Francisco Examiner,* May 26, 1999.

50. See http://www.80-20initiative.net.

51. Quoted in Elaine Woo, "How to Beat a Bad Rap: With Money and Votes," *Los Angeles Times,* April 23, 2000.

52. Sam Chu Lin, "80-20 Initiative Endorses Al Gore," *AsianWeek,* September 7, 2000.

53. Connie Kang, "Asian Americans Lean to Democrats, Poll Says," *Los Angeles Times,* November 10, 2000.

54. John Wildermuth, "68% of State's Latino Voters Back Gore," *San Francisco Chronicle,* November 14, 2000.

55. Don Philipps, "Mineta Brings Pro-Transit Views, Pragmatic Outlook," *Washington Post,* January 4, 2001; and David E. Sanger, "In A Swift Action, Bush Names Choice for Labor Dept.," *New York Times,* January 12, 2001.

56. Sam Chu Lin, "Chao Time in Prime Time," *AsianWeek,* August 26, 2004.

57. Sandip Roy, "Indian Americans Moving Into the GOP Camp?" *AsianWeek,* November 18, 2004.

58. See http://www.aapi.gov/president/factsheet.htm.

59. Keith Umemoto, "A Shift of 10,000 APA Voters Could Have . . . " *AsianWeek,* July 22, 2004.

60. Sam Chu Lin, "Bucks for Kerry, But APAs Hunger for More Substance," *AsianWeek,* July 22, 2004.

61. *New California Media,* "National Survey of Asian and Pacific Islander Likely Voters in the United States" (September 2004) at http://www.ncmonline.com/media/pdf/polls/apia_presentation.pdf.

62. Asian American Legal Defense and Education Fund, "The Asian American Vote: A Report on the Multilingual Exit Poll in the 2004 Presidential Election" (2005) at http://www.aaldef.org/images/04-20-05_exit_poll_report.pdf.

63. Don T. Nakanishi, James S. Lai, Daphne Kwock (eds.), *National Asian Pacific American Political Almanac* (Los Angeles: UCLA Asian American Studies Center, 2005), pp. 42–46.

64. "Election 2004/The State: Times California Poll Results," *Los Angeles Times*, November 4, 2004, p. B9; also see 80-20 Initiative Web site at http://www.80-20initiative.net/APAvote 2004 .html#main.

65. Pei-te Lien, Christian Collet, Janelle Wong, and S. Karthick Ramakrishnan, "Asian Pacific American Public Opinion and Political Participation," *Political Science & Politics* 34:3 (September 2001): 625–630.

66. Stewart Kwoh and Mindy Hui, "Empowering Our Communities: Political Policy," *The State of Asian Pacific America: Policy Issues to the Year 2020* (Los Angeles: LEAP Asian Pacific American Public Policy Institute and UCLA Asian American Studies Center, 1993), pp. 189–197.

67. Samuel R. Cacus, "NYC Civil Rights Group Scores First Victory on Bilingual Voting Rights," *AsianWeek*, June 20, 1994; and Samuel R. Cacus, "NYC Agrees to Translate Candidates' Names into Chinese on Voting Ballots," *AsianWeek*, September 2, 1994.

68. National Asian Pacific American Legal Consortium, "Sound Barriers: Asian Americans and Language Access in Election 2004" (2005), pp. 9–10 at http:// www.advancingequality .org/files/sound_barriers.pdf.

69. *Ibid.*, pp. 10–11.

70. *Ibid.*, p. 11.

71. *Ibid.*, pp. 13–15.

72. Leland T. Saito, "Asian Americans and Latinos in San Gabriel Valley, California: Ethnic Political Cooperation and Redistricting 1990–1992," *Amerasia Journal* 19:2 (1993): 55–68.

73. *Ibid.*, p. 61.

74. For more details on redistricting and coalition politics see Leland T. Saito, *Race and Politics: Asian Americans, Latinos, and Whites in a Los Angeles Suburb* (Urbana and Chicago: University of Illinois Press, 1998).

75. Leland Saito, "Asian Americans and Multiracial Political Coalitions: New York City's Chinatown and Redistricting, 1990–2001," in Gordon Chang, *Asian Americans and Politics: Perspectives, Experiences, Prospects* (Stanford, CA: Stanford University Press, 2001), pp. 383–408; and Leland Saito, "Asian Pacific Americans and Redistricting Changes in 2001," in *2001–02 National Asian Pacific American Political Almanac* (Los Angeles, CA: UCLA Asian American Studies Center Press, 2001), pp. 130–140.

76. Quoted in David Cogan, "Oakland's Stormy Redistricting Fight," *East Bay Express*, May 28, 1993.

77. Steve Stallone, "White Noise," *The Bay Guardian*, July 21, 1993.

78. William Wong, "Unseemly Tactics in Redistricting Fight," *Oakland Tribune*, July 16, 1993.

79. Saito, "Ethnic Political Cooperation" (1993), p. 64, *op. cit.*

80. Quoted in Asian Pacific American Legal Center, "Coalition of Asian Pacifics for Fair Representation" at http://www.apalc.org/pdffiles/capafrsum.pdf.

81. See Fact Sheet on the Commission at http://cpr.ca.gov/updates/archives/pdf/ 09_27_2004/Special%20Order%20Panel/HUI.pdf.

82. Maeley Tom, "Winning for Dummies," *AsianWeek*, July 22, 2004.

83. Gary Locke, "The One-Hundred Year Journey: From Houseboy to the Governor's Mansion," in Don Nakanishi and James Lai (eds.), *Asian American Politics: Law, Participation, and Policy* (Lanham, MD: Rowman & Littlefied, 2003), pp. 359–364.

84. Stephen Magagnini, "Profile: Mee Moua, From the Mountains of Laos to Halls of State Government," *Sacramento Bee*, September 14, 2004.

85. Quoted in Rodney Foo and Throng Phuoc Khanh, "Madison Nguyen Romps to Win," *San Jose Mercury News*, September 14, 2005.

86. "Madison Nguyen: Rising Star Has Much To Prove in Dist. 7: To Be Effective, She'll Have to Reach Beyond the Vietnamese Community," *San Jose Mercury News*, September 15, 2005.

87. Lani Guinier, *The Tyranny of the Majority* (New York: The Free Press, 1994), pp. 7–8.

88. Anne S. Kim, "A Bigger and Better Political Force," *AsianWeek*, October 5, 2000.

89. Leland T. Saito and Edward J. W. Park, "Multiracial Collaborations and Coalitions," in Paul Ong, ed., *Transforming Race Relations: A Public Policy Report* (Los Angeles: LEAP Asian American Public Policy Institute and UCLA Asian American Studies Center, 2000), pp. 435–474.

9

———

Conclusion: Coming Full Circle

VISIBILITY AND INVISIBILITY

Asian Americans are no longer a silent minority. All demographic projections call for the continued growth of the Asian American population, and this will bring greater attention to this extremely diverse panethnic group. Attention to Asian Americans is also a result of the combined efforts by Asian American scholars, journalists, artists, and community activists who come together to bring an awareness of Asian Americans to the national forefront. In short, it is the multifaceted process of population growth, research, *and* social activism that will continue to move Asian Americans from being a mostly invisible entity to a visible force that must be recognized. This book shows that the Asian American experience is a highly complex combination of many different experiences that defy easy explanation, that go far beyond traditional race relations theories or the simple model minority stereotypes.

There is no doubt that each of the issues raised in the previous chapters deserve more attention and detail than can be provided in just one book. Fortunately, new research studies about the contemporary Asian American experience are continually being published and are adding to the information available. The constantly changing Asian American experience brings forth many challenges. One way I attempt to confront this challenge is to center this book on the new thinking in Asian American studies as an academic discipline, and on the Asian American movement as a political force. Both have undergone a great amount of self-examination in recent years, and fundamental to this has been a critique of the basic assumptions about the pre-1965 Asian American experience and its applicability to the post-1965 Asian American experience.

Both can be seen in "paradigm shifts" described by Shirly Hune in the introduction of this book. Hune calls for race relations in the United States to be viewed beyond the simple black-white paradigm of the past. New thinking on race relations looks more broadly to include today's multiracial reality, along with important class and gender factors that cut across racial lines. Within this, relations between various racial groups are seen as extremely fluid with periods of relative harmony as well as periods of bitter conflict, depending on the social, political, and economic conditions at the time. The new paradigms Hune describes also acknowledge the very real diversity among Asian Americans, the willingness of Asian Americans to fight against injustice (agency), and the significance of the immigrant experience for both foreign-born and native-born Asians in the United States.

BEYOND THE MODEL MINORITY

The key question must now be asked: What is the future for Asians in America? Some have suggested that the future for Asian Americans is bright. As a group they will be much more successful at assimilating socially, culturally, and politically into the American mainstream. This perspective maintains that Asian cultures will be more accepted and that anti-Asian sentiment will decline as the population of Asians in America grows. There are, however, ample reasons to believe these projections may be overly optimistic and simplistic.

First of all, the optimistic outlook is solidly based on the old European immigrant analogy paradigm that sees race and ethnic relations as linear and progressive (i.e., things will always get better over time). This is a paradigm that Hune argues needs to be changed. Many examples in this book show how race relations fluctuate over time and context. For example, the insecurity in the United States created by global economic restructuring has helped to promulgate increased anti-Asian sentiment and "Asian bashing" across the nation. Economic instability has historically been powerful fodder for increased social conflict, racial antagonism, and hostility toward immigrants.

Second, the optimistic outlook understates the impact of the continued flow of immigrants and capital from Asia to the United States. On one hand, this will be an overall benefit to the U.S. economy. At the same time, however, the diverse population of immigrants is a double-edged sword for Asian Americans. New immigrants and refugees quickly became the source of great animosity among many in the general public. The affluent Asian immigrants are resented for their wealth and education, while poorer immigrants and refugees are resented for receiving welfare benefits and other government supports. In addition, the image of the perpetual foreigner and the stereotypes that go with large immigrant populations will continue to be reinforced among many non-Asians. This does not deny that there will indeed be a large segment of second-generation Asian Americans who will be more assimilated then their first-generation parents. Unfortunately, as we often see in this book, many non-Asians can't tell the difference between an immigrant and an American-born Asian, nor do they care about the distinctions.

Third, the overly optimistic projection overlooks the relative lack of political representation and empowerment among Asian Americans. The lack of political power on the national level can leave Asian Americans vulnerable to broadly targeted attacks. Historical examples include harsh laws limiting immigration from Asia, as well as the massive forced relocation of Japanese American citizens during World War II. More recently, this is seen in the investigations into illegal political contributions by a few wealthy Asian influence peddlers, and their chilling effect on Asian American participation in electoral politics. The relative lack of political power can also be seen in the drawn out persecution of scientist Wen Ho Lee and Chaplin James Yee, both accused of being threats against the U.S. government and military security. Many Asian Americans have expressed deep concern that attention to these investigations scapegoat Asians and Asian Americans rather than focusing on the more fundamental issue of campaign finance reform, national security, and racial profiling.

NEW DIRECTIONS IN ASIAN AMERICAN STUDIES

The optimistic projections into the future of Asian America are not totally incorrect, but they must be examined openly and critically. As an academic discipline, Asian American studies must change and grow in order to keep up with the continual change and growth of Asian America itself. The writings of various Asian American scholars stand out as important works addressing this concern for the future. Chalsa Loo's provocative essay "The 'Middle-Aging' of Asian American Studies" (1988) calls for the maturation of Asian American studies. She borrows from psychologist Erik Erikson's eight stages of human development and focuses her attention on stage seven, "Generativity versus Self- Absorption and Stagnation." According to Erikson, this stage generally occurs between ages 25 and 65, which is quite appropriate as the Asian American studies discipline was "born" in 1969. This stage is primarily concerned with turning outward from the self and establishing and guiding the next generation. With regard to Asian American studies, Loo writes, "We must care for the welfare of our collectivity, exceed the limitless bounds of creativity, and prepare a second generation to be more courageous, risk-taking and bold than ourselves."[1]

Michael Omi's essay "It Just Ain't the Sixties No More: The Contemporary Dilemmas of Asian American Studies" (1988) agrees with Loo's interest in generativity. However, he warns that the second generation of Asian American scholars, activists, and artists will not, and should not, be clones of their predecessors. Omi recalls a conversation with a colleague who said the people involved in the social activism of the 1960s were greatly influenced and shaped during this unique period of history. The colleague emphasized that although it is important to pass the lessons learned to succeeding generations, it is impossible to re-create these experiences. "While acquainting students with our collective 'buried past' and stressing the need for them to be political participants, we should not expect to create them in our image," Omi writes. "We need to start exploring some new directions."[2] The process of exploration may be transformative, but it will not be easy." The key to continued growth of Asian American studies, he believes, is to develop a conceptual framework to analyze the contemporary Asian American experience.

This new conceptual framework is advanced by Lisa Lowe's seminal essay, "Heterogeneity, Hybridity, and Multiplicity: Marking Asian American Differences" (1991). Lowe describes the need for Asian Americanists to look beyond the dominant "modernist" perspective in social sciences and the humanities that posits society has an inherent and consistent underlying order that can be studied and understood. Lowe offers a "postmodern" analysis that reveals the complexity of Asian American life and warns against an overreliance on traditional thinking. "In the 1990s, we can diversify our political practices to include a more heterogeneous group and to enable crucial alliances with other groups— ethnicity-based, class-based, gender-based, and sexually-based," she writes. "I want to suggest that essentializing Asian American identity and suppressing our differences ... risks particular dangers: not only does it underestimate the differences and hybridities among Asians, but it also inadvertently supports the racist discourse that constructs Asians as a homogeneous group, that implies we are 'all alike' and conform to 'types.'"[3]

Lowe's analysis is sharpened by Keith Osajima in his essay "Postmodern Possibilities: The Theoretical and Political Directions for Asian American Studies" (1995). He cautions against focusing solely on differences because he understands political unity is a necessary element for Asian American social, economic, and political empowerment. Osajima calls for an "oppositional postmodernism," that recognizes the need to expand and to incorporate the divergent elements that more broadly make up the new realities of the Asian American experience. This approach harks back to the fundamental position of Asian American studies to develop knowledge to inform political action. "For Asian American studies, an oppositional postmodernism requires us to pay serious attention to the multiplicity, complexity, and hybridity of the Asian American experience," he writes. "It requires that our analyses not end at the moment of critique, but, attendant to the history of Asian American studies, also includes ways for turning postmodern analyses into concrete strategies for change."[4]

Another direction of Asian American studies is to give greater attention to global and diasporic studies. This is not intended to privilege Asian studies at the expense of Asian American studies. Nor is it intended to have Asian Americans reminisce about their "roots," or entertain romanticized visions of a far-off homeland to which they wish to return or visit for the first time. The most important reason for incorporating a global perspective is aimed at better understanding, analyzing, and addressing the experiences of Asians in the United States. Wong warns against any possible misplaced intentions of global and diasporic studies in her essay "Denationalization Reconsidered: Asian American Cultural Criticism at a Theoretical Crossroads" (1996), and expresses concern over what may happen with an uncritical acceptance of global and diasporic studies. "To Asian Americans the term 'roots' could evoke contradictory meanings: either 'origin,' where one or one's family hails in Asia; or else commitment to the place where one resides," Wong writes.[5] She emphasizes the second meaning should be the future direction for Asian Americanists, because it expands on the ideals upon which Asian American studies was founded.

In a similar description of the new directions in Asian American studies, Kent Ono's *Asian American Studies After Critical Mass* (2005) explores what he calls the "two phases" of Asian American studies. Phase one is deeply rooted in the experiences and analysis developed within the context of the civil rights movement in the late 1960s and early 1970s. According to Ono, "Asian American studies surfaced as a countercultural, counterhegemonic formation with an explicit purpose of dismantling oppressive educational and institutional structures, while simultaneously creating racially specific alternatives not only within colleges and universities but also in communities. And it did so by employing grassroots political participatory models for social change." Phase one concentrated primarily on domestic issues facing Asians in the United State, with particular emphasis on racial and gender oppression and inequality. Phase two of Asian American studies maintains a foundational base in the earlier phase but is more expansive; it is additionally concerned with "transnationalism, the effects of the globalization of capital products and labor, the affective dimensions of experiences of minoritized subjects, neo- and postcoloniality, queer studies, multiraciality, theories of representation, comparative and critical race studies, cultural studies, critical feminist studies, and the like."[6] Ono's book includes essays such as "Asian American Studies Through (Somewhat) Asian Eyes: Integrating 'Mixed Race' into Asian American Discourse" by Cynthia L. Nakashima, "Planet Youth: Asian American Youth Cultures, Citizenship, and Globalization," by Sunaina Mar Maira, and "A Gay World Make-Over? An Asian American Queer Critique" by Martin F. Manalansan IV.

THE NEXT STEPS

These ideas are used to help shape more realistic, desirable, and positive prospects for Asians in the United States. This final section draws upon the new directions in Asian American studies and broadly summarizes actions and ideals needed to enhance the social, cultural, economic, and political well being for Asian Americans, and for the nation as a whole.

Speak Out, Act Up

First and foremost, there is a conscious emphasis in this book for Asian Americans to transition away from their isolation and invisibility. Both Loo and Omi realize that now is the time for a new generation of Asian American scholars, activists, artists, and students to assert themselves, step out, and confront the various issues discussed in previous chapters. These issues may be viewed from a very different lens by this new generation. There may be a new set of priorities, and maybe even the emergence of completely new issues. Chapter 7 highlights issues of changing families, intermarriage, biraciality, and sexuality as examples of areas of interest not often touched upon by earlier Asian Americanists. These all should be seen as important and vital parts of "generativity."

Embrace Diversity and Change

It is up to the new generation to fully and creatively engage the broad diversity that is Asian America. Lowe argues that the denial of the diverse Asian American reality is highly problematic and ultimately self-defeating. Earlier Asian Americanists focused primarily on the experiences of Chinese and Japanese Americans, and, to a lesser degree, Filipino Americans. Today and in the future, there is and will be much greater attention to Korean Americans, Asian Indian Americans, Vietnamese, Cambodian, Laotian, and Hmong Americans, as well as other emerging groups considered Asian Americans. Diversity and multiculturalism are not unique concerns to Asian Americans. They can be seen across the nation in cities confronting rapid demographic change, and on many college campuses creating a stage on which difference, equality, and community are brought to the forefront. Asian Americans are part of, not separate from, the increasing pluralization of U.S. society. There are those who fear that diversity and multiculturalism lead only to conflict and disunity. These fears fail to recognize the generative role that geographically and historically separated communities play when they come together and establish ongoing relations.

Work Together and with Others

The new directions in Asian American studies are part of a broader social, political, and academic movement that recognizes we have reached the limits of the monocultural, monochromatic, and individualistic concept of American society. For Asian Americans, this means celebrating their distinctiveness, but at the same time, finding the points of unity among themselves and with others. For Osajima, political organizing involves two steps, which develop when people understand another person's unique struggles and recognize the areas of shared experience. The first step usually entails forming pan-Asian coalitions that bridge diverse groups of Asian Americans to work on a specific goals of mutual importance. The second step involves building alliances with others beyond the pan-Asian group. Alliance-building is most often based on broader issues, such as working for a more just and fair society, rather than on narrow ethnic concerns. These steps in action can be seen around the issue of anti-Asian violence. Asian American activists skillfully rallied to raise awareness of increasing anti-Asian violence, and eventually joined forces with other groups to confront the broader issue of rising hate violence in the United States.

Think Globally, Act Locally

It is vitally important that Asian Americans recognize the powerful influence of globalization, or "transnational" interaction, on their lives. This influence can be seen in areas such as global economic restructuring, changing patterns of immigration and settlement, and the emergence of new Asian American communities detailed in the beginning of this book. This also includes the fluidity of material culture (i.e., films, books, food, etc.) and the shifting family patterns across national boundaries. Within this, Wong discusses the distinctions between diasporic and domestic perspectives in the contemporary and future Asian American experience. Her emphasis on "roots" meaning a commitment to where one resides shows that attention to globalization must include a local (or domestic) focus for political action. The impact of global economic restructuring, the global context and domestic impact of the 1996 campaign fundraising scandal, the Wen Ho Lee and James Yee cases, and the rise in hate crimes and anti-immigrant sentiments following 9/11 highlight this point. Recognizing how global events and politics impact Asian Americans here at home is key to understanding many of the issues raised in this book.

New Thinking and Teaching

The new directions in Asian American studies are reflected in the increasing attention given to the importance of teaching and learning about the Asian American experience. Lane Hirabayashi's *Teaching Asian America: Diversity & the Problem of Community* (1998) is the first book-length volume that specifically focuses on this topic.[7] This anthology features personal accounts of twenty university professors and their responses to the challenges teaching Asian American studies courses. In the introduction, Hirabayashi acknowledges how those who teach Asian American studies must struggle to bring together academic theory and its application to the everyday lives of their students. Another tension comes from the commonly seen separation between ideas discussed in the university classroom and the realities faced in the "outside" community. In his essay "Pedagogical Considerations in Asian American Studies" (1998), Keith Osajima is explicit in his belief that community service learning outside of the four walls of a classroom should be a central element of any Asian American studies course. "Incorporating community-based projects is the most direct way to promote student political involvement," he writes. "This means working with groups or organizations to identify their needs and matching those needs with the skills of the students and the curricular focus and logistics of the class."[8] Asian American studies scholar and university administrator Kenyon Chan shares a similar but more inclusive view of teaching and community service work in his essay "Rethinking the Asian American Studies Project: Bridging the Divide Between Campus and Community" (2000). He argues that the university is itself a legitimate community site, and that teaching is important community work: "Through teaching, faculty challenge students to be ethical, critical, and contributing members of our communities. . . . It is how faculty make use of this role, how they define it, and act on it, that makes the difference between teaching as strictly a campus phenomenon versus teaching as a transformative and empowering form of community work."[9] Both Osajima and Chan are encouraged that the Association for Asian American Studies, the professional organization for the discipline, has initiated regular "teaching sessions" at its annual conferences. These teaching sessions provide faculty members an opportunity to discuss teaching experiences, share innovative teaching methods and strategies, and problem-solve classroom and community challenges.

CONCLUSION

This book provides a broad overview and a basic groundwork for greater under-standing of the contemporary Asian American experience. The extensive use of real-life examples, personal profiles, and theoretical concepts in this book high-light the dynamics that complicate the simple notion of Asian Americans as the "model minority." No one can predict the future with authority. However, enlightened individuals and groups can make informed choices about their future, rather than blindly have the future determined for them.

The issues discussed are fundamental to the Asian American experience, and they will continue to emerge and redevelop. Also fundamental is the need for Asian Americans to work together and with other groups. Asian Americans, like all Americans, cannot continue to live in either self-imposed or externally contrived isolation.

Asian Americans must be willing to enter what African American philoso-pher, theologian, and activist Cornel West calls "the public square." West writes: "We must focus our attention on the public square—the common good that undergirds our national and global destinies. The vitality of any public square ultimately depends on how much we care about the quality of our lives together."[10] Today, the United States is in a new period of pluralistic democracy at home and globalization. This requires, among many things, greater attention to societal restructuring, self-examination, and negotiation. This period also calls for clear and thoughtful dialogue, historical awareness, and a willingness to listen to diverse populations and ideas as we contemplate the future. Asian Americans are an essential part of this process.

NOTES

1. Chalsa Loo, "The 'Middle-Aging' of Asian American Studies," in Gary Y. Okihiro et al. (eds.), *Reflections on Shattered Windows: Promise and Prospects for Asian American Studies* (Pullman, WA: Washington State University Press, 1988), pp. 16–23.
2. Michael Omi, "It Just Ain't the Sixties No More: The Contemporary Dilemmas of Asian American Studies," in *Ibid.*, pp. 31–36.
3. Lisa Lowe, "Heterogeneity, Hybridity, Multiplicity: Marking Asian American Differences," *Diaspora* (Spring 1991), pp. 24–44.
4. Keith Osajima, "Postmodern Possibilities: The Theoretical and Political Directions for Asian American Studies," *Amerasia Journal* 21:1 & 2 (1995): 79–87.
5. Sau-Ling C. Wong, "Denationalization Reconsidered: Asian American Cultural Criticism at a Theoretical Crossroads," *Amerasia Journal* 21:1 & 2 (1995): 1–27.
6. Kent A. Ono, *Asian American Studies After Critical Mass* (Maldin, MA: Blackwell Publishing, Ltd., 2005), pp. 2–3.
7. Lane Ryo Hirabayashi, Teaching Asian America: Diversity & the Problem of Community (Boulder, CO: Roman & Littlefield Publishers, Inc., 1998).
8. Keith Osajima, "Pedagogical Considerations in Asian American Studies," *Journal of Asian American Studies* 1:3 (1998): 269–292.
9. Kenyon Chan, "Rethinking the Asian American Studies Project: Bridging the Divide Between Campus and Community," *Journal of Asian American Studies* 3:1 (2000): 17–36.
10. Cornel West, *Race Matters* (Boston: Beacon Press, 1993), p. 6.

Bibliography

"4 Face Charges in Attack." *Los Angeles Times* 6 Jun. 1991.

80-20 Initiative. Online at http://www.80-20initiative.net.

"The A 100: 100 Most Influential Asian Americans of the Decade." *A Magazine* 30 Nov. 1999.

"A Knife Honed by Hate?" *Los Angeles Times* 1 Aug. 2001.

"AAHOA—Asian American Hotel Owners Association—Selects GenaRes as the Preferred Reservation Service for its 6,300 Independent Hotels: AAHOA Members can now use GenaRes for CRS, GDS, Internet and Voice Reservations." *Business Wire* 10 May 2005.

"Abdul Backs Bill for Cleaner Nail Salons." *San Francisco Chronicle* 28 June 2005.

ABATE, TOM. "Heavy Load for Silicon Valley Workers." *San Francisco Examiner* 23 May 1993.

ABELMAN, NANCY, and JOHN LIE. *Blue Dreams: Korean Americans and the Los Angeles Riots.* Cambridge, MA: Harvard University Press, 1995.

Abu–Near, Donna. "Multiracials Want Own Category." *San Francisco Examiner* 21 Jul. 1996.

Act of 14 Jul. 1870. Stat. 16.256.

"After the Guilty Verdict." *Wisconsin State Journal,* Spectrum Section, 22 Sep. 2005.

AIWA News 14:2 (September 1998).

AKAKA, DANIEL. "From the Senate Floor." *AsianWeek* 28 Mar. 1997.

ALLEN, WALTER R. "The Search for Applicable Theories of Black Family Life." *Journal of Marriage and the Family* 40:1 (1978): 117–129.

ALMIROL, EDWIN B. *Ethnic Identity and Social Negotiation: A Study of a Filipino Community in California.* New York: AMS P, 1985.

"Also Known As." Online at http://www.alsoknownas.org/.

American Civil Liberties Union of Northern California. *Caught in the Backlash: Stories from Northern California.* San Francisco, CA, 2002.

ANCHETA, ANGELO. *Race, Rights, and the Asian American Experience.* New Brunswick: Rutgers University Press, 1998.

ANDERSON, STUART. "The Contributions of Legal Immigration to the Social Security System." Online at http://www.aila.org/content/default.aspx?docid=12396.

ANWAR, YASMIN. "UC Berkeley Puts to Rest Tenure Suit." *Oakland Tribune* 9 Jan. 1996.

AOKI, GUY, and PHILIP W. CHUNG. " 'Rising Sun,' Hollywood and Asian Stereotypes." *Los Angeles Times* 3 May 1993.

APPLEBAUM, RICHARD P., and GARY GEREFFI. "Power and Profits in the Apparel Commodity Chain." *Global Production: The Apparel Industry in the Pacific Rim.* Edna Bonacich et al., eds. Philadelphia: Temple University Press, 1994. 42–62.

ARIFUKU, ISAMI, et al. "Culture Counts: How Five Community-Based Organizations Serve Asian and Pacific Islander Youth" (2003). Online at http://www.api-center.org/documents/culture_counts.pdf.

338   *Bibliography*

ASAKASHI, KIYOSHI, and MIHALY CSIKSZENTMIHALYI. "The Quality of Experience of Asian American Adolescents in Activities Related to Future Goals." *Journal of Youth and Adolescence* 27:2 (1998): 141–164.

ASHOK, MALA. "On the Road to Success." *The Hindu* 17 Jan. 2004.

"The Asian American Dream?" *A Magazine* Dec. 1993: 70.

Asian American Legal Defense and Education Fund. "The Asian American Vote: A Report on the Multilingual Exit Poll in the 2004 Presidential Election" (2005). Online at http://www.aaldef.org/images/04-20-05_exit_poll_report.pdf.

"Asian Americans: Be Assertive." *Wisconsin State Journal,* Opinion Section, 20 Sep. 2005.

"Asian Americans Going for the Gold." *AsianWeek* 14 Sept. 2000.

Asian American Students Association of Brown University. "Asian American Admission at Brown University." 11 Oct. 1993.

"Asian American Women Struggling to Move Past Cultural Expectations." *New York Times* 23 Jan. 1994.

Asian and Pacific Islander Coalition on HIV/AIDS. Online at http://www.apicha.org/apicha/pages/education/index.htm.

Asian and Pacific Islander Institute on Domestic Violence. Online at www.apiahf.org/apidvinstitute.

Asian and Pacific Islander Institute on Domestic Violence. "Fact Sheet: Domestic Violence in Asian and Pacific Islander Communities." Dec. 2002. Online at http://www.apiahf.org/apidvinstitute/ResearchAndPolicy/factsheet.htm.

"Asian Athlete." Online at http://www.asianathlete.com.

Asian Immigrant Women Advocates. Letter and Press Release. 20 Mar. 1996.

Asian Media Watch. "Hot 97 Radio Hosts Sing 'Africans Drowning,' 'Screaming Chinks,' and 'Chinamen' Tsunami Victims." Online at http://www.asianmedia watch.net/missjones.

Asian Pacific American Education Advisory Committee. "Asian Pacific Americans in the CSU: A Follow-Up Report." Aug. 1994.

Asian Pacific American Labor Association. "APALA Convention Elects New Officers; Action Plan to Organize APA's into Unions." APALA Press Release. 6 Sep. 2005. Online at http://www.apalanet.org/pr_090605.html.

———. "APALA Convention Elects New Officers." 6 Sep. 2005.

Asian Pacific American Legal Center, "Coalition of Asian Pacifics for Fair Representation." Online at http://www.apalc.org/pdffiles/capafrsum.pdf.

———. "Garment Workers Victorious in Ninth Circuit Sweatshop Decision Against Forever 21." Press Release. 10 Mar. 2004. Online at http://apalc.org/pressr_ march_10_2004.htm.

Asian Pacific Islander Legislative Caucus. Online at http://democrats.assembly.ca.gov/apilegcaucus/history.htm.

"Asian SportsNet." Online at http://www.asiansportsnet.com.

ASIMOV, NANETTE. "A Hard Lesson in Diversity." *San Francisco Chronicle* 19 Jun. 1995.

———. "Single Standard for Admissions at Lowell High." *San Francisco Chronicle* 28 Feb. 1996.

ASIMOV, NANETTE, and TARA SHIOYA. "A Test for the Best Public Schools." *San Francisco Chronicle* 21 Jun. 1995.

Assembly Member Judy Chu. "'Kenny's Law' Signed by Governor Schwarzenegger; New Law Will Provide Additional Rights for Hate Crime Victims." Press Release. 29 Sep. 2004.

AWANOHARA, SUSUMU. "Spicier Melting Pot: Asian Americans Come of Age Politically." *Far Eastern Economic Review* 22 Nov. 1990: 30+.

AWANOHARA, SUSUMU, and JONATHAN BURTON. "More Money than Votes." *Far Eastern Economic Review* 29 Oct. 1992: 29+.

BAILEY, ERIC, and ERIC SLATER. "'Racial' Shooting Rampage Kills Five." *Sacramento Bee* 29 Apr. 2000.

BAILEY, STAN. "English-only Driver Test Likely to Fail, Lawyers Say." *Birmingham News* 20 May 2005.

BAKER, DAVID. "China Walks Away." *San Francisco Chronicle* 3 Aug. 2005.

BALLON, MARC. "A Hole in Their Dreams." *Los Angeles Times* 7 Apr. 2002.

BANFIELD, EDWARD. *The Unheavenly City.* Boston: Little, Brown and Co. 1970.

BANKS, SANDY. "UCLA Is Cleared in Bias Case." *Los Angeles Times* 27 Aug. 1993.

BARRINGER, HERBERT R., ROBERT W. GARDNER, and MICHAEL J. LEVINE, eds. *Asian and Pacific Islanders in the United States.* New York: Russell Sage Foundation, 1993.

BASS, THOMAS A. *Vietnamerica: The War Comes Home.* New York: Soho Press, Inc., 1996.

BAU, IGNATIUS. "APAs and AIDS: We Are Not Immune." *AsianWeek* 5 Jan. 1996.

————. "Immigrant Rights: A Challenge to Asian Pacific American Political Influence." *Asian American Policy Review* 5 (1995): 7–44.

BAZAR, EMILY. "Ex-Spy Suspect Receives Award, Hero's Welcome," *Sacramento Bee* 22 Nov. 2004.

BECKER, GARY S. *Human Capital: A Theoretical and Empirical Analysis,* 2nd ed. Chicago: University of Chicago Press, 1980.

BECKER, JO, and PHUONG LY. "Sikhs Campaign Against Hate." *Washington Post* 24 Sep. 2001.

BEINART, PETER. "The Lee Route: How the GOP Lost Asian Americans." *The New Republic* 5 Jan. 1998.

BELL, DAVID. "An American Success Story: The Triumph of Asian Americans." *New Republic* Jul. 1985: 24+.

BENEDICT, RUTH. *Race: Science and Politics.* New York: Viking Press, 1959.

BERESTEIN, LESLIE. "Nursing Home Rule Starts War of Words." *Los Angeles Times* 27 Feb. 1995.

BERG, JUDITH, DAISY RODRIGUEZ, VALERIE KADING, and CAROLINA DE GUZMAN. "Demographic Study of Filipino American Nurses." *Nursing Administration Quarterly* 29:3 (July–Sept., 2004): 199–207.

BERNSTEIN, RICHARD, and ROSS H. MUNRO. *The Coming Conflict With China.* New York: Vintage Books, 1999.

BINDER, DAVID, and CATHERINE LEW. "Asian/Pacific Vote '92: An Analysis of the Northern California Asian/Pacific Islander Vote." Oakland, CA: Larry Tramutola & Associates, 1992.

BISHOFF, TONYA, and JO RANKIN eds. *Seeds of a Silent Tree.* Glendale, CA: Pandal Press, 1997.

Board of Trustees of the Federal Old-Age and Survivors Insurance and Disability Insurance Trust Fund. *2004 Annual Report of the Board of Trustees of the Federal Old-Age and Survivors Insurance and Disability Insurance Trust Fund.* Transmitted to Congress 23 Mar. 2004. Online at www.ssa.gov/OACT/TR/TR04.

BONACICH, EDNA. "The Social Costs of Immigrant Entrepreneurship." *Amerasia Journal* 14:1 (1988): 119–128.

BONACICH, EDNA, et al., eds. *Global Production: The Apparel Industry in the Pacific Rim.* Philadelphia: Temple University Press, 1994.

BONACICH, EDNA, and IVAN LIGHT. *Immigrant Entrepreneurs: Koreans in Los Angeles.* Berkeley and Los Angeles: University of California Press, 1988.

BONACICH, EDNA, and JOHN MODELL. *The Economic Basis of Ethnic Solidarity: Small Business in the Japanese American Community.* Berkeley and Los Angeles: University of California Press, 1980.

BORGER, JULIAN. "September 11 Revenge Killer to Die for Shooting Sikh." *The Guardian* 11 Oct. 2003.

BOUVIER, LEON, and PHILLIP MARTIN. *Population Change and California's Education System.* Washington, DC: Population Reference Bureau, Inc., 1987.

BOUVIER, LEON, and ROSEMARY JENKS. "Doctors and nurses: a demographic profile." Online at http://www.cis.org/article/1998/DocsandNurses.html.

BOYD, MONICA. "Oriental Immigration: The Experience of Chinese, Japanese, and Filipino Populations in the United States." *International Migration Review* 10 (1976): 48–60.

BRAND, DAVID. "The New Whiz Kids." *Time* 31 Aug. 1987.

BRAUN, STEPHEN, and JOHN BECKHAM. "On Hate-Filled Web Sites, 'Wake-Up' Call Gets a Volatile, Divided Reaction." *Los Angeles Times* 15 Aug. 1999.

"Braves' Rocker Expresses Regret After Comments Spark Outrage." *Washington Post* 23 Dec. 1999.

BRAZIL, ERIC. "SF Housing Agency Settles Asian Bias Suit." *San Francisco Examiner* 19 Jul. 1999.

BREMMER, BRIAN, and KATHLEEN KERWIN. "Here Come Chinese Cars." *BusinessWeek* 6 Jun. 2005.

BRESLAUER, JAN. "After the Fall." *Los Angeles Times* 13 Jan. 1991, Calendar Section.

———. "Hues and Cries." *Los Angeles Times* 7 Jul. 1991, Calendar Section.

BROWN, CLIFFORD. "Stephenson Apologizes For Remarks on Asians." *New York Times* 12 Oct. 2003.

BROWNING, E. S. "A New Chinatown Grows in Brooklyn." *Wall Street Journal* 31 May 1994.

BUAKEN, MANUEL. "Life in the Armed Forces." *New Republic* 109 (1943): 279+.

BUNZEL JOHN H., and JEFFREY K. D. AU. "Diversity or Discrimination? Asian Americans in College." *The Public Interest* 87 (Spring 1987): 56.

BUTTERFIELD, FOX. "Why Asians Americans Are Going to the Head of the Class." *New York Times Magazine* 3 Aug. 1986.

CACAS, SAMUEL R. "Accent Discrimination Case by Five Filipino American Security Guards Is Settled." *AsianWeek* 10 June 1994.

———. "Fall River Trial Ends with Murder Conviction." *AsianWeek* 23 Sep. 1994.

———. "Language Rights Hotline Established." *Rafu Shimpo* 8 Feb. 1995.

———. "New Census Category for Multiracial Persons?" *AsianWeek* 15 Jul. 1994.

———. "NYC Agrees to Translate Candidates' Names into Chinese on Voting Ballots." *AsianWeek* 2 Sep. 1994.

———. "NYC Civil Rights Group Scores First Victory on Bilingual Voting Rights." *AsianWeek* 20 Jun. 1994.

———. "Vietnamese American Man Charges Police Brutality in Defense Trial." *AsianWeek* 30 Sep. 1994.

California Advisory Committee for the United States Commission on Civil Rights. "Community Concerns About Law Enforcement in Sonoma County." Dec. 1999. Online at http://www.pressdemo.com/evergreen/review/commission.html.

California Attorney General's Asian Pacific Advisory Committee. *Final Report*. Dec. 1988.

California Commission on Asian Pacific Islander American Affairs. Online at http://cpr.ca.gov/updates/archives/pdf/09_27_2004/Special%20Order%20Panel/HUI.pdf.

California Department of Education. "Language Census Summary Report 1998–1999." Online at http://www.cde.ca.gov/ds/sd/lc/reports.asp#s.

California Department of Justice. *Hate Crimes in California, 1999*. Sacramento, CA: Division of Criminal Justice Information Services, 2000.

———. *Hate Crimes in California, 1995*. Sacramento: Div. of Criminal Justice Information Services, 1996. Table 1, p. 7.

California State Assembly. Online at http://www.assembly.ca.gov.

"Camp Moon-Hwa." Online at http://hometown.aol.com/Moonhwa//.

CAPLAN, NATHAN, MARCELLA H. CHOY, and JOHN K. WHITMORE. *Children of the Boat People: A Study of Educational Success*. Ann Arbor: University of Michigan Press, 1991.

CAPLAN, NATHAN, JOHN K. WHITMORE, and MARCELLA H. CHOY. *The Boat People and Achievement in America: A Study of Economic and Educational Success*. Ann Arbor: University of Michigan Press, 1989.

CARLSEN, WILLIAM. "Teng Voting Plan Faces Criticism." *San Francisco Chronicle* 7 Feb. 1996.

CARREA, JOHN WILLSHIRE. *New Voices: Immigrant Students in U.S. Public Schools*. Boston: National Coalition of Advocates for Students, 1988.

CASS, DANIELLE. "Unfriendly Skies' Slurs Launch Suit." *Oakland Tribune* 27 Oct. 1994.

CAUDILL, WILLIAM, and GEORGE DeVos. "Achievement, Culture and Personality: The Case of Japanese Americans." *American Anthropologist* 58 (1956): 1102–1126.

CAUVIN, HENRI E., and BILL HUTCHINSON. "Disappointed Louima Hopes His Case Will Change System." *New York Times* 9 June 1999.

CAVOSORA, RICHARD J. P. "Discrimination Spoken Here." *Filipinas* Jul. 1993: 16+.

CBS News. "Look of Abercrombie & Fitch." 24 Nov. 2004. Online at http://www.cbsnews.com/stories/2003/12/05/60minutes/main587099.shtml.

"CCSF Launches First At-risk APA Student Center. *AsianWeek*, 21 Oct. 2004.

"Census Bureau Projects Tripling." *U.S. Census Bureau News* 18 Mar. 2004. Online at http://www.census.gov/Press-Release/www/releases/archives/population/001720.html.

Center for Global Change. "Wan-Joon Yoon Memorial Scholarship." Online at http://www.indiana.edu/~global/yoonscholarship.htm.

Center for Immigration Studies. Online at www.cis.org.

Center for Integration and Improvement of Journalism. *News Watch: A Critical Look at Coverage of People of Color*. San Francisco: San Francisco State University, 1994.

"Chamber Declines to Remove Hu." *Oakland Tribune* 24 May 1994.

CHAMI, RAMI. "Indiana U. Students, Community Responds to Hate Crimes." *Indiana Daily Student* 11 Jul. 2005.

CHAN, CONNIE S. "Issues of Identity Development Among Asian-American Lesbians and Gay Men." *Journal of Counseling and Development* 68 (Sep.–Oct. 1989): 16–20.

CHAN, ANITA. "'Mr. Wong' Cartoon To Continue Airing Despite Mounting Criticism." aonline.com 22 Jun. 2000.

CHAN, ERIN. "A Loser's Success and a Winner's Failure." *Detroit Free Press* 7 May 2004.

CHAN, KENYON. "Rethinking the Asian American Studies Project: Bridging the Divide Between Campus and Community. *Journal of Asian American Studies* 3:1 (2000): 17–36.

CHAN, SUCHENG. *Asian Californians*. San Francisco: MTL/Boyd & Fraser, 1991.

———. "Beyond Affirmative Action." *Change* Nov.–Dec. 1989: 48–51.

CHANG, EDWARD T. "America's First Multiethnic 'Riots.'" In Karin Aguilar-San Juan, ed. *The State of Asian America: Activism and Resistance in 1990s*. Boston: South End Press, 1994.

———. "New Urban Crisis: Intra-Third World Conflict." *Perspectives*. Shirley Hune et al., eds. Pullman, WA: Washington State University Press, 1991.

CHANG, EDWARD T., and JEANNETTE DIAZ-VEIZADES. *Ethnic Peace in the American City: Building Community in Los Angeles and Beyond*. New York: New York University Press, 1999.

CHANG, IRENE. "Asian, Latino Activists Seek Ethnic Harmony at Schools." *Los Angeles Times* 22 Sep. 1991.

CHANG, JACK. "Indian American's Powerful Tech Presence." *AsianWeek* 20 Apr. 2000.

CHANG, JEFF. "On the Wrong Side: Chinese Americans Win Anti-Diversity Settlement and Lose in the End." *Colorlines* Summer 1999.

CHANSANCHAI, ATHIMA. "Shedding Light on Exploitation Exhibit Looks at Violence Against Asian Women." *Seattle Post-Intelligencer* 20 Apr. 2005.

CHAO, JULIE. "Getting a Handle on Hate Crimes." *San Francisco Examiner* 14 Jan. 1998.

———. "Asian Man's Shooting by Police Spurs Three Probes." *San Francisco Examiner* 25 May 1997.

———. "Outrage at Killing by Cop in North Bay." *San Francisco Examiner* 21 May 1997.

CHARNY, BEN. "Mental Health Center Targets the Asian Community." *Oakland Tribune* 17 Oct. 1994.

CHEN, STANFORD. "It's a Matter of Visibility." *Quill* Apr. 1993: 33–34.

CHENG, CLIFF, and TOJO JOSEPH THATCHENKERY. *The Journal of Applied Behavioral Science* 33:3 (1997).

CHIA, ROSINA. "Pilot Study: Family Values of American versus Chinese American Parents." *Journal of Asian American Psychological Association* 13:1 (1989): 8–11.

CHIN, ERIN. "An Asian Voice Raised Against Abuse." *Detroit Free Press* 2 May 2005.

CHIN, STEVEN A. "Asians Terrorized in Housing Projects." *San Francisco Chronicle* 17 Jan. 1993.

———. "Garment Workers Fight for Back Pay." *San Francisco Examiner* 16 Feb. 1994.

———. "The World of B. D. Wong." *Image* 5 Sep. 1993: 6+.

"The China Syndrome." *Mirabella* Mar. 1994: 58+.

CHISWICK, BARRY. *Income Inequality.* New York: Columbia University Press, 1974.

CHO, SUMI. "Conflict and Construction." *Reading Rodney King: Reading Urban Uprising.* Robert Goodings-Williams, ed. New York: Routledge, 1993.

CHOATE, PAT. *Agents of Influence.* New York: Alfred A. Knopf, 1990.

CHOW, MAY. "CCSF Wins Excellence Award for Immigrant Work." *AsianWeek* 6 May 2004.

CHOY, CATHERINE CENIZA. *Empire of Care: Nursing and Migration in Filipino American History.* Durham and London: Duke University Press, 2003.

CHRISTMAN, ROY, and JAMES FAY. "Growing Clout of Asians in California." *Sacramento Bee* 29 Jun. 1994.

———. "A New Electorate Gains Power." *Los Angeles Times* 4 Nov. 1991.

CHU, LEONORA. "A Coveted Market." *AsianWeek* 23 Mar. 2000.

CHU LIN, SAM. "80-20 Initiative Endorses Al Gore." *AsianWeek* 7 Sept. 2000.

CHUNG, L. A. "How Asian American Groups Voted." *San Francisco Chronicle* 6 Nov. 1992.

———. "The Year of the Asian American." *San Francisco Chronicle* 31 Oct. 1992.

CHUNG, PHILIP W. "Asiandudes to Hollywood." *AsianWeek* 29 Jul. 2004.

———. "Better Luck Today." *AsianWeek* 24 Apr. 2003.

———. "Beyond Asian Chic." *A Magazine* Summer 1994: 22.

"Citizenship Applications Soaring Among Legal Immigrants." *New York Times* 2 Apr. 1995.

City College of San Francisco. Online at www.ccsf.edu.

CLARY, MIKE. "Rising Toll of Hate Crimes." *Los Angeles Times* 10 Oct. 1992.

COAKLEY, JAY J. *Sport in Society: Issues and Controversies.* St. Louis, MO: Mosby, 1994.

COGAN, DAVID. "Oakland's Stormy Redistricting Fight." *East Bay Express* 28 May 1993.

COLIVER, VICTORIA. "Clinton Cuts 'Sweatshop-free' Deal." *Oakland Tribune* 3 Aug. 1996.

COOPERMAN, ALAN. "Sept. 11 Backlash Murders and the State of Hate." *Washington Post* 20 Jan. 2002.

"Confucian Work Ethic." *Time* 28 Mar. 1983.

Committee of 100, "Asian Pacific American (APA) Corporate Board Report Card." Online at http://www.committee100.org/publications/initiative_corporate.htm.

CONNER, JOHN. *A Study of the Marital Stability of Japanese War Brides.* San Francisco: R & E Research Assocs., 1976.

"A Conversation with David Henry Hwang." *Bearing Dreams, Shaping Visions: Asian Pacific American Perspectives.* Linda A. Revilla et al., eds. Pullman, WA: Washington State University Press, 1993. 185–191.

CORLISS, RICHARD. "Pacific Overtures." *Time* 13 Sep. 1993: 68–70.

CORNITCHER, DAWN. "Explosive Growth of Ethnic Media in the United States." *Mediaweek* 17 May 1999.

Council of Islamic American Relations (CAIR). *The Status of Muslim Civil Rights in the United States, 2002 Executive Summary.* Online at http://www.cair-net.org/asp/execsum2001.asp.

CRAWFORD, JAMES. *Bilingual Education: History, Politics, Theory, and Practice.* Trenton, NJ: Crane, 1989.

CRICHTON, MICHAEL. *Rising Sun.* New York: Ballantine, 1992.

CROWE, JERRY. "Wie Starts Life as a Money Player." *Los Angeles Times* 13 Oct. 2005.

CRUMPACKER, JOHN. "Kwan Is Feeling the Heat." *San Francisco Chronicle* 18 Jan. 2001.

CUNNINGHAM, DWIGHT. "One Size Does." *Mediaweek* 15 Nov. 1999.

CURTIS, JAKE. "Ping-Pong Wizard." *San Francisco Chronicle* 16 June 2000.

"D'Amato Apologizes for Spoof of Judge Ito." *Newsday* 6 Apr. 1995.

DANG, JANET. "Anti-Asian Hate Crimes on the Rise." *AsianWeek* 11 Jan. 2001.

———. "Asian Law Caucus Settles Housing Suit." *AsianWeek* 22 July 1999.

———. "UC's Connerly, Takaki Debate Race." *AsianWeek* 1 Oct. 1998.

DANIEL, CHRISTOPHER. "Diminishing Returns from Statistical Analysis: Detecting Discrimination in Public Employment (a response to Pan Suk Kim and Gregory B. Lewis)." *Public Administration Review* 57:3 (1997): 264–267.

DANIELS, ROGER. *Asian Americans: Chinese and Japanese in the United States.* Seattle: University of Washington Press, 1988.

———. *Coming to America.* New York: Harper, 1990.

———. *Concentration Camps: North America Japanese in the United States and Canada During World War II.* Malabar, FL: Robert A. Kreiger, 1981.

———. *Concentration Camps, U.S.A.* New York: Holt, 1971.

"The Dark Side of the Sun." *Entertainment Weekly* 6 Aug. 1993: 26+.

DARLIN, DAMON. "The East Is Technicolor." *Forbes* 8 Nov. 1993: 318.

DAS, RAJANKI K. *Hindustani Workers on the Pacific Coast.* Berlin: Walter De Bruyter, 1923.

"Daughter Finally Finds GI Dad." *San Francisco Chronicle* 24 Dec. 1994.

DAY, JENNIFER C, and AVALAURA L. GAITHER. "Voting and Registration in the Election of November 1998." Washington, DC: U.S. Census Bureau, 2000.

"Deaf Killer's Fate Rests on Mental Health." *Los Angeles Times* 21 Sep. 2003.

DER, HENRY. "Affirmative Action Policy." *The State of Asian Pacific America: Policy Issues to the Year 2020.* Los Angeles: LEAP Asian Pacific American Public Policy Institute and UCLA Asian American Studies Center, 1993: 215–232.

———. "Clash Between Race-Conscious Remedies and Merit: School Desegregation and the San Francisco Chinese American Community." *Asian American Policy Review* 4 (1994): 65–91.

DER, HENRY, et al. *The Broken Ladder '92: Asian Americans in City Government.* San Francisco: Chinese for Affirmative Action, 1992.

"Diamond in the Rough." *AsianWeek* 30 Oct. 1997.

DIN, GRANT. "An Analysis of Asian/Pacific American Registration and Voting Patterns in San Francisco." Masters Thesis. Claremont Graduate School, 1984.

———. "A Comparison of Chinese American Voter Registration in 1983 and 1992." The Repeal and Its Legacy, a Conference on the 50th Anniversary of the Repeal of the Chinese Exclusion Acts. San Francisco. 13 Nov. 1993.

DIVOKY, DIANE. "The Model Minority Goes to School." *Phi Delta Kappan* Nov. 1988: 219–222.

DO, AHN. "Viet Manicurists Leave Southern California to Start Salons Elsewhere." *Los Angeles Times* 25 Oct. 1999.

DOYLE, JIM. "High Court Lets English-Only Job Rules Stand." *San Francisco Chronicle* 21 Jun. 1994.

"Dr. Sammy Lee." Online at: http//www.viscom.apnet.org.

D'SOUZA, KAREN. "Some Foresee Era of Intolerance." *Oakland Tribune* 26 Dec. 1994.

DUKE, LYNNE. "Panel Finds Japan-Bashing, Violence." *Washington Post* 29 Feb. 1992.

DUTKA, ELAINE. "Asian Americans: Rising Furor Over 'Rising Sun.'" *Los Angeles Times* 28 Jul. 1993.

DYNES, WAYNE R., and STEPHEN DONALDSON, eds. *Asian Homosexuality.* New York: Garland Press, 1992.

EBERT, ROGER. "No Place For Political Correctness in Films." *Chicago Sun-Times* 18 Jan. 2002.

EDWARDS, HARRY. *Sociology of Sport.* Homewood, IL: The Dorsey Press, 1973.

EFFRON, SETH. "Racial Slayings Prompt Fear, Anger in Raleigh." *Greensboro News and Record* 24 Sep. 1989.

EGELKO, BOB. "S.F. Gay Marriages Head to Court." *San Francisco Chronicle* 21 Dec. 2005.

EITZEN, STANLEY D., and GEORGE H. SAGE. *The Sociology of North American Sport.* Madison, WI: Brown & Benchmark, 1993.

"Election 2004/The State: Times California Poll Results." *Los Angeles Times* 4 Nov. 2004.

"Election Watch No. 5." *San Francisco Chronicle* 6 Oct. 2000.

EL-GHOBASHI, TAMER. "Sikh Files Suit vs. 5 in Bias Attack." *New York Daily News* 13 Jul. 2005.

ELJERA, BERT. "An Emerging Political Force." *Los Angeles Times* 22 Dec. 1992.

———. "APA Unionists Voice Optimism." *AsianWeek* 8 Aug. 1997.

———. "DNC Investigates APA Contributors." *AsianWeek* 29 Jan. 1997.

———. "Mixed Reactions on Immigration Moves." *AsianWeek* 3 Mar. 1996.

———. "Police Clear Officer in Kao Shooting." AsianWeek 15 Aug. 1997.

ENG, DAVID L., and ALICE Y. HOM. *Q & A: Queer in Asian America.* Philadelphia: Temple University Press, 1998.

ESPIRITU, YEN LE. *Asian American Panethnicity: Bridging Institutions and Identities* Philadelphia: Temple University Press, 1992.

EVANGELISTA, BENNY. "Eyeing Asian American E-Shoppers. *San Francisco Chronicle* 19, June 2000.

"Fallout and Damage Control." *AsianWeek* 24 Feb. 2000.

FALLOWS, JAMES M. *More Like Us: Making America Great Again.* Boston: Houghton, 1989.

FARAUDO, JEFF. "Chow Takes Silver Medal." *Oakland Tribune* 29 Jul. 1996.

———. "Silence Is Golden for Reluctant Hero Chow." *Oakland Tribune* 24 Jul. 1996.

FARQUHAR, KIDOTJ, and MARY L. DOI. "Bruce Lee vs. Fu Manchu: Kung Fu Films and Asian American Stereotypes in America." *Bridge: An Asian American Perspective* 6:3 (Fall 1978): 23–40.

FAWCETT, JAMES T., and BENJAMIN V. CARINO, eds. *Pacific Bridges: The New Immigration from Asia and the Pacific Islands.* Staten Island, NY: Center for Migration Studies, 1987.

FEAGIN, JOE R., and CLAIRECE BOOHER FEAGIN. *Racial and Ethnic Relations.* 4th ed. Englewood Cliffs, NJ: Prentice Hall, 1994.

Federal Asian Pacific American Council. Online at http://www.fapac.org.

FEIGELMAN, WILLIAM, and ARNOLD SILVERMAN. *Chosen Children.* New York: Praeger, 1983.

———. "The Long-Term Effects of Transracial Adoption." *Social Service Review* 58 (1983): 588–602.

FEIGEN, JOHNATHAN. "Rockets Summary." *Houston Chronicle* 19 Jan. 2003.

FENG, PETER. *Identities in Motion: Asian American Film & Video.* Durham, NC: Duke University Press, 2002.

FERNANDEZ, JAY A. "Controversy Gives A Push." *USA Today* 14 Apr. 2003.

FERNANDEZ, MARILYN. "Asian Indian Americans in the Bay Area and the Glass Ceiling." *Sociological Perspectives* 41:1 (Spring 1998): 119–150.

FERRELL, DAVID, and K. CONNIE KANG. "'Rising Sun' Opens to Charges of Racism." *Los Angeles Times* 31 Jul. 1993.

FIMRITE, PETER. "$1 Million Deal in UC Bias Suit." *San Francisco Chronicle* 9 Jan. 1996.

"First Person Plural." Online at: www.pbs.org/pov/firstpersonplural.

FLYNN, JOHN. "Success the Old Fashioned Way." *San Francisco Examiner* 30 Apr. 1995.

FONG, COLLEEN, and JUDY YUNG. "In Search of the Right Spouse: Interracial Marriage Among Chinese and Japanese Americans." *Amerasia Journal* 21:3 (1995): 77–98.

FONG, TIM. "Yamaguchi's Gold Won't Deter Hate Crimes." *San Jose Mercury News* 25 Feb. 1992.

FONG, TIMOTHY P. *The First Suburban Chinatown: The Remaking of Monterey Park, California.* Philadelphia: Temple University Press, 1994.

FONG-TORRES, BEN. "Why There Are No Male Asian Anchors." *San Francisco Chronicle* 13 Jul. 1986, Datebook Section: 51–55.

FOO, RODNEY. "Vietnamese Find Unity, Voice in Wake of Fatal S. J. Shooting." *San Jose Mercury News* 12 Jul. 2004.

FOO, RODNEY, and THRONG PHUOC KHANH. "Madison Nguyen Romps to Win." *San Jose Mercury News* 14 Sep. 2005.

FOX, DAVID. "Neuropsychology, Achievement, and Asian-American Culture: Is Relative Functionalism Oriented Times Three?" *American Psychologist* 46:8 (1991): 877–878.

FRANKS, JOEL. *Crossing Sidelines, Crossing Cultures: Sport and Asian Pacific American Cultural Citizenship* (New York: University Press of America, Inc., 2000).

FREEBERG, LOUIS. "Citizenship Wave Surprises INS." *San Francisco Chronicle* 13 Apr. 1995.

———. "Feinstein Fails to Limit Legal Immigration." *San Francisco Chronicle* 26 Apr. 1996.

FUJIMURA, GUY. "Message from the President: APALA Convention Returns to Washington, D.C." *APALA News* Summer 1999.

FUJITA, STEPHEN S., and MARILYN FERNANDEZ. "Asian American Admissions to an Elite University: A Multivariate Case Study of Harvard." *Asian American Policy Review* 5 (1995): 45–62.

FULWOOD, SAM III. "Japan-Bashing Condemned by Rights Panel." *San Francisco Chronicle* 29 Jan. 1992.

FURILLO, ANDY, and STEPHEN MAGANINI. "Leaders Say Deaths Show Hmong Needs." *Sacramento Bee* 7 Dec. 1999.

"Furrow Gets 5 Life Terms for Racial Rampage." *Los Angeles Times* 27 Mar. 2001

"Furrow Spared by His Mental Illness." *Los Angeles Times* 25 Jan. 2001.

GALBRAITH, JANE. "Group Takes 'Rising Sun' Protest Public." *Los Angeles Times* 7 Apr. 1993.

Garcia v. Gloor. 618 Fed.2d 264, 270 (1981).

"Garment Workers Victorious in Ninth Circuit Sweatshop Decision Against Forever 21." Asian Pacific American Legal Center. Press Release. 10 Mar. 2004. Online at http://apalc.org/pressr_march_10_2004.htm.

GATHRIGHT, ALAN. "Vietnamese Community Rallies." *San Francisco Chronicle* 17 Jul. 2003

GERON, TOMIO. "APA Activism, New York Style." *AsianWeek* 5 Apr. 1996.

———. "N.Y.P.D. Settles APA Complaints." *AsianWeek* 1 Mar. 1996.

———. "Voter Drives on in N.Y." *AsianWeek* 19 Jul. 1996.

GEISSINGER, STEVE. "Asian Caucus to Fete Former Accused Spy: New Patriotic Group Upset with Lawmakers Honoring Wen Ho Lee." *Alameda Times-Star* 4 June 2004.

GIPSON, MARGARET. *Accomodation Without Assimilation: Sikh Immigrants in an American High School.* Ithaca, NY: Cornell University Press, 1988.

GOCK, TERRY S. "Acquired Immunodeficiency Syndrome." *Confronting Critical Health Issues of Asian and Pacific Islander Americans.* Nolan W. S. Zane, David T. Takeuchi, and Kathleen N. J. Young, eds. Thousand Oaks, CA: Sage Press, 1994. 247–265.

GODWIN, D. D., and J. SCANZONI. "Couple Consensus During Marital Joint Decision-Making: A Context, Process, Outcome Model." *Journal of Marriage and the Family* 51 (1989): 943–956.

GONZALES, JUAN L. *Racial and Ethnic Groups in America.* 2nd ed. Dubuque, Iowa: Kendall/Hunt, 1993.

———. *Racial and Ethnic Families in America.* 2nd ed. Dubuque, Iowa: Kendall/Hunt, 1993.

GOODING-WILLIAMS, ROBERT, ed. *Reading Rodney King: Reading Urban Uprising.* New York: Routledge, 1993.

GORDON, MILTON M. *Assimilation in American Life: The Role of Race Religion, and National Origins.* New York: Oxford University Press, 1964.

GORMAN, CHRISTINE. "The Disease Detective." *Time* 30 Dec. 1996.

GOSSETT, THOMAS F. *Race: The History of an Idea in America.* New York: Schocken Books, 1965.

GOTANDA, NEIL. "Re- Producing the Model Minority Stereotype: Judge Joyce Karlin's Sentencing Colloquy in *People v. Soon Ja Du." Reviewing Asian America: Locating Diversity.* Wendy L. Ng et al., eds. Pullman, WA: Washington State University Press, 1995.

GOULD, STEPHEN JAY. "Curveball." *New Yorker* 28 Nov. 1994: 139–149.

"Gouw Gets Warner Bros. to Pull Offensive Cartoon." *AsianWeek* 17 Feb. 1995.

"Governor Wilson Vetoes Garment Manufacturers' Joint Liability Bill." *AIWA News* 10:2 (Fall 1994): 7.

GRAHAM, JEFFERSON. "Actor's Chance to Part a Racial and Cultural Curtain." *USA Today* 13 Sep. 1994.

GRAHAM, TIM. "A Letter from the Editor of the Oakland Tribune." *Oakland Tribune* 1 Apr. 1996.

GREENHOUSE, STEVE. "Foreign Workers at Highest Level in Seven Decades. *New York Times* 4 Sept. 2000.

GREY, MARK. "Sports and Immigrant, Minority, and Anglo Relations in Gardner City High School." *Sociology of Sport Journal* 9:3 (1992): 255–270.

GROVE, KWA JULIENNE. "Identity Development in Interracial, Asian/White Late Adolescents: Must It Be So Problematic?" *Journal of Youth and Adolescence* 20:6 (1991): 617–628.

GUEY, EMILY. "Child Abuse Among Asian Americans." Online at http://model minority.com/article469.html.

GUILLERMO, EMIL. "Asian Americans Have Become Political Pariahs." *Oakland Tribune* 22 May 1997.

———. "Being White and Right in S.F. Hate-Crime Sentence." *AsianWeek* 4 Nov. 2004.

———. "Condemning the Devil in Jones." *AsianWeek* 3 Feb. 2005.

———. "From Miss America to Mr. President." *AsianWeek* 19 Oct. 2000.

———. "Glaring Omissions of Masterpiece History." *AsianWeek* 25 Nov. 2004.

———. "Hung As Buckwheat." Special to SF Gate.com. 20 Apr. 2005 at http://www.sfgate.com.

———. "Slur Away, Parcells." *AsianWeek* 17 Jun. 2004.

———. " The William Hung Joke." *AsianWeek* 15 Apr. 2005.

———. "You've Got Hate." *AsianWeek* 4 Feb. 1998.

GUINIER, LANI. *The Tyranny of the Majority.* New York: The Free Press, 1994.

GUTHRIE, JULIAN. "Bridging the Language Gap: Immigrants Put Teachers to the Test." *San Francisco Examiner* 12 May 1997.

H., PAMELA. "Asian American Lesbians: An Emerging Voice in the Asian American Community." *Making Waves.* Asian Women United, eds. Boston: Beacon Press, 1989.

HAMAMOTO, DARRELL Y. *Monitored Peril: Asian Americans and the Politics of TV Representation.* Minneapolis: University of Minnesota Press, 1994.

HAMAMOTO, DARRELL, and SANDRA LIU, eds. *Countervisions: Asian American Film Criticism.* Philadelphia: Temple University Press, 2000.

HAMILL, PETE. "New Race Hustle." *Esquire* Sep. 1990: 77–80.

HAMILTON, DENISE. "6 Accused in Ethnic Fight on Campus." *Los Angeles Times* 18 Feb. 1995.

HANSEN, MARCUS LEE. The Problems of the Third Generation. Rock Island, IL: Augustana Historical Soc., 1938.

HARLIN, HEATHER. "NYC Prosecutor Drops Charges Against Cop." *AsianWeek* 10 Sept. 1998.

———. "Storeowners Sue NYPD Over Arrest." *AsianWeek* 4 June 1998.

———. "SUNY Binghamton Wrestler Pleads Guilty to Attempted Assault." *AsianWeek* 8 June 2000.

"Harlemm Lee." Online at http://www.harlemmlee.com.

"Harlemm Lee: Winner of the Ultimate Talent Search—Fame." Online at http://www .aarising.com/aprofiler/harlemm.htm.

Harvard University Enrollment Information. Online at http://search.harvard. edu: 8765/query.html?qt=undergraduate+enrollment+by+ethnicity.

"Have Skills, Will Travel—Home." *Businessweek* 18 Nov. 1994: 164–165.

HAYS, CONSTANCE. "Asian-American Groups Call for Breslin's Ouster Over Racial Slurs." *New York Times* 7 May 1990.

HEIZER, ROBERT F., and ALAN F. ALMQUIST. *The Other Californians: Prejudice and Discrimination Under Spain, Mexico, and the United States to 1920.* Berkeley and Los Angeles: University of California Press, 1971.

"Helping Asians Climb Through Bamboo Ceiling." *Wall Street Journal* 13 Dec. 1991.

HENRY, SARAH. "Fighting Words." *Los Angeles Times Magazine* 10 Jun. 1990: 10+.

———. "Labor & Lace." *San Francisco Chronicle* 5 Sep. 1993.

HERBERT, SOLOMON J. "Why African-Americans Vented Anger at the Korean Community During the LA Riots." *Crisis* Aug.–Sep. 1992: 5+.

HERRNSTEIN, RICHARD J., and CHARLES MURRAY. *The Bell Curve: Intelligence and Class Structure in American Life.* New York: The Free Press, 1994.

HINCH, BRET. *Passions of the Cut Sleeve: The Male Homosexual Traditions in China.* Berkeley and Los Angeles: University of California Press, 1990.

HING, ALEX. "Organizing Asian Pacific American Workers in the AFL-CIO: New Opportunities." *Amerasia Journal* 18:1 (1992): 141–154.

HING, BILL ONG. *Defining America Through Immigration Policy.* Philadelphia: Temple University Press, 2004.

———. *Making and Remaking Asian America Through Immigration Policy, 1850–1990.* Stanford, CA: Stanford University Press, 1993.

HIRABAYASHI, LANE RYO. "Back to the Future: Re-framing Community-Based Research." *Amerasia Journal.* 21:1&2 (1995): 118.

———. "How a Death threat Became an Opportunity to Connect With My Students." *Chronicle of Higher Education* 12 May 2000.

———. *Teaching Asian America: Diversity & the Problem of Community.* Boulder, CO: Rowman and Littlefield, 1998.

HOLGUIN, RICK, and JOHN LEE. "Boycott of Store Where Man Was Killed Is Urged." *Los Angeles Times* 18 Jun. 1991.

HIRAHARA, NAOMI. *Distinguished Asian American Business Leaders.* Westport, CN: Greenwood Press, 2003.

HOLMES, STEVEN A. "Survey Finds Minorities Resent One Another Almost as Much as They Do Whites." *New York Times* 3 Mar. 1994.

HOFFER, THOMAS. "Employment Sector, Salaries, Publishing and Patenting Activities of S&E Doctorate Holders." *InfoBrief,* NSF 04-328/June 2004. Online at http://www.nsf.gov/ statistics/infbrief/nsf04328/.

HOM, ALICE Y. "Stories from the Homefront: Perspectives of Asian American Parents with Lesbian Daughters and Gay Sons." *Amerasia Journal* 20:1 (1994): 19–32.

HONG, HOWARD. "Asian Americans Welcome Bush with Open Arms." *AsianWeek* 21 Jun. 1991.

HORTON, JOHN. *The Politics of Diversity: Immigration, Resistance, and Change in Monterey Park, California.* Philadelphia: Temple University Press, 1995.

HOSOKAWA, BILL. *Nisei: The Quiet Americans.* New York: W. Morrow, 1969.

HOUSTON, VELINA HASU. "It's Time to Overcome the Legacy of Racism in Theater." *Los Angeles Times* 18 Aug. 1990.

"How Los Angeles Reached the Crisis Point Again, Chapter 5." *Los Angeles Times* 11 May 1992, Special Report: T10.

"How to Tell Your Friends from the Japs." *Time* 22 Dec. 1941: 33.

HSIA, JAYJIA. "Asian Americans Fight the Myth of the Super Student." *Educational Record* Fall 1987–Winter 1988: 94–97.

HUA, VANESSA. "Asian American Entertainers Find Demand For Their Talent Overseas Very Rewarding." *San Francisco Chronicle* 27 Nov. 2005.

———. "Coats Being Collected for Hurricane Victims." *San Francisco Chronicle* 8 Oct. 2005.

———. "Korean-born in U.S. Return to a Home They Never Knew." *San Francisco Chronicle* 11 Sep. 2004

———. "Teen Tied to Hate Crime Must Do Public Service: White Student Assaulted Group of Asian Americans." *San Francisco Chronicle* 22 Oct. 2004.

HUDDLE, DONALD. *The Cost of Immigration.* Washington, DC: Carrying Capacity Network, 1993.

HUGHES, BETH. "Ethnic Formula for Success." *San Francisco Examiner* 28 Jan. 1990.

Human Rights Watch. *We Are Not the Enemy.* Washington, DC, 2002.

HUMPHREYS, JEFFERY M. "Buying Power at the Beginning of a New Century: Projections for 2000 and 2001." University of Georgia Selig Center for Economic Growth, 2000.

———. "The Multicultural Economy 2004: America's Minority Buying Power." *Georgia Business and Economic Conditions.* University of Georgia: Selig Center for Economic Growth, Vol. 64, No. 3, Third Quarter 2004.

HUNE, SHIRLEY. "Rethinking Race: Paradigms and Policy Formation." *Amerasia Journal* 21:1&2 (1995): 29–40.

"Hung Jury in Ocean Shores Stabbing." *Seattle Post-Intelligencer* 14 Dec. 2000.

HUYNH, CRAIG TRINH-PHAT. "Vietnamese-Owned Manicure Businesses in Los Angeles." *Reframing the Immigration Debate.* Bill Ong Hing and Ronald Lee, eds. Los Angeles: LEAP Asian Pacific American Policy Institute and UCLA Asian American Studies Center, 1996. 195–203.

HUYNH, CUONG QUY, and GERALDINE V. PADILLA. "Vietnamese Knowledge and Attitudes about HIV/AIDS." Association for Asian American Studies Conference. Washington, DC. 29 May–2 June, 1996.

HWANG, DAVID HENRY. "A New Musical by Rogers and Hwang." *New York Times* 13 Oct. 2002.

———. *M. Butterfly.* New York: Penguin Books, 1988.

ICHIOKA, YUJI. *The Issei: The World of the First Generation Japanese Immigrants, 1885–1924.* New York: The Free Press, 1988.

IGNACIO, ABRAHAM F., JR., and H. C. TORIBIO. "The House of Pain." *Filipinas* Sept. 1994: 19.

IGNATIUS, DAVID. *A Firing Offense.* New York: Random House, 1998.

"Indian American Woman Youngest Rhodes Scholar." *AsianWeek* 19 Dec. 2002.

The IndUS Entrepreneurs [a.k.a. TiE]. Online at http://www.tie.org

Intel Science Talent Search Finalist (2004–05). Online at http://www.sciserv.org/sts/64sts/finalists.asp.

"Intel Science Talent Search $100,000 Scholarship Awarded to 17-Year-Old Female High School Senior from New York." *Science Service: Intel Science Talent Search.* Press Release. 13 Mar. 2000.

Intercollegiate Department of Asian American Studies: The Claremont Colleges. On line at http://www.idaas.pomona.edu.

"Interracial Children Pose Challenge for Classifiers." *Wall Street Journal* 27 Jan. 1993.

"Interracial Married Couples: 1960 to Present." Online at http://www.census.gov/populations/socdemo/ms-la/tabms-3.txt.

IRITANI, EVELYN. "China Showing Bigger Interest in U.S." *Los Angeles Times* 22 Jun. 2005.

ISSACS, HAROLD. *Images of Asia: American Views of China and India.* New York: Harper, 1972.

JACKSON, PETER A. *Male Homosexuality in Thailand: An Interpretation of Contemporary Thai Sources.* Elmhurst, NY: Global Academic Press, 1989.

JACOBUS, PATRICIA. "Oakland's Council's 'Asian Seat' Not a Sure Thing." *San Francisco Chronicle* 24 May 1994.

JACOBY, RUSSELL, and NAOMI GLAUBERMAN, eds. *The Bell Curve Debate: History, Documents, Opinions.* New York: Random House, 1995.

"Jan Stephenson Sparks LPGA Debate." Online at http://www.worldgolf.com/features/stephenson-letters.htm.

"Japanese American Basball History Project." Online at http://www.nikkeiheritage.org.

Japanese American Citizen's League. "JACL Bitterly Disappointed and Deeply Offended by Parcells' Use of 'Jap' and 'Orientals.'" Press Release. 8 Jun. 2004. Online at http://www.jacl.org/current_prs/040608.html.

JASCHIK, SCOTT. "Affirmative-Action Ruling on Connecticut Called a 'Big Step' for Asian Americans." *The Chronicle of Higher Education* 19 May 1993.

JENSEN, ARTHUR. *Educability and Group Difference.* New York: Harper, 1973.

JENSEN, JOAN. *Passage from India: Asian Indian Immigrants in North America.* New Haven: Yale University Press, 1988.

"Jessica McClintock Just Doesn't Get It." *New York Times* 14 Feb. 1994.

JOHNSON, CLARENCE. "2nd Choice Easily Wins Key SF Job." *San Francisco Chronicle* 28 Mar. 1995.

JORDAN, WINTHROP D. *White Over Black.* Baltimore: Penguin Books, 1969.

JOSEPH, RAYMOND. "American Men Find Asian Brides Fill the Unliberated Bill." *Wall Street Journal* 25 Jan. 1984.

"Judge Imposes 100 Hours, Probation for Anti-Asian Gang Assault." *AsianWeek* 28 Oct. 2004.

KABRIA, NAZLI. *Family Tightrope: The Changing Lives of Vietnamese Americans.* Princeton: Princeton University Press, 1993.

KALITA, MITRA. "A Dollar in Any Language." *Washington Post* 10 June 2005.

KAM, KATHERINE. "A False and Shattered Peace." *California Tomorrow* Summer 1989: 8–21.

KANG, K. CONNIE. "Asian Americans Lean to Democrats, Poll Says." *Los Angeles Times* 10 Nov. 2000.

———. "Korean Americans Return to District Torn By Riots." *Los Angeles Times* 29 Apr. 2000.

———. "No Longer 'Work, Work, Work.'" *Los Angeles Times* 22 Oct. 1994.

KANTROWITZ, BARBARA. "The Ultimate Assimilation." *Newsweek* 24 Nov. 1986: 80.

KAO, GRACE, and MARTA TIENDA. "Optimism and Achievement: The Educational Performance of Immigrant Youth." *Social Science Quarterly* 76:1 (1995): 1–19.

KAR, SNEHENDU B., ARMANDO JIMENEZ, KEVIN CAMPBELL, and FELICIA SZE. "Acculturation and Quality of Life: A Comparative Study of Japanese-American and Indo-Americans." *Amerasia Journal* 24:1 (1998): 129–142.

KAR, SNEHENDU B., KEVIN CAMPBELL, ARMANDO JIMENEZ, and SANGEETA R. GUPTA. "Invisible Americans: An Exploration of Indo-American Quality of Life." *Amerasia Journal* 21:3 (Winter 1995–1996): 25–52.

KARKABI, BARBARA. "Betty Waki: Sharpstown Teacher Devoted to Easing School's Racial Tension." *Houston Chronicle* 24 Apr. 1989.

KARLINS, MARVIN, THOMAS L. COFFMAN, AND GARY WALTERS. "On the Fading of Social Stereotypes: Studies of Three Generations of College Students." *Journal of Personality and Psychology* 13 (1990): 4–5.

KARNOW, STANLEY. "Apathetic Asian Americans?" *Washington Post* 29 Nov. 1992.

———. *Vietnam: A History.* New York: Penguin Books, 1991.

KARNOW, STANLEY, and NANCY YOSHIHARA. *Asian Americans in Transition.* New York: The Asia Society, 1992.

KATZ, JESSE, and JOHN H. LEE. "Conflict Brings Tragic End to Similar Dreams of Life." *Los Angeles Times* 8 Apr. 1991.

KAUFMAN, JONATHAN. "How Cambodians Came to Control California Doughnuts." *Wall Street Journal* 22 Feb. 1995.

KEMPSKY, NELSON. *A Report to Attorney General John K. Van de Kamp on Edward Patrick Purdy and the Cleveland School Killings.* Sacramento: California Department of Justice, 1989.

KENWORTHY, TOM. "Wis. Suspect Says He Was Taunted." *USA Today* 24 Nov. 2005.

KESSLER, PETER. "Jan Stephenson: LPGA's Original Siren Still Making Waves." *Golf Magazine* 1 Nov. 2003,

KHANH, TRUONG PHUOC. "In Shooting, Probes to Deal in the Details." *San Jose Mercury News* 27 Jul. 2003.

KIANG, PETER NIEN-CHA. *We Could Shape It: Organizing for Asian Pacific American Student Empowerment.* University of Boston: Institute for Asian American Studies, 1996.

KIBRIA, NAZLI. *Becoming Asian American: Second Generation Chinese and Korean American Identities.* Baltimore, MD: Johns Hopkins University Press, 2002.

———. *Family Tightrope: The Changing Lives of Vietnamese Americans.* Princeton, NJ: Princeton University Press, 1993.

KIM, ANNIE. "A Bigger and Better Political Force." *AsianWeek* 5 Oct. 2000.

KIM, BOK–LIM. "Asian Wives of U.S. Servicemen: Women in Shadows." *Amerasia Journal* 4:1 (1977): 91–116.

———. "Casework with Japanese and Korean Wives of Americans." *Social Casework* 53 (1972): 242–279.

KIM, ELAINE, and EUI-YOUNG YU. "Asian Americans and American Popular Culture." *Dictionary of Asian American History.* Chicago: University of Chicago Press, 1986.

———. *East to America: Korean-American Life Stories.* New York: New Press, 1996.

———. "They Armed in Self-Defense." *Newsweek* 18 May 1992.

KIM, ILLSOO. *New Urban Immigrants: The Korean Community in New York.* Princeton, NJ: Princeton University Press, 1981.

KIM, JA YOP, and KYU-TAIK SUNG. "Conjugal Violence in Korean American Families: A Residue of the Cultural Tradition." *Journal of Family Violence* 15:4 (December 2000): 331–345.

KIM, MIMI. "The Critique: API Response to the Standardized Models of Domestic Violence Intervention" in *Innovative Strategies to Address Domestic Violence in Asian and Pacific Islander Communities: Examining Themes, Models, and Interventions.* San Francisco: Asian & Pacific Islander Institute on Domestic Violence, 2002. Online at http:// www.apiahf.org/ apidvinstitute/GenderViolence/innovative_exec.htm.

———. *The Community Engagement Continuum: Outreach, Mobilization Organizing, and Accountability to Address Domestic Violence in Asian & Pacific Islander Communities.* San Francisco, Asian & Pacific Islander Institute on Domestic Violence, 2005. Online at http:// www.apiahf.org/apidvinstitute/PDF/Community_Engagement_Report.pdf.

KIM, PAN SUK, and GREGORY B. LEWIS. "Asian Americans in Public Service: Success, Diversity, and Discrimination." *Public Administration Review* 54:3 (May–Jun. 1994): 285–290.

KIM, RONALD. "The Myth and Realities of Ethnic Studies." *AsianWeek* 16 Feb. 1996.

KIM, RYAN. "$1 Million Settlement in Slaying by Rohnert Park Police." *San Francisco Chronicle* 16 Aug. 2001.

KIM, WARREN Y. *Koreans in America.* Seoul: Po Chin Chai Printing, 1971.

KING, REBECCA CHIYOKO. "Multiraciality Reigns Supreme?: Mixed Race Japanese Americans and the Cherry Blossom Queen Pagent." *Amerasia Journal* 23:1 (1997): 113–128.

———. "Racialization, Recognition, and Rights: Lumping and Splitting Multiracial Asian Americans in the 2000 Census." *Journal of Asian American Studies* 3:2 (June 2000): 191–217.

KITANO, HARRY. "Japanese-American Mental Illness." *Changing Perspectives on Mental Illness.* Stanley Plog and Robert Edgerton, eds. New York: Holt, 1969.

KITANO, HARRY, and LYNN CHAI. "Korean Interracial Marriage." *Marriage and Family Review* 5 (1982): 75–89.

KITANO, HARRY H. L., and ROGER DANIELS. *Asian Americans: Emerging Minorities.* 2nd ed. Englewood Cliffs, NJ: Prentice Hall, 1995.

KITANO, HARRY H. L., and WAI-TSANG YEUNG. "Chinese Interracial Marriage." *Marriage and Family Review* 5 (1982): 35–48.

KITANO, HARRY H. L., Wai-Tsang Yeung, Lynn Chai, and Herbert Hatanaka. "Asian-American Interracial Marriage." *Journal of Marriage and the Family* 46 (1984): 179–190.

KITCH, GEORGE KITAHARA. "The Developmental Process of Asserting Biracial, Bicultural Identity." *Racially Mixed People in America.* Maria Root, ed. Newbury Park, CA: Sage Press, 1992. 304–317.

"Korean Adoptees Gather." *Baltimore Sun* 10 Sept. 1999.

KORNBLUM, JANET. "Rational Rantings Return After Rampage." *USA Today* 4 May 2000.

KOSAREFF, JASON. "Chu Bill Aims to Protect Victims." *San Gabriel Valley Tribune* 21 May 2004.

KOTKIN, JOEL. *California: A Twenty-First Century Prospectus.* Denver, CO: Center for the New West, 1996.

KUMASHIRO, KEVIN K. *Restoried Selves: Autobiographies of Queer Asian Pacific American Activists.* New York: Harrington Park Press, 2004.

———. *Troubled Intersections Between Race and Sexuality: Queer Students of Color and Anti-Oppressive Education.* Landham, MD: Rowman and Littlefield Publishers, Inc., 2001.

KWOH, STEWART, and MINDY HUI. "Empowering Our Communities: Political Policy." *The State of Asian Pacific America: Policy Issues to the Year 2020.* Los Angeles: LEAP Asian Pacific American Public Policy Institute and UCLA Asian American Studies Center, 1993. 189–197.

KWON, CHRIS. "Seeds of a Silent Tree." *Korea Times* 28 Feb. 1998.

LA BRACK, BRUCE. "Occupational Specialization Among Rural California Sikhs: The Interplay of Culture and Economics," *Amerasia Journal* 9:2 (1982): 29–56.

LAI, JAMES S., ed. *2000–2001 National Asian Pacific American Political Almanac.* Los Angeles: UCLA Asian American Studies Center, 2000.

LAIT, MATT, and NORMA ZAMICHOW. "Valley Shooting Suspect Surrenders, Confesses." *Los Angeles Times* 12 Aug. 1999.

LAM, MAY. "Hate Crime Surfaces in Affluent Neighborhood." *AsianWeek* 2 Apr. 1995.

LAT, EMELYN CRUZ. "Widow Files Lawsuit in Rohnert Park Death." *San Francisco Examiner* 3 Feb. 1998.

LAVELLA, STACEY. "Arizona Youth's Suicide Questioned: Fight with Whites, Latinos Preceded Vietnamese American's Death." *AsianWeek* 25 Nov. 1998.

LE, NGOAN. "The Case of the Southeast Asian Refugees: Policy for a Community 'At-Risk.'" *The State of Asian Pacific America: Policy Issues to the Year 2020.* Los Angeles: LEAP Asian Pacific American Public Policy Institute and UCLA Asian American Studies Center. 167–188.

LE, THAO. "Delinquency Among Asian/Pacific Islanders: Review of Literature and Research." *The Justice Professional* 15:1 (2002): 57–70.

LE, THUY-DOAN, and GARANCE BURKE. "Getting a Toehold Cleaning Nails Opens Doors for Many Vietnamese." *Sacramento Bee* 12 Sept. 2004.

"Leadership Training Wraps Up." *AIWA News* 10:2 (Fall 1994): 3.

"Lee Clash Angers Caucus: Group Had Planned to Honor Lab Scientist." *San Francisco Chronicle* 9 June 2004.

LEE, BILL LANN. Quoted on the Travis Smiley Show 18 Nov. 2004. Online at http://www.npr.org/templates/story/story.php?storyId=4176534.

———. "Young Wing and the Americanization of China." *Amerasia Journal* 1:1 (1971): 25–32.

LEE, CARMEN. "Bethel Rally Puts Hatred on Hit List." *Pittsburgh Post-Gazette* 13 Aug. 2001.

LEE, ELISA. "Asian American Men Bare More Than Greetings in 'Double A' Cards." *AsianWeek* 11 Nov. 1994.

———. "Martin Luther King, Jr. Scholarship Recipients Depart for Seoul." *AsianWeek* 17 Jun. 1994.

————. "Silicon Valley Study Finds Asian Americans Hitting the Glass Ceiling." *AsianWeek* 8 Oct. 1993.

LEE, JOANN. "A Look at Asians as Portrayed in the News." *Editor & Publisher* 30 Apr. 1994: 46.

LEE, JENNIFER, and MIN ZHOU, eds. *Asian American Youth: Culture, Identity, and Ethnicity.* New York: Routledge, 2004.

LEE, JOSEPHINE. *Performing Asian America: Race and Ethnicity on the Contemporary Stage.* Philadelphia: Temple University Press, 1999.

LEE, LEE C, and GINNY ZHAN. "Psychosocial Status of Children and Youths." *Handbook of Asian American Psychology.* Lee C. Lee and Nolan W. S. Zane, eds. Thousand Oaks, CA: Sage Publications, 1998. 137–164.

LEE, MEI JYU- CHWANG. *An Extreme Asian-American Upbringing.* Authorhouse, 2003.

LEE, ROBERT G. *Orientals: Asian Americans in Popular Culture.* Philadelphia: Temple University Press, 1999.

LEE, SHARON M., and MARILYN FERNANDEZ. "Trends in Asian American Racial/Ethnic Intermarriage: A Comparison of 1980 and 1990 Census Data." *Sociological Perspectives* 41:2 (1998): 323–343.

LEE, SHARON M., MARILYN FERNANDEZ, and KEIKO YAMANAKA. "Patterns of Asian American Intermarriage and Marital Assimilation." *Journal of Comparative Family Studies* 21 (1990): 227–305.

LEE, STACEY J. *Unraveling the Model Minority Stereotype: Listening to Asian American Youth.* New York: Teachers College Press, 1996.

LEE, TOM. "Bill Lan Lee Named Assistant Attorney General." *AsianWeek* 10 Aug. 2000.

"Legislation to Improve Higher Education for APAs." *AsianWeek* 16 Jan. 2003.

LELAND, JOHN, and JOHN MCCORMICK. "The Quiet Race War." *Newsweek* 8 Apr. 1996: 38.

LEONARD, KAREN. *Ethnic Choices: California's Punjabi-Mexican Americans.* Philadelphia: Temple University Press, 1991.

LEONG, RUSSELL, ed. *Moving the Image: Independent Asian Pacific American Media Arts.* Los - Angeles: UCLA Asian American Studies Center, 1991.

LEONG, RUSSELL C, and DON T. NAKANISHI. *Asian Americans On War & Peace.* Los Angeles, CA: UCLA Asian American Studies Center Press, 2002.

LEWIS, GREGORY, and PAN SUK KIM. "Asian Americans in the Federal Service: Education, Occupational Choice, and Perceptions of Discrimination: a Reply." *Public Administration Review* 57:3 (1997): 267–270.

LEWIS, NEIL A. "Wen Ho Lee Case Exposes Flaws in Racial Profiling." *New York Times* 17 Sept. 2000.

LI, DAVID K. "Don't Stereotype Asians, Panel Tells Journalists." *Oakland Tribune* 1 Aug. 1994.

————. "Rarely Used Voting Style Advocated." *Oakland Tribune* 27 Nov. 1995.

LIAUH, WAYNE. Statement. *Roundtable Conference on Asian American Civil Rights Issues for the 1990s.* U.S. Commission on Civil Rights. Washington, DC. 27 May 1989.

LICHTBLAU, ERIC. "Racial Writings Linked to Rampage." *Los Angeles Times* 30 Apr. 2000.

LIEN, PEI-TI, CHRISTIAN COLLET, JANELLE WONG, and S. KARTHICK RAMAKRISHNAN. "Asian Pacific American Public Opinion and Political Participation." *Political Science & Politics* 34:3 (September 2001): 625–630.

LIGHT, IVAN. *Ethnic Enterprise in America.* Berkeley and Los Angeles: University of California Press, 1972.

LIM, GERARD. "JACL Formally Adopts Same-Sex Marriages." *AsianWeek* 12 Aug. 1994.

————. "Lawsuit Over Chinese American HS Enrollment: Class Warfare by the Bay?" *AsianWeek* 19 Aug. 1994.

LIM, JI HYUN. "Report Released on Plight of the Asian Pacific American Worker." *AsianWeek* 15 Aug. 2005.

LIN, CHIN-YAU, and VICTORIA FU. "A Comparison of Child-Rearing Practices of American Chinese, Immigrant Chinese, and Caucasian-American Parents." *Child Development* 61:1 (1990): 429–433.

LIN, JAN. "Globalization and the Revalorization of Ethnic Places in Immigration Gateway Cities." *Urban Affairs Review* 34:2 (1998): 313–339.

LIN, SAM CHU. "Bucks for Kerry, But APAs Hunger for More Substance." *AsianWeek* 22 Jul. 2004.

———. "Chao Time in Prime Time." *AsianWeek* 26 Aug. 2004.

———. "Norm Chow Leads USC's National Football Title." *AsianWeek* 8 Jan. 2004.

———. "Parcells Apologizes for 'Jap Remark.'" *AsianWeek* 10 Jun. 2004.

———. "Radio Tirade." *AsianWeek* 5 Apr. 1996.

LINDREN, KRISTINA. "UC Irvine Asian-American Studies Demanded." *Los Angeles Times* 23 Apr. 1993.

LINDSEY, ROBERT. "Colleges Accused of Bias to Stem Asian's Gains." *New York Times* 21 Jan. 1987.

LIU, TED W. "Americans in All Colors." *San Francisco Chronicle* 25 June 1999.

LOCKE, GARY. "The One-Hundred Year Journey: From Houseboy to the Governor's Mansion." In Don Nakanishi and James Lai, eds., *Asian American Politics: Law, Participation, and Policy*. Lanham, MD: Rowman & Littlefied, 2003. 359–364.

LOEB, VERNON. "China Spy Report Ignites Outcry. *Washington Post* 26 May, 1999.

———. "Los Alamos Scientist Released." *Washington Post* 14 Sep. 2000.

LOEWEN, JAMES W. *The Mississippi Chinese: Between Black and White*. Cambridge, MA: Harvard University Press, 1971.

"Lofgren Introduces Citizenship Bill for Children Born in Vietnam to American Servicemen and Vietnamese Women During the Vietnam War." Press Release. 22 Oct. 2003. Online at http://www.house.gov/lofgren/news/2003/pr_031022_Amerasian.html.

LOO, CHALSA. "M. Butterfly: A Feminist Perspective." *Bearing Dreams, Shaping Visions: Asian Pacific American Perspectives*. Linda A. Revilla et al., eds. Pullman, WA: Washington State University Press, 1993. 177–180.

———. "The 'Middle-Aging' of Asian American Studies." *Reflections on Shattered Windows: Promise and Prospects for Asian American Studies*. Gary Y. Okihiro et al., eds. Pullman, WA: Washington State University Press, 1988. 16–23.

LOO, CHALSA, and DON MAR. "Research and Asian Americans: Social Change or Empty Prize?" *Amerasia Journal* 12:2 (1985–1986): 85–93.

LOUIE, MIRIAM CHING. "After Sewing, Laundry, Cleaning and Cooking, I Have No Breath Left to Sing." *Amerasia Journal* 18:1 (1992): 1–26.

LOWE, JUSTIN. "All or Nothing." *AsianWeek* 10 Apr. 2003.

———. "'Better Luck Tomorrow' Makes Box Office History." *AsianWeek* 17 Apr. 2003.

LOWE, LISA. "Heterogeneity, Hybridity, Multiplicity: Marking Asian American Differences." *Diaspora* Spring 1991: 24–44.

LYMAN, STANFORD. *Chinese Americans*. New York: Random House, 1974.

LYNCH, APRIL, and MARC SANDALOW. "Spotlight on Asian Americans." *San Francisco Chronicle* 12 Mar. 1997.

LYNN, RICHARD. *Educational Achievement in Japan*. London: Macmillan, 1988.

———. "The Intelligence of Mongoloids: A Psychometric Evolutionary and Neurological Theory." *Personality and Individual Differences* 8:6 (1987): 813–844.

———. "IQ in Japan and in the United States Shows Great Disparity." *Nature* 297 (1982): 222–226.

MA, JASON. "Campaign-Finace Probe Fizzling Out." *AsianWeek* 25 Aug. 1999.

———. "East Bay Youths Fight Violence Together." *AsianWeek* 23 Sept. 1999.

———. "'Hate' Was There All The Time." *AsianWeek* 11 Nov. 1999.

———. "Korean Suffers Cracked Skull in Hate Crime." *AsianWeek* 30 Mar. 2000.

———. "McCain Apologizes for 'Gook' Comment." *AsianWeek* 24 Feb. 2000.

———. "Whose Oakland Is It?" *AsianWeek* 20 Apr. 2000.

MA, JASON, and JOYCE NISHIOKA. "SFUSD Overseer Sends Mixed Signals on Race," *AsianWeek* 11 Nov. 1999.

"Madison Nguyen: Rising Star Has Much To Prove in Dist. 7: To Be Effective, She'll Have to Reach Beyond the Vietnamese Community." *San Jose Mercury News* 15 Sep. 2005.

MAGAGNINI, STEPHEN. "Profile: Mee Moua, From the Mountains of Laos to Halls of State Government." *Sacramento Bee* 14 Sep. 2004.

MAGNER, DENISE K. "Colleges Faulted for Not Considering Differences in Asian-American Groups." *Chronicle of Higher Education,* 10 Feb. 1993: A32+.

MAGWILI, DOM. "Makibaka! Asian-American Artists Should Struggle—and Not Be Afraid." *Los Angeles Times* 13 Aug. 1990.

"MANAA's Official Statement on the Movie 'Rising Sun.'" Mar. 1993.

MANDEL, MICHAEL J., and CHRISTOPHER FARRELL. "The Immigrants: How They're Helping to Revitalize the US Economy." *BusinessWeek* 13 Jul. 1992: 114+.

MANGAOANG, GIL. "From the 1970s to the 1990s: Perspective of a Gay Filipino American Activist." *Amerasia Journal* 20:1 (1994): 33–44.

MANGIAFICO, LUCIANO. *Contemporary American Immigrants: Patterns of Filipino, Korean, and Chinese Settlement in the United States.* New York: Praeger, 1988.

"Man in Racial Killing Ruled Insane. *Los Angeles Times* 26 Sep. 2003.

MAR, DON. "Another Look at the Enclave Economy Thesis." *Amerasia Journal* 17:3 (1991): 5–21.

MARECH, RONA. "Asians to Rally in Favor of Same-Sex Marriage." *San Francisco Chronicle* 7 Aug. 2004.

MARCHETTI, GINA. *Romance and the "Yellow Peril": Race, Sex and Discursive Strategies in Hollywood Films.* Berkeley and Los Angeles: University of California Press, 1993.

MARGONELLI, LISA. "Asian Activists Give UC Berkeley Politics a New Spin." *Pacific News Service* 2–6 Jan. 1993: 3.

MARIA. "Coming Home." *A Lotus of Another Color: An Unfolding of the South Asian Gay and Lesbian Experience.* Rakesh Ratti, ed. Boston: Alyson Press, 1993.

"Marine Wins Bars After Fight Over Bias." *San Francisco Chronicle* 19 Mar. 1994.

MARK, DIANE, and GINGER CHIH. *A Place Called Chinese America.* San Francisco: The Organization of Chinese Americans, 1982.

MARK, GREGORY YEE. "Director's Report" *API Currents Newsletter.* April 2001. 1, 4.

MATHEWS, LINDA. "When Being Best Isn't Good Enough." *Los Angeles Times Magazine* 19 Jul. 1987: 22–28.

MATIER, PHILLIP, and ANDREW ROSS. "'Dog' Comment Bites the S.F. Housing Chief." *San Francisco Chronicle* 17 Jul. 1995.

MAXIE, DARRYL. "Another Shocker by Rocker." *Atlantic Constitution* 22 Dec. 1999.

MAY, MEREDITH, and MAI HOANG. "Crossing Color Barriers a Tough Path for Asians." *Oakland Tribune* 12 Feb. 1995.

MAZUMDAR, SUCHETA. "South Asians in the United States with a Focus on Asian Indians: Policy on New Communities." *State of Asian Pacific America: Policy Issues to the Year 2020.* Los Angeles: LEAP Asian Pacific American Public Policy Institute and UCLA Asian American Studies Center, 1993. 283–301.

McBEE, SUSANNA. "Asian Merchants Find Ghettos Full of Peril." *U.S. News and World Report* 24 Nov. 1986.

"McClintock Attacks Free Speech Rights." *AIWA News* 10:2 (Fall 1994): 1+.

McCORMICK, ERIN. "Filipino Guards Sue Over 'Accent Discrimination.'" *San Francisco Examiner* 15 Apr. 1993.

McCUNN, RUTHANN LUM. *Thousand Pieces of Gold.* San Francisco: Design Enterprises, 1981.

McFadden, Robert D. "Blacks Attack Vietnamese; One Hurt Badly." *New York Times* 14 May 1990.

McKelvey, Robert S. *The Dust of Life: America's Children Abandoned in Vietnam.* Seattle: University of Washington Press, 1999.

McKinnon, Jim. "Baumhammers To Be Sentenced: Judge to Affirm Jury's May Decree of Death." *Pittsburgh Post-Gazette* 6 Sep. 2001.

———. "Death for Baumhammers: Jury Verdict Brings Tears and Cheers." *Pittsburgh Post-Gazette* 12 May 2001.

McLeod, Ramon G. "Elderly Immigrants Swell Welfare Roles." *San Francisco Chronicle* 20 Apr. 1996.

McNamara, Victoria. "Battling the Bamboo Ceiling." *Houston Post* 31 May 1993.

McPhereson, Barry D., James E. Curtis, and John W. Loy. *The Significance of Sport.* Champaign, IL: Human Kinetics Books, 1989.

McQueen, Michael. "Voters' Response to Poll Disclose Huge Chasm Between Social Attitudes of Blacks and Whites." *Wall Street Journal* 17 May 1991.

Meier, Dani I. "Cultural Identity and Place in Adult Korean-American Intercountry Adoptees." *Adoption Quarterly* 3:1 (1999): 15–48.

Melegrito, Jon. "Freedom Riders Demand Justice, Mobilize Support." APALA Press Release. 5 Oct. 2003. Online at http://www.apalanet.org/pr_100503.html.

Melendy, H. Brett. "Filipinos in the United States." *The Asian American: The Historical Experience.* Norris Hundley, Jr., ed. Santa Barbara: Cleo, 1977.

Mendez, Carlos. "A Fighter for Gay Rights." *AsianWeek* 22 Jul. 1994.

———. " 'Vanishing Son': No Plans to Disappear." *AsianWeek* 3 Feb. 1995.

Meyer, Jeremy. "Workings Fighting English-only Rules." *Denver Post* 18 Nov. 2004.

Mickelson, Roslyn Arlin. "The Attitude-Achievement Paradox Among Black Adolescents. *Sociology of Education* 56 (1990): 44–61.

Milborn, Todd. "Tasty Treats Build Dreams: Mr. T's Doughnuts are Key to Family's Success." *Modesto Bee* 2 August 2004.

Miller, Bill. "Fund-Raising Friend of Gore Guilty in Scam." *Sacramento Bee* 3 Mar. 2000.

Miller, John J. "Asian Americans and the Republicans: A Natural Fit or a Party in Turmoil?" *AsianWeek* 16 Sep. 1994.

———. "Asian Americans Head for Politics: What Horse Will They Ride?" *AsianWeek* 7 Apr. 1995. Reprinted from the Mar.–Apr. 1995 issue of *The American Enterprise.*

Miller, Susan Katz. "Asian Americans Bump Against Glass Ceilings." *Science* 13 Nov. 1992: 1225.

Miller v. Johnson. 115 S.Ct. 2475 (1995).

Mills, C. Wright. *The Sociological Imagination.* New York: Oxford University Press, 1959.

Milvy, Erika. "Asian American, Berkeley Rep Join Hands." *San Francisco Examiner/Chronicle* 21 Nov. 1993, Datebook Section: 21–22.

Min, Pyong Gap, ed. *Asian Americans: Contemporary Trends and Issues.* Thousand Oaks, CA: Sage Press, 1995.

———. "Cultural and Economic Boundaries of Korean Ethnicity: A Comparative Analysis." *Ethnic and Racial Studies* 14 (1991): 225–241.

———. *Ethnic Business Enterprise: Korean Small Business in Atlanta.* New York: Center for Migration Studies, 1988.

———. "The Korean Family." *Ethnic Families in America.* Charles H. Mindel, Robert W. Habenstein, and Roosevelt Wright, Jr., eds. New York: Elsevier, 1989. 199–229.

———. "Korean Immigrant Wives' Overwork." *Korean Journal of Population and Development* 21 (1992): 23–36.

———. "The Social Costs of Immigrant Entrepreneurship: A Response to Edna Bonacich." *Amerasia Journal* 15:2 (1989): 187–194.

MIN, PYONG GAP, and ROSE KIM, eds. *Struggle for Identity: Narratives by Asian American Professionals.* Walnut Creek, CA: AltaMira Press, 1999.

MIN, PYONG GAP, and KYEYOUNG PARK, eds. "Second Generation Asian Americans' Ethnic Identity" *Amerasia Journal* 25:1 (1999).

MINTON, TORRI. "Quiet Marin Confronts Hate Crimes." *San Francisco Chronicle* 29 Nov. 1995.

"Mixed Folks." Online at http://www.mixedfolks.com/aothers.htm.

"Monte Jade." Online at http://www.mtjade.org.

MOORE, MARTHA. "Conners' new Racket: Ad Spokesman." *USA Today* 4 Sep. 1991.

MORROW, LANCE. "Japan in the Mind of America." *Time* 10 Feb. 1992: 17–21.

MOY, JAMES S. *Marginal Sights: Staging the Chinese in America.* Iowa City: University of Iowa Press, 1993.

"Mr. Wong." Online at http://www.icebox.com/icebox/shows/show_54/show_frameset.html.

MUNOZ, LORENZO. "60 Years Later, It's a Sensitive Topic." *Los Angeles Times* 22 May 2001.

MURATSUCHI, ALBERT Y. "Voter Registration in the Oakland Pacific American Communities: An Agenda for the 1990s." San Francisco: The Coro Foundation, 1990.

MYDANS, SETH. "New Unease for Japanese Americans." *New York Times* 4 Mar. 1992.

MYERS, LAURA. "Spelling Bee Sweep." *AsianWeek* 7 Jun. 1996.

"N.C. Congressman Says Internment of Japanese- Americans During World War II was Appropriate." Associated Press State and Local Wire. 5 Feb. 2003.

NAGATA, DONNA. *Legacy of Injustice: Exploring the Cross-Generational Impact of the Japanese American Internment.* New York: Plenum Press, 1993.

NAKANISHI, DON T. "Asian American Politics: An Agenda for Research." *Amerasia Journal* 12:2 (1985–1986): 1–27.

———. "The Next Swing Vote? Asian Pacific Americans and California Politics." *Racial and Ethnic Politics in California.* Bryan O. Jackson and Michael B. Preston, eds. Berkeley: IGS Press, 1991. 25–54.

———. "UCLA Asian Pacific American Voter Registration Study." Sponsored by the Asian Pacific American Legal Center, 1986.

NAKANISHI, DON T., and JAMES S. LAI, eds. *1996 National Asian Pacific American Political Almanac.* Los Angeles: UCLA Asian American Studies Center, 1997.

NAKANISHI, DON T., JAMES S. LAI, and DAPHNE KWOCK, eds. *National Asian Pacific American Political Almanac.* Los Angeles: UCLA Asian American Studies Center, 2005.

NAKANO, ANNIE. "Asian Americans Fear Backlash." *San Francisco Examiner* 26 May 1999.

———. "Asian Americans Vote Big." *San Francisco Examiner* 15 Dec. 1996.

———. "Forgiving Shaq is a Tall Order to Fill." *San Francisco Chronicle* 21 Jan. 2003.

NAKASHIMA, CYNTHIA L. "An Invisible Monster: The Creation and Denial of Mixed-Race People in America." *Racially Mixed People in America.* Maria P. P. Root, ed. Newbury Park, CA: Sage Press, 1992. 162–178.

———. "Voices from the Movement: Approaches to Multiraciality." *The Multiracial Experience: Racial Borders as the New Frontier.* Maria P. P. Root, ed. Thousand Oaks, CA: Sage Publications, 1996. 79–97.

NAMKOONG, FRANCES M. "Stereotyping Is Holding Asian-Americans Back." *Cleveland Plain Dealer* 17 May 1994.

NARIKIYO, TRUDY, and VELMA KAMEOKA. "Attributions of Mental Illness and Judgments About Help Seeking Among Japanese American and White Students." *Journal of Counseling Psychology* 39:3 (1992): 363–369.

NASH, J. MADELEINE. "Tigers in the Lab." *Time* 21 Nov. 1994: 86–87.

NASH, PHIL TAJITSU, and FRANK WU. "Asian-Americans under Glass: Where the Furor Over the President's Fundraising has Gone Wrong—and Racist." *The Nation* 24:12 (31 Mar. 1997): 15+.

National Asian Pacific American Legal Consortium. *1993 Audit of Violence Against Asian Pacific Americans.* First Annual Report. Washington, DC, 1994.

———. *1994 Audit of Violence Against Asian Pacific Americans.* Second Annual Report. Washington, DC, 1995.

———. *1995 Audit of Violence Against Asian Pacific Americans.* Third Annual Report. Washington, DC, 1996.

———. *1996 Audit of Violence Against Asian Pacific Americans.* Fourth Annual Report. Washington, DC, 1997.

———. *1997 Audit of Violence Against Asian Pacific Americans.* Fifth Annual Report. Washington, DC, 1998.

———. *1998 Audit of Violence Against Asian Pacific Americans.* Sixth Annual Report. Washington, DC, 1999.

———. *1999 Audit of Violence Against Asian Pacific Americans,* Seventh Annual Report. Washington, DC, 2000.

———. 2000 *Audit of Violence Against Asian Pacific Americans,* Eighth Annual Report. Washington, DC, 2001.

———. *2001 Audit of Violence Against Asian Pacific Americans.* Ninth Annual Report. Washington DC, 2002.

———. "Asian Americans in Prime Time: Lights, Camera, and Little Action." 2005. Online at http://www.advancingequality.org/files/NAPALC_report_final.pdf.

———. "Civil Rights Groups Horrified by Another Wave of Hate Crimes Against Asian Pacific Americans in Pittsburgh." Press Release. 2 May 2000.

———. "Sound Barriers: Asian Americans and Language Access in Election 2004." 2005. Online at http://www.advancingequality.org/files/sound_barriers.pdf.

National Asian Pacific Islander American Scholarship Fund. Online at www.apiasf.org.

National Center for Education Statistics. *Digest of Educational Statistics, 1995.* Washington, DC: U.S. Department of Education, Office of Research and Improvement, 1995. Tables 138, 136.

National Coalition for Equity in Public Service. Online at http://www.fapac.org/m_partners.php.

National Immigration Forum. Online at www.immigrationforum.org.

National Science Foundation, Division of Science Resource Statistics. *Women, Minorities, and Persons With Disabilities in Science and Engineering: 2004,* NSF 04-317. Arlington, VA, 2004.

———. *Women, Minorities, and Persons with Disabilities in Science and Engineering: 1998.* Washington, DC: GPO, 1999.

———. *Women and Minorities in Science and Engineering.* Washington, DC: GPO, 1990.

Naturalization Act of 1790, I Stat. 103 (1790).

NAVARRETTE, RUBEN JR. "Illegal Immigrants and Social Security." *San Diego Union-Tribune* 10 April 2005.

NEE, VICTOR G., and BRETT DE BARY NEE. *Longtime Californ': A Documentary Study of an American Chinatown.* Boston: Houghton, 1974.

"New California Media Expo 2005." Online at http://expo.ncmonline.com/news/.

"New Gifford Sweatshop Charge." *San Francisco Examiner* 6 Dec. 1997.

NEIWERT, DAVID. *Death on the Fourth of July.* New York: Palgrave Macmillan, 2004.

NEUMEISTER, LARRY. "Asian Officers Allege Discrimination in Lawsuit Against Bi-State Agency." *Associated Press* 15 Apr. 2005.

NEVIUS, C. W., MARC SANDALOW, and JOHN WILDERMUTH. "McCain Criticized for Slur." *San Francisco Chronicle* 18 Feb. 2000.

New California Media. "National Survey of Asian and Pacific Islander Likely Voters in the United States." Sep. 2004. Online at http://www.ncmonline.com/media/pdf/polls/apia_presentation.pdf.

NEWMAN, MARIA. "Restaurant is Ordered to Pay Ex-Waitresses $3.4 Million." *New York Times* 27 Sep. 2003.

NGIN, CHOR-SWAN. "The Acculturation Pattern of Orange County's Southeast Asian Refugees." *Journal of Orange County Studies.* 3:4 (Fall 1989–Spring 1990): 46–53.

NJERI, ITABARI. "Power Elite Turns Out a Bitter Brew." *Los Angeles Times* 29 Nov. 1991.

NIHU, T. T. "Area Cambodian Doughnut Shops Add Bagels to Menu." *San Jose Mercury News* 22 Jun. 1999.

NIIYA, BRIAN, ed. *More Than a Game: Sport in the Japanese American Community.* Los Angeles: Japanese American National Museum, 2000.

NISHIOKA, JOYCE. "Fresno Factory Workers Allege Language Bias." *AsianWeek* 8 Apr. 1999.

———. "Workers Protest English-Only Rule." *AsianWeek* 18 Mar. 1999.

———. "Young, Gay and APA." *AsianWeek* 17 Jun. 1999.

NOGAWA, H., and S. J. SUTTIE. "A Japanese-American Basketball League and the Assimilation of Its Members Into the Mainstream of United States Society." *Review for the Sociology of Sport* 19 (1984): 259–271.

NOLTE, CARL. "Racism Charge Over Mariners Sale." *San Francisco Chronicle* 7 Feb. 1992.

———. "Slam-Dunk Memories." *San Francisco Chronicle* 28 May 1999.

"North American Chinese Basketball Tournament." Online at: http//www.asianhoops.com.

"North American Chinese Invitational Volleyball Tournament." Online at http//www .nacivt.com.

NORTON, DEE. "Anniversary Vigil Highlights Domestic Violence: 15 Groups Remember Those Killed in Courthouse Shootings." *Seattle Times* 2 Mar. 1996.

"Nuprin's Smash Hit: Conners Ad Leads Brand to 23% Gain." *Advertising Age* 14 Oct. 1991.

Oakland, City of. "Asian Advisory Committee on Crime." Police Dept.: Community Services Div., 1996.

OAKS, LARRY. "Vang Tells of Confrontation in the Woods." *Star Tribune* 10 Jun. 2005.

OGBU, JOHN, and MARIA MATUTE-BIANCHI. "Understanding Sociocultural Factors: Knowledge, Identity, and School Adjustment." *Beyond Language: Social and Cultural Factors in Schooling Language Minority Students.* California State Department of Education. Los Angeles: California State Department of Education, 1986. 73–142.

OKAMURA, RAYMOND. "Farewell to Manzanar: A Case of Subliminal Racism." *Counterpoint: Perspectives on Asian America.* Emma Gee, ed. Los Angeles: UCLA Asian American Studies Center, 1976. 280–283.

OKIHIRO, GARY Y. *Margins and Mainstreams: Asian American History and Culture.* Seattle: University of Washington Press, 1994.

OLSEN, LAURIE. *Crossing the Schoolhouse Border: Immigrant Students and the California Public Schools.* San Francisco: California Tomorrow, 1988.

OLIVER, RICHARD. "Spencer Slams Toyota Entry: Veteran Driver Uses Pearl Harbor Reference In His Remarks." *San Antonio Express-News* 29 Jan. 2004.

OMATSU, GLEN. "Expansion of Democracy." *Amerasia Journal* 18:1 (1992): v–xix.

OMI, MICHAEL. "It Just Ain't the Sixties No More: The Contemporary Dilemmas of Asian American Studies." *Reflections on Shattered Windows: Promise and Prospects for Asian American Studies.* Gary Y. Okihiro, et al., eds. Pullman, WA: Washington State University Press, 1988. 31–36.

OMI, MICHAEL, and HOWARD WINANT. *Racial Formation in the United States: From the 1960s to the 1980s.* New York: Routledge, 1986.

———. *Racial Formation in the United States: From the 1960s to the 1990s.* 2nd ed. New York: Routledge, 1994.

ONG, PAUL, and TANIA AZORES. "Health Professionals on the Front-Line." *The State of Asian Pacific America: Economic University, Issues & Policies.* Paul Ong, ed. Los Angeles: LEAP

Asian Pacific American Public Policy Institute and UCLA Asian American Studies Center, 1994. 139–164.

———. "The Migration and Incorporation of Filipino Nurses." *The New Asian Immigration in Los Angeles and Global Restructuring*. Paul Ong et al., eds. Philadelphia: Temple University Press, 1994.

ONG, PAUL, and EVELYN BLUMENBERG. "Scientists and Engineers." *The State of Asian Pacific America: Economic Diversity, Issues & Policies*. Paul Ong, ed. Los Angeles: LEAP Asian Pacific American Public Policy Institute and UCLA Asian American Studies Center, 1994. 165–192.

———. "Welfare and Work Among Southeast Asians." *The State of Asian Pacific America: Economic Diversity, Issues & Policies*. Paul Ong, ed. Los Angeles: LEAP Asian Pacific American Public Policy Institute and UCLA Asian American Studies Center, 1994. 113–138.

ONG, PAUL, EDNA BONACICH, and LUCIE CHENG, eds. *The New Asian Immigration in Los Angeles and Global Restructuring*. Philadelphia: Temple University Press, 1994.

ONG, PAUL, and SUZANNE J. HEE. "The Growth of the Asian Pacific American Population: Twenty Million in 2020." *The State of Asian Pacific America: Policy Issues to the Year 2020*. Los Angeles: LEAP Asian Pacific American Public Policy Institute and UCLA Asian American Studies Center, 1993. 11–24.

———. "Work Issues Facing Asian Pacific Americans: Labor Policy." *The State of Asian Pacific American: Policy Issues to the Year 2020*. Los Angeles: LEAP Asian Pacific American Public Policy Institute and UCLA Asian American Studies Center, 1993. 141–152.

ONG, PAUL, and DON NAKANISHI. "Becoming Citizens, Becoming Voters: The Naturalization and Political Participation of Asian Pacific Immigrants." *Reframing the Immigration Debate*. Bill Ong Hing and Ronald Lee, eds. Los Angeles: LEAP Asian Pacific American Policy Institute and UCLA Asian American Studies Center, 1996. 292–293.

ONO, KENT A. *Asian American Studies After Critical Mass*. Maldin, MA: Blackwell Publishing, Ltd., 2005.

"Opponent Calls Senate Candidate a Japanese Agent." *San Francisco Chronicle* 27 Oct. 1990.

ORONDA, TRINITY. "In Our Own Way." *Amerasia Journal* 20:1 (1994): 137–147.

OSAJIMA, KEITH. "Asian Americans as the Model Minority: An Analysis of the Popular Press Image in the 1960s and 1980s." *Reflections on Shattered Windows: Promises and Prospects for Asian American Studies*. Gary Y. Okihiro et al., eds. Pullman, WA: Washington State University Press, 1988. 165–174.

———. "Pedagogical Considerations in Asian American Studies." *Journal of Asian American Studies* 1:3 (1998): 269–292.

———. "Postmodern Possibilities: The Theoretical and Political Directions for Asian American Studies." *Amerasia Journal* 21:1&2 (1995): 79–87.

OSUMI, MEGUMI DICK. "Asians and California's Anti-Miscegenation Laws." *Asian and Pacific American Experiences: Women's Perspectives*. Nobuya Tsuchida, ed. Minneapolis, MN: Asian/Pacific American Learning Resource Center, University of Minnesota, 1982. 1–37.

OTT, MICHELE. "The Incidences of Anti-Asian Violence in High Schools." Honors Thesis prepared for Bates College, 1994.

OXFORD-CARPENTER, REBECCA, et al. *Demographic Projections of Non-English-Language-Background and Limited-English-Proficient Persons*. Rosslyn, VA: InterAmerica Research Associates, 1984.

Ozawa v. United States. 260 US 178 (1922).

PAIK, FELICIA. "Say Anything." *A Magazine* Feb.–Mar. 1995: 34.

PARISH, RIC, JAMES SAKAKURA, BRIAN GREEN, JOEL B. TAN, and ROBERT VASZQUEZ PACHECO. "Communion: A Collaboration on AIDS." *Asian American Sexualities: Dimensions of Gay & Lesbian Experience*. Russell Leong, ed. New York: Routledge, 1996. 202–203.

PARK, EDWARD JANG-WOO. "Asians Matter: Asian American Entrepreneurs in the Silicon Valley High Technology Industry." *Reframing the Immigration Debate*. Bill Ong Hing and Ronald Lee, eds. Los Angeles: LEAP Asian Pacific American Public Policy Institute and UCLA Asian American Studies Center, 1996. 155–178.

PARK, JOHN S. W. *Elusive Citizenship: Immigration, Asian Americans and the Paradox of Civil Rights*. New York: NYU Press, 2004.

PASSEL, JEFFERY S. "Immigrants and Taxes: A Reappraisal of Huddle's 'The Cost of Immigrants.'" Washington, DC: Program for Research on Immigration Policy, The Urban Institute, Jan. 1994.

PEARLMAN, JEFF. "At Full Blast." *Sports Illustrated* 27 Dec. 2000.

PENG, SAMUEL, et al. "School Experiences and Performance of Asian American High School Students." Paper presented at the Annual Meeting of the American Educational Research Association, New Orleans. Apr. 1984.

PENG, SAMUEL S., and DEEANN WRIGHT. "Explanation of Academic Achievement of Asian American Students." *Journal of Educational Research* 87:6 (1994): 346–352.

PETERS, NICK. "A Silver Star Emerges." *Sacramento Bee* 25 Aug. 2004.

PETERSEN, WILLIAM. *Japanese Americans*. New York: Random House, 1971.

———. "Success Story, Japanese-American Style." *New York Times Magazine* 9 Jan. 1966: 20+.

PHILIPPS, DON. "Mineta Brings Pro-Transit Views, Pragmatic Outlook." *Washington Post* 4 Jan. 2001.

PHINNEY, JEAN. "Stages of Ethnic Identity Development in Minority Group Adolescents." *Journal of Early Adolescence* 9 (1989): 34–49.

PICKEL, MARY LOU. "Ruling Backs Somali Refugees Fired at Airport." *Atlanta Journal-Constitution* 20 Jul. 2005.

PYKE, KAREN. "'Generation Deserters' and 'Black Sheep': Acculturative Differences Among Siblings in Asian Immigrant Families. *Journal of Family Issues* 26:4 (May 2005): 1–27.

PYKE, KAREN D., and DENISE L. JOHNSON. "Asian American Women and Racialized Femininities: 'Doing' Gender Across Cultural Worlds. *Gender and Society* 17:1 (February 2003): 33–55.

PIMENTEL, BENJAMIN. "'All-American Girl' Stirs Debate Among Asians." *San Francisco Chronicle* 1 Nov. 1994.

———. "One Man's War Against Marines." *San Francisco Chronicle* 5 Feb. 1994.

PIMENTEL, BENJAMIN, and CHARLES BURRESS. "Oakland Tribune Fires Respected Columnist Wong." *San Francisco Chronicle* 26 Mar. 1996.

POOLE, SHEILA M. "Between Cultures: Vietnamese Amerasians Find a Refuge in Atlanta from Taunts that Plagued Their Childhood." *Atlanta Journal-Constitution* 18 May 2005.

POPE, LISA. "Asian American Businesses Targeted." *Los Angeles Daily News* 1 May 1992.

PORTER, DAVID. "Asian American Groups Call for Boycott over 'Bigoted' Remarks." *Associated Press* 28 Apr. 2005.

PORTES, ALEJANDRO, and ROBERT BACH. *Latin Journey: Cuban and Mexican Immigrants in the United States*. Berkeley and Los Angeles: University of California Press, 1985.

PORTES, ALEJANDRO, and RUBÉN G. RUMBAUT. *Immigrant America: A Portrait*. Berkeley and Los Angeles: University of California Press, 1990.

———. *Immigrant America: A Portrait*, 2nd ed. Berkeley and Los Angeles: University of California Press, 1996.

POSADAS, BARBARA M. "Crossed Boundaries in Interracial Chicago: Filipino American Families Since 1925." *Amerasia Journal* 8:2 (1981): 31–52.

PRESTONOWITZ, CLYDE V. *Trading Places: How We Are Giving Our Future to Japan and How to Reclaim It*. New York: Basic Books, 1989.

Princeton University Enrollment Information. Online at http://registrar1.princeton.edu/data/oe_items/ug_by_race_ethn.pdf.

Profile of Jerry Yang. Online at http://docs.yahoo.com/docs/pr/executives/yang.html.

"The Push to 'Buy American.'" *Newsweek* 3 Feb. 1992: 32–35.

PYE, LUCIEN. *Asian Power and Politics: The Cultural Dimensions of Authority.* Cambridge, MA: Belknap Press, 1985.

"Questions and Answers on Lowell High Series." *San Francisco Chronicle* 29 Jun. 1995.

QUINONES, SAM. "From Sweet Success to Bitter Tears." *Los Angeles Times* 19 Jan. 2005.

RABALAIS, SCOTT. "Toyota Takes On American Sport." *State-Times/Morning Advocate* 14 Feb. 2004.

"Racist Convicted in Firebombings Faces New Trial." *San Francisco Chronicle* 1 Sep. 1994.

"Racist Leader Credits Furrow as Mourners Gather." *Oakland Tribune* 15 Aug. 1999.

"Radio Hosts Apologize for Remarks about Asian American Candidate." *Associated Press* 26 May 2005.

"Radio Show's Staff Pulled Over Tsunami Parody Song." *San Francisco Chronicle* 27 Jan. 2005.

RAGAZA, ANGELO. "All of the Above." *A Magazine* 3:1 (1994): 76.

RANDOLPH, ELEANOR. "In N.Y., the Breslin Backlash: Asians Demanded Ouster after Newsday Tirade." *Washington Post* 8 May 1990.

RASHBAUM, WILLIAM K. "Marchers Protest Diallo Verdict, Taunting Police Along the Way." *New York Times* 26 Feb. 2000.

RATTI, RAKESH, ed. *A Lotus of Another Color: An Unfolding of the South Asian Gay and Lesbian Experience.* Boston: Alyson Press, 1993.

RAUM, TOM. "Republicans Capitalize on Espionage Allegations." *AsianWeek* 1 Apr. 1999.

"Reality Check on Domestic Front." *Hindustan Times* 13 Mar. 2005.

REED, CHERYL. "One Child Genius to Another." *Chicago Sun-Times* 20 Jan. 2004.

REICH, ROBERT B. *The Work of Nations.* New York: Alfred A. Knopf, 1991.

REILLY, RICK. "Heaven Help Her." *Sports Illustrated* 20 May 1996: 77–78.

REINHOLD, ROBERT. "Buying American Is No Cure-All, U.S. Economists Say." *New York Times* 27 Jan. 1992.

"Rep. Coble Reneges on Agreement to Meet." Japanese American Citizen's League. Press Release. 10 Jul. 2003.

RICHMOND, RAY. "ABC Gives Innovation 'All-American Try.'" *Los Angeles Daily News* 14 Sep. 1994.

RIGDON, JOHN E. "Asian-American Youth Suffer a Rising Toll From Heavy Pressures." *Wall Street Journal* 10 Jul. 1991.

"Rising Toll of Hate Crimes Cited in Student's Slaying." *Los Angeles Times* 10 Oct. 1992.

RIVERA, CARLA. "Asians Say They Fare Better Than Other Minorities." *Los Angeles Times* 20 Aug. 1993.

ROGERS, CARROLL. "A Day of Healing for Rocker; Meeting, Apologies Clear Air on Return." *The Atlantic Journal and Constitution* 3 Mar. 2000.

"Rohnert Park Man Fatally Shot by Cops." *San Francisco Chronicle* 30 Apr. 1997.

ROJAS, AURELIA. "Turning A Blind Eye To Hate Crimes." *San Francisco Chronicle* 22 Oct. 1996.

ROOT, MARIA P. P. "A Bill of Rights for Mixed Race People." Online at http://www.mixedfolks.com/rights.htm.

ROSENBAUM, DAVID, and ROBIN TONER. "To Social Security Debate, Add Variable: Immigration." *New York Times* 16 Feb. 2005.

ROSENBLATT, ROBERT A. "'Glass Ceiling' Still Too Hard to Break, U.S. Panel Finds." *Los Angeles Times* 16 Mar. 1995.

ROTHENBERG, STUART. "The Invisible Success Story." *National Review* 15 Sep. 1989: 43–45.

ROY, SANDIP. "Indian Americans Moving Into the GOP Camp?" *AsianWeek* 18 Nov. 2004.

RUMBAUT, RUBÉN. "Mental Health and the Refugee Experience. *Southeast Asian Mental Health: Treatment, Prevention, Services, Training and Research.* Tom C. Owen, ed. Rockville, MD: National Institute of Mental Health, 1985. 433–486.

———. "Vietnamese, Laotian, and Cambodian Americans." *Asian Americans: Contemporary Trends and Issues.* Pyong Gap Min, ed. Thousand Oaks, CA: Sage Publications, 1985.

RUMBAUT, RUBÉN G., and KENJI IMA. *The Adaptation of Southeast Asian Refugee Youth: A Comparative Study, Final Report to the U.S. Department of Health and Human Services, Office of Refugee Resettlement.* Jan. 1988.

RUMBAUT, RUBÉN, and J. R. WEEKS. "Fertility and Adaptation: Indochinese Refugees in the United States." *International Migration Review* 20:2 (1986): 428–466.

RUTTIN, TIM. "A New Kind of Riot." *The New York Review* 11 Jun. 1992.

RYAN, JOAN. "Colorado Horror Evokes Painful Memories of '89." *San Francisco Chronicle* 24 Apr. 1999.

SAAD, LYDIA. "Americans Divided on Immigration." *Gallop Poll News Service* 22 Jul. 2004.

SAID, EDWARD. *Orientalism.* New York: Pantheon Books, 1978.

SAITO, LELAND T. "Asian Americans and Latinos in San Gabriel Valley, California: Ethnic Political Cooperation and Redistricting 1990–1992." *Amerasia Journal* 19:2 (1993): 55–68.

———. "Asian Americans and Multiracial Political Coalitions: New York City's Chinatown and Redistricting, 1990–2001." In Gordon Chang, *Asian Americans and Politics: Perspectives, Experiences, Prospect.* Stanford, CA: Stanford University Press, 2001. 383–408.

———. "Asian Pacific Americans and Redistricting Changes in 2001." In *2001–02 National Asian Pacific American Political Almanac.* Los Angeles, CA: UCLA Asian American Studies Center Press, 2001. 130–140.

———. *Race and Politics: Asian Americans, Latinos, and Whites in a Los Angeles Suburb.* Urbana and Chicago: University of Illinois Press, 1998.

SAITO, LELAND, and EDWARD J. W. PARK. "Multiracial Collaborations and Coalitions." *Transforming Race Relations: A Public Policy Report.* Paul Ong, ed. Los Angeles: LEAP Asian American Public Policy Institute and UCLA Asian American Studies Center, 2000. 435–474.

SANDERS, JIMY, and VICTOR NEE. "Limits of Ethnic Solidarity in the Enclave Economy." *American Sociological Review* 52 (1987): 745–767.

SANGER, DAVID E. "In A Swift Action, Bush Names Choice for Labor Dept." *New York Times* 12 Jan. 2001.

SANTOS, BIENVENIDO. "Filipinos in War." *Far Eastern Survey* 11 (1942): 249–250.

SAVAGE, DAVID G. "Study Finds U.S. Asians Get More School, Less Pay." *Los Angeles Times* 18 Sep. 1992.

SAXENIAN, ANNALEE. *Silicon Valley's New Immigrant Entrepreneurs.* San Francisco, CA: Public Policy Institute of California, 1999.

SAXENIAN, ANNALEE, with YASUYUKI MOTOYAMA and XIAOHONG QUAN. *Local and Global Networks of Immigrant Professionals in Silicon Valley.* San Francisco, CA: Public Policy Institute of California, 2002.

SCHAPIRO, WALTER. "Japan Bashing on the Campaign Train." *Time* 10 Feb. 1992: 23–24.

SCHEVITZ, TANYA. "A Natural Love of Learning: 12-Year-Old Boy to Enter UC Davis as a Junior." *San Francisco Chronicle* 4 May 1999.

———. "UC May Seek Diversity Via Admission Changes." *San Francisco Chronicle* 15 Dec. 2000.

———. "UC System Struggles to Attract Minorities. *San Francisco Chronicle* 5 May 2005.

SCHLOSSER, JIM. "Groups Call on Cobel to Resign Chair: The Greensboro Congressman says He Won't Apologize for Comments About Japanese Americans and Arab Americans." *Greensboro News & Record* 8 Feb. 2003.

SCHMIDT, ERIC. "Asian-American Proves Marine Bias." *New York Times* 21 Jan. 1994.

SCHNIDER, BARBARA, and YOUNGSOOK LEE. "A Model for Academic Success: The School and Home Environment of East Asian Students." *Anthropology & Education Quarterly* 21:4 (1990): 358–377.

SCHNIDER, WILLIAM. "Asian Americans Will Matter More." *National Journal* 14 Aug. 1999.

SCHUETZ, LISA. "Accused Killer: Victim Shot First." *Wisconsin State Journal* 24 Nov. 2004.

SCHUYLER, NINA. "Asian Women Come Out Swinging." *The Progressive* May 1993: 14.

SCHWARTZ, MARY ANN, and BARBARA MARLIENE SCOTT. *Marriages and Families: Diversity and Change*. Englewood Cliffs, NJ: Prentice Hall, 1994.

"Science Prodigy Mixes Biochemistry, Music and Laughter." *Oakland Tribune* 26 Mar. 1995.

SCOTT, WILLIAM, and RUTH SCOTT. *Adaptation of Immigrants: Individual Differences and Determinants*. Oxford: Pergamon, 1989.

SENGUPTA, SOMINI. "Charlie Chan, Retooled for the '90s," *New York Times* 5 Jan. 1997.

SEYMOUR, GENE. "When Simple Isn't Good Enough." *Los Angeles Times* 25 Jul. 1993.

"S.F. Schools Assignment Controversy Continues." *AsianWeek* 17 April 2003.

SHEER, ROBERT. "The Wen Ho Lee 'Case' is Quickly Evaporating." *Sacramento Bee* 13 Jul. 2000.

SHEPARD, NATHANIEL. "Racist Hate Groups Are Thriving on the Internet." *Racism: Current Controversies*. San Diego, CA: Greenhaven Press, Inc., 1998.

SHIN, EUI-HANG, and SHIN-KAP HAN. "Korean Immigrant Small Businesses in Chicago: An Analysis of the Resource Mobilization Process." *Amerasia Journal* 16:1 (1990): 39–60.

SHIN, PAUL H. B. "Journey of Discovery for Korean Adoptees." *Daily News* 8 Jul. 1998.

SHINAGAWA, LARRY H. "Asian Pacific Electoral Participation in the San Francisco Bay Area: A Study of the Exit Poll Results of the November 8, 1994 Elections for the Cities of Daly City, San Francisco, and Oakland." San Francisco: Asian Law Caucus, 1995.

SHINAGAWA, LARRY H., and GIN Y. PANG. "Asian American Pan-Ethnicity and Intermarriage." *Amerasia Journal* 22:2 (1996): 127–152.

———. "Marriage Patterns of Asian Americans in California, 1980." *Income and Status Differences Between White and Minority Americans*. Sucheng Chan, ed. Lewiston, NY: Edwin Mellon Press, 1990: 225–282.

SHIOYA, TARA. "For the Lys, American Is an Ongoing Journey." *San Francisco Chronicle* 9 Dec. 1994.

———. "Recalling Insights—and Slights." *San Francisco Chronicle* 20 Jun. 1995.

SILVA, CHRISTINA M., and RAJA MISHRA. "Umpire's Call Gets Unheard-Of Result: Youth Baseball Tam Told to Speak English." Boston Globe 30 Jul. 2005.

SIM, SHARON YEN-LING. "Parent's Wishes and Children's Dreams Are Sources of Conflict." *AsianWeek* 2 Sep. 1995.

SIM, SUSAN K. "Why No Outrage Over Slur of Asians?" *Atlanta Journal-Constitution* 5 Nov. 2003.

SIMON, JULIAN L. *Immigration: The Demographic and Economic Facts*. Washington, DC: The Cato Institute and the National Immigration Forum, 1995.

———. "Studies on Immigrants Prove They'd Rather Give Than Receive." Letter to the Editor. *New York Times* 26 Feb. 1994.

SINGH, GURDIAL. "East Indians in the United States." *Sociology and Social Research* 30:3 (1946): 209–216.

SINHA, TITO. "P.R. Elections in N.Y.C.: Effects of Preference Voting on Asian-American Participation." *National Civic Review* 83:1 (Winter–Spring 1994): 80–83.

SIRAK, RON. "On Asians and Racism." *Golf World* 26 Aug. 2005. Online at http://www.golfdigest.co.za/stories/df_On_Asians_and_racism541.php.

SKINNER, RICHARD, and PHILIP A. KLINKNER. "Black, White, Brown and Cajun: The Racial Dynamics of the 2003 Louisiana Gubernatorial Election." *The Forum* 2:1 (2004), Article 3. Online at http://www.bepress.com/forum/vol2/iss1/art3.

SLATER, ERIC, and JOHN BECKHAM. "Shooter Cultivated His Racist Views in College." *Los Angeles Times* 6 Jul. 1999.

SMITH, LYNN. "Time to Add His Political Voice." *Los Angeles Times* 4 Nov. 2004.

SONG, KYUNG M. "Workers Accuse Boeing of Discrimination." *Seattle Times* 14 Oct. 1999.

SONG, YOUNG I. *Silent Victims: Battered Women in Korean Immigrant Families.* San Francisco: Oxford Press, 1987.

SOUNG-AH, CHOI. "Korean Adoptees Gather in Seoul." *Korean Herald* 6 Aug. 2005.

SOWELL, THOMAS. *The Economics and Politics of Race: An International Perspective.* New York: Quill, 1983.

———. *Ethnic America.* New York: Basic Books, 1981.

———. *Race and Culture: A World View.* New York: Basic Books, 1994.

STAATS, CRAIG. "Council Candidate Exaggerated Credentials." *Oakland Tribune* 20 May 1994.

———. "Hu and Her Supporters Can't Agree on Stand." *Oakland Tribune* 17 May 1994.

STALLONE, STEVE. "Crossing Lines." *San Francisco Bay Guardian* 8 Dec. 1993.

———. "Was Stabbing a Racist Attack or Merely Self-Defense?" *Seattle Post-Intelligencer* 13 Dec. 2000.

———. "White Noise." *The Bay Guardian* 21 Jul. 1993.

STAMMER, LARRY. "Turbans Make Sikhs Easy Targets." *Los Angeles Times* 20 Sep. 2001.

Stanford University Enrollment Information. Online at http://www.stanford.edu/home/stanford/facts/undergraduate.html.

STANTON, SAM, and GARY DELSOHN. "Violent Ideology Spred on Web." *Sacramento Bee* 11 Jun. 2000.

STAPLES, ROBERT, and ALFREDO MIRANDE. "Racial and Cultural Variations Among American Families: A Decennial Review of the Literature on Minority Families." *Journal of Marriage and the Family* 42:4 (1980): 887–903.

"State Wide Exit Poll." *Los Angeles Times* 10 Nov. 1994.

STEINBERG, LAURENCE, et al. "Ethnic Differences in Adolescent Achievement: An Ecological Perspective." *American Psychologist* 47:6 (1992): 723–729.

STEINBERG, STEPHEN. *The Ethnic Myth: Race, Ethnicity, and Class in America.* Boston: Beacon Press, 1981.

STEINER, STAN. *Fushang: The Chinese Who Built America.* New York: Harper, 1979.

STERBA, JAMES P. "Indians in U.S. Prosper in Their New Country, and Not Just in Motels." *Wall Street Journal* 27 Jan. 1987.

STEVENSON, HAROLD W., et al. "Cognitive Performance and Academic Achievement of Japanese, Chinese, and American Children." *Child Development* 56 (1985): 718–734.

STINNETT, PEGGY. "Checking Your Civil Rights at the Airline Gate." *Oakland Tribune* 29 Oct. 1997.

———. "Civil Rights Activist Finds Hate-Crime Justice Elusive." *Oakland Tribune* 12 Mar. 1999.

———. "Racism Is in the Air, Literally and Otherwise." *Oakland Tribune* 30 Oct. 1994.

STRAND, PAUL J., and WOODROW JONES, JR. *Indochinese Refugees in America: Problems of Adaptation and Assimilation.* Durham, NC: Duke University Press, 1985.

STRASBERG, JENNY. "Abercrombie & Glitch—Asian Americans rip retailer for stereotypes on T-shirts" *San Francisco Chronicle* 18 Apr. 2002.

STRAUSS, ASELM. "Strain and Harmony in American-Japanese War-bride Marriages." *Marriage and Family Living* 16 (1954): 99–106.

———. "Student 9, in College." *Sacramento Bee* 2 Oct. 2000.

———. "Success Story of One Minority Group in the U.S." *U.S. News and World Report* 26 Dec. 1966: 73–78.

SUE, STANLEY. "Mental Health Policy." *The State of Asian Pacific America: Policy Issues to the Year 2020.* Los Angeles: LEAP Asian Pacific American Policy Institute and UCLA Asian American Studies Center, 1993. 79–94.

SUE, STANLEY, and HARRY KITANO. "Stereotypes as a Measure of Success." *Journal of Social Issues* 29 (1973): 83–98.

SUE, STANLEY, and SUMIE OKAZAKI. "Asian-American Educational Achievements: A Phenomenon in Search of an Explanation." *American Psychologist* 46:8 (1990): 913–920.

———. "Explanations for Asian-American Achievements: A Reply." *American Psychologist* 46:8 (1991): 878–880.

SUNG, BETTY LEE. *The Adjustment Experience of Chinese Immigrant Children in New York City.* New York: Center for Migration Studies, 1987.

———. *Chinese American Intermarriage.* New York: Center for Migration Studies, 1990.

———. *The Story of the Chinese in America.* New York: Macmillan, 1967.

"Sunnyhills High School." Online at http://www.sunnyhills.net/School Description.pdf.

"A 'Superminority' Tops Out." *Newsweek* 11 May 1987: 48–49.

"Support for JACL Decision." *AsianWeek* 12 Aug. 1994.

SURO, ROBERT. "Study of Immigrants Finds Asians at Top in Science and Medicine." *The Washington Post* 18 Apr. 1994.

SUZUKI, BOB H. "Education and the Socialization of Asian Americans: A Revisionist Analysis of the 'Model Minority' Thesis." *Amerasia Journal* 4:2 (1977): 23–51.

SWORD, SUSAN. "New SF Police Chief Is Widely Respected." *San Francisco Chronicle* 9 Jan. 1996.

TCHEN, JOHN KUO WEI. "Critics Clueless About Emergent American Sensibility." *AsianWeek* 12 Dec. 2002.

TAJAMI, RENEE. "Moving the Image: Asian American Independent Filmmaking 1970–1980." *Moving the Image: Independent Asian Pacific American Media Arts.* Russell Leong, ed. Los Angeles: UCLA Asian American Studies Center and Visual Communications, Southern California Asian American Studies Central, Inc., 1991: 10–33.

TAKAGI, DANA Y. "Maiden Voyage: Excursion into Sexuality and Identity Politics in Asian America." *Amerasia Journal* 20:1 (1994): 1–18.

———. *The Retreat from Race* New Brunswick, NJ: Rutgers University Press, 1992.

TAKAKI, RONALD. *Strangers from a Different Shore.* Boston: Little, Brown and Co., 1989.

TAMAKI, JULIE. "Claims of Racism in Assembly Contest." *Los Angeles Times* 10 Oct. 2000.

TANG, IRWIN. "APA Community Should Tell Shaquille O'Neal to 'Come down to Chinatown.'" *AsianWeek* 2 Jan. 2003.

TANG, JOYCE. *Doing Engineering: The Career Attainment and Mobility of Caucasian, Black, and Asian American Engineers.* Boulder, CO: Rowman & Littlefield Press, 2000.

TANSEY, BERNADETTE. "9 Asians At Lab File Bias Claim." *San Francisco Chronicle* 24 Dec. 1999.

TANZER, ANDREW. "Tiger Woods Played Here." *Forbes* 10 Mar. 1997.

TAYLOR, CHARLES R., and BARBARA S. STEIN. "Asian Americans: Television Advertising and the 'Model Minority' Stereotype." *Journal of Advertising* 26:2 (1997): 47–62.

TAYLOR, DANIEL B. "Asian-American Test Scores: They Deserve a Closer Look." *Education Week* 17 Oct. 1990: 23.

TAYLOR, RONALD L. "Black American Families." *Minority Families in the United States: A Multicultural Approach.* Ronald L. Taylor, ed. Englewood Cliffs, NJ: Prentice Hall, 1994. 19–24.

TENBROEK, JACOBUS, EDWARD N. BARNHART, and FLOYD W. MATSON. *Prejudice, War, and the Constitution.* Berkeley and Los Angeles: University of California Press, 1970.

TENG, MABEL. "We Have Won Before and We Will Win Again." *AsianWeek* 18 Mar. 2004.

"Tentative Settlement of Asian Scientists and Engineer Class Action." *Lawrence Livermore National Laboratory Public Affairs* 11 Mar. 2005. Online at http://www.llnl.gov/pao/news/news_releases/2005/NR-05-03-06.html.

TJADEN, PATRICIA, and NANCY THOENES. "Extent, Nature, and Consequences of Intimate Partner Violence: Research Report." Washington, DC: National Institute of Justice and the Centers for Disease Control and Prevention. Jul. 2000. Online at www.ncjrs.org/ txtfiles1/nij/181867.txt.

"Timmy Chang Scouting Report." Online at http://www.nfl.com/draft/profiles/2005/ chang_timmy.

"Tolerance of Bigotry Has Run Out." *Los Angeles Times* 11 May 1990.

TOM, MAELEY. "Winning for Dummies." *AsianWeek* 22 Jul. 2004.

TOMLINSON, TOMMY. *Hard Work and High Expectations: Motivating Students to Learn.* Washington, DC: GPO, 1992.

TORASSA, ULYSSES. "Thousands Protest Legalizing Same-Sex Marriages. *San Francisco Chronicle* 26 Apr. 2004.

TRAN, MAI, and CLAIRE LUNA. "Katrina's Aftermath: Vietnamese in O.C. Fear for Gulf Relatives." *Los Angeles Times* 3 Sep. 2003.

TRAN, TINI. "War Orphans Return to Vietnam 25 Years Later." *AsianWeek* 13 Apr. 2000.

TRENKA, JANE JEONG. *The Language of Blood: A Memoir.* St. Paul, MN: Borealis Books, 2003.

TROST, ANN-MARIE. "Korean Adoptees Share Experiences Through Documentary." *Asian Pages* 14 Apr. 1998.

TRUEBA, HENRY T., LILLY CHENG, and KENJI IMA. *Myth or Reality: Adaptive Strategies of Asian Americans in California.* Washington, DC: The Falmer Press, 1993.

TSAI, SHIH-SHAN HENRY. *The Chinese Experience in America.* Bloomington: Indiana University Press, 1986.

TSANG, DANIEL C. "Founder of First Gay and Lesbian Asian Group Succumbs to AIDS." *AsianWeek* 2 Sep. 1994.

———. "Jury Awards Vietnamese American Bashing Victim $1.1 Million Sum." *AsianWeek* 24 Mar. 1995.

TSENG, WEN-SHING, JOHN MCDERMOTT, and THOMAS MARETZKI. *Adjustment in Intercultural Marriage.* Hawaii: University Press of Hawaii, 1977.

TUAN, MAI. "On Asian American Ice Queens and Multigenerational Asian Ethnics." *Amerasia Journal* 25 (1999): 181–186.

———. *Forever Foreigners or Honorary Whites? The Asian American Experience Today.* New Brunswick, NJ: Rutgers University Press, 1998.

"Tung Case Pries Open Secret Tenure Review." *The Berkeley Graduate* Apr. 1990.

UBA, LAURA. *Asian Americans: Personality Patterns, Identity, and Mental Health.* New York: Guilford Press, 1994.

"UC Berkeley Apologizes for Policy that Limited Asians." *Los Angeles Times* 7 Apr. 1989.

UDESKY, LAURIE. "Sweatshops Behind the Labels." *The Nation* 16 May 1994: 665–668.

UHLANDER, CAROL, BRUCE CAIN, and D. RODERICK KIEWIET. "Political Participation of Ethnic Minorities in the 1980s." *Political Behavior* 11:3 (1989): 195–231.

UMEMOTO, KAREN. " 'On Strike!' San Francisco State College Strike, 1968–1969." *Amerasia Journal* 15:1 (1991): 3–41.

UMEMOTO, KEITH. "A Shift of 10,000 APA Voters Could Have . . ." *AsianWeek* 22 Jul. 2004.

United States. Bureau of the Census. *1990 Census of the Population, Asians and Pacific Islanders in the United States.* Washington, DC: GPO, 1993.

———. *1990 Census of the Population, Social and Economic Characteristics, Metropolitan Areas.* Washington, DC: GPO, 1994.

———. *1993 Statistical Yearbook of the Immigration and Naturalization Service.* Washington, DC: GPO, 1994.

———. *1994 Statistical Yearbook of the Immigration and Naturalization Service.* Washington, DC: GPO, 1996.

———. *1998 Statistical Yearbook of the Immigration and Naturalization Service.* Washington, DC: GPO, 1999.

———. *2002 Crimes in the United States.* Online at http://www.fbi.gov/ucr/02cius.htm.

———. *Adopted Children and Stepchildren: 2000.* Oct. 2003. Online at http://www.census.gov/prod/2003pubs/censr-6.pdf.

———. *Annual Report on the Employment of Minorities, Women and Handicapped Individuals in the Federal Government.* Washington, DC: GPO, 1990.

———. "Central Station Casino To Pay $1.5 Million in EEOC Settlement for National Origin Bias." 18 Jul. 2003. Online at http://www.eeoc.gov/press/7-18-03a.html.

———. *Characteristics of Business Owners, 1992.* Washington, DC: GPO, 1992.

———. Commission on Civil Rights. *Civil Rights Issues Facing Asian Americans in the 1990s.* Washington, DC: GPO, 1992.

———. Commission on Wartime Relocation and Internment of Civilians. *Personal Justice Denied.* Washington, DC: GPO, 1982.

———. Committee for Refugees. *Cambodians in Thailand: People on the Edge.* Washington, DC: GPO, 1985.

———. Dept. of Commerce. *Statistical Abstract of the United States, 1995.* Washington, DC: GPO, 1995.

———. Dept. of Commerce. *Statistical Abstract of the United States, 2004–2005.* Washington, DC: GPO, 2005.

———. Dept. of Education. *The Condition of Bilingual Education in the Nation, 1982: A Report from the Secretary of Education to the President and the Congress.* Washington, DC: GPO, 1982.

———. Dept. of Education Office of English Language Acquisition. "Executive Summary of Title III LEP Biennial Evaluation Report to Congress." 2005. Online at http://www.ed.gov/about/offices/list/oela/index.html.

———. Dept. of Energy. Final Report: Task Force on Racial Profiling. Jan. 2000. Online at http://www.fas.org/irp/news/2000/01/rprofilerpt.pdf.

———. Dept. of Justice. Immigration and Naturalization Service. *2003 Statistical Yearbook of the Immigration and Naturalization Service.* Washington, DC: GPO, 2004.

———. Dept. of Labor. "Projections of Occupational Employment, 1988–2000." *BLS Monthly Labor Review* May. 1989: 51–59.

———. "EEOC Agrees to Landmark Resolution of Discrimination Case Against Abercrombie & Fitch." 18 Nov. 2004. Online at http://www.eeoc.gov/press/11-18-04.html.

———. Equal Employment Opportunity Commission. "National Origin Discrimination." 2 Mar. 2000. Online at http://www.eeoc.gov/origin/index.html.

———. Federal Bureau of Investigation. *Uniform Crime Report, 2002.* Online at http://www.fbi.gov/ucr/hatecrime2002.pdf.

———. Federal Communications Commission. "1995 Broadcast and Cable Employment Report." Washington, DC: GPO. 12 Jun. 1996.

———. The Foreign-Born population in the united states, March 2000. Washington DC: GPO 2000.

———. Office for Civil Rights. "Statement of Findings." (For Compliance Review No. 01–88–6009 on Harvard University.) Washington, DC: GPO, 4 Oct. 1990.

———. *Overview of Race and Hispanic Origin, 2000.* Washington, DC: GPO, 2001.

———. "Profile of Selected Social Characteristics: 2000 (Census Summary File 4, DP-2)."

———. *Refugees from Laos: In Harm's Way.* Washington, DC: GPO, 1986.

———. "Richardson Releases Task Force Against Racial Profiling Report and Announces 8 Immediate Actions." Jan. 2000. Press release online at http://www.fas.org/irp/news/2000/01/000119-pr00011.htm.

———. *Survey of Minority-Owned Business Enterprises: Asian Americans, American Indians, and Other Minorities.* Washington, DC: GPO, Jun. 1991.

———. *Uncertain Harbors: The Plight of Vietnamese Boat People.* Washington, DC: GPO, 1987.

United States v. Ronald Ebans 800 F.2nd. 1422 (1986 6th Cir.).

United States v. Bhagat Singh Thind. 261 U.S. 204 (1923).

University of California, Berkeley, Enrollment Information. Online at http://www.berk ley.edu/news/media/releases/2004/12/02_enroll_table.shtml.

University of California, San Francisco. "What Are Asian and Pacific Islander HIV Prevention Needs?" Online at http://www.apiahf.org/programs/hivcba/resources/facts/ apifs.pdf.

"Up from Inscrutable." *Fortune* 6 Apr. 1992: 120.

VALVERDE, KIEU-LINH CAROLINE. "From Dust to Gold: The Amerasian Experience." *Racially Mixed People in America.* Maria Root, ed. Newbury Park, CA: Sage Publications, 1992. 144–161.

VAN WOLFEN, KARL. *The Enigma of Japanese Power.* New York: Alfred A. Knopf, 1989.

VAN SAINT, WILL. "One Step Forward, Two Steps Back." *National Journal* 8 May 1999.

VARTABEDIAN, RALPH. "Aerospace Careers in Low Orbit." *Los Angeles Times* 16 Nov. 1992.

VAUGHN, CHRIS. "Vietnamese Children of U.S. Soldiers Struggle to Make New Lives in America." *Fort Worth Star-Telegram* 10 Nov. 2003.

VILLAPANDO, VENNY. "The Business of Selling Mail-Order Brides." *Making Waves.* Asian Women United, eds. Boston: Beacon Press, 1989.

"Vision for the 21st Century." *AsianWeek* 24 May 1996.

VISWANATHAN, VINESH. "Seeing the Person, Not the Color." *San Francisco Chronicle* 17 May 1995.

VIVIANO, FRANK. "Strangers in the Promised Land." *Image* 31 Aug. 1986: 15+.

WACHS, ESTER. "The East Is Hot." *Far Western Review* 23 Dec. 1993: 34–35.

WAIN, BARRY L. *The Refused: The Agony of Indochina Refugees.* New York: Simon & Schuster, 1981.

WALDINGER, ROGER. "Immigrant Enterprise and the Structure of the Labor Market." *New Approaches to Economic Life.* Bryan Roberts et al., eds. Manchester: Manchester University Press, 1985.

WALSH, EDWARD. "Midwest Gun Spree Suspect Is Dead, Man Shot Himself, Pursuing Police Say." *Washington Post* 5 Jul. 1999.

———. "Racial Issues Dog GOP Foes; McCain Won't Fire Aide; Bush Pressed On Bob Jones, Flag." *Washington Post* 17 Feb. 2000.

———. "Racial Slayer Killed Himself in Struggle." *Washington Post* 6 Jul. 1999.

WALSH, JOAN. "Asian Women, Caucasian Men." *Image* 2 Dec. 1990: 11–17.

WANG, L. LING-CHI. "Foreign Money Is No Friend of Ours." *AsianWeek* 8 Nov. 1996.

———. "Lau v. Nichols: History of a Struggle for Equal and Quality Education." *Amerasia Journal* 2:2 (1974): 16–45.

———. "Meritocracy and Diversity in Higher Education: Discrimination Against Asian Americans in the Post-Bakke Era." *The Urban Review* 20:3 (1991): 202–203.

———. "The Politics of Ethnic Identity and Empowerment: The Asian American Community Since the 1960s." *Asian American Policy Review* 2 (Spring 1991): 43–56.

———. "Race, class, Citizenship and Extraterritorality: Asian Americans and the 1996 Campaign Finance Scandal." *Amerasia Journal* 24:1 (1998): 1–21.

———. "Trends in Admissions for Asian Americans in Colleges and Universities: Higher Education Policy." *The State of Asian Pacific America: Policy Issues to the Year 2020.* Los Angeles: LEAP Asian Pacific American Public Policy Institute and UCLA Asian American Studies Center, 1993. 49–60.

WASHINGTON, FRANK S. "Asians are Prime Prospects but Automakers Ignore Them." *Automotive News* 20 Apr. 1999.

WAT, ERIC. *The Making of a Gay Asian Community: An Oral History of Pre-AIDS Los Angeles.* Landham, MD: Rowman and Littlefield Publishers, Inc., 1998.

WATANABE, MYRNA E. "Asian American Investigators Decry 'Glass Ceiling' In Academic Administration." *The Scientist* 29 May 1995.

WATANABE, TSUNEO, and JUN'ICHI IVATA. Translated by Dr. R. Roberts. *The Love of the Samurai: A Thousand Years of Japanese Homosexuality.* London: Gay Men's Press, 1989.

WAUGH, DEXTER. "Stanford Lacks Asian American Studies." *San Francisco Examiner* 25 Feb. 1994.

WAUGH, DEXTER, and STEVEN A. CHIN. "Daly City: New Manila." *San Francisco Examiner* 17 Sep. 1989.

WAYNE, LESLIE. "Infamous Political Commercial Is Turned on Gore." *Los Angeles Times* 27 Oct. 2000.

WEI, WILLIAM. *The Asian American Movement.* Philadelphia: Temple University Press, 1993.

WELLS, JANET. "Racial Divide In Boom Time, Study Reports." *San Francisco Chronicle* 5 Sep. 2000.

WEST, CORNEL. *Race Matters.* Boston: Beacon Press, 1993.

WESTHOFF, CHARLES F., and NOREEN GOLDMAN. "Figuring the Odds in the Marriage Market." *Current Issues in Marriage and the Family.* J. Gipson Wells, ed. New York: Macmillan, 1988. 39–46.

White House Initiative on Asian Americans and Pacific Islanders. Online at http://www.aapi .gov/president/factsheet.htm.

"Why They Count: Immigrant Contributions to the Golden State." Claremont, CA: Tomas Rivera Center, 1996.

WILDERMUTH, JOHN. "68% of State's Latino Voters Back Gore." *San Francisco Chronicle* 14 Nov. 2000.

WILGOREN, JODI. "High Pressure High." *Los Angeles Times* 4 Dec. 1994.

WILKINSON, HEI SOOK PARK. *Birth is More Than Once: The Inner World of Adopted Korean Children.* Detroit, MI: Harlo Press, 1985.

WILL, GEORGE F. "The Lunacy of Punishing Those Who Try to Excel." *Los Angeles Times* 16 Apr. 1989.

"William Hung." Online at http:/www.williamhung.net.

WILLIAMS, DENNIS. "A Formula for Success." *Newsweek* 23 Apr. 1984: 77–78.

WILLIAMS, TERESA K. "Marriage Betwen Japanese Women and U.S. Servicemen Since World War II." *Amerasia Journal* 17:1 (1991): 135–154.

WILLIAMS-LEON, TERESA, and CYNTHIA NAKASHIMA, eds. *The Sum of Our Part: Mixed Heritage Asian Americans.* Philadelphia: Temple University Press, 2001.

WILLIAMSON, B. C. CHANG. "M. Butterfly: Passivity, Deviousness, and the Invisibility of the Asian American Male." *Bearing Dreams, Shaping Visions: Asian Pacific American Perspectives.* Linda A. Revilla et al., eds. Pullman, WA: Washington State University Press, 1993. 181–184.

WILSON, YUMI. "Consent Decree Ends Asians' Housing Bias." *San Francisco Chronicle* 19 Jul. 1999.

———. "Designer's Largesse Questioned." *San Francisco Chronicle* 16 Feb. 1994.

Yick Wo v. Hopkins. 118 U.S. 356 (1886).

WONG, BILL. "Human Cargo." *AsianWeek* 26 Apr. 1996.

———. "Sweatshop Fame." *AsianWeek* 21 Jun. 1996.

WONG, DIANE YEN-MEI. "Will the Real Asian Pacific American Please Stand Up?" *The State of Asian Pacific America: Policy Issues to the Year 2020.* Los Angeles: LEAP Asian Pacific American Public Policy Institute and UCLA Asian American Studies Center, 1993. 270–273.

WONG, KENT. "Building an Asian Pacific Labor Alliance: A New Chapter in Our History." *The State of Asian America: Activism and Resistance in the 1990s.* Karin Aguilar-San Juan, ed. Boston: South End Press, 1994. 335–349.

WONG, MORRISON G. "The Chinese American Family." *Ethnic Families in America.* Charles H. Mindel, Robert W. Habenstein, and Roosevelt Wright, Jr., eds. New York: Elsevier, 1989. 230–257.

WONG, SAU-LING, C. "Denationalization Reconsidered: Asian American Cultural Criticism at a Theoretical Crossroads." *Amerasia Journal* 21:1&2 (1995): 1–27.

WONG, WILLIAM. "A Disappointing 'All-American Girl.'" *Oakland Tribune* 9 Oct. 1994.

———. "Election Exposes Chinatown Issues." *Oakland Tribune* 25 May 1994.

———. "Loser Helps Winner: What a Concept." *Oakland Tribune* 5 Jul. 1995.

———. "Unseemly Tactics in Redistricting Fight." *Oakland Tribune* 16 Jul. 1993.

WOO, ELAINE. "How to Beat a Bad Rap: With Money and Votes." *Los Angeles Times* 23 Apr. 2000.

WOOD, DANIEL B. "As Korean Americans Become Visible, They Seek Understanding." *Christian Science Monitor* 27 Jul. 1993.

"Writings May Indicate Hate Motive in Spree." *Seattle Times* 30 Apr. 2000.

WU, DIANA TING LIU. *Asian Pacific Americans in the Workplace.* Walnut Creek, CA: Alta Mira Press, 1997.

WU, FELICIA. "15 APIs Elected to NYC School Board." *AsianWeek* 29 Jul. 1999.

WU, FRANK. "Campaign of Our Own." *AsianWeek* 22 Mar. 1996.

———. "China: The New Scapegoat." *AsianWeek* 6 May 1999.

———. "Fundraising Investigation Targets APA's." *AsianWeek* 7 Mar. 1997.

———. "Push for Citizenship." *AsianWeek* 21 Jun. 1996.

XING, JUNE. *Asian America Through the Lens.* Walnut Creek, CA: AltaMira Press, 1998.

YAMAMOTO, J. K. "Cho Watch." *San Francisco Bay Guardian* 7 Dec. 1994.

YANG, CATHERINE. "In Any Language, It's Unfair." *BusinessWeek* 21 Jun. 1993: 110, 111.

YANG, SANDY. "Man Sentenced to Death for Killing Sikh Immigrant." *Associated Press* 10 Oct. 2003.

"Yao Ming Scouting Report." Online at http://nbadraft.net/profiles/yaoming.htm.

YICK, ALICE. "Predictors of Physical Spousal/Intimate Violence in Chinese American Families." *Journal of Family Violence* 15:3 (Sep. 2000): 246–267.

YIP, ALTHEA. "Asian Votes Shift to the Left." *AsianWeek* 11 Nov. 1996.

———. "ROTC Rebel." *AsianWeek* 23 Feb. 1996.

———. "S.F. Initiative Seeks Vote for Noncitizens." *AsianWeek* 3 May 1996.

———. "Talk of the Town." *AsianWeek* 29 Mar. 1996.

YIP, JEFF. "A Heroic Leading Role for One Asian 'Son.'" *Los Angeles Times* 25 Mar. 1995.

YOO, PAULA. "Troubled Waters." *A Magazine* 1:4 (1992): 14+.

YOON, IN-JIN, *On My Own: Korean Immigration Entrepreneurship, and Korean-Black Relations in Chicago and Los Angeles.* Chicago: University of Chicago Press, 1996.

YOSHIKAWA, HIROKAZU. "Network-, Setting-, and Community-Level HIV Prevention Strategies for Asian/Pacific Islanders: Data from Peer Educators at the Asian Pacific Islander Coalition on HIV/AIDS." Online at http://www.apiahf.org/programs/hivcba/resources/archives/apichareport5.pdf.

YOSHIKAWA, YOKO. "The Heat Is on 'Miss Saigon' Coalition: Organizing Across Race and Sexuality." *The State of Asian America: Activism and Resistance in the 1990s.* Karin Aguilar-San Juan, ed. Boston: South End Press, 1994. 275–294.

YOUNG, LINDSEY. "NASCAR Stirred by Toyota's Entry." *Chattanooga Times Free Press* 13 Feb. 2004.

YU, ELENA S. H. "Filipino Migration and Community Organization in the United States." *California Sociologist* 3:2 (1980): 76–102.

Yu, Winifred. "Asian-Americans Charge Prejudice Slows Climb to Management Ranks." *Wall Street Journal* 11 Sep. 1985.

Zeigler, Mark. "Ump Out—Told Massachusetts Little Leaguers: English Only." *San Diego Union* 30 Jul. 2005.

Zelnick, Straus. "To Guy Aoki." Letter. 23 Mar. 1993.

Zhao, John. "A Parent's Fight Against S.F. Schools." *AsianWeek* 29 May 2003.

Zheng, Zen T. C. "Mall First Stop for Evacuees; Many Finding Food, Clothing, Guidance, and Care." *Houston Chronicle* 8 Sep. 2005.

Zhou, Min. *Chinatown: The Socioeconomic Potential of an Urban Enclave.* Philadelphia: Temple University Press, 1992.

———. "Coming of Age: The Current Situation of Asian American Children." In Pyong Gap Min and Kyeyoung Park, eds. *Amerasia Journal* 25:1 (1999): 1–27.

Zhou, Min, and Carl Bankston III. *How Vietnamese Children Adapt to Life in the United States.* New York: Russell Sage Foundation, 1998.

Zinn, Laura. "To Marketers, Kristi Yamaguchi Isn't as Good as Gold." *BusinessWeek* 9 Mar. 1992: 40.

Zinn, Maxine Baca. "Adaptation and Continuity in Mexican-Origin Families." *Minority Families in the United States: A Multicultural Approach.* Ronald L. Taylor, ed. Upper Saddle River, NJ: Prentice Hall, 1994. 70–75.

Zinsmeister, Karl. "Asians and Blacks: Bittersweet Success." *Current* Feb. 1988: 9–15.

Index